NEW PERSPECTIVES

SHAFFER | PINARD

Microsoft® Office 365®
Word
2019

Comprehensive

 CENGAGE

Australia • Brazil • Canada • Mexico • Singapore • United Kingdom • United States

**New Perspectives Microsoft® Office 365®
Word 2019 Comprehensive**
Ann Shaffer and Katherine T. Pinard

SVP, GM Skills & Global Product Management:
  Jonathan Lau

Product Director: Lauren Murphy

Product Assistant: Veronica Moreno-Nestojko

Executive Director, Content Design: Marah
  Bellegarde

Director, Learning Design: Leigh Hefferon

Learning Designer: Courtney Cozzy

Vice President, Marketing - Science, Technology,
  and Math: Jason R. Sakos

Senior Marketing Director: Michele McTighe

Marketing Manager: Timothy J. Cali

Director, Content Delivery: Patty Stephan

Content Manager: Christina Nyren

Digital Delivery Lead: Jim Vaughey

Designer: Lizz Anderson

Text Designer: Althea Chen

Cover Designer: Lizz Anderson

Cover Template Designer: Wing-Ip Ngan,
  Ink Design, Inc.

Cover Image: mycteria/ShutterStock.com

For product information and technology assistance, contact us at
**Cengage Customer & Sales Support, 1-800-354-9706 or
support.cengage.com.**

For permission to use material from this text or product,
submit all requests online at **www.cengage.com/permissions.**

Library of Congress Control Number: 2019936776

Student Edition ISBN: 978-0-357-02618-2
*Looseleaf available as part of a digital bundle

Cengage
200 Pier 4 Boulevard
Boston, MA 02210
USA

Cengage is a leading provider of customized learning solutions with employees residing in nearly 40 different countries and sales in more than 125 countries around the world. Find your local representative at
www.cengage.com.

To learn more about Cengage platforms and services,
visit **www.cengage.com.**

To register or access your online learning solution or purchase materials for your course, visit **www.cengage.com.**

Notice to the Reader

Printed at CLDPC, USA, 04-21

BRIEF CONTENTS

TABLE OF CONTENTS

Module 5 Working with Templates, Themes, and Styles
Creating a Summary Report . . . . **WD 5-1**

Module 6 Using Mail Merge
Creating a Form Letter, Mailing Labels, and a Phone Directory . . . . **WD 6-1**

Getting to Know Microsoft Office Versions

Cengage is proud to bring you the next edition of Microsoft Office. This edition was designed to provide a robust learning experience that is not dependent upon a specific version of Office.

Microsoft supports several versions of Office:

- **Office 365:** A cloud-based subscription service that delivers Microsoft's most up-to-date, feature-rich, modern productivity tools direct to your device. There are variations of Office 365 for business, educational, and personal use. Office 365 offers extra online storage and cloud-connected features, as well as updates with the latest features, fixes, and security updates.

- **Office 2019:** Microsoft's "on-premises" version of the Office apps, available for both PCs and Macs, offered as a static, one-time purchase and outside of the subscription model.

- **Office Online:** A free, simplified version of Office web applications (Word, Excel, PowerPoint, and OneNote) that facilitates creating and editing files collaboratively.

Office 365 (the subscription model) and Office 2019 (the one-time purchase model) had only slight differences between them at the time this content was developed. Over time, Office 365's cloud interface will continuously update, offering new application features and functions, while Office 2019 will remain static. Therefore, your onscreen experience may differ from what you see in this product. For example, the more advanced features and functionalities covered in this product may not be available in Office Online or may have updated from what you see in Office 2019.

For more information on the differences between Office 365, Office 2019, and Office Online, please visit the Microsoft Support site.

Cengage is committed to providing high-quality learning solutions for you to gain the knowledge and skills that will empower you throughout your educational and professional careers.

Thank you for using our product, and we look forward to exploring the future of Microsoft Office with you!

Using SAM Projects and Textbook Projects

SAM and *MindTap* are interactive online platforms designed to transform students into Microsoft Office and Computer Concepts masters. Practice with simulated SAM Trainings and MindTap activities and actively apply the skills you learned live in Microsoft Word, Excel, PowerPoint, or Access. Become a more productive student and use these skills throughout your career.

If your instructor assigns SAM Projects:

1. Launch your SAM Project assignment from SAM or MindTap.
2. Click the links to download your **Instructions file**, **Start file**, and **Support files** (when available).
3. Open the Instructions file and follow the step-by-step instructions.
4. When you complete the project, upload your file to SAM or MindTap for immediate feedback.

To use SAM Textbook Projects:

1. Launch your SAM Project assignment from SAM or MindTap.
2. Click the links to download your **Start file** and **Support files** (when available).
3. Locate the module indicated in your book or eBook.
4. Read the module and complete the project.

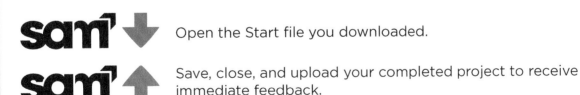

sam ⬇ Open the Start file you downloaded.

sam ⬆ Save, close, and upload your completed project to receive immediate feedback.

IMPORTANT: To receive full credit for your Textbook Project, you must complete the activity using the Start file you downloaded from SAM or MindTap.

Creating and Editing a Document

Writing a Business Letter and Formatting a Flyer

OBJECTIVES

Session 1.1
- Create and save a document
- Enter text and correct errors as you type
- Use AutoComplete and AutoCorrect
- Select text and move the insertion point
- Undo and redo actions
- Adjust paragraph spacing, line spacing, and margins
- Preview and print a document
- Create an envelope

Session 1.2
- Open an existing document
- Use the Editor pane
- Change page orientation, font, font color, and font size
- Apply text effects and align text
- Copy formatting with the Format Painter
- Insert a paragraph border and shading
- Delete, insert, and edit a photo
- Add a page border
- Create bulleted and numbered lists
- Use Microsoft Word Help

Case | *Water Resources Department*

David Alzacar is the communications director for the Water Resources Department in Portland, Oregon. As part of his outreach efforts, he has produced a set of brochures promoting the city's water conservation efforts. David has asked you to create a cover letter to accompany the brochures he is sending to the organizers of a national sustainability conference. He has also asked you to create an envelope for sending a water quality report to an environmental engineering publication. Next, he wants your help creating a flyer encouraging community members to join a citizen advisory panel. Finally, he would like to add bulleted and numbered lists to the minutes of a recent advisory panel meeting.

You will create the letter and flyer using **Microsoft Office Word 2019** (or simply **Word**), a full-featured word processing app that lets you create professional-looking documents and revise them easily. You'll start by opening Word and saving a new document. Then you'll type the text of the cover letter and print it. In the process of entering the text, you'll learn several ways to correct typing errors and how to adjust paragraph and line spacing. When you create the envelope, you'll learn how to save it as part of a document for later use. As you work on the flyer, you will learn how to open an existing document, change the way text is laid out on the page, format text, add a page border, and insert and resize a photo. Finally, you'll add bulleted and numbered lists to a document, and then learn how to use Microsoft Word Help.

STARTING DATA FILES

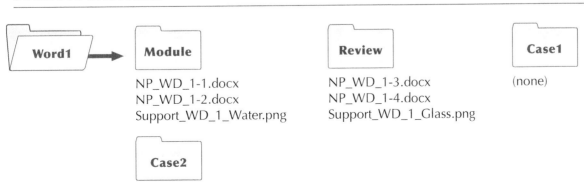

Word1 → **Module**

NP_WD_1-1.docx
NP_WD_1-2.docx
Support_WD_1_Water.png

Review

NP_WD_1-3.docx
NP_WD_1-4.docx
Support_WD_1_Glass.png

Case1

(none)

Case2

NP_WD_1-5.docx
Support_WD_1_Sign.jpg

Session 1.1 Visual Overview:

The **Quick Access Toolbar** is a collection of buttons that provides one-click access to commonly used commands, such as Save, Undo, and Repeat; you might see additional buttons here.

Each **tab** includes commands related to particular activities or tasks. The Home tab includes options for formatting and editing text.

The **title bar** displays the name of the open file and the program.

The **ribbon** is the main set of buttons and other tools you can use to complete tasks. It is organized into tabs and groups.

The **insertion point** shows where characters will appear when you start typing.

The dark gray areas on the ruler represent the document's margins. **Margins** are the blank spaces around the edges of a document's content.

Buttons for related commands are organized on a tab in **groups**. The buttons in this group can be used to change the appearance of a paragraph.

The **paragraph mark** indicates the end of a paragraph. It is visible only if nonprinting characters are turned on. **Nonprinting characters** appear on the screen but not on the printed page.

You can choose to display the rulers, which help you position elements in a document.

The **status bar** provides information about the current document, such as the current page and number of words in the document; it also contains buttons and other controls for working with the document.

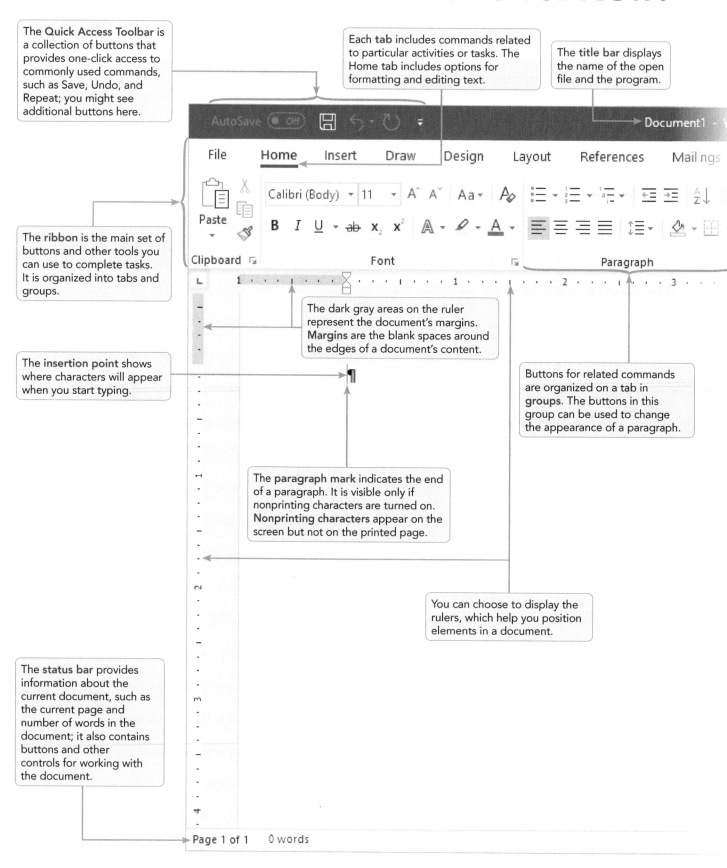

The Word Window

The Show/Hide button is selected, meaning that nonprinting characters are displayed in the document.

You can click the Ribbon Display Options button to display a menu with options for how the ribbon looks. If the ribbon is hidden, click Show Tabs and Commands in this menu to redisplay it.

You use the Minimize button to reduce the Word window to an icon in the taskbar, which you can click later to display the Word window again.

You use the Restore Down button to reduce the Word window to a smaller size; the Restore Down button is then replaced with the Maximize button, which you can click to restore the Word window to its full size.

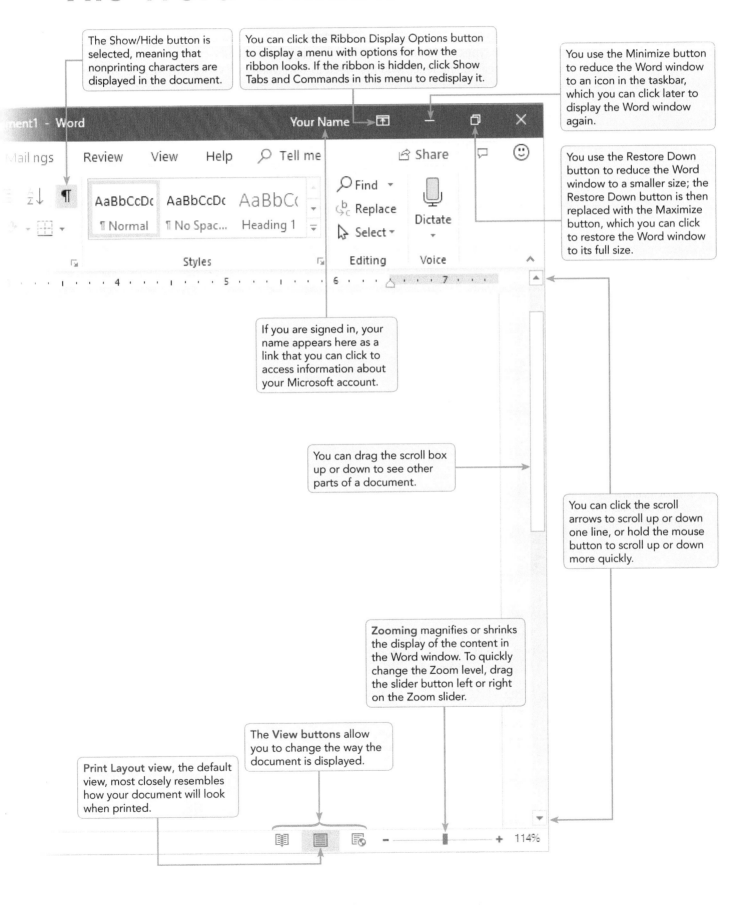

If you are signed in, your name appears here as a link that you can click to access information about your Microsoft account.

You can drag the scroll box up or down to see other parts of a document.

You can click the scroll arrows to scroll up or down one line, or hold the mouse button to scroll up or down more quickly.

Zooming magnifies or shrinks the display of the content in the Word window. To quickly change the Zoom level, drag the slider button left or right on the Zoom slider.

The View buttons allow you to change the way the document is displayed.

Print Layout view, the default view, most closely resembles how your document will look when printed.

Starting Word

With Word, you can quickly create polished, professional documents. You can type a document, adjust margins and spacing, create columns and tables, add graphics, and then easily make revisions and corrections. In this session, you will create one of the most common types of documents—a block-style business letter.

To begin creating the letter, you first need to start Microsoft Word and then set up the Word window.

To start Word:

▶ 1. **sam⁷** ↓ On the Windows taskbar, click the **Start** button ⊞. The Start menu opens.

▶ 2. On the Start menu, scroll the list of apps, and then click **Word**. Word starts and displays the Recent screen in Backstage view. Backstage view provides access to various screens with commands that allow you to manage files and Word options. See Figure 1–1.

Figure 1–1	Recent screen in Backstage view

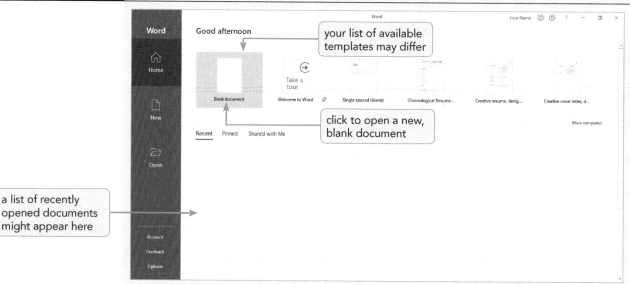

▶ 3. Click **Blank document**. The Word window opens, with the ribbon displayed.

Trouble? If you don't see the ribbon, click the Ribbon Display Options button ⊞, as shown in the Session 1.1 Visual Overview, and then click Show Tabs and Commands.

Don't be concerned if your Word window doesn't match the Session 1.1 Visual Overview exactly. You'll have a chance to adjust its appearance shortly.

Working in Touch Mode

You can interact with the Word screen using a mouse, or, if you have a touchscreen, you can work in Touch Mode, using a finger instead of the pointer. In **Touch Mode**, extra space around the buttons on the ribbon makes it easier to tap the specific button you need. The figures in this text show the screen with Mouse Mode on, but it's helpful to learn how to switch back and forth between Touch Mode and Mouse Mode.

Note: The steps in this module assume that you are using a mouse. If you are instead using a touch device, please read these steps but don't complete them so that you remain working in Touch Mode.

To switch between Touch and Mouse Mode:

▶ **1.** On the Quick Access Toolbar, click the **Customize Quick Access Toolbar** button ▼ to open the menu. The Touch/Mouse Mode command near the bottom of the menu does not have a checkmark next to it, indicating that it is currently not selected.

   Trouble? If the Touch/Mouse Mode command has a checkmark next to it, press ESC to close the menu, and then skip to Step 3.

▶ **2.** On the menu, click **Touch/Mouse Mode**. The menu closes, and the Touch/Mouse Mode button 👆 appears on the Quick Access Toolbar.

▶ **3.** On the Quick Access Toolbar, click the **Touch/Mouse Mode** button 👆 . A menu opens with two options—Mouse and Touch. The icon next to Mouse is shaded gray to indicate it is selected.

   Trouble? If the icon next to Touch is shaded gray, press ESC to close the menu and skip to Step 5.

▶ **4.** On the menu, click **Touch**. The menu closes, and the ribbon increases in height so that there is more space around each button on the ribbon. See Figure 1–2.

Figure 1–2   **Word window in Touch Mode**

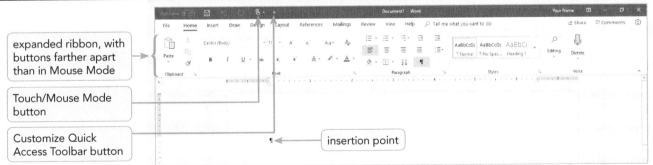

- expanded ribbon, with buttons farther apart than in Mouse Mode
- Touch/Mouse Mode button
- Customize Quick Access Toolbar button
- insertion point

   Trouble? If you are working with a touchscreen and want to use Touch Mode, skip Steps 5 and 6.

▶ **5.** On the Quick Access Toolbar, click the **Touch/Mouse Mode** button 👆 , and then click **Mouse**. The ribbon changes back to its Mouse Mode appearance, as shown in the Session 1.1 Visual Overview.

▶ **6.** On the Quick Access Toolbar, click the **Customize Quick Access Toolbar** button ▤, and then click **Touch/Mouse Mode** to deselect it. The Touch/Mouse Mode button is removed from the Quick Access Toolbar.

Setting Up the Word Window

Before you start using Word, you should make sure you can locate and identify the different elements of the Word window, as shown in the Session 1.1 Visual Overview. In the following steps, you'll make sure your screen matches the Visual Overview.

To set up your Word window to match the figures in this book:

▶ **1.** If the Word window does not fill the entire screen, click the **Maximize** button ▢ in the upper-right corner of the Word window.

The insertion point on your computer should be positioned about an inch from the top of the document, as shown in Figure 1–2, with the top margin visible.

Trouble? If the insertion point appears at the top of the document, with no white space above it, position the pointer between the top of the document and the horizontal ruler, until it changes to ⊞, double-click, and then scroll up to top of the document.

▶ **2.** On the ribbon, click the **View** tab. The ribbon changes to show options for changing the appearance of the Word window.

▶ **3.** In the Show group, click the **Ruler** check box to insert a checkmark, if necessary. If the rulers were not displayed, they are displayed now.

Next, you'll change the Zoom level to a setting that ensures that your Word window will match the figures in this book. To increase or decrease the screen's magnification, you could drag the slider button on the Zoom slider in the lower-right corner of the Word window. But to choose a specific Zoom level, it's easier to use the Zoom dialog box.

> **TIP**
>
> Changing the Zoom level affects only the way the document is displayed on the screen; it does not affect the document itself.

▶ **4.** In the Zoom group, click the **Zoom** button to open the Zoom dialog box. Double-click the current value in the **Percent** box to select it, type **120**, and then click **OK** to close the Zoom dialog box.

▶ **5.** On the status bar, click the **Print Layout** button 🗏 to select it, if necessary. As shown in the Session 1.1 Visual Overview, the Print Layout button is the middle of the three View buttons located on the right side of the status bar. The Print Layout button in the Views group on the View tab is also now selected.

Before typing a document, you should make sure nonprinting characters are displayed. Nonprinting characters provide a visual representation of details you might otherwise miss. For example, the (¶) character marks the end of a paragraph, and the (•) character marks the space between words.

To verify that nonprinting characters are displayed:

▶ **1.** On the ribbon, click the **Home** tab.

▶ **2.** In the blank Word document, look for the paragraph mark (¶) in the first line of the document, just to the right of the blinking insertion point.

> **Trouble?** If you don't see the paragraph mark, click the Show/Hide ¶ button ¶ in the Paragraph group.

In the Paragraph group, the Show/Hide ¶ button should be highlighted in gray, indicating that it is selected, and the paragraph mark (¶) should appear in the first line of the document, just to the right of the insertion point.

Saving a Document

Before you begin working on a document, you should save it with a new name. When you use the Save button on the Quick Access Toolbar to save a document for the first time, Word displays the Save As screen in Backstage view. In the Save As screen, you can select the location where you want to store your document. After that, when you click the Save button, Word saves your document to the same location you specified earlier and with the same name.

To save the document:

▶ **1.** On the Quick Access Toolbar, click the **Save** button 🖫. Word switches to the Save As screen in Backstage view, as shown in Figure 1–3.

| **Figure 1–3** | Save As screen in Backstage view |

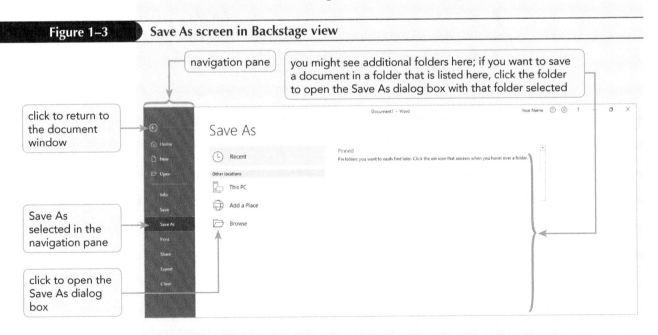

navigation pane

you might see additional folders here; if you want to save a document in a folder that is listed here, click the folder to open the Save As dialog box with that folder selected

click to return to the document window

Save As selected in the navigation pane

click to open the Save As dialog box

Because a document is now open, more commands are available in Backstage view than when you started Word. The **navigation pane** on the left contains commands for working with the open document and for changing settings that control how Word works.

▶ **2.** Click the **Browse** button. The Save As dialog box opens.

Trouble? If your instructor wants you to save your files to your OneDrive account, click OneDrive, and then log in to your account.

▶ **3.** Navigate to the location specified by your instructor. The default file name, "Doc1," appears in the File name box. You will change that to something more descriptive. See Figure 1–4.

Figure 1–4 | **Save As dialog box**

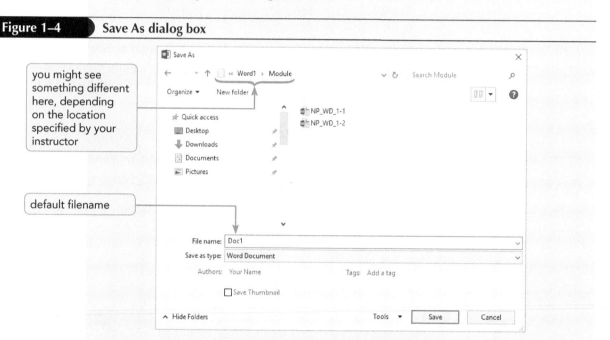

you might see something different here, depending on the location specified by your instructor

default filename

▶ **4.** Click the **File name** box, and then type **NP_WD_1_Letter**. The text you type replaces the selected text in the File name box.

▶ **5.** Click **Save**. The file is saved, the dialog box and Backstage view close, and the document window appears again, with the new file name in the title bar.

Now that you have saved the document, you can begin typing the letter. David has asked you to type a block-style letter to accompany some water conservation brochures that will be sent to Carla Zimmerman. Figure 1–5 shows the block-style letter you will create in this module.

Figure 1–5   Completed block-style letter

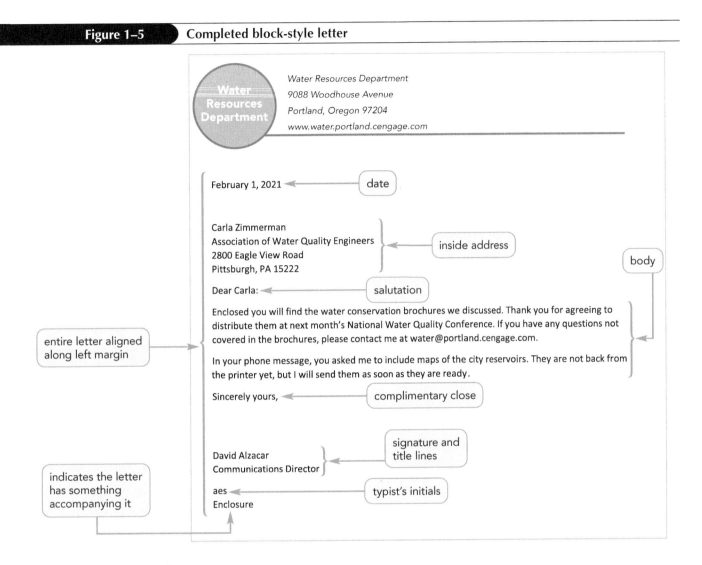

Written Communication: Creating a Business Letter

PROSKILLS

Several styles are considered acceptable for business letters. The main differences among the styles have to do with how parts of the letter are indented from the left margin. In the block style, which you will use in this module, each line of text starts at the left margin. In other words, nothing is indented. Another style is to indent the first line of each paragraph. The choice of style is largely a matter of personal preference, or it can be determined by the standards used in a particular business or organization. To further enhance your skills in writing business correspondence, you should consult an authoritative book on business writing that provides guidelines for creating a variety of business documents, such as *Business Communication: Process & Product*, by Mary Ellen Guffey and Dana Loewy.

Entering Text

The letters you type in a Word document appear at the current location of the blinking insertion point.

Inserting a Date with AutoComplete

The first item in a block-style business letter is the date. David plans to send the letter to Carla on February 1, so you need to insert that date into the document. To do so, you can take advantage of **AutoComplete**, a Word feature that automatically suggests dates and other regularly used items for you to insert. In this case, you can type the first few characters of the month and let Word insert the rest.

To insert the date:

▶ **1.** Type **Febr** (the first four letters of "February"). A ScreenTip appears above the letters, as shown in Figure 1–6, suggesting "February" as the complete word.

Figure 1–6   AutoComplete suggestion

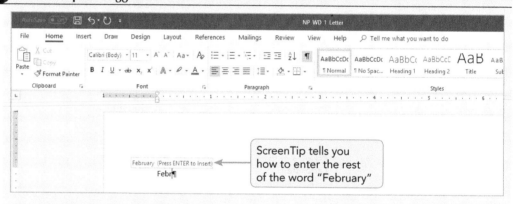

A **ScreenTip** is a label with descriptive text or an explanation about what to do next.

If you wanted to type something other than "February," you could continue typing to complete the word. In this case, you want to accept the AutoComplete suggestion.

▶ **2.** Press **ENTER**. The rest of the word "February" is inserted in the document. Note that AutoComplete works for long month names like February but not shorter ones like May, because "Ma" could be the beginning of many words besides "May."

▶ **3.** Press **SPACEBAR**, type **1, 2021** and then press **ENTER** twice, leaving a blank paragraph between the date and the line where you will begin typing the inside address, which contains the recipient's name and address. Notice the nonprinting character (•) after the word "February" and before the number "1," which indicates a space. Word inserts this nonprinting character every time you press SPACEBAR.

Trouble? If February happens to be the current month, you will see a second AutoComplete suggestion displaying the current date after you press SPACEBAR. To ignore that AutoComplete suggestion, continue typing the rest of the date, as instructed in Step 3.

Note that you can also insert the current date (as well as the current time) by using the Insert Date and Time button in the Text group on the Insert tab. This opens the Date and Time dialog box, where you can select from a variety of date and time formats. If you want Word to update the date or time automatically each time you re-open the document, select the Update automatically check box. In that case, Word inserts the date and time as a special element called a field, which you'll learn more about as you become a more experienced Word user. However, for typical correspondence, it makes more sense to deselect the Update automatically check box so the date and time are inserted in the document as ordinary text.

Continuing to Type the Block-Style Letter

In a block-style business letter, the inside address appears below the date, with one blank paragraph in between. Some style guides recommend including even more space between the date and the inside address. But in the short letter you are typing, more space would make the document look out of balance.

To insert the inside address:

▶ **1.** Type the following information, pressing **ENTER** after each item:

Carla Zimmerman

Association of Water Quality Engineers

2800 Eagle View Road

Pittsburgh, PA 15222

Remember to press ENTER after you type the zip code. Your screen should look like Figure 1–7. Don't be concerned if the lines of the inside address seem too far apart. You'll use the default spacing for now, and then adjust it after you finish typing the letter.

Figure 1–7	Letter with inside address

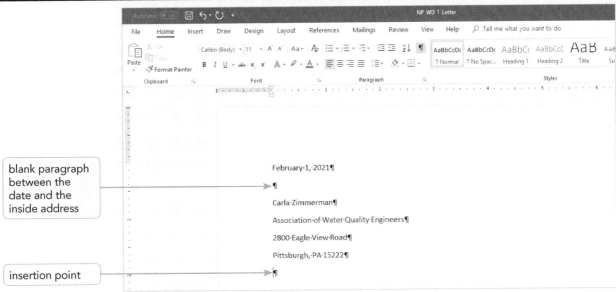

blank paragraph between the date and the inside address

insertion point

Trouble? If you make a mistake while typing, press BACKSPACE to delete the incorrect character, and then type the correct character.

Now you can move on to the salutation and the body of the letter. As you type the body of the letter, notice that Word automatically moves the insertion point to a new line when the current line is full.

To type the salutation and the body of the letter:

▶ 1. Type **Dear Carla:** and then press **ENTER** to start a new paragraph for the body of the letter.

▶ 2. Type the following sentence, including the period: **Enclosed you will find the sustainability brochures we discussed.**

▶ 3. Press **SPACEBAR**. Note that you should only include one space between sentences.

▶ 4. Type the following sentence, including the period: **Thank you for agreeing to distribute them at next month's National Water Quality Conference.**

▶ 5. On the Quick Access Toolbar, click the **Save** button 🖫 . Word saves the document as **NP_WD_1_Letter** to the same location you specified earlier.

The next sentence you need to type includes David's email address.

Typing a Hyperlink

When you type an email address and then press the SPACEBAR or ENTER, Word converts it to a hyperlink, with blue font and an underline. A **hyperlink** is a specially formatted word, phrase, or graphic which, when clicked or tapped, lets you display a webpage on the Internet, another file, an email, or another location within the same file; it is sometimes called hypertext or a link. Hyperlinks are useful in documents that you plan to distribute via email. In printed documents, where blue font and underlines can be distracting, you'll usually want to convert a hyperlink back to regular text.

To add a sentence containing an email address:

▶ 1. Press **SPACEBAR**, and then type the following sentence, including the period: **If you have any questions not covered in the brochures, please contact me at water@portland.cengage.com.**

▶ 2. Press **ENTER**. Word converts the email address to a hyperlink, with blue font and an underline. The same thing would happen if you pressed SPACEBAR instead of ENTER.

▶ 3. Position the pointer over the hyperlink. A ScreenTip appears, indicating that you could press and hold CTRL and then click the link to follow it—that is, to open an email message addressed to the Water Resources Department.

▶ 4. With the pointer positioned over the hyperlink, right-click—that is, press the right mouse button. A shortcut menu opens with commands related to working with hyperlinks.

You can right-click many items in the Word window to display a **shortcut menu** with commands related to the item you right-clicked. The **Mini toolbar** also appears when you right-click or select text, giving you easy access to the buttons and settings most often used when formatting text. See Figure 1–8.

Figure 1–8   Shortcut menu

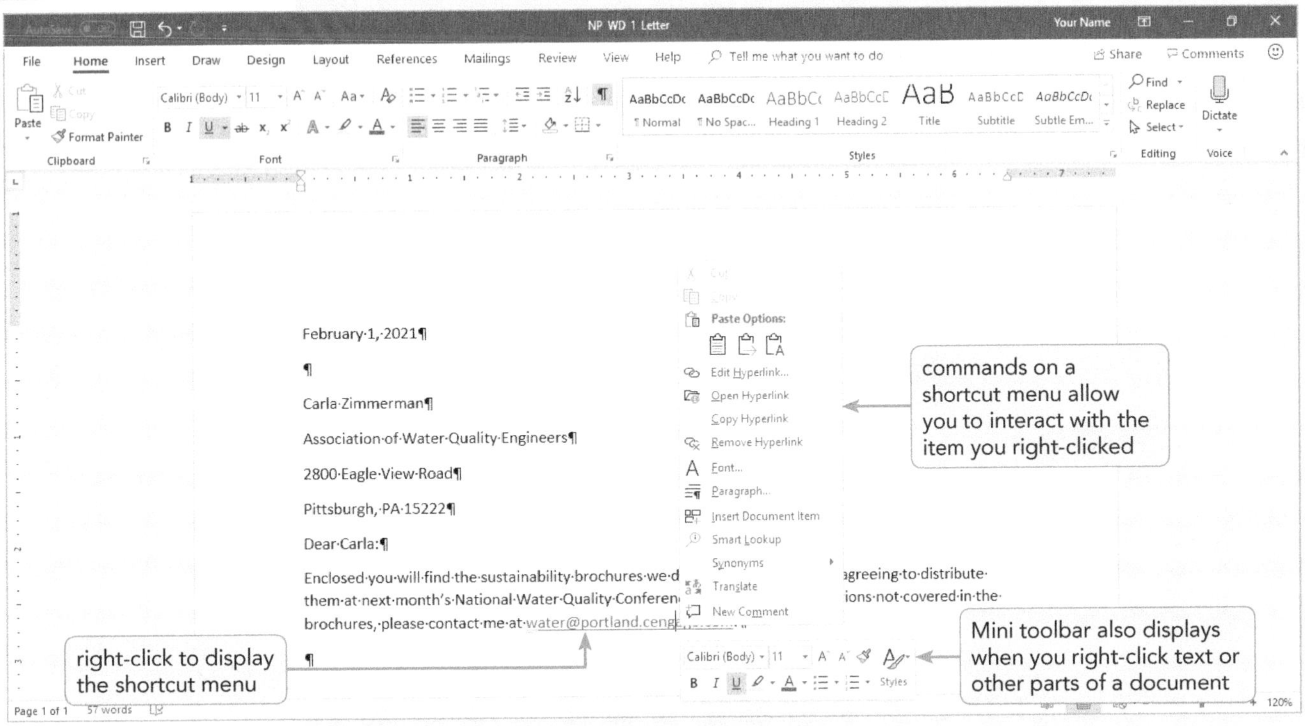

February·1,·2021¶

¶

Carla·Zimmerman¶

Association·of·Water·Quality·Engineers¶

2800·Eagle·View·Road¶

Pittsburgh,·PA·15222¶

Dear·Carla:¶

Enclosed·you·will·find·the·sustainability·brochures·we·d... ...agreeing·to·distribute·
them·at·next·month's·National·Water·Quality·Conferen... ...ions·not·covered·in·the·
brochures,·please·contact·me·at·water@portland.cenge...

commands on a shortcut menu allow you to interact with the item you right-clicked

right-click to display the shortcut menu

Mini toolbar also displays when you right-click text or other parts of a document

5. Click **Remove Hyperlink** in the shortcut menu. The shortcut menu and the Mini toolbar are no longer visible. The email address is now formatted in black, like the rest of the document text.

6. On the Quick Access Toolbar, click the **Save** button.

Using the Undo and Redo Buttons

When you first open Word, you see the Undo button and the Repeat button in the Quick Access Toolbar. To undo (or reverse) the last thing you did in a document, you can click the Undo button on the Quick Access Toolbar. Once you click the Undo button, the Repeat button is replaced with the Redo button. To restore your original change, click the Redo button, which reverses the action of the Undo button (or redoes the undo). To undo more than your last action, you can continue to click the Undo button, or you can click the Undo arrow on the Quick Access Toolbar to open a list of your most recent actions. When you click an action in the list, Word undoes every action in the list up to and including the action you clicked.

David asks you to change "sustainability" to "water conservation" in the first sentence you typed. You'll make the change now. If David decides he doesn't like it after all, you can always undo it. To delete a character, space, or blank paragraph to the right of the insertion point, you press DEL, or to delete an entire word, you can press CTRL+DEL. To delete a character, space, or blank paragraph to the left of the insertion point, you press BACKSPACE, or to delete an entire word, you can press CTRL+BACKSPACE.

To change the word "sustainability":

▸ **1.** Press the ↑ key twice and then press the ← key as necessary to move the insertion point to the left of the first "s" in the word "sustainability."

▸ **2.** Press and hold **CTRL**, and then press **DEL** to delete the word "sustainability."

▸ **3.** Type **water conservation** as a replacement, and then press **SPACEBAR**. After reviewing the sentence, David decides he prefers the original wording, so you'll undo the change.

▸ **4.** On the Quick Access Toolbar, click the **Undo** button ↶. The phrase "water conservation" is removed from the sentence.

▸ **5.** Click the **Undo** button ↶ again to restore the word "sustainability."

David decides that he does want to use "water conservation" after all. Instead of retyping it, you'll redo the undo.

TIP

You can also press CTRL+Z to execute the Undo command, and press CTRL+Y to execute the Redo command.

▸ **6.** On the Quick Access Toolbar, click the **Redo** button ↷ twice. The phrase "water conservation" replaces "sustainability" in the document, so that the phrase reads "…the water conservation brochures we discussed."

▸ **7.** Press and hold **CTRL**, and then press **END** to move the insertion point to the blank paragraph at the end of the document.

Trouble? If you are working on a small keyboard, you might need to press and hold a key labeled "Function" or "FN" before pressing END.

▸ **8.** On the Quick Access Toolbar, click the **SAVE** button 🖫. Word saves your letter with the same name and to the same location you specified earlier.

In the previous steps, you used the arrow keys and a key combination to move the insertion point to specific locations in the document. For your reference, Figure 1–9 summarizes the most common keystrokes for moving the insertion point in a document.

Figure 1–9   **Keystrokes for moving the insertion point**

To Move the Insertion Point	Press
Left or right one character at a time	← or →
Up or down one line at a time	↑ or ↓
Left or right one word at a time	CTRL+ ← or CTRL+ →
Up or down one paragraph at a time	CTRL+ ↑ or CTRL+ ↓
To the beginning or to the end of the current line	HOME or END
To the beginning or to the end of the document	CTRL+HOME or CTRL+END
To the previous screen or to the next screen	PAGE UP or PAGE DOWN
To the top or to the bottom of the document window	ALT+CTRL+PAGE UP or ALT+CTRL+PAGE DOWN

Correcting Errors as You Type

As you have seen, you can press BACKSPACE or DEL to remove an error, and then type a correction. In many cases, however, the AutoCorrect feature will do the work for you. Among other things, **AutoCorrect** automatically detects and corrects common typing errors, such as typing "adn" instead of "and." For example, you might have noticed AutoCorrect at work if you forgot to capitalize the first letter in a sentence as you typed the letter. After you type this kind of error, AutoCorrect automatically corrects it when you press SPACEBAR, TAB, or ENTER.

Word draws your attention to other potential errors by marking them with underlines. If you type a word that doesn't match the correct spelling in the Word dictionary, or if a word is not in the dictionary at all, a wavy red line appears beneath it. A wavy red underline also appears if you mistakenly type the same word twice in a row. Misused words (for example, "you're" instead of "your") are underlined with a double blue line, as are problems with punctuation, and potential grammar errors, such as a singular verb used with a plural subject. Possible wordiness is marked with a dotted brown underline, although keep in mind that this feature does not produce consistent results. Word might mark a phrase as wordy in one document, but then not mark the same phrase in a different document. This feature can be a helpful guide, but ultimately you'll need to make your own decisions about whether a phrase could be more concise.

You'll see how this works as you continue typing the letter and make some intentional typing errors.

To learn more about correcting errors as you type:

▌ 1. Type the following sentence, including the errors: **in you're phone mesage, you asked me me to include maps of teh city reservoirres. They are not back from the printer yet, but I will send them as soon as they are actually ready.**

As you type, AutoCorrect changes the lowercase "i" at the beginning of the sentence to uppercase. It also changes "mesage" to "message" and "teh" to "the." Also, the incorrectly used word "you're" is marked with a double blue underline. The second "me" and the spelling error "reservoirres" are marked with wavy red underlines.

▌ 2. Press **ENTER**. One additional error is now visible—the phrase "actually ready" is marked with a dotted brown underline, indicating a lack of conciseness. See Figure 1–10.

Figure 1–10   Errors marked in the document

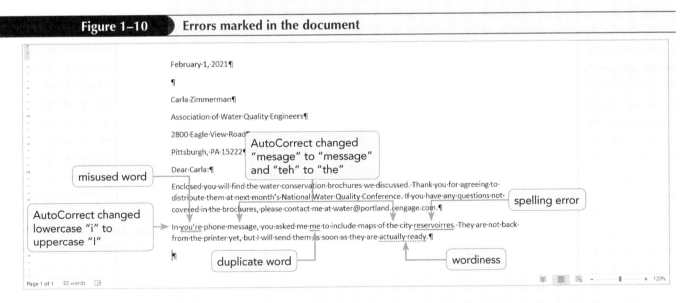

To correct an error marked with an underline, you can right-click the error and then click a replacement in the shortcut menu. If you don't see the correct word in the shortcut menu, click anywhere in the document to close the menu, and then type the correction yourself. You can also bypass the shortcut menu entirely and simply delete the error and type a correction.

To correct the spelling, grammar, and wordiness errors:

▶ **1.** Right-click **you're** to display the shortcut menu shown in Figure 1–11.

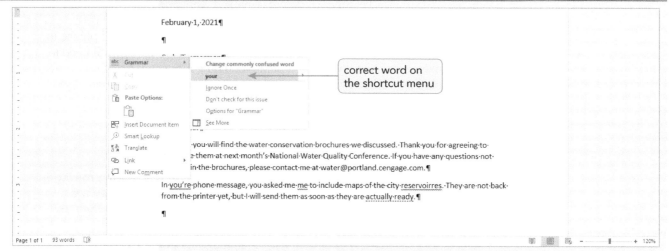

Trouble? If you see a shortcut menu other than the one shown in Figure 1–11, you didn't right-click exactly on the word "you're." Press ESC to close the menu, and then repeat Step 1.

▶ **2.** On the shortcut menu, click **your**. The correct word is inserted into the sentence, and the shortcut menu closes.

▶ **3.** Use a shortcut menu to replace the spelling error "reservoirres" with the correct word "reservoirs."

You could use a shortcut menu to remove the second instance of "me," but in the next step you'll try a different method—selecting the word and deleting it.

TIP

To deselect highlighted text, click anywhere in the document.

▶ **4.** Double-click anywhere in the underlined word **me**. The word and the space following it are highlighted in gray, indicating that they are selected. The Mini toolbar is also visible, but you can ignore it.

Trouble? If the entire paragraph is selected, you triple-clicked the word by mistake. Click anywhere in the document to deselect it, and then repeat Step 4.

▶ **5.** Press **DEL**. The second instance of "me" and the space following it are deleted from the sentence. Finally, you need to correct the error related to concise language.

▶ **6.** Right-click the phrase **actually ready** and use the shortcut menu to choose the more concise option, **ready**.

▶ **7.** On the Quick Access Toolbar, click the **Save** button 🖫.

You can see how quick and easy it is to correct common typing errors with AutoCorrect and the multicolored underlines, especially in a short document that you are typing yourself. If you are working on a longer document or a document typed by someone else, you'll also want to have Word check the entire document for errors. You'll learn how to do this in Session 1.2.

Next, you'll finish typing the letter.

To finish typing the letter:

▶ **1.** Press **CTRL+END**. The insertion point moves to the end of the document.

▶ **2.** Type **Sincerely yours,** (including the comma).

▶ **3.** Press **ENTER** three times to leave space for the signature.

▶ **4.** Type **David Alzacar** and then press **ENTER**. Because David's last name is not in the Word dictionary, a wavy red line appears below it. You can ignore this for now.

▶ **5.** Type your first, middle, and last initials in lowercase, and then press **ENTER**. AutoCorrect wrongly assumes your first initial is the first letter of a new sentence and changes it to uppercase. If your initials do not form a word, a red wavy underline appears beneath them. You can ignore this for now.

▶ **6.** On the Quick Access Toolbar, click the **Undo** button ↺. Word reverses the change, replacing the uppercase initial with a lowercase one.

▶ **7.** Type **Enclosure** so your screen looks like Figure 1–12.

TIP

You need to include your initials in a letter only if you are typing it for someone else.

Figure 1–12   **Letter to Carla Zimmerman**

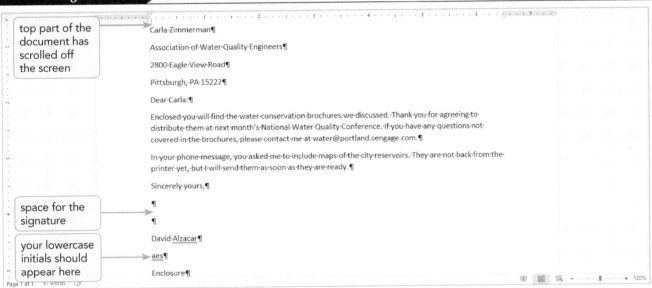

top part of the document has scrolled off the screen

Carla·Zimmerman¶

Association·of·Water·Quality·Engineers¶

2800·Eagle·View·Road¶

Pittsburgh,·PA·15222¶

Dear·Carla:¶

Enclosed·you·will·find·the·water·conservation·brochures·we·discussed.·Thank·you·for·agreeing·to·distribute·them·at·next·month's·National·Water·Quality·Conference.·If·you·have·any·questions·not·covered·in·the·brochures,·please·contact·me·at·water@portland.cengage.com.¶

In·your·phone·message,·you·asked·me·to·include·maps·of·the·city·reservoirs.·They·are·not·back·from·the·printer·yet,·but·I·will·send·them·as·soon·as·they·are·ready.¶

Sincerely·yours,¶

space for the signature

¶

¶

David·Alzacar¶

your lowercase initials should appear here

aes¶

Enclosure¶

Page 1 of 1   97 Words   ⊡₂   120%

Notice that as you continue to add lines to the letter, the top part of the letter scrolls off the screen. For example, in Figure 1–12, you can no longer see the date. Don't be concerned if more or less of the document has scrolled off the screen on your computer.

▶ **8.** Save the document.

Now that you have finished typing the letter, you need to proofread it.

Proofreading a Document

After you finish typing a document, you need to proofread it carefully from start to finish. Part of proofreading a document in Word is removing all wavy underlines, either by correcting the text or by telling Word to ignore the underlined text because it isn't really an error. For example, David's last name is marked as an error, when in fact it is spelled correctly. You need to tell Word to ignore "Alzacar" wherever it occurs in the letter. You need to do the same for your initials.

To proofread and correct the remaining marked errors in the letter:

▶ **1.** Right-click **Alzacar**. A shortcut menu opens.

▶ **2.** On the shortcut menu, click **Ignore All** to indicate that Word should ignore the word "Alzacar" each time it occurs in this document. (The Ignore All option can be particularly helpful in a longer document.) The wavy red underline disappears from below David's last name.

▶ **3.** If you see a wavy red underline below your initials, right-click your initials. On the shortcut menu, click **Ignore All** to remove the red wavy underline. To choose to ignore something just once in a document, you could click See More in the shortcut menu, and then click Ignore Once in the Editor pane. You'll learn how to use the Editor pane in Session 1.2.

▶ **4.** Read the entire letter to proofread it for typing errors. Correct any errors using the techniques you have just learned.

▶ **5.** Scroll up, if necessary, so you can see the complete inside address, which you'll work on next, and then save the document.

The text of the letter is finished. Now you need to think about its appearance—that is, you need to think about the document's **formatting**. First, you need to adjust the spacing in the inside address.

Adjusting Paragraph and Line Spacing

When typing a letter, you might need to adjust two types of spacing—paragraph spacing and line spacing. **Paragraph spacing** is the space that appears directly above and below a paragraph. In Word, any text that ends with a paragraph mark symbol (¶) is a paragraph. So, a **paragraph** can be a group of words that is many lines long, a single word, or even a blank line, in which case you see a paragraph mark alone on a single line. A paragraph can also contain a picture instead of text. Paragraph spacing is measured in points; a **point** is 1/72 of an inch. The default setting for paragraph spacing in Word is 0 points before each paragraph and 8 points after each paragraph. When laying out a complicated document, resist the temptation to simply press ENTER to insert extra space between paragraphs. Changing the paragraph spacing gives you much more control over the final result.

Line spacing is the space between lines of text within a paragraph. Word offers a number of preset line spacing options. The 1.0 setting, which is often called **single-spacing**, allows the least amount of space between lines. All other line spacing options are measured as multiples of 1.0 spacing. For example, 2.0 spacing (sometimes called **double-spacing**) allows for twice the space of single-spacing. The default line spacing setting is 1.08, which allows a little more space between lines than 1.0 spacing.

Now consider the line and paragraph spacing in the letter. The four lines of the inside address are too far apart. That's because each line of the inside address is actually a separate paragraph. Word inserted the default 8 points of paragraph spacing after each of these separate paragraphs. See Figure 1–13.

Figure 1–13   **Line and paragraph spacing in the letter to Carla Zimmerman**

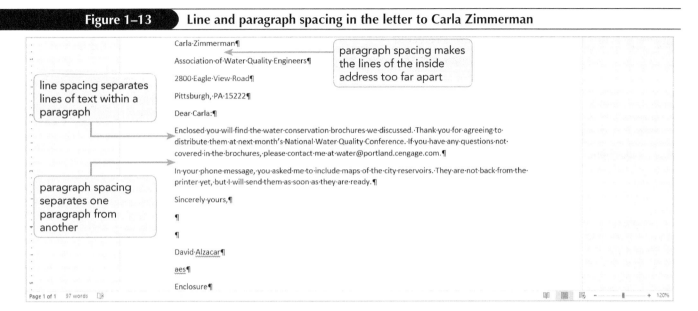

To follow the conventions of a block-style business letter, the four paragraphs that make up the inside address should have the same spacing as the lines of text within a single paragraph—that is, they need to be closer together. You can accomplish this by removing the 8 points of paragraph spacing after the first two paragraphs in the inside address. To conform to the block-style business letter format, you also need to close up the spacing between your initials and the word "Enclosure" at the end of the letter.

To adjust paragraph and line spacing in Word, you use the Line and Paragraph Spacing button in the Paragraph group on the Home tab. Clicking this button displays a menu of preset line spacing options (1.0, 1.15, 2.0, and so on). The menu also includes two paragraph spacing options that allow you to add 12 points before a paragraph or remove the default 8 points of space after a paragraph.

Next you'll adjust the paragraph spacing in the inside address and after your initials. In the process, you'll also learn some techniques for selecting text in a document.

To adjust the paragraph spacing in the inside address and after your initials:

1. Move the pointer to the white space just to the left of "Carla Zimmerman" until it changes to a right-pointing arrow ⟰.

2. Click the mouse button. The entire name, including the paragraph symbol after it, is selected.

   Trouble? If the Mini toolbar obscures your view of Carla's name, move the pointer away from the address to close the Mini toolbar.

3. Press and hold the mouse button, drag the pointer down to select the next two paragraphs of the inside address as well, and then release the mouse button.

   Carla's name, the name of her organization, and the street address are selected as well as the paragraph marks at the end of each paragraph. You did not select the paragraph containing the city, state, and zip code because you do not need to change its paragraph spacing. See Figure 1–14.

TIP

The white space in the left margin is sometimes referred to as the selection bar because you can click it to select text.

Figure 1–14 Inside address selected

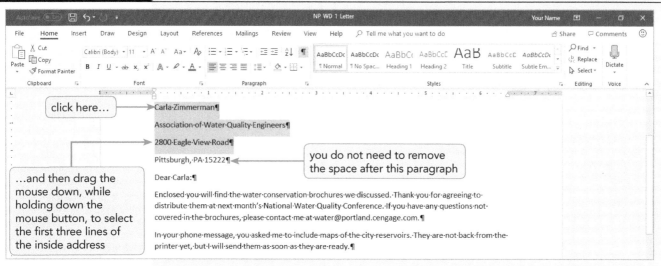

4. Make sure the Home tab is selected on the ribbon.

5. In the Paragraph group on the Home tab, click the **Line and Paragraph Spacing** button. A menu of line spacing options appears, with two paragraph spacing options at the bottom. See Figure 1–15.

Figure 1–15 Line and paragraph spacing options

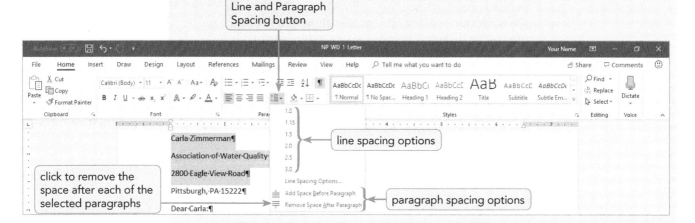

At the moment, you are interested only in the paragraph spacing options. Your goal is to remove the default 8 points of space after the first two paragraphs in the inside address.

6. Click **Remove Space After Paragraph**. The menu closes, and the paragraphs are now closer together.

7. Double-click your initials to select them and the paragraph symbol after them.

8. In the Paragraph group, click the **Line and Paragraph Spacing** button, click **Remove Space After Paragraph**, and then click anywhere in the document to deselect your initials.

Another way to compress lines of text is to press SHIFT+ENTER at the end of a line. This inserts a **manual line break**, also called a **soft return**, which moves the insertion point to a new line without starting a new paragraph. You will use this technique now as you add David's title below his name in the signature line.

To use a manual line break to move the insertion point to a new line without starting a new paragraph:

▶ **1.** Click to the right of the "r" in "Alzacar."

▶ **2.** Press **SHIFT+ENTER**. Word inserts a small arrow symbol ↵, indicating a manual line break, and the insertion point moves to the line below David's name.

▶ **3.** Type **Communications Director**. David's title now appears directly below his name with no intervening paragraph spacing, just like the lines of the inside address.

▶ **4.** Save the document.

INSIGHT

Understanding Spacing between Paragraphs

When discussing the correct format for letters, many business style guides talk about single-spacing and double-spacing between paragraphs. In these style guides, to single-space between paragraphs means to press ENTER once after each paragraph. Likewise, to double-space between paragraphs means to press ENTER twice after each paragraph. With the default paragraph spacing in Word 2019, however, you need to press ENTER only once after a paragraph. The space Word adds after a paragraph is not quite the equivalent of double-spacing, but it is enough to make it easy to see where one paragraph ends and another begins. Keep this in mind if you're accustomed to pressing ENTER twice; otherwise, you could end up with more space than you want between paragraphs.

As you corrected line and paragraph spacing in the previous set of steps, you used the mouse to select text. Word provides multiple ways to select, or highlight, text as you work. Figure 1–16 summarizes these methods and explains when to use them most effectively. Note that there are multiple ways to select each element in a document. Three especially useful options are: 1) selecting an entire paragraph by triple-clicking it; 2) selecting nonadjacent text by pressing and holding CTRL, and then dragging the mouse pointer to select multiple blocks of text; and 3) selecting an entire document by pressing CTRL+A.

Figure 1–16   Methods for selecting text

To Select	Mouse	Keyboard	Mouse and Keyboard
A word	Double-click the word	Move the insertion point to the beginning of the word, press and hold CTRL+SHIFT, and then press →	
A line	Click in the white space to the left of the line	Move the insertion point to the beginning of the line, press and hold SHIFT, and then press ↓	
A sentence	Click at the beginning of the sentence, then drag the pointer until the sentence is selected		Press and hold CTRL, then click any location within the sentence
Multiple lines	Click and drag in the white space to the left of the lines	Move the insertion point to the beginning of the first line, press and hold SHIFT, and then press ↓ until all the lines are selected	
A paragraph	Double-click in the white space to the left of the paragraph, or triple-click at any location within the paragraph	Move the insertion point to the beginning of the paragraph, press and hold CTRL+SHIFT, and then press ↓	
Multiple paragraphs	Click in the white space to the left of the first paragraph you want to select, and then drag to select the remaining paragraphs	Move the insertion point to the beginning of the first paragraph, press and hold CTRL+SHIFT, and then press ↓ until all the paragraphs are selected	
An entire document	Triple-click in the white space to the left of the document text	Press CTRL+A	Press and hold CTRL, and click in the white space to the left of the document text
A block of text	Click at the beginning of the block, then drag the pointer until the entire block is selected		Click at the beginning of the block, press and hold SHIFT, and then click at the end of the block
Nonadjacent blocks of text			Press and hold CTRL, then drag the mouse pointer to select multiple blocks of nonadjacent text

Adjusting the Margins

Another important aspect of document formatting is the amount of margin space between the document text and the edge of the page. You can check the document's margins by changing the Zoom level to display the entire page.

To change the Zoom level to display the entire page:

▶ **1.** On the ribbon, click the **View** tab.

▶ **2.** In the Zoom group, click the **One Page** button. The entire document is now visible in the Word window. See Figure 1–17.

Figure 1–17 ▶ **Document zoomed to show entire page**

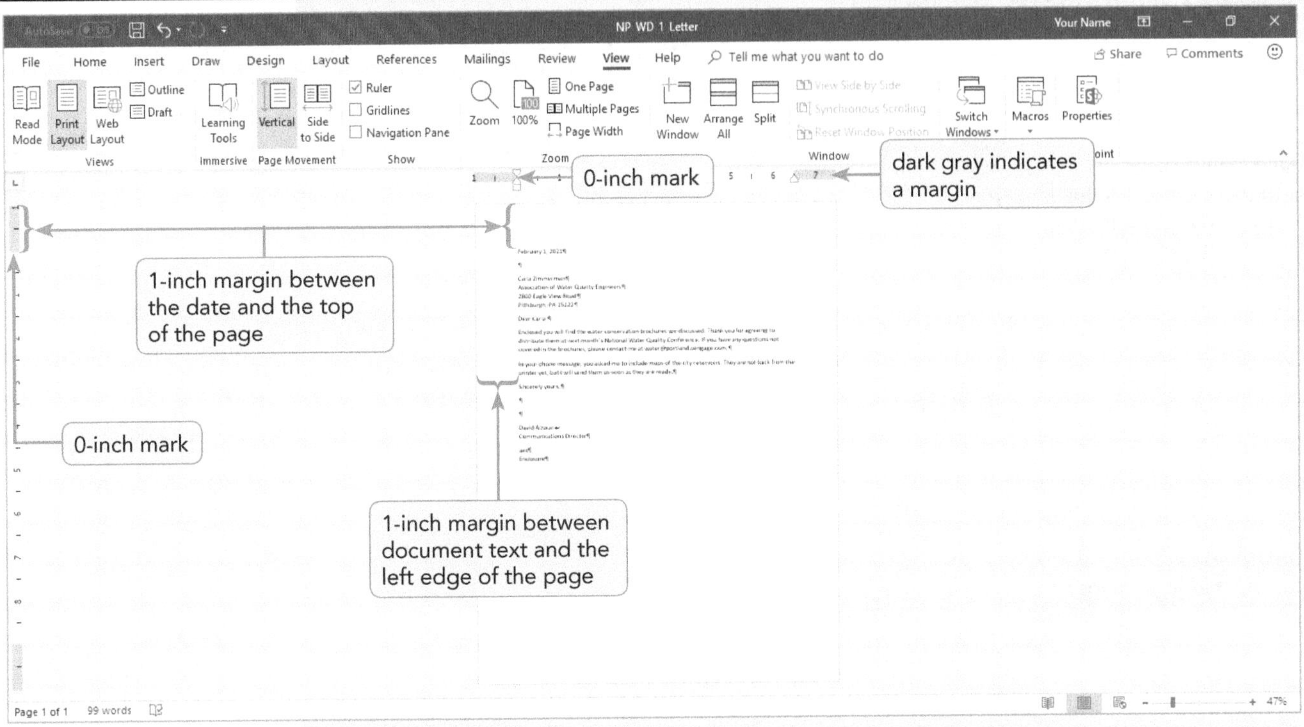

On the rulers, the margins appear dark gray. By default, Word documents include 1-inch margins on all sides of the document. By looking at the vertical ruler, you can see that the date in the letter, the first line in the document, is located 1 inch from the top of the page. Likewise, the horizontal ruler indicates the document text begins 1 inch from the left edge of the page.

Reading the measurements on the rulers can be tricky at first. On the horizontal ruler, the 0-inch mark is like the origin on a number line. You measure from the 0-inch mark to the left or to the right. On the vertical ruler, you measure up or down from the 0-inch mark.

David plans to print the letter on the Water Resources Department letterhead, which includes a graphic and the department's address. To allow more blank space for the letterhead, and to move the text down so that it doesn't look so crowded at the top of the page, you need to increase the top margin. The settings for changing the page margins are located on the Layout tab on the ribbon.

To change the page margins:

▶ **1.** On the ribbon, click the **Layout** tab. The Layout tab displays options for adjusting the layout of your document.

▶ **2.** In the Page Setup group, click the **Margins** button. The Margins gallery opens, as shown in Figure 1–18.

Figure 1–18   Margins gallery

most recent margin settings selected via the Custom Margins option; you may not see this

predefined, commonly used margin settings

click to access the custom margin settings

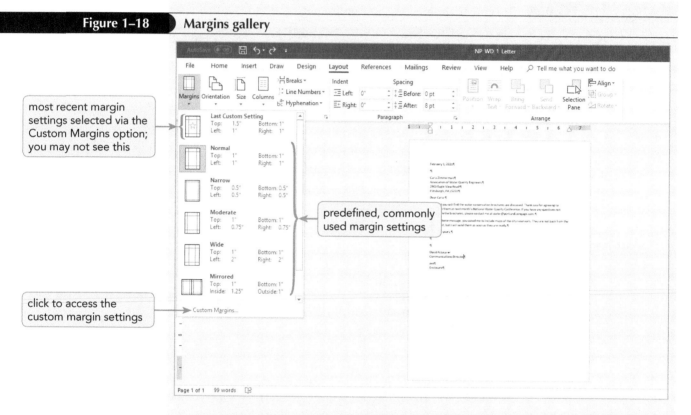

In the Margins gallery, you can choose from a number of predefined margin options, or you can click the Custom Margins command to select your own settings. After you create custom margin settings, the most recent set appears as an option at the top of the menu. For the current document, you will create custom margins.

▶ **3.** Click **Custom Margins**. The Page Setup dialog box opens with the Margins tab displayed. The default margin settings are displayed in the boxes at the top of the Margins tab. The top margin of 1" is already selected, ready for you to type a new margin setting.

▶ **4.** In the Top box in the Margins section, type **2.5**. You do not need to type an inch mark ("). See Figure 1–19.

Figure 1–19   Creating custom margins in the Page Setup dialog box

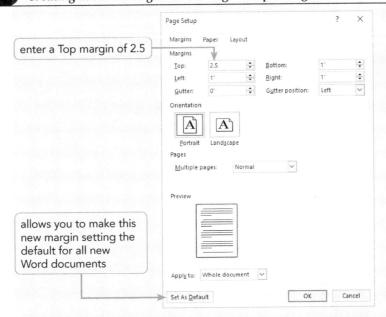

enter a Top margin of 2.5

allows you to make this new margin setting the default for all new Word documents

> **5.** Click **OK**. The text of the letter is now lower on the page. The page looks less crowded, with room for the company's letterhead.

> **6.** Change the Zoom level back to **120%**, and then save the document.

For most documents, the Word default of 1-inch margins is fine. In some professional settings, however, you might need to use a particular custom margin setting for all your documents. In that case, define the custom margins using the Margins tab in the Page Setup dialog box, and then click the Set As Default button to make your settings the default for all new documents. Keep in mind that most printers can't print to the edge of the page; if you select custom margins that are too narrow for your printer's specifications, Word alerts you to change your margin settings.

Previewing and Printing a Document

To make sure the document is ready to print, and to avoid wasting paper and time, you should first review it in Backstage view to make sure it will look right when printed. Like the One Page zoom setting you used earlier, the Print option in Backstage view displays a full-page preview of the document, allowing you to see how it will fit on the printed page. However, you cannot actually edit this preview. It simply provides one last opportunity to look at the document before printing.

To preview the document:

> **1.** Proofread the document one last time and correct any remaining errors.

> **2.** Click the **File** tab to display Backstage view.

> **3.** In the navigation pane, click **Print**.
>   The Print screen displays a full-page version of your document, showing how the letter will fit on the printed page. The Print settings to the left of the preview allow you to control a variety of print options. For example, you can change the number of copies from the default setting of "1." The 1 Page Per

Sheet button opens a menu where you can choose to print multiple pages on a single sheet of paper or to scale the printed page to a particular paper size. You can also use the navigation controls at the bottom of the screen to display other pages in a document. See Figure 1–20.

Figure 1–20 Print settings in Backstage view

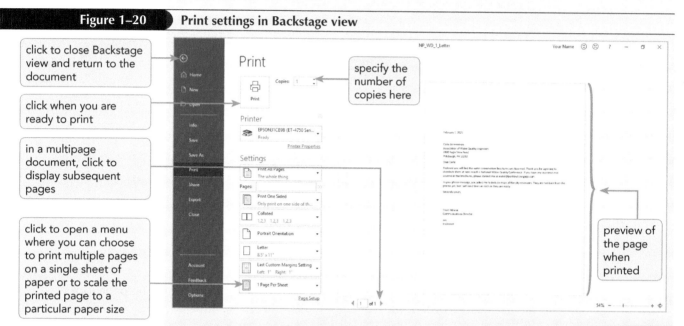

click to close Backstage view and return to the document

click when you are ready to print

in a multipage document, click to display subsequent pages

click to open a menu where you can choose to print multiple pages on a single sheet of paper or to scale the printed page to a particular paper size

specify the number of copies here

preview of the page when printed

4. Review your document and make sure its overall layout matches that of the document in Figure 1–20. If you notice a problem with paragraph breaks or spacing, click the **Back** button ⊙ at the top of the navigation pane to return to the document, make any necessary changes, and then start again at Step 2.

At this point, you can print the document or you can leave Backstage view and return to the document in Print Layout view. In the following steps, you should print the document only if your instructor asks you to. If you will be printing the document, make sure your printer is turned on and contains paper.

To leave Backstage view or to print the document:

1. Click the **Back** button ⊙ at the top of the navigation pane to leave Backstage view and return to the document in Print Layout view, or click the **Print** button. Backstage view closes, and the letter prints if you clicked the Print button.

2. **sam**↑ Click the **File** tab, and then click **Close** in the navigation pane to close the document without closing Word.

Next, David asks you to create an envelope he can use to send a water quality report to an environmental engineering publication.

Creating an Envelope

Before you can create the envelope, you need to open a new, blank document. To create a new document, you can start with a blank document—as you did with the letter to Carla Zimmerman—or you can start with one that already contains formatting and generic text commonly used in a variety of professional documents, such as a fax cover sheet or a memo. These preformatted files are called **templates**. You could use a template to create a formatted envelope, but to create a basic envelope for a business letter, it's better to start with a new, blank document.

To create a new document for the envelope:

▶ **1.** Click the **File** tab, and then click **New** in the navigation pane. The New screen is similar to the one you saw when you first started Word, with a blank document in the upper-left corner, along with a variety of templates. See Figure 1–21.

Figure 1–21   **New options in Backstage view**

use this search box to find even more templates online

document templates; your list of available templates may differ

scroll down to see more templates

click to create a blank document

▶ **2.** Click **Blank document**. A new document named Document2 opens in the document window, with the Home tab selected on the ribbon.

▶ **3.** If necessary, change the Zoom level to **120%**, and display nonprinting characters and the rulers.

▶ **4.** Save the new document as **NP_WD_1_Envelope** in the location specified by your instructor.

To create the envelope:

▶ **1.** On the ribbon, click the **Mailings** tab. The ribbon changes to display the various Mailings options.

▶ **2.** In the Create group, click the **Envelopes** button. The Envelopes and Labels dialog box opens, with the Envelopes tab displayed. The insertion point appears in the Delivery address box, ready for you to type the recipient's address. Depending on how your computer is set up, and whether you are working on your own computer or a school computer, you might see an address in the Return address box.

3. In the Delivery address box, type the following address, pressing **ENTER** to start each new line:

Belinda Harper

Journal of Urban Environmental Engineering

600 East Kelda Street

San Antonio, TX 78205

Because David will be using the department's printed envelopes, you don't need to print a return address on this envelope.

4. Click the **Omit** check box to insert a checkmark, if necessary.

At this point, if you had a printer stocked with envelopes, you could click the Print button to print the envelope. To save an envelope for printing later, you need to add it to the document. Your Envelopes and Labels dialog box should match the one in Figure 1–22.

Figure 1–22 Envelopes and Labels dialog box

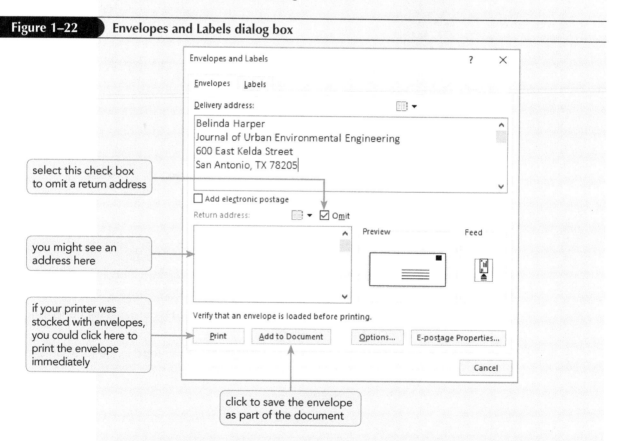

5. Click **Add to Document**. The dialog box closes, and you return to the document window. The envelope is inserted at the top of your document, with 1.0 line spacing. The double line with the words "Section Break (Next Page)" is related to how the envelope is formatted and will not be visible when you print the envelope. The envelope will print in the standard business envelope format. In this case, you added the envelope to a blank document, but you could also add an envelope to a completed letter, in which case Word adds the envelope as a new page before the letter.

▶ **6.** Save the document. David will print the envelope later, so you can close the document now.

▶ **7.** Click the **File** tab, and then click **Close** in the navigation pane. The document closes, but Word remains open.

You're finished creating the cover letter and the envelope. In the next session, you will modify a flyer by formatting the text and adding a photo.

INSIGHT

Creating Documents with Templates

Microsoft offers predesigned templates for all kinds of documents, including calendars, reports, and thank-you cards. You can use the scroll bar on the right of the New screen (shown earlier in Figure 1–21) to scroll down to see more templates, or you can use the Search for online templates box in the New screen to search among thousands of other options available at Office.com. When you open a template, you actually open a new document containing the formatting and text stored in the template, leaving the original template untouched. A typical template includes placeholder text that you replace with your own information.

Templates allow you to create stylish, professional-looking documents quickly and easily. To use them effectively, however, you need to be knowledgeable about Word and its many options for manipulating text, graphics, and page layouts. Otherwise, the complicated formatting of some Word templates can be more frustrating than helpful. As you become a more experienced Word user, you'll learn how to create your own templates.

REVIEW

Session 1.1 Quick Check

1. What Word feature automatically inserts dates and other regularly used items for you?

2. Explain how to display nonprinting characters.

3. In a block-style letter, does the inside address appear above or below the date?

4. Explain how to use a hyperlink in a Word document to open a new email message.

5. Define the term "paragraph spacing."

6. Explain how to display a shortcut menu with options for correcting a word with a wavy red underline.

Session 1.2 Visual Overview:

Alignment buttons control the text's **alignment** —that is, the way it lines up horizontally between the left and right margins. Here, the Center button is selected because the text containing the insertion point is center-aligned.

You can click the Clear All Formatting button to restore selected text to the default font, font size, and color.

Clicking the Format Painter button displays the Format Painter pointer, which you can use to copy formatting from the selected text to other text in the document.

The Font group on the Home tab includes the Font box and the Font size box for setting the font and the font size, respectively. A **font** is a set of characters that uses the same typeface.

You click the Shading arrow to apply a colored background to a selected paragraph.

This document has a landscape orientation, meaning it is wider than it is tall.

You can insert a photo or another type of picture in a document by using the **Pictures button** located on the Insert tab of the ribbon. After you insert a photo or another picture, you can format it with a style that adds a border or a shadow or changes its shape.

The white font color used on this text is an example of **character formatting** because it affects individual characters.

The boldface and blue font color applied to this text are examples of formatting that you should use sparingly to draw attention to a specific part of a document.

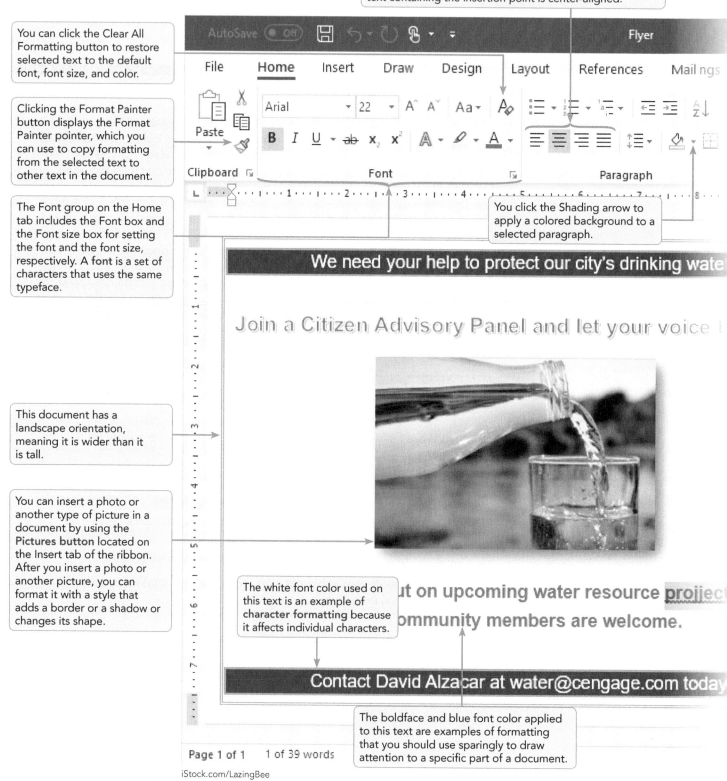

Page 1 of 1   1 of 39 words

iStock.com/LazingBee

Formatting a Document

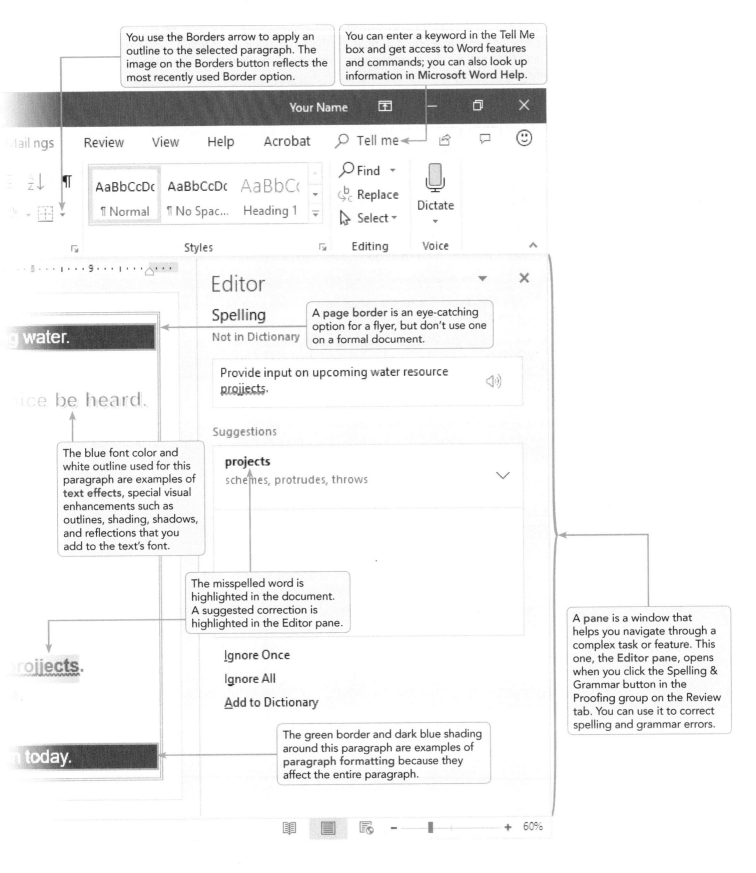

You use the Borders arrow to apply an outline to the selected paragraph. The image on the Borders button reflects the most recently used Border option.

You can enter a keyword in the Tell Me box and get access to Word features and commands; you can also look up information in Microsoft Word Help.

A page border is an eye-catching option for a flyer, but don't use one on a formal document.

The blue font color and white outline used for this paragraph are examples of **text effects**, special visual enhancements such as outlines, shading, shadows, and reflections that you add to the text's font.

The misspelled word is highlighted in the document. A suggested correction is highlighted in the Editor pane.

A pane is a window that helps you navigate through a complex task or feature. This one, the Editor pane, opens when you click the Spelling & Grammar button in the Proofing group on the Review tab. You can use it to correct spelling and grammar errors.

The green border and dark blue shading around this paragraph are examples of **paragraph formatting** because they affect the entire paragraph.

Your Name

Mailings   Review   View   Help   Acrobat   Tell me

AaBbCcDc   AaBbCcDc   AaBbCc

¶ Normal   ¶ No Spac...   Heading 1

Styles

Find
Replace
Select

Dictate

Editing   Voice

Editor

Spelling

Not in Dictionary

Provide input on upcoming water resource projjects.

Suggestions

projects
schemes, protrudes, throws

Ignore Once

Ignore All

Add to Dictionary

60%

Opening an Existing Document

In this session, you'll complete a flyer encouraging community members to join a citizen advisory panel. David has already typed the text of the flyer, inserted a photo into it, and saved it as a Word document. He would like you to check the document for spelling and grammar errors, format the flyer to make it eye-catching and easy to read, and then replace the current photo with a new one. You'll start by opening the document.

To open the flyer document:

▶ **1.** **sam** ⬇ On the ribbon, click the **File** tab to open Backstage view, and then verify that **Open** is selected in the navigation pane. On the left side of the Open screen is a list of places you can go to locate other documents, and on the right is a list of recently opened documents.

   Trouble? If you closed Word at the end of the previous session, start Word now, click Open Other Documents at the bottom of the navigation pane in Backstage view, and then begin with Step 2.

▶ **2.** Click the **Browse** button. The Open dialog box opens.

   Trouble? If your instructor asked you to store your files to your OneDrive account, click OneDrive, and then log in to your account.

▶ **3.** Navigate to the **Word1 > Module** folder included with your Data Files, click **NP_WD_1-1.docx** in the file list, and then click **Open**. The document opens with the insertion point blinking in the first line of the document.

Before making changes to David's document, you will save it with a new name. Saving the document with a different file name creates a copy of the file and leaves the original file unchanged in case you want to work through the module again.

To save the document with a new name:

▶ **1.** On the ribbon, click the **File** tab.

▶ **2.** In the navigation pane in Backstage view, click **Save As**. Save the document as **NP_WD_1_Flyer** in the location specified by your instructor. Backstage view closes, and the document window appears again with the new file name in the title bar. The original NP_WD_1-1.docx document closes, remaining unchanged.

PROSKILLS

Decision Making: Creating Effective Documents

Before you create a new document or revise an existing document, take a moment to think about your audience. Ask yourself these questions:

- Who is your audience?
- What do they know?
- What do they need to know?
- How can the document you are creating change your audience's behavior or opinions?

Every decision you make about your document should be based on your answers to these questions. To take a simple example, if you are creating a flyer to announce an upcoming seminar on college financial aid, your audience would be students and their parents. They probably all know what the term "financial aid" means, so you don't need to explain that in your flyer. Instead, you can focus on telling them what they need to know—the date, time, and location of the seminar. The behavior you want to affect, in this case, is whether your audience will show up for the seminar. By making the flyer professional looking and easy to read, you increase the chance that they will.

You might find it more challenging to answer these questions about your audience when creating more complicated documents, such as corporate reports. But the focus remains the same—connecting with the audience. As you are deciding what information to include in your document, remember that the goal of a professional document is to convey the information as effectively as possible to your target audience.

Before revising a document for someone else, it's a good idea to familiarize yourself with its overall structure.

To review the document:

▶ 1. Verify that the document is displayed in Print Layout view and that nonprinting characters and the rulers are displayed. For now, you can ignore the wavy underlines that appear in the document.

▶ 2. Change the Zoom level to **120%**, if necessary, and then scroll down, if necessary, so that you can read the last line of the document.

At this point, the document is very simple. By the time you are finished, it will look like the document shown in the Session 1.2 Visual Overview, with the spelling and grammar errors corrected. Figure 1–23 summarizes the tasks you will perform.

Figure 1-23 **Formatting changes requested by David**

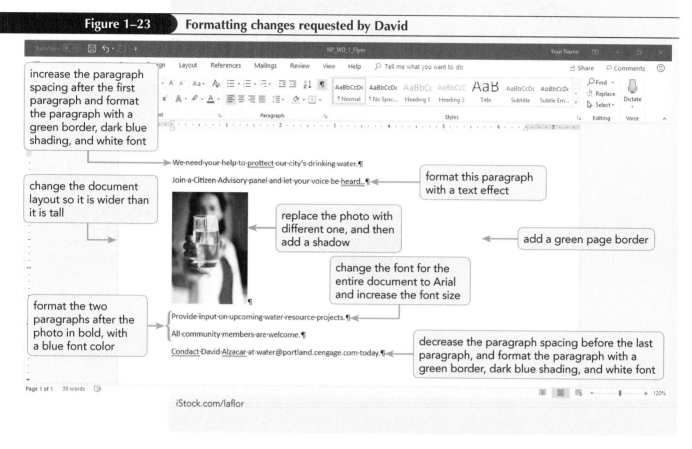

iStock.com/laflor

You will start by correcting the spelling and grammar errors.

Using the Editor Pane

As you type, Word marks possible spelling and grammatical errors, as well as wordiness, with underlines so you can quickly go back and correct those errors. A more thorough way of checking the spelling in a document is to use the Editor pane to check a document word by word for a variety of errors. You can customize the spelling and grammar settings to add or ignore certain types of errors.

David asks you to use the Editor pane to check the flyer for mistakes. Before you do, you'll review the various Spelling and Grammar settings.

To review the Spelling and Grammar settings:

1. On the ribbon, click the **File** tab, and then click **Options** in the navigation pane. The Word Options dialog box opens. You can use this dialog box to change a variety of settings related to how Word looks and works.

2. In the left pane, click **Proofing**.

   Note the three selected options in the "When correcting spelling and grammar in Word" section. These options tell you that Word will check for misspellings, grammatical errors, and frequently confused words as you type, marking them with wavy underlines as necessary.

3. In the "When correcting spelling and grammar in Word" section, click **Settings**. The Grammar Settings dialog box opens. Here you can control the

types of grammar errors Word checks for. All of the boxes in the Grammar section are selected by default, which is what you want. See Figure 1–24.

Figure 1–24   **Grammar Settings dialog box**

click to display settings related to proofing a document

click to recheck words that you chose to ignore in a previous spelling and grammar check

click to display the Grammar Settings dialog box

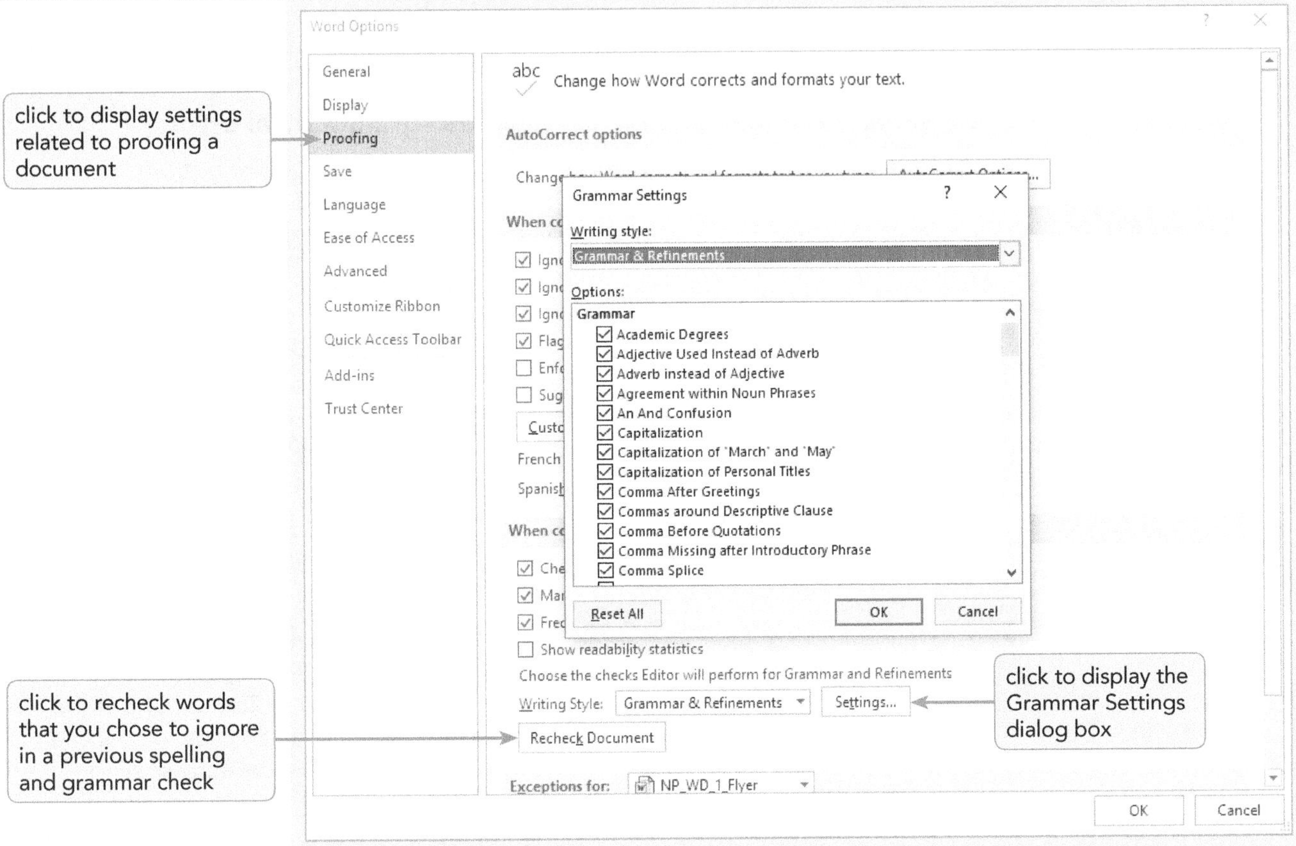

▶ **4.** Scroll down in the Grammar Settings dialog box to display the Clarity and Conciseness settings. By default, only Nominalizations and Wordiness are selected.

▶ **5.** Click **Cancel** to close the Grammar Settings dialog box and return to the Word Options dialog box.

Note that the results of the Spelling and Grammar checker are sometimes hard to predict. For example, in some documents Word will mark a misused word or duplicate punctuation as errors and then fail to mark the same items as errors in another document. Also, if you choose to ignore a misspelling in a document, and then, without closing Word, type the same misspelled word in another document, Word will probably not mark it as an error. Sometimes, if you change a document's line or paragraph spacing, Word will mark text as errors that it previously did not. These issues can be especially problematic when working on a document typed by someone else. So to ensure that you get the best possible results, it's a good idea to click Recheck Document in the Word Options dialog box before you use the Spelling and Grammar checker.

▶ **6.** Click the **Recheck Document** button, and then click **Yes** in the warning dialog box.

▶ **7.** In the Word Options dialog box, click **OK** to close the dialog box. You return to the document.

Now you are ready to check the document's spelling and grammar. All errors marked with red underlines are considered spelling errors, while all errors marked with blue underlines are considered grammatical errors. Errors marked with brown dotted underlines are considered errors related to a lack of conciseness. To begin checking the document, you'll use the Check Document button in the Proofing group on the Review tab. Note that in some installations of Word, this button might be called the "Spelling & Grammar" button instead.

To check the document for spelling and grammatical errors:

▶ 1. Press **CTRL+HOME**, if necessary, to move the insertion point to the beginning of the document, to the left of the "W" in "We." By placing the insertion point at the beginning of the document, you ensure that Word will check the entire document from start to finish, without having to go back and check an earlier part.

▶ 2. On the ribbon, click the **Review** tab. The ribbon changes to display reviewing options.

▶ 3. In the Proofing group, click the **Check Document** button. The Editor pane opens on the right side of the Word window, indicating that the document contains three spelling errors, one grammar error, and no clarity and conciseness errors.

   Trouble? If you see the Spelling & Grammar button instead of the Check Document button, click the Spelling & Grammar button.

▶ 4. Near the top of the Editor pane, click **4 Results**. Now the Editor pane displays information about the first error. As in the document, the word "prottect" is underlined in red as a possible spelling error. To the right of the sentence in the Editor pane is a speaker icon, which you can click to hear the sentence read aloud. Below, in the Suggestions box, the correctly spelled word "protect" appears along with its definition. You might also see some other suggestions. The incorrectly spelled word "prottect" is also highlighted in gray in the document. See Figure 1–25.

Figure 1–25 **Editor pane**

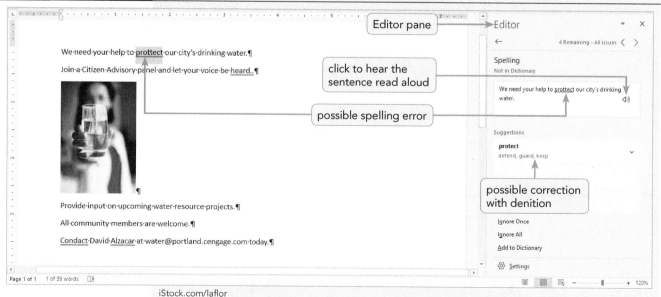

iStock.com/laflor

Trouble? If you don't see "4 Results" at the top of the Editor pane, that's fine. Everything else in Step 4 should still match what you see on your screen.

5. In the Editor pane, click the **protect** suggestion. The misspelled word "prottect" is replaced with "protect."

Next Word highlights the last word in the second sentence, indicating another possible error. The explanation near the top of the pane indicates that Word has detected a redundant punctuation mark—that is, an extra period.

6. In the Suggestions list, click **heard.** (with one period).

The first word of the last sentence is now highlighted in the document. You could correct this misspelling by clicking an option in the Editor pane, but this time you'll try typing directly in the document.

7. In the document, click to the right of the "d" in "Condact," press **BACKSPACE**, type **t**, and then click **Resume** in the Editor pane. David's last name is now highlighted in the document. Although the Editor pane doesn't recognize "Alzacar" as a word, it is spelled correctly, so you can ignore it. Note that if his name appeared repeatedly in the document, you could click Ignore All to ignore all instances of it.

Trouble? If you see "Resume" in the Editor pane instead of "Resume checking all results," click "Resume" instead.

8. In the Editor pane, click **Ignore Once**. A dialog box opens, indicating that the spelling and grammar check is complete.

Trouble? If you do not see the dialog box mentioned in Step 8, skip Step 9.

9. Click **OK** to close the dialog box.

10. Close the Editor pane.

PROSKILLS

Written Communication: Proofreading Your Document

Although the Editor pane is a useful tool, it won't always catch every error in a document, and it sometimes flags "errors" that are actually correct. This means there is no substitute for careful proofreading. Always take the time to read through your document to check for errors the Editor pane might have missed. Keep in mind that the Editor pane cannot pinpoint inaccurate phrases or poorly chosen words. You'll have to find those yourself. To produce a professional document, you must read it carefully several times. It's a good idea to ask one or two other people to read your documents as well; they might catch something you missed.

You still need to proofread the document. You'll do that next.

To proofread the document:

1. Review the document text for any remaining errors. In the second paragraph, change the lowercase "p" in "panel" to an uppercase "P."

2. In the last line of text, replace "David Alzacar" with your first and last names, and then save the document. Including your name in the document will make it easier for you to find your copy later if you print it on a shared printer.

Now you're ready to begin formatting the document. You will start by turning the page so it is wider than it is tall. In other words, you will change the document's **orientation**.

Changing Page Orientation

Portrait orientation, with the page taller than it is wide, is the default page orientation for Word documents because it is the orientation most commonly used for letters, reports, and other formal documents. However, David wants you to format the flyer in **landscape orientation**—that is, with the page turned so it is wider than it is tall—to better accommodate the photo. You can accomplish this task by using the Orientation button located on the Layout tab on the ribbon. After you change the page orientation, you will select narrower margins so you can maximize the amount of color on the page.

To change the page orientation:

1. Change the document Zoom level to **One Page** so that you can see the entire document.

2. On the ribbon, click the **Layout** tab. The ribbon changes to display options for formatting the overall layout of text and images in the document.

3. In the Page Setup group, click the **Orientation** button, and then click **Landscape** on the menu. The document changes to landscape orientation.

4. In the Page Setup group, click the **Margins** button, and then click the **Narrow** option on the menu. The margins shrink from 1 inch to .5 inch on all four sides. See Figure 1–26.

Figure 1–26   **Document in landscape orientation with narrow margins**

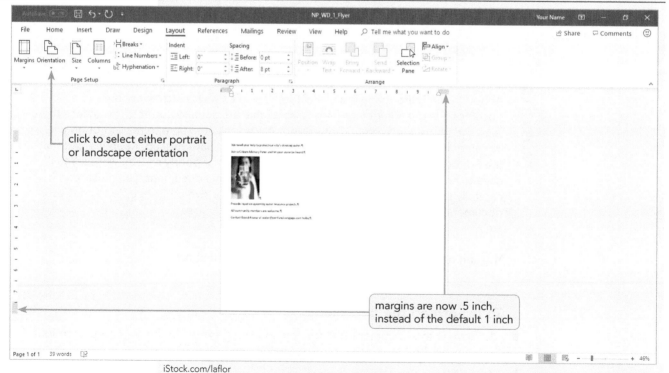

click to select either portrait or landscape orientation

margins are now .5 inch, instead of the default 1 inch

iStock.com/laflor

Changing the Font and Font Size

David typed the document in the default font size, 11 point, and the default font, Calibri, but he would like to switch to the Arial font instead. Also, he wants to increase the size of all five paragraphs of text. To apply these changes, you start by selecting the text you want to format. Then you select the options you want in the Font group on the Home tab.

To change the font and font size:

▶ **1.** Change the document Zoom level to **120%**.

▶ **2.** On the ribbon, click the **Home** tab.

▶ **3.** To verify that the insertion point is located at the beginning of the document, press **CTRL+HOME**.

▶ **4.** Press and hold **SHIFT**, and then click to the right of the second paragraph marker, at the end of the second paragraph of text. The first two paragraphs of text are selected, as shown in Figure 1–27.

Figure 1–27   **Selected text, with default font displayed in Font box**

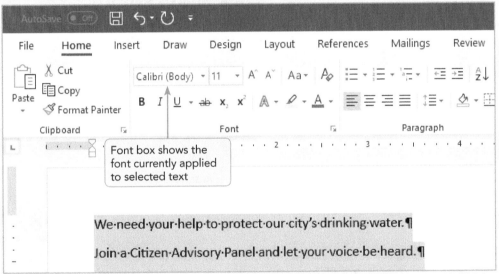

iStockPhoto.com/laflor

The Font box in the Font group displays the name of the font applied to the selected text, which in this case is Calibri. The word "Body" next to the font name indicates that the Calibri font is intended for formatting body text. **Body text** is ordinary text, as opposed to titles or headings.

▶ **5.** In the Font group on the Home tab, click the **Font arrow**. A list of available fonts appears, with Calibri Light and Calibri at the top of the list. Calibri is highlighted in gray, indicating that this font is currently applied to the selected text. The word "Headings" next to the font name "Calibri Light" indicates that Calibri Light is intended for formatting headings.

Below Calibri Light and Calibri, you might see a list of fonts that have been used recently on your computer, followed by a complete alphabetical list of all available fonts. (You won't see the list of recently used fonts if you just installed Word.) You need to scroll the list to see all the available fonts. Each name in the list is formatted with the relevant font. For example, the name "Arial" appears in the Arial font. See Figure 1–28.

Figure 1–28   Font list

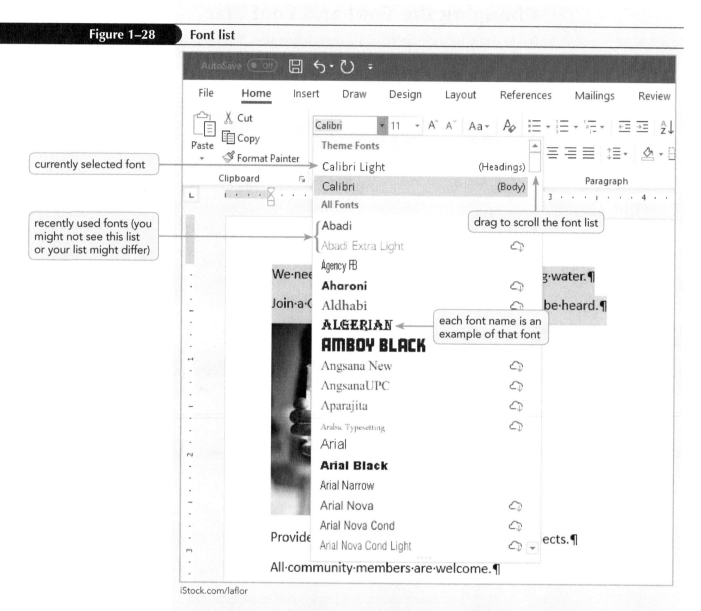

currently selected font

recently used fonts (you
might not see this list
or your list might differ)

drag to scroll the font list

each font name is an
example of that font

iStock.com/laflor

▶ **6.** Without clicking, move the pointer over a dramatic-looking font in the
font list, such as Algerian or Arial Black, and then move the pointer over
another font.

The selected text in the document changes to show a Live Preview of the
font the pointer is resting on. **Live Preview** shows the results that would
occur in your document if you clicked the option you are pointing to.

▶ **7.** When you are finished reviewing the Font list, click **Arial**. The Font menu
closes, and the selected text is formatted in Arial.

Next, you will make the text more eye-catching by increasing the font size.
The Font Size box currently displays the number "11," indicating that the
selected text is formatted in 11-point font.

▶ **8.** Verify that the first two paragraphs are still selected, and then click the **Font
Size arrow** in the Font group to display a menu of font sizes. As with the
Font menu, you can move the pointer over options in the Font Size menu to
see a Live Preview of that option.

▶ **9.** On the Font Size menu, click **22**. The selected text increases significantly in size, and the Font Size menu closes.

▶ **10.** Select the three paragraphs of text below the photo, format them in the Arial font, and then increase the paragraph's font size to 22 points.

▶ **11.** Click a blank area of the document to deselect the text, and then save the document.

Keep in mind that to restore selected text to its default appearance, you can click the Clear All Formatting button in the Font group on the Home tab.

David examines the flyer and decides he would like to apply more character formatting, which affects the appearance of individual characters, in the middle three paragraphs. After that, you can turn your attention to paragraph formatting, which affects the appearance of the entire paragraph.

Applying Text Effects, Font Colors, and Font Styles

For formal, professional documents, you typically only need to use **bold** or *italic* to make a word or paragraph stand out. Occasionally you might need to underline a word. To apply these forms of character formatting, select the text you want to format, and then click the Bold, Italic, or Underline button in the font group on the Home tab. To really make text stand out, you can use text effects. You access these options by clicking the Text Effects and Typography button in the Font group on the Home tab. Keep in mind that text effects can be very dramatic.

David suggests applying text effects to the second paragraph.

To apply text effects to the second paragraph:

▶ **1.** Scroll up, if necessary, to display the beginning of the document, and then click in the selection bar to the left of the second paragraph. The entire second paragraph is selected.

▶ **2.** In the Font group on the Home tab, click the **Text Effects and Typography** button ⟦A ⌄⟧.

A gallery of text effects appears. Options that allow you to fine-tune a particular text effect, perhaps by changing the color or adding an even more pronounced shadow, are listed below the gallery. A **gallery** is a menu or grid that shows a visual representation of the options available when you click a button.

▶ **3.** In the middle of the bottom row of the gallery, place the pointer over the blue letter "A." This displays a ScreenTip with the text effect's full name: Fill: Blue, Accent color 5; Outline: White, Background color 1; Hard Shadow: Blue, Accent color 5. A Live Preview of the effect appears in the document. See Figure 1–29.

Figure 1–29   **Live Preview of a text effect**

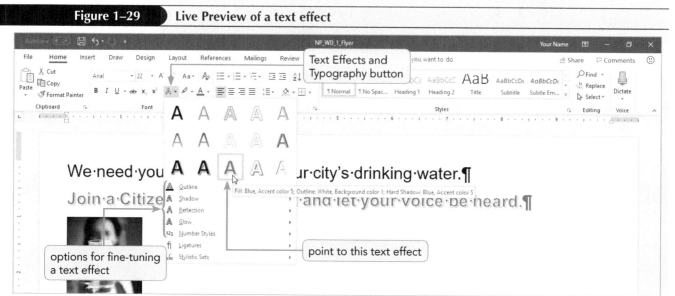

iStock.com/laflor

4. In the bottom row of the gallery, click the blue letter "A." The text effect is applied to the selected paragraph, and the Text Effects gallery closes. The second paragraph is formatted in blue, as shown in the Session 1.2 Visual Overview. On the ribbon, the Bold button in the Font group is now highlighted because bold formatting is part of this text effect.

Next, to make the text stand out a bit more, you'll increase the font size. This time, instead of using the Font Size button, you'll use a different method.

5. In the Font group, click the **Increase Font Size** button $A^{^}$. The font size increases from 22 points to 24 points, which is the next higher font size on the Font menu.

6. Click the **Increase Font Size** button $A^{^}$ again. The font size increases to 26 points, which is the next higher font size on the Font menu. If you need to decrease the font size of selected text, you can use the Decrease Font Size button. Each time you click the Decrease Font Size button, the font decreases to the next lower font size on the Font menu.

David asks you to emphasize the third and fourth paragraphs by adding bold and a blue font color.

To apply a font color and bold:

1. Select the third and fourth paragraphs of text, which contain the text "Provide input on upcoming water resource projects. All community members are welcome."

2. In the Font group on the Home tab, click the **Font Color arrow** $\boxed{A \cdot}$. A gallery of font colors appears. Black is the default font color and appears at the top of the Font Color gallery, with the word "Automatic" next to it.

The options in the Theme Colors section of the menu are complementary colors that work well when used together in a document. The options in the Standard Colors section are more limited. For more advanced color options, you could use the More Colors or Gradient options. David prefers a simple blue.

Trouble? If the third and fourth paragraphs turned red, you clicked the Font Color button ⬛ instead of the arrow next to it. On the Quick Access Toolbar, click the Undo button ↺, and then repeat Step 2.

▶ **3.** In the Theme Colors section, place the pointer over the square that's second from the right in the top row. A ScreenTip with the color's name, "Blue, Accent 5," appears. A Live Preview of the color appears in the document, where the text you selected in Step 1 now appears formatted in blue. See Figure 1–30.

Figure 1–30   **Font Color gallery showing a Live Preview**

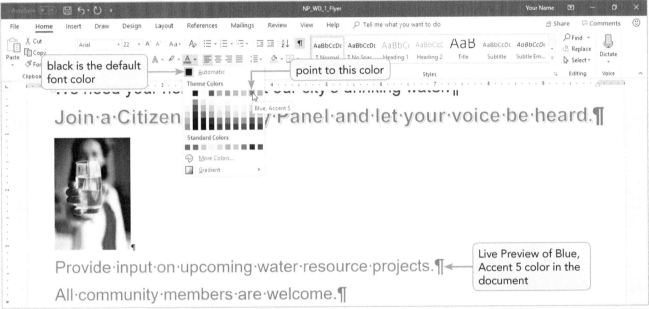

iStock.com/laflor

▶ **4.** Click the **Blue, Accent 5** square. The Font color gallery closes, and the selected text is formatted in blue. On the Font Color button, the bar below the letter "A" is now blue, indicating that if you select text and click the Font Color button, the text will automatically change to blue.

▶ **5.** In the Font group, click the **Bold** button ⬛. The selected text is now formatted in bold, with thicker, darker lettering.

Next, you will complete some paragraph formatting, starting with paragraph alignment.

Aligning Text

Alignment refers to how text and graphics line up between the page margins. By default, text is **left-aligned** in Word. That is, the text is flush with the left margin, with the text along the right margin **ragged**, or uneven. By contrast, **right-aligned** text is aligned along the right margin and is ragged along the left margin. **Centered** text is positioned evenly between the left and right margins and is ragged along both the left and right margins. Finally, with **justified alignment**, full lines of text are spaced between both the left and the right margins, and no text is ragged. Text in newspaper columns is often justified. See Figure 1–31.

| Figure 1–31 | Varieties of text alignment |

left alignment The term "alignment" refers to the way a paragraph lines up between the margins. The term "alignment" refers to the way a paragraph lines up between the margins.	**right alignment** The term "alignment" refers to the way a paragraph lines up between the margins. The term "alignment" refers to the way a paragraph lines up between the margins.
center alignment The term "alignment" refers to the way a paragraph lines up between the margins.	**justified alignment** The term "alignment" refers to the way a paragraph lines up between the margins. The term "alignment" refers to the way a paragraph lines up between the margins.

The Paragraph group on the Home tab includes a button for each of the four major types of alignment described in Figure 1–31: the Align Left button, the Center button, the Align Right button, and the Justify button. To align a single paragraph, click anywhere in that paragraph, and then click the appropriate alignment button. To align multiple paragraphs, select the paragraphs first, and then click an alignment button.

You need to center all the text in the flyer now. You can center the photo at the same time.

To center-align the text:

Use CTRL+A to select the entire document, instead of dragging the pointer. It's easy to miss part of the document when you drag the pointer.

1. Make sure the Home tab is still selected, and press **CTRL+A** to select the entire document.

2. In the Paragraph group, click the **Center** button ☰, and then click a blank area of the document to deselect the selected paragraphs. The text and photo are now centered on the page, similar to the centered text shown earlier in the Session 1.2 Visual Overview.

3. Save the document.

Adding a Paragraph Border and Shading

A **paragraph border** is an outline that appears around one or more paragraphs in a document. You can choose to apply only a partial border—for example, a bottom border that appears as an underline under the last line of text in the paragraph—or an entire box around a paragraph. You can select different colors and line weights for the border as well, making it more or less prominent as needed. You apply paragraph borders using the Borders button in the Paragraph group on the Home tab. **Shading** is background color that you can apply to one or more paragraphs and can be used in conjunction with a border for a more defined effect. You apply shading using the Shading button in the Paragraph group on the Home tab.

Now you will apply a border and shading to the first paragraph, as shown earlier in the Session 1.2 Visual Overview. Then you will use the Format Painter to copy this formatting to the last paragraph in the document.

To add shading and a paragraph border:

▶ **1.** Scroll up if necessary and select the first paragraph. Be sure to select the paragraph mark at the end of the paragraph.

▶ **2.** On the Home tab, in the Paragraph group, click the **Borders arrow** ⊞ . A gallery of border options appears, as shown in Figure 1–32. To apply a complete outline around the selected text, you use the Outside Borders option.

Figure 1–32	Border gallery

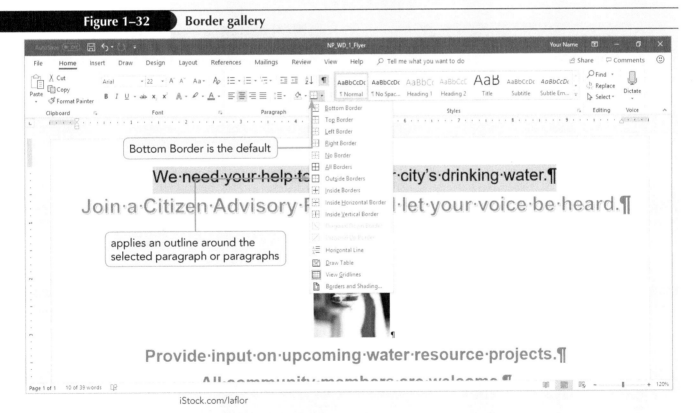

iStock.com/laflor

Trouble? If the gallery does not open and instead the paragraph becomes underlined with a single underline, you clicked the Borders button ⊞ instead of the arrow next to it. On the Quick Access Toolbar, click the Undo button ↶ , and then repeat Step 2.

▶ **3.** In the Border gallery, click **Outside Borders**. The menu closes and a black border appears around the selected paragraph, spanning the width of the page. In the Paragraph group, the Borders button ⊞ changes to show the Outside Borders option.

Trouble? If the border around the first paragraph doesn't extend all the way to the left and right margins and instead encloses only the text, you didn't select the paragraph mark as directed in Step 1. Click the Undo button ↺ repeatedly to remove the border, and begin again with Step 1.

▶ 4. In the Paragraph group, click the **Shading arrow** ⟨◇ ⌄⟩. A gallery of shading options opens, divided into Theme Colors and Standard Colors. You will use a shade of dark blue in the fifth column from the left.

▶ 5. In the bottom row in the Theme Colors section, move the pointer over the square in the fifth column from the left to display a ScreenTip that reads "Blue, Accent 1, Darker 50%." A Live Preview of the color appears in the document. See Figure 1–33.

Figure 1–33	Shading gallery with a Live Preview displayed

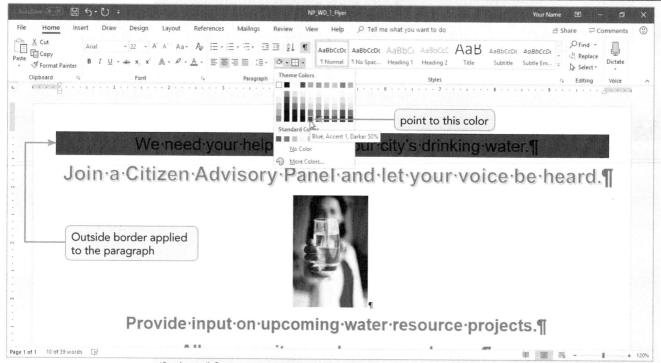

iStock.com/laflor

▶ 6. Click the **Blue, Accent 1, Darker 50%** square to apply the shading to the selected text.

On a dark background like the one you just applied, a white font creates a striking effect. David asks you to change the font color for this paragraph to white.

▶ 7. Make sure the Home tab is still selected.

▶ 8. In the Font group, click the **Font Color arrow** ⟨A ⌄⟩ to open the Font Color gallery, and then click the **white** square in the top row of the Theme Colors. The Font Color gallery closes, and the paragraph is now formatted with white font.

The black paragraph border is hard to see with the dark blue shading, so you will change the border to a different color. To make more advanced changes to borders or paragraph shading, you need to use the Borders and Shading dialog box.

▶ 9. Click the **Borders arrow** ⟨▦ ⌄⟩ and then, at the bottom of the menu, click **Borders and Shading**. The Borders and Shading dialog box opens with the Borders tab displayed.

▶ **10.** Click the **Color arrow** to open the Color gallery, and then click the **Green, Accent 6** square, which is the right-most square in the top row of the Theme Colors section.

Next, to make the border more noticeable, you will increase its width.

▶ **11.** Click the **Width arrow**, and then click **3 pt**. At this point, the settings in your Borders and Shading dialog box should match the settings in Figure 1–34.

Figure 1–34   **Borders and Shading dialog box**

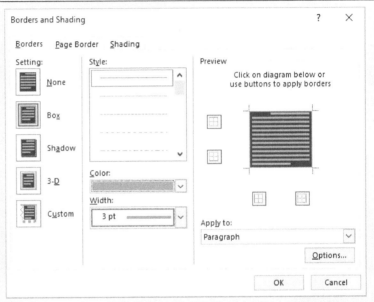

▶ **12.** Click **OK** to close the Borders and Shading dialog box and return to the document.

▶ **13.** Click a blank area of the document to deselect the text, review the change, and then save the document. The first paragraph is now formatted with a green border, a dark blue background, and white text as shown in the Session 1.2 Visual Overview.

To add balance to the flyer, David suggests formatting the last paragraph in the document with the same shading, border, and font color as the first paragraph. You'll do that next.

Copying Formatting with the Format Painter

You could select the last paragraph and then apply the border, shading, and font color one step at a time. But it's easier to copy all the formatting from the first paragraph to the last paragraph using the Format Painter button in the Clipboard group on the Home tab.

REFERENCE

Using the Format Painter

- Select the text whose formatting you want to copy.
- On the Home tab, in the Clipboard group, click the Format Painter button, or to copy formatting to multiple sections of nonadjacent text, double-click the Format Painter button.
- The pointer changes to the Format Painter pointer, the I-beam pointer with a paintbrush.
- Click the words you want to format, or drag to select and format entire paragraphs.
- When you are finished formatting the text, click the Format Painter button again to turn off the Format Painter.

You'll use the Format Painter now.

To use the Format Painter:

1. Change the document Zoom level to One Page so you can easily see both the first and last paragraphs.

2. Select the first paragraph, which is formatted with the dark blue shading, the green border, and the white font color.

3. On the ribbon, click the **Home** tab.

4. In the Clipboard group, click the **Format Painter** button to activate, or turn on, the Format Painter.

5. Move the Format Painter pointer over the document. The pointer changes to the Format Painter pointer when you move the pointer near an item that can be formatted. See Figure 1–35.

Figure 1–35   **Format Painter**

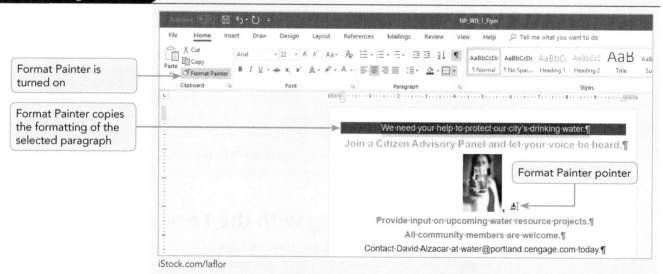

Format Painter is turned on

Format Painter copies the formatting of the selected paragraph

We·need·your·help·to·protect·our·city's·drinking·water.¶

Join·a·Citizen·Advisory·Panel·and·let·your·voice·be·heard.¶

Format Painter pointer

Provide·input·on·upcoming·water·resource·projects.¶
All·community·members·are·welcome.¶
Contact·David·Alzacar·at·water@portland.cengage.com·today.¶

iStock.com/laflor

TIP

To turn off the Format Painter without using it, press ESC.

6. Click and drag the Format Painter pointer to select the last paragraph in the document. The paragraph is now formatted with dark blue shading, a green border, and white font. The pointer returns to its original I-beam shape.

   Trouble? If the text in the newly formatted paragraph wrapped to a second line, replace your full name with your first name, or, if necessary, use only your initials so the paragraph is only one-line long.

7. Click anywhere in the document to deselect the text, review the change, and then save the document.

Your next task is to increase the paragraph spacing below the first paragraph and above the last paragraph. This will give the shaded text even more weight on the page. To complete this task, you will use the settings on the Layout tab, which offer more options than the Line and Paragraph Spacing button on the Home tab.

To increase the paragraph spacing below the first paragraph and above the last paragraph:

1. Click anywhere in the first paragraph, and then click the **Layout** tab. On this tab, the Paragraph group contains settings that control paragraph spacing. Currently, the paragraph spacing for the first paragraph is set to the default 0 points before the paragraph and 8 points after.

2. In the Paragraph group, click the **After** box to select the current setting, type **42**, and then press **ENTER**. The added space causes the second paragraph to move down 42 points.

3. Click anywhere in the last paragraph.

4. On the Layout tab, in the Paragraph group, click the **Before** box to select the current setting, type **42**, and then press **ENTER**. The added space causes the last paragraph to move down 42 points.

INSIGHT

Formatting Professional Documents

In more formal documents, use color and special effects sparingly. The goal of letters, reports, and many other types of documents is to convey important information, not to dazzle the reader with fancy fonts and colors. Such elements only serve to distract the reader from your main point. In formal documents, it's a good idea to limit the number of colors to two and to stick with left alignment for text. In a document like the flyer you're currently working on, you have a little more leeway because the goal of the document is to attract attention. However, you still want it to look professional.

Next, David wants you to replace the photo with one that will look better in the document's new landscape orientation. You'll replace the photo, and then you'll resize it so that the flyer fills the entire page.

Inserting a Picture and Adding Alt Text

A **picture** is a photo or another type of image that you insert into a document. To work with a picture, you first need to select it. Once a picture is selected, a contextual tab—the Picture Tools Format tab—appears on the ribbon, with options for editing the picture and adding effects such as a border, a shadow, a reflection, or a new shape. A **contextual tab** appears on the ribbon only when an object is selected. It contains commands related to the selected object so that you can manipulate, edit, and format the selected object. You can also use the mouse to resize or move a selected picture. To insert a new picture, you use the Pictures button in the Illustrations group on the Insert tab.

To delete the current photo and insert a new one:

▶ **1.** Click the photo to select it.

The circles, called **sizing handles**, around the edge of the photo indicate the photo is selected. The Layout Options button, to the right of the photo, gives you access to options that control how the document text flows around the photo. You don't need to worry about these options now. Finally, note that the Picture Tools Format tab appeared on the ribbon when you selected the photo. See Figure 1–36.

Figure 1–36   Selected photo

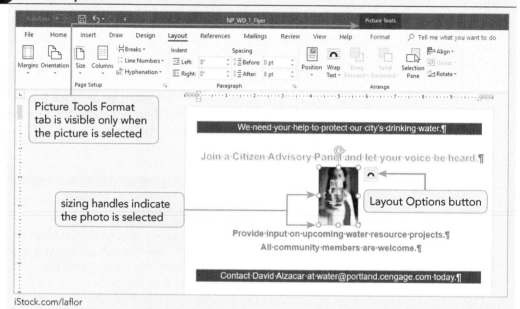

iStock.com/laflor

▶ **2.** Press **DEL**. The photo is deleted from the document. The insertion point blinks next to the paragraph symbol.

Now you are ready to insert the new photo in the paragraph containing the insertion point. When you do, you will briefly see a gray box at the bottom of the photo containing a description of the image. This description, which is called **alternative text** (or **alt text**, for short), makes it possible for a screen-reading device to read a description of the image aloud. This is useful for people with vision impairment, who would otherwise find it difficult or impossible to read a document.

Word automatically creates alt text for most photos, although it is often too generic to be really helpful (for example, "Two people"). To refine alt text created by Word so that it accurately describes an image, click the Alt Text button in the Accessibility group on the Picture Tools Format tab. This opens the Alt Text pane, where you can edit the existing alt text. As you become a more experienced Word user, you'll have the chance to create new alt text for charts, tables, and other items. Before you can use alt text, you need to make sure intelligent services are turned on in the Word Options dialog box.

To turn on intelligent services, insert a new photo, and edit its alt text:

1. Click **File**, and then click **Options** to open the Word Options dialog box with the General tab displayed.

2. In the "Office intelligent services" section, click the **Enable** services check box to insert a checkmark, if necessary, and then click **OK** to close the Word Option dialog box.

3. On the ribbon, click the **Insert** tab. The ribbon changes to display the Insert options.

4. In the Illustrations group, click the **Pictures** button. The Insert Picture dialog box opens.

5. Navigate to the **Word1 > Module** folder included with your Data Files, and then click **Support_WD_1_Water.png** to select the file. The name of the selected file appears in the File name box.

6. Click the **Insert** button to close the Insert Picture dialog box and insert the photo. An image of water pouring from a bottle into a glass appears in the document, below the second paragraph. The photo is selected, as indicated by the sizing handles on its border, and the Picture Tools Format tab is displayed. After a pause, a gray box with the text "Alt Text: A glass of water" appears as shown in Figure 1–37, remains on the screen for about five seconds, and then disappears.

Figure 1–37   Newly inserted photo with alt text visible

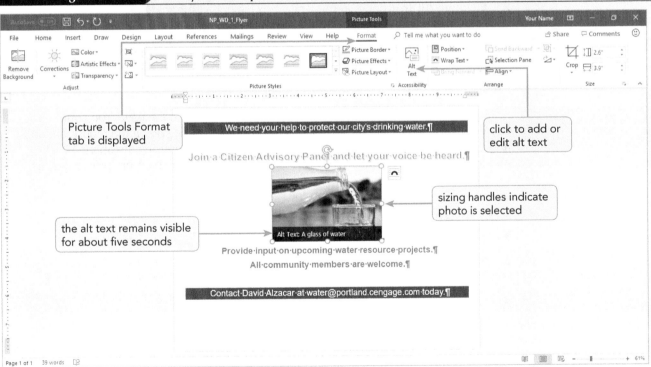

iStock.com/LazingBee

Trouble? If you see a blue message box explaining how alt text works, click Got It to close the message box.

7. In the Accessibility group on the ribbon, click the **Alt Text** button to display the Alt Text pane, which displays the current alt text, "A glass of water" as well as a note indicating the likelihood that this description is correct. See Figure 1–38.

Figure 1–38 Alt Text pane

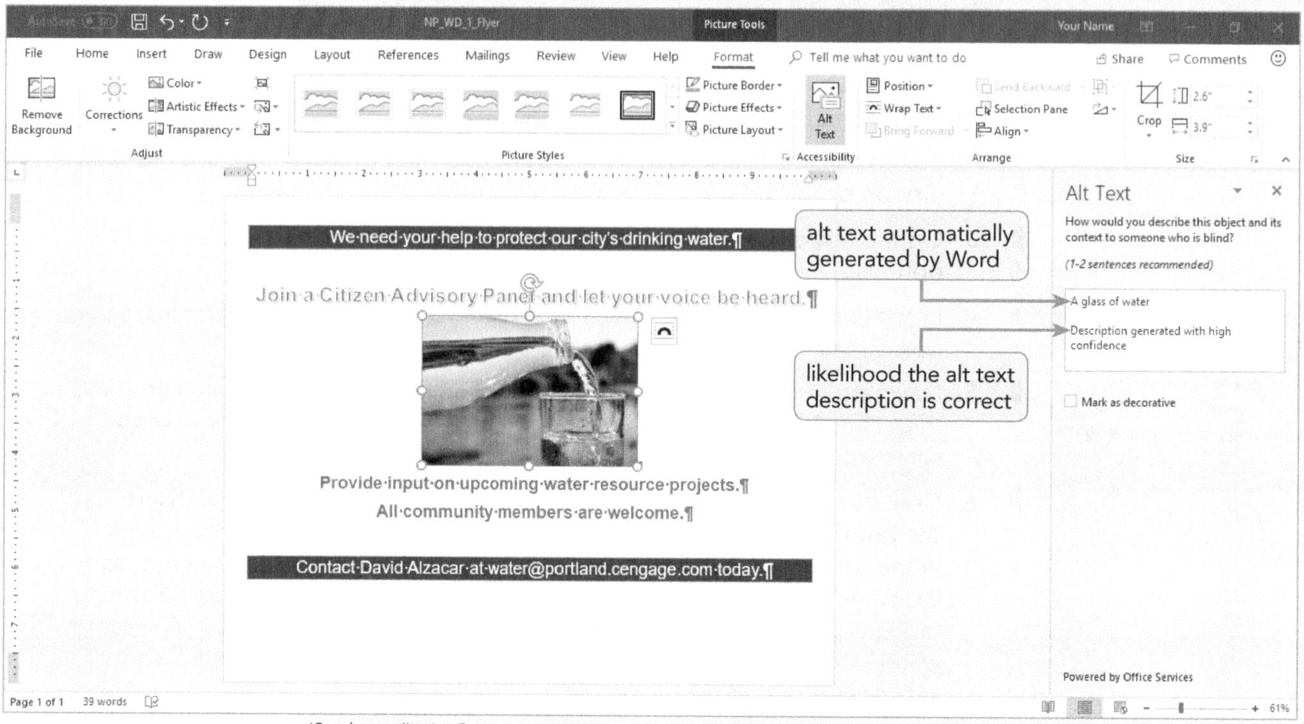

iStock.com/LazingBee

8. In the Alt Text pane, in the white box, select all the text, including the phrase "Description generated with high confidence."

9. Type **Water pouring from a bottle into a glass, with a lake in the background** and then click the **Close** button [X] to close the Alt Text pane.

TIP

For images that require no screen reader narration, you can select the Mark as decorative check box in the Alt Text pane.

Now you need to resize the photo so it fills more space on the page. You could do so by clicking one of the picture's corner sizing handles, holding down the mouse button, and then dragging the sizing handle to resize the picture. But using the Shape Height and Shape Width boxes on the Picture Tools Format tab gives you more precise results.

To resize the photo:

1. Make sure the Picture Tools Format tab is still selected on the ribbon.
2. In the Size group on the far-right edge of the ribbon, locate the Shape Height box, which indicates that the height of the selected picture is currently 2.6". The Shape Width box indicates that the width of the picture is 3.9". As you'll see in the next step, when you change one of these measurements, the other changes accordingly, keeping the overall shape of the picture the same. See Figure 1–39.

| Figure 1–39 | Shape Height and Shape Width boxes |

iStock.com/LazingBee

▶ **3.** Click the **up arrow** in the Shape Height box in the Size group. The photo increases in size slightly. The measurement in the Shape Height box increases to 2.7", and the measurement in the Shape Width box increases to 4.05".

▶ **4.** Click the **up arrow** in the Shape Height box repeatedly until the picture is 3.2" tall and 4.8" wide.

Finally, to make the photo more noticeable, you can add a **picture style**, which is a collection of formatting options, such as a frame, a rounded shape, and a shadow. You can apply a picture style to a selected picture by clicking the style you want in the Picture Styles gallery on the Picture Tools Format tab. Note that to return a picture to its original appearance, you can click the Reset Picture button in the Adjust group on the Picture Tools Format tab. In the following steps, you'll start by displaying the Picture Styles gallery.

To add a style to the photo:

▶ **1.** Make sure the Picture Tools Format tab is still selected on the ribbon.

▶ **2.** In the Picture Styles group, click the **More** button ▾ to the right of the Picture Styles gallery to open the gallery and display more picture styles. Some of the picture styles simply add a border, while others change the picture's shape. Other styles combine these options with effects such as a shadow or a reflection.

▶ **3.** Place the pointer over various styles to observe the Live Previews in the document, and then place the pointer over the Drop Shadow Rectangle style, which is the middle style in the top row. See Figure 1–40.

Figure 1–40   Previewing a picture style

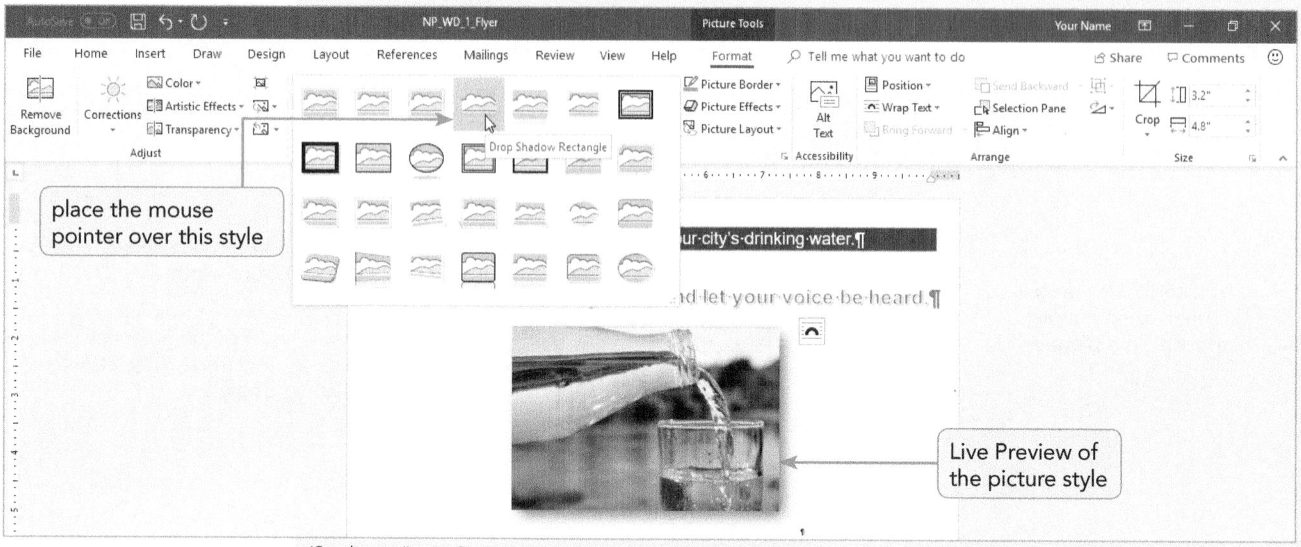

place the mouse
pointer over this style

Drop Shadow Rectangle

Live Preview of
the picture style

iStock.com/LazingBee

TIP

To return a picture to its
original appearance, click
the Reset Picture button
in the Adjust group on the
Picture Tools Format tab.

4. In the gallery, click the **Drop Shadow Rectangle** style to apply it to the
   photo and close the gallery. The photo is formatted with a shadow on the
   bottom and right sides, as shown earlier in the Session 1.2 Visual Overview.

5. Click anywhere outside the photo to deselect it, and then save the
   document.

INSIGHT

Working with Inline Pictures

By default, when you insert a picture in a document, it is treated as an inline object,
which means its position changes in the document as you add or delete text. Also,
because it is an inline object, you can align the picture just as you would align text,
using the alignment buttons in the Paragraph group on the Home tab. Essentially, you
can treat an inline picture as just another paragraph.

When you become a more advanced Word user, you'll learn how to wrap text
around a picture so that the text flows around the picture—with the picture maintaining
its position on the page no matter how much text you add to or delete from the
document. The alignment buttons don't work on pictures that have text wrapped
around them. Instead, you can drag the picture to the desired position on the page.

To complete the flyer, you need to add a border around the page.

Adding a Page Border

As with a paragraph border, the default style for a page border is a simple black line
that forms a box around each page in the document. However, you can choose more
elaborate options, including a dotted line, double lines, and, for informal documents, a
border of graphical elements, such as stars or trees.

To insert a border around the flyer:

▶ **1.** On the ribbon, click the **Design** tab.

▶ **2.** In the Page Background group, click the **Page Borders** button. The Borders and Shading dialog box opens with the Page Border tab displayed. You can use the Setting options on the left side of this tab to specify the type of border you want. Because a document does not normally have a page border, the default setting is None. The Box setting is the most professional and least distracting choice, so you'll select that next.

It's important to select the Box setting before you select other options for the border. Otherwise, when you click OK, your document won't have a page border, and you'll have to start over.

▶ **3.** In the Setting section, click the **Box** setting. Selecting this option would add a simple line page border, but David prefers a different line style.

▶ **4.** In the Style box, scroll down and click the **double-line style**. Now you can select a different line color, just as you did when creating a paragraph border.

▶ **5.** Click the **Color arrow** to open the Color gallery, and then click the **Green, Accent 6** square, which is the right-most square in the top row of the Theme Colors section. The Color gallery closes and the Green, Accent 6 color is displayed in the Color box. At this point, you could change the line width as well, but David prefers the default setting. See Figure 1–41.

Figure 1–41	Adding a border to the flyer

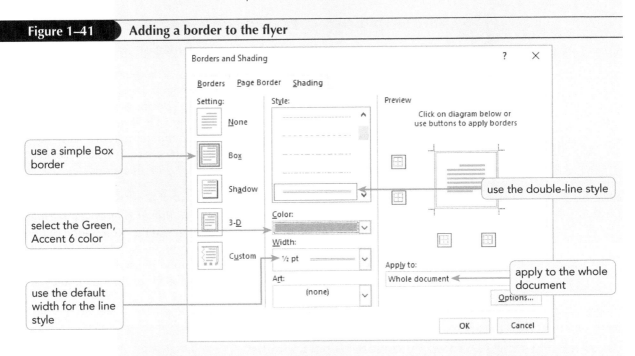

▶ **6.** In the lower-right corner of the Borders and Shading dialog box, click the **Options** button. The Border and Shading Options dialog box opens.

By default, the border is positioned 24 points from the edges of the page. If you plan to print your document on an older printer, it is sometimes necessary to change the Measure from setting to Text, so that the border is positioned relative to the outside edge of the text rather than the edge of the page. Alternatively, you can increase the settings in the Top, Bottom, Left, and Right boxes to move the border closer to the text. For most modern printers, however, the default settings are fine.

▶ **7.** In the Border and Shading Options dialog box, click **Cancel**, and then click **OK** in the Borders and Shading dialog box. The flyer now has a double-line green border, as shown earlier in the Session 1.2 Visual Overview.

▶ **8.** Save the document.

▶ **9.** Close the document without closing Word.

David needs your help with one last task—adding bulleted and numbered lists to a document containing the minutes of the Citizen Advisory Panel's May meeting. After you finish formatting the document, David can make the minutes available to the public through the department's website.

Creating Bulleted and Numbered Lists

A **bulleted list** is a group of related paragraphs with a black circle or other character to the left of each paragraph. For a group of related paragraphs that have a particular order (such as steps in a procedure), you can use consecutive numbers instead of bullets to create a **numbered list**. If you insert a new paragraph, delete a paragraph, or reorder the paragraphs in a numbered list, Word adjusts the numbers to make sure they remain consecutive.

PROSKILLS

Written Communication: Organizing Information in Lists

Bulleted and numbered lists are both great ways to draw the reader's attention to information. But it's important to know how to use them. Use numbers when your list contains items that are arranged by priority in a specific order. For example, in a document reviewing the procedure for performing CPR, it makes sense to use numbers for the sequential steps. Use bullets when the items in the list are of equal importance or when they can be accomplished in any order. For example, in a resume, you could use bullets for a list of professional certifications.

To add bullets to a series of paragraphs, you use the Bullets button in the Paragraph group on the Home tab. To create a numbered list, you use the Numbering button in the Paragraph group instead. Both the Bullets button and the Numbering button have arrows you can click to open a gallery of bullet or numbering styles.

David asks you to add two bulleted lists and a numbered list to the minutes of the last meeting of the Citizen Advisory Panel.

To apply bullets to paragraphs:

▶ **1.** Open the document **NP_WD_1-2.docx** located in the Word1 > Module folder, and then save the document as **NP_WD_1_Minutes** in the location specified by your instructor.

▶ **2.** Verify that the document is displayed in Print Layout view and that the rulers and nonprinting characters are displayed. Make sure the Zoom level is set to **120%**.

▶ **3.** On page 1, select the complete list of members in attendance, starting with Tomeka Newcomb, and concluding with Jeffrey Holmes.

   4. On the ribbon, click the **Home** tab, if necessary.

   5. In the Paragraph group, click the **Bullets** button ⊞. Black circles appear as bullets before each item in the list. Also, the bulleted list is indented, and the paragraph spacing between the items is reduced.

   After reviewing the default, round bullet in the document, David decides he would prefer square bullets.

   6. In the Paragraph group, click the **Bullets arrow** ⊞ ˅. A gallery of bullet styles opens. See Figure 1–42.

Figure 1–42   **Bullets gallery**

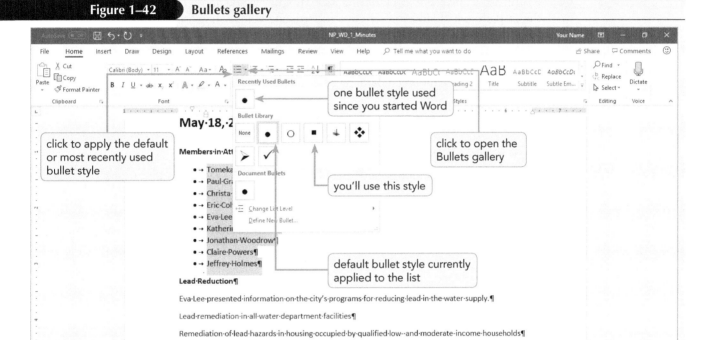

The Recently Used Bullets section appears at the top of the gallery of bullet styles; it displays the bullet styles that have been used since you started Word, which, in this case, is just the round black bullet style that was applied by default when you clicked the Bullets button. The **Bullet Library**, which offers a variety of bullet styles, is shown below the Recently Used Bullets. To create your own bullets from a picture file or from a set of predesigned symbols including diamonds, hearts, or Greek letters, click Define New Bullet, and then click Symbol or Picture in the Define New Bullet dialog box.

   7. Move the pointer over the bullet styles in the Bullet Library to see a Live Preview of the bullet styles in the document. David prefers the black square style.

   8. In the Bullet Library, click the **black square**. The round bullets are replaced with square bullets.

Next, you need to format the list of lead-reduction programs with square bullets. When you first start Word, the Bullets button applies the default, round bullets you saw earlier. But after you select a new bullet style, the Bullets button applies the last bullet style you used. So, to add square bullets to the lead-reduction programs list, you just have to select the list and click the Bullets button.

To add bullets to the list of lead-reduction programs:

▶ **1.** Scroll down in the document, and select the paragraphs describing the department's lead-reduction programs, starting with "Lead remediation in all water department facilities" and ending with "Workshop 2: Children and Lead Paint Hazards."

▶ **2.** In the Paragraph group, click the **Bullets** button ⊞. The list is now formatted with square black bullets.

The list is finished except for one issue. Below "Workshops co-sponsored with the Department of Housing" are two subordinate items listing the workshop titles. However, that's not clear because of the way the list is currently formatted.

To clarify this information, you can use the Increase Indent button in the Paragraph group to indent the last two bullets. When you do this, Word inserts a different style bullet to make the indented paragraphs visually subordinate to the bulleted paragraphs above.

To indent the last two bullets:

▶ **1.** In the list of lead-reduction programs, select the last two paragraphs.

▶ **2.** In the Paragraph group, click the **Increase Indent** button ⊞. The two paragraphs move to the right, and the black square bullets are replaced with open circle bullets. Note that to remove the indent from selected text, you could click the Decrease Indent button in the Paragraph group.

Next, you will format the agenda items as a numbered list.

To apply numbers to the list of agenda items:

▶ **1.** Scroll down, if necessary, until you can see the last paragraph in the document.

▶ **2.** Select all the paragraphs below the "Agenda for Next Meeting" heading, starting with "Opening remarks, public comments, and minutes" and ending with "Report on upcoming projects...."

▶ **3.** In the Paragraph group, click the **Numbering** button ⊞. Consecutive numbers appear in front of each item in the list. See Figure 1–43.

Figure 1–43   **Numbered list**

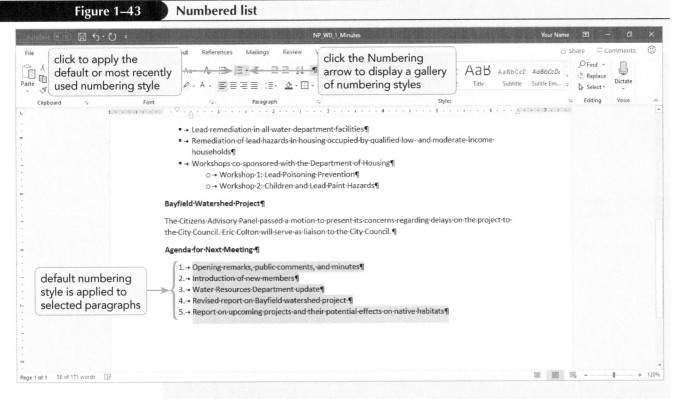

4. Click anywhere in the document to deselect the numbered list.

5. sam⬆ Save the document.

As with the Bullets arrow, you can click the Numbering arrow, and then select from a library of numbering styles. You can also indent paragraphs in a numbered list to create an outline, in which case the indented paragraphs will be preceded by lowercase letters instead of numbers. To apply a different list style to the outline (for example, with Roman numerals and uppercase letters), select the list, click the Multilevel List button in the Paragraph group, and then click a multilevel list style. Keep in mind that you can always add items to a bulleted or numbered list by moving the insertion point to the end of the last item in the list and pressing ENTER. The Bullets button is a **toggle button**, which means you can click it to add or remove bullets from selected text. The same is true of the Numbering button.

The document is complete and ready for David to post to the department's website. Because David is considering creating a promotional brochure that would include numerous photographs, he asks you to look up more information about inserting pictures. You can do that using Word Help.

Getting Help

TIP

To display a menu of recent and suggested Help topics, click the Tell me box and wait for the menu to appear.

To get the most out of Word Help, your computer must be connected to the Internet so it can access the reference information stored at Office.com. The quickest way to look up information is to use the Tell Me box—which displays the text "Tell me what you want to do"—on the ribbon. You can also use the Tell Me box to quickly access Word features.

To look up information in Word Help:

1. Verify that your computer is connected to the Internet, and then, on the ribbon, click the **Tell Me** box, and type **insert picture**. A menu of Help topics related to inserting pictures opens. You could click one of the items in the top part of the menu to access the relevant dialog box, menu, or other word tool. For example, you could click Insert Picture to open the Insert Picture dialog box. To open a submenu of relevant Help articles, point to the Get Help on "insert picture" command. If you prefer to expand your search to the entire web, you could click the Smart Lookup command at the bottom of the menu to open the Smart Lookup pane with links to articles from Wikipedia and other sources. See Figure 1–44.

Figure 1–44 | **Word Help menu**

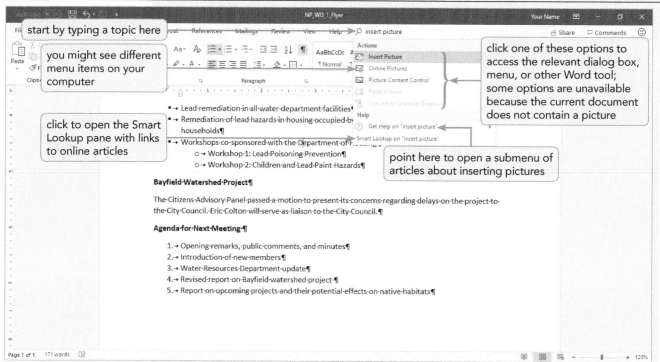

2. Click **Get Help on "insert picture."** A menu of articles about inserting pictures appears.

3. Click the first item in the menu to open the Help pane with information about inserting pictures.

4. Scroll down in the Help pane to read all the information. Note that you can use the Search help box at the top of the Help pane to look up information on other topics.

5. Click the **Close** button ☒ in the upper-right corner to close the Help pane.

6. Click the **File** tab, and then click **Close** in the navigation pane to close the document without closing Word.

Word Help is a great way to learn about and access Word's many features. Articles and videos on basic skills provide step-by-step guides for completing tasks, while more elaborate, online tutorials walk you through more complicated tasks. Be sure to take some time on your own to explore Word Help so you can find the information and features you want when you need it.

REVIEW

Session 1.2 Quick Check

1. Explain how to accept a spelling correction suggested by the Editor pane.
2. What orientation should you choose if you want your document to be wider than it is tall?
3. What is the default font size?
4. What is a gallery?
5. What is the default text alignment?
6. Explain two important facts about a picture inserted as an inline object.
7. What is the default shape for bullets in a bulleted list?

Review Assignments

Data Files needed for the Review Assignments: NP_WD_1-3.docx, NP_WD_1-4.docx, Support_WD_1_Glass.png

David asks you to write a cover letter to Roberto Campos at the New Day Neighborhood Center to accompany a pamphlet on water quality that will be used in an upcoming workshop. After that, he wants you to create an envelope for the letter, and then format a flyer announcing free educational tours of Portland's water resource facilities. Finally, he needs you to add bulleted and numbered list to the minutes for the Citizen Advisory Panel's July meeting. Change the Zoom level as necessary while you are working. Complete the following steps:

1. Open a new, blank document and then save the document as **NP_WD_1_CamposLetter** in the location specified by your instructor.

2. Type the date **February 15, 2021** using AutoComplete for "February."

3. Press ENTER twice, and then type the following inside address, using the default paragraph spacing and pressing ENTER once after each line:
   Roberto Campos
   New Day Neighborhood Center
   6690 Sullivan Circle
   Portland, OR 97203

4. Type **Dear Roberto:** as the salutation, press ENTER, and then type the following two paragraphs as the body of the letter:
   Enclosed you will find the water quality pamphlet we discussed. I hope the young people taking part in your sustainability workshop find this information useful. Additional data on our city's water supply is available at www.water.portland.cengage.com.
   Keep in mind that we also offer free educational tours of our water resources facilities. We can accommodate groups as large as thirty.

5. Press ENTER, type **Sincerely yours,** as the complimentary closing, press ENTER three times, type **David Alzacar** as the signature line, insert a manual line break, and type **Communications Director** as his title.

6. Press ENTER, type your initials, insert a manual line break, and then use the Undo button to make your initials all lowercase, if necessary.

7. Type **Enclosure** and save the document.

8. Scroll to the beginning of the document and proofread your work. Remove any wavy underlines by using a shortcut menu or by typing a correction yourself. Remove the hyperlink formatting from the web address.

9. Remove the paragraph spacing from the first three lines of the inside address.

10. Change the top margin to 2.75 inches. Leave the other margins at their default settings.

11. Save your changes to the letter, preview it, print it if your instructor asks you to, and then close it.

12. Create a new, blank document, and then create an envelope. Use Roberto Campos's address (from Step 3) as the delivery address. Use your school's name and address for the return address. Add the envelope to the document. If you are asked if you want to save the return address as the new return address, click No.

13. Save the document as **NP_WD_1_CamposEnvelope** in the location specified by your instructor, and then close the document.

14. Open the document **NP_WD_1-3.docx**, located in the Word1 > Review folder included with your Data Files, and then check your screen to make sure your settings match those in the module.

15. Save the document as **NP_WD_1_DrinkingWater** in the location specified by your instructor.

16. Use the Recheck Document button in the Word Options dialog box to reset the Spelling and Grammar checker, and then use the Editor pane to correct any errors. Ignore any items marked as errors that are in fact correct, and accept any suggestions regarding clarity and conciseness. If the Editor pane does not give you the opportunity to correct all the errors marked in the document, close the Editor pane and correct the errors using shortcut menus.

17. Proofread the document and correct any other errors. Be sure to change "Today" to **today** in the last paragraph.

18. Change the page orientation to Landscape and the margins to Narrow.

19. Format the document text in 22-point Times New Roman font.

20. Center the text and the photo.

21. Format the first paragraph with an outside border using the default style, and change the border color to Gold, Accent 4, and the border width to 1 ½ pt. Add blue shading to the paragraph, using the Blue, Accent 5 color in the Theme Colors section of the Shading gallery. Format the paragraph text in white.

22. Format the last paragraph in the document using the same formatting you applied to the first paragraph.

23. Increase the paragraph spacing after the first paragraph to 42 points. Increase the paragraph spacing before the last paragraph in the document to 42 points.

24. Format the second paragraph with the Gradient Fill: Gold, Accent color 4; Outline: Gold, Accent color 4 text effect. Increase the paragraph's font size to 26 points.

25. Format the text in the third and fourth paragraphs (the first two paragraphs below the photo) using the Blue, Accent 5 font color, and then add bold and italic.

26. Delete the photo and replace it with the **Supprt_WD_1_Glass.png** photo, located in the Word1 > Review folder.

27. Delete the existing alt text and the text indicating the degree of confidence that the alt text is correct, and then type **Water pouring into a glass**. (Do not include the period after "glass.")

28. Resize the new photo so that it is 3.8" tall, and then add the Soft Edge Rectangle style in the Pictures Styles gallery.

29. Add a page border using the Box setting, a double-line style, the default width, and the Gold, Accent 4 color.

30. Save your changes to the flyer, preview it, and then close it.

31. Open the document **NP_WD_1-4.docx**, located in the Word1 > Review folder, and then check your screen to make sure your settings match those in the module.

32. Save the document as **NP_WD_1_JulyMinutes** in the location specified by your instructor.

33. Format the list of members in attendance as a bulleted list with square bullets, and then format the list of lawn-care initiatives with square bullets (starting with "Alternate-day watering…" and ending with "Workshop 2: Drought-Tolerant Gardening"). Indent the paragraphs for Workshop 1 and Workshop 2 so they are formatted with open circle bullets.

34. Format the five paragraphs below the "Agenda for Next Meeting" heading as a numbered list.

35. Use Word Help to look up the topic **work with pictures**. Read the first article, return to the Help home page, and then close Help.

Case Problem 1

There are no Data Files needed for this Case Problem.

Laufer Commercial Real Estate   You are a real estate agent at Laufer Commercial Real Estate, in St. Louis, Missouri. You recently sold a building and need to forward an extra key to the building's new owner. Create a cover letter to accompany the key by completing the following steps. Because your office is currently out of letterhead, you'll start the letter by typing a return address. As you type the letter, remember to include the appropriate number of blank paragraphs between the various parts of the letter. Complete the following steps:

1. Open a new, blank document, and then save the document as **NP_WD_1_Kettering** in the location specified by your instructor. If necessary, change the Zoom level to 120%.

2. Type the following return address, using the default paragraph spacing and replacing [Your Name] with your first and last names:

   [Your Name]

   Laufer Commercial Real Estate

   3996 Pepperdine Avenue, Suite 10

   St. Louis, MO 63105

3. Type **November 9, 2021** as the date, leaving a blank paragraph between the last line of the return address and the date.

4. Type the following inside address, using the default paragraph spacing and leaving the appropriate number of blank paragraphs after the date:

   Sam Kettering

   Marshall-Hempstead Properties

   4643 Jillian Drive

   Columbia, MO 65201

5. Type **Dear Mr. Kettering:** as the salutation.

6. To begin the body of the letter, type the following two paragraphs: **Enclosed please find the extra office key for the apartment building you recently purchased at 362 Neuhauser Road. The previous owner found it when he was cleaning out his desk and asked me to send it to you.**

   It was a pleasure working with you. In order to improve our service, I would be grateful if you would review the following questions, and then email me your answers at kettering@laufer. cengage.com.

7. Remove the hyperlink formatting from the email address.

8. Add the following questions as separate paragraphs, using the default paragraph spacing:

   Did you find our staff helpful and well-informed?

   Were you satisfied with the service provided during your real estate transaction?

   Would you recommend Laufer Commercial Real Estate to others?

   Can you suggest any ways to improve our service?

9. Insert a new paragraph after the last question, and then type the complimentary closing **Sincerely,** (including the comma).

10. Leave the appropriate amount of space for your signature, type your full name, insert a manual line break, and then type **Licensed Real Estate Agent**.

11. Type **Enclosure** in the appropriate place.

12. Use the Editor pane to correct any errors. Ignore any items marked as errors that are in fact correct (such as the word "Neuhauser"), and accept any suggestions regarding clarity and conciseness. Instruct the Editor pane to ignore the recipient's name. If the Editor pane does not give you the opportunity to correct all the errors marked in the document, close the Editor pane and correct the errors using shortcut menus.

13. Italicize the four paragraphs containing the questions.

14. Format the list of questions as a bulleted list with square bullets.

15. Remove the paragraph spacing from the first three lines of the return address. Do the same for the first three paragraphs of the inside address.

16. Center the four paragraphs containing the return address, format them in 16-point font, and then add the Fill: Blue, Accent color 1; Shadow text effect.

17. Deselect any selected text, and then create an envelope in the current document. Use Sam Kettering's address (from Step 4) as the delivery address. Edit the delivery address as necessary to remove any incorrect text. Use the return address shown in Step 2. Add the envelope to the NP_WD_1_Kettering.docx document. If you are asked if you want to save the return address as the default return address, click No.

18. Save the document, preview it, and close it.

Case Problem 2

CREATE

Data Files needed for this Case Problem: NP_WD_1-5.docx, Support_WD_1_Sign.jpg

Newland Health Care   You work as a marketing coordinator for Newland Health Care. You need to create a flyer promoting the weekly flu shot clinics that will be held in November. Complete the following steps:

1. Open the document **NP_WD_1-5.docx** located in the Word1 > Case2 folder included with your Data Files, and then save the document as **NP_WD_1_Flu** in the location specified by your instructor.

2. In the document, replace "Student Name" with your first and last names.

3. Use the Editor pane to correct any errors. Instruct the Editor pane to ignore your name if Word marks it with a wavy underline. If the Editor pane does not give you the opportunity to correct all the errors marked in the document, close the Editor pane and correct the errors using shortcut menus.

4. Change the page margins to Narrow.

5. Complete the flyer as shown in Figure 1–45. Use the photo **Support_WD_1_Sign.jpg** located in the Word1 > Case2 folder. Use the default line spacing and paragraph spacing unless otherwise specified in Figure 1–45.

Figure 1–45   **Formatted Newland Health Care flyer**

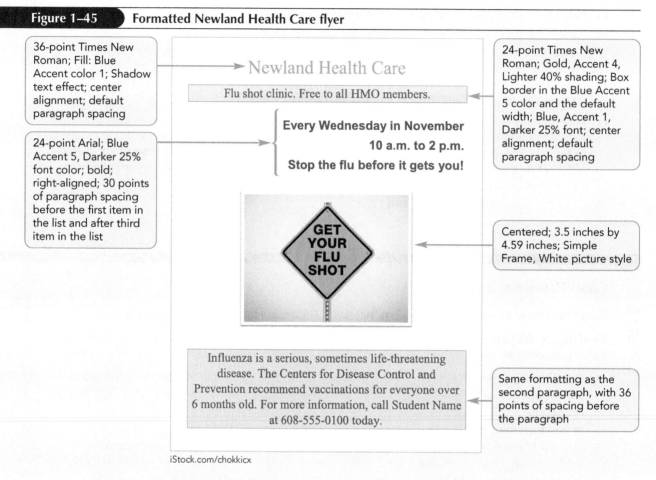

36-point Times New Roman; Fill: Blue Accent color 1; Shadow text effect; center alignment; default paragraph spacing

24-point Arial; Blue Accent 5, Darker 25% font color; bold; right-aligned; 30 points of paragraph spacing before the first item in the list and after third item in the list

24-point Times New Roman; Gold, Accent 4, Lighter 40% shading; Box border in the Blue Accent 5 color and the default width; Blue, Accent 1, Darker 25% font; center alignment; default paragraph spacing

Centered; 3.5 inches by 4.59 inches; Simple Frame, White picture style

Same formatting as the second paragraph, with 36 points of spacing before the paragraph

Newland Health Care

Flu shot clinic. Free to all HMO members.

Every Wednesday in November

10 a.m. to 2 p.m.

Stop the flu before it gets you!

GET YOUR FLU SHOT

Influenza is a serious, sometimes life-threatening disease. The Centers for Disease Control and Prevention recommend vaccinations for everyone over 6 months old. For more information, call Student Name at 608-555-0100 today.

iStock.com/chokkicx

6. Delete the existing alt text and the text indicating the degree of confidence that the alt text is correct, and then type **A sign with the message "GET YOUR FLU SHOT"**. (Do not include the period after the quotation mark.)

7. Save the document, preview it, and then close it.

WORD

OBJECTIVES

Session 2.1
- Read, reply to, delete, and add comments
- Move text using drag and drop
- Cut and paste text
- Copy and paste text
- Navigate through a document using the Navigation pane
- Find and replace text
- Format text with styles

Session 2.2
- Review the MLA style for research papers
- Indent paragraphs
- Insert and modify page numbers
- Create footnotes and endnotes
- Create citations
- Create and update a bibliography
- Modify a source

Navigating and Formatting a Document

Editing an Academic Document According to MLA Style

Case | *Cedar Hills Community College*

Sabrina Desantes, a student at Cedar Hills Community College, is doing a student internship at Prairie Savings and Loan. She has written a handout for first-time homebuyers that explains the process of getting a mortgage. She asks you to help her finish the handout. The text needs some reorganization and other editing, as well as some formatting so the finished document looks professional and is easy to read.

Sabrina is also taking an American history class and is writing a research paper on Alexander Hamilton, the first Secretary of the Treasury and the founder of the Bank of the United States. To complete the paper, she needs to follow a set of very specific formatting and style guidelines for academic documents.

Sabrina has asked you to help her edit these two very different documents. In Session 2.1, you will review and respond to some comments in the handout and then revise and format that document. In Session 2.2, you will review the MLA style for research papers and then format Sabrina's research paper to match the MLA specifications.

STARTING DATA FILES

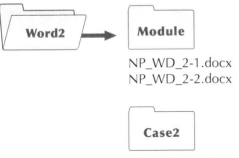

Word2 → **Module**

NP_WD_2-1.docx
NP_WD_2-2.docx

 Review

NP_WD_2-3.docx
NP_WD_2-4.docx

 Case1

NP_WD_2-5.docx

Case2

NP_WD_2-6.docx

Session 2.1 Visual Overview:

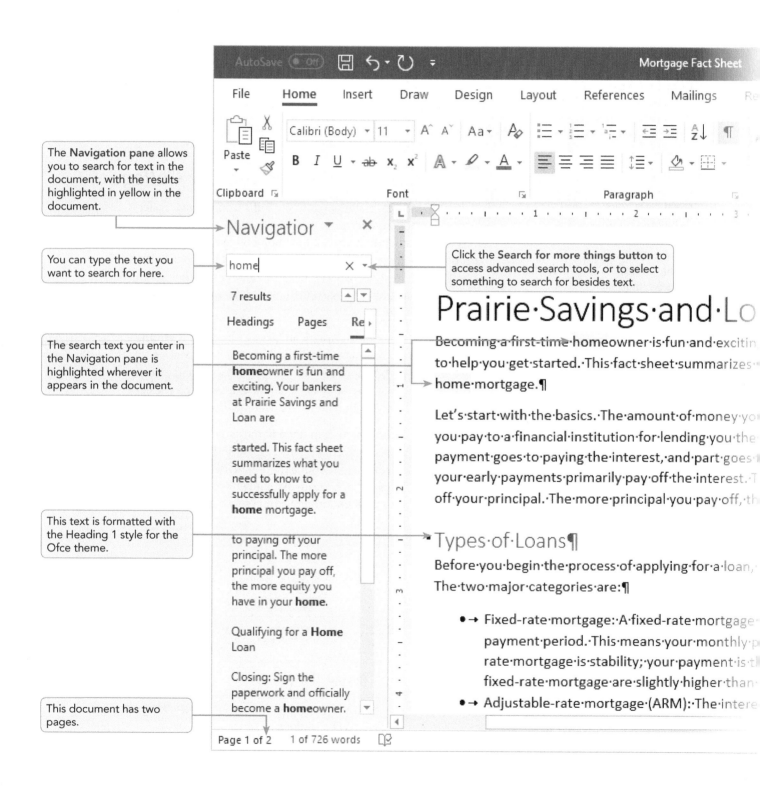

The **Navigation pane** allows you to search for text in the document, with the results highlighted in yellow in the document.

You can type the text you want to search for here.

Click the **Search for more things button** to access advanced search tools, or to select something to search for besides text.

The search text you enter in the Navigation pane is highlighted wherever it appears in the document.

This text is formatted with the Heading 1 style for the Ofce theme.

This document has two pages.

The Navigation Pane and Styles

Text styles allow you to apply a set of paragraph and character formatting options with one click in the Style Gallery.

Mortgage Fact Sheet   Your Name

Mailings   Review   View   Help   🔎 Tell me   🖉 Share

AaBbCcDc   AaBbCcDc   AaBbCc

¶ Normal   ¶ No Spac...   Heading 1

Styles

🔎 Find   ⌄
ᵇ꜀ Replace
Select ⁻

Editing

Dictate

Voice

To open the Navigation pane, click the Find button.

You can click the More button to expand the Style Gallery to see more style options.

You can click a group's Dialog Box Launcher to open a dialog box or pane that gives you access to advanced settings.

s·and·Loan·Mortgage·Facts¶

This text is formatted with the Title style for the Ofce theme.

er·is·fun·and·exciting.·Your·bankers·at·Prairie·Savings·and·Loan·are·eager·
sheet·summarizes·what·you·need·to·know·to·successfully·apply·for·a·

mount·of·money·you·borrow·is·known·as·the·principal,·and·the·money·
for·lending·you·the·money·is·the·interest.·Part·of·your·monthly·
rest,·and·part·goes·to·paying·off·the·principal.·With·most·mortgages,·
ay·off·the·interest.·Then,·over·time,·more·of·your·payments·go·to·paying·
cipal·you·pay·off,·the·more·equity·you·have·in·your·home.¶

The search text you enter in the Navigation pane appears highlighted wherever it appears in the document.

applying·for·a·loan,·you·need·to·understand·the·various·types·of·loans.·

fixed-rate·mortgage·maintains·the·same·rate·throughout·the·entire·
eans·your·monthly·payment·will·never·change.·The·advantage·of·a·fixed-
y··your·payment·is·the·same·every·month.·However,·interest·rates·for·a·
slightly·higher·than·for·other·types·of·loans.¶
e·(ARM):·The·interest·rate·for·an·adjustable-rate·mortgage·changes·

110%

Reviewing the Document

Before revising a document for someone else, it's a good idea to familiarize yourself with its overall structure and the revisions that need to be made. Take a moment to review Sabrina's notes, which are shown in Figure 2–1.

Figure 2–1 **Draft of handout with Sabrina's notes (page 1)**

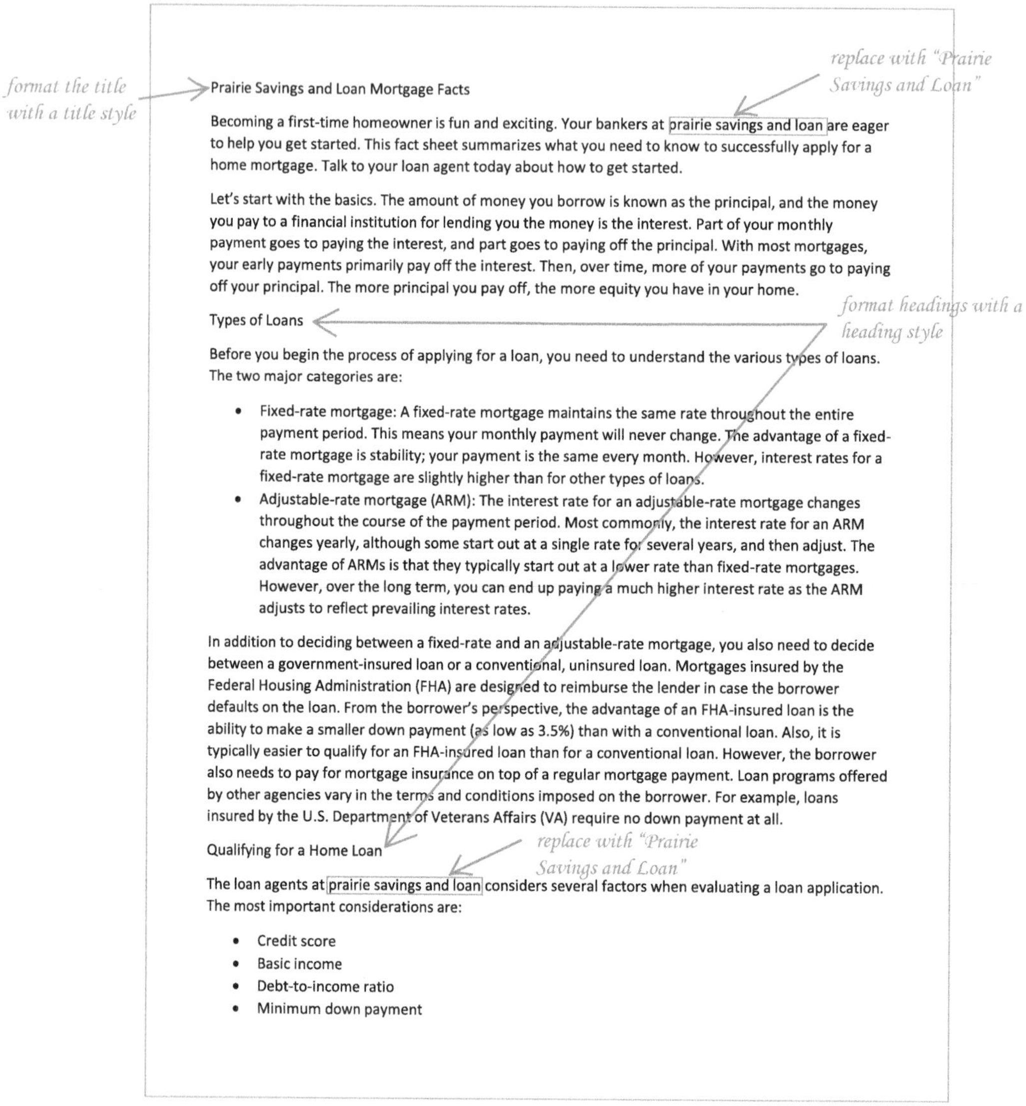

format the title with a title style →

replace with "Prairie Savings and Loan"

Prairie Savings and Loan Mortgage Facts

Becoming a first-time homeowner is fun and exciting. Your bankers at prairie savings and loan are eager to help you get started. This fact sheet summarizes what you need to know to successfully apply for a home mortgage. Talk to your loan agent today about how to get started.

Let's start with the basics. The amount of money you borrow is known as the principal, and the money you pay to a financial institution for lending you the money is the interest. Part of your monthly payment goes to paying the interest, and part goes to paying off the principal. With most mortgages, your early payments primarily pay off the interest. Then, over time, more of your payments go to paying off your principal. The more principal you pay off, the more equity you have in your home.

format headings with a heading style

Types of Loans

Before you begin the process of applying for a loan, you need to understand the various types of loans. The two major categories are:

- Fixed-rate mortgage: A fixed-rate mortgage maintains the same rate throughout the entire payment period. This means your monthly payment will never change. The advantage of a fixed-rate mortgage is stability; your payment is the same every month. However, interest rates for a fixed-rate mortgage are slightly higher than for other types of loans.
- Adjustable-rate mortgage (ARM): The interest rate for an adjustable-rate mortgage changes throughout the course of the payment period. Most commonly, the interest rate for an ARM changes yearly, although some start out at a single rate for several years, and then adjust. The advantage of ARMs is that they typically start out at a lower rate than fixed-rate mortgages. However, over the long term, you can end up paying a much higher interest rate as the ARM adjusts to reflect prevailing interest rates.

In addition to deciding between a fixed-rate and an adjustable-rate mortgage, you also need to decide between a government-insured loan or a conventional, uninsured loan. Mortgages insured by the Federal Housing Administration (FHA) are designed to reimburse the lender in case the borrower defaults on the loan. From the borrower's perspective, the advantage of an FHA-insured loan is the ability to make a smaller down payment (as low as 3.5%) than with a conventional loan. Also, it is typically easier to qualify for an FHA-insured loan than for a conventional loan. However, the borrower also needs to pay for mortgage insurance on top of a regular mortgage payment. Loan programs offered by other agencies vary in the terms and conditions imposed on the borrower. For example, loans insured by the U.S. Department of Veterans Affairs (VA) require no down payment at all.

replace with "Prairie Savings and Loan"

Qualifying for a Home Loan

The loan agents at prairie savings and loan considers several factors when evaluating a loan application. The most important considerations are:

- Credit score
- Basic income
- Debt-to-income ratio
- Minimum down payment

| Figure 2–1 | Draft of handout with Sabrina's notes (page 2) |

To verify information on income and debt, we request numerous supporting items as part of your application. You will need to provide:

- Social Security number
- Proof of employment history for the last three years
- Pay stubs
- Tax documents for the last two years
- W-2 statements
  - Tax returns
  - Proof of current residence
- Bank account information
- Credit report
- Real estate contract
- Letters documenting any financial gifts from family or friends that will help fund your house purchase
- Itemized list of monthly expenses

If you are CONSIDERING buying a rental property, you will likely need to provide additional documentation. Please see your loan agent at prairie savings and loan for details.

replace with "Prairie Savings and Loan"

Loan-Approval Process

The steps in the loan-approval process are:

1. Supporting documents: Supply the required documentation.
2. Preapproval: Get preapproved for a specific amount.
3. Preclosing: Work with your loan agent and real estate agent to prepare for the closing, providing additional information as necessary.
4. Application: Complete the online form.
5. Closing: Sign the paperwork and officially become a homeowner.

format headings with a heading style

move paragraph up

Even before you find a home you want to buy, it's a good idea to fill out an application so your loan agent can preapprove you for a certain amount. That way you'll know *exactly* how much you can afford to spend as you begin looking at properties.

Getting Started

The staff of Prairie Savings and Loan is ready to make your dream of home ownership a reality.

Prepared by:

Sabrina also included additional guidance in some comments she added to the document file. A **comment** is like an electronic sticky note attached to a word, phrase, or paragraph in a document. Comments appear in the margin, along with the name of the person who added them. Within a single document, you can add new comments, reply to existing comments, and delete comments.

You will open the document now, save it with a new name, and then review Sabrina's comments in Word.

To open and rename the document:

1. **sam** ⬇ Open the document **NP_WD_2-1.docx** located in the Word2 > Module folder included with your Data Files.

2. Save the document as **NP_WD_2_Mortgage** in the location specified by your instructor.

3. Verify that the document is displayed in Print Layout view, that the Zoom level is set to **120%**, and that the rulers and nonprinting characters are displayed.

4. On the ribbon, click the **Review** tab to display the tools used for working with comments. Comments can be displayed in several different ways, so your first step is to make sure the comments in the document are displayed to match the figures in this book—using Simple Markup view.

▶ **5.** In the Tracking group, click the **Display for Review arrow**, and then click **Simple Markup** to select it, if necessary. At this point, you might see comment icons to the right of the document text, or you might see the full text of each comment.

▶ **6.** In the Comments group, click the **Show Comments** button several times to practice displaying and hiding the comments, and then, when you are finished, make sure the Show Comments button is selected so the full text of each comment is displayed.

▶ **7.** At the bottom of the Word window, drag the horizontal scroll bar all the way to the right, if necessary, so you can read the full text of each comment. See Figure 2–2. Note that the comments on your screen might be a different color than the ones shown in the figure.

Figure 2–2   **Comments displayed in the document**

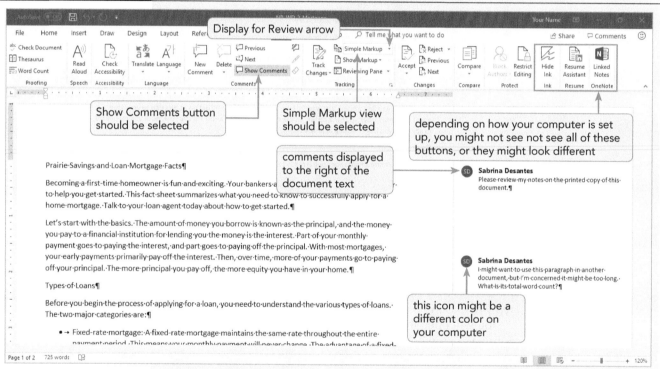

Keep in mind that when working on a small monitor, it can be helpful to switch the document Zoom level to Page Width, in which case Word automatically reduces the width of the document to accommodate the comments on the right.

▶ **8.** Read the document, including the comments. The handout includes the title "Prairie Savings and Loan Mortgage Facts" at the top, as well as headings (such as "Types of Loans" and "Qualifying for a Home Loan") that divide the document into parts. Right now, the headings are hard to spot because they don't look different from the surrounding text. Sabrina used the default font size, 11-point, and the default font, Calibri (Body), for all the text in the document.

▶ **9.** Scroll down until you can see the first line on page 2 (which begins "To verify information…"), and then click anywhere in that sentence. The message "Page 2 of 2" in the status bar, in the lower-left corner of the Word window, tells you that the insertion point is currently located on page 2 of the two-page document. The shaded space between the first and second pages of the document indicates a page break. To hide the top and bottom margins in a document, as well as the space between pages, you can double-click the shaded space between any two pages.

▶ **10.** Position the pointer over the shaded space between page 1 and page 2 until the pointer changes to the hide white space pointer ⊞, and then double-click. The shaded space disappears. Instead, the two pages are now separated by a gray, horizontal line.

Trouble? If the Header & Footer Tools Design contextual tab appears on the ribbon, you double-clicked the top or bottom of one of the pages, instead of in the space between them. Click the Close Header and Footer button on the Header & Footer Tools Design tab, and then repeat Step 10.

▶ **11.** Use the show white space pointer ⊞ to double-click the gray horizontal line between pages 1 and 2. The shaded space between the two pages is redisplayed.

Working with Comments

Now that you are familiar with Sabrina's handout, you can review and respond to her comments. The Comment group on the Review tab includes helpful tools for working with comments.

REFERENCE

Working with Comments

- On the ribbon, click the Review tab.
- To display comments in an easy-to-read view, in the Tracking group, click the Display for Review arrow, and then click Simple Markup.
- Use the Show Comments button in the Comments group to display or hide the text of the comments.
- To move the insertion point to the next or previous comment in the document, click the Next button or the Previous button in the Comments group.
- To delete a comment, click anywhere in the comment, and then click the Delete button in the Comments group.
- To delete all the comments in a document, click the Delete arrow in the Comments group, and then click Delete All Comments in Document.
- To add a new comment, select the document text you want to comment on, click the New Comment button in the Comments group, and then type the comment text.
- To reply to a comment, click the Reply button to the right of the comment, and then type your reply.
- To indicate that a comment or an individual reply to a comment is no longer a concern, click Resolve. To mark a comment and all of the replies attached to it as resolved, click Resolve in the original comment.
- To respond to a resolved comment, click Reopen in the comment, and then type your reply.

To review and respond to the comments in the document:

▶ **1.** Press **CTRL+HOME** to move the insertion point to the beginning of the document.

▶ **2.** On the Review tab, in the Comments group, click the **Next** button. The first comment now has an outline, indicating that it is selected. See Figure 2–3.

Figure 2–3	Comment attached to document text

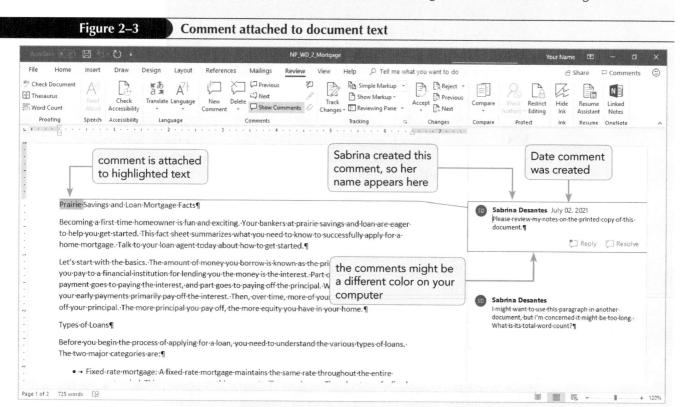

In the document, the text "Prairie" is highlighted. A line connects the comment to "Prairie," indicating that the comment is attached to that text. Because Sabrina created the comment, her name appears at the beginning of the comment. The insertion point blinks at the beginning of the comment and is ready for you to edit the comment if you want.

▶ **3.** Read the comment, and then in the Comments group, click the **Next** button to select the next comment. According to this comment, Sabrina wants to know the total word count of the paragraph the comment is attached to. You can get this information by selecting the entire paragraph and locating the word count in the status bar.

▶ **4.** Triple-click anywhere in the second paragraph of the document (which begins "Let's start with the basics...") to select the paragraph. In the status bar, the message "89 of 725 words" tells you that 89 of the document's 725 words are currently selected. So the answer to Sabrina's question is 89.

Trouble? Don't be concerned if you see a slightly different word count in the status bar. No matter what you see, type the number indicated in Step 5.

▶ **5.** Point to the second comment to select it again, click the **Reply** button, and then type **89**. Your reply appears below Sabrina's original comment.

Trouble? If you do not see the Reply button in the comment box, drag the horizontal scroll bar at the bottom of the Word window to the right until you can see it.

If you are logged in, the name that appears in your reply comment is the name associated with your Microsoft account. If you are not logged in, the name in the Reply comment is taken from the User name box on the General tab of the Word Options dialog box.

▶ **6.** In the Comments group, click the **Next** button to move the insertion point to the next comment, which asks you to insert your name after "Prepared by:" at the end of the document.

▶ **7.** Click after the colon in "Prepared by:", press **SPACEBAR**, and then type your first and last names. To indicate that you have complied with Sabrina's request by adding your name, you could click anywhere in the comment in the margin, and then click Resolve. However, in this case, you'll simply delete the comment. Sabrina also asks you to delete the first comment in the document.

▶ **8.** Click anywhere in the final comment, and then in the Comments group, click the **Delete** button.

▶ **9.** In the Comments group, click the **Previous** button three times to select the comment at the beginning of the document, and then click the **Delete** button to delete the comment. Note that to delete all the comments in the document, you could click the Delete arrow in the Comments group, and then click Delete All Comments in Document.

INSIGHT

Changing the Username

To change the username associated with your copy of Word, click the Dialog Box Launcher in the Tracking group on the Review tab, and then click Change User Name. From there, you can change the username and the initials associated with your copy of Word. To override the name associated with your Microsoft account and use the name that appears in the User name box in the Word Options dialog box instead, select the "Always use these values regardless of sign in to Office" check box. However, there is no need to change these settings for this module, and you should never change them on a shared computer at school unless specifically instructed to do so by your instructor.

As you reviewed the document, you might have noticed that, on page 2, a word appears in all uppercase letters. This is probably just a typing mistake. You can correct it and then add a comment that points out the change to Sabrina.

To correct the mistake and add a comment:

▶ **1.** Scroll down to the middle of page 2, and then, in the paragraph above the "Loan Approval Process" heading, select the text **CONSIDERING**.

▶ **2.** On the ribbon, click the **Home** tab.

▶ **3.** In the Font group, click the **Change Case** button Aa▾ , and then click **lowercase**. The text changes to read "considering." Note that you could select Capitalize Each Word to make the first letter in each word you have selected uppercase.

▶ **4.** Verify that the text is still selected, and then click the **Review** tab on the ribbon.

▶ **5.** In the Comments group, click the **New Comment** button. A new comment appears, with the insertion point ready for you to begin typing.

▶ **6.** In the new comment, type **I assumed you didn't want this in all uppercase letters, so I changed it to lowercase.** and then save the document.

You can now hide the text of the comments because you are finished working with them.

▶ **7.** In the Comments group, click the **Show Comments** button. A "See comments" icon now appears in the document margin rather than on the right side of the Word screen. The "See comments" icon alerts you to the presence of a comment without taking up all the space required to display the comment text. You can click a comment icon to read a particular comment without displaying the text of all the comments.

▶ **8.** Click the **See comments** icon 🗩. The comment icon is highlighted, and the full comment is displayed, as shown in Figure 2–4.

Figure 2–4   **Document with the See comments icon**

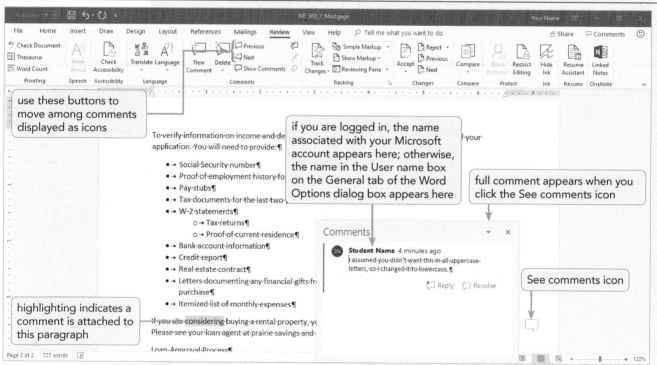

▶ **9.** Click anywhere outside the comment to close it.

Moving Text in a Document

One of the most useful features of a word-processing program is the ability to move text easily. For example, Sabrina wants to reorder the information in the numbered list on page 2. You could do this by deleting a paragraph and then retyping it at a new location. However, it's easier to select and then move the text. Word provides several ways to move text—drag and drop, cut and paste, and copy and paste.

Dragging and Dropping Text

To move text with **drag and drop**, you select the text you want to move, press and hold the mouse button while you drag the selected text to a new location, and then release the mouse button.

In the numbered list on page 2, Sabrina wants you to move up the paragraph that reads "Application: Complete the online form" so it is the first item in the list.

To move text using drag and drop:

1. Scroll down to display the numbered list on page 2.

2. Triple-click to select the fourth paragraph in the numbered list, "Application: Complete the online form." Take care to include the paragraph marker at the end. The number 4 remains unselected because it's not actually part of the paragraph text.

3. Position the pointer over the selected text. The pointer changes to a left-pointing arrow ⌕.

4. Press and hold the mouse button, and move the pointer slightly until the drag-and-drop pointer ⌕ appears. A dark black insertion point appears within the selected text.

5. Without releasing the mouse button, drag the pointer to the beginning of the list until the insertion point is positioned to the left of the first "S" in "Supporting documents: Supply the required documentation." Use the insertion point, rather than the pointer, to guide the text to its new location. See Figure 2–5.

Figure 2–5   Moving text with the drag-and-drop pointer

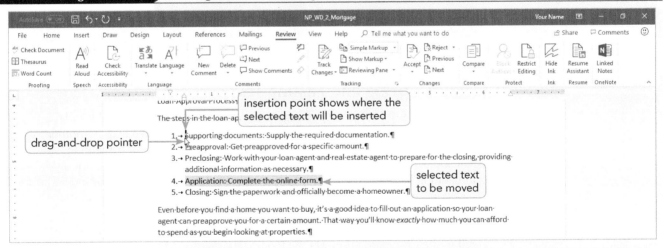

6. Release the mouse button, and then click a blank area of the document to deselect the text. The first item in the list is now "Application: Complete the online form." The remaining paragraphs have been renumbered as paragraphs 2 through 5. See Figure 2–6.

Figure 2–6 **Text in new location**

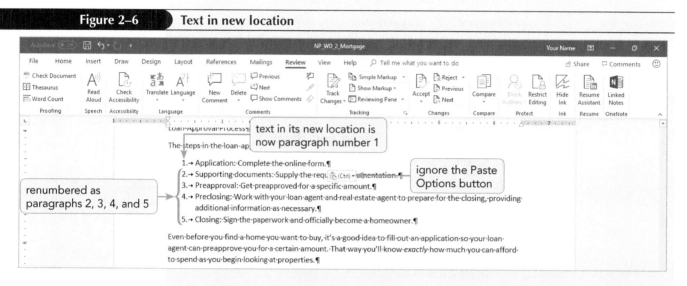

The Paste Options button appears near the newly inserted text, providing access to more advanced options related to pasting text. You don't need to use the Paste Options button right now; it will disappear when you start performing another task.

Trouble? If the selected text moves to the wrong location, click the Undo button ↩ on the Quick Access Toolbar, and then repeat Steps 3 through 6.

▶ **7.** Save the document.

Dragging and dropping works well when you are moving text a short distance. When you are moving text from one page to another, it's easier to cut, copy, and paste text using the Clipboard.

Cutting or Copying and Pasting Text Using the Clipboard

The **Office clipboard** is a temporary storage area on your computer that holds objects such as text or graphics until you need them. To **cut** means to remove text or another item from a document and place it on the Clipboard. Once you've cut something, you can paste it somewhere else. To **copy** means to copy a selected item to the Clipboard, leaving the item in its original location. To **paste** means to insert a copy of whatever is on the Clipboard into the document, at the insertion point. When you paste an item from the Clipboard into a document, the item remains on the Clipboard so you can paste it again somewhere else if you want. The buttons for cutting, copying, and pasting are located in the Clipboard group on the Home tab.

By default, Word pastes text in a new location in a document with the same formatting it had in its old location. To select other ways to paste text, you can use the Paste Options button, which appears next to newly pasted text, or the Paste arrow in the Clipboard group. Both buttons display a menu of paste options. Two particularly useful paste options are Merge Formatting, which combines the formatting of the copied text with the formatting of the text in the new location, and Keep Text Only, which inserts the text using the formatting of the surrounding text in the new location.

When you need to keep track of multiple pieces of cut or copied text, it's helpful to open the **Clipboard pane**, which displays the contents of the Clipboard. You open the Clipboard pane by clicking the Clipboard Dialog Box Launcher in the Clipboard group on the Home tab. When the Clipboard pane is displayed, the Clipboard can store up to 24 text items. When the Clipboard pane is not displayed, the Clipboard can hold only the most recently copied item.

Sabrina would like to move the last sentence in the second paragraph (the paragraph below the title "Prairie Savings and Loan Mortgage Facts"). You'll use cut and paste to move this sentence to a new location.

To move text using cut and paste:

1. Make sure the Home tab is selected on the ribbon.

2. Scroll up until you can see the second paragraph in the document, just below the "Prairie Savings and Loan Mortgage Facts" title.

3. Press and hold **CTRL**, and then click anywhere in the last sentence of the second paragraph, which reads "Talk to your loan agent today about how to get started." The entire sentence is selected, but not the space before it.

4. In the Clipboard group, click the **Cut** button. The selected text is removed from the document and copied to the Clipboard. The space that originally appeared before the sentence remains, so you have to delete it.

5. Press **BACKSPACE** to delete the space.

6. Scroll down to the bottom of page 2, and then click at the end of the second-to-last paragraph in the document, just to the right of the period after "reality."

7. In the Clipboard group, click the **Paste** button. The sentence appears in the new location. Note that Word also inserts a space before the sentence. The Paste Options button appears near the newly inserted sentence.

    Trouble? If a menu opens below the Paste button, you clicked the Paste arrow instead of the Paste button. Press ESC to close the menu, and then repeat Step 7, taking care not to click the arrow below the Paste button.

8. Save the document.

Sabrina explains that she'll be using some text from the mortgage fact sheet as the basis for another department handout. She asks you to copy that information and paste it into a new document. You can do this using the Clipboard pane.

To copy text to paste into a new document:

1. In the Clipboard group, click the **Clipboard Dialog Box Launcher**. The Clipboard pane opens on the left side of the document window, as shown in Figure 2–7.

TIP

You can also press CTRL+X to cut selected text. Press CTRL+V to paste the most recently copied item.

Figure 2–7 Clipboard pane

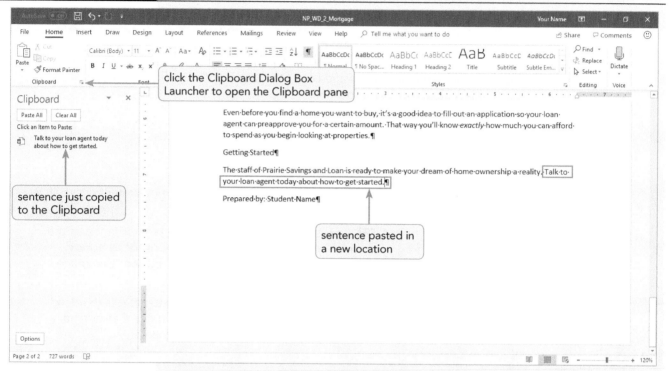

Notice the Clipboard contains the sentence you copied in the last set of steps. Now you can copy another sentence to the Clipboard.

2. Scroll up slightly, if necessary, and then locate the last sentence in the paragraph above the "Getting Started" heading.

3. Press and hold **CTRL**, and then click anywhere in the sentence, which begins "That way you'll know *exactly* how much...." The sentence and the space following it are selected. Notice that the word "exactly" is italicized for emphasis.

4. In the Clipboard group, click the **Copy** button. The sentence appears at the top of the Clipboard pane, as shown in Figure 2–8. You can also copy selected text by pressing CTRL+C.

Figure 2–8 Items in the Clipboard pane

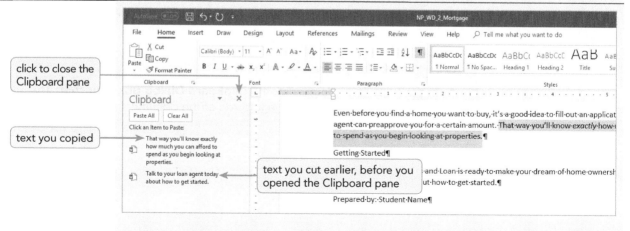

Now you can use the Clipboard pane to insert the copied text into a new document.

To insert the copied text into a new document:

1. Open a new, blank document. Open the Clipboard pane, if necessary. At this point, you could click the Paste All button in the Clipboard pane to paste the entire contents of the Clipboard into the document, but Sabrina wants to paste one item at a time.

2. In the Clipboard pane, click the first item in the list of copied items, which begins "That way you'll know exactly how much...." The text is inserted in the document and the word "exactly" retains its italic formatting.

   Sabrina doesn't want to keep the italic formatting in the newly pasted text. You can remove this formatting by using the Paste Options button, which is visible just below the pasted text.

3. Click the **Paste Options** button 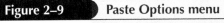 in the document. The Paste Options menu opens, as shown in Figure 2–9.

Figure 2–9   **Paste Options menu**

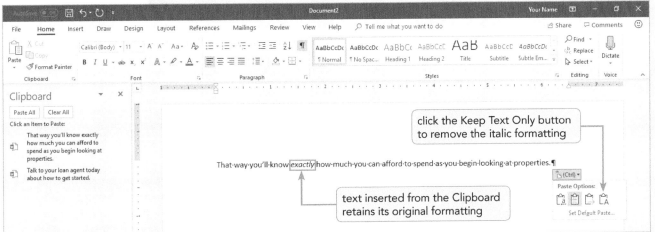

To paste the text without the italic formatting, you can click the Keep Text Only button.

TIP

To select a paste option before pasting an item, click the Paste arrow in the Clipboard group, and then click the paste option you want.

4. Click the **Keep Text Only** button. Word removes the italic formatting from "exactly."

5. Press **ENTER** to start a new paragraph, and then click the second item in the Clipboard pane, which begins "Talk to your loan agent...." The text is inserted as the second paragraph in the document.

6. Save the document as **NP_WD_2_Handout** in the location specified by your instructor, and then close it. You return to the NP_WD_2_Mortgage.docx document, where the Clipboard pane is still open.

7. In the Clipboard pane, click the **Clear All** button. The copied items are removed from the Clipboard.

8. In the Clipboard pane, click the **Close** button. The Clipboard pane closes.

9. Click anywhere in the document to deselect the paragraph, and then save the document.

Using the Navigation Pane

The Navigation pane simplifies the process of moving through a document page by page. You can also use the Navigation pane to locate a particular word or phrase. You start by typing the text you're searching for—the **search text**—in the Search box at the top of the Navigation pane. As shown in the Session 2.1 Visual Overview, Word highlights every instance of the search text in the document. At the same time, a list of the **search results** appears in the Navigation pane. You can click a search result to go immediately to that location in the document.

To become familiar with the Navigation pane, you'll use it to navigate through the document page by page. You'll start by moving the insertion point to the beginning of the document.

To navigate through the document page by page:

▶ **1.** Press **CTRL+HOME** to move the insertion point to the beginning of the document, making sure the Home tab is still selected on the ribbon.

▶ **2.** In the Editing group, click the **Find** button. The Navigation pane opens on the left side of the Word window.

In the box at the top, you can type the text you want to find. The three links below the Search document box—Headings, Pages, and Results—allow you to navigate through the document in different ways. As you become a more experienced Word user, you'll learn how to use the Headings link; for now, you'll ignore it. To move quickly among the pages of a document, you can use the Pages link.

▶ **3.** In the Navigation pane, click the **Pages** link. The Navigation pane displays thumbnail icons of the document's two pages, as shown in Figure 2–10. You can click a page in the Navigation pane to display that page in the document window.

Trouble? If you see the page icons displayed side by side in the Navigation pane, position the mouse pointer over the right border of the Navigation pane until it turns into a two-sided arrow ⇔, click the left mouse button, and then drag the border left until the page icons are as shown in Figure 2–10.

| Figure 2–10 | Document pages displayed in the Navigation pane |

- click to display page thumbnails
- Search document box
- page 1
- page 2

4. In the Navigation pane, click the **page 2** thumbnail. Page 2 is displayed in the document window, with the insertion point blinking at the beginning of the page.

5. In the Navigation pane, click the **page 1** thumbnail to move the insertion point back to the beginning of the document.

Sabrina thinks she might have mistakenly used "prairie savings and loan" in some parts of the document when she actually meant to use "Prairie Savings and Loan." She asks you to use the Navigation pane to find all instances of "prairie savings and loan."

To search for "prairie savings and loan" in the document:

1. In the Navigation pane, click the **Results** link, click the **Search document** box, and then type **prairie savings and loan**. You do not have to press ENTER.

Every instance of the text "prairie savings and loan" is highlighted in yellow in the document. The yellow highlight is only temporary; it will disappear as soon as you begin to perform any other task in the document. A full list of the five search results is displayed in the Navigation pane. Some of the search results contain "Prairie Savings and Loan" (with "P," "S," and "L" in uppercase letters), while others contain "prairie savings and loan" (with all lowercase letters). To narrow the search results, you need to tell Word to match the case of the search text.

2. In the Navigation pane, click the **Search for more things** button ▼ . This displays a two-part menu. In the bottom part, you can select other items to search for, such as graphics or tables. The top part provides more advanced search tools. See Figure 2–11.

Figure 2–11   Navigation pane with Search for more things menu

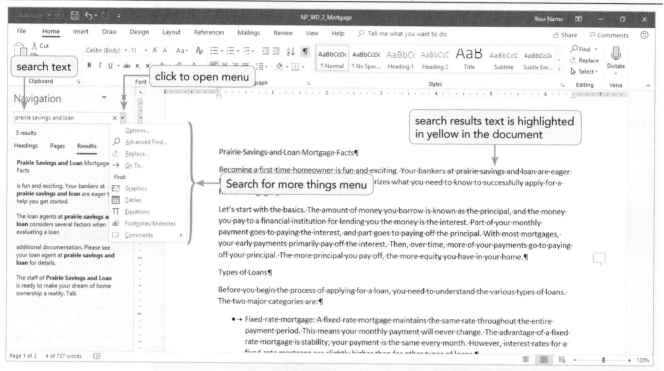

3. At the top of the Search for more things menu, click **Options** to open the Find Options dialog box.

   The check boxes in this dialog box allow you to fine-tune your search. For example, to ensure that Word finds the search text only when it appears as a separate word and not when it appears as part of another word, you could select the Find whole words only check box. Right now, you are concerned only with making sure the search results have the same case as the search text.

4. Click the **Match case** check box to select it, and then click **OK** to close the Find Options dialog box. Now you can search the document again.

5. Press **CTRL+HOME** to move the insertion point to the beginning of the document, click the **Search document** box in the Navigation pane, and then type **prairie savings and loan**. This time, only three search results appear in the Navigation pane, and they contain the lowercase text "prairie savings and loan."

   To move among the search results, you can use the up and down arrows in the Navigation pane.

6. In the Navigation pane, click the **down arrow** button ▼. Word selects the first instance of "prairie savings and loan" in the Navigation pane, as indicated by a blue outline. Also, in the document, the first instance has a gray selection highlight over the yellow highlight. See Figure 2–12.

Figure 2–12   **Navigation pane with the first search result selected**

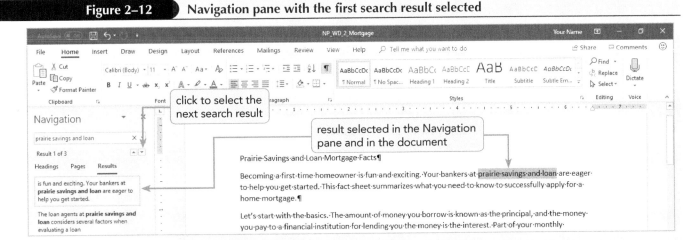

Trouble? If the second instance of "prairie savings and loan" is selected in the Navigation pane, then you pressed ENTER key after typing "prairie savings and loan" in Step 5. Click the up arrow button ▲ to select the first instance.

7. In the Navigation pane, click the **down arrow** button ▼. Word selects the second instance of "prairie savings and loan" in the document and in the Navigation pane.

8. Click the **down arrow** button ▼ again to select the third search result, and then click the **up arrow** button ▲ to select the second search result again.

   You can also select a search result in the document by clicking a search result in the Navigation pane.

9. In the Navigation pane, click the third search result (which begins "additional documentation. Please see…"). The third search result is selected in the document and in the Navigation pane.

After reviewing the search results, Sabrina decides she would like to replace the three instances of "prairie savings and loan" with "Prairie Savings and Loan." You can do that by using the Find and Replace dialog box.

Finding and Replacing Text

To open the Find and Replace dialog box from the Navigation pane, click the Search for more things button, and then click Replace. This opens the **Find and Replace dialog box**, with the Replace tab displayed by default. The Replace tab provides options for finding a specific word or phrase in the document and replacing it with another word or phrase. To use the Replace tab, type the search text in the Find what box, and then type the text you want to substitute in the Replace with box. You can also click the More button on the Replace tab to display the Search Options section, which includes the same options you saw earlier in the Find Options dialog box, including the Find whole words only check box and the Match case check box.

After you have typed the search text and selected any search options, you can click the Find Next button to select the first occurrence of the search text; you can then decide whether to substitute the search text with the replacement text.

REFERENCE

Finding and Replacing Text

- Press CTRL+HOME to move the insertion point to the beginning of the document.
- In the Editing group on the Home tab, click the Replace button, or in the Navigation pane, click the Search for more things button, and then click Replace.
- In the Find and Replace dialog box, click the More button, if necessary, to display the Search Options section of the Replace tab.
- In the Find what box, type the search text.
- In the Replace with box, type the replacement text.
- Select the appropriate check boxes in the Search Options section of the dialog box to narrow your search.
- Click the Find Next button.
- Click the Replace button to substitute the found text with the replacement text and find the next occurrence.
- Click the Replace All button to substitute all occurrences of the found text with the replacement text without reviewing each occurrence. Use this option only if you are absolutely certain that the results will be what you expect.

You'll use the Find and Replace dialog box now to replace three instances of "prairie savings and loan" with "Prairie Savings and Loan."

To replace three instances of "prairie savings and loan" with "Prairie Savings and Loan":

1. Press **CTRL+HOME** to move the insertion point to the beginning of the document.

2. In the Navigation pane, click the **Search for more things** button ▼ to open the menu, and then click **Replace**. The Find and Replace dialog box opens with the Replace tab on top.

   The search text you entered earlier in the Navigation pane, "prairie savings and loan," appears in the Find what box. If you hadn't already conducted a search, you would need to type your search text now. Because you selected the Match case check box earlier in the Find Options dialog box, "Match Case" appears below the Find what box.

3. In the lower-left corner of the dialog box, click the **More** button ▼ to display the search options. Because you selected the Match case check box earlier in the Find Options dialog box, it is selected here.

   Trouble? If you see the Less button instead of the More button, the search options are already displayed.

4. Click the **Replace with** box, and then type **Prairie Savings and Loan**.

5. Click the **Find Next** button. Word highlights the first instance of "prairie savings and loan" in the document. See Figure 2–13.

Figure 2–13 Find and Replace dialog box

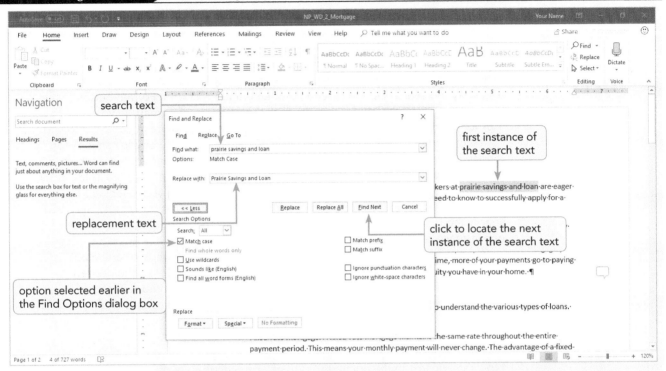

6. Click the **Replace** button. Word replaces "prairie savings and loan" with "Prairie Savings and Loan" and then selects the next instance of "prairie savings and loan." If you do not want to make a replacement, you can click the Find Next button to skip the current instance of the search text and move onto the next. In this case, however, you do want to make the replacement.

7. Click the **Replace** button. Word selects the last instance of "prairie savings and loan."

8. Click the **Replace** button. Word makes the substitution and then displays a message box telling you that Word has finished searching the document.

9. Click **OK** to close the message box, and then in the Find and Replace dialog box, click **Close**.

You are finished with the Navigation pane, so you can close it. But first you need to restore the search options to their original settings. It's a good practice to restore the original search settings so that future searches are not affected by any settings you used for an earlier search.

To restore the search options to their original settings:

1. In the Navigation pane, open the **Find Options** dialog box, deselect the **Match case** check box, and then click **OK** to close the Find Options dialog box.

2. Click the **Close** button ☒ in the upper-right corner of the Navigation pane.

3. Save the document.

INSIGHT

Searching for Formatting

You can search for formatting just as you can search for text. For example, you might want to check a document to look for text formatted in bold and the Arial font. To search for formatting from within the Navigation pane, click the Search for more things button to display the menu, and then click Advanced Find. The Find and Replace dialog box opens with the Find tab displayed. Click the More button, if necessary, to display the Search Options section of the Find tab. Click the Format button at the bottom of the Search Options section, click the category of formatting you want to look for (such as Font or Paragraph), and then select the formatting you want to find.

You can look for formatting that occurs only on specific text, or you can look for formatting that occurs anywhere in a document. If you're looking for text formatted in a certain way (such as all instances of "Prairie Savings and Loan" that are bold), enter the text in the Find what box, and then specify the formatting you're looking for. To find formatting on any text in a document, leave the Find what box empty, and then specify the formatting. Use the Find Next button to move through the document, from one instance of the specified formatting to another.

You can follow the same basic steps on the Replace tab to replace one type of formatting with another. First, click the Find what box and select the desired formatting. Then click the Replace with box and select the desired formatting. If you want, type search text and replacement text in the appropriate boxes. Then proceed as with any Find and Replace operation.

Now that the text in the document is final, you will turn your attention to styles, which affect the look of the entire document.

Working with Styles

A style is a set of formatting options that you can apply by clicking an icon in the Style gallery on the Home tab. Each style is designed for a particular use. For example, the Title style is intended for formatting the title at the beginning of a document.

All the text you type in a document has a style applied to it. By default, text is formatted in the Normal style, which applies 11-point Calibri font, left alignment, 1.08 line spacing, and a small amount of extra space between paragraphs. In other words, the Normal style applies the default formatting you learned about when you first began typing a Word document.

There are two types of styles—character and paragraph. A **paragraph style** is a named set of paragraph and character format settings, such as line spacing, text alignment, and borders, that can be applied to a paragraph to format it all at once. The Normal, Heading, and Title styles all apply paragraph-level formatting. A **character style** is a named group of character format settings; character styles are set up to format only individual characters or words (for example, emphasizing a phrase by adding italic formatting and changing the font color).

One row of the Style gallery is always visible on the Home tab. To display the entire Style gallery, click the More button in the Styles group. After you begin applying styles in a document, the visible row of the Style gallery changes to show the most recently used styles.

You are ready to use the Style gallery to format the document title.

To display the entire Style gallery and then format the document title with a style:

▶ **1.** Make sure the Home tab is still selected and locate the More button in the Styles group, as shown earlier in the Session 2.1 Visual Overview.

▶ **2.** In the Styles group, click the **More** button ⏷. The Style gallery opens, displaying a total of 16 styles arranged in three rows, as shown in Figure 2–14. If your screen is set at a lower resolution than the screenshots in this book, the Style gallery on your screen might contain less than three rows.

Figure 2–14	Displaying the Style gallery

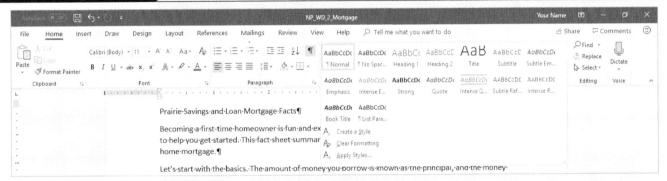

You don't actually need any of the styles in the bottom row now, so you can close the Style gallery.

▶ **3.** Press **ESC** to close the Style gallery.

▶ **4.** Scroll up, if necessary, and click anywhere in the first paragraph, "Prairie Savings and Loan Mortgage Facts," if necessary, and then point to (but don't click) the **Title** style, which is the fifth style from the left in the top row of the gallery. The ScreenTip "Title" is displayed, and a Live Preview of the style appears in the paragraph containing the insertion point, as shown in Figure 2–15. The Title style changes the font to 28-point Calibri Light.

Figure 2–15	Title style in the Style gallery

▶ **5.** Click the **Title** style. The style is applied to the paragraph. After you apply a style you can always add additional formatting. In this case, Sabrina would like you to center the title.

▶ **6.** In the Paragraph group, click the **Center** button ≡. The title is centered in the document.

Next, you will format the document headings using the heading styles, which have different levels. The highest level, Heading 1, is used for the major headings in a document, and it applies the most noticeable formatting using a larger font than the other heading styles. (In heading styles, the highest, or most important, level has the lowest number.) The Heading 2 style is used for headings that are subordinate to the highest level headings; it applies slightly less dramatic formatting than the Heading 1 style.

The handout only has one level of headings, so you will apply only the Heading 1 style.

To format text with the Heading 1 style:

1. Click anywhere in the "Types of Loans" paragraph.

2. On the Home tab, in the Style gallery, click the **Heading 1** style. The paragraph is now formatted in blue, 16-point Calibri Light. The Heading 1 style also inserts some paragraph space above the heading.

3. Scroll down, click anywhere in the "Qualifying for a Home Loan" paragraph, and then click the **Heading 1** style in the Style gallery.

4. Repeat Step 3 to apply the Heading 1 style to the "Loan Approval Process" paragraph, and the "Getting Started" paragraph. When you are finished, scroll up to the beginning of the document to review the new formatting. See Figure 2–16.

5. **sam**⬆ Save your changes and close the document.

Figure 2–16   **Document with Title and Heading 1 styles**

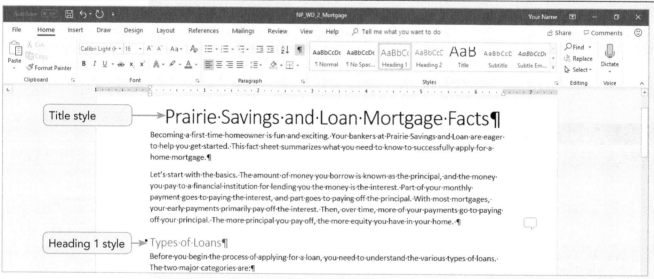

By default, the Style gallery offers 16 styles, each designed for a specific purpose. As you gain more experience with Word, you will learn how to use a wider array of styles. You'll also learn how to create your own styles. Styles allow you to change a document's formatting in an instant. But the benefits of heading styles go far beyond attractive formatting. Heading styles allow you to reorganize a document or generate a table of contents with a click of the mouse. Also, heading styles are set up to keep a heading and the body text that follows it together, so a heading is never separated from its body text by a page break. Each Word document includes nine levels of heading styles, although only the Heading 1 and Heading

2 styles are available by default in the Style gallery. Whenever you use the lowest heading style in the Style gallery, the next-lowest level is added to the Style gallery. For example, after you use the Heading 2 style, the Heading 3 style appears in the Styles group in the Style gallery.

INSIGHT

Creating a Resume with the Resume Assistant

Word Styles are particularly useful when formatting a resume. For additional help in creating a resume, you can use the Resume Assistant pane, which allows you to look for ideas on what to include in your resume. If Word detects that you are working on a document that is formatted like a resume, you might see a suggestion box with the heading "Working on a Resume?" If so, you can click See resume suggestions to open the Resume Assistant. Otherwise, to open it manually, click the Resume Assistant button in the Resume group on the Review tab. This opens the Resume Assistant pane, where you can click Get started to search for tips and examples provided by LinkedIn.

On the first line, type the name of the job (role) you are looking for, and then enter the industry that interests you. For example, you might type "Loan Agent" on the first line and "Banking", on the second line. As you type text in the Resume Assistant, a menu appears where you can click possible search terms. After you've entered your role and industry, you'll see a list of examples. (You might have to click See examples first.) Click Read more in any example to display the full resume. To look for resumes for different jobs, click the Back button, delete the role and industry you entered previously, and type new ones. You can scroll down in the Resume Assistant pane to see a list of top skills for the role you searched on, as well as suggested jobs and articles about resume writing.

Sabrina's mortgage fact sheet is now finished. She will review it, delete the comments, and have copies printed for new homebuyers.

REVIEW

Session 2.1 Quick Check

1. Explain how to insert a comment in a document.
2. Which paste option inserts copied text using the formatting of the surrounding text?
3. How can you ensure that the Navigation pane will find instances of "Prairie Savings and Loan" instead of "prairie savings and loan"?
4. Which style is applied to all text in a new document by default?
5. What are the two types of styles?

Session 2.2 Visual Overview:

Use an easy-to-read font, such as the default Calibri, set to 12 point.

An MLA-style research paper does not require a separate title page; instead, type your name, your instructor's name, the course number, and the date in the upper-left corner of the rst page.

An MLA-style research paper requires 1-inch margins.

Center the title. Do not add any other special formatting unless your title includes the title of another work, in which case you should italicize the title of the other work.

The entire document is double-spaced with no extra space between paragraphs.

Indent the first line of each paragraph, except for the headings.

The text is left-justied, with a ragged right margin.

Include only one space between the end of a sentence and the beginning of the next.

Include citations to tell your readers that you are referring to information from a book, a journal, or some other source. This citation includes the author's last name and the page number.

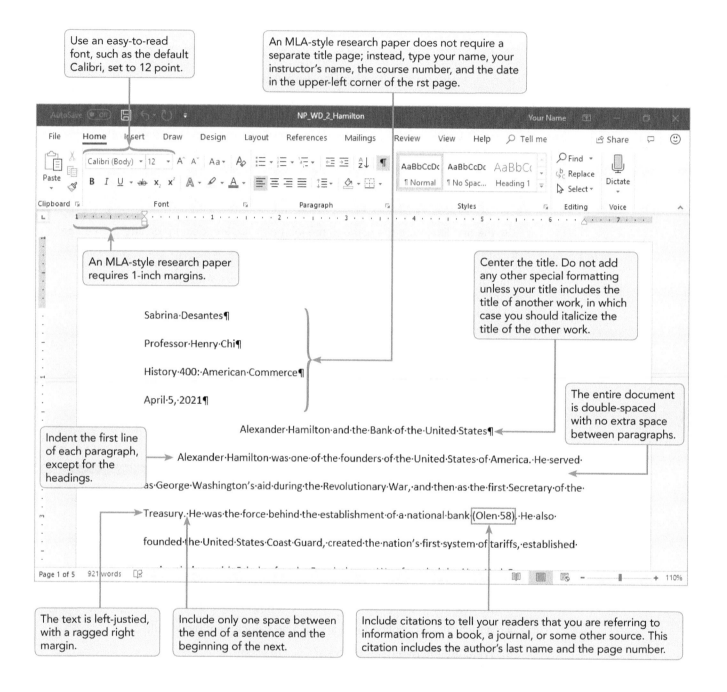

MLA Formatting Guidelines

The References tab includes options that help you create a research paper.

In the Style box, specify the style of research paper you are creating. For college research papers, the MLA style is commonly used.

After you create all the citations, click the Bibliography button to create a list of all the sources mentioned in your citations. This list is known as a **bibliography** or, in the MLA style, a **works cited list**.

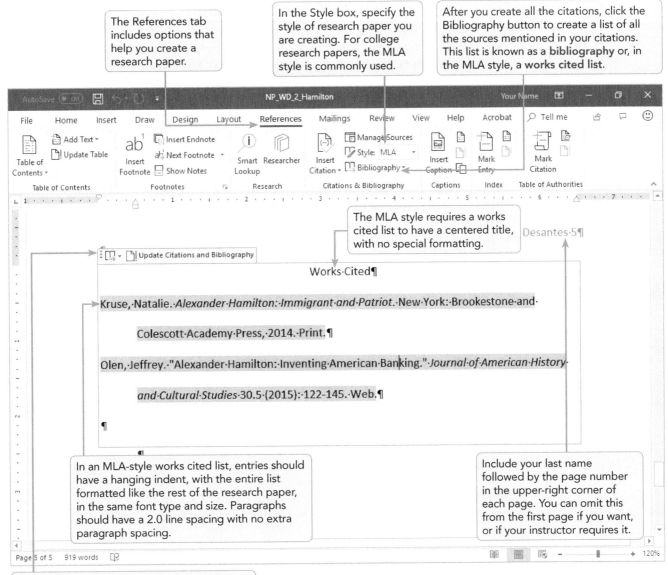

The MLA style requires a works cited list to have a centered title, with no special formatting.

Desantes·5¶

Works·Cited¶

Kruse,·Natalie.·*Alexander·Hamilton:·Immigrant·and·Patriot*.·New·York:·Brookestone·and· Colescott·Academy·Press,·2014.·Print.¶

Olen,·Jeffrey.·"Alexander·Hamilton:·Inventing·American·Banking."·*Journal·of·American·History· and·Cultural·Studies*·30.5·(2015):·122-145.·Web.¶

In an MLA-style works cited list, entries should have a hanging indent, with the entire list formatted like the rest of the research paper, in the same font type and size. Paragraphs should have a 2.0 line spacing with no extra paragraph spacing.

Include your last name followed by the page number in the upper-right corner of each page. You can omit this from the first page if you want, or if your instructor requires it.

Word inserts a bibliography, or works cited list, contained in a special feature, known as a **content control**, used to display information that is inserted automatically and that may need to be updated later. You can use the buttons in the content control tab to make changes to material inside the content control.

Reviewing the MLA Style

A **style guide** is a set of rules that describe the preferred format and style for a certain type of writing. People in different fields use different style guides, with each style guide designed to suit the needs of a specific discipline. For example, journalists commonly use the *Associated Press Stylebook*, which focuses on the concise writing style common in magazines and newspapers. In the world of academics, style guides emphasize the proper way to create a **citation**, which is a formal reference to the work of others that appears in parentheses at the end of a sentence. Researchers in the social and behavioral sciences use the **American Psychological Association (APA) style**, which is designed to help readers scan an article quickly for key points and emphasizes the date of publication in citations. Other scientific and technical fields have their own specialized style guides.

In the humanities, the **Modern Language Association (MLA) style** is widely used. This is the style Sabrina has used for her research paper. She followed the guidelines specified in the *MLA Handbook for Writers of Research Papers*, published by the Modern Language Association of America. These guidelines focus on specifications for formatting a research document and citing the sources used in research conducted for a paper. The major formatting features of an MLA-style research paper are illustrated in the Session 2.2 Visual Overview. Compared to style guides for technical fields, the MLA style is very flexible, making it easy to include citations without disrupting the natural flow of the writing. MLA-style citations of other writers' works take the form of a brief parenthetical entry, with a complete reference to each item included in the alphabetized bibliography, also known as the works cited list, at the end of the research paper.

INSIGHT

Formatting an MLA-Style Research Paper

The MLA guidelines were developed, in part, to simplify the process of transforming a manuscript into a journal article or a chapter of a book. The style calls for minimal formatting; the simpler the formatting in a manuscript, the easier it is to turn the text into a published document. The MLA guidelines were also designed to ensure consistency in documents, so that all research papers look alike. Therefore, you should apply no special formatting to the text in an MLA-style research paper. Headings should be formatted like the other text in the document, with no bold or heading styles.

Sabrina has started writing a research paper on Alexander Hamilton for her class. You'll open the draft of Sabrina's research paper and determine what needs to be done to make it meet the MLA style guidelines for a research paper.

To open the document and review it for MLA style:

▶ 1. **sam** ⬇ Open the document **NP_WD_2-2.docx** located in the Word2 > Module folder included with your Data Files, and then save the document as **NP_WD_2_Hamilton** in the location specified by your instructor.

▶ 2. Verify that the document is displayed in Print Layout view, and that the rulers and nonprinting characters are displayed. Make sure the Zoom level is set to **120%**.

▶ 3. Review the document to familiarize yourself with its structure. First, notice the parts of the document that already match the MLA style. Sabrina included a block of information in the upper-left corner of the first page, giving her name, her instructor's name, the course name, and the date. The title at the top of the first page also meets the MLA guidelines in that it is centered and does not have any special formatting. The headings ("Early Life," "Revolutionary War," "The Federalist Papers," and "Building a New Economy") have no special formatting; but unlike the title, they are left-aligned. Finally, the body text is left-aligned with a ragged right margin, and the entire document is formatted in the same font, Calibri, which is easy to read.

What needs to be changed in order to make Sabrina's paper consistent with the MLA style? Currently, the entire document is formatted using the default settings, which are the Normal style for the Office theme. To transform the document into an MLA-style research paper, you need to complete the checklist shown in Figure 2–17.

Figure 2–17   **Checklist for formatting a default Word document to match the MLA style**

✓ Double-space the entire document.

✓ Remove extra paragraph spacing from the entire document.

✓ Increase the font size for the entire document to 12 points.

✓ Indent the first line of each body paragraph .5 inch from the left margin.

✓ Add the page number (preceded by your last name) in the upper-right corner of each page. If you prefer, you can omit this from the first page.

You'll take care of the first three items in the checklist now.

To begin applying MLA formatting to the document:

1. Press **CTRL+A** to select the entire document.

2. Make sure the Home tab is selected on the ribbon.

3. In the Paragraph group, click the **Line and Paragraph Spacing** button and then click **2.0**.

4. Click the **Line and Spacing** button again, and then click **Remove Space After Paragraph**. The entire document is now double-spaced, with no paragraph spacing, and the entire document is still selected.

5. In the Font group, click the **Font Size arrow**, and then click **12**. The entire document is formatted in 12-point font.

6. Click anywhere in the document to deselect the text.

7. In the first paragraph of the document, replace Sabrina's name with your first and last names, and then save the document.

Now you need to indent the first line of each body paragraph.

Indenting a Paragraph

Word offers a number of options for indenting a paragraph. You can move an entire paragraph to the right, or you can create specialized indents, such as a **hanging indent**, where all lines except the first line of the paragraph are indented from the left margin. As you saw in the Session 2.2 Visual Overview, all the body paragraphs (that is, all the paragraphs except the information in the upper-left corner of the first page, the title, and the headings) have a first-line indent in MLA research papers. Figure 2-18 shows some examples of other common paragraph indents.

Figure 2-18   Common paragraph indents

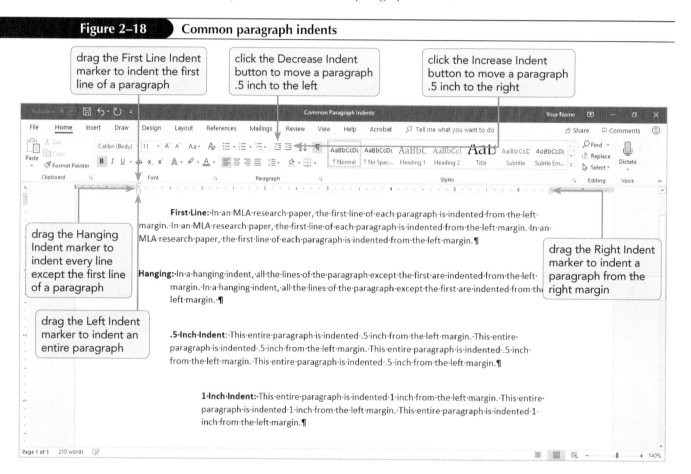

To quickly indent an entire paragraph .5 inch from the left, position the insertion point in the paragraph you want to indent, and then click the Increase Indent button in the Paragraph group on the Home tab. You can continue to indent the paragraph in increments of .5 inch by repeatedly clicking the Increase Indent button. To move an indented paragraph back to the left .5 inch, click the Decrease Indent button.

To create first-line, hanging, or right indents, you can use the indent markers on the ruler. First, click in the paragraph you want to indent or select multiple paragraphs. Then drag the appropriate indent marker to the left or right on the horizontal ruler. The indent markers are small and can be hard to see. As shown in Figure 2-18, the **First Line Indent marker** is triangle-shaped and looks like the top half of an hourglass; the **Hanging Indent marker** looks like the bottom half. The rectangle below the Hanging Indent marker is the **Left Indent marker**. The **Right Indent marker** looks just like the Hanging Indent marker except that it is located on the far-right side of the horizontal ruler.

Note that when you indent an entire paragraph using the Increase Indent button, the three indent markers move as a unit along with the paragraphs you are indenting. If you prefer, instead of dragging indent markers to indent a paragraph, you can click the Dialog Box Launcher in the Paragraph group on the Home tab, and then adjust the Indentation settings in the Paragraph dialog box.

In Sabrina's paper, you will indent the first lines of the body paragraphs .5 inch from the left margin, as specified by the MLA style.

To indent the first line of each paragraph:

▶ 1. On the first page of the document, just below the title, click anywhere in the first main paragraph, which begins "Alexander Hamilton was…."

▶ 2. On the horizontal ruler, position the pointer over the First Line Indent marker ▽. When you see the ScreenTip that reads "First Line Indent," you know the mouse is positioned correctly.

▶ 3. Press and hold the mouse button as you drag the **First Line Indent** marker ▽ to the right, to the .5-inch mark on the horizontal ruler. As you drag, a vertical guideline appears over the document, and the first line of the paragraph moves right. See Figure 2–19.

| Figure 2–19 | Dragging the First Line Indent marker |

First Line Indent marker

.5-inch mark

guideline appears as you drag the indent marker and the first line of the paragraph moves right

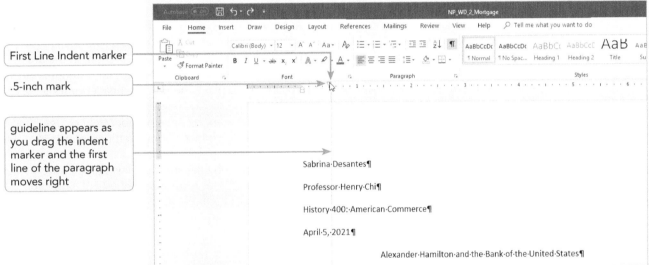

▶ 4. When the First Line Indent marker ▽ is positioned at the .5-inch mark on the ruler, release the mouse button. The first line of the paragraph containing the insertion point indents .5 inch, and the vertical guideline disappears.

▶ 5. Scroll down, if necessary, click anywhere in the next paragraph in the document (which begins "All told, Alexander Hamilton…"), and then drag the **First Line Indent** marker ▽ to the right, to the .5-inch mark on the horizontal ruler. As you move the indent marker, you can use the vertical guideline to ensure that you match the first-line indent of the preceding paragraph.

You could continue to drag the indent marker to indent the first line of the remaining body paragraphs, but it's faster to use the Repeat button on the Quick Access Toolbar.

▶ 6. Scroll down and click in the paragraph below the "Early Life" heading, and then on the Quick Access Toolbar, click the **Repeat** button ↻. Note that, on most computers, you can press F4 instead to repeat an action, if you prefer.

▶ **7.** Click in the next paragraph, at the top of page 2 (which begins "He soon began to desire…"), and then click the **Repeat** button ↻.

▶ **8.** Continue using the **Repeat** button ↻ to indent the first line of all of the remaining body paragraphs, including the paragraph on page 4. Take care not to indent the headings, which in this document are formatted just like the body text.

▶ **9.** Scroll to the top of the document, verify that you have correctly indented the first line of each body paragraph, and then save the document.

Next, you need to insert page numbers.

Inserting and Modifying Page Numbers

When you insert page numbers in a document, you don't have to type a page number on each page. Instead, you can insert a **page number field**, which is an instruction that tells Word to insert a page number on each page, no matter how many pages you eventually add to the document. Word inserts page number fields above the top margin, in the blank area known as the **header**, or below the bottom margin, in the area known as the **footer**. You can also insert page numbers in the side margins, although for business or academic documents, it's customary to place them in the header or footer.

After you insert a page number field, Word switches to Header and Footer view. In this view, you can add your name or other text next to the page number field or use the Header & Footer Tools Design contextual tab to change various settings related to headers and footers.

The MLA style requires a page number preceded by the student's last name in the upper-right corner of each page. If you prefer (or if your instructor requests it), you can omit the page number from the first page by selecting the Different First Page check box on the Header & Footer Tools Design tab.

To add page numbers to the research paper:

▶ **1.** Press **CTRL+HOME** to move the insertion point to the beginning of the document.

▶ **2.** On the ribbon, click the **Insert** tab. The ribbon changes to display the Insert options, including options for inserting page numbers.

▶ **3.** In the Header & Footer group, click the **Page Number** button to open the Page Number menu. Here you can choose where you want to position the page numbers in your document—at the top of the page, at the bottom of the page, in the side margins, or at the current location of the insertion point. To remove page numbers from a document, you can click the Remove Page Numbers command on the Page Number menu.

▶ **4.** Point to **Top of Page**. A gallery of page number styles opens. You can scroll the list to review the many styles of page numbers. Because the MLA style calls for a simple page number in the upper-right corner, you will use the Plain Number 3 style. See Figure 2–20.

Figure 2-20   **Gallery of page number styles**

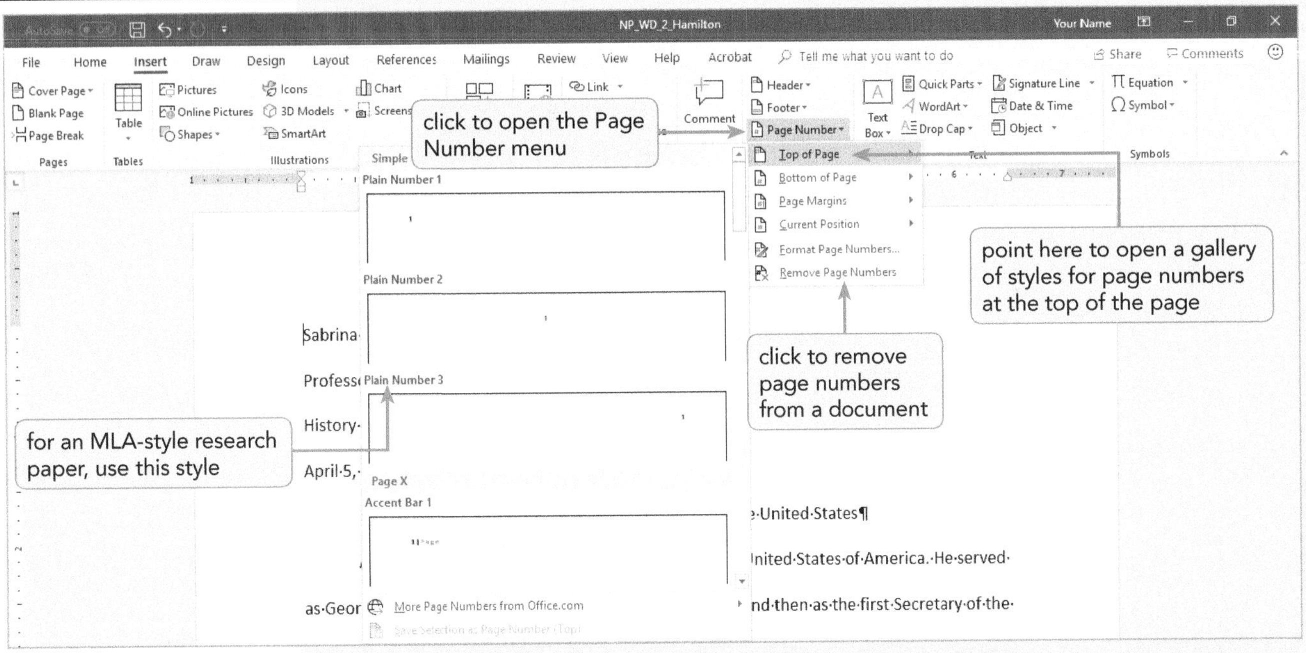

5. In the gallery, click the **Plain Number 3** style. The Word window switches to Header and Footer view, with the page number for the first page in the upper-right corner. The page number has a gray background, indicating that it is actually a page number field and not simply a number that you typed.

The Header & Footer Tools Design tab is displayed on the ribbon, giving you access to a variety of formatting options. The insertion point blinks to the left of the page number field, ready for you to add text to the header if you wish. Note that in Header and Footer view, you can type only in the header or footer areas. The text in the main document area is a lighter shade of gray, indicating that it cannot be edited in this view.

6. Type your last name, and then press **SPACEBAR**. If you see a wavy red line below your last name, right-click your name, and then click **Ignore All** on the Shortcut menu.

7. Select your last name and the page number field.

8. In the Mini toolbar, click the **Font Size arrow**, click **12**, and then click anywhere in the header to deselect the text. Now the header's font size matches the font size of the rest of the document. This isn't strictly necessary in an MLA research paper, but some instructors prefer it. The page number no longer has a gray background, but it is still a field, which you can verify by clicking it.

9. Click the **page number field** to display its gray background. See Figure 2-21.

Figure 2-21 Last name inserted next to the page number field

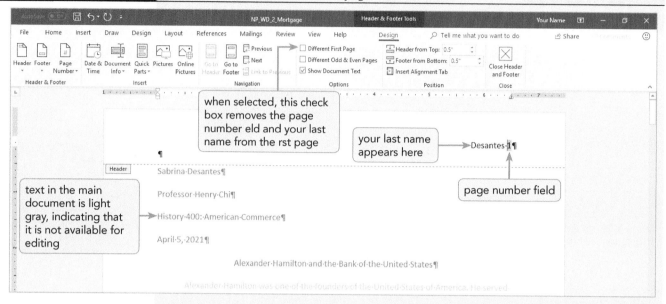

10. Scroll down and observe the page number (with your last name) at the top of pages 2, 3, and 4. As you can see, whatever you insert in the header on one page appears on every page of the document by default.

11. Scroll up to return to the header on the first page.

12. On the Header & Footer Tools Design tab, in the Options group, click the **Different First Page** check box to insert a check. The page number field and your last name are removed from the first page header. The insertion point blinks at the header's left margin in case you want to insert something else for the first page header. In this case, you don't.

TIP

After you insert page numbers, you can reopen Header and Footer view by double-clicking a page number in Print Layout view.

13. In the Close group, click the **Close Header and Footer** button. You return to Print Layout view, and the Header & Footer Tools Design tab is no longer displayed on the ribbon.

14. Scroll down to review your last name and the page number in the headers for pages 2, 3, and 4. In Print Layout view, the text in the header is light gray, indicating that it is not currently available for editing.

You have finished all the tasks related to formatting the MLA-style research paper. Now Sabrina would like to add a footnote to provide some extra information.

Creating a Footnote

A **footnote** is an explanatory comment or reference that appears at the bottom of a page. When you create a footnote, Word inserts a small, superscript number (called a **reference marker**) in the text. The term **superscript** means that the number is raised slightly above the line of text. Word then inserts the same number in the page's bottom margin and positions the insertion point next to it so you can type the text of the footnote. **Endnotes** are similar, except that the text of an endnote appears at the end of a document. By default, the reference marker for an endnote is a lowercase Roman numeral, and the reference marker for a footnote is an ordinary, Arabic numeral.

Word automatically manages the reference markers for you, keeping them sequential from the beginning of the document to the end, no matter how many times you add, delete, or move footnotes or endnotes. For example, if you move a paragraph containing footnote 4 so that it falls before the paragraph containing footnote 1, Word renumbers all the footnotes in the document to keep them sequential.

REFERENCE

Inserting a Footnote or an Endnote

- Click the location in the document where you want to insert a footnote or an endnote.
- On the ribbon, click the References tab.
- In the Footnotes group, click the Insert Footnote button or the Insert Endnote button.
- Type the text of the footnote in the bottom margin of the page, or type the text of the endnote at the end of the document.
- When you are finished typing the text of a footnote or an endnote, click in the body of the document to continue working on the document.

Sabrina asks you to insert a footnote that provides additional information about Alexander Hamilton's writing skills.

To add a footnote to the research paper:

1. Use the Navigation pane to find the phrase "made him invaluable" on page 2, and then click to the right of the period after "invaluable."

2. Close the Navigation pane.

3. On the ribbon, click the **References** tab.

4. In the Footnotes group, click the **Insert Footnote** button. A superscript "1" is inserted to the right of the period after "invaluable." Word also inserts the number "1" in the bottom margin below a separator line. The insertion point is now located next to the number in the bottom margin, ready for you to type the text of the footnote.

5. Type **A digital archive of his letters maintained by the New York Public Library testifies to his excellent handwriting.** See Figure 2–22.

Figure 2–22   **Inserting a footnote**

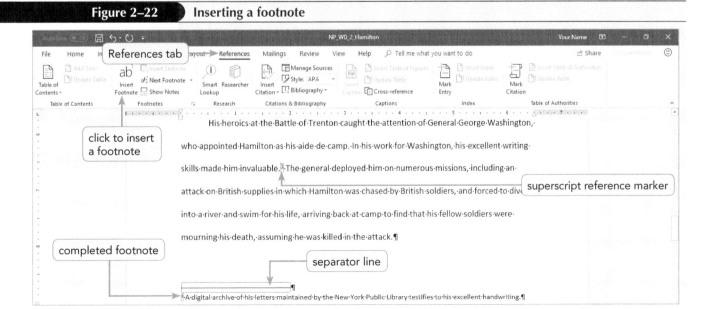

Now, Sabrina would like you to insert a second footnote.

To insert a second footnote:

▶ **1.** Scroll up to the third line of page 2, locate the phrase "send Hamilton to New York to be educated" and then click to the right of the period after "educated."

▶ **2.** In the Footnotes group, click the **Insert Footnote** button, and then type **The letter impressed a local newspaper owner, who decided to publish it.** Because this footnote is placed earlier in the document than the one you just created, Word inserts a superscript "1" for this footnote and then renumbers the other footnote as "2." See Figure 2–23. You can easily move back and forth between superscript footnote numbers and footnote text, as you'll see in the next two steps.

Figure 2–23	Inserting a second footnote

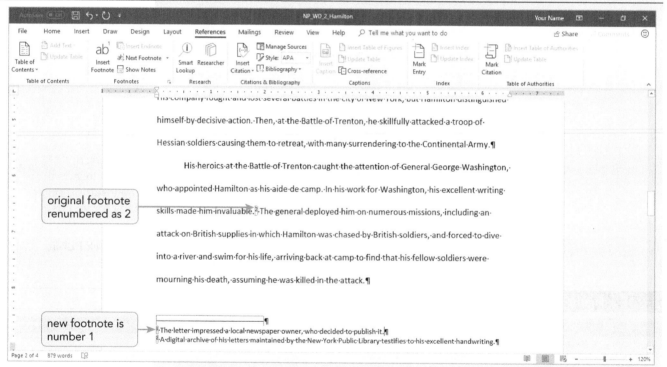

▶ **3.** Scroll up to the first paragraph of page 2 and double-click the superscript **1** after the word "educated." The screen scrolls down to display the footnote at the bottom of the page.

▶ **4.** Double-click the **1** at the beginning of the footnote. The screen scrolls up to display the superscript number 1 in the first paragraph on page 2.

▶ **5.** Save the document.

Inserting endnotes is similar to inserting footnotes, except that the notes appear at the end of the document. To insert an endnote, click where you want to insert it, and then click the Insert Endnote button in the Footnotes group on the References tab. You can double-click endnote numbers to move back and forth between the superscript numbers in the document and the notes at the end of the document.

Next Sabrina wants your help with creating the essential parts of any research paper—the citations and the bibliography.

Creating Citations and a Bibliography

A bibliography (or, as it is called in the MLA style, the works cited list) is an alphabetical list of all the books, magazine articles, websites, movies, and other works referred to in a research paper. The items listed in a bibliography are known as **sources**. The entry for each source includes information such as the author, the title of the work, the publication date, and the publisher.

Within the research paper itself, you include a parenthetical reference, or citation, every time you summarize, quote, or refer to a source. Every source included in your citations then has a corresponding entry in the works cited list. A citation should include enough information to identify the quote or referenced material, so the reader can easily locate the source in the accompanying works cited list. The exact form for a citation varies depending on the style guide you are using and the type of material you are referencing.

Some style guides are very rigid about the form and location of citations, but the MLA style offers quite a bit of flexibility. Typically, though, you insert an MLA citation at the end of a sentence in which you quote or refer to material from a source. For books or journals, the citation itself usually includes the author's last name and a page number. However, if the sentence containing the citation already includes the author's name, you need to include only the page number in the citation. Figure 2–24 provides some sample MLA citations; the format shown could be used for books or journals. For detailed guidelines, you can consult the *MLA Handbook, Eighth Edition*.

Figure 2–24 MLA guidelines for citing a book or journal

Citation Rule	Example
If the sentence includes the author's name, the citation should only include the page number.	Peterson compares the opening scene of the movie to a scene from Shakespeare (188).
If the sentence does not include the author's name, the citation should include the author's name and the page number.	The opening scene of the movie has been compared to a scene from Shakespeare (Peterson 188).

Note that Word's citation and bibliography tools correspond to the seventh edition of the *MLA Handbook*. The main difference between the seventh and eighth editions is better guidance on citing digital sources in the eighth edition. See this webpage for a summary of what's new in the eighth edition: www.mla.org/MLA-Style/What-s-New-in-the-Eighth-Edition. For quick guidelines and examples, go to the MLA Style Center at https://style.mla.org.

Word greatly simplifies the process of creating citations and a bibliography. You specify the style you want to use, and then Word takes care of setting up the citation and the works cited list appropriately. Every time you create a citation for a new source, Word prompts you to enter the information needed to create the corresponding entry in the works cited list. If you don't have all of your source information available, Word also allows you to insert a temporary, placeholder citation, which you can replace later with a complete citation. When you are finished creating your citations, Word generates the bibliography automatically. Note that placeholder citations are not included in the bibliography.

PROSKILLS

Written Communication: Acknowledging Your Sources

A research paper is a means for you to explore the available information about a subject and then present this information, along with your own understanding of the subject, in an organized and interesting way. Acknowledging all the sources of the information presented in your research paper is essential. If you fail to do this, you might be subject to charges of plagiarism, or trying to pass off someone else's thoughts as your own. Plagiarism is an extremely serious accusation for which you could suffer academic consequences ranging from failing an assignment to being expelled from school.

To ensure that you don't forget to cite a source, you should be careful about creating citations in your document as you type. In this module, you will insert citations into completed paragraphs as practice, but in real life you should insert citations as you type your document. It's easy to forget to go back and cite all your sources correctly after you've finished typing a research paper. Failing to cite a source could lead to accusations of plagiarism and all the consequences that entails. If you don't have the complete information about a source available when you are typing your paper, you should at least insert a placeholder citation. But take care to go back later and substitute complete citations for any placeholders.

Creating Citations

Before you create citations, you need to select the style you want to use, which in the case of Sabrina's paper is the MLA style. Then, to insert a citation, you click the Insert Citation button in the Citations & Bibliography group on the References tab. If you are citing a source for the first time, Word prompts you to enter all the information required for the source's entry in the bibliography or works cited list. If you are citing an existing source, you simply select the source from the Insert Citation menu.

By default, an MLA citation includes only the author's name in parentheses. However, you can use the Edit Citation dialog box to add a page number. You can also use the Edit Citation dialog box to remove, or suppress, the author's name, so only the page number appears in the citation. However, in an MLA citation, Word will replace the suppressed author name with the title of the source, so you need to suppress the title as well, by selecting the Title check box in the Edit Citation dialog box.

REFERENCE

Creating Citations

- On the ribbon, click the References tab. In the Citations & Bibliography group, click the Style arrow, and then select the style you want.
- Click in the document where you want to insert the citation. Typically, a citation goes at the end of a sentence, before the ending punctuation.
- To add a citation for a new source, click the Insert Citation button in the Citations & Bibliography group, click Add New Source, enter information in the Create Source dialog box, and then click OK.
- To add a citation for an existing source, click the Insert Citation button, and then click the source.
- To add a placeholder citation, click the Insert Citation button, click Add New Placeholder, and then, in the Placeholder Name dialog box, type placeholder text, such as the author's last name, that will serve as a reminder about which source you need to cite. Note that a placeholder citation cannot contain any spaces.
- To add a page number to a citation, click the citation in the document, click the Citation Options button, click Edit Citation, type the page number, and then click OK.
- To display only the page number in a citation, click the citation in the document, click the Citation Options button, and then click Edit Citation. In the Edit Citation dialog box, select the Author and Title check boxes to suppress this information, and then click OK.

So far, Sabrina has referenced information from two different sources in her research paper. You'll select a style and then begin adding the appropriate citations.

To select a style for the citation and bibliography:

▶ **1.** On the ribbon, click the **References** tab. The ribbon changes to display references options.

▶ **2.** In the Citations & Bibliography group, click the **Style arrow**, and then click **MLA Seventh Edition** if it is not already selected.

▶ **3.** Press **CTRL+F** to open the Navigation pane.

▶ **4.** Use the Navigation pane to find the phrase "However, as at least one historian," which appears on page 3, and then click in the document at the end of that sentence (between the end of the word "him" and the closing period).

▶ **5.** Close the **Navigation** pane, and then click the **References** tab on the ribbon, if necessary. You need to add a citation that informs the reader that historian Natalia Cruz made the observation described in the sentence. See Figure 2–25.

Be sure to select the correct citation and bibliography style before you begin.

Figure 2-25 **MLA style selected and insertion point positioned for new citation**

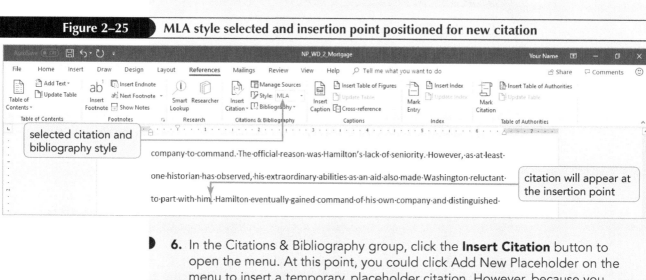

▶ **6.** In the Citations & Bibliography group, click the **Insert Citation** button to open the menu. At this point, you could click Add New Placeholder on the menu to insert a temporary, placeholder citation. However, because you have all the necessary source information, you can go ahead and create a complete citation.

▶ **7.** On the menu, click **Add New Source**. The Create Source dialog box opens, ready for you to add the information required to create a bibliography entry for Natalia Cruz's book.

▶ **8.** If necessary, click the **Type of Source arrow**, scroll up or down in the list, and then click **Book**.

▶ **9.** In the Author box, type **Natalia Cruz**.

▶ **10.** Click in the **Title** box, and then type **Alexander Hamilton: Immigrant and Patriot**.

▶ **11.** Click in the **Year** box, and then type **2014**. This is the year the book was published. Next, you need to enter the name and location of the publisher.

▶ **12.** Click the **City** box, type **New York**, click the **Publisher** box, and then type **Brookstone and Colescott Academy Press**.

Finally, you need to indicate the medium used to publish the book. In this case, Sabrina used a printed copy, so the medium is "Print." For books or journals published online, the correct medium would be "Web."

▶ **13.** Click the **Medium** box, and then type **Print**. See Figure 2-26.

Figure 2-26 **Create Source dialog box with information for the first source**

▶ **14.** Click **OK**. Word inserts the parenthetical "(Cruz)" at the end of the sentence in the document.

Trouble? If the Researcher pane opens, close it.

Although the citation looks like ordinary text, it is actually contained inside a content control, a special feature used to display information that is inserted automatically and that may need to be updated later. You can see the content control itself only when it is selected. When it is unselected, you simply see the citation. In the next set of steps, you will select the content control and then edit the citation to add a page number.

To edit the citation:

▶ **1.** In the document, click the citation **(Cruz)**. The citation appears in a content control, which is a box with a tab on the left and an arrow button on the right. The arrow button is called the Citation Options button.

▶ **2.** Click the **Citation Options** button. A menu of options related to editing a citation opens, as shown in Figure 2–27.

Figure 2–27   **Citation Options menu**

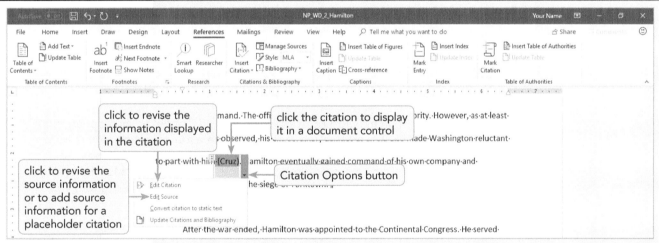

To edit the information about the source, you click Edit Source. To change the information that is displayed in the citation itself, you use the Edit Citation option.

▶ **3.** On the Citation Options menu, click **Edit Citation**. The Edit Citation dialog box opens, as shown in Figure 2–28.

Figure 2–28   **Edit Citation dialog box**

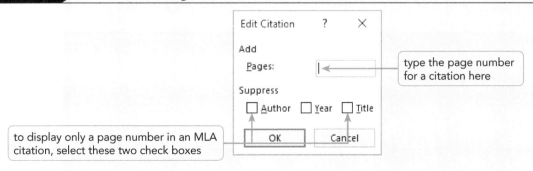

To add a page number for the citation, you type the page number in the Pages box. If you want to display only the page number in the citation (which would be necessary if you already mentioned the author's name in the same sentence in the text), then you would also select the Author and Title check boxes in this dialog box to suppress this information.

4. Type **37** to insert the page number in the Pages box, click **OK** to close the dialog box, and then click anywhere in the document outside the citation content control. The revised citation now reads "(Cruz 37)."

Note that if you need to delete a citation, you can click the citation to display the content control, click the tab on the left side of the content control, and then press DEL. Next, you will add two more citations, both for the same journal article.

To insert two more citations:

1. Scroll down to the second-to-last paragraph on page 3, and then click at the end of the last sentence in that paragraph (which begins "According to historian Jeffrey Olen…"), between the word "powers" and the period. This sentence mentions historian Jeffrey Olen; you need to add a citation to one of his journal articles.

2. In the Citations & Bibliography group, click the **Insert Citation** button to open the Insert Citation menu. Notice that Natalia Cruz's book is now listed as a source on this menu. You could click Cruz's book on the menu to add a citation to it, but right now you need to add a new source.

3. Click **Add New Source** to open the Create Source dialog box, click the **Type of Source arrow**, and then click **Journal Article**.

   The Create Source dialog box displays the boxes, or fields, appropriate for a journal article. The information required to cite a journal article differs from the information you entered earlier for the citation for the Cruz book. For journal articles, you are prompted to enter the page numbers for the entire article. If you want to display a particular page number in the citation, you can add it later.

   By default, Word displays boxes, or fields, for the information most commonly included in a bibliography. In this case, you also want to include the volume and issue numbers for Jeffrey Olen's article, so you need to display more fields.

4. In the Create Source dialog box, click the **Show All Bibliography Fields** check box to select this option. The Create Source dialog box expands to allow you to enter more detailed information. Red asterisks highlight the fields that are recommended, but these recommended fields don't necessarily apply to every source.

5. Enter the following information, scrolling down to display the necessary boxes:

Author: **Jeffrey Olen**

Title: **Alexander Hamilton: Inventing American Banking**

Journal Name: **Journal of American History and Cultural Studies**

Year: **2015**

Pages: **122–145**

Volume: **30**

Issue: **5**

Medium: **Web**

When you are finished, your Create Source dialog box should look like the one shown in Figure 2–29.

| Figure 2–29 | Create Source dialog box with information for the journal article |

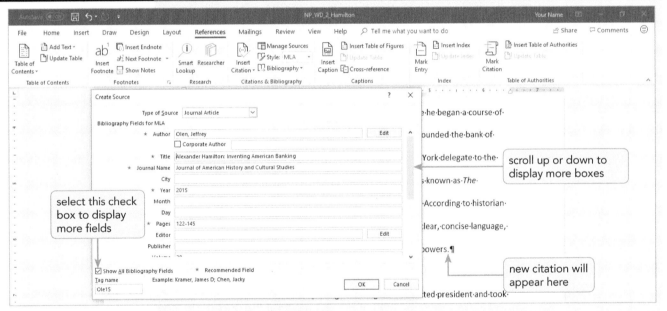

6. Click **OK**. The Create Source dialog box closes, and the citation "(Olen)" is inserted in the text. Because the sentence containing the citation already includes the author's name, you will edit the citation to include the page number and suppress the author's name.

7. Click the **(Olen)** citation to display the content control, click the **Citation Options** button ⬇, and then click **Edit Citation** to open the Edit Citation dialog box.

8. In the Pages box, type **142**, and then click the **Author** and **Title** check boxes to select them. You need to suppress both the author's name and the title because otherwise Word will replace the suppressed author name with the title. When using the MLA style, you don't ever have to suppress the year because the year is never included as part of an MLA citation. When working in other styles, however, you might need to suppress the year.

▶ **9.** Click **OK** to close the Edit Citation dialog box, and then click anywhere outside the content control to deselect it. The end of the sentence now reads "…separation of powers (142)."

▶ **10.** Scroll down to the last sentence in the document. Click at the end of the sentence, to the left of the period after "1811."

▶ **11.** On the References tab, in the Citations & Bibliography group, click the **Insert Citation** button, and then click the **Olen, Jeffrey** source in the menu. You want the citation to refer to the entire article instead of just one page, so you will not edit the citation to add a specific page number.

▶ **12.** Save the document.

You have entered the source information for two sources.

INSIGHT

Understanding Endnotes, Footnotes, and Citations

It's easy to confuse footnotes with endnotes, and endnotes with citations. Remember, a footnote appears at the bottom, or foot, of a page and always on the same page as its reference marker. You might have one footnote at the bottom of page 3, three footnotes at the bottom of page 5, and one at the bottom of page 6. By contrast, an endnote appears at the end of the document, with all the endnotes compiled into a single list. Both endnotes and footnotes can contain any kind of information you think might be useful to your readers. Citations, however, are only used to list specific information about a book or other source you refer to or quote from in the document. A citation typically appears in parentheses at the end of the sentence containing information from the source you are citing, and the sources for all of the document's citations are listed in a bibliography, or a list of works cited, at the end of the document.

Inserting a Page Break

Once you have created a citation for a source in a document, you can generate a bibliography. In the MLA style, the bibliography (or works cited list) starts on a new page. So your first step is to insert a manual page break. A **manual page break** is one you insert at a specific location; it doesn't matter if the previous page is full or not. To insert a manual page break, use the Page Break button in the Pages group on the Insert tab.

To insert a manual page break:

▶ **1.** Press **CTRL+END** to move the insertion point to the end of the document.

▶ **2.** On the ribbon, click the **Insert** tab.

▶ **3.** In the Pages group, click the **Page Break** button. Word inserts a new, blank page at the end of the document, with the insertion point blinking at the top. Note that you could also use the CTRL+ENTER keyboard shortcut to insert a manual page break. To insert a new, blank page in the middle of a document, you would use the Blank Page button in the Pages group instead.

▶ **4.** Scroll up to see the dotted line with the words "Page Break" at the bottom of the text on page 4. You can delete a manual page break just as you would delete any other nonprinting character, by clicking immediately to its left and then pressing DEL. See Figure 2–30.

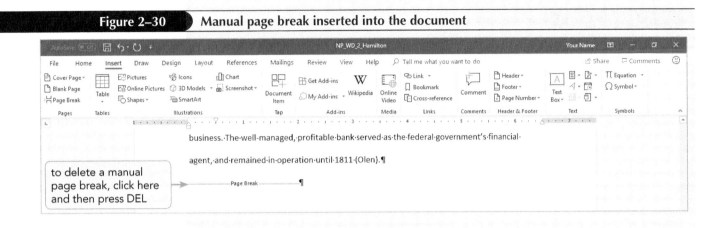

Figure 2-30   Manual page break inserted into the document

Now you can insert the bibliography on the new page 5.

Generating a Bibliography

When you generate a bibliography, Word scans all the citations in the document, collecting the source information for each citation, and then it creates a list of information for each unique source. The format of the entries in the bibliography will reflect the style you specified when you created your first citation, which in this case is the MLA style. The bibliography itself is a **field**, similar to the page number field you inserted earlier in this session. In other words, it is really an instruction that tells Word to display the source information for all the citations in the document. Because it is a field and not actual text, you can easily update the bibliography later to reflect any new citations you might add.

You can choose to insert a bibliography as a field directly in the document, or you can insert a bibliography enclosed within a content control that also includes the heading "Bibliography" or "Works Cited." Inserting a bibliography enclosed in a content control is best because the content control includes a useful button that you can use to update your bibliography if you make changes to the sources.

To insert the bibliography:

▶ **1.** Scroll down so you can see the insertion point at the top of page 5.

▶ **2.** On the ribbon, click the **References** tab.

▶ **3.** In the Citations & Bibliography group, click the **Bibliography** button. The Bibliography menu opens, displaying three styles with preformatted headings—"Bibliography," "References," and "Works Cited." The Insert Bibliography command at the bottom inserts a bibliography directly in the document as a field, without a content control and without a preformatted heading. See Figure 2-31.

Figure 2–31 **Bibliography menu**

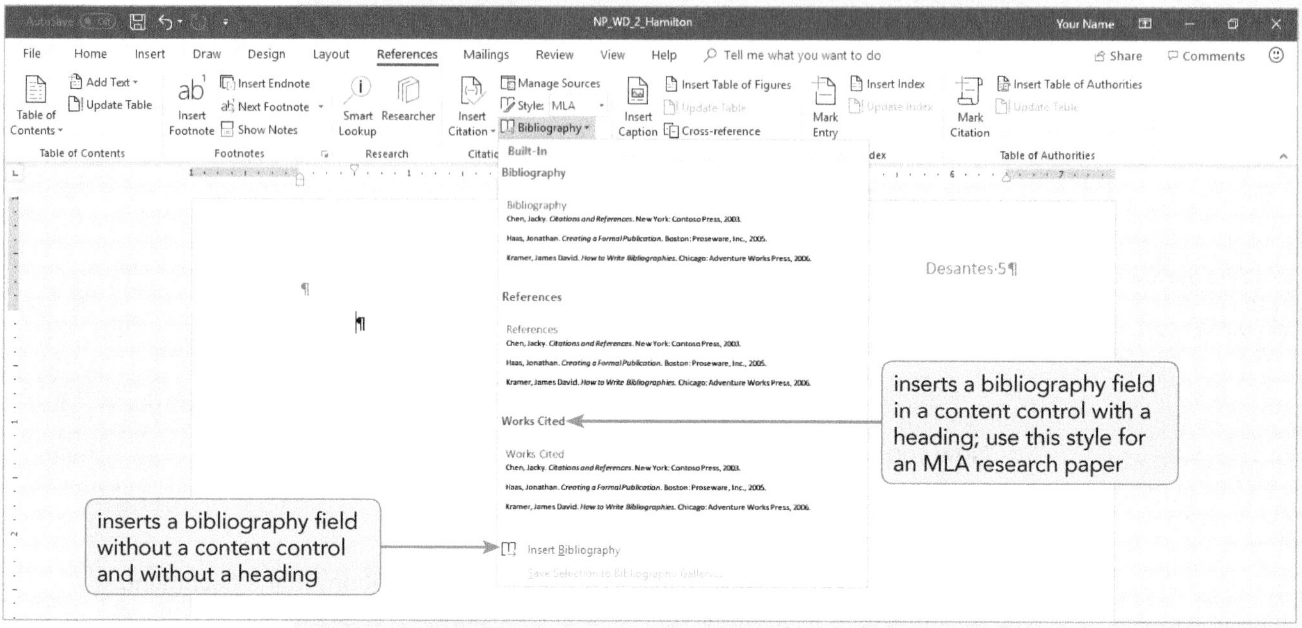

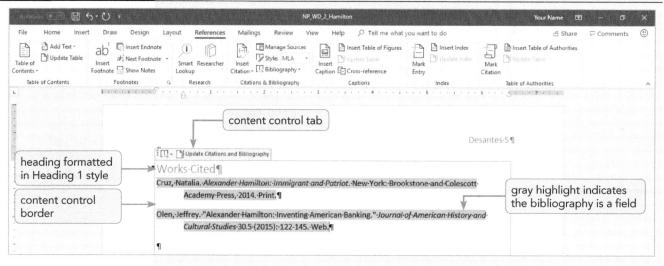

inserts a bibliography field in a content control with a heading; use this style for an MLA research paper

inserts a bibliography field without a content control and without a heading

4. Click **Works Cited**. Word inserts the bibliography, with two entries, below the "Works Cited" heading. The bibliography text is formatted in Calibri, the default font for the Office theme. The "Works Cited" heading is formatted with the Heading 1 style.

To see the content control that contains the bibliography, you need to select it.

5. Click anywhere in the bibliography. Inside the content control, the bibliography is highlighted in gray, indicating that it is a field and not regular text. The content control containing the bibliography is also now visible in the form of a rectangular border and a tab with two buttons. See Figure 2–32.

Figure 2–32 **Bibliography displayed in a content control**

content control tab

heading formatted in Heading 1 style

content control border

gray highlight indicates the bibliography is a field

As Sabrina looks over the works cited list, she realizes that she misspelled the last name of one of the authors. You'll correct the error now and then update the bibliography.

Managing Sources

When you create a source, Word adds it to a Master List of all the sources created on your computer. Word also adds each new source to the Current List of sources for that document. Both the Master List and the Current List are accessible via the Source Manager dialog box, which you open by clicking the Manage Sources button in the Citations & Bibliography group on the References tab. Using this dialog box, you can copy sources from the Master List into the Current List and vice versa. As you begin to focus on a particular academic field and turn repeatedly to important works in your chosen field, you'll find this ability to reuse sources very helpful.

Modifying an Existing Source

TIP

To transform a placeholder citation into a regular citation, click the Citation Options button, click Edit Source, and then enter source information.

To modify information about a source, you click a citation to that source in the document, click the Citation Options button on the content control, and then click Edit Source. Depending on how your computer is set up, after you are finished editing the source, Word may prompt you to update the Master List and the source information in the current document. In almost all cases, you should click Yes to ensure that the source information is correct in all the places it is stored on your computer.

To edit a source in the research paper:

1. Click in the blank paragraph below the bibliography content control to deselect the bibliography.

2. Scroll up to display the top of page 3, and then click the **(Cruz 37)** citation you entered earlier in the sixth line from the top of the page. The content control appears around the citation.

3. Click the **Citation Options** button ⌄, and then click **Edit Source**. The Edit Source dialog box opens. Note that Word displays the author's last name first in the Author box, just as it would appear in a bibliography.

4. In the **Author** box, double-click **Cruz** to select the author's last name, and then type **Kruse**. The author's name now reads "Kruse, Natalia."

5. Click **OK**. The revised author name in the citation now reads "(Kruse 37)." A message dialog box appears, asking if you want to update the master source list and the current document. You need to click Yes so that Word makes the change both in the list of sources for the current document, and in the master list of all sources created in your copy of Word.

6. Click **Yes** to close the message box and return to the document.

7. Click anywhere on the page to deselect the citation content control.

8. Save the document.

You've edited the document text and the citation to include the correct spelling of "Kruse," but now you need to update the bibliography to correct the spelling.

Updating and Finalizing a Bibliography

The bibliography does not automatically change to reflect edits you make to existing citations or to show new citations. To incorporate the latest information stored in the citations, you need to update the bibliography. To update a bibliography in a content control, click the bibliography, and then, in the content control tab, click Update Citations and Bibliography. To update a bibliography field that is not contained in a content control, right-click the bibliography, and then click Update Field on the shortcut menu.

To update the bibliography:

▶ **1.** Scroll down to page 5, and click anywhere in the works cited list to display the content control.

▶ **2.** In the content control tab, click **Update Citations and Bibliography**. The works cited list is updated, with "Cruz" changed to "Kruse" in the first entry.

Sabrina still has a fair amount of work to do on her research paper. After she finishes writing it and adding all the citations, she will update the bibliography again to include all her cited sources. At that point, you might think the bibliography would be finished. However, a few steps remain to ensure that the works cited list matches the MLA style. To finalize Sabrina's works cited list to match the MLA style, you need to make the changes shown in Figure 2–33.

Figure 2–33 **Steps for finalizing a Word bibliography to match MLA guidelines for the works cited list**

1. Format the "Works Cited" heading to match the formatting of the rest of the text in the document.
2. Center the "Works Cited" heading.
3. Double-space the entire works cited list, including the heading, and remove extra space after the paragraphs.
4. Change the font size for the entire works cited list to 12 points.

To format the bibliography as an MLA-style works cited list:

▶ **1.** Click in the **Works Cited** heading, and then click the **Home** tab on the ribbon.

▶ **2.** In the Styles group, click the **Normal** style. The "Works Cited" heading is now formatted in Calibri body font like the rest of the document. The MLA style for a works cited list requires this heading to be centered.

▶ **3.** In the Paragraph group, click the **Center** button ▤.

▶ **4.** Select the entire works cited list, including the heading. Change the font size to **12** points, change the line spacing to **2.0**, and then remove the paragraph spacing after each paragraph.

▶ **5.** Click below the content control to deselect the works cited list, and then review your work. See Figure 2–34.

Figure 2–34   MLA-style Works Cited list

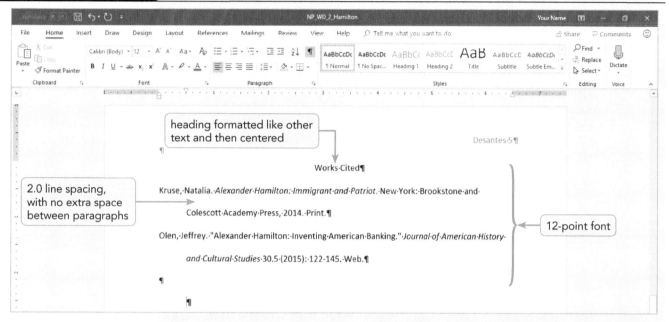

▶ 6. **sam** Save the document and close it.

Sabrina's research paper now meets the MLA style guidelines.

Session 2.2 Quick Check

REVIEW

1. List the five tasks you need to perform to make a default Word document match the MLA style.

2. How can you quickly repeat the action you just performed?

3. Explain how to remove a page number from the first page of a document.

4. What is the default form of an MLA citation in Word?

5. Explain how to edit a citation to display only the page number.

6. Explain how to generate a works cited list.

PRACTICE

Review Assignments

Data Files needed for the Review Assignments: NP_WD_2-3.docx, NP_WD_2-4.docx

Because the home mortgage fact sheet turned out so well, Sabrina has been asked to create a fact sheet describing the process for refinancing a home mortgage. Sabrina asks you to help her revise and format the document. She also asks you to create a document listing the issues loan agents consider when evaluating a refinancing application. Finally, Sabrina is working on another research paper on the history of situation comedies for a media history class she is taking. She asks you to help her format the paper according to the MLA style and to create some citations and a bibliography. She has inserted the uppercase word "CITATION" wherever she needs to insert a citation. Complete the following steps:

1. Open the document **NP_WD_2-3.docx** located in the Word2 > Review folder included with your Data Files, and then save the document as **WD_2_Refinance** in the location specified by your instructor.

2. Read the first comment, which provides an overview of the changes you will be making to the document in the following steps. Perform the task described in the second comment, and then delete both comments.

3. In the third paragraph on page 1, change the text TERMINOLOGY to all lowercase. Attach a comment to the word that explains the change.

4. In the numbered list on page 2, move the first item in the list ("Prepare for closing.") down to make it the fourth item in the list.

5. Replace all three instances of "Mortgage" with "mortgage"—making sure to match the case.

6. Format the title "Refinancing at Prairie Savings and Loan" using the Title style. Format the following headings with the Heading 1 style: "Choosing a Type of Loan," "Qualifying to Refinance," and "Refinancing Process."

7. Display the Clipboard pane. On page 1, copy the bulleted list of the three major considerations (which begins "Credit score") to the Clipboard, and then copy the "Qualifying to Refinance" heading to the Clipboard. To ensure that you copy the heading formatting, be sure to select the paragraph mark after "Qualifying to Refinance" before you click the Copy button.

8. Open a new, blank document, and then save the document as **NP_WD_2_Qualify** in the location specified by your instructor.

9. At the beginning of the document, paste the "Qualifying to Refinance" heading and then, from the Paste Options menu, apply the Keep Text Only option. Below the heading, paste the list of considerations. If necessary, reapply the bulleted list formatting to the last item in the list.

10. At the end of the document, type **Prepared by:** followed by your first and last names.

11. Save the NP_WD_2_Qualify.docx document and close it.

12. In the NP_WD_2_Refinance.docx document, clear the contents of the Clipboard pane, close the Clipboard pane, save the document, and then close it.

13. Open the document **NP_WD_2-4.docx** located in the Word2 > Review folder.

14. Save the document as **NP_WD_2_Comedy** in the location specified by your instructor.

15. In the first paragraph, replace Sabrina's name with your own.

16. Adjust the font size, line spacing, paragraph spacing, and paragraph indents to match the MLA style.

17. Insert your last name and a page number on every page except the first. Use the same font size as in the rest of the document.

18. On page 2, locate the third sentence after the "Physical Comedy" heading, which begins "The term 'slapstick' derives from…." Insert a footnote at the end of the sentence that reads: **Many images of slapsticks are available on the web. Search for the term "wooden slapstick noisemaker."**

19. If necessary, select MLA Seventh Edition as the citations and bibliography style.

20. Use the Navigation pane to highlight all instances of the uppercase word "CITATION." Keep the Navigation pane open so you can continue to use it to find the locations where you need to insert citations in Steps 21–25.

21. Delete the first instance of "CITATION" and the space before it, and then create a new source with the following information:

    Type of Source: **Book**
    Author: **Cleo Jantsch**
    Title: Modern Comedy: **A History in Words and Photos**
    Year: **2018**
    City: **Cambridge**
    Publisher: **New Media Press**
    Medium: **Print**

22. Edit the citation to add **106** as the page number. Display only the page number in the citation.

23. Delete the second instance of "CITATION" and the space before it, and then create a new source with the following information:

    Type of Source: **Journal Article**
    Author: **Frieda Robbins**
    Title: **Physical Comedy in Early American Television**
    Journal Name: **Media Signpost Quarterly: Criticism and Comment**
    Year: **2016**
    Pages: **68–91**
    Volume: **10**
    Issue: **2**
    Medium: **Web**

24. Edit the citation to add **75** as the page number.

25. Delete the third instance of "CITATION" and the space before it, and then insert a citation for the book by **Cleo Jantsch**.

26. At the end of the document, start a new page and insert a bibliography in a content control with the heading "Works Cited."

27. In the second source you created, change "**Robbins**" to "**Robbinson**" and then update the bibliography.

28. Finalize the bibliography to create an MLA-style works cited list.

29. Save the document and close it.

30. Close any other open documents.

Case Problem 1

Data File needed for this Case Problem: NP_WD_2-5.docx

Paralegal Ester Ashkan has more than a decade of experience as a paralegal. After moving to New Mexico, she is looking for a job at one of the many law firms in Albuquerque. She has asked you to edit and format her resume. As part of the application process, she will have to upload her resume to employee recruitment websites. Because these sites typically request a simple page design, Ester plans to rely primarily on heading styles to organize her information. When the resume is complete, she wants you to remove any color applied by the heading styles. She also needs help beginning a separate document that lists some of her current affiliations and certifications. Complete the following steps:

1. Open the document **NP_WD_2-5.docx** located in the Word2 > Case1 folder included with your Data Files, and then save the file as **NP_WD_2_Resume** in the location specified by your instructor.

2. If you see a box at the top of the Word window with the heading "Working on a resume?", click See resume suggestions, and review some examples in the Resume Assistant pane. If you do not see the box at the top of the Word window, open the Resume Assistant and review some examples in the Resume Assistant pane. When you are finished, close the Resume Assistant pane.

3. Read the comment included in the document, and then perform the task it specifies.

4. Respond to the comment with the response **If you like, I can show you how to remove hyperlink formatting the next time we meet.**, and then mark Ester's comment as resolved.

5. Replace all occurrences of "SarasotaFlorida" with **Sarasota, Florida**.

6. Format the document with styles as follows:
   - Ester's name:
     - Title style
   - Ester's address, phone number, and email address:
     - Subtitle style, 0 points of paragraph spacing
   - The "Summary," "Experience," "Education," and "Affiliations and Certifications" headings:
     - Heading 1 style; Black, Text 1 font color; all uppercase
   - The paragraphs containing the names of the three law firms where Ester used to work:
     - Heading 2 style; Black, Text 1 font color

7. In the bulleted list for Beckett, Hunter, and Lawrence, move the bullet that begins "Managed documents for cases…" up to make it the second bullet in the list.

8. Copy the "AFFILIATIONS AND CERTIFICATIONS" heading to the Clipboard, and then copy the last two bullets in the list of affiliations and certifications to the Clipboard.

9. Open a new, blank document, and then save the document as **NP_WD_2_Affiliations** in the location specified by your instructor.

10. Paste the heading in the document as text only, and then paste the bulleted list.

11. At the end of the document, type **Prepared by:** followed by your first and last names.

12. Save the NP_WD_2_Affiliations.docx document and close it.

13. In the **NP_WD_2_Resume.docx** document, clear the contents of the Clipboard pane, and close the Clipboard pane.

14. In the email address, replace "ester_ashkan" with your first and last names in all lowercase, separated by an underscore, and then save the document and close it.

15. Save and close the document.

Case Problem 2

Data File needed for this Case Problem: NP_WD_2-6.docx

Albertine State College   Xavier Jackson is a student at Albertine State College. He's working on a research paper about modern architecture for an history of architecture course, taught by Professor Linda Liu. The research paper is only partly finished, but before he does more work on it, he asks you to help format this early draft to match the MLA style. He also asks you to help create some citations, add a placeholder citation, and manage his sources. Complete the following steps:

1. Open the document **NP_WD_2-6.docx** located in the Word2 > Case2 folder included with your Data Files, and then save the document as **NP_WD_2_Modern** in the location specified by your instructor.

2. Revise the paper to match the MLA style, seventh edition. Instead of Xavier's name, use your own. Also, use the current date. Use the same font size for the header as for the rest of the document.

3. Locate the sentences in which the authors Thomas Cohn and Haley Bowerman are mentioned. At the end of the appropriate sentence, add a citation for page 123 in the following book and one for page 140 in the following journal article:

Cohn, Thomas. *Frank Lloyd Wright: Wisconsin Boy, Titan of Modernism*. New York: Domicile Academy Press, 2010. Print.

Bowerman, Haley. "Bauhaus Style and Structure in the Western World." Journal of Modernist Architecture and Domestic Arts (2018): 133-155. Web.

4. At the end of the second-to-last sentence in the document, insert a placeholder citation that reads "Wesley." At the end of the last sentence in the document, insert a placeholder citation that reads "Zhang."

✦ **Explore** 5. Use Word Help to look up the topic "Add citations in a Word document," and then, within that article, read the section titled "Find a source." Then read the section "Edit a source," which includes a note about editing a placeholder.

✦ **Explore** 6. Open the Source Manager, and search for the name "Cohn." From within the Current List in the Source Manager, edit the Thomas Cohn citation to change "Titan" to "King" so the book title reads "Frank Lloyd Wright: Wisconsin Boy, King of Modernism." After you make the change, update the source in both lists. When you are finished, delete "Cohn" from the Search box to redisplay all the sources in both lists.

✦ **Explore** 7. From within the Source Manager, copy a source not included in the current document from the Master List to the Current List. Examine the sources in the Current List, and note the checkmarks next to the two sources for which you have already created citations and the question marks next to the placeholder sources. Sources in the Current list that are not actually cited in the text have no symbol next to them. For example, if you copied a source from the Master List into your Current List, that source has no symbol next to it in the Current List.

8. Close the Source Manager, create a bibliography on a new page with a "Works Cited" heading, and note which works appear in it.

✦ **Explore** 9. Open the Source Manager, and then edit the Wesley placeholder source to include the following information about a journal article:

Wesley, Jamal. "Le Corbusier and the International Style." Modernism International Journal (2018): 72–89. Web.

10. Update the bibliography.

✦ **Explore** 11. Open Microsoft Edge, and use the web to research the difference between a works cited list and a works consulted list. If necessary, open the Source Manager, and then delete any uncited sources from the Current List to ensure that your document contains a true works cited list, as specified by the MLA style, and not a works consulted list. (Xavier will create a full citation for the "Zhang" placeholder later.)

12. Update the bibliography, finalize it so it matches the MLA style, save the document, and close it.

Creating Tables and a Multipage Report

Writing a Recommendation

OBJECTIVES

Session 3.1
- Review document headings in the Navigation pane
- Reorganize document text using the Navigation pane
- Collapse and expand body text in a document
- Create and edit a table
- Sort rows in a table
- Modify a table's structure
- Format a table
- Merge cells and add a formula

Session 3.2
- Set tab stops
- Turn on automatic hyphenation
- Divide a document into sections
- Create a SmartArt graphic
- Create headers and footers
- Insert a cover page
- Change the document's theme
- Review a document in Read Mode

Case | *Spruce & Cooper*

Eboni Wheatley is the new IT manager at Spruce & Cooper, an online gourmet gift basket business that is expanding rapidly.

She has written a multiple-page report for the company's leadership team summarizing basic information about wireless site surveys. She has asked you to finish formatting the report. Eboni also needs your help with adding a table and a diagram to the end of the report.

In this module, you'll use the Navigation pane to review the document headings and reorganize the document. You will also insert a table and modify it by changing the structure and formatting, merging table cells, and adding a formula. Next, you'll set tab stops, hyphenate the document, and insert a section break. In addition, you'll create a SmartArt graphic and add headers and footers. Finally, you will insert a cover page, change the theme, and review the document in Read Mode.

STARTING DATA FILES

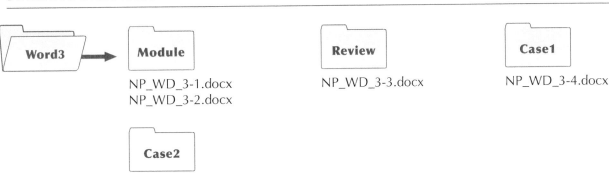

Word3 → Module

NP_WD_3-1.docx
NP_WD_3-2.docx

Review

NP_WD_3-3.docx

Case1

NP_WD_3-4.docx

Case2

(none)

Session 3.1 Visual Overview:

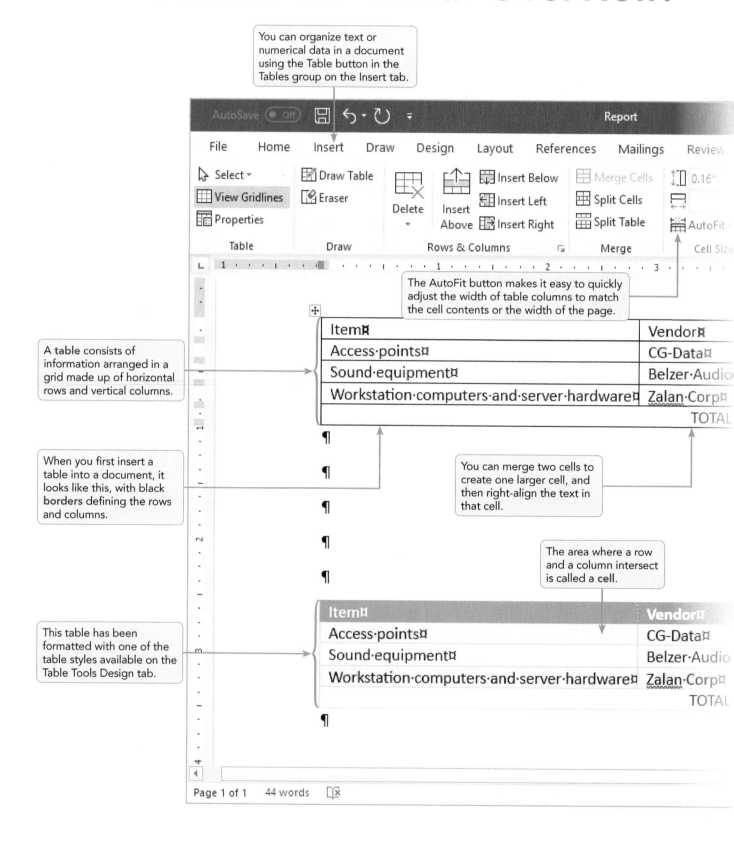

You can organize text or numerical data in a document using the Table button in the Tables group on the Insert tab.

The AutoFit button makes it easy to quickly adjust the width of table columns to match the cell contents or the width of the page.

A **table** consists of information arranged in a grid made up of horizontal **rows** and vertical **columns**.

When you first insert a table into a document, it looks like this, with black **borders** defining the rows and columns.

You can merge two cells to create one larger cell, and then right-align the text in that cell.

The area where a row and a column intersect is called a **cell**.

This table has been formatted with one of the table styles available on the Table Tools Design tab.

Item¤	Vendor¤
Access·points¤	CG-Data¤
Sound·equipment¤	Belzer·Audio
Workstation·computers·and·server·hardware¤	Zalan·Corp
	TOTAL

Item¤	Vendor¤
Access·points¤	CG-Data¤
Sound·equipment¤	Belzer·Audio
Workstation·computers·and·server·hardware¤	Zalan·Corp¤
	TOTAL

Page 1 of 1   44 words

Organizing Information in Tables

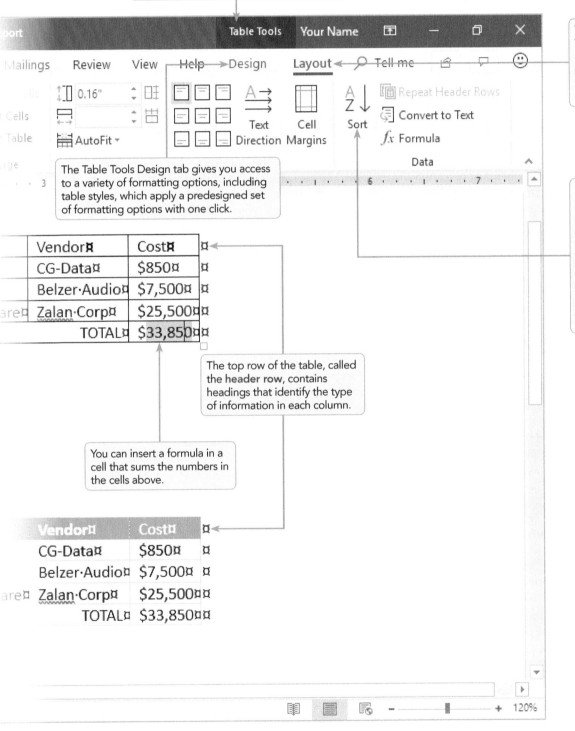

The Table Tools contextual tabs are visible when the insertion point is located inside a table cell or when the table or part of the table is selected.

The options on the Table Tools Layout tab help you control both the overall structure of the table and the arrangement of data inside the table cells.

The Table Tools Design tab gives you access to a variety of formatting options, including table styles, which apply a predesigned set of formatting options with one click.

You can use the Sort button to rearrange the rows of a table according to the contents of a particular column. For example, you could sort the table shown here alphabetically by the contents of the "Item" column or numerically by the contents of the "Cost" column.

The top row of the table, called the header row, contains headings that identify the type of information in each column.

You can insert a formula in a cell that sums the numbers in the cells above.

Vendor¤	Cost¤
CG-Data¤	$850¤
Belzer·Audio¤	$7,500¤
Zalan·Corp¤	$25,500¤¤
TOTAL¤	$33,850¤¤

Vendor¤	Cost¤
CG-Data¤	$850¤
Belzer·Audio¤	$7,500¤
Zalan·Corp¤	$25,500¤¤
TOTAL¤	$33,850¤¤

Working with Headings in the Navigation Pane

When used in combination with the Navigation pane, Word's heading styles make it easier to navigate through a long document and to reorganize a document. You start by formatting the document headings with heading styles, displaying the Navigation pane, and then clicking the Headings link. This displays a hierarchy of all the headings in the document, allowing you to see, at a glance, an outline of the document headings.

Paragraphs formatted with the Heading 1 style are considered the highest-level headings and are aligned at the left margin of the Navigation pane. Paragraphs formatted with the Heading 2 style are considered subordinate to Heading 1 paragraphs and are indented slightly to the right below the Heading 1 paragraphs. Subordinate headings are often referred to as **subheadings**. Each successive level of heading styles (Heading 3, Heading 4, and so on) is indented farther to the right. To simplify your view of the document outline in the Navigation pane, you can choose to hide lower-level headings from view, leaving only the major headings visible.

From within the Navigation pane, you can **promote** a subordinate heading to the next level up in the heading hierarchy. For example, you can promote a Heading 2 paragraph to a Heading 1 paragraph. You can also do the opposite—that is, you can **demote** a heading to a subordinate level. You can also click and drag a heading in the Navigation pane to a new location in the document's outline. When you do so, any subheadings—along with their subordinate body text—move to the new location in the document.

REFERENCE

Working with Headings in the Navigation Pane

- Format the document headings using Word's heading styles.
- On the ribbon, click the Home tab.
- In the Editing group, click the Find button, or press CTRL+F, to display the Navigation pane.
- In the Navigation pane, click the Headings link to display a list of the document headings, and then click a heading to display that heading in the document window.
- In the Navigation pane, click a heading, and then drag it up or down in the list of headings to move that heading and the body text below it to a new location in the document.
- In the Navigation pane, right-click a heading, and then click Promote to promote the heading to the next-highest level. To demote a heading, right-click it, and then click Demote.
- To hide subheadings in the Navigation pane, click the collapse triangle next to the higher level heading above them. To redisplay the subheadings, click the expand triangle next to the higher-level heading.

Eboni saved the draft of her report as a Word document. You will use the Navigation pane to review the outline of Eboni's report and make some changes to its organization.

To review the document headings in the Navigation pane:

▶ 1. **sam** ⬇ Open the document **NP_WD_3-1.docx** located in the Word3 > Module folder included with your Data Files, and then save the file with the name **NP_WD_3_Wireless** in the location specified by your instructor.

2. Verify that the document is displayed in Print Layout view and that the rulers and nonprinting characters are displayed.

3. Make sure the Zoom level is set to **120%**, and that the Home tab is selected on the ribbon.

4. Press **CTRL+F**. The Navigation pane opens to the left of the document.

5. In the Navigation pane, click the **Headings** link. The document headings are displayed in the Navigation pane, as shown in Figure 3–1. The blue highlighted heading ("Summary") indicates that part of the document currently contains the insertion point.

Figure 3–1   **Headings displayed in the Navigation pane**

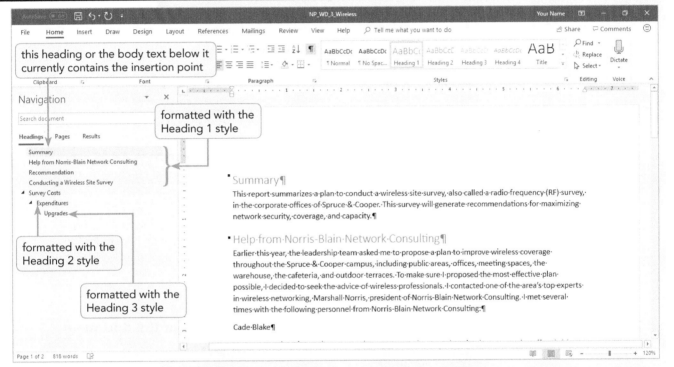

6. In the Navigation pane, click the **Recommendation** heading. Word displays the heading in the document window, with the insertion point at the beginning of the heading. The "Recommendation" heading is highlighted in blue in the Navigation pane.

7. In the Navigation pane, click the **Survey Costs** heading. Word displays the heading in the document window. In the Navigation pane, you can see that there are subheadings below this heading.

8. In the Navigation pane, click the **collapse** triangle ◢ next to the "Survey Costs" heading. The subheadings below this heading are no longer visible in the Navigation pane. This has no effect on the text in the actual document. See Figure 3–2.

Figure 3–2   Heading 2 and Heading 3 text hidden in Navigation pane

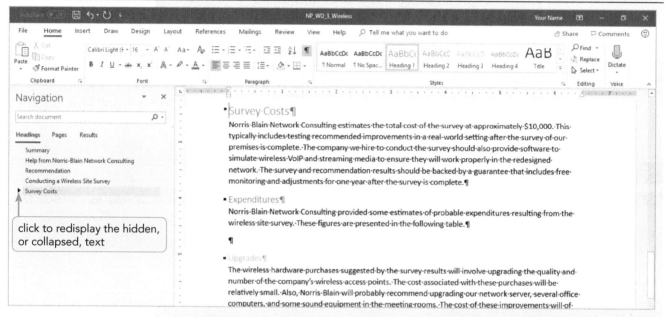

9. In the Navigation pane, click the **expand** triangle ▶ next to the "Survey Costs" heading. The subheadings are again visible in the Navigation pane.

Now that you have had a chance to review the report, you need to make a few organizational changes. Eboni wants to promote the Heading 3 text "Upgrades" to Heading 2 text. Then she wants to move the "Upgrades" heading and its body text up, so it precedes the "Expenditures" section.

To use the Navigation pane to reorganize text in the document:

1. In the Navigation pane, right-click the **Upgrades** heading to display the shortcut menu.

2. Click **Promote**. The heading moves to the left in the Navigation pane, aligning below the "Expenditures" heading. In the document window, the text is now formatted with the Heading 2 style, with its slightly larger font.

3. In the Navigation pane, click and drag the **Upgrades** heading up. As you drag the heading, the pointer changes to ↖, and a blue guideline is displayed. You can use the guideline to position the heading in its new location.

4. Position the guideline directly below the "Survey Costs" heading, as shown in Figure 3–3.

Figure 3–3	Moving a heading in the Navigation pane

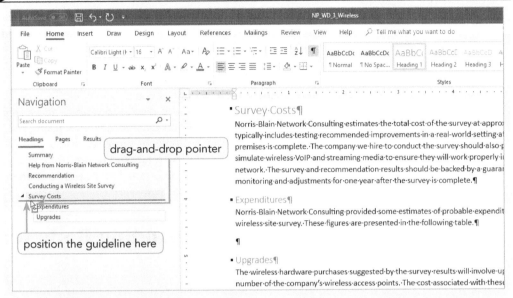

5. Release the mouse button. The "Upgrades" heading is displayed in its new position in the Navigation pane, as the second-to-last heading in the outline. The heading and its body text are displayed in their new location in the document, before the "Expenditures" heading. See Figure 3–4.

Figure 3–4	Heading and body text in new location

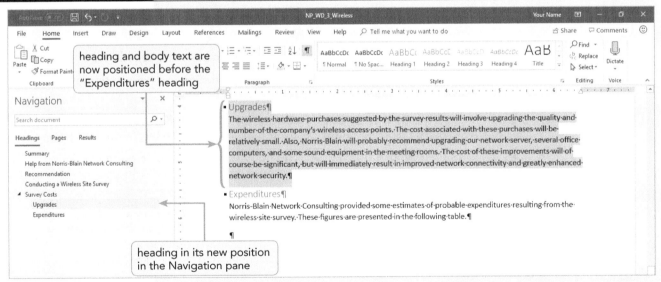

6. Click anywhere in the document to deselect the text, and then save the document.

Eboni also wants you to move the "Recommendation" heading and its accompanying body text. You'll do that in the next section, using a different method.

Promoting and Demoting Headings

When you promote or demote a heading, Word applies the next higher- or lower-level heading style to the heading paragraph. You could accomplish the same thing by using the Style gallery to apply the next higher- or lower-level heading style, but it's easy to lose track of the overall organization of the document that way. By promoting and demoting headings from within the Navigation pane, you ensure that the overall document outline is right in front of you as you work.

You can also use Outline view to display, promote, and demote headings and to reorganize a document. Turn on Outline view by clicking the View tab, and then clicking the Outline button in the Views group to display the Outlining contextual tab on the ribbon. To hide the Outlining tab and return to Print Layout view, click the Close Outline View button on the ribbon or the Print Layout button in the status bar.

Collapsing and Expanding Body Text in the Document

Because the Navigation pane gives you an overview of the entire document, dragging headings within the Navigation pane is the best way to reorganize a document. However, you can also reorganize a document from within the document window, without using the Navigation pane, by first hiding, or collapsing, the body text below a heading in a document. After you collapse the body text below a heading, you can drag the heading to a new location in the document. When you do, the body text moves along with the heading, just as if you had dragged the heading in the Navigation pane. You'll use this technique now to move the "Recommendation" heading and its body text.

To collapse and move a heading in the document window:

▶ 1. In the Navigation pane, click the **Recommendation** heading to display it in the document window.

▶ 2. In the document window, place the pointer over the **Recommendation** heading to display the gray collapse triangle ◢ to the left of the heading.

▶ 3. Click the **collapse** triangle ◢. The body text below the "Recommendation" heading is now hidden. The collapse triangle is replaced with an expand triangle.

▶ 4. Collapse the body text below the "Conducting a Wireless Site Survey" heading. The body text below that heading is no longer visible. Collapsing body text can be helpful when you want to hide details in a document temporarily, so you can focus on a particular part. See Figure 3–5.

Figure 3–5	Body text collapsed in the document

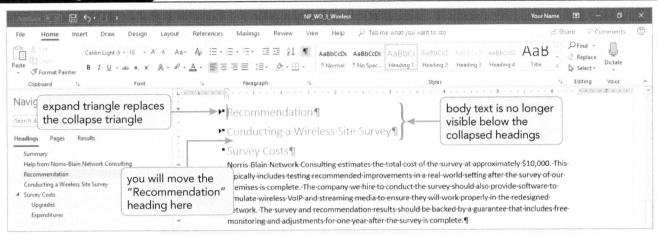

5. In the document, select the **Recommendation** heading, including the paragraph mark at the end of the paragraph.

6. Click and drag the heading down. As you drag, a dark black insertion point moves along with the pointer.

7. Position the dark black insertion point to the left of the "S" in the "Survey Costs" heading, and then release the mouse button. The "Recommendation" heading and its body text move to the new location, before the "Survey Costs" heading.

Finally, you need to expand the body text below the two collapsed headings.

8. Click anywhere in the document to deselect the text.

9. Click the **expand** triangle ▶ to redisplay the body text below the heading.

10. Click to the **expand** triangle ▶ to the left of the "Conducting a Wireless Site Survey" heading to redisplay the body text below the heading.

11. Save the document.

The document is now organized the way Eboni wants it. Next, you need to create a table summarizing her data on probable expenditures.

INSIGHT

Using Learning Tools

Hiding body text in a document makes it easy to focus on important material as you read and edit the document. But at times you might find you need even more help reading a document. In that case, you can take advantage of Word options specifically designed to help with reading fluency and comprehension. To get started, click the View tab, and then, in the Immersive group, click the Learning Tools button. This displays the Immersive Learning Tools tab, which includes the following five options:

- The Column Width button allows you to alter the line length. For some people, reading short lines of text is easier than reading text that extends across the full width of the document.
- The Page Color button gives you the option of choosing alternate page colors, which can help reduce eye strain.
- The Text Spacing button adds more space between words, characters, and lines. Depending on your needs, you might find that this makes a block of text easier to read.
- The Syllables button inserts breaks between syllables, making it easier to pronounce unfamiliar words.
- The Read Aloud button begins an automated reading of the document text. As each word is pronounced, it is highlighted in the text.

The Immersive Learning Tools tab stays visible as long as the current document is open. To hide it, click the Close Learning Tools button.

The Dictate button in the Voice group on the Home tab is an extremely useful accessibility option that can also increase writing fluency for some people. It allows you to add text to a document by speaking rather than typing. Of course, it only works on computers with microphones installed.

To get started, click the Dictate button, and wait for the button icon to change into white microphone with a red circle next to it. Then speak clearly into your computer's microphone. The sentences you speak are immediately translated into document text. Note that you'll probably need to edit the text when you are finished dictating, but with practice, you can learn how to dictate in a way that produces fewer and fewer errors. Exactly how fast you need to talk, and how precisely, will vary from one microphone to another.

Inserting a Blank Table

TIP

The terms "table," "field," and "record" are also used to refer to information stored in database programs, such as Microsoft Access.

A table is a useful way to present information that is organized into categories, or **fields**. For example, you could use a table to organize contact information for a list of clients. For each client, you could include information in the following fields: first name, last name, street address, city, state, and zip code. The complete set of information about a particular client is called a **record**. In a typical table, each column is a separate field, and each row is a record. A header row at the top contains the names of each field.

The sketch in Figure 3–6 shows what Eboni wants the table in her report to look like.

Figure 3–6   Table sketch

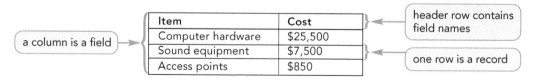

Eboni's table includes two columns, or fields: "Item" and "Cost." The header row contains the names of these two fields. The three rows below contain the records.

Creating a table in Word is a three-step process. First, you use the Table button on the Insert tab to insert a blank table structure. Then you enter information into the table. Finally, you format the table to make it easy to read.

Before you begin creating the table, you'll insert a page break before the "Expenditures" heading. This will move the heading and its body text to a new page, with plenty of room below for the new table. As a general rule, you should not use page breaks to position a particular part of a document at the top of a page. If you add or remove text from the document later, you might forget that you inserted a manual page break, and you could end up with a document layout you didn't expect. By default, Word heading styles are set up to ensure that a heading always appears on the same page as the body text paragraph below it, so you'll never need to insert a page break just to move a heading to the same page as its body text. However, in this case, a page break is appropriate because you need the "Expenditures" heading to be displayed at the top of a page with room for the table below.

To insert a page break and insert a blank table:

1. In the Navigation pane, click **Expenditures** to display the heading in the document, with the insertion point to the left of the "E" in "Expenditures."

2. Close the Navigation pane, and then press **CTRL+ENTER** to insert a page break. The "Expenditures" heading and the body text following it move to a new, third page.

3. Scroll to position the "Expenditures" heading at the top of the Word window, and then press **CTRL+END** to move the insertion point to the blank paragraph at the end of the document.

4. On the ribbon, click the **Insert** tab.

5. In the Tables group, click the **Table** button. A table grid opens, with a menu at the bottom.

6. Use the pointer to point to the **upper-left cell** of the grid, and then move the pointer down and across the grid to highlight two columns and four rows. (The outline of a cell turns orange when it is highlighted.) As you move the pointer across the grid, Word indicates the size of the table (columns by rows) at the top of the grid. A Live Preview of the table structure is displayed in the document. See Figure 3–7.

TIP

You can use the Quick Tables option to choose from preformatted tables that contain placeholder text.

Figure 3–7   Inserting a blank table

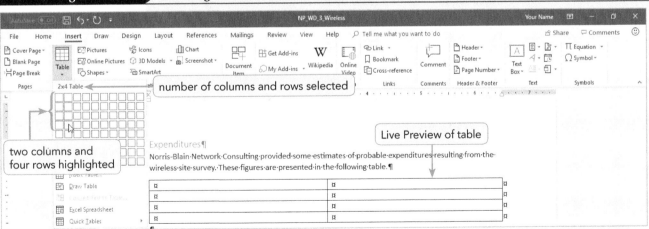

7. When the table size is 2×4, click the lower-right cell in the block of selected cells. An empty table consisting of two columns and four rows is inserted in the document, with the insertion point in the upper-left cell. See Figure 3–8.

Figure 3-8   Blank table inserted in document

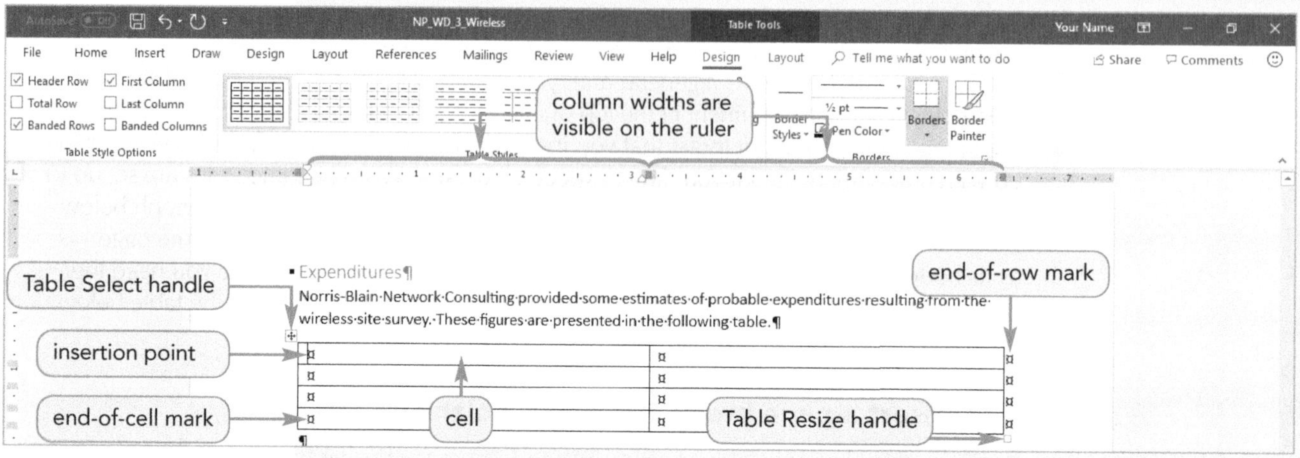

The two columns are of equal width. Because nonprinting characters are displayed in the document, each cell contains an end-of-cell mark, and each row contains an end-of-row mark, which are important for selecting parts of a table. The Table Select handle ⊞ is displayed at the table's upper-left corner. You can click the Table Select handle ⊞ to select the entire table, and you can drag it to move the table. You can drag the Table Resize handle □, which is displayed at the lower-right corner, to change the size of the table. The Table Tools Design and Layout contextual tabs are displayed on the ribbon.

Trouble? If you inserted a table with the wrong number of rows or columns, click the Undo button ⟳ on the Quick Access Toolbar to remove the table, and then repeat Steps 4 through 7.

The blank table is ready for you to begin entering information.

Entering Data in a Table

You can enter data in a table by moving the insertion point to a cell and typing. If the data takes up more than one line in the cell, Word automatically wraps the text to the next line and increases the height of that row. To move the insertion point to another cell in the table, you can click in that cell, use the arrow keys, or press TAB.

To enter information in the header row of the table:

▶ 1. Verify that the insertion point is located in the upper-left cell of the table.

▶ 2. Type **Item**. As you type, the end-of-cell mark moves right to accommodate the text.

▶ 3. Press **TAB** to move the insertion point to the next cell to the right.

   Trouble? If Word created a new paragraph in the first cell rather than moving the insertion point to the second cell, you pressed ENTER instead of TAB. Press BACKSPACE to remove the paragraph mark, and then press TAB to move to the second cell in the first row.

▶ 4. Type **Cost** and then press **TAB** to move to the first cell in the second row.

You have finished entering the header row—the row that identifies the information in each column. Now you can enter the information about the various expenditures.

To continue entering information in the table:

▶ **1.** Type **computer hardware** and then press **TAB** to move to the second cell in the second row. Notice that the "c" in "computer" is capitalized, even though you typed it in lowercase. By default, AutoCorrect capitalizes the first letter in a cell entry.

▶ **2.** Type **$25,500** and then press **TAB** to move the insertion point to the first cell in the third row.

▶ **3.** Enter the following information in the bottom two rows, pressing **TAB** to move from cell to cell:

Sound equipment; **$7,500**

Access points; **$850**

At this point, the table consists of a header row and three records. Eboni realizes that she needs to add one more row to the table. You can add a new row to the bottom of a table by pressing TAB when the insertion point is in the rightmost cell in the bottom row.

To add a row to the table:

▶ **1.** Verify that the insertion point is in the lower-right cell (which contains the value "$850"), and then press **TAB**. A new, blank row is added to the bottom of the table.

▶ **2.** Type **Servers**, press **TAB**, type **$15,000**, and then save the document. When you are finished, your table should look like the one shown in Figure 3–9.

Figure 3–9   **Table with all data entered**

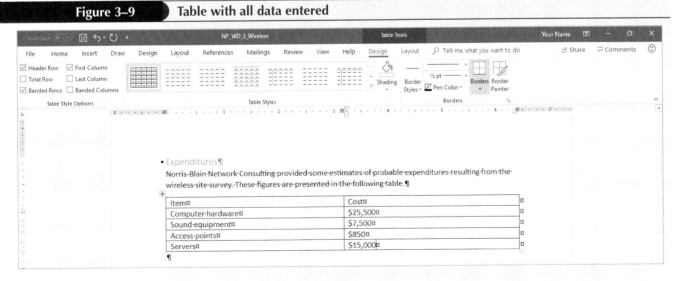

Trouble? If a new row is added to the bottom of your table, you pressed TAB after entering "$15,000". Click the Undo button ↺ on the Quick Access Toolbar to remove the extra row from the table.

The table you've just created presents information about expenditures in an easy-to-read format. To make it even easier to read, you can format the header row in bold so it stands out from the rest of the table. To do that, you need to first select the header row.

Selecting Part of a Table

When selecting part of a table, you need to make sure you select the end-of-cell mark in a cell or the end-of-row mark at the end of a row. If you don't, the formatting changes you make next might not have the effect you expect. The foolproof way to select part of a table is to click in the cell, row, or column you want to select; click the Select button on the Table Tools Layout contextual tab; and then click the appropriate command—Select Cell, Select Column, or Select Row. Or click Select Table to select the entire table. To select a row, you can also click in the left margin next to the row. Similarly, you can click just above a column to select it. After you've selected an entire row, column, or cell, you can drag the mouse to select adjacent rows, columns, or cells.

Note that in the following steps, you'll position the pointer until it takes on a particular shape so that you can then perform the task associated with that type of pointer. Pointer shapes are especially important when working with tables and graphics; in many cases, you can't perform a task until the pointer is the right shape. It takes some patience to get accustomed to positioning the pointer until it takes on the correct shape, but with practice you'll grow to rely on the pointer shapes as a quick visual cue to the options currently available to you.

To select and format the header row:

▶ **1.** Position the pointer in the selection bar, to the left of the header row. The pointer changes to a right-pointing arrow.

▶ **2.** Click the mouse button. The entire header row, including the end-of-cell mark in each cell and the end-of-row mark, is selected. See Figure 3–10.

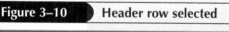

Figure 3–10   **Header row selected**

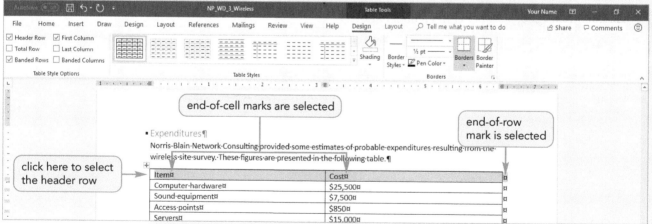

▶ **3.** Press **CTRL+B** to apply bold to the text in the header row. You can also use the formatting options on the Home tab to format selected text in a table, including adding italic formatting, changing the font, aligning text within cells, or applying a style. However, text in a table that is formatted with a heading style will not show up as a heading in the Navigation pane.

▶ **4.** Click anywhere in the table to deselect the header row, and then save the document.

Note that, in some documents, you might have a long table that extends across multiple pages. To make a multipage table easier to read, you can format the table header row to appear at the top of every page. To do so, click in the header row, click the Table Tools Layout tab, and then click the Properties button in the Table group. In the Table Properties dialog box, click the Row tab, and then select the "Repeat as header row at the top of each page" check box.

Now that you have created a very basic table, you can sort the information in it and improve its appearance.

Sorting Rows in a Table

The term **sort** refers to the process of rearranging information in alphabetical, numerical, or chronological order. You can sort a series of paragraphs, including the contents of a bulleted list, or you can sort the rows of a table.

When you sort a table, you arrange the rows based on the contents of one of the columns. For example, you could sort the table you just created based on the contents of the "Item" column—either in ascending alphabetical order (from A to Z) or in descending alphabetical order (from Z to A). Alternatively, you could sort the table based on the contents of the "Cost" column—either in ascending numerical order (lowest to highest) or in descending numerical order (highest to lowest).

Clicking the Sort button in the Data group on the Table Tools Layout tab opens the Sort dialog box, which provides a number of options for fine-tuning the sort, including options for sorting a table by the contents of more than one column. This is useful if, for example, you want to organize the table rows by last name and then by first name within each last name. By default, Word assumes your table includes a header row that should remain at the top of the table—excluded from the sort.

REFERENCE

Sorting the Rows of a Table

- Click anywhere within the table.
- On the ribbon, click the Table Tools Layout tab.
- In the Data group, click the Sort button.
- In the Sort dialog box, click the Sort by arrow, and then select the header for the column you want to sort by.
- In the Type box located to the right of the Sort by box, select the type of information stored in the column you want to sort by; you can choose Text, Number, or Date.
- To sort in alphabetical, chronological, or numerical order, verify that the Ascending option button is selected. To sort in reverse order, click the Descending option button.
- To sort by a second column, click the Then by arrow, and then select a column header. If necessary, specify the type of information stored in the Then by column, and then confirm the sort order.
- At the bottom of the Sort dialog box, make sure the Header row option button is selected. This indicates that the table includes a header row that should not be included in the sort.
- Click OK.

Eboni would like you to sort the contents of the table in ascending numerical order based on the contents of the "Cost" column.

To sort the information in the table:

▶ **1.** Make sure the insertion point is located somewhere in the table.

▶ **2.** On the ribbon, click the **Table Tools Layout** tab.

▶ **3.** In the Data group, click the **Sort** button. The Sort dialog box opens. Take a moment to review its default settings. The leftmost column in the table, the "Item" column, is selected in the Sort by box, indicating the sort will be based on the contents in this column. Because the "Item" column contains text, "Text" is selected in the Type box. The Ascending option button is selected by default, indicating that Word will sort the contents of the "Item" column from A to Z. The Header row option button is selected in the lower-left corner of the dialog box, ensuring the header row will not be included in the sort.

   You want to sort the column by the contents of the "Cost" column, so you need to change the Sort by setting.

▶ **4.** Click the **Sort by arrow**, and then click **Cost**. Because the "Cost" column contains numbers, the Type box now displays "Number". The Ascending button is still selected, indicating that Word will sort the numbers in the "Cost" column from lowest to highest. At this point, if you wanted to sort by a second column, you could click the Then by arrow, and then select the Item header. See Figure 3–11.

Figure 3–11   **Sort dialog box**

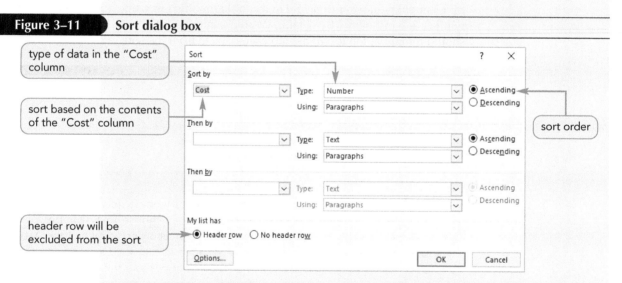

▶ **5.** Click **OK** to close the Sort dialog box, and then click anywhere in the table to deselect it. Rows 2 through 5 are now arranged numerically from lowest to highest, according to the numbers in the "Cost" column, with the "Computer hardware" row at the bottom. See Figure 3–12.

Figure 3–12   Table after being sorted

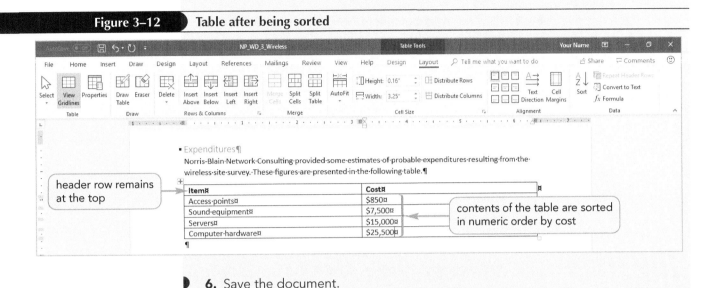

6. Save the document.

Eboni decides that the table should also include the cost for installing each item. She asks you to insert an "Installation Cost" column.

Inserting Rows and Columns in a Table

To add a column to a table, you can use the tools in the Rows & Columns group on the Table Tools Layout tab, or you can use the Add Column button in the document window. To use the Add Column button, make sure the insertion point is located somewhere within the table. When you position the pointer at the top of the table, pointing to the border between two columns, the Add Column button is displayed. When you click that button, a new column is inserted between the two existing columns.

To insert a column in the table:

1. Verify that the insertion point is located anywhere in the table.

2. Position the pointer at the top of the table, so that it points to the border between the two columns. The Add Column button ⊕ appears at the top of the border. A blue guideline shows where the new column will be inserted. See Figure 3–13.

Figure 3–13   Inserting a column

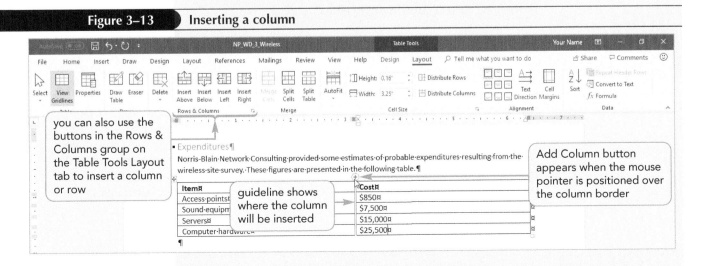

▶ **3.** Click the **Add Column** button ⊕. A new, blank column is inserted between the "Item" and "Cost" columns. The three columns in the table are narrower than the original two columns, but the overall width of the table remains the same.

▶ **4.** Click in the top cell of the new column, and then enter the following header and data. Use the ↓ key to move the insertion point down through the column.

Installation Cost

$600

$1,000

$1,250

$900

Your table should now look like the one in Figure 3–14.

Figure 3–14   New "Installation Cost" column

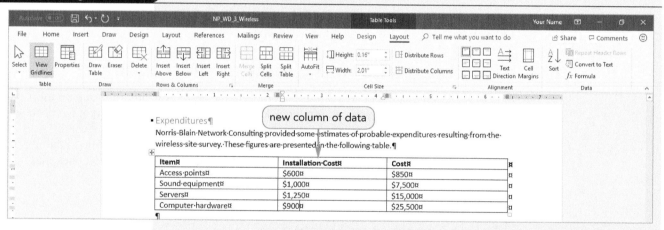

Because you selected the entire header row when you formatted the original headers in bold, the newly inserted header, "Installation Cost," is also formatted in bold.

Eboni just learned that the costs listed for computer hardware actually cover both ordinary work station computers and new servers. Therefore, she would like you to delete the "Servers" row from the table.

Deleting Rows and Columns

When you consider deleting a row, you need to be clear about whether you want to delete just the contents of the row, or both the contents and the structure of the row. You can delete the contents of a row by selecting the row and pressing DEL. This removes the information from the row but leaves the row structure intact. The same is true for deleting the contents of an individual cell, a column, or the entire table. To delete the structure of a row, a column, or the entire table—including its contents—you select the row (or column or the entire table), and then use the Delete button on the Mini toolbar or in the Rows & Columns group on the Table Tools Layout tab. To delete multiple rows or columns, start by selecting all the rows or columns you want to delete.

Before you delete the "Servers" row, you need to edit the contents in the last cell of the first column to indicate that the items in that row include servers.

To delete the "Servers" row:

▶ 1. Triple-click the cell containing the text "Computer hardware" to select it and type **Workstation computers and server hardware**. Part of the text wraps to a second line within the cell. Note that you could also click anywhere in a cell, and then use BACKSPACE or DEL to delete text, and then type new text. In other words, you can edit text in a table just as you would edit ordinary text in a document.

Next, you can delete the "Servers" row, which is no longer necessary.

▶ 2. Click in the selection bar to the left of the **Servers** row. The row is selected, with the Mini toolbar displayed on top of the selected row.

▶ 3. On the Mini toolbar, click the **Delete** button. The Delete menu opens, displaying options for deleting cells, columns, rows, or the entire table. See Figure 3–15.

| Figure 3–15 | Deleting a row |

▶ 4. Click **Delete Rows**. The "Servers" row is removed from the table, and the Mini toolbar disappears.

▶ 5. Save your work.

The table now contains all the information Eboni wants to include. Next, you'll adjust the widths of the three columns.

Changing Column Widths and Row Heights

Word offers many ways to change the size of columns and rows. While it's good to know how to adjust row heights, in most cases you'll only need to focus on column widths, because columns that are too wide for the material they contain can make a table hard to read.

You can change a column's width by dragging the column's right border to a new position. Or, if you prefer, you can double-click a column border to make the column width adjust automatically to accommodate the widest entry in the column. A more precise option is to click in the column you want to adjust, click the Table Tools Layout tab, and then change the setting in the Width box, just as you would adjust the width of a picture. To adjust the width of all the columns to match their widest entries, click anywhere in the table, click the AutoFit button in the Cell Size group on the Table Tools Layout tab, and then click AutoFit Contents.

You can also adjust the height of rows and the width of the entire table. To change the height of a row, position the pointer over the bottom row border and drag the border up or down, or click in the row and change the setting in the Height box on the Table Tools Layout tab. You can change the width of the entire table by changing the width of all the columns and the height of all the rows at one time. To do this, drag the Table Resize handle (shown in Figure 3–8) or select the entire table and then adjust the settings in the Height and Width boxes on the Table Tools Layout tab. As a final option, you can adjust the width of the entire table to span the width of the page by clicking the AutoFit button and then clicking AutoFit Window.

You'll adjust the columns in Eboni's table by double-clicking the right column border. You need to start by making sure that no part of the table is selected. Otherwise, when you double-click the border, only the width of the selected part of the table will change.

> When resizing a column, be sure that no part of the table is selected. Otherwise, you'll resize just the selected part.

To change the width of the columns in the table:

▶ **1.** Verify that no part of the table is selected, and then position the pointer over the right border of the "Installation Cost" column until the pointer changes to ◀╫▶. See Figure 3–16.

| Figure 3–16 | Adjusting the column width |

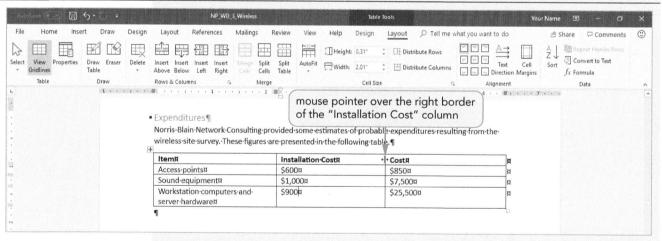

▶ **2.** Double-click the mouse button. The right column border moves left so that the "Installation Cost" column is just wide enough to accommodate the widest entry in the column.

▶ **3.** Verify that no part of the table is selected, and that the insertion point is located in any cell in the table.

▶ **4.** Make sure the Table Tools Layout tab is selected on the ribbon.

▶ **5.** In the Cell Size group, click the **AutoFit** button, and then click **AutoFit Contents**. All of the table columns adjust so that each is just wide enough to accommodate its widest entry. The text "Workstation computers and server hardware" in row 4 no longer wraps to a second line.

▶ **6.** Save the document.

To finish the table, you will add some formatting to improve the table's appearance.

Formatting Tables with Styles

To adjust a table's appearance, you can use any of the formatting options available on the Home tab. To change a table's appearance more dramatically, you can use table styles, which allow you to apply a collection of formatting options, including shading, color, borders, and other design elements, with a single click.

By default, a table is formatted with the Table Grid style, which includes only black borders between the rows and columns, no paragraph spacing, no shading, and the default black font color. You can select a more colorful table style from the Table Styles group on the Table Tools Design tab. Whatever table style you choose, you'll give your document a more polished look if you use the same style consistently in all the tables in a single document.

Some table styles format rows in alternating colors, called **banded rows**, while others format the columns in alternating colors, called **banded columns**. You can choose a style that includes different formatting for the header row than for the rest of the table. Or, if the first column in your table is a header column—that is, if it contains headers identifying the type of information in each row—you can choose a style that instead applies different formatting to the first column.

REFERENCE

Formatting a Table with a Table Style

- Click in the table you want to format.
- On the ribbon, click the Table Tools Design tab.
- In the Table Styles group, click the More button to display the Table Styles gallery.
- Position the pointer over a style in the Table Styles gallery to see a Live Preview of the table style in the document.
- In the Table Styles gallery, click the style you want.
- To apply or remove style elements (such as special formatting for the header row, banded rows, or banded columns), select or deselect check boxes as necessary in the Table Style Options group.

Eboni wants to use a table style that emphasizes the header row with special formatting, does not include column borders, and uses color to separate the rows.

To apply a table style to the Expenditures table:

▶ **1.** Click anywhere in the table, and then scroll to position the table at the very bottom of the Word window. This will make it easier to see the Live Preview in the next few steps.

▶ **2.** On the ribbon, click the **Table Tools Design** tab. In the Table Styles group, the plain Table Grid style is highlighted, indicating that it is the table's current style.

▶ **3.** In the Table Styles group, click the **More** button ⬇. The Table Styles gallery opens. The default Table Grid style now appears under the heading "Plain Tables." The more elaborate styles appear below, in the "Grid Tables" section of the gallery.

4. Use the gallery's vertical scroll bar to view the complete collection of table styles. When you are finished, scroll up until you can see the "Grid Tables" heading again.

5. Move the pointer over the style located in the fourth row of the Grid Tables section, first column on the right. See Figure 3–17.

Figure 3–17   Table styles gallery

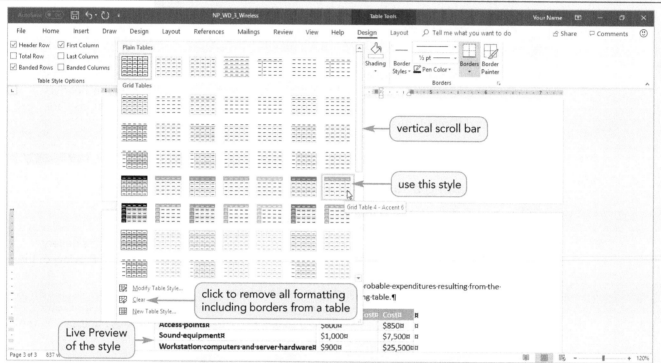

A ScreenTip displays the style's name, "Grid Table 4 - Accent 6." The style consists of a dark green heading row, with alternating rows of light green and white below. A Live Preview of the style is visible in the document.

6. Click the **Grid Table 4 - Accent 6** style. The Table Styles gallery closes.

7. Scroll to position the table at the top of the Word window, so you can review it more easily. The table's header row is formatted with dark green shading and white text. The rows below appear in alternating colors of light green and white.

The only problem with the newly formatted table is that the text in the first column is formatted in bold. In tables where the first column contains row headers, bold would be appropriate—but this isn't the case with Eboni's table. You'll fix this by deselecting the First Column check box in the Table Style Options group on the Table Tools Design tab.

To remove the bold formatting from the first column:

▶ **1.** In the Table Style Options group, click the **First Column** check box to deselect this option. The bold formatting is removed from the entries in the "Item" column. Note that the Header Row check box is selected. This indicates that the table's header row is emphasized with special formatting (dark green shading with white text). The Banded Rows check box is also selected because the table is formatted with banded rows of green and white. To remove the banded rows, you could deselect the Banded Rows checkbox. To apply or remove banded columns, you could select or deselect the Banded Columns checkbox. Figure 3-18 shows the finished table.

Figure 3-18   **Completed table**

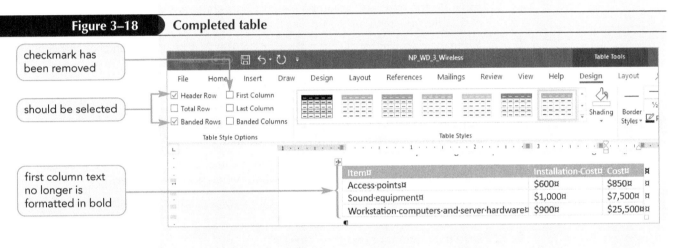

- checkmark has been removed
- should be selected
- first column text no longer is formatted in bold

▶ **2.** Save the document.

After you apply a table style, it's helpful to know how to remove it in case you want to start over from scratch. The Clear option on the menu below the Table Styles gallery removes the current style from a table, including the borders between cells. When a table has no borders, the rows and columns are defined by **gridlines**, which are useful as guidelines but do not appear when you print the table.

In the following steps, you'll experiment with clearing the table's style, displaying and hiding the gridlines, and removing the table's borders.

To experiment with table styles, gridlines, and borders:

▶ **1.** In the Table Styles group, click the **More** button ⬇, and then click **Clear** in the menu below the gallery. The green shading and borders are removed from the table. Next, you need to make sure the table gridlines are displayed.

▶ **2.** On the ribbon, click the **Table Tools Layout** tab.

▶ **3.** In the Table group, click the **View Gridlines** button, if necessary, to select it. The table now looks much simpler, with no shading or font colors. Instead of the table borders, dotted gridlines separate the rows and columns. The text in the table is spaced farther apart because removing the table style restored the default paragraph and line spacing of the Normal style. The bold formatting that you applied earlier, which is not part of a table style, is visible again.

It is helpful to clear a table's style and view only the gridlines if you want to use a table to lay out text and graphics on a page, but you want no visible indication of the table itself.

Another option is to remove only the table borders, leaving the rest of the table style applied to the table. To do this, you have to select the entire table. But first you need to undo the style change.

▶ **4.** On the Quick Access Toolbar, click the **Undo** button ↺ to restore the Grid Table 4 - Accent 6 style, so that your table looks like the one in Figure 3–18.

▶ **5.** In the upper-left corner of the table, click the **Table Select** handle ⊞ to select the entire table, and then click the **Table Tools Design** tab.

▶ **6.** In the Borders group, click the **Borders arrow** to open the Borders gallery, click **No Border**, and then click anywhere in the table to deselect it. The borders are removed from the table, leaving only the nonprinting gridlines to separate the rows and columns. To add borders of any color to specific parts of a table, you can use the Border Painter.

▶ **7.** In the Borders group, click the **Border Painter** button, and then click the **Pen Color** button to open the Pen Color gallery.

▶ **8.** In the Pen Color gallery, click the **Orange, Accent 2** square in the sixth column of the first row of the gallery.

▶ **9.** Use the Border Painter pointer to click any gridline in the table. An orange border is added to the cell where you clicked.

▶ **10.** Continue experimenting with the Border Painter pointer 🖌, and then press **ESC** to turn off the Border Painter pointer when you are finished.

▶ **11.** Reapply the Grid Table 4 - Accent 6 table style to make your table match the one shown earlier in Figure 3–18.

▶ **12.** Save the document and then close it.

PROSKILLS

Problem Solving: Fine-Tuning Table Styles

After you apply a table style to a table, you might like the look of the table but find that it no longer effectively conveys your information or is not quite as easy to read. To solve this problem, you might be inclined to go back to the Table Styles gallery to find another style that might work better. Another method to correct problems with a table style is to identify the table elements with problematic formatting, and then manually make formatting adjustments to only those elements using the options on the Table Tools Design tab. For example, you can change the thickness and color of the table borders using the options in the Borders group, and you can add shading using the Shading button in the Table Styles group. Also, if you don't like the appearance of table styles in your document, consider changing the document's theme (as explained later in this module) and previewing the table styles again. The table styles have a different appearance in each theme. When applying table styles, remember there are many options for attractively formatting the table without compromising the information being conveyed.

Adding Formulas

Now that the Expenditures table is finished, Eboni would like your help finishing a table containing her estimates for the cost of the servers and workstations. She might add it to the report later, but for now it's stored in a separate document. The table is almost complete, but she still needs to add a formula field that calculates and displays the total cost of the new hardware.

The Formula button in the Data group on the Table Tools Layout tab allows you to insert a field that performs mathematical operations such as addition, subtraction, or division. By default, it inserts a formula field that sums the numbers in the rows above the cell containing the formula field. You'll see how that works in the following steps. In the process, you'll learn how to insert formulas that perform other operations.

To open the document and add a formula:

▶ 1. Open the document **NP_WD_3-2.docx** located in the Word3 > Module folder, and then save the file with the name **NP_WD_3_Hardware** in the location specified by your instructor.

▶ 2. Verify that the document is displayed in Print Layout view and that the rulers and nonprinting characters are displayed.

▶ 3. Make sure the Zoom level is set to 120%. Eboni wants you to insert a formula that sums the three dollar amounts in the right-hand column.

▶ 4. Click the blank cell below "$14,000."

▶ 5. Click the **Table Tools Layout** tab, and then click the **Formula** button in the Data group. The Formula dialog box opens. By default, the Formula box contains =SUM(ABOVE), which tells Word to add together all the numbers in the cells above the cell that contains the insertion point, and then display the result of that calculation in the cell that contains the insertion point. You can use the Number format arrow to determine how the result of the formula will look in the cell. For example, you can choose to display it with no decimal places, with or without a dollar sign, or with a percentage sign. In this case, Eboni wants the result of the calculation to display with no decimal places to match the dollar amounts in the cells above.

▶ 6. Click the **Number format arrow**, and then click **#,##0**. If you wanted to perform a calculation other than summing numbers, you could type a new formula in the Formula box, or you could select an option using the Paste function arrow. Using formulas other than the default SUM formula is an advanced skill, but you can learn how to incorporate them into your documents by searching Help for information on adding formulas to tables. See Figure 3–19.

Figure 3–19   Formula dialog box

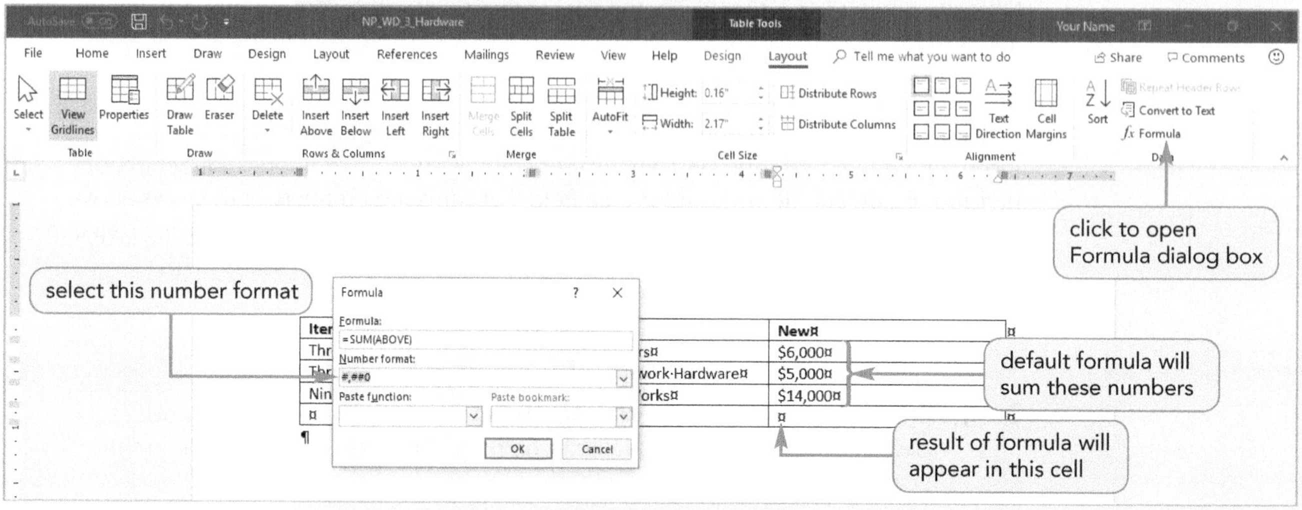

> **7.** Click **OK**. The Formula dialog box closes, and the result of the calculation, 25,000, appears in the right-most cell in the bottom row. Next, you need to add a dollar sign to match the entries in the cells above.

> **8.** Click to the left of the "2" in "25,000" and type **$**. When you click in the cell, gray shading appears behind the result of the formula. The shading indicates that the value is actually the result of a formula field rather than plain text.

> **9.** Save the document.

The beauty of a formula field is that you can edit the numbers in a table, and then quickly update the result of the calculation. In this case, Eboni wants to change the cost of the new workstations from $14,000 to $14,500.

To change the cost of the new workstations and then update the formula:

> **1.** Click the cell containing "$14,000," use the → or ← keys to move the insertion point to the left of the first "0," press DEL, and then type **5** to change the amount to $14,500. Now you need to update the formula to reflect the higher cost.

> **2.** Right-click the cell containing the formula field, which currently displays the value $25,000. A shortcut menu opens, as shown in Figure 3–20. If the gray shading around the value $25,000 did not appear earlier, it appears now.

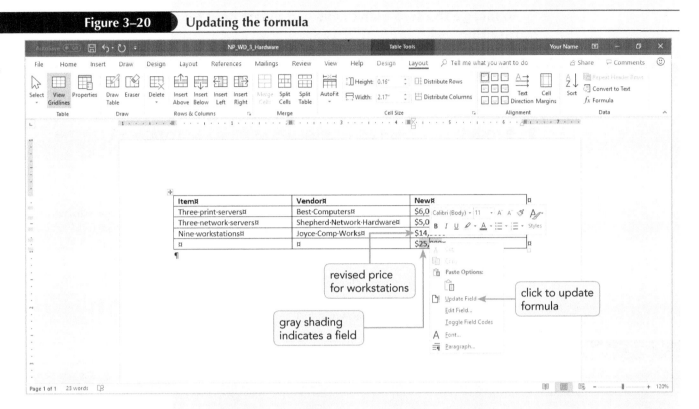

Figure 3–20   Updating the formula

> **3.** Click **Update Field** in the shortcut menu. The shortcut menu closes, and the value displayed in the cell changes to $25,500.

To finish the table, Eboni would like to add "TOTAL" next to the cell containing the formula field.

Merging Cells

Currently the table contains two blank cells in the bottom row. Eboni could insert "TOTAL" in the cell next to the one containing the formula, but the table will look more polished if she combines, or **merges**, the two blank cells, and then inserts the text in the resulting new, larger cell. To merge one or more cells, select the cells, and then click the Merge Cells button in the Merge group on the Table Tools Layout tab. Note that you can also split one cell into multiple cells by clicking the cell you want to split, clicking the Split Cells button in the Merge group to open the Split Cells dialog box, and then specifying the desired number of rows and column you want to divide the cell into.

To merge the two blank cells and insert new text in the resulting cell:

▶ **1.** Click and drag the mouse to select the two blank cells in the table's bottom row.

▶ **2.** In the Merge group, click the **Merge Cells** button. The border dividing the two cells disappears, leaving one, larger cell.

▶ **3.** Click the new, larger cell to deselect it, and then type **TOTAL** in the cell. The new text is aligned on the left border of the cell. To move it closer to the cell containing the formula field, you need to right-align it.

▶ **4.** Verify that the insertion point is located in the new, merged cell.

▶ **5.** Click the **Home** tab, and then in the Paragraph group, click the **Align Right** button ☰. The text moves to the right side of the merge cell. Finally, to make the new text and formula easier to spot, you should format the bottom row in bold.

▶ **6.** Select the bottom row, click the **Bold** button ⬚B⬚ in the Font group, then click anywhere in the document to deselect the row. Your completed table should now look like the one shown in Figure 3–21.

Figure 3–21 ▶ **Table with merged cell and right-aligned text**

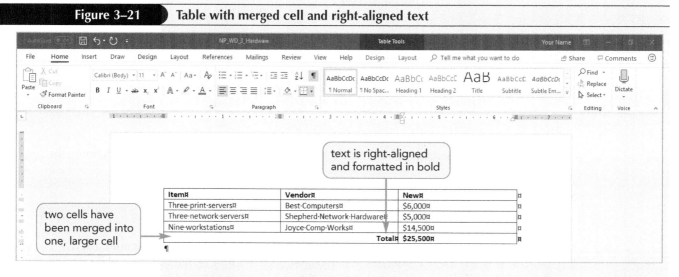

▶ **7.** Save the document and then close it.

INSIGHT

Using the Draw Table Pointer

Instead of inserting a blank table grid as a starting point, you can draw a table structure using the Draw Table pointer. This is especially useful when you want to use a table as a way to lay out the contents of a flyer or other specially formatted documents. You can insert titles, graphics, and other elements in the table cells, apply formatting to the cells, and then, when you are finished, remove all borders and hide the gridlines.

To get started, click the Insert tab, click the Table button in the Tables group, and then click Draw Table. This displays the Draw Table pointer, which looks like a pencil. You can click the mouse button and drag the Draw Table pointer to draw horizontal and vertical lines on the page. You can put row and column borders anywhere you want; there's no need to make all the cells in the table the same size. When you are finished drawing the table, turn off the Draw Table pointer by pressing ESC. To delete a border, click the Eraser button in the Draw group on the Table Tools Layout tab, and click anywhere on the border you want to erase. Click the Eraser button again to turn it off.

In the next session, you'll complete the rest of the report by organizing information using tab stops, dividing the document into sections, inserting headers and footers, inserting a cover page, and, finally, changing the document's theme.

REVIEW

Session 3.1 Quick Check

1. What kind of style must you apply to a paragraph to make the paragraph appear as a heading in the Navigation pane?

2. What are the three steps involved in creating a table in Word?

3. Explain how to insert a new column in a table.

4. After you enter data in the last cell in the last row in a table, how can you insert a new row?

5. When sorting a table, is the header row included by default?

6. To adjust the width of a table's column to span the width of the page, would you use the AutoFit Contents option or the AutoFit Window option?

Session 3.2 Visual Overview:

You can click the Go to Header and Go to Footer buttons to move easily between the headers and footers in your document.

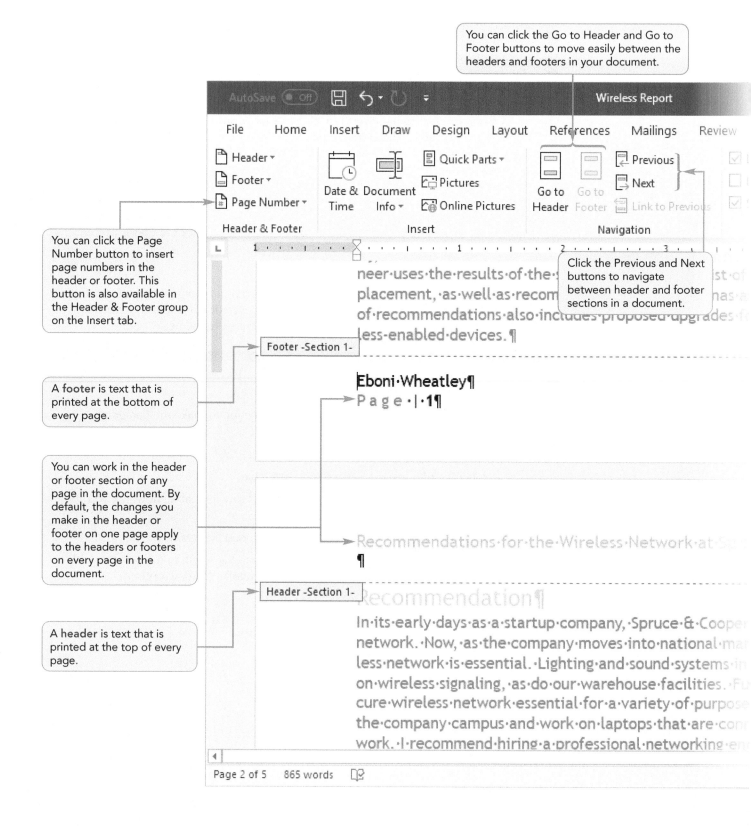

You can click the Page Number button to insert page numbers in the header or footer. This button is also available in the Header & Footer group on the Insert tab.

Click the Previous and Next buttons to navigate between header and footer sections in a document.

A footer is text that is printed at the bottom of every page.

You can work in the header or footer section of any page in the document. By default, the changes you make in the header or footer on one page apply to the headers or footers on every page in the document.

A header is text that is printed at the top of every page.

Working with Headers and Footers

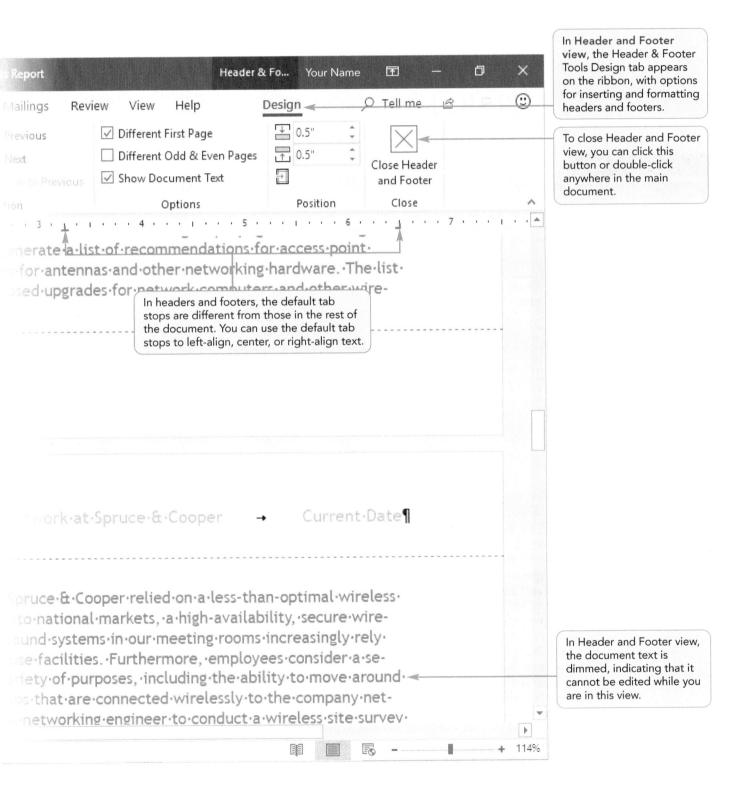

In Header and Footer view, the Header & Footer Tools Design tab appears on the ribbon, with options for inserting and formatting headers and footers.

To close Header and Footer view, you can click this button or double-click anywhere in the main document.

In headers and footers, the default tab stops are different from those in the rest of the document. You can use the default tab stops to left-align, center, or right-align text.

In Header and Footer view, the document text is dimmed, indicating that it cannot be edited while you are in this view.

Setting Tab Stops

A **tab stop** (often called a **tab**) is a location on the horizontal ruler where the insertion point moves when you press TAB. You can use tab stops to align small amounts of text or data. By default, a document contains tab stops every one-half inch on the horizontal ruler. There's no mark on the ruler indicating these default tab stops, but in the document you can see the nonprinting Tab character that appears every time you press TAB. (Of course, you need to have the Show/Hide ¶ button selected to see these nonprinting characters.) A nonprinting tab character is just like any other character you type; you can delete it by pressing BACKSPACE or DEL.

The five major types of tab stops are Left, Center, Right, Decimal, and Bar, as shown in Figure 3–22. The default tab stops on the ruler are all left tab stops because that is the tab style used most often.

Figure 3–22	Tab stop alignment styles

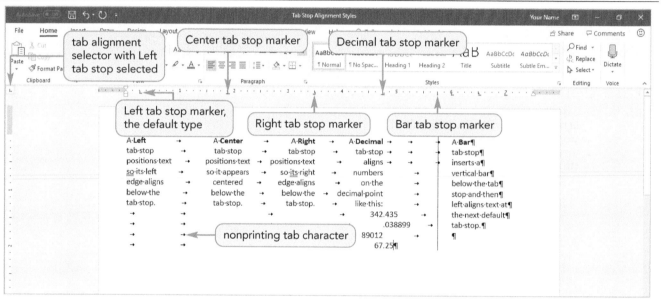

You can use tab stops a few different ways. The simplest is to press TAB until the insertion point is aligned where you want it, and then type the text you want to align. Each time you press TAB, the insertion point moves right to the next default tab stop, with the left edge of the text aligning below the tab stop. To use a different type of tab stop, or to use a tab stop at a location other than the default tab stop locations (every half-inch on the ruler), first select an alignment style from the tab alignment selector, located at the left end of the horizontal ruler, and then click the horizontal ruler where you want to insert the tab stop. This process is called setting a tab stop. When you set a new tab stop, all of the default tab stops to its left are removed. This means you have to press TAB only once to move the insertion point to the newly created tab stop. To set a new tab stop in text you have already typed, select the text, including the nonprinting tab stop characters, and then set the tab stop by selecting a tab alignment style and clicking on the ruler where you want to set the tab stop.

To create more complicated tab stops, you can use the Tabs dialog box. Among other things, the Tabs dialog box allows you to insert a **dot leader**, which is a row of dots (or other characters) between tabbed text. A dot leader makes it easier to read a long list of tabbed material because the eye can follow the dots from one item to the next. You've probably seen dot leaders used in the table of contents in a book, where the dots separate the chapter titles from the page numbers.

To create a left tab stop with a dot leader, click the Dialog Box Launcher in the Paragraph group on the Home tab, click the Indents and Spacing tab, if necessary, and then click the Tabs button at the bottom of the dialog box. In the Tab stop position box in the Tabs dialog box, type the location on the ruler where you want to insert the tab. For example, to insert a tab stop at the 4-inch mark, type 4. Verify that the Left option button is selected in the Alignment section, and then, in the Leader section, click the option button for the type of leader you want. Click the Set button, and then click OK.

Setting, Moving, and Clearing Tab Stops

- To set a tab stop, click the tab alignment selector on the horizontal ruler until the appropriate tab stop alignment style is displayed, and then click the horizontal ruler where you want to position the tab stop.
- To move a tab stop, drag it to a new location on the ruler. If you have already typed text that is aligned by the tab stop, select the text before dragging the tab stop to a new location.
- To clear a tab stop, drag it off the ruler.

In the report you have been working on for Eboni, you need to type the list of consultants and their titles. You can use tab stops to quickly format this small amount of information in two columns. As you type, you'll discover whether Word's default tab stops are appropriate for this document or whether you need to set a new tab stop. Before you get started working with tabs, you'll take a moment to explore Word's Resume Reading feature.

To enter the list of consultants using tabs:

1. Open the **NP_WD_3_Wireless.docx** document. The document opens with the "Summary" heading at the top of the Word window. In the lower-right corner, a "Welcome back!" message is displayed briefly and is then replaced with the Resume Reading button [⬚].

2. Point to the **Resume Reading** button [⬚] to expand its "Welcome back!" message. See Figure 3–23.

Figure 3–23   "Welcome back!" message displayed in reopened document

3. Click the **Welcome back!** message. The document window scrolls down to display the table, which you were working on just before you closed the document.

4. Scroll up to display the "Help from Norris-Blain Network Consulting" heading on page 1.

5. Confirm that the ruler and nonprinting characters are displayed, and that the document is displayed in **Print Layout** view, zoomed to **120%**.

6. Click to the right of the last "e" in "Cade Blake."

7. Press **TAB**. An arrow-shaped tab character appears, and the insertion point moves to the first tab stop after the last "e" in "Blake." This tab stop is the default tab located at the 1-inch mark on the horizontal ruler. See Figure 3–24.

Figure 3–24 Tab character

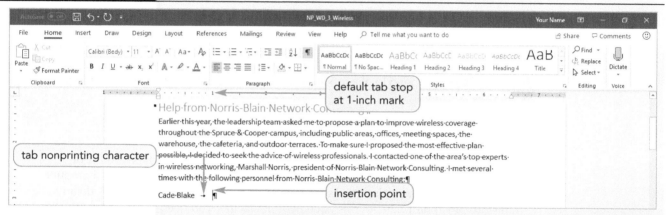

8. Type **Senior Consultant**, and then press **ENTER** to move the insertion point to the next line.

9. Type **Samuel J. Iglesias**, and then press **TAB**. The insertion point moves to the next available tab stop, this time located at the 1.5-inch mark on the ruler.

10. Type **Senior Consultant**, and then press **ENTER** to move to the next line. Notice that Samuel J. Iglesias's title does not align with Cade Blake's title on the line above it. You'll fix this after you type the last name in the list.

11. Type **Beverly Sheffield-McCoy**, press **TAB**, and then type **Project Manager**. See Figure 3–25.

Figure 3–25 List of consultants

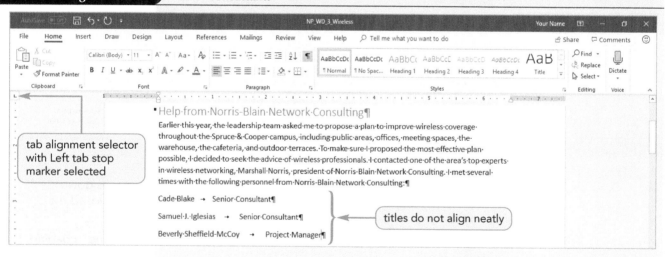

The list of names and titles is not aligned properly. You could fix this by dragging a tab stop to a new location. However, you would have to select the list of names and positions before dragging the tab stop. In this case, it's easier to insert a new tab stop.

To add a new tab stop to the horizontal ruler:

1. Make sure the Home tab is displayed on the ribbon, and then select the list of consultants and their titles.

2. On the horizontal ruler, click at the 2.5-inch mark. Because the current tab stop alignment style is Left tab, Word inserts a left tab stop at that location.

Remember that when you set a new tab stop, all the default tab stops to its left are removed. The column of titles shifts to the new tab stop. Note that if you needed to remove a tab stop, you could drag it off the ruler. See Figure 3–26.

Figure 3–26   **Titles aligned at new tab stop**

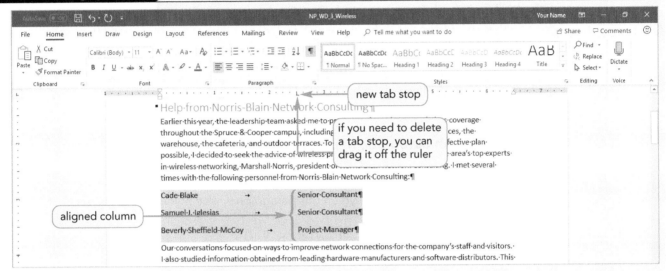

To complete the list, you need to remove the paragraph spacing after the first two paragraphs in the list, so the list looks like it's all one paragraph. You can quickly reduce paragraph and line spacing to 0 points by clicking the No Spacing style in the Styles group. In this case, you want to reduce only the paragraph spacing to 0 points, so you'll use the Line and Paragraph Spacing button instead.

3. Select the first two paragraphs in the list, which contain the names and titles for Cade and Samuel.

4. In the Paragraph group, click the **Line and Paragraph Spacing** button, and then click **Remove Space After Paragraph**.

5. Click anywhere in the document to deselect the list, and then save your work.

PROSKILLS

Decision Making: Choosing Between Tabs and Tables

When you have information that you want to align in columns in your document, you need to decide whether to use tabs or tables. Whatever you do, don't try to align columns of data by adding extra spaces by pressing SPACEBAR. Although the text might seem precisely aligned on the screen, it probably won't be aligned when you print the document. Furthermore, if you edit the text, the spaces you inserted to align your columns will be affected by your edits; they get moved just like regular text, ruining your alignment.

So what is the most efficient way to align text in columns? It depends. Inserting tabs works well for aligning small amounts of information in just a few columns and rows, such as two columns with three rows, but tabs become cumbersome when you need to organize a lot of data over multiple columns and rows. In that case, using a table to organize columns of information is better. Unlike with tabbed columns of data, it's easy to add data to tables by inserting columns. You might also choose tables over tab stops when you want to take advantage of the formatting options available with table styles. As mentioned earlier, if you don't want the table structure itself to be visible in the document, you can clear its table style and then hide its gridlines.

Now you're ready to address some other issues with the document. First, Eboni has noticed that the right edges of most of the paragraphs in the document are uneven, and she'd like you to try to smooth them out. You'll correct this problem in the next section.

Hyphenating a Document

By default, hyphenation is turned off in Word documents. That means if you are in the middle of typing a word and you reach the end of a line, Word moves the entire word to the next line instead of inserting a hyphen and breaking the word into two parts. This can result in ragged text on the right margin. To ensure a smoother right margin, you can turn on automatic hyphenation—in which case, any word that ends within the last quarter-inch of a line will be hyphenated.

To turn on automatic hyphenation in the document:

▶ **1.** Review the paragraph below the "Help from Norris-Blain Network Consulting" heading. The text on the right side of this paragraph is uneven. Keeping an eye on this paragraph will help you see the benefits of hyphenation.

▶ **2.** On the ribbon, click the **Layout** tab.

▶ **3.** In the Page Setup group, click the **Hyphenation** button to open the Hyphenation menu, and then click **Automatic**. The Hyphenation menu closes. The document text shifts to account for the insertion of hyphens in words that break near the end of a line. For example, in the paragraph below the "Help from Norris-Blain Network Consulting" heading, the words "throughout" and "networking" are now hyphenated. See Figure 3–27.

Figure 3–27 **Hyphenated document**

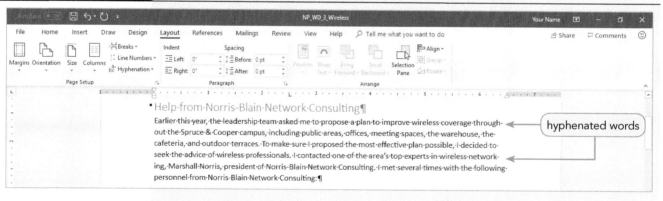

▶ **4.** Save the document.

Eboni plans to post a handout in the company dining room to illustrate the benefits of improving the corporate network, and she wants to include a sample handout in the report. Before you can add the sample handout, you need to divide the document into sections.

Formatting a Document into Sections

TIP

If you insert an endnote in a document with sections, the endnote will appear at the end of the section containing the superscript endnote number, not at the end of the document.

A **section** is a part of a document that can have its own page orientation, margins, headers, footers, and so on. In other words, each section is like a document within a document. To divide a document into sections, you insert a **section break**. You can select from a few different types of section breaks. One of the most useful is a Next page section break, which inserts a page break and starts the new section on the next page. Another commonly used kind of section break, a Continuous section break, starts the section at the location of the insertion point without changing the page flow. To insert a section break, you click the Breaks button in the Page Setup group on the Layout tab and then select the type of section break you want to insert.

Eboni wants to format the handout in landscape orientation, but the report is currently formatted in portrait orientation. To format part of a document in an orientation different from the rest of the document, you need to divide the document into sections.

To insert a section break below the table:

▶ **1.** Press **CTRL+END** to move the insertion point to the end of the document, just below the table.

▶ **2.** In the Page Setup group, click the **Breaks** button. The Breaks gallery opens, as shown in Figure 3–28.

Figure 3–28	Breaks gallery

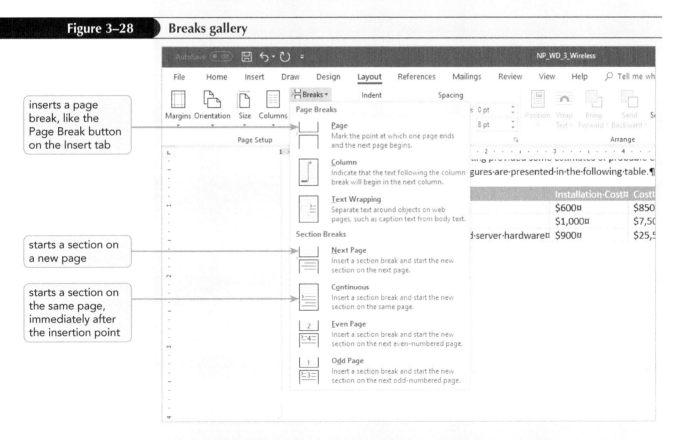

inserts a page break, like the Page Break button on the Insert tab

starts a section on a new page

starts a section on the same page, immediately after the insertion point

The Page Breaks section of the gallery includes options for controlling how the text flows from page to page. The first option, Page, inserts a page break. It has the same effect as clicking the Page Break button on the Insert tab or pressing CTRL+ENTER. The Section Breaks section of the gallery includes four types of section breaks. The two you'll use most often are Next Page and Continuous.

3. Under "Section Breaks," click **Next Page**. A section break is inserted in the document, and the insertion point moves to the top of the new page 4.

4. Scroll up, if necessary, until you can see the double dotted line and the words "Section Break (Next Page)" below the table on page 3. This line indicates that a new section begins on the next page.

5. Save the document.

TIP

To delete a section break, click to the left of the line representing the break, and then press DEL.

You've created a new page that is a separate section from the rest of the report. The sections are numbered consecutively. The first part of the document is section 1, and the new page is section 2. Now you can format section 2 in landscape orientation without affecting the rest of the document.

To format section 2 in landscape orientation:

1. Scroll down and verify that the insertion point is positioned at the top of the new page 4.

2. On the ribbon, click the **View** tab.

3. In the Zoom group, click the **Multiple Pages** button, and then change the Zoom level to **30%** so you can see all four pages of the document displayed side by side.

4. On the ribbon, click the **Layout** tab.

5. In the Page Setup group, click the **Orientation** button, and then click **Landscape**. Section 2, which consists solely of page 4, changes to landscape orientation, as shown in Figure 3–29. Section 1, which consists of pages 1 through 3, remains in portrait orientation.

Figure 3–29 **Page 4 formatted in landscape orientation**

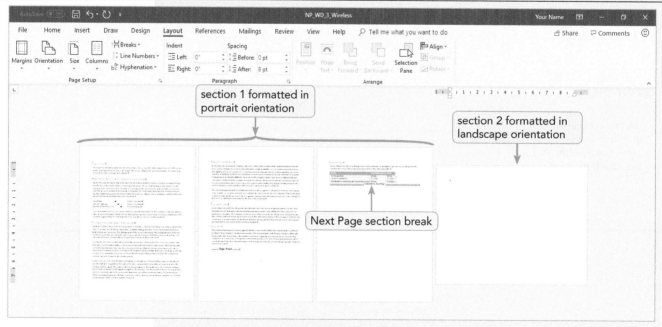

6. Change the Zoom level back to **120%**, and then save the document.

Page 4 is now formatted in landscape orientation, ready for you to create Eboni's handout, which will consist of a graphic that shows the benefits of improving the company's wireless network. You'll use Word's SmartArt feature to create the graphic.

Creating SmartArt

A **SmartArt** graphic is a diagram of shapes, such as circles, squares, or arrows. A well-designed SmartArt graphic can illustrate concepts that might otherwise require several paragraphs of explanation. To create a SmartArt graphic, you switch to the Insert tab and then, in the Illustrations group, click the SmartArt button. This opens the Choose a SmartArt Graphic dialog box, where you can select from eight categories of graphics, including graphics designed to illustrate relationships, processes, and hierarchies. Within each category, you can choose from numerous designs. Once inserted into your document, a SmartArt graphic contains placeholder text that you replace with your own text. When a SmartArt graphic is selected, the SmartArt Tools Design and Format tabs appear on the ribbon.

To create a SmartArt graphic:

▶ **1.** Verify that the insertion point is located at the top of page 4, which is blank.

▶ **2.** On the ribbon, click the **Insert** tab.

▶ **3.** In the Illustrations group, click the **SmartArt** button. The Choose a SmartArt Graphic dialog box opens, with categories of SmartArt graphics in the left panel. The middle panel displays the graphics associated with the category currently selected in the left panel. The right panel displays a larger image of the graphic that is currently selected in the middle panel, along with an explanation of the graphic's purpose. By default, All is selected in the left panel.

▶ **4.** Explore the Choose a SmartArt Graphic dialog box by selecting categories in the left panel and viewing the graphics displayed in the middle panel.

▶ **5.** In the left panel, click **Relationship**, and then scroll down in the middle panel and click the **Converging Radial** graphic (in the first column, seventh row from the top), which shows three rectangles with arrows pointing to a circle. In the right panel, you see an explanation of the Converging Radial graphic. See Figure 3–30.

Figure 3–30   Selecting a SmartArt graphic

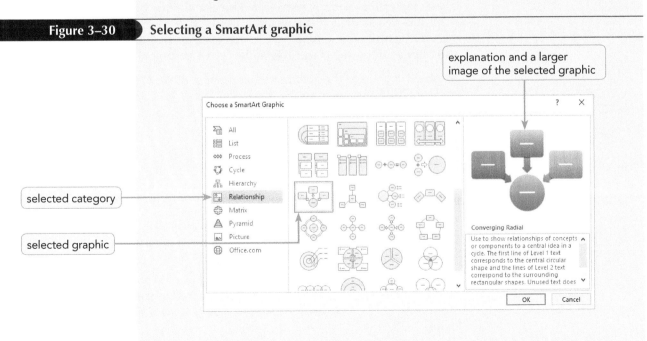

> **6.** Click **OK**. The Converging Radial graphic, with placeholder text, is inserted at the top of page 4. The graphic is surrounded by a rectangular border, indicating that it is selected. The SmartArt Tools contextual tabs appear on the ribbon. To the left of the graphic, you also see the Text pane, a small window with a title bar that contains the text "Type your text here." See Figure 3–31.

Figure 3–31	SmartArt graphic with text pane displayed

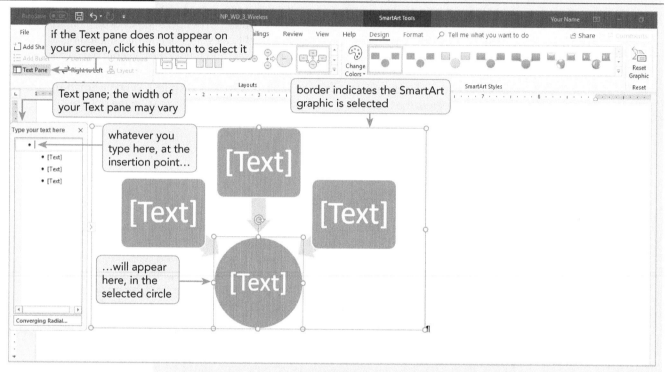

Trouble? If you do not see the Text pane, click the Text Pane button in the Create Graphic group on the SmartArt Tools Design tab to select it.

The insertion point is blinking next to the first bullet in the Text pane, which is selected with an orange rectangle. The circle at the bottom of the SmartArt graphic is also selected, as indicated by the border with sizing handles. At this point, anything you type next to the selected bullet in the Text pane will also appear in the selected circle in the SmartArt graphic.

Trouble? If you see the Text pane but the first bullet is not selected as shown in Figure 3–31, click next to the first bullet in the Text pane to select it.

Now you are ready to add text to the graphic.

To add text to the SmartArt graphic:

> **1.** Type **Better Connectivity**. The new text is displayed in the Text pane and in the circle in the SmartArt graphic. Now you need to insert text in the three rectangles.

> **2.** Press the ↓ key to move the insertion point down to the next placeholder bullet in the Text pane, and then type **Hardware Upgrades**. The new text is displayed in the Text pane and in the blue rectangle on the left. See Figure 3–32.

Figure 3–32	New text in text pane and in SmartArt graphic

3. Press the ↓ key to move the insertion point down to the next placeholder bullet in the Text pane, and then type **Wireless Site Survey**. The new text appears in the middle rectangle and in the Text pane. You don't need the third rectangle, so you'll delete it.

4. Click the blank rectangle, on the right side of the SmartArt image, to select it. Make sure to click in the blue area and not on any letters. Then, press DEL. The rectangle on the right is deleted from the SmartArt graphic. The two remaining rectangles and the circle enlarge and shift position. Note that if you wanted to add a shape to the diagram, you could click a shape in the SmartArt graphic, click the Add Shape arrow in the Create Graphic group on the SmartArt Tools Design tab, and then click a placement option.

5. Make sure the SmartArt Tools Design tab is still selected on the ribbon.

6. In the Create Graphic group, click the **Text Pane** button to deselect it. The Text pane closes.

7. Click the white area inside the SmartArt border to ensure that none of the individual shapes are selected.

Next, you need to resize the SmartArt graphic so it fills the page.

To adjust the size of the SmartArt graphic:

1. Zoom out so you can see the entire page. As you can see on the ruler, the SmartArt is currently 6 inches wide. You could drag the SmartArt border to resize it, just as you can with any graphic, but you will get more precise results using the Size button on the SmartArt Tools Format tab.

▶ 2. On the ribbon, click the **SmartArt Tools Format** tab.

▶ 3. On the right side of the SmartArt Tools Format tab, click the **Size** button to display the Height and Width boxes.

▶ 4. Click the **Height** box, type **6.5**, click the **Size** button again if necessary, click the **Width** box, type **9**, and then press **ENTER**. The SmartArt graphic resizes, so that it is now 9 inches wide and 6.5 inches high, taking up most of the page. See Figure 3–33.

Figure 3–33   Resized SmartArt

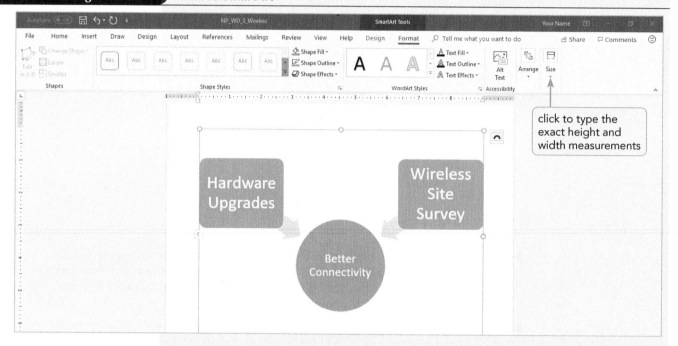

click to type the exact height and width measurements

Trouble? If one of the shapes in the SmartArt graphic was resized, rather than the entire SmartArt graphic, the insertion point was located within the shape rather than in the white space. On the Quick Access Toolbar, click the Undo button ↶, click in the white area inside the SmartArt border, and then repeat Steps 3 and 4.

▶ 5. Click outside the SmartArt border to deselect it, and then review the graphic centered on the page.

TIP

To add a border to a SmartArt graphic, click the SmartArt Tools Format tab, click the Shape Outline button in the Shape Styles group, and select an outline color.

Next, you need to insert a header at the top of each page in the report and a footer at the bottom of each page in the report.

Adding Headers and Footers

The first step to working with headers and footers is to open Header and Footer view. You can do that in three ways: (1) insert a page number using the Page Number button in the Header & Footer group on the Insert tab; (2) double-click in the header area (in a page's top margin) or in the footer area (in a page's bottom margin); or (3) click the Header button or the Footer button on the Insert tab.

By default, Word assumes that when you add something to the header or footer on any page of a document, you want the same text to appear on every page of the document. To create a different header or footer for the first page, you select the Different First Page check box in the Options group on the Header & Footer Tools Design tab. When a document is divided into sections, like Eboni's report, you can create a different header or footer for each section.

For a simple header or footer, double-click the header or footer area, and then type the text you want directly in the header or footer area, formatting the text as you would any other text in a document. To choose from a selection of predesigned header or footer styles, use the Header and Footer buttons on the Header & Footer Tools Design tab (or on the Insert tab). These buttons open galleries that you can use to select from a number of header and footer styles, some of which include page numbers and graphic elements such as horizontal lines or shaded boxes.

Some styles also include document controls that are similar to the kinds of controls that you might encounter in a dialog box. Any information that you enter in a document control is displayed in the header or footer as ordinary text, but it is also stored in the Word file so that Word can easily reuse it in other parts of the document. For example, later in this module you will create a cover page for Eboni's report. Word's predefined cover pages include document controls similar to those found in headers and footers. So if you use a document control to enter the document title in the header, the same document title will show up on the cover page; there's no need to retype it.

In the following steps, you'll create a footer for the whole document (sections 1 and 2) that includes the page number and your name. As shown in Eboni's plan in Figure 3–34, you'll also create a header for section 1 only (pages 1 through 3) that includes the document title and the date. You'll leave the header area for section 2 blank.

| Figure 3–34 | Plan for headers and footers in Eboni's report |

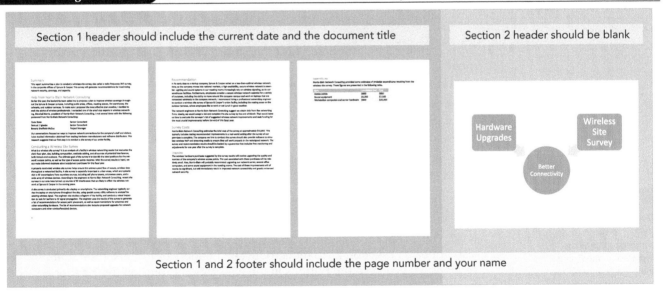

First you will create the footer on page 1.

To create a footer for the entire document:

▶ **1.** Change the Zoom level to **120%**, and then scroll up until you can see the bottom of page 1 and the top of page 2.

▶ **2.** Double-click in the white space at the bottom of page 1. The document switches to Header and Footer view. The Header & Footer Tools Design tab is displayed on the ribbon. The insertion point is positioned on the left side of the footer area, ready for you to begin typing. The label "Footer -Section 1-"

tells you that the insertion point is located in the footer for section 1. The document text is gray, indicating that you cannot edit it in Header and Footer view. The header area for section 1 is also visible at the top of page 2. The default footer tab stops (which are different from the default tab stops in the main document) are visible on the ruler. See Figure 3–35.

Figure 3–35 Creating a footer

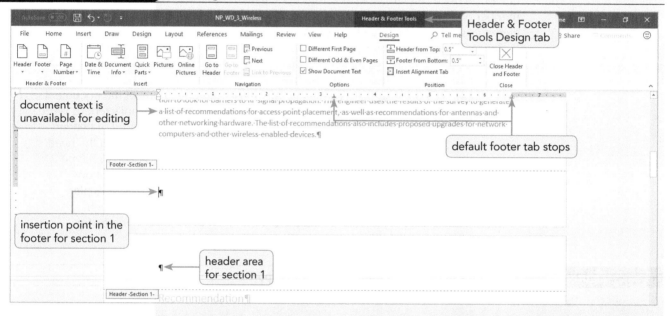

3. Type your first and last names, and then press **ENTER**. The insertion point moves to the second line in the footer, aligned along the left margin. This is where you will insert the page number.

4. In the Header & Footer group, click the **Page Number** button. The Page Number menu opens. Because the insertion point is already located where you want to insert the page number, you'll use the Current Position option.

5. Point to **Current Position**. A gallery of page number styles opens. Eboni wants to use the Accent Bar 2 style.

6. Click the **Accent Bar 2** style (the third style from the top). The word "Page," a vertical bar, and the page number are inserted in the footer.

   Next, you'll check to make sure that the footer you just created for section 1 also appears in section 2. To move between headers or footers in separate sections, you can use the buttons in the Navigation group on the Header & Footer Tools Design tab.

7. In the Navigation group, click the **Next** button. Word displays the footer for the next section in the document—that is, the footer for section 2, which appears at the bottom of page 4. The label at the top of the footer area reads "Footer -Section 2-" and it contains the same text (your name and the page number) as in the section 1 footer. Word assumes, by default, that when you type text in one footer, you want it to appear in all the footers in the document.

TIP

To change the numbering style or to specify a number to use as the first page number, click the Page Number button in the Header & Footer group, and then click Format Page Numbers.

Now you need to create a header for section 1. Eboni does not want to include a header in section 2 because it would distract attention from the SmartArt graphic. So you will first separate the header for section 1 from the header for section 2.

To separate the headers for section 1 and section 2:

▶ **1.** Verify that the insertion point is located in the section 2 footer area at the bottom of page 4 and that the Header & Footer Tools Design tab is selected on the ribbon. To switch from the footer to the header in the current section, you can use the Go to Header button in the Navigation group.

▶ **2.** In the Navigation group, click the **Go to Header** button. The insertion point moves to the section 2 header at the top of page 4. See Figure 3–36.

Figure 3–36	Section 2 header is currently the same as the previous header, in section 1

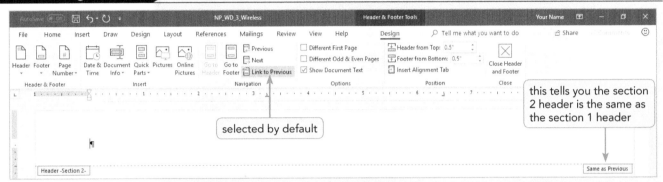

this tells you the section 2 header is the same as the section 1 header

selected by default

Notice that in the Navigation group, the Link to Previous button is selected. In the header area in the document window, the gray tab on the right side of the header border contains the message "Same as Previous," indicating that the section 2 header is set up to display the same text as the header in the previous section, which is section 1. To make the section 2 header a separate entity, you need to break the link between the section 1 and section 2 headers.

TIP

When you create a header for a section, it doesn't matter what page you're working on as long as the insertion point is located in a header in that section.

▶ **3.** In the Navigation group, click the **Link to Previous** button to deselect it. The Same as Previous tab is removed from the right side of the section 2 header border.

▶ **4.** In the Navigation group, click the **Previous** button. The insertion point moves up to the nearest header in the previous section, which is the section 1 header at the top of page 3. The label "Header -Section 1-" identifies this as a section 1 header.

▶ **5.** In the Header & Footer group, click the **Header** button. A gallery of header styles opens.

▶ **6.** Scroll down and review the various header styles, and then click the **Grid** style (eighth style from the top). The placeholder text "[Document title]" is aligned at the left margin. The placeholder text "[Date]" is aligned at the right margin.

▶ **7.** Click the **[Document title]** placeholder text. The placeholder text is now selected within a document control. See Figure 3–37.

Figure 3–37   Adding a header to section 1

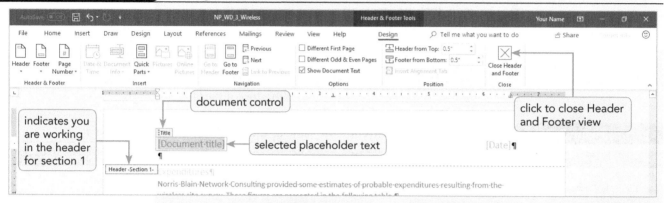

8. Type **Recommendations for the Wireless Network at Spruce & Cooper**. The text you just typed is now displayed in the document control instead of the placeholder text. Next, you need to add the date. The header style you selected includes a date picker document control, which allows you to select the date from a calendar.

9. Click the **[Date]** placeholder text to display an arrow in the document control, and then click the arrow. A calendar for the current month appears, as shown in Figure 3–38. In the calendar, the current date is outlined in dark blue.

Figure 3–38   Adding a date to the section 1 header

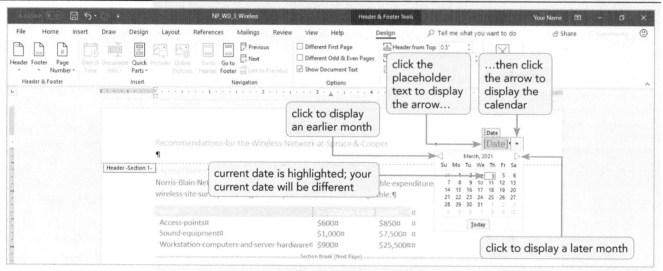

10. Click the current date. The current date, including the year, is inserted in the document control.

11. Scroll up slightly and click anywhere in the section 1 footer (on the preceding page) to deselect the date document control. You are finished creating the header and footer for Eboni's report, so you can close Header and Footer view and return to Print Layout view.

12. In the Close group, click the **Close Header and Footer** button, or double-click anywhere in the main document, and then save your work.

13. On the ribbon, click the **View** tab.

▶ **14.** In the Zoom group, click the **Multiple Pages** button, and then change the Zoom level to **30%** so you can see all four pages of the document, including the header at the top of pages 1 through 3 and the footer at the bottom of pages 1 through 4. Take a moment to compare your completed headers and footers with Eboni's plan for the headers and footers shown earlier in Figure 3–34.

Next, you need to insert a cover page for the report.

Inserting a Cover Page

A report's cover page typically includes the title and the name of the author. Some people also include a summary of the report on the cover page, which is commonly referred to as an abstract. In addition, you might include the date, the name and possibly the logo of your company or organization, and a subtitle. A cover page should not include the document header or footer.

To insert a preformatted cover page at the beginning of the document, you use the Cover Page button on the Insert tab. You can choose from a variety of cover page styles, all of which include document controls in which you can enter the document title, the document's author, the date, and so on. These document controls are linked to any other document controls in the document. For example, you already entered "Recommendations for the Wireless Network at Spruce & Cooper" into a document control in the header of Eboni's report. So if you use a cover page that contains a similar document control, "Recommendations for the Wireless Network at Spruce & Cooper" will be displayed on the cover page automatically. Note that document controls sometimes display information entered when either Word or Windows was originally installed on your computer. If your computer has multiple user accounts, the information displayed in some document controls might reflect the information for the current user. In any case, you can easily edit the contents of a document control.

To insert a cover page at the beginning of the report:

▶ **1.** Verify that the document is still zoomed so that you can see all four pages, and then press **CTRL+HOME**. The insertion point moves to the beginning of the document.

▶ **2.** On the ribbon, click the **Insert** tab.

▶ **3.** In the Pages group, click the **Cover Page** button. A gallery of cover page styles opens.

Notice that the names of the cover page styles match the names of the preformatted header styles you saw earlier. For example, the list includes a Grid cover page, which is designed to match the Grid header used in this document. To give a document a uniform look, it's helpful to use elements with the same style throughout.

▶ **4.** Scroll down the gallery to see the cover page styles, and then locate the Grid cover page style.

TIP

To delete a cover page that you inserted from the Cover Page gallery, click the Cover Page button in the Pages group, and then click Remove Current Cover Page.

5. Click the **Grid** cover page style. The new cover page is inserted at the beginning of the document.

6. Change the Zoom level to **120%**, and then scroll down to display the report title in the middle of the cover page. The only difference between the title "Recommendations for the Wireless Network at Spruce & Cooper" here and the title you entered in the document header is that here the title is displayed in all uppercase letters. The entire title is right-aligned. The cover page also includes document controls for a subtitle and an abstract. See Figure 3–39.

Figure 3–39	Newly inserted cover page

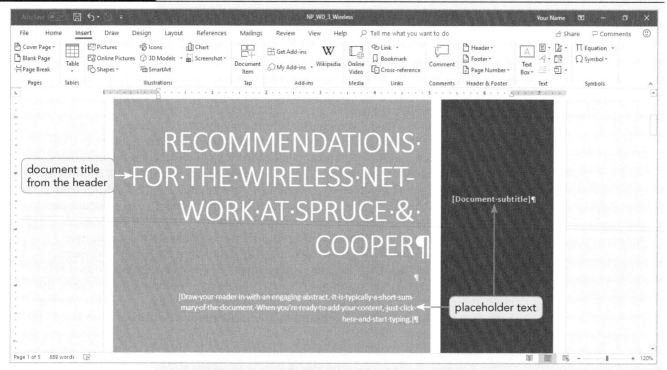

The word "NETWORK" is hyphenated, which looks awkward in a title that is formatted in all capital letters. You can fix that by changing the document's hyphenation settings.

7. On the ribbon, click the **Layout** tab.

8. In the Page Setup group, click the **Hyphenation** button, and then click **Hyphenation Options**.

9. In the Hyphenation dialog box, click the **Hyphenate words in CAPS** check box to remove the checkmark, and then click **OK**. The word "NETWORK" moves to the third line, so the hyphen is no longer necessary.

Next, you need to type a subtitle in the subtitle document control on the right side of the page.

10. Click the **[Document subtitle]** placeholder text, and then type **Prepared by Eboni Wheatley**. Next, you will remove the abstract document control because you do not need an abstract for this report.

11. Below the document title, right-click the placeholder text that begins **[Draw your reader in...** to display the shortcut menu, and then click **Remove Content Control**. The content control is removed from the cover page.

12. Save the document.

Working with Themes

A **theme** is a coordinated collection of fonts, colors, and other visual effects designed to give a document a cohesive, polished look. A variety of themes are installed with Word, with more available online at Templates.office.com. When you open a new, blank document in Word, the Office theme is applied by default. To change a document's theme, you click the Themes button, which is located in the Document Formatting group on the Design tab, and then click the theme you want. Pointing to the Themes button displays a ScreenTip that tells you what theme is currently applied to the document.

The **theme colors** are the colors you see in the Theme Colors section of any color gallery, such as the Font Color gallery. Theme colors are used in the document's styles to format headings, body text, and other elements. When applying color to a document, you usually have the option of selecting a color from a palette of colors designed to match the current theme or from a palette of standard colors. For instance, recall that the colors in the Font Color gallery are divided into Theme Colors and Standard Colors. When you select a Standard Color, such as Dark Red, that color remains the same no matter which theme you apply to the document. But when you click one of the Theme Colors, you are essentially telling Word to use the color located in that particular spot on the Theme Colors palette. Then, if you change the document's theme later, Word substitutes a color from the same location on the Theme Colors palette. This ensures that all the colors in a document are drawn from a group of colors coordinated to look good together. So as a rule, if you are going to use multiple colors in a document (perhaps for paragraph shading and font color), it's a good idea to stick with the Theme Colors.

A similar substitution takes place with fonts when you change the theme. However, to understand how this works, you need to understand the difference between headings and body text. Eboni's document includes the headings "Summary," "Help from Norris-Blain Network Consulting," "Conducting a Wireless Site Survey," "Recommendation," "Survey Costs," "Upgrades," and "Expenditures"—all of which are formatted with heading styles. The text below the headings is considered body text. For example, the paragraph below the "Summary" heading is body text.

To ensure that your documents have a harmonious look, each theme assigns a font for headings and a font for body text. These two fonts are known as the document's **theme fonts**. They are used in the document's styles and appear at the top of the font list when you click the Font arrow in the Font group on the Home tab.

Typically, in a given theme, the same font is used for both headings and body text, but not always. In the Office theme, for instance, they are slightly different; the heading font is Calibri Light, and the body font is Calibri. These two fonts appear at the top of the Font list as "Calibri Light (Headings)" and "Calibri (Body)" when you click the Font arrow in the Font group on the Home tab. When you begin typing text in a new document with the Office theme, the text is formatted as body text with the Calibri font by default.

When applying a font to selected text, you can choose one of the two theme fonts at the top of the Font list, or you can choose one of the other fonts in the Font list. If you choose one of the other fonts and then change the document theme, that font remains the same. But if you use one of the theme fonts and then change the document theme, Word substitutes the appropriate font from the new theme. When you paste text into a document that has a different theme, Word applies the theme fonts and colors of the new document. To retain the original formatting, use the Keep Source Formatting option in the Paste Options menu.

Figure 3–40 compares elements of the default Office theme with the Integral theme. The Integral theme was chosen for this example because, like the Office theme, it has different heading and body fonts.

Figure 3–40   Comparing the Office theme to the Integral theme

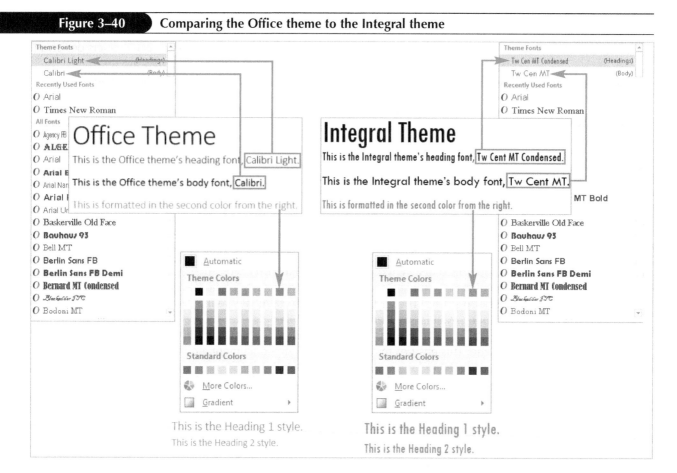

Because Eboni has not yet selected a new theme, the Office theme is currently applied to the document. However, she thinks the Facet theme might be more appropriate for the document. She asks you to apply it now.

To change the document's theme:

▶ **1.** If necessary, scroll to display the title on the cover page. This will allow you to quickly see how the document changes when you change the theme. Note that currently one section of the cover page is formatted with a blue background and the other is formatted with a blue-gray background.

▶ **2.** On the ribbon, click the **Design** tab.

▶ **3.** In the Document Formatting group, point to the **Themes** button. A ScreenTip appears containing the text "Current: Office Theme" as well as general information about themes.

▶ **4.** In the Document Formatting group, click the **Themes** button. The Themes gallery opens. Because Microsoft occasionally updates the available themes, you might see a different list than the one shown in Figure 3–41.

Figure 3–41   **Themes gallery**

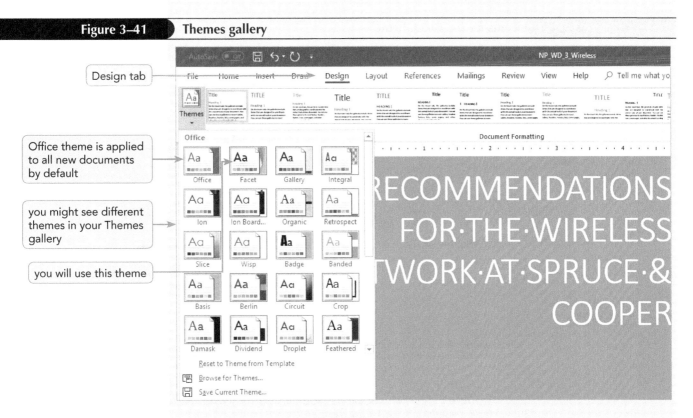

Design tab

Office theme is applied to all new documents by default

you might see different themes in your Themes gallery

you will use this theme

5. Move the pointer (without clicking it) over the various themes in the gallery to see a Live Preview of each theme in the document. The heading and body fonts as well as the heading colors change to reflect the fonts associated with the various themes.

6. In the Themes gallery, click the **Facet** theme, and then scroll down to review the document's new look. One section of the cover page now has a green background, and the other has a dark gray background. The table is formatted in shades of brown, and the SmartArt is green. The document text is now formatted in the body and heading fonts of the Facet theme, with the headings formatted in green.

   Trouble? If you do not see the Facet theme in your Themes gallery, click a different theme.

7. In the Document Formatting group, point to the **Fonts** button. A ScreenTip appears, listing the currently selected theme (Facet), the heading font (Trebuchet MS), and the body font (Trebuchet MS). See Figure 3–42.

Figure 3–42   **Fonts for the Facet theme**

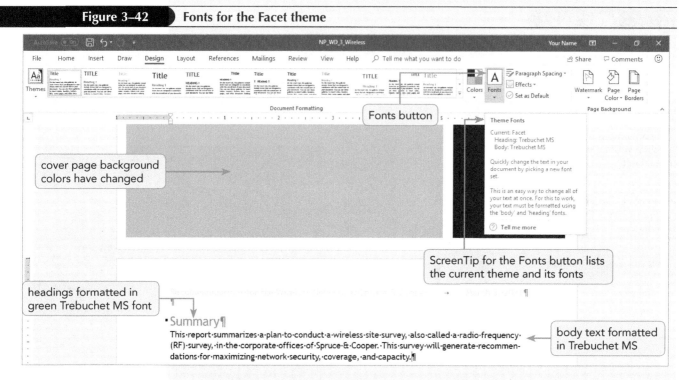

cover page background colors have changed

Fonts button

ScreenTip for the Fonts button lists the current theme and its fonts

Theme Fonts

Current: Facet
   Heading: Trebuchet MS
   Body: Trebuchet MS

Quickly change the text in your document by picking a new font set.

This is an easy way to change all of your text at once. For this to work, your text must be formatted using the 'body' and 'heading' fonts.

? **Tell me more**

headings formatted in green Trebuchet MS font

Summary¶
This·report·summarizes·a·plan·to·conduct·a·wireless·site·survey,·also·called·a·radio·frequency·(RF)·survey,·in·the·corporate·offices·of·Spruce·&·Cooper.·This·survey·will·generate·recommen-dations·for·maximizing·network·security,·coverage,·and·capacity.¶

body text formatted in Trebuchet MS

Trouble? If a menu appears, you clicked the Fonts button instead of pointing to it. Press ESC, and then repeat Step 7.

Note that if you wanted to select a different set of theme fonts, you could click the Fonts button and then select a set of fonts. You could also click the Colors button and select a different set of theme colors. However, the fonts and colors in a theme have been paired by designers who have a lot of experience selecting options that, together, create a coherent look. So for professional documents, you should avoid changing the theme fonts and colors.

▶ 8. **sam**↟ Save your changes.

Personalizing the Word Interface

The Word Options dialog box allows you to change the look of the Word interface. For starters, you can change the Office Theme from the default setting (Colorful) to Dark Gray or White. Note that in this context, "Office Theme" refers to the colors of the Word interface, and not the colors and fonts used in a Word document. You can also use the Office Background setting to add graphic designs, such as clouds or stars, to the Word interface. To get started, click the File tab, click Options in the navigation pane, make sure the General tab is displayed, and then select the options you want in the Personalize your copy of Microsoft Office section of the Word Options dialog box.

Your work on the report is finished. You should preview the report before closing it.

To preview the report:

▶ **1.** On the ribbon, click the **File** tab.

▶ **2.** In the navigation pane, click the **Print** tab. The cover page of the report is displayed in the document preview in the right pane.

▶ **3.** Examine the document preview, using the arrow buttons at the bottom of the pane to display each page.

▶ **4.** If you need to make any changes to the report, return to Print Layout view, edit the document, preview the document again, and then save the document.

▶ **5.** Display the document in Print Layout view.

▶ **6.** Change the Zoom level back to **120%**, and then press **CTRL+HOME** to make sure the insertion point is located on the first page.

Reviewing a Document in Read Mode

The members of Spruce & Cooper's leadership team could choose to print the report, but some might prefer to read it on their computers instead. In that case, they can take advantage of **Read Mode**, a document view designed to make reading on a screen as easy as possible. Unlike Print Layout view, which mimics the look of the printed page with its margins and page breaks, Read Mode focuses on the document's content. Read Mode displays as much content as possible on the screen at a time, with buttons that allow you to display more. Note that you can't edit text in Read Mode. To do that, you need to switch back to Page Layout view.

To display the document in Read Mode:

▶ **1.** In the status bar, click the **Read Mode** button 📖. The document switches to Read Mode, with a reduced version of the cover page on the left and the first part of the document text on the right. On the left edge of the status bar, the message "Screens 1–2 of 9" explains that you are currently viewing the first two screens out of a total of 9.

Trouble? If your status bar indicates that you have a different number of screens, you may be using a computer with a different screen resolution than the resolution used to create the figures in this book. Change the Zoom level as needed so that the document is split into 9 screens.

The title page on the left is screen 1. The text on the right is screen 2. To display more of the document, you can click the arrow button on the right. See Figure 3–43.

Figure 3–43	Document displayed in Read Mode

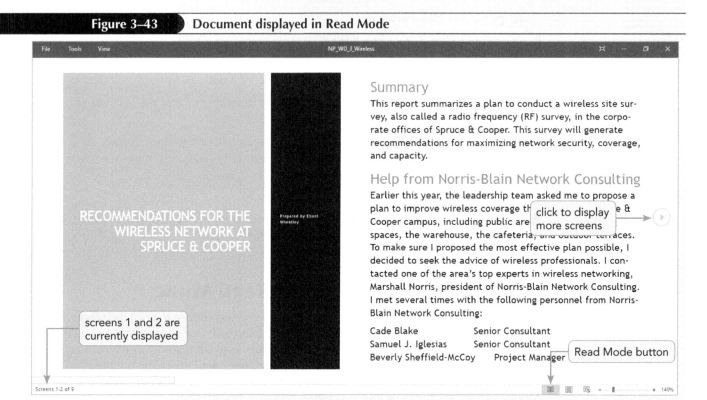

File   Tools   View   NP_WD_3_Wireless

Summary

This report summarizes a plan to conduct a wireless site survey, also called a radio frequency (RF) survey, in the corporate offices of Spruce & Cooper. This survey will generate recommendations for maximizing network security, coverage, and capacity.

Help from Norris-Blain Network Consulting

Earlier this year, the leadership team asked me to propose a plan to improve wireless coverage th[click to display more screens]e & Cooper campus, including public are spaces, the warehouse, the cafeteria, and outdoor terraces. To make sure I proposed the most effective plan possible, I decided to seek the advice of wireless professionals. I contacted one of the area's top experts in wireless networking, Marshall Norris, president of Norris-Blain Network Consulting. I met several times with the following personnel from Norris-Blain Network Consulting:

Cade Blake   Senior Consultant
Samuel J. Iglesias   Senior Consultant
Beverly Sheffield-McCoy   Project Manager

RECOMMENDATIONS FOR THE WIRELESS NETWORK AT SPRUCE & COOPER

Prepared by Eboni Wheatley

screens 1 and 2 are currently displayed

Read Mode button

Screens 1-2 of 9   140%

Trouble? If the pages on your screen are not laid out as shown in Figure 3–43, click View on the menu bar, point to Layout, and then click Column Layout.

2. Click the **right arrow** button on the right to display screens 3 and 4. A left arrow button is now displayed on the left side of the screen. You could click it to move back to the previous screens.

TIP

To zoom in on a SmartArt graphic, you can double-click it. Click anywhere outside the object zoom window to return to the Read Mode screens.

3. Click the **right arrow** button to display screens 5 and 6, then screens 7 and 8, and then screen 9.

4. Click the **left arrow** button on the left as necessary to return to screens 1 and 2, and then click the **Print Layout** button in the status bar to return to Page Layout view.

5. Close the document.

You now have a draft of the document, including a cover page, the report text, a nicely formatted table, and the SmartArt graphic (in landscape orientation).

PROSKILLS

Written Communication: Taking Notes

The process of writing a report or other long document usually involves taking notes. It's essential to organize your notes in a way that allows you to write about your topic logically and coherently. It's also important to retain your notes after you finish a first draft, so that you can incorporate additional material from your notes in subsequent drafts.

Clicking the Linked Notes button on the Review tab opens Microsoft OneNote in a window on the right side of the screen. (If you don't see the Linked Notes button, click the File tab to display Backstage view. Click Options in the navigation pane, and then click Add-ins. Click the arrow button in the Manage box, select Com Add-ins, if necessary, and then click the Go button. In the Com Add-ins dialog box, select OneNote Linked Notes Add-In, and then click OK.) In the Microsoft OneNote window, you can take notes that are linked to your Microsoft Word account. Every time you start Word and click the Linked Notes button, your notes are displayed in the OneNote window. You can copy material from a Word document and paste it in OneNote, and vice versa.

To get started, open a Word document, save it, make sure you are logged into your Microsoft account, click the Review tab, and then, in the OneNote group, click the Linked Notes button. This opens the Select Location in OneNote dialog box, where you can select a notebook. OneNote works best if you use a notebook stored on OneDrive, so unless you have a compelling reason to do otherwise, select a notebook stored on OneDrive. Now you're ready to take notes. Start by typing a title for your notebook page at the insertion point, then click in the blank space below the title, and start taking notes. To display the OneNote ribbon, with a selection of tools for working with notes, click the ellipses at the top of the OneNote window. Click the Close button in the upper-right corner of the OneNote window pane when you are finished.

REVIEW

Session 3.2 Quick Check

1. What is the default tab stop style?

2. Explain how to configure Word to hyphenate a document automatically.

3. What is the first thing you need to do if you want to format part of a document in an orientation different from the rest of the document?

4. Explain how to create separate headers for a document with two sections.

5. Explain how to insert a preformatted cover page.

6. What is the default theme in a new document?

PRACTICE

Review Assignments

Data File needed for the Review Assignments: NP_WD_3-3.docx

The wireless site survey has been completed, and the Spruce & Cooper wireless network has been upgraded. Now Eboni Wheatley is focusing on the second phase of her work on the network—improving security. She has begun working on a report for the leadership team that outlines information about conducting security training classes and installing network security software. You need to format the report, add a table at the end containing a preliminary schedule, add a formula to another table that summarizes costs associated with subscriptions for network security protection, and create a sample graphic that Eboni could use in a handout announcing the security training.

Complete the following steps:

1. Open the document **NP_WD_3-3.docx** located in the Word3 > Review folder included with your Data Files, and then save it as **NP_WD_3_Security** in the location specified by your instructor.
2. Promote the "Schedule" and "Planning for Level 1 Sessions" headings from Heading 2 text to Heading 1 text, and then move the "Planning for Level 1 Sessions" heading and its body text up above the "Schedule" heading.
3. Insert a page break before the "Schedule" heading. On the new page 2, in the blank paragraph before the "Network Security Subscription Costs" heading, insert a table using the information shown in Figure 3–44. Format the header row in bold.

Figure 3–44 **Level 1 training schedule**

Date	Topic
8/6/2021	Social engineering
5/21/2021	Introduction to cybersecurity
10/5/2021	Mobile security
7/20/2021	Cloud-based threats
6/16/2021	Data protection

4. Sort the table by the contents of the "Date" column in ascending order.
5. In the appropriate location in the table, insert a new row for an **Endpoint security** class on **9/3/2021**.
6. Delete the "Mobile security" row from the table.
7. Modify the widths of both columns to accommodate the widest entry in each.
8. Apply the Grid Table 4 - Accent 4 style to the table, and then remove the special formatting for the first column.
9. Locate the table in the "Network Security Subscription Costs" section of the document. In the table's lower-right cell, add a formula field that sums the total cost per month and displays the result in a format that matches the other numbers in the table, including a dollar sign ($).
10. Change the cost for DNS Protection to **$650.00** and then update the formula.
11. Merge the two blank cells, insert **TOTAL** in the new, merged cell, right-align the text in the cell, and then format the contents of the bottom row in bold.
12. Apply the Grid Table 4 - Accent 4 style to the table, and then remove the special formatting for the first column.
13. On page 1, replace the text "[instructor names]" with a tabbed list of instructors and their specialties, using the following information: **Suzette Carrington-Brewster**, **Malware**; **Lia Kim**, **Server security**; **Leopold R. Coia**, **Social engineering**. Insert a tab after each name, and don't include any punctuation in the list.

14. Use a left tab stop to align the instructors' specialties 2.5 inches from the left margin, and then adjust the list's paragraph spacing so it appears to be a single paragraph.

15. Turn on automatic hyphenation.

16. After the second table on page 2, insert a section break that starts a new, third page, and then format the new page in landscape orientation.

17. Insert a SmartArt graphic that illustrates the two parts of upgrading Spruce & Cooper's network security. Use the Circle Process graphic from the Process category, and, from left to right, include the following text in the SmartArt diagram: **Security Training**, **Web Secure Portal Plus**, and **Secure Network**. Do not include any punctuation in the SmartArt. Size the SmartArt graphic to fill the page.

18. Create a footer for sections 1 and 2 that aligns your first and last names at the left margin. Insert the page number, without any design elements and without the word "Page," below your name.

19. Separate the section 2 header from the section 1 header, and then create a header for section 1 using the Retrospect header style. Enter **IMPROVING NETWORK SECURITY AT SPRUCE & COOPER** as the document title, and select the current date. Note that the document title will be displayed in all uppercase no matter how you type it.

20. Insert a cover page using the Retrospect style. If you typed the document title in all uppercase in the header, it will be displayed in all uppercase here. If you used a mix of uppercase and lowercase in the header, you'll see a mix here. Revise the document title if necessary to make it all uppercase, change the hyphenation options so "NETWORK" is no longer hyphenated, and then add the following subtitle: **PREPARED BY *YOUR NAME***, replacing *YOUR NAME* with your first and last name. Delete the Author document control. Also delete the Company Name and Company Address document controls, as well as the vertical bar character between them.

21. Change the document theme to Slice, then save and preview the report. Eboni will be adding more text to page 3, so don't be concerned that most of that page is blank.

22. Close the document.

Case Problem 1

Data File needed for this Case Problem: NP_WD_3-4.docx

LEED Landscape Design Association   You are the business manager of the LEED Landscape Design Association, a professional organization for LEED landscape designers in Atlanta, Georgia, and the surrounding area. LEED, which is short for Leadership in Energy and Environmental Design, is a certification system designed to encourage environmentally friendly construction and design, as well as sustainable landscape design. Landscapers join the LEED Landscape Design Association to make professional contacts with like-minded vendors and customers. You have been asked to help prepare an annual report for the board of directors. The current draft is not complete, but it contains enough for you to get started.

Complete the following steps:

1. Open the document **NP_WD_3-4.docx** located in the Word3 > Case1 folder included with your Data Files, and then save it as **NP_WD_3_LEED** in the location specified by your instructor.

2. Adjust the heading levels so that the "LEED Sustainable Landscape Fair" and "LEED Tech Fest" headings are formatted with the Heading 2 style.

3. Move the "New Members" heading and its body text down to the end of the report.

4. Format the Board of Directors list using a left tab stop with a dot leader at the 2.2-inch mark. (*Hint:* Use the Dialog Box Launcher in the Paragraph group on the Layout tab to open the Paragraph dialog box, and then click the Tabs button at the bottom of the Indents and Spacing tab to open the Tabs dialog box.)

5. Insert a page break that moves the "New Members" heading to the top of a new page, and then, below the body text on the new page, insert a table consisting of three columns and four rows.

6. In the table, enter the information shown in Figure 3–45. Format the column headings in bold.

Figure 3–45   Information for membership table

Type	Fee	Members
Vendor	$500	225
Enterprise	$200	125
Individual	$175	200

7. Sort the table in ascending order by type.

8. In the appropriate location in the table, insert a row for a **Student** membership type, with a **$25** fee, and **170** members.

9. Adjust the column widths so each column accommodates the widest entry.

10. Add a new row to the bottom of the table, and then insert a formula that sums the total number of members. Make sure the formula displays the result in the appropriate format.

11. Merge the two blank cells, add the right-aligned text **TOTAL** to the new, merged cell, and then format the bottom row in bold.

12. Format the table using the Grid Table 4 - Accent 3 table style without banded rows or bold formatting in the first column.

13. Turn on automatic hyphenation.

14. Insert a Blank footer, and then type your name to replace the selected placeholder text in the footer's left margin. In the right margin, insert a page number using the Large Color style. (*Hint*: Press TAB twice to move the insertion point to the right margin before inserting the page number, and then insert the page number at the current location.)

15. Insert a cover page using the Semaphore style. Select the current date. Enter the document title, **LEED LANDSCAPE DESIGN ASSOCIATION** in the appropriate document control. If necessary, change the Hyphenation options so "ASSOCIATION" appears on one line. In the subtitle document control, enter **Prepared by [Your Name]**, but replace "[Your Name]" with your first and last names). (Note that the text you type is formatted in a special font format called small caps.) Delete the remaining document controls.

16. Change the document theme to Facet.

17. Save, preview, and then close the document.

Case Problem 2

There are no Data Files needed for this Case Problem.

York Pickup and Delivery   Rory York owns a small pickup and delivery company in Birmingham, Alabama. A professional contact has just emailed him a list of potential corporate customers. Rory asks you to create and format a table containing the list of customers. When you're finished with that project, you'll create a table detailing some of his recent repair expenses in the garage where he houses his fleet of trucks.

Complete the following steps:

1. Open a new, blank document, and then save it as **NP_WD_3_Corporate** in the location specified by your instructor.

2. Create the table shown in Figure 3–46.

Figure 3–46   Corporate customers table

Company	Contact	Phone
Walnut Springs Coffee Imports	Krystal Winford	205-555-0100
CDX Creative Partners	Tobias Forster	205-555-0107
Blue Diamond Construction Supply	Layla Jordan	205-555-0114
Cornerstone and Woodward Partners Incorporated	Mohammed Khan	205-555-0121
Carbon Wear Unlimited	Huey McGrath	205-555-0128

For the table style, start with the Grid Table 4 - Accent 4 table style, make any necessary changes, and then change the theme to a theme that uses TW Cen MT (Condensed) for the heading font and TW Cen MT for the body font, and that formats the heading row with the Green, Accent 4 shading color. (Note that the text in the heading row is formatted with the theme's body font, which means it is displayed in TW CEN MT after you change the theme.) The final table should be about 5 inches wide and about 2.5 inches tall, as measured on the horizontal and vertical rulers. (*Hint*: Remember that you can drag the Table Resize handle to increase the table's overall size.)

3. Replace "Huey McGrath" with your first and last names.

4. Add a new blank paragraph below the corporate customers table, and then, in that new paragraph, create the table shown in Figure 3–47, using the same table style and modifications you used for the corporate customers table. Use a formula for the total with a number format that includes a dollar sign but no decimal places. (*Hint*: You can edit the number format in the Formula dialog box to delete both instances of a decimal place with two trailing zeros.) The final table should be about 5.5 inches wide and about 2 inches tall, as measured on the horizontal and vertical rulers.

Figure 3–47   Garage repair table

Repair	Completion Date	Cost
Install new overhead lights	3/4/2021	$450
Replace deadbolts on front and back doors	3/15/2021	$125
Fix broken screens	3/21/2021	$50
	TOTAL	$ 625

5. Save, preview, and then close the document.

Enhancing Page Layout and Design

Creating a Newsletter

Case | *Metropolitan Library System*

Vassily Gogol is a librarian for the Metropolitan Library System in Indianapolis, Indiana. He has decided to begin publishing a monthly newsletter with articles about the latest events at the system's many branches. He has already written the text of the first newsletter. Now he needs you to transform the text into an eye-catching publication with a headline, pictures, drop caps, and other desktop-publishing elements. Vassily's budget doesn't allow him to hire a professional graphic designer to create the document using desktop-publishing software. But there's no need for that because you can do the work for him using the formatting, graphics, and page layout tools in Word. After you finish the newsletter, Vassily wants you to save the newsletter as a PDF so he can email it to the printing company. You also need to review a document that is currently available only as a PDF.

OBJECTIVES

Session 4.1
- Use continuous section breaks for page layout
- Format text in columns
- Insert symbols and special characters
- Distinguish between inline and floating objects
- Wrap text around an object
- Insert and format text boxes
- Insert drop caps

Session 4.2
- Create and modify WordArt
- Crop a picture
- Search for online pictures and 3-D models
- Rotate and adjust a picture
- Remove a picture's background
- Insert and format an icon
- Balance columns
- Add a page border
- Save a document as a PDF
- Open a PDF in Word

STARTING DATA FILES

Word4 → **Module**

NP_WD_4-1.docx
Support_WD_4_Bookmobile.png
Support_WD_4_Cupcakes.png
Support_WD_4_Festival.docx
Support_WD_4_Hours.docx
Support_WD_4_Listening.pdf

Review

NP_WD_4-2.docx
Support_WD_4_Island.png
Support_WD_4_Retirement.png
Support_WD_4_Schedule.docx
Support_WD_4_Volunteers.docx

Case1

NP_WD_4-3.docx
Support_WD_4_Bins.docx
Support_WD_4_Earth.png
Support_WD_4_Sorting .png

Case2

(none)

Session 4.1 Visual Overview:

This picture is an example of an **object**—that is, something you can manipulate independently of the text. The bookmobile picture, the headphone icon, the WordArt headline, and the text boxes are also objects. To edit an object, you first have to click it to select it.

This specially formatted text is an example of **WordArt**, which is created using the WordArt button in the Text group on the Insert tab.

These are examples of text boxes, which are like mini documents within a document.

This bookmobile picture was inserted from a file, but you can also use the Online Pictures button in the Illustrations group on the Insert tab to search for photos and other illustrations on the web.

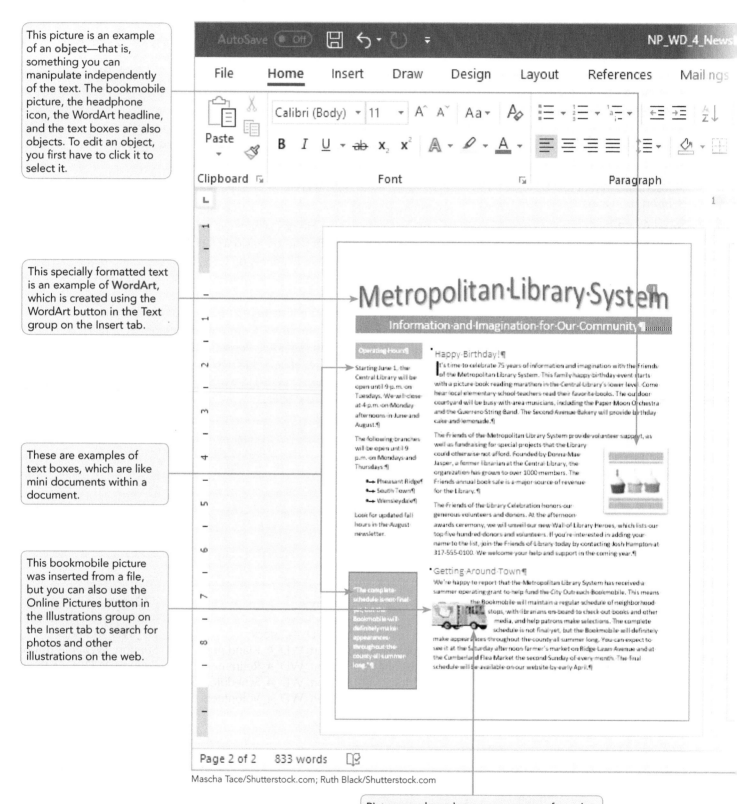

Mascha Tace/Shutterstock.com; Ruth Black/Shutterstock.com

Pictures and text boxes are separate from the document text; you need to adjust the way text flows, or **wraps**, around those elements. Here, the Tight text wrap option is used to make text flow as closely as possible around the shape of the bookmobile.

Elements of Desktop Publishing

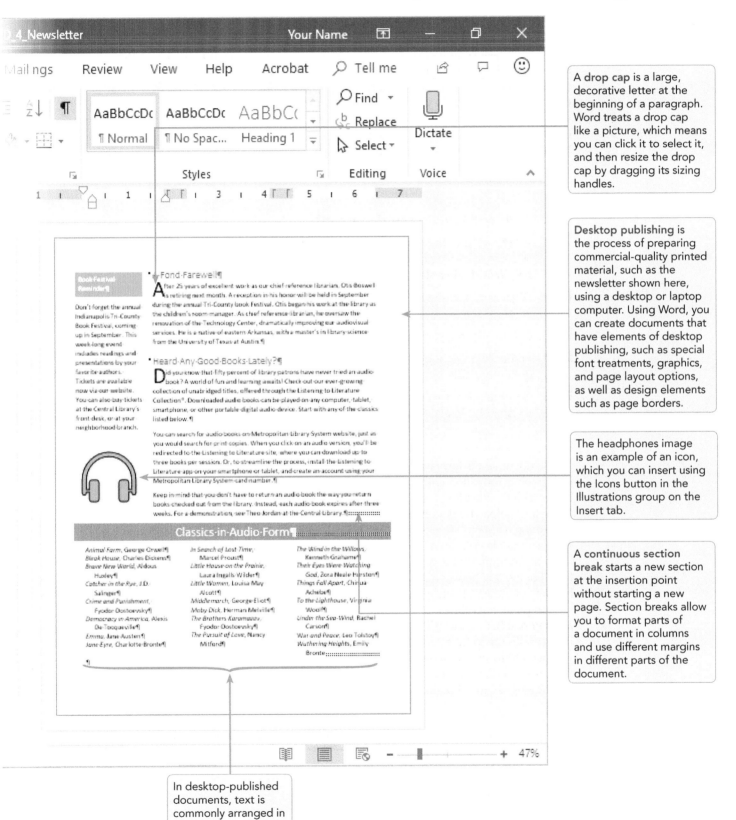

A **drop cap** is a large, decorative letter at the beginning of a paragraph. Word treats a drop cap like a picture, which means you can click it to select it, and then resize the drop cap by dragging its sizing handles.

Desktop publishing is the process of preparing commercial-quality printed material, such as the newsletter shown here, using a desktop or laptop computer. Using Word, you can create documents that have elements of desktop publishing, such as special font treatments, graphics, and page layout options, as well as design elements such as page borders.

The headphones image is an example of an **icon**, which you can insert using the Icons button in the Illustrations group on the Insert tab.

A **continuous section break** starts a new section at the insertion point without starting a new page. Section breaks allow you to format parts of a document in columns and use different margins in different parts of the document.

In desktop-published documents, text is commonly arranged in two or more **columns**.

Using Continuous Section Breaks to Enhance Page Layout

Newsletters and other desktop-published documents often incorporate multiple section breaks, with the various sections formatted with different margins, page orientations, column settings, and other page layout options. Continuous section breaks, which start a new section without starting a new page, are especially useful when creating a newsletter because they allow you to apply different page layout settings to different parts of a single page. To create the newsletter shown in the Session 4.1 Visual Overview, the first step is to insert a series of section breaks that will allow you to use different margins for different parts of the document. Section breaks will also allow you to format some of the text in multiple columns.

You'll start by opening and reviewing the document.

To open and review the document:

▶ **1.** **sam** ⬇ Open the document **NP_WD_4-1.docx** from the Word4 > Module folder included with your Data Files, and then save the file as **NP_WD_4_Newsletter** in the location specified by your instructor.

▶ **2.** Display nonprinting characters and the rulers, and switch to Print Layout view, if necessary.

▶ **3.** On the ribbon, click the **View** tab.

▶ **4.** In the Zoom group, click **Multiple Pages** so you can see both pages of the document side by side.

▶ **5.** Compare the document to the completed newsletter shown in the Session 4.1 Visual Overview.

The document is formatted with the Office theme, using the default margins. The first paragraph is formatted with the Title style, and the remaining headings are formatted either with the Heading 1 style or with blue paragraph shading, center alignment, and white font color. The document doesn't yet contain any text boxes or other desktop-publishing elements. The list of audio books at the end of the document appears as a standard, single column of text.

To make room for the text boxes, you need to change the left margin to 2.5 inches for all of the text between the "Information and Imagination for our Community" heading and the "Classics in Audio Form" heading. To accomplish this, you'll insert a section break after the "Information and Imagination for our Community" heading and another one before the "Classics in Audio Form" heading. You'll eventually format the list of audio books, at the end of the document, in three columns. To accomplish that, you need to insert a third section break after the "Classics in Audio Form" heading. Because you don't want any of the section breaks to start new pages, you will use continuous sections breaks for all three. See Figure 4–1.

| Figure 4–1 | Newsletter document before adding section breaks |

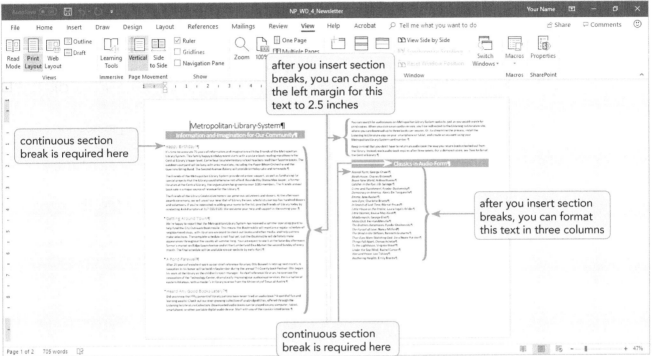

To insert continuous section breaks in the document:

1. Change the Zoom level to **120%**.

2. In the document, click at the beginning of the third paragraph, which contains the heading "Happy Birthday!"

3. On the ribbon, click the **Layout** tab.

4. In the Page Setup group, click the **Breaks** button, and then click **Continuous**. A short dotted line, indicating a continuous section break, appears in the blue shading at the end of the preceding paragraph, although you might find it hard to see. If there was more white space to the right of the line of text, you would see a longer line with the words "Section Break (Continuous)." You'll be able to see the section break text more clearly when you insert the next one.

5. Scroll down to page 2, click at the beginning of the shaded paragraph "Classics in Audio Form," and then insert a continuous section break. A dotted line with the words "Section Break (Continuous)" appears at the end of the preceding paragraph.

6. Click at the beginning of the next paragraph, which contains the text "*Animal Farm*, George Orwell," and then insert a continuous section break. A dotted line with the words "Section Break (Continuous)" appears in the blue shading at the end of the preceding paragraph.

Now that you have created sections within the newsletter document, you can format the individual sections as if they were separate documents. In the following steps, you'll format the first and third sections by changing their left and right margins to .75 inch. Then, you'll format the second section by changing its left margin to 2.5 inches.

To set custom margins for sections 1, 2, and 3:

▶ **1.** Press **CTRL+HOME** to position the insertion point in section 1.

▶ **2.** In the Page Setup group, click the **Margins** button, and then click **Custom Margins** to open the Page Setup dialog box with the Margins tab displayed.

▶ **3.** Change the Left and Right margin settings to **.75** inch, and then click **OK**. The blue shading expands slightly on both sides of the paragraph.

▶ **4.** On page 1, click anywhere in the "Happy Birthday!" heading to position the insertion point in section 2.

▶ **5.** In the Page Setup group, click the **Margins** button, and then click **Custom Margins** to open the Page Setup dialog box.

▶ **6.** Change the Left margin setting to **2.5** inches, and then click **OK**. The text in section 2 shifts to the right.

▶ **7.** Scroll down to page 2, click in the shaded heading "**Classics in Audio Form**" to position the insertion point in section 3, and then change the Left and Right margin settings to **.75** inch.

▶ **8.** On the ribbon, click the **View** tab.

▶ **9.** In the Zoom group, click **Multiple Pages** so you can see both pages of the document side by side. See Figure 4–2.

Figure 4–2	**Sections 1, 2, and 3 with new margins**

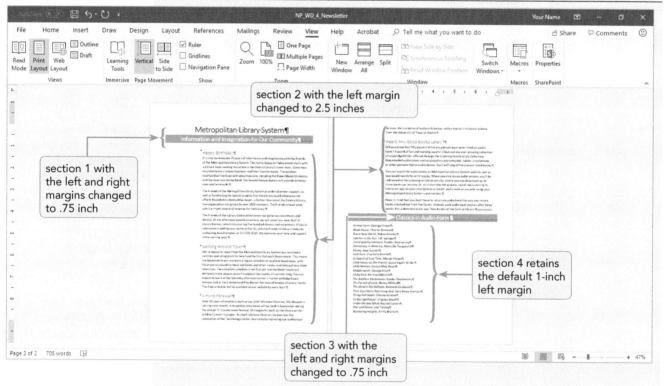

section 2 with the left margin changed to 2.5 inches

section 1 with the left and right margins changed to .75 inch

section 4 retains the default 1-inch left margin

section 3 with the left and right margins changed to .75 inch

▶ **10.** Save the document.

In addition to allowing you to format parts of a document with different margins, section breaks allow you to format part of a document in columns. You'll add some columns to section 4 next.

Formatting Text in Columns

TIP

When working with large amounts of text formatted in columns, it's helpful to hyphenate the document to avoid excessive white space caused by short lines.

Text meant for quick reading is often laid out in columns, with text flowing down one column, continuing at the top of the next column, flowing down that column, and so forth. To get started, click the Columns button in the Page Setup group on the Layout tab, and then click the number of columns you want in the Columns gallery. For more advanced column options, you can use the More Columns command to open the Columns dialog box. In this dialog box, you can adjust the column widths and the space between columns and choose to format either the entire document in columns or just the section that contains the insertion point.

As shown in the Session 4.1 Visual Overview, Vassily wants section 4 of the newsletter document, which consists of the audio books list, to be formatted in three columns.

To format section 4 in three columns:

▶ **1.** Click anywhere in the list of audio books at the end of the document to position the insertion point in section 4.

▶ **2.** On the ribbon, click the **Layout** tab.

▶ **3.** In the Page Setup group, click the **Columns** button to display the Columns gallery. At this point, you could simply click Three to format section 4 in three columns of equal width. However, it's helpful to take a look at the columns dialog box so you can get familiar with some more advanced column options.

▶ **4.** Click **More Columns** to open the Columns dialog box, and then in the Presets section, click **Three**. See Figure 4–3.

Figure 4–3   Columns dialog box

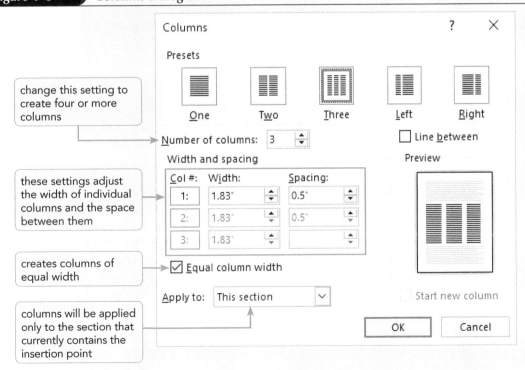

To format text in four or more columns, you can change the setting in the Number of columns box instead of selecting an option in the Presets section. By default, the Apply to box, in the lower-left corner, displays "This section," indicating that the three-column format will be applied only to the current section. To apply columns to the entire document, you could click the Apply to arrow and then click Whole document. To change the width of the individual columns or the spacing between the columns, you can use the settings in the Width and spacing section of the Columns dialog box.

▶ **5.** Click **OK**. Section 4 is now formatted in three columns of the default width, although the third column is currently blank. This will change when you add more formatting elements to the newsletter. See Figure 4–4.

Figure 4–4 **Section 4 formatted in three columns**

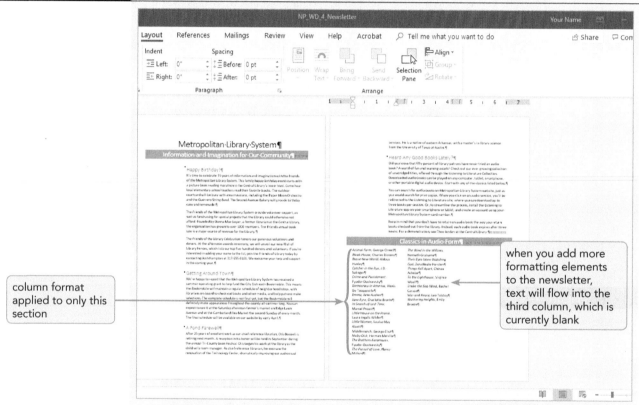

column format applied to only this section

when you add more formatting elements to the newsletter, text will flow into the third column, which is currently blank

▶ **6.** Change the document Zoom level to **120%**, scroll down so you can see the entire list of audio books, and then save the document.

Keep in mind that you can restore a document or a section to its original format by formatting it as one column. You can also adjust paragraph indents within columns, just as you would in normal text. In fact, Vassily would like you to format the columns in section 4 with hanging indents so that it's easier to read the audio book titles that take up more than one line.

To indent the audio book titles, you first need to select the three columns of text. Selecting columns of text by dragging the mouse can be tricky. It's easier to use the SHIFT+click method instead.

To format the columns in section 4 with hanging indents:

▶ **1.** Make sure the **Layout** tab is selected on the ribbon.

▶ **2.** Click at the beginning of the first audio book title and author name ("*Animal Farm*, George Orwell"), press and hold **SHIFT**, and then click at the end of the last audio book title and author name ("*Wuthering Heights*, Emily Bronte"). The entire list of audio books is selected.

▶ **3.** In the Paragraph group, click the **Paragraph Dialog Box Launcher** to open the Paragraph dialog box with the Indents and Spacing tab displayed.

▶ **4.** In the Indentation section, click the **Special** arrow, click **Hanging**, and then change the By setting to **0.2"**.

▶ **5.** Click **OK** to close the Paragraph dialog box, and then click anywhere in the list to deselect it. The list of audio books and authors is now formatted with a hanging indent, so the second line of each paragraph is indented .2 inches. See Figure 4–5.

| Figure 4–5 | Text formatted in columns with hanging indent |

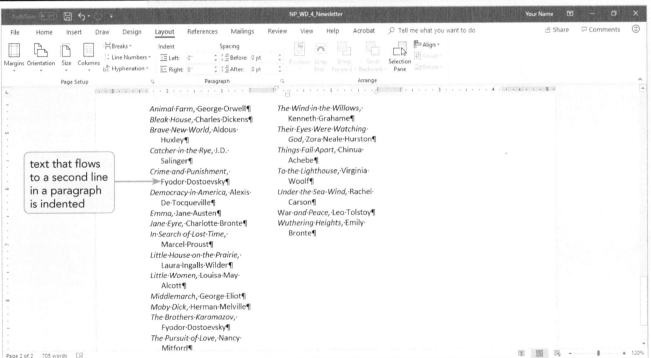

text that flows to a second line in a paragraph is indented

Inserting Symbols and Special Characters

When creating documents in Word, you can change some of the characters available on the standard keyboard into special characters or symbols called **typographic characters**. The AutoCorrect feature in Word automatically converts some standard characters into typographic characters as you type. In some cases, you need to press SPACEBAR and type more characters before Word inserts the appropriate typographic character. If Word inserts a typographic character that you don't want, you can click the Undo button to revert to the characters you originally typed. See Figure 4–6.

Figure 4–6   Common typographic characters

To Insert This Symbol or Character	Type	Word Converts To
Em dash	word--word	word—word
Smiley face	:)	☺
Copyright symbol	(c)	©
Trademark symbol	(tm)	™
Registered trademark symbol	(r)	®
Fractions	1/2, 1/4	½, ¼
Arrows	<-- or -->	← or →

Most of the typographic characters in Figure 4–6 can also be inserted using the Symbol button on the Insert tab, which opens a gallery of commonly used symbols, and the More Symbols command, which opens the Symbol dialog box. The Symbol dialog box provides access to all the symbols and special characters you can insert into a Word document.

REFERENCE

Inserting Symbols and Special Characters from the Symbol Dialog Box

- Move the insertion point to the location in the document where you want to insert a particular symbol or special character.
- On the ribbon, click the Insert tab.
- In the Symbols group, click the Symbol button.
- If you see the symbol or character you want in the Symbol gallery, click it to insert it in the document. For a more extensive set of choices, click More Symbols to open the Symbol dialog box.
- In the Symbol dialog box, locate the symbol or character you want on either the Symbols tab or the Special Characters tab.
- Click the symbol or special character you want, click the Insert button, and then click Close.

Vassily forgot to include a registered trademark symbol (®) after "Listening to Literature Collection" on page 2. He asks you to add one now. After you do, you'll explore the Symbol dialog box.

To insert the registered trademark symbol and explore the Symbol dialog box:

▶ 1. Use the Navigation pane to find **the Listening to Literature Collection** in the document, and then close the Navigation pane.

▶ 2. Click at the end of the word "Collection" to position the insertion point between the "n" at the end of "Collection" and the period.

▶ 3. Type **(r)**. AutoCorrect converts the "r" in parentheses into the superscript ® symbol.

   If you don't know which characters to type to insert a symbol or special character, you can review the AutoCorrect replacements in the AutoCorrect: English (United States) dialog box.

▶ 4. On the ribbon, click the **File** tab.

▶ 5. In the navigation pane, click **Options** to open the Word Options dialog box.

6. In the left pane, click **Proofing**, and then click the **AutoCorrect Options** button. The AutoCorrect: English (United States) dialog box opens, with the AutoCorrect tab displayed.

7. Review the table at the bottom of the AutoCorrect tab. The column on the left shows the characters you can type, and the column on the right shows what AutoCorrect inserts as a replacement. See Figure 4–7.

Figure 4–7   **AutoCorrect: English (United States) dialog box**

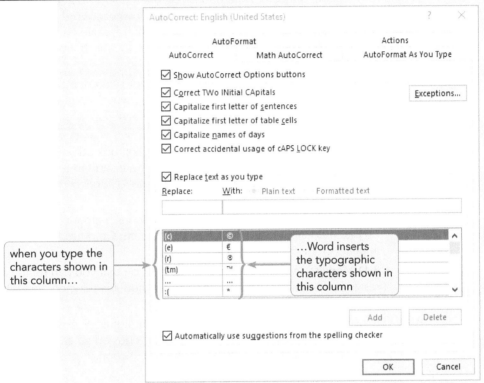

8. Scroll down to review the AutoCorrect replacements, click **Cancel** to close the AutoCorrect: English (United States) dialog box, and then click **Cancel** to close the Word Options dialog box.

Now you can explore the Symbol dialog box, which offers another way to insert symbols and special characters.

9. On the ribbon, click the **Insert** tab.

10. In the Symbols group, click the **Symbol** button, and then click **More Symbols**. The Symbol dialog box opens with the Symbols tab displayed.

11. Scroll down the gallery of symbols on the Symbols tab to review the many symbols you can insert into a document. To insert one, you would click it, and then click the Insert button.

12. Click the **Special Characters** tab. The characters available on this tab are often used in desktop publishing. Notice the shortcut keys that you can use to insert many of the special characters.

13. Click **Cancel** to close the Symbol dialog box.

Introduction to Working with Objects

An object is something that you can manipulate independently of the document text. In desktop publishing, you use objects to illustrate the document or to enhance the page layout. To complete the newsletter for Vassily, you'll need to add some text boxes, drop caps, and pictures. These are all examples of objects in Word.

Inserting Graphic Objects

The Insert tab is the starting point for adding all types of illustrations to a document. People who work in online or print publishing often refer to objects used for illustration purposes as **graphic objects**, or simply **graphics**. However, Word has more specific vocabulary for the various types of illustrations, with separate contextual tabs for formatting each type. The following list summarizes the illustrations most commonly used in newsletters:

- **Picture**—A line drawing, screenshot, or photo stored as an electronic file, and sometimes downloaded from an online site; when a picture is selected, the Picture Tools Format tab appears on the ribbon.
- **Shape**—A simple, geometric object, like a rectangle or a circle, created using the Shapes command on the Insert tab; a text box added to a document via the Text Box button in the Text group on the Insert tab is also considered a shape. When a shape is selected, the Drawing Tools Format tab appears on the ribbon.
- **Graphic**—A line drawing inserted via the Icons button in the Illustrations group on the Insert tab; when an icon is selected, the Graphics Tools Format tab appears on the ribbon.
- **3-D Models**—A three-dimensional illustration that you can rotate, and also resize by zooming in or out; when a 3-D model is selected, the 3D Model Tools tab appears on the ribbon.

After you insert an illustration, you typically need to adjust its position on the page. Your ability to control the position of an object depends on whether it is an inline object or a floating object, as you'll see in the next section.

Distinguishing Between Inline and Floating Objects

An **inline object** behaves as if it were text. Like an individual letter, it has a specific location within a line of text, and its position changes as you add or delete text. You can align an inline object just as you would align text, using the alignment buttons in the Paragraph group on the Home tab. In a simple document like a letter, inline objects are a good choice. However, in more complicated documents, inline objects are difficult to work with because every time you add or remove paragraphs of text, the object moves to a new position.

In contrast, you can position a **floating object** anywhere on the page, with the text flowing, or wrapping, around it. Unlike an inline object, which has a specific position in a line of text, a floating object has a more fluid connection to the document text. It is attached, or **anchored**, to an entire paragraph—so if you delete that paragraph, you will also delete the object. However, you can also move the object independently of that paragraph. An anchor symbol next to an object tells you that the object is a floating object rather than an inline object, as illustrated in Figure 4–8. As a general rule, you'll usually want to transform inline objects into floating objects, because floating objects are far more flexible.

Figure 4–8   An inline object compared to a floating object

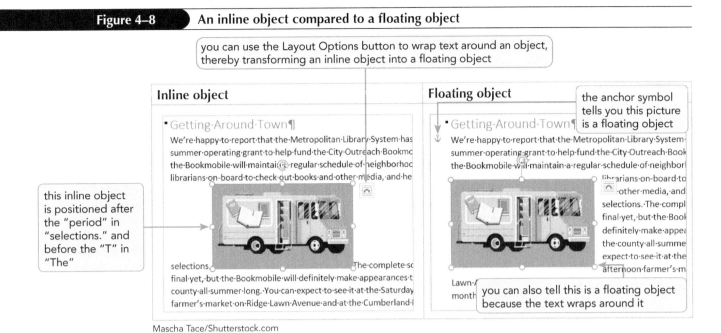

you can use the Layout Options button to wrap text around an object, thereby transforming an inline object into a floating object

Inline object

Floating object

the anchor symbol tells you this picture is a floating object

this inline object is positioned after the "period" in "selections." and before the "T" in "The"

Getting·Around·Town¶
We're·happy·to·report·that·the·Metropolitan·Library·System·has summer·operating·grant·to·help·fund·the·City·Outreach·Bookmc the·Bookmobile·will·maintai⊙·regular·schedule·of·neighborhoc librarians·on·board·to·check·out·books·and·other·media,·and·he

selections
final·yet,·but·the·Bookmobile·will·definitely·make·appearances·t county·all·summer·long.·You·can·expect·to·see·it·at·the·Saturday farmer's·market·on·Ridge·Lawn·Avenue·and·at·the·Cumberland·l

Getting·Around·Town¶
We're·happy·to·report·that·the·Metropolitan·Library·System· summer·operating·grant·to·help·fund·the·City·Outreach·Book the·Bookmobile·will·maintain·a·regular·schedule·of·neighbor librarians·on·board·to ·other·media,·and· selections.·The·compl final·yet,·but·the·Book definitely·make·appea the·county·all·summe expect·to·see·it·at·the afternoon·farmer's·m

Lawn·/ month

you can also tell this is a floating object because the text wraps around it

Mascha Tace/Shutterstock.com

Wrapping Text Around an Object

To transform an inline object into a floating object, you apply a **text wrapping setting** to it. First, click the object to select it, click the Layout Options button next to the object, and then click an option in the Layout Options gallery. For example, you can select Square text wrapping to make the text follow a square outline as it flows around the object, or you can select Tight text wrapping to make the text follow the shape of the object more exactly. Figure 4–9 describes the different types of wrapping. Note that you can also transform a floating object into an inline object by selecting the Inline with Text option in the Layout Options gallery.

Figure 4–9   Text wrapping options in the Layout Options gallery

Menu Icon	Type of Wrapping	Description
	Inline with Text	The object behaves as if it were text, and has a specific position within a paragraph. You can align inline objects using the alignment buttons on the Home tab, just as you would align text.
	Square	Text flows in a square outline around the object, regardless of the shape of the object; by default, Square text wrapping is applied to preformatted text boxes inserted via the Text Box button on the Insert tab.
	Tight	Text follows the exact outline of the object; if you want the text to flow around an object, this is usually the best option.
	Through	Text flows through the object, filling up any open areas; this type is similar to Tight text wrapping.
	Top and Bottom	Text stops above the object and then starts again below the object.
	Behind Text	The object is layered behind the text, with the text flowing over it.
	In Front of Text	The object is layered in front of the text, with the text flowing behind it; if you want to position an object in white space next to the text, this option gives you the greatest control over its exact position. By default, In Front of Text wrapping is applied to any shapes inserted via the Shapes button in the Illustrations group on the Insert tab.

Most graphic objects, including photos and SmartArt, are inline by default; however, all text boxes and shapes are floating by default. Objects that are inserted as floating objects by default have a specific text wrapping setting assigned to them, but you can change the default setting to any text wrapping setting you want.

Displaying Gridlines

When formatting a complicated document such as a newsletter, you'll often have to adjust the position of objects on the page until everything looks the way you want. To make it easier to see the relative position of objects, you can display the document's gridlines. These vertical and horizontal lines are not actually part of the document. They are simply guidelines you can use when positioning text and objects on the page. By default, when gridlines are displayed, objects align with, or snap to, the nearest intersection of a horizontal and vertical line. The figures in this module do not show gridlines because they would make the figures difficult to read. To display gridlines, click the View tab on the ribbon, and then click the Gridlines check box to insert a check.

Inserting Text Boxes

You can choose to add a preformatted text box to a document, or you can create your own text box from scratch and adjust its appearance. To insert a preformatted text box, you use the Text Box button in the Text group on the Insert tab. Text boxes inserted this way include placeholder text that you can replace with your own text. Preformatted text boxes come with preset font and paragraph options that are designed to match the text box's overall look. However, you can change the appearance of the text in the text box by using the options on the Home tab, just as you would for ordinary text. The text box, as a whole, is designed to match the document's current theme. You could alter its appearance by using the Shape Styles options on the Drawing Tools Format tab, but there's typically no reason to do so.

Because the preformatted text boxes are so professional looking, they are usually a better choice than creating your own. However, if you want a very simple text box, you can use the Shapes button in the Illustrations group to draw a text box. After you draw the text box, you can adjust its appearance by using the Shape Styles options on the Drawing Tools Format tab. You can type any text you want inside the text box at the insertion point. When you are finished, you can format the text using the options on the Home tab. Note that you can actually use any shape as a text box. Simply draw a shape (for example, a star) in the document, and then, while the shape is selected, type any text you want. You can format text inside a shape just as you would format ordinary text.

REFERENCE

Inserting a Text Box

To insert a preformatted, rectangular text box, click in the document where you want to insert the text box.

- On the ribbon, click the Insert tab.
- In the Text group, click the Text Box button to open the Text Box gallery, and then click a text box style to select it.
- In the text box in the document, delete the placeholder text, type the text you want to include, and then format the text using the options on the Home tab.

or

- To insert and format your own rectangular text box, click the Insert tab on the ribbon.
- In the Illustrations group, click the Shapes button to open the Shapes gallery, and then click Text Box.
- In the document, position the pointer where you want to insert the text box, press and hold the mouse button, and then drag the pointer to draw the text box.
- In the text box, type the text you want to include, and then format the text using the options on the Home tab.
- Format the text box using the options in the Shape Styles group on the Drawing Tools Format tab.

Inserting a Preformatted Text Box

Vassily's newsletter requires three text boxes. You need to insert the first text box on page 1, to the left of the "Happy Birthday!" heading. For this text box, you'll insert one that is preformatted to work as a sidebar. A **sidebar** is a text box designed to look good positioned to the side of the main document text. A sidebar is typically used to draw attention to important information.

To insert a preformatted text box in the document:

▶ **1.** Scroll up to the top of page 1, and then click anywhere in the "Happy Birthday!" heading.

▶ **2.** Change the Zoom level to **Multiple Pages** so you can see both pages of the document.

▶ **3.** On the ribbon, click the **Insert** tab.

▶ **4.** In the Text group, click the **Text Box** button to display the Text Box gallery, and then use the scroll bar to scroll down the gallery to locate the Ion Sidebar 1 text box.

▶ **5.** Click **Ion Sidebar 1**. The text box is inserted in the left margin of page 1. See Figure 4–10.

Figure 4–10   **Text box inserted on page 1**

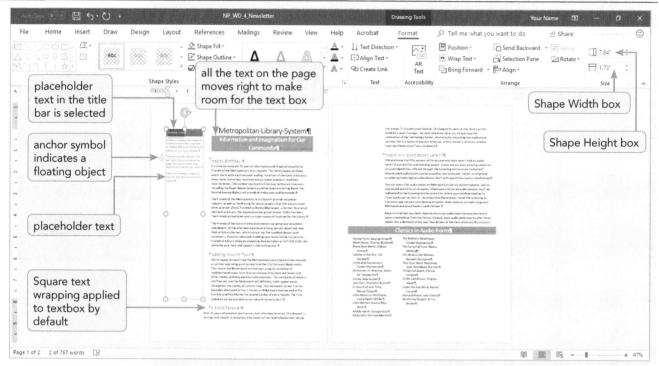

Most of the text on page 1 moves right to make room for the text box because Square text wrapping is applied to the text box by default. Later, after you resize and move the text box, the first two paragraphs will resume their original positions, centered at the top of the page. The anchor symbol next to the text box tells you it is a floating object.

The text box consists of a blue title bar at the top that contains placeholder text, with additional placeholder text below the title bar. The dotted outline with sizing handles indicates the borders of the text box. When you first insert a text box, the placeholder text in the title bar is selected, ready for you to type your own title. In this case, however, before you add any text, you'll resize and reposition the text box.

▶ **6.** On the ribbon, click the **Drawing Tools Format** tab, if necessary.

▶ **7.** In the Size group, click the **Shape Height** box, type **4.3**, click the **Shape Width** box, type **1.5**, and then press **ENTER**. The text box is now shorter and narrower.

▶ **8.** Change the Zoom level to **120%**.

Next, you need to drag the text box down below the first two paragraphs. To make this easier, you will make use of Word's alignment guides to help you position the text box. You will verify that those guides are turned on next.

▶ **9.** In the Arrange group, click the **Align** button, and then click **Use Alignment Guides**, if necessary, to insert a check, or, if it is already checked, press **ESC** to close the menu. Now you are ready to move the text box, but first you need to select the entire text box. Currently, only the placeholder text in the text box title bar is selected.

▶ **10.** Position the pointer somewhere over the text box border until the pointer changes to ⌖.

▶ **11.** Click the **text box border** to select the entire text box. The text box border changes from dotted to solid, and the Layout Options button ⌃ appears to the right of the text box.

▶ **12.** With the ⬚ pointer positioned over the border, press and hold the **mouse button**, and then drag the text box down so that the top of the text box aligns with the first line of text below the "Happy Birthday!" heading. The left edge of the text box should align with the left edge of the blue shaded heading "Happy Birthday!" as indicated by the green alignment guide that appears when you have the text box aligned with the left margin of the blue-shaded heading. Alignment guides appear when you move an object close to a margin. The anchor symbol will likely remain in its original position, next to the blue shaded paragraph, although on your computer it might move to a different location, or not be visible at all as you drag the text box. When you are sure the text box is positioned as shown in Figure 4–11, release the mouse button.

Figure 4–11	Resized and repositioned text box

▶ **13.** If necessary, drag the anchor icon to position it to the left of the blue shaded paragraph.

After you insert a text box or other object, you usually need to adjust its relationship to the surrounding text; that is, you need to adjust its text wrapping setting.

Changing the Text Wrapping Setting for the Text Box

A preformatted text box inserted via the Text Box button on the Insert tab is, by default, a floating object formatted with Square text wrapping. You will verify this when you open the Layout Options gallery in the following steps. Then you'll select the In Front of Text option instead to gain more control over the exact position of the text box on the page.

To open the Layout Options gallery and change the wrapping option:

1. Change the Zoom level to **70%** so you can see the text box's position relative to the text on page 1.

2. Click the **Layout Options** button . The Layout Options gallery opens with the Square option selected. See Figure 4–12.

Figure 4–12 │ **Square text wrapping currently applied to text box**

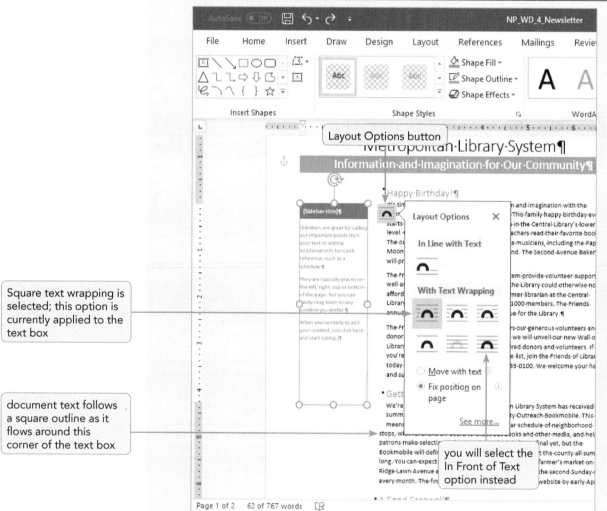

Square text wrapping is currently applied to the text box. You can see evidence of Square text wrapping where the document text flows around the lower-right corner of the text box. You'll have a chance to see some more dramatic examples of text wrapping later in this module, but it's important to be able to identify subtle examples of it.

3. Click any of the other options in the Layout Options gallery, and observe how the document text and the text box shift position. Continue exploring the Layout Options gallery, trying out several of the options.

4. Click the **In Front of Text** option , and then click the **Close** button ⊠ in the upper-right corner of the Layout Options gallery to close the gallery. The document text shifts so that it now flows directly down the left margin, without wrapping around the text box.

Your next formatting task is to make sure the text box is assigned a fixed position on the page. You could check this setting using the Layout Options button, but you'll use the Wrap Text button in the Arrange group on the Drawing Tools Format tab instead.

▶ **5.** On the ribbon, click the **Drawing Tools Format** tab, if necessary.

▶ **6.** In the Arrange group, click the **Wrap Text** button. The Wrap Text menu gives you access to all the options in the Layout Options gallery, plus some more advanced settings.

▶ **7.** Verify that **Fix Position on Page** has a checkmark next to it. This setting helps ensure that the text box will remain in its position on page 1, even if you add text above the paragraph it is anchored to. However, if you add so much text that the paragraph moves to page 2, then the text box will also move to page 2, but it will be positioned in the same location on the page that it occupied on page 1. To avoid having graphic objects move around unexpectedly on the page as you add or delete other elements, it's a good idea to check this setting either in the Wrap Text menu or in the Layout Options menu for every graphic object.

▶ **8.** Click anywhere in the document to close the gallery, and then save the document.

Adding Text to a Text Box

TIP

If you want to work on a document's layout before you've finished writing the text, you can insert placeholder text by inserting a new paragraph, typing =lorem() and then pressing ENTER.

Now that the text box is positioned where you want it, with the correct text wrapping, you can add text to it. In some documents, text boxes are used to present new information, while others highlight a quote from the main document. A direct quote from a document formatted in a text box is known as a **pull quote**. To create a pull quote text box, you can copy the text from the main document, and then paste it into the text box, or you can simply type text in a text box. You can also insert text from another Word document by using the Object arrow on the Insert tab.

To insert text in the text box:

▶ **1.** Change the Zoom level to **120%**, and then scroll as necessary so you can see the entire text box.

▶ **2.** In the text box's title bar, click the placeholder text **[Sidebar title]** to select it, if necessary, and then type **Operating Hours** as the new title

▶ **3.** Click the placeholder text below the title bar to select it. See Figure 4–13.

Figure 4–13 Text box with placeholder text selected

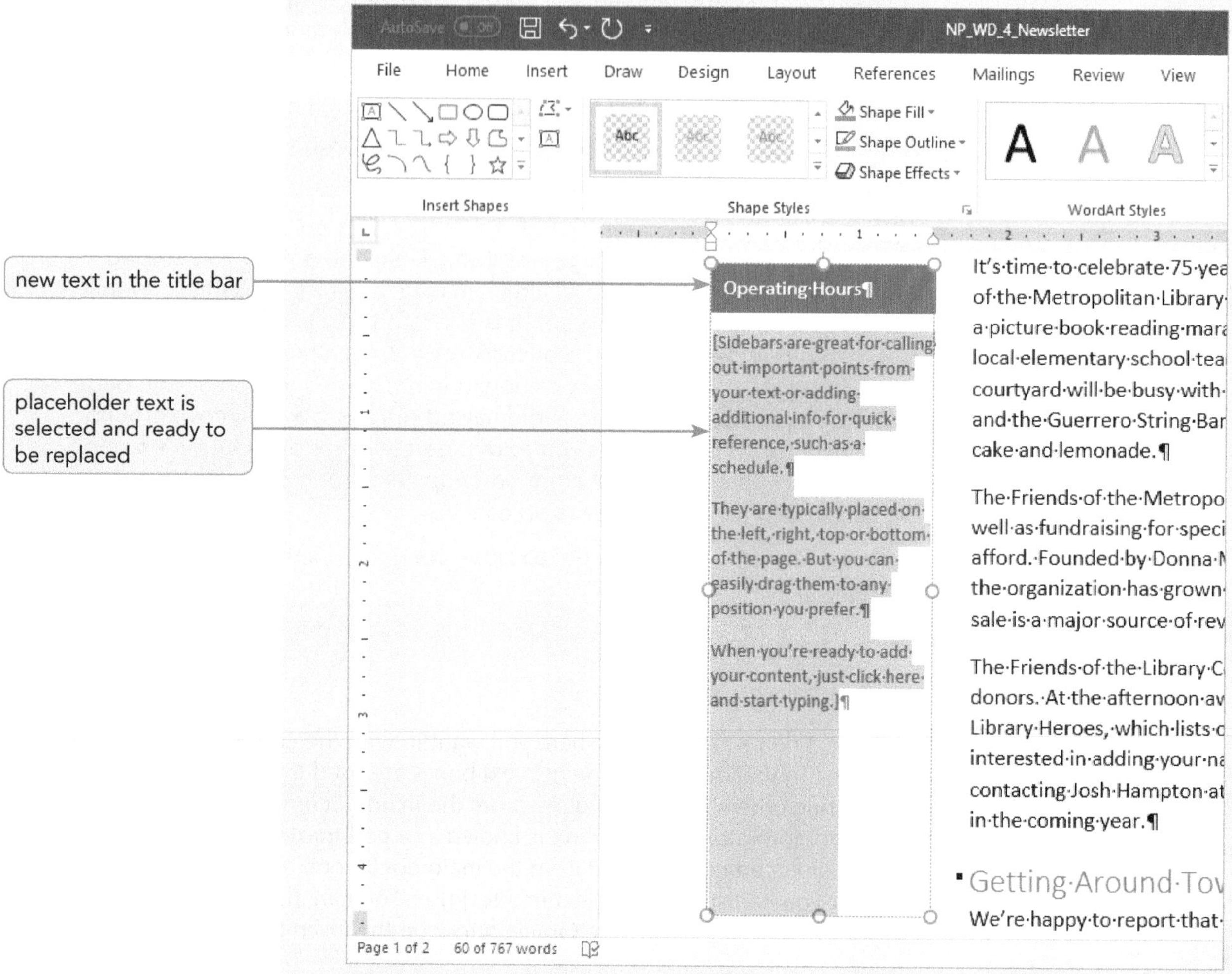

new text in the title bar

placeholder text is selected and ready to be replaced

4. Press **DEL** to delete the placeholder text. Now you can insert new text from another Word document.

5. On the ribbon, click the **Insert** tab.

6. In the Text group, click the **Object arrow** 🔲 ▾ to open the Object menu, and then click **Text from File**. The Insert File dialog box opens. Selecting a Word document to insert is just like selecting a document in the Open dialog box.

7. Navigate to the **Word4 > Module** folder, click **Support_WD_4_Hours.docx** to select the file, and then click the **Insert** button. The operating hours information is inserted directly into the text box. The inserted text was formatted in 9-point Calibri in the Support_WD_4_Hours.docx document, and it retains that formatting when you paste it into the newsletter document. To make the text easier to read, you'll increase the font size to 11 points.

8. With the insertion point located in the last paragraph in the text box (which is blank), press **BACKSPACE** to delete the blank paragraph, and then click and drag the pointer to select all the text in the text box, including the title in the shaded title box.

9. On the ribbon, click the **Home** tab.

10. In the Font group, click the **Font Size** arrow, and then click **11**. The size of the text in the text box increases to 11 points. See Figure 4–14.

Figure 4–14   **Operating hours information inserted in text box**

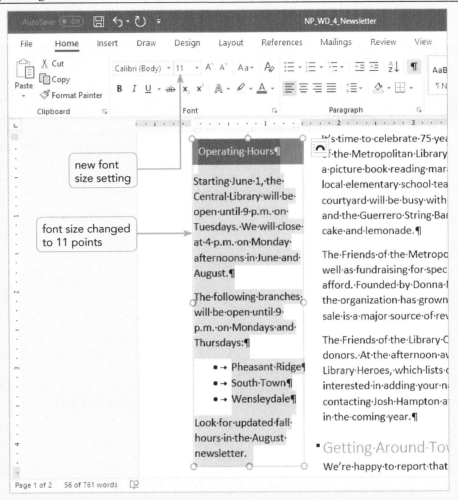

Trouble? Don't be concerned if the text in your text box wraps slightly differently from the text shown in Figure 4–14. The same fonts can vary slightly from one computer to another, causing slight differences in the way text wraps within and around text boxes.

▶ **11.** Click anywhere outside the text box to deselect it, and then save the document.

The first text box is complete. Now you need to add one more on page 1 and another on page 2. Vassily wants the second text box on page 1 to have a different look from the first one, so he asks you to use the Shapes button to draw a text box.

Drawing and Formatting a Text Box Using the Shapes Menu

A text box is considered a shape, just like the other shapes you can insert via the Shapes button on the Insert tab. This is true whether you insert a text box via the Text Box button or via the Shapes button. While text boxes are typically rectangular, you can turn any shape into a text box. Start by using the Shapes button to draw a shape of your choice, and then, with the shape selected, type any text you want. You won't see an insertion point inside the shape, but you can still type text inside it and then format it. You can format the shape itself by using the Shape Styles options on the Drawing Tools Format tab.

To draw and format a text box:

▶ **1.** Scroll down to display the bottom half of page 1.

▶ **2.** On the ribbon, click the **Insert** tab.

▶ **3.** In the Illustrations group, click the **Shapes** button to display the Shapes gallery. See Figure 4–15.

Figure 4–15   **Shapes gallery**

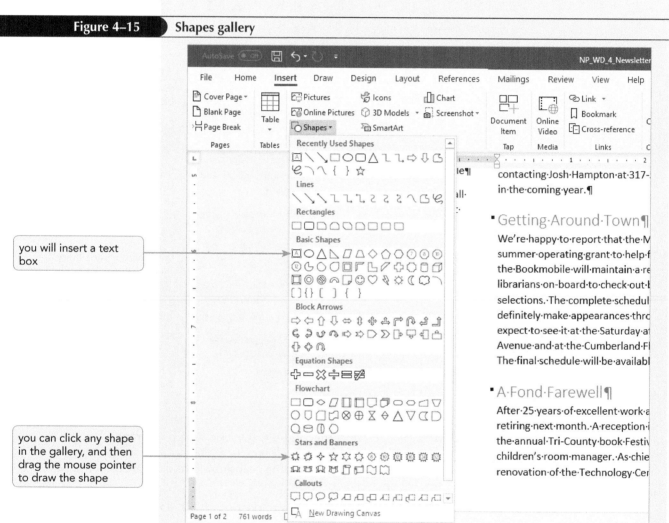

you will insert a text box

you can click any shape in the gallery, and then drag the mouse pointer to draw the shape

At this point, you could click any shape in the gallery, and then drag the pointer in the document to draw that shape. Then, after you finish drawing the shape, you could start typing in the selected shape to insert text.

▶ **4.** In the Basic Shapes section of the Shapes gallery, click the **Text Box** icon. The gallery closes, and the pointer turns into a black cross $+$.

▶ **5.** Position the pointer in the blank area in the left margin at about the 6-inch mark (according to the vertical ruler), and then click and drag down and to the right to draw a text box approximately 1.5 inches wide and 2.5 inches tall. When you are satisfied with the text box, release the mouse button.

Don't be concerned about the text box's exact dimensions or position on the page. For now, just make sure it fits in the blank space to the left of the last two paragraphs on the page.

The new text box is selected, with sizing handles on its border and the insertion point blinking inside. The Layout Options button is visible, and the text box's anchor symbol is positioned to the left of the paragraph below the "Getting Around Town" heading. By default, a shape is always anchored to the nearest paragraph that begins above the shape's top border. It doesn't matter where the insertion point is located.

6. Use the Shape Height and Shape Width boxes on the Drawing Tools Format tab to set the height to **2.5** inches and the width to **1.5** inches.

7. Drag the text box as necessary to align its bottom border with the last line of text on the page and its left border with the left edge of the text box above. See Figure 4–16.

| Figure 4–16 | **Text box created using the Shapes button** |

Now you need to add some text to the blank text box. Instead of inserting text from another Word document, you will copy a sentence from the newsletter and paste it into the text box to create a pull quote. After you add the text, you'll format the text box to make it match the one shown earlier in the Session 4.1 Visual Overview.

To copy text from the newsletter and paste it into the text box:

1. Select the third sentence after the "Getting Around Town" heading (which begins "The complete schedule is not final yet. . ."), and then press **CTRL+C** to copy it to the Office Clipboard.

2. Click in the blank text box, and then press **CTRL+V** to paste the copied sentence into the text box. The newly inserted sentence is formatted in 11-point Calibri, just as it was in the main document.

▶ **3.** Add quotation marks at the beginning and end of the sentence, so it's clear the text box is a pull quote. Your next task is to center the sentence between the top and bottom borders of the text box. Then you'll add some color.

▶ **4.** On the ribbon, click the **Drawing Tools Format** tab, if necessary.

▶ **5.** In the Text group, click the **Align Text** button to display the Align text menu, and then click **Middle**. The text is now centered between the top and bottom borders of the text box. Note that you can use also the Text Direction button in the Text group to rotate text within a text box. Next, you need to change the text's font color and add a background color. But first you'll make sure the text box is positioned so that you can see a Live Preview when you open the Shape Styles gallery.

▶ **6.** Scroll down, if necessary, so that the bottom of the text box is positioned just above the bottom of the Word screen.

▶ **7.** In the Shape Styles group, click the **More** button ⤓ to display the Shape Styles gallery. Like the text styles you have used to format text, shape styles allow you to apply a collection of formatting options, including font color and shading, with one click.

▶ **8.** Move the pointer over the various options in the Shape Styles gallery, and observe the Live Previews in the document. When you are finished, position the pointer over the **Colored Fill - Blue, Accent 5** style, which is a dark blue box, the second from the right in the second row. See Figure 4–17.

| Figure 4–17 | **Shape Styles gallery** |

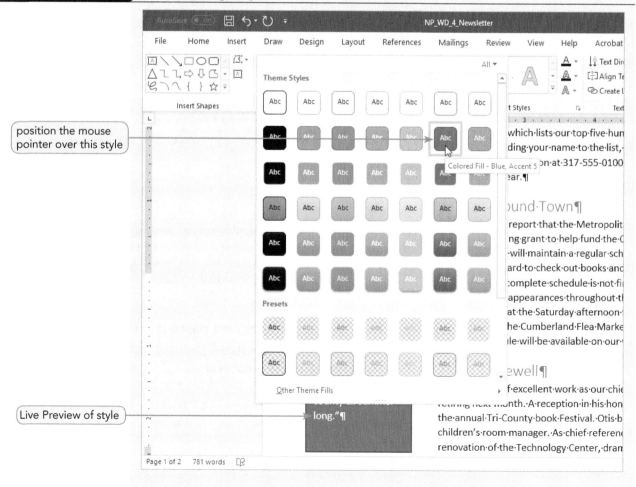

▶ **9.** In the Shape Styles gallery, click the **Colored Fill - Blue, Accent 5** style. The style is applied to the text box, and the Shape Styles gallery closes.

Now, you need to make sure the text box is located in a fixed position on the page. In the following steps, you'll also experiment with the text box's anchor symbol. It's important to understand the role the anchor symbol plays in the document's overall layout.

To fix the text box's position on the page and experiment with the anchor symbol:

▶ **1.** Verify that the text box is still selected, with the Drawing Tools Format tab displayed on the ribbon.

▶ **2.** In the Arrange group, click the **Wrap Text** button. A checkmark appears next to Move with Text because that is the default setting for shapes.

▶ **3.** Click **Fix Position on Page** to add a checkmark and close the Wrap Text menu.

If you select the entire paragraph to which the text box is anchored, you will also select the text box, as you'll see in the next step.

▶ **4.** Triple-click the paragraph below the "Getting Around Town" heading. The entire paragraph and the text box are selected. If you pressed DEL at this point, you would delete the paragraph of text and the text box. If you ever need to delete a paragraph but not the graphic object that is anchored to it, you should first drag the anchor to a different paragraph.

▶ **5.** Click anywhere in the document to deselect the text and the text box, and then save the document.

You've finished creating the second text box on page 1. Vassily wants you to add a third text box at the top of page 2. For this text box, you'll again use the preformatted Ion Side Bar 1 text box.

To insert another preformatted text box:

▶ **1.** Scroll down to display the top half of page 2, and then click in the first line on page 2.

▶ **2.** On the ribbon, click the **Insert** tab.

▶ **3.** In the Text group, click the **Text Box** button to display the menu, scroll down, and then click **Ion Sidebar 1**.

▶ **4.** Click the **text box border** to select the entire text box and display the Layout Options button.

▶ **5.** Click the **Layout Options** button ⌃, click the **In Front of Text** option ⌃, if necessary, verify that the **Fix position on page** button is selected, and then close the Layout Options gallery.

▶ **6.** Drag the text box left so its left side aligns with the left edge of the blue-shaded paragraph below, with the top of the text box aligned with the first line of text below the heading "A Fond Farewell" on page 2. A green alignment guide might appear if you try to position the right border of the text box too close to the document text.

▶ **7.** Change the text box's height to **3.5** inches and the width to **1.5** inches.

8. In the title bar, replace the placeholder text with **Book Festival Reminder**.

9. In the main text box, click the **placeholder text** to select it, and then press **DEL**.

10. On the ribbon, click the **Insert** tab.

11. In the Text group, click the **Object arrow** , and then click **Text from File**.

12. Navigate to the **Word4 > Module** folder, if necessary, and then insert the document named **Support_WD_4_Festival.docx**.

13. Delete the extra paragraph at the end of the text box, increase the font size for the text and title to **11** points, click anywhere inside the text box to deselect the text, and then make sure your text box is positioned like the one shown in Figure 4–18.

| Figure 4–18 | Completed text box on page 2 |

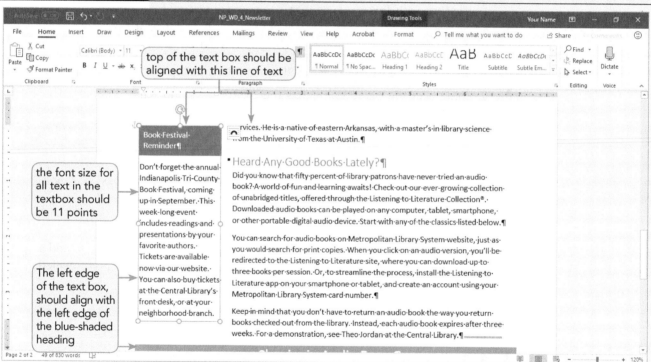

14. Click anywhere in the document to deselect the text box, and then save the document.

INSIGHT

Linking Text Boxes

If you have a large amount of text that you want to place in different locations in a document, with the text continuing from one text box to another, you can use linked text boxes. For example, in a newsletter, you might have an article that starts in a text box on page 3 of the newsletter and continues in a text box on page 4. To flow the text automatically from one text box to a second, blank text box, click the first text box to select it (this text box should already contain some text). Next, on the ribbon, click the Drawing Tools Format tab, click the Create Link button in the Text group, and then click the empty text box. The text boxes are now linked. You can resize the first text box without worrying about how much text fits in the box. The text that no longer fits in the first text box is moved to the second text box. Note that you'll find it easier to link text boxes if you use simple text boxes without title bars.

To make the main document text look more polished, you will add some drop caps.

Inserting Drop Caps

As you saw in the Session 4.1 Visual Overview, a drop cap is a large decorative letter that replaces the first letter of a paragraph. Drop caps are commonly used in newspapers, magazines, and newsletters to draw the reader's attention to the beginning of an article. You can place a drop cap in the margin or next to the paragraph, or you can have the text of the paragraph wrap around the drop cap. By default, a drop cap extends down three lines, but you can change that setting in the Drop Cap dialog box.

Vassily asks you to create a drop cap for some of the paragraphs that follow the headings. He wants the drop cap to extend two lines into the paragraph, with the text wrapping around it.

To insert drop caps in the newsletter:

1. Scroll up to page 1, and then click anywhere in the paragraph below the "Happy Birthday!" heading.

2. On the ribbon, click the **Insert** tab.

3. In the Text group, click the **Add a Drop Cap** button [A≡▾]. The Drop Cap gallery opens.

4. Move the pointer over the **Dropped** option and then the **In margin** option, and observe the Live Preview of the two types of drop caps in the document. The default settings applied by these two options are fine for most documents. Clicking Drop Cap Options, at the bottom of the menu, allows you to select more detailed settings. In this case, Vassily wants to make the drop cap smaller than the default. Instead of extending down through three lines of text, he wants the drop cap to extend only two lines.

5. Click **Drop Cap Options**. The Drop Cap dialog box opens.

6. Click the **Dropped** icon, click the **Lines to drop** box, and then change the setting to **2**. See Figure 4–19.

Figure 4–19   **Drop Cap dialog box**

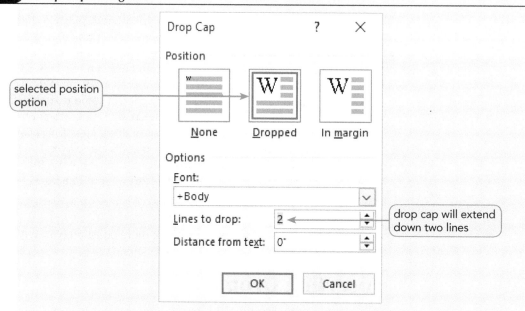

selected position option

drop cap will extend down two lines

TIP

To delete a drop cap, click the paragraph that contains it, open the Drop Cap dialog box, and then click None.

7. Click **OK**. Word formats the first character of the paragraph as a drop cap "A," as shown in the Session 4.1 Visual Overview. The dotted box with selection handles around the drop cap indicates it is selected.

8. Near the bottom of page 1, insert a similar drop cap in the paragraph following the "A Fond Farewell" heading. You skipped the paragraph following the "Getting Around Town" heading because you'll eventually insert a graphic there. Including a drop cap there would make the paragraph look too cluttered.

9. On page 2, insert a similar drop cap in the paragraph following the "Heard Any Good Books Lately?" heading.

10. Click anywhere in the text to deselect the drop cap, and then save your work.

PROSKILLS

Written Communication: Writing for a Newsletter

Pictures, WordArt, and other design elements can make a newsletter very appealing to readers. They can also be a lot of fun to create and edit. But don't let the design elements in your desktop-published documents distract you from the most important aspect of any document—clear, effective writing. Because the newsletter format feels less formal than a report or letter, some writers are tempted to use a casual, familiar tone. If you are creating a newsletter for friends or family, that's fine. But in most other settings—especially in a business or academic setting—you should strive for a professional tone, similar to what you find in a typical newspaper. Avoid jokes; you can never be certain that what amuses you will also amuse all your readers. Worse, you risk unintentionally offending your readers. Also, space is typically at a premium in any printed document, so you don't want to waste space on anything unessential. Finally, keep in mind that the best writing in the world will be wasted in a newsletter that is overburdened with too many design elements. You don't have to use every element covered in this module in a single document. Instead, use just enough to attract the reader's attention to the page, and then let the text speak for itself.

REVIEW

Session 4.1 Quick Check

1. Explain how to format a document in three columns of the default width.

2. What should you do if you don't know which characters to type to insert a symbol or special character?

3. What does the anchor symbol indicate?

4. How do you convert an inline object into a floating object?

5. What is a pull quote?

6. How many lines does a drop cap extend by default?

Session 4.2 Visual Overview:

You can use the Remove Background button to remove a picture's background.

You can click the Crop button arrow to access more advanced cropping options, including cropping to a shape such as an oval or an arrow.

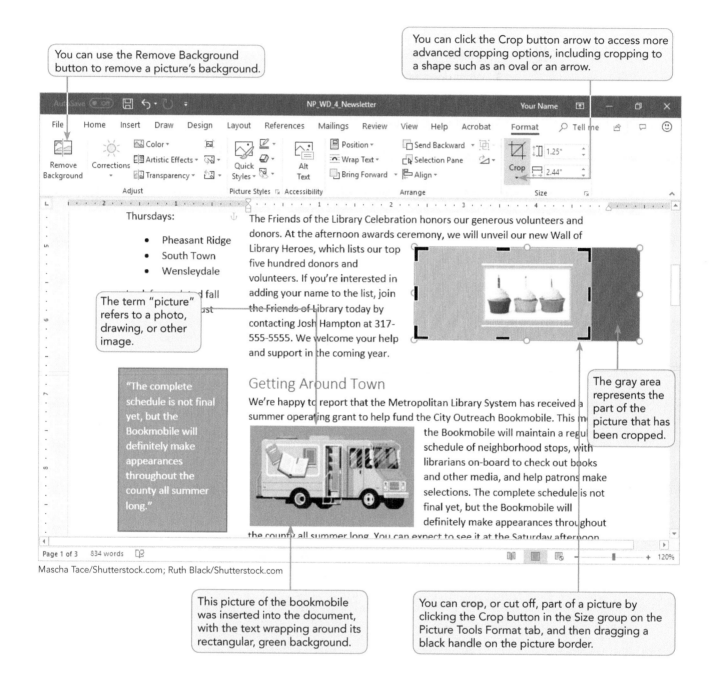

The term "picture" refers to a photo, drawing, or other image.

The gray area represents the part of the picture that has been cropped.

Mascha Tace/Shutterstock.com; Ruth Black/Shutterstock.com

This picture of the bookmobile was inserted into the document, with the text wrapping around its rectangular, green background.

You can **crop**, or cut off, part of a picture by clicking the Crop button in the Size group on the Picture Tools Format tab, and then dragging a black handle on the picture border.

Editing Pictures

Clicking the Remove Background button in the Adjust group on the Picture Tools Format tab displays the Background Removal tab, with tools for removing a picture's background.

You can use these buttons to mark areas in the picture that you want to keep and to mark areas that you want to remove along with the rest of the picture's background.

Mascha Tace/Shutterstock.com; Ruth Black/Shutterstock.com

The purple area is the part of the picture that Word considers part of the background.

The picture of the bookmobile is displayed here with its background removed, which allows the text to wrap around the shape of the bookmobile itself.

Formatting Text with WordArt

To create special text elements such as a newspaper headline, you can use decorative text known as WordArt. Essentially, WordArt is text in a text box that is formatted with a text effect. Before you move on to learning about WordArt, it's helpful to review the formatting options available with text effects.

To begin applying a text effect, you select the text you want to format. Then you can choose from several preformatted text effects via the Text Effects and Typography button in the Font group on the Home tab. You can also modify a text effect by choosing from the options on the Text Effects and Typography menu. For example, you can add a shadow or a glow effect. You can also change the **outline color** of the characters—that is, the exterior color of the characters—and you can change the style of the outline by making it thicker or breaking it into dashes, for example. To change the character's **fill color**—that is, the interior color of the characters—you select a different font color via the Font Color button in the Font group, just as you would with ordinary text.

All of these text effect options are available with WordArt. However, the fact that WordArt is in a text box allows you to add some additional effects. You can add rounded, or **beveled**, edges to the letters in WordArt, format the text in 3-D, and transform the text into waves, circles, and other shapes. You can also rotate WordArt text so it lies vertically on the page. In addition, because WordArt is in a text box, you can use page layout and text wrap settings to place it anywhere you want on a page, with text wrapped around it.

To start creating WordArt, you can select the text you want to transform into WordArt, and then click the WordArt button in the Text group on the Insert tab. Alternatively, you can start by clicking the WordArt button without selecting text first. In that case, Word inserts a text box with placeholder WordArt text, which you can then replace with something new. In the following steps, you'll select the first paragraph and format it as WordArt to create the newsletter title Vassily wants.

To create the title of the newsletter using WordArt:

1. If you took a break after the last session, make sure the **NP_WD_4_Newsletter.docx** is open and zoomed to **120%**, with the rulers and nonprinting characters displayed.

2. On page 1, select the entire paragraph containing the "Metropolitan Library System" heading, including the paragraph mark.

   To avoid unexpected results, you should start by clearing any formatting from the text you want to format as WordArt, so you'll do that next.

3. On the ribbon, click the **Home** tab, if necessary.

4. In the Font group, click the **Clear All Formatting** button ⒜. The paragraph reverts to the Normal style. Now you can convert the text into WordArt.

5. On the ribbon, click the **Insert** tab.

6. In the Text group, click the **Insert WordArt** button ⒜·. The WordArt gallery opens.

7. Position the pointer over the WordArt style that is second from the left in the top row. A ScreenTip describes some elements of this WordArt style—"Fill: Blue, Accent color 1; Shadow." See Figure 4–20.

Be sure to select the paragraph mark so the page layout in your newsletter matches the figures.

Figure 4–20   WordArt gallery

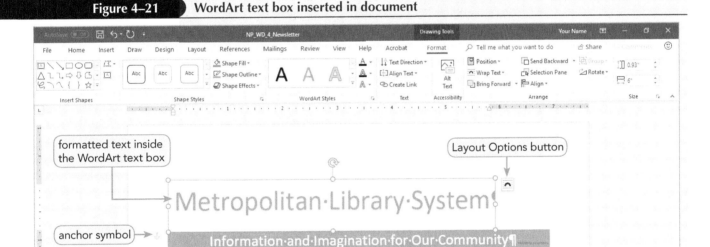

8. Click the WordArt style **Fill: Blue, Accent color 1; Shadow**. The gallery closes, and a text box containing the formatted text is displayed in the document. See Figure 4–21.

Figure 4–21   WordArt text box inserted in document

The Drawing Tools Format tab appears as the active tab on the ribbon, displaying a variety of tools that you can use to edit the WordArt. Before you change the look of the WordArt, you need to fix its position on the page and change its text wrap setting. You will use the Top and Bottom option, which is only available via the Wrap Text button in the Wrap Text group.

9. Make sure the **Drawing Tools Format** tab is selected on the ribbon.

10. In the Arrange group, click the **Wrap Text** button to open the Wrap Text menu, then click **Top and Bottom**. Note that for a WordArt text box that contains fewer characters, you might find that the Square text wrap option works better. When wrapping text around an object on a page, it's often necessary to experiment until you find the best option.

11. Click the **Wrap Text** button again and then click **Fix Position on Page** to insert a check.

12. If necessary, drag the WordArt text box up to position it above the shaded paragraph, using the top and left green guidelines as necessary.

13. Save the document.

Next, you will modify the WordArt in several ways.

Modifying WordArt

Your first task is to resize the WordArt. When resizing WordArt, you need to consider both the font size of the text and the size of the text box that contains the WordArt. You change the font size for WordArt text just as you would for ordinary text—by selecting it and then choosing a new font size using the Font Size box in the Font group on the Home tab. If you choose a large font for a headline, you might also need to resize the text box to ensure that the resized text appears on a single line. Vassily is happy with the font size of the new WordArt headline, so you only need to adjust the size of the text box so it spans the width of the page. The larger text box will make it possible for you to add some more effects.

To resize the WordArt text box and add some effects:

1. Make sure the **Drawing Tools Format** tab is selected on the ribbon.

2. Change the width of the text box to **7** inches. The text box height should remain at the default 0.93 inches.

   By default, the text is centered within the text box, which is what Vassily wants. Note, however, that you could use the alignment buttons on the Home tab to align the text any way you wanted within the text box borders. You could also increase the text's font size so that it expands to span the full width of the text box. Instead, you will take advantage of the larger text box to apply a transform effect, which will expand and change the overall shape of the WordArt text. Then you'll make some additional modifications.

3. Make sure the border of the **WordArt** text box is a solid line, indicating that the text box is selected.

4. In the WordArt Styles group, click the **Text Effects** button [A ⁃] to display the Text Effects gallery, and then point to **Transform**. The Transform gallery displays options for changing the WordArt's shape.

5. Move the pointer over the options in the Transform gallery and observe the Live Previews in the WordArt text box. Note that you can always remove an effect that has been previously applied by clicking the None option at the top of a gallery. For example, to remove a transform effect, you could click the None option in the No Transform section at the top of the gallery. When you are finished, position the pointer over the **Chevron: Up** effect. See Figure 4–22.

Figure 4–22   **Applying a transform text effect**

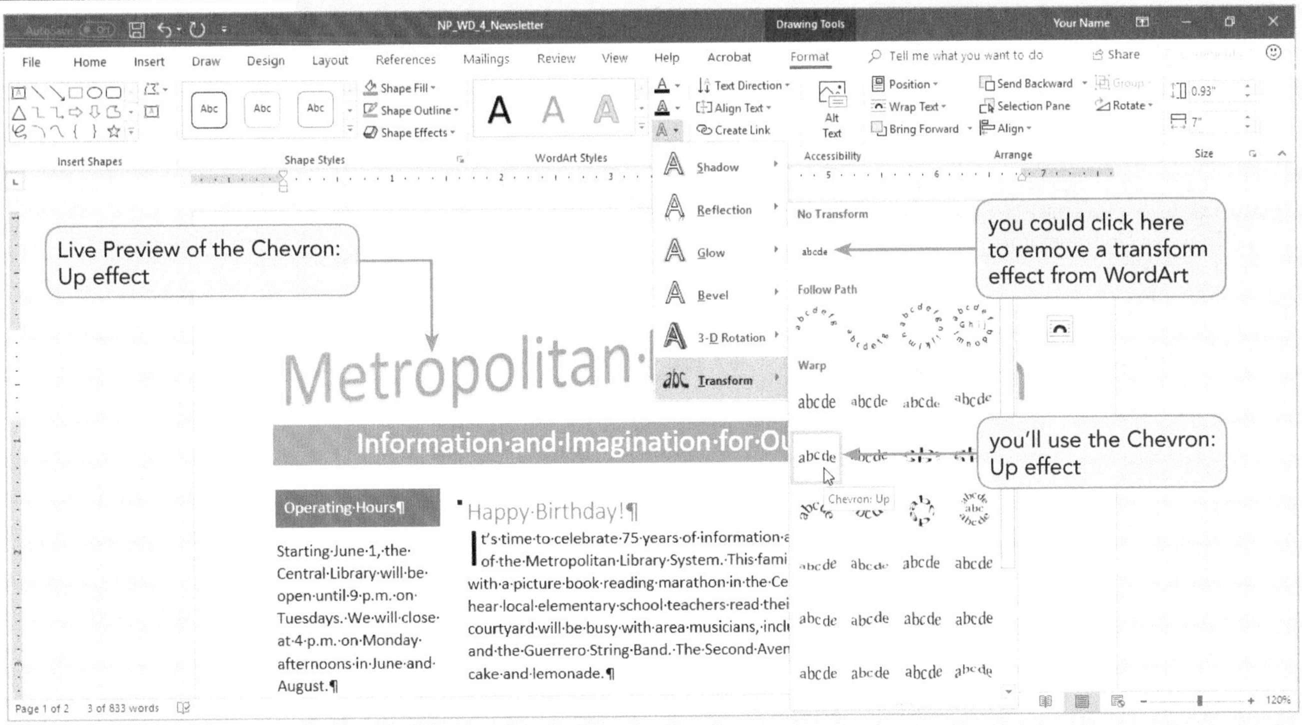

Live Preview of the Chevron: Up effect

you could click here to remove a transform effect from WordArt

you'll use the Chevron: Up effect

Metropolitan·l

Information·and·Imagination·for·Ou

Operating·Hours¶

Starting·June·1,·the· Central·Library·will·be· open·until·9·p.m.·on· Tuesdays.·We·will·close· at·4·p.m.·on·Monday· afternoons·in·June·and· August.¶

·Happy·Birthday!¶

t's·time·to·celebrate·75·years·of·information·a of·the·Metropolitan·Library·System.·This·fami with·a·picture·book·reading·marathon·in·the·Ce hear·local·elementary·school·teachers·read·thei courtyard·will·be·busy·with·area·musicians,·incl and·the·Guerrero·String·Band.·The·Second·Aven cake·and·lemonade.¶

▶ **6.** Click the **Chevron: Up** effect. The Transform menu closes, and the effect is applied to the WordArt. Now you will make some additional changes using the options in the WordArt Styles group. You'll start by changing the fill color.

▶ **7.** In the WordArt Styles group, click the **Text Fill arrow** to display the Text Fill color gallery.

▶ **8.** In the Theme Colors section of the gallery, click the square that is fifth from the left in the second row from the bottom to select the **Blue, Accent 1, Darker 25%** color. The Text Fill gallery closes, and the WordArt is formatted in a darker shade of blue. Next, you'll add a shadow to make the headline more dramatic.

▶ **9.** In the WordArt Styles group, click the **Text Effects** button to display the Text Effects gallery, and then point to **Shadow** to display the Shadow gallery, which is divided into several sections.

▶ **10.** In the Outer section, point to the top-left option to display a ScreenTip that reads "Offset: Bottom Right."

▶ **11.** Click the **Offset: Bottom Right** shadow style. A shadow is added to the WordArt text. See Figure 4–23.

Figure 4–23 Completed WordArt headline

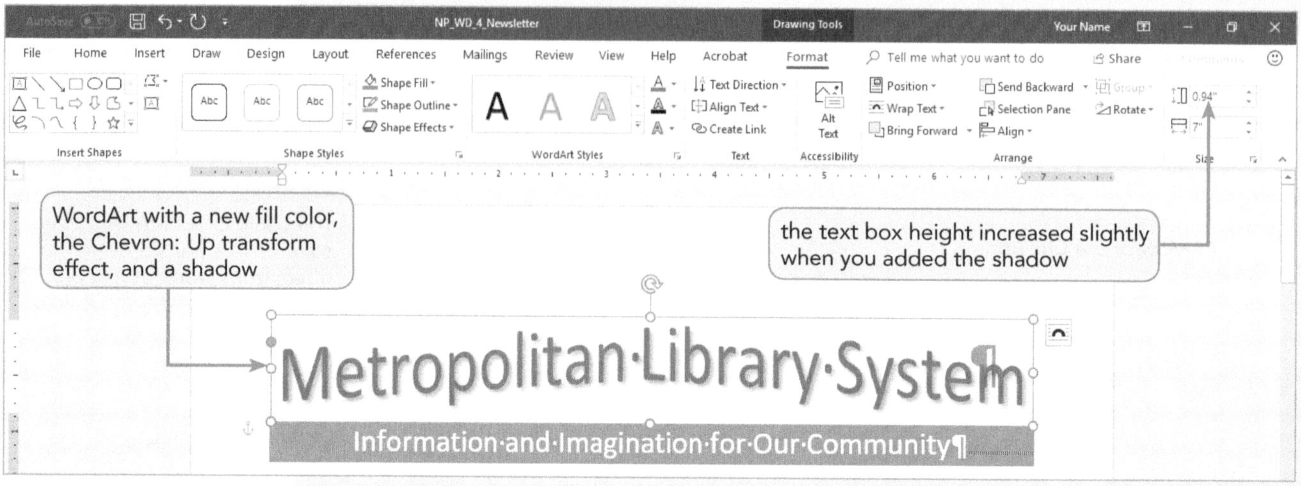

WordArt with a new fill color, the Chevron: Up transform effect, and a shadow

the text box height increased slightly when you added the shadow

Metropolitan·Library·System

Information·and·Imagination·for·Our·Community¶

Note that the height of the text box that contains the WordArt increased slightly, to 0.94 inches.

12. Click a blank area of the document to deselect the WordArt, and then save the document.

The WordArt headline is complete. Your next job is to add some pictures to the newsletter.

Working with Pictures

In Word, a picture is a photo, drawing, icon, or other image. Although you can copy and paste pictures into a document from other documents, you'll typically insert pictures via either the Pictures button or the Online Pictures button, both of which are located in the Illustrations group on the Insert tab. You use the Pictures button to insert a picture from a file stored on your computer. You use the Online Pictures button to insert images that you find online using Bing Image Search or that you have stored on OneDrive. As you saw in the Session 4.1 Visual Overview, the final version of the newsletter will contain a photograph, a drawing, and an icon.

After you insert a picture into a document, it functions as an object that you can move, resize, wrap text around, and edit in other ways using the appropriate contextual tab on the ribbon. In general, the skills you used when modifying text boxes apply to pictures as well.

Note that you can also use the Online Video button in the Media group on the Insert tab to insert an online video into your document from YouTube or elsewhere on the web. However, you should use videos sparingly in professional documents.

And be aware that inserting an online video introduces code that hackers could manipulate to import malware into your computer.

Written Communication: Understanding Copyright Laws

The ownership of all forms of media, including text, drawings, photographs, and video, is governed by copyright laws. You should assume that anything you find on the web is owned by someone who has a right to control its use. It's your responsibility to make sure you understand copyright laws and to abide by them. The U.S. Copyright Office maintains a Frequently Asked Questions page that should answer any questions you might have: www.copyright.gov/help/faq.

Generally, copyright laws allow a student to reuse a photo, drawing, or other item for educational purposes, on a one-time basis, without getting permission from the owner. However, to avoid charges of plagiarism, you need to acknowledge the source of the item in your work. You don't ever want to be accused of presenting someone else's work as your own. Businesses face much more stringent copyright restrictions. To reuse any material, you must request permission from the owner, and you will often need to pay a fee.

When you search for images using the Online Pictures button in the Illustrations group on the Insert tab, all of the images that initially appear as a result of your search will be licensed under a Creative Commons license. (You'll learn more about using the Online Pictures button later in this module.) There are several types of Creative Commons licenses. One type allows you to use an image for any reason, including commercial use, and to modify the image, as long as the photographer is credited or attributed (similar to the credits under the photos in some figures in this book). Another type of license allows you to use an image with an attribution as long as it is not for commercial purposes and as long as you do not modify the image. Even if an image has a Creative Commons license, you must still review the exact license on the website on which the image is stored. When you point to an image in the search results in the Online Pictures window, the More information and actions button appears in the lower-right corner of the image. Click the icon to display more information about the image, including its website. Note that you can also click the Learn more here link, at the bottom of the Online Pictures dialog box, to read an in-depth explanation of copyright regulations.

Cropping a Picture

Vassily wants to insert a photo of cupcakes into the newsletter on page 1. He has the illustration saved as a PNG file named Support_WD_4_ Cupcakes.png, so you can insert it using the Pictures button in the Illustrations group. Keep in mind that whenever you insert a picture in a document, you should add Alt text, or revise the default Alt text, as necessary.

To insert the picture on page 1:

1. On page 1, click at the end of the first paragraph below the "Happy Birthday" heading to position the insertion point between "…and lemonade." and the paragraph mark. Normally, there's no need to be so precise about where you click before inserting a picture, but doing so here will ensure that your results match the results described in these steps exactly.

2. On the ribbon, click the **Insert** tab.

3. In the Illustrations group, click the **Pictures** button to open the Insert Picture dialog box.

4. Navigate to the **Word4 > Module** folder included with your Data Files, and then insert the picture file named **Support_WD_4_Cupcakes.png**. The picture is inserted in the document as an inline object. It is selected, and the

Picture Tools Format tab is displayed on the ribbon. For a few seconds, the default alt text appears at the bottom of the picture. It is not correct, so you need to create new alt text.

▶ **5.** In the Accessibility group, click the **Alt Text** button to open the Alt Text pane, delete the alt text and the sentence below it, type **Three cupcakes with candles**, and then close the Alt Text pane.

▶ **6.** Scroll down if necessary so you can see the entire picture.

The picture is wider than it needs to be and would look better as a square. So you'll need to cut off, or crop, part of it. In addition to being able to crop part of a picture, Word offers several more advanced cropping options. One option is to crop to a shape, which means trimming the edges of a picture so it fits into a star, an oval, an arrow, or another shape. You can also crop to a specific ratio of height to width.

Whatever method you use, once you crop a picture, the part you cropped is hidden from view. However, it remains a part of the picture in case you change your mind and want to restore the cropped picture to its original form.

Before you crop off the sides of the picture, you'll try cropping it to a specific shape.

To crop the picture:

▶ **1.** In the Size group, click the **Crop arrow** to display the Crop menu, and then point to **Crop to Shape**. A gallery of shapes is displayed, similar to the gallery you saw in Figure 4-15.

▶ **2.** In the Basic Shapes section of the gallery, click the **Lightning Bolt** shape ⚡ (third row down, sixth from the right). The picture takes on the shape of a lightning bolt, with everything outside the lightning bolt shape cropped off.

Obviously, this isn't a useful option for the picture, but cropping to shapes can be very effective with pictures in informal documents, such as party invitations or posters, especially if you then use the Behind Text wrapping option, so that the document text flows over the picture.

▶ **3.** Press **CTRL+Z** to undo the cropping.

▶ **4.** In the Size group, click the **Crop** button (not the Crop arrow). Dark black sizing handles appear around the picture borders.

▶ **5.** Position the pointer directly over the middle sizing handle on the right border. The pointer changes to ⊢.

▶ **6.** Press and hold down the mouse button, and drag the pointer slightly left. The pointer changes to ┼.

▶ **7.** Drag the pointer toward the left until the picture border aligns with the 4-inch mark on the horizontal ruler, as shown in Figure 4-24.

Figure 4–24   **Cropping a picture**

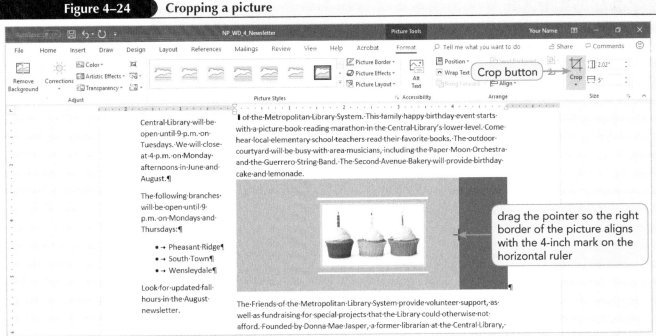

Ruth Black/Shutterstock.com

8. When the picture looks like the one shown in Figure 4–24, release the mouse button. The right portion of the picture is no longer visible. You can ignore the text wrapping for now. The original border remains, indicating that the cropped portion is still saved as part of the picture in case you want to undo the cropping.

9. Drag the middle sizing handle on the left border to the right until the left border aligns with the 1.5-inch mark on the horizontal ruler.

    The picture now takes up much less space, but it's not exactly a square. To ensure a specific ratio, you can crop the picture by changing its **aspect ratio**—that is, the ratio of width to height. You'll try that next. But first, you'll restore the picture to its original state.

10. In the Adjust group, click the **Reset Picture arrow** to display the Reset Picture menu, and then click **Reset Picture & Size**. The picture returns to its original state.

11. In the Size group, click the **Crop arrow**, and then point to **Aspect Ratio** to display the Aspect Ratio menu, which lists various ratios of width to height. A square has a 1-to-1 ratio of width to height.

12. Under "Square," click **1:1**. The picture is cropped to a square shape. See Figure 4–25.

Figure 4–25 **Figure 4–25**   **Picture cropped to a 1:1 aspect ratio**

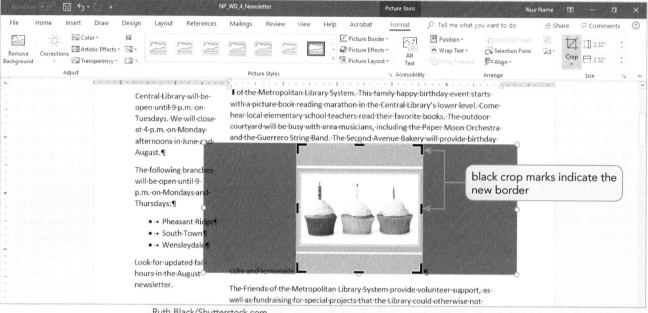

Ruth Black/Shutterstock.com

▶ **13.** Click anywhere outside the picture to deselect it and complete the cropping procedure.

Next, you need to change the picture from an inline object to a floating object by wrapping text around it. You also need to position it on the page. You can complete both of these tasks at the same time by using the Position button in the Arrange group.

To change the picture's position and wrapping:

▶ **1.** Change the Zoom level to **One Page**, and then click the **picture** to select it.

▶ **2.** On the ribbon, click the **Picture Tools Format** tab.

▶ **3.** In the Arrange group, click the **Position** button to display the Position gallery. You can click an icon in the "With Text Wrapping" section to move the selected picture to one of nine preset positions on the page. As with any gallery, you can see a Live Preview of the options before you actually select one.

▶ **4.** Move the pointer over the various icons, and observe the changing Live Preview in the document, with the picture moving to different locations on the page and the text wrapping around it.

▶ **5.** Point to the icon in the middle row on the far right side to display a ScreenTip that reads "Position in Middle Right with Square Text Wrapping," and then click the **Position in Middle Right with Square Text Wrapping** icon . The picture moves to the middle of the page along the right margin. By default, it is formatted with Square text wrapping, so the text wraps to its left, following its square outline. Next, you'll add a picture style.

▶ **6.** In the Pictures Styles group, click the **Simple Frame, White** style, which is the left-most style in the visible row of the Picture Styles gallery. A frame and a shadow are applied to the picture. See Figure 4–26.

Figure 4–26   Picture style added to cupcake picture

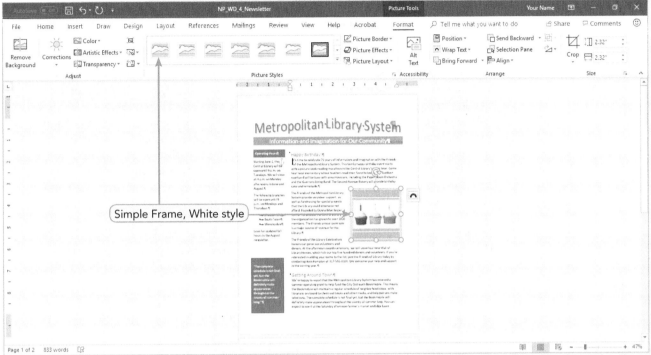

Simple Frame, White style

Ruth Black/Shutterstock.com

Your final step is to resize the picture to make it a bit smaller.

▶ 7. In the Size group, click the **Shape Height** box, type **1.3**, and then press **ENTER**. The settings in both the Shape Height and Shape Width boxes change to 1.3 inches. For most types of graphics, the aspect ratio is locked, meaning that when you change one dimension, the other changes to match. In this case, because the aspect ratio of the picture is 1:1, when you changed the height to 1.3 inches, the width also changed to 1.3 inches, ensuring that the picture retained its square shape.

▶ 8. Click anywhere in the document to deselect the picture, and then save the document.

INSIGHT

Aligning Graphic Objects and Using the Selection Pane

The steps in this module provide precise directions about where to position graphic objects in the document. However, when you are creating a document on your own, you might find it helpful to use the Align button in the Arrange group on the Picture Tools Format tab to align objects relative to the margin or the edge of the page. Aligning a graphic relative to the margin, rather than the edge of the page, is usually the best choice because it ensures that you don't accidentally position a graphic outside the page margins, causing the graphic to get cut off when the page is printed.

After you choose whether to align to the page or margin, you can open the Align menu again and choose an alignment option. For example, you can align the top of an object at the top of the page or align the bottom of an object at the bottom of the page. You can also choose to have Word distribute multiple objects evenly on the page. To do this, it's helpful to open the Selection pane first by clicking the Layout tab and then clicking Selection Pane in the Arrange group. Press and hold CTRL, and then in the Selection pane, click the objects you want to select. After the objects are selected, there's no need to switch back to the Picture Tools Format tab. Instead, you can take advantage of the Align button in the Arrange group on the Layout tab to open the Align menu, where you can then click Distribute Horizontally or Distribute Vertically.

The cupcake picture is finished. Next, Vassily asks you to insert a picture of a bookmobile near the bottom of page 1.

Searching for and Inserting Online Pictures and 3-D Models

TIP

Be mindful of copyright restrictions for online pictures. For more on this, see the ProSkills box "Written Communication: Understanding Copyright Laws."

If you don't already have the pictures you need for a document stored as image files, you can look for pictures online. You can also look for **3-D models**, which are illustrations created using 3-D animation techniques that you can rotate in three dimensions. The first step in using online pictures or 3-D models is finding the picture or model you want. Most image websites include a search box where you can type some descriptive keywords to help you narrow the selection down to a smaller range. To search for images from within Word, click the Online Pictures button in the Illustrations group on the Insert tab. This opens the Online Pictures window, shown in Figure 4–27, where you can use the Search Bing box at the top to look for images, or click categories such as "Animals" to see a collection of related images.

Figure 4–27 | **Inserting an online picture**

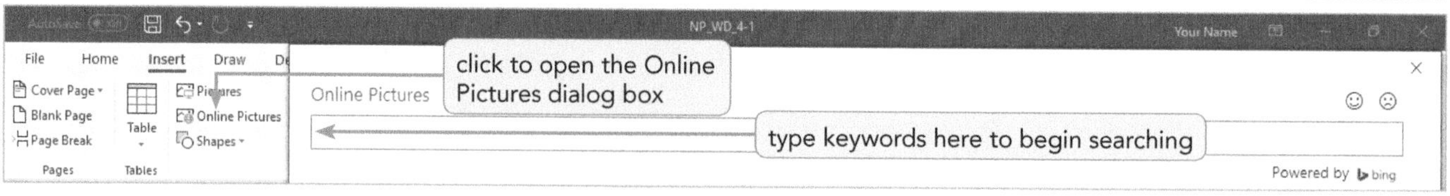

To start a search, you would type keywords, such as "walking a dog," in the search box, and then press ENTER. Images from all over the web that have the keywords "walking a dog" and that are licensed under Creative Commons would appear below the search box. Typically, the search results include photos and premade pictures known as **clip art**, which can be used to illustrate a wide variety of publications. To insert one of those images, you would click it, and then click the Insert button. To widen your search to all the images on the web (the vast majority of which are subject to strict copyright restrictions), you could click the Creative Commons only check box to deselect it.

To insert a 3-D model in a document, click the 3D Models button in the Illustrations group on the Insert tab. This opens the Online 3D Models dialog box, where you can type some key words, or click categories such as "Animals" to see a collection of related 3-D models. Click the model you want, click the Insert button, and then use the handles on the image in the document to resize or rotate it. You can wrap text around a 3-D model just as you would wrap text around any type of picture. Like other pictures, 3-D models are typically copyright protected. After you insert a 3-D model, you can use the tools on the 3D Model Tools tab to select other options and to add alt text. You can use the Scenes button in the Play 3D group to choose from a variety of animated scenes for your model. For example, you could choose to display an astronaut 3D model with hands down, or with one hand raised in a wave.

Because results from an online search are unpredictable, in the following steps you will insert a picture included with your Data Files.

To insert a picture in the newsletter:

1. Zoom in so you can read the document text at the bottom of page 1, and then click at the end of the paragraph below the "Getting Around Town" heading to position the insertion point between "early April." and the paragraph mark.

2. Change the Zoom level to **Multiple Pages** so you can see the entire document.

3. On the ribbon, click the **Insert** tab.

4. In the Illustrations group, click the **Pictures** button to display the Insert Picture dialog box, and then navigate to the **Word4 > Module** folder.

5. Click the image **Support_WD_4_Bookmobile.png**, and then click the **Insert** button. The dialog box closes, and the picture of a bookmobile is inserted as an inline object at the current location of the insertion point. The picture has a vertical orientation, so it looks like it is driving up the page. See Figure 4–28.

Figure 4–28   **Picture inserted as inline object**

Ruth Black/Shutterstock.com; Mascha Tace/Shutterstock.com

6. Change the alt text for the image to **Bookmobile**, and then close the Alt Text pane.

   Because the picture is too large to fit on page 1, the line that contains the insertion point jumps to page 2, with the picture displayed below the text. The rest of the document text starts below the picture on page 2 and flows to page 3. The picture is selected, as indicated by its border with handles. The Picture Tools Format tab is displayed on the ribbon. Now you can wrap text around the picture, and position it on the page.

7. In the Arrange group, click the **Wrap Text** button, and then click **Tight**. The picture is now a floating object and has moved back to page 1.

8. Drag the picture to the bottom of page 1, and position it so the "Getting Around Town" heading wraps above the picture and the text below the heading wraps to the right of the picture. See Figure 4–29. The anchor symbol for the picture is only partially visible because it's covered by the blue text box.

Figure 4–29   **Resized picture as a floating object**

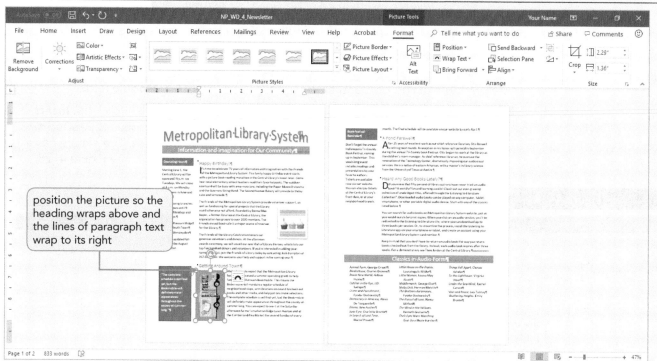

Ruth Black/Shutterstock.com; Mascha Tace/Shutterstock.com

Trouble? Don't be concerned if you can't get the text to wrap around the picture exactly as shown in Figure 4–29.

9. Click the **Layout Options** button, click **Fix position on page**, and then close the Layout Options gallery.

Vassily likes the picture, but he asks you to make a few changes. First, he wants you to rotate the bookmobile to the right, so it appears to be driving across the page instead of up the page. Also, Vassily wants to remove the green background, and to make the picture a bit smaller.

INSIGHT

Using the Draw Tab

You can use the tools on the Draw tab to draw on a touch screen, using your finger or a stylus. If you do not have a touch screen, you can use the mouse instead. When the Draw with Touch button is selected, you can choose to draw with a pen, a pencil, or a highlighter. For each drawing tool, you can choose from different colors, and you can adjust any of the drawing tools to create a wider or more narrow line. You can select different effects, such as Galaxy, which creates a glitter effect. To begin selecting an effect, click a pen in the Pens group on the Draw tab, and then click the down arrow button on the pen's icon in the Pens group to display a menu of options. The Ink Editor button lets you incorporate hand-drawn text edits (including common copy-editing symbols such as an inverted V to indicate an insertion) into regular document text. Likewise, you can use the Ink to Math button to convert hand-drawn mathematical equations into document text, which you can then edit using the Equation Tools Design tab. After you have finished drawing, you can "replay" the drawing action and watch the characters and shapes you drew get redrawn in the document. To hide anything you have drawn in a document, click the Hide Ink button in the Ink group on the Review tab.

Rotating a Picture

You can quickly rotate a picture by dragging the Rotation handle that appears on the picture's border when the picture is selected. To access some preset rotation options, you can click the Rotate Objects button in the Arrange group on the Picture Tools Format tab to open the Rotate menu. To quickly rotate a picture 90 degrees, click Rotate Right 90° or Rotate Left 90° in the Rotate menu. You can also flip a picture, as if the picture were printed on both sides of a card and you wanted to turn the card over. To do this, click Flip Vertical or Flip Horizontal in the Rotate menu.

Vassily only wants to rotate the picture 90 degrees to the right. You could do that quickly by clicking the Rotate Objects button in the Arrange group, and then clicking Rotate Right 90°. But it's helpful to know how to rotate a picture by dragging the Rotation handle, so you'll use that method in the following steps.

To rotate the picture:

▶ **1.** Change the document Zoom level to **120%**, and then scroll down so you can see the bottom half of page 1.

▶ **2.** Click the **bookmobile picture**, if necessary, to select it, and then position the pointer over the circular rotation handle above the middle of the picture's top border. The pointer changes to ⟳.

▶ **3.** Drag the pointer down and to the right, until the bookmobile rotates to a horizontal position. Release the mouse button. The picture is displayed in the new, rotated position, but, depending on where you positioned it earlier, part of the picture might overlap the blue text box. See Figure 4–30.

Figure 4–30	Dragging the Rotation handle

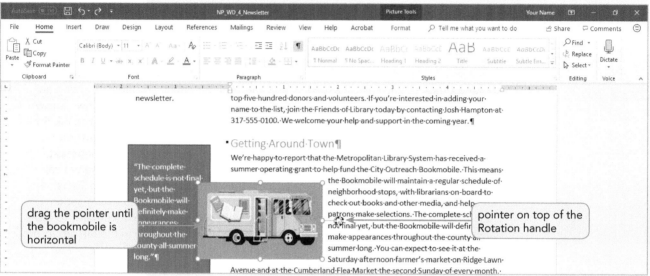

Mascha Tace/Shutterstock.com

▶ **4.** Drag the bookmobile picture right, so its left edge aligns below the left edge of the "Getting Around Town" heading, and two lines of paragraph text wrap above it.

▶ **5.** Save the document.

You're almost finished editing the bookmobile picture. Your next task is to remove its background, but first you'll explore the options in the Adjust group.

Adjusting a Picture

The Adjust group on the Picture Tools Format tab provides several tools for adjusting a picture's overall look. You'll explore some of these options in the following steps.

To try out some options in the Adjust group:

▶ **1.** Make sure that the **bookmobile picture** is still selected, and that the **Picture Tools Format** tab is selected on the ribbon.

▶ **2.** In the Adjust group, click the **Corrections** button, and then move the pointer over the various options in the Corrections gallery and observe the Live Preview in the document. You can use the Corrections gallery to sharpen or soften a picture's focus or to adjust its brightness.

▶ **3.** Press **ESC** to close the Corrections gallery.

▶ **4.** In the Adjust group, click the **Color** button, and then move the pointer over the options in the Color gallery, and observe the Live Preview in the document. You can adjust a picture's color saturation and tone. You can also use the Recolor options to completely change a picture's colors.

▶ **5.** Press **ESC** to close the Color gallery.

▶ **6.** In the Adjust group, click the **Artistic Effects** button, and then move the pointer over the options in the Artistic Effects gallery, and observe the Live Preview in the document.

▶ **7.** Press **ESC** to close the Artistic Effects gallery.

▶ **8.** In the Adjust group, click the **Compress Pictures** button ⊞ to open the Compress Pictures dialog box. In the Resolution portion of the dialog box, you can select the option that reflects the purpose of your document. Compressing pictures reduces the file size of the Word document but can result in some loss of detail. To compress all the pictures in a document, deselect the Apply only to this picture check box.

▶ **9.** Click **Cancel** to close the Compress Pictures dialog box.

Now you are ready to remove the green background from the bookmobile picture.

Removing a Picture's Background

Removing a picture's background can be tricky, especially if you are working on a photo with a background that is not clearly differentiated from the foreground image. For example, you might find it difficult to remove a white, snowy background from a photo of an equally white snowman. Removing a background from a drawing, like the bookmobile picture, is usually much easier than removing a background from a photo. You start by clicking the Remove Background button in the Adjust group, and then making changes to help Word distinguish between the background that you want to exclude and the image you want to keep.

REFERENCE

Removing a Picture's Background

- Select the picture, and then on the Picture Tools Format tab, in the Adjust group, click the Remove Background button.
- To mark areas to keep, click the Mark Areas to Keep button in the Refine group on the Background Removal tab, and then use the drawing pointer to select areas of the picture to keep.
- To mark areas to remove, click the Mark Areas to Remove button in the Refine group on the Background Removal tab, and then use the drawing pointer to select areas of the picture to remove.
- Click the Keep Changes button in the Close group.

You'll start by zooming in so you can clearly see the picture as you edit it.

To remove the green background from the bookmobile picture:

▶ **1.** On the Zoom slider, drag the slider button to change the Zoom level to **180%**, and then scroll as necessary to display the selected bookmobile picture.

▶ **2.** In the Adjust group, click the **Remove Background** button. See Figure 4–31.

Figure 4-31 **Removing a picture's background**

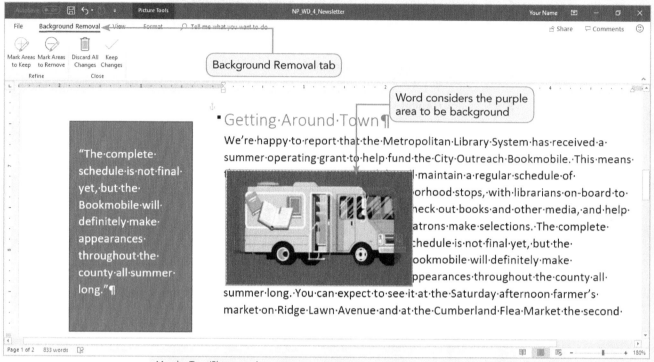

Mascha Tace/Shutterstock.com

The part of the picture that Word considers to be the background turns purple, and the Background Removal tab appears on the ribbon. Notice that the front and back ends of the bookmobile are purple, indicating that Word considers them to be part of the background. If you have trouble distinguishing colors, note that the front and back ends of the bookmobile are obscured by shading. The shading indicates that Word considers that part of the bookmobile to be background.

3. On the Background Removal tab, click the **Mark Areas to Keep** button in the Refine group to select it, if necessary, and then move the drawing pointer over the bookmobile. You can use this pointer to click any areas you want to keep.

4. Move the pointer over a purple area on the left side of the bookmobile. See Figure 4-32.

Figure 4–32   **Marking an area to keep**

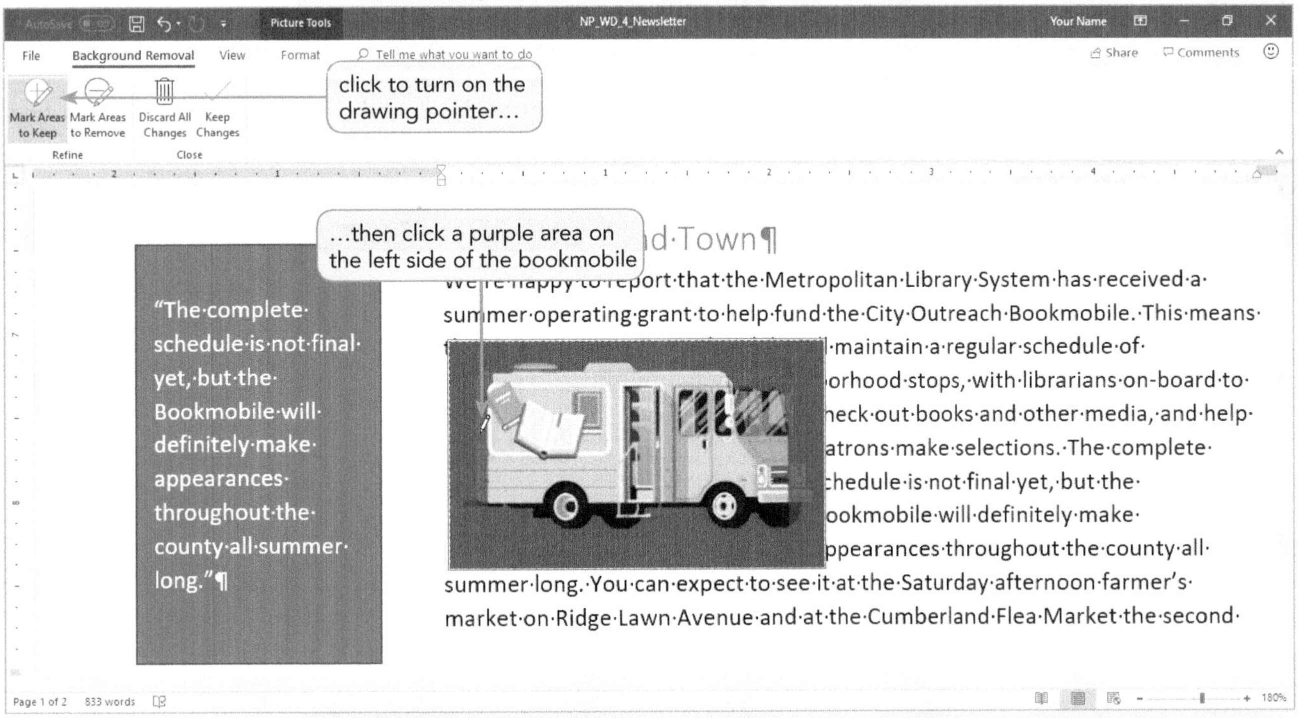

Mascha Tace/Shutterstock.com

> **5.** Click the mouse button. The area you clicked loses the shading, so you can see the bookmobile clearly. To give the image a clean line on the left, do not click the bump at the back of the bookmobile.

> **6.** Click the other major shaded spots on the right side of the bookmobile, including the front bumper and the headlight. You might need to click once, or you might need to click multiple times to convert all of the bookmobile from background to foreground. Also click the step below the door. It's fine if a little of the green background is visible here and there. Feel free to use CTRL+Z to undo changes and start again as necessary. Removing a picture's background can be tricky, and it often takes several tries to get it right.

> Note that you could click the Mark Areas to Remove button and then use the pointer in a similar way to mark parts of the picture that you want to remove, rather than retain. In an image with a larger background, you could also click and drag the Mark Areas to Remove pointer or the Mark Areas to Keep pointer to select a larger area of the picture for deletion or retention.

> Now you will accept the changes you made to the picture.

> **7.** In the Close group, click the **Keep Changes** button. The background is removed from the picture, leaving only the image of the bookmobile, with no green background. Now the text wrapping follows the curved shape of the bookmobile, although the bookmobile might overlap some letters. Depending on exactly where you positioned the bookmobile, some of the text might now wrap to its left.

Position the bookmobile picture carefully, so it doesn't overlap any text

8. Change the Zoom level to **100%** so that you can see the entire bookmobile, as well as the top of page 2.

9. Change the picture's height to 1.5 inches, and then drag the bookmobile as necessary so the text wraps similarly to the text shown in Figure 4–33, and then click anywhere in the document to deselect the bookmobile picture.

| Figure 4–33 | Bookmobile picture with background removed |

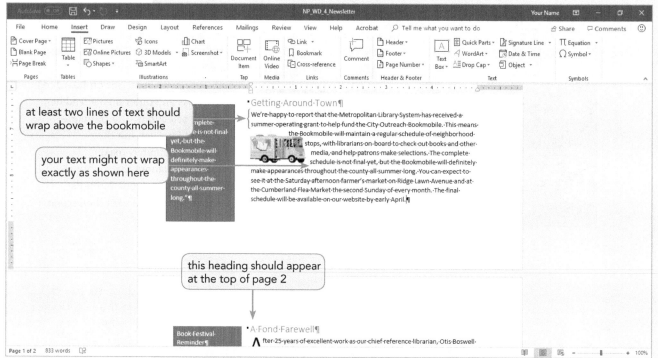

Mascha Tace/Shutterstock.com

Don't be concerned if you can't get the text wrapping to match exactly. The most important thing is that when you are finished, the heading "A Fond Farewell" should be positioned at the top of page 2. Also, at least two lines of text should wrap above the bookmobile. Finally, you might need to adjust the bookmobile's position slightly so it doesn't overlap any text.

10. Click outside the picture to deselect it, and then save the document.

You're finished with your work on the bookmobile picture. Now Vassily asks you to add a picture illustrating the article about audio books.

Adding an Icon

Vassily doesn't have a particular image in mind for the audio books article. You could search for an illustration online, but sometimes it's easier to use the streamlined drawings, known as icons, available via the Icons button in the Illustrations group on the Insert tab. After you add an icon to a document, you can fine-tune it by changing its fill and outline colors. Note that to work with icons, your computer must be connected to the Internet.

To insert an icon:

▶ **1.** Change the Zoom level to **120%**, and then scroll to display the middle of page 2. You'll insert the icon in the blank space in the margin, below the text box.

▶ **2.** Click at the end of the paragraph below the "Heard Any Good Books Lately?" heading to position the insertion point between "…listed below." and the paragraph mark.

▶ **3.** On the ribbon, click the **Insert** tab.

▶ **4.** In the Illustrations group, click the **Icons** button. The Insert Icons dialog box opens, with a list of icon categories on the left, and a gallery of icons for the selected category on the right.

▶ **5.** Explore the options in the Insert Icons gallery, scrolling up and down, and selecting various categories.

▶ **6.** In the category list, click **Technology and electronics**, and then click the headphones icon in the second row, third icon from the right. A border around the icon and a checkmark indicates that the icon is selected, as shown in Figure 4–34.

   Trouble? Don't be concerned if you see different icons than the ones shown in Figure 4–34. If you don't see a headphones icon, click another option.

Figure 4–34 **Icon selected in the Insert Icons dialog box**

TIP

To edit an icon using the tools on the Drawing Tools Format tab, select the icon, click the Convert to Shape button in the Change group on the Graphic Tools Format tab, and then click Yes.

▶ **7.** Click the **Insert** button. The headphones icon is inserted as an inline object at the end of the paragraph, with the Graphics Tools Format tab displayed. The alt text, "Headphones," is correct so you don't need to change it.

   Next, you need to wrap text around the icon, and position it on the page.

▶ **8.** In the Arrange group, click the **Wrap Text** button to open the Wrap Text menu. The In Line with Text option is selected. Because the icon is still an inline picture, the Move with Text and Fix Position on Page options are grayed out, indicating that they are not available.

▶ **9.** Click **In Front of Text** to select it, and then close the Wrap Text menu.

▶ **10.** Click the **Wrap Text** button again, and then click **Fix Position on Page**. The picture appears layered on top of the document text. Keep in mind that even though you selected Fix Position on Page, the picture is not stuck in one place. You can drag it anywhere you want. The point of the Fix Position on Page setting is that it prevents the picture from moving unexpectedly as you make changes to other parts of the document.

▶ **11.** Drag the icon to the left, to center it in the white space below the text box in the margin.

To make the icon more eye-catching, Vassily would like to change its fill and outline colors. You could do that by using the Graphics Fill button and the Graphics Outline button in the Graphics Styles group on the Graphics Tools Format tab. You can also change both options at once by applying a graphics style. You'll try that option next, and then you'll enlarge the icon to make it more noticeable.

To apply a graphics style and enlarge the icon:

▶ **1.** In the Graphics Styles group, click the **More** button ⬛ to open the Graphics Styles gallery, point to some of the style icons and view the Live Previews in the document, and then click the **Colored Fill - Accent 5, Dark 1 Outline** style, which is in the second row from the bottom, second style from the right. The style applies a blue fill with a black outline to the icon.

▶ **2.** In the Graphics Styles group, click the **Graphics Effects** button to open the Graphics Effects menu, point to **Glow** to open the Glow Effects gallery, and then point to the **Glow: 8 point; Orange, Accent color 2** effect, which is in the second row of the Glow Variations section, second effect from the left. A Live Preview appears in the document, as shown in Figure 4–35.

Figure 4–35   **Icon with Live Preview of graphics style**

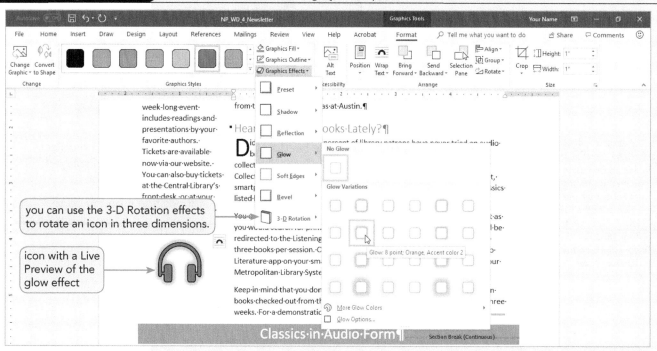

▶ **3.** Click the **Glow 8 point: Orange; Accent color 2** effect. An orange glow appears around the icon in the document.

▶ **4.** In the Size group, change the icon's height to 1.5 inches. Because the icon has a square aspect ratio, its width also changes to 1.5 inches.

▶ **5.** Drag the icon as necessary to make sure it is centered in the white space below the text box in the margin, click anywhere in the document to deselect the icon, and then save the document.

INSIGHT

Working with Digital Picture Files

Digital picture files come in two main types—vector graphics and raster graphics. A vector graphics file stores an image as a mathematical formula, which means you can increase or decrease the size of the image as much as you want without affecting its overall quality. Vector graphics are often used for line drawings and, because the file sizes tend to be small, are widely used on the web. File types for vector graphics are often proprietary, which means they work only in specific graphics programs. In Word, you will sometimes encounter files with the .wmf file extension, which is short for Windows Metafiles. A WMF file is a type of vector graphics file created specifically for Windows. In most cases, though, you'll work with raster graphics, also known as bitmap graphics. A **bitmap** is a grid of square colored dots, called **pixels**, that form a picture. A bitmap graphic, then, is essentially a collection of pixels. The most common types of bitmap files are:

- **BMP**—These files, which have the .bmp file extension, tend to be very large, so it's best to resave them in a different format before using them in a Word document.
- **EPS**—These files, which have the .eps file extension, are created by Adobe Illustrator and can contain text as graphics.
- **GIF**—These files are suitable for most types of simple line art, without complicated colors. A GIF file is compressed, so it doesn't take up much room on your computer. A GIF file has the file extension .gif.
- **JPEG**—These files are suitable for photographs and drawings. Files stored using the JPEG format are even more compressed than GIF files. A JPEG file has the file extension .jpg. If conserving file storage space is a priority, use JPEG graphics for your document.
- **PNG**—These files are similar to GIF files but are suitable for art containing a wider array of colors. A PNG file has the file extension .png.
- **TIFF**—These files are commonly used for photographs or scanned images. TIFF files are usually much larger than GIF or JPEG files but smaller than BMP files. A TIFF file has the file extension .tif.

Now that you are finished inserting and formatting the graphic elements in the newsletter, you need to make sure the columns are more or less the same length.

Balancing Columns

To **balance** columns on a page—that is, to make them equal length—you insert a continuous section break at the end of the last column. Word then adjusts the flow of content between the columns so they are of equal or near-equal length. The columns remain balanced no matter how much material you remove from any of the columns later. The columns also remain balanced if you add material that causes the columns to flow to a new page; the overflow will also be formatted in balanced columns.

To balance the columns:

▶ **1.** Press **CTRL+END** to move the insertion point to the end of the document.

▶ **2.** Insert a continuous section break. See Figure 4–36.

Figure 4–36 **Newsletter with balanced columns**

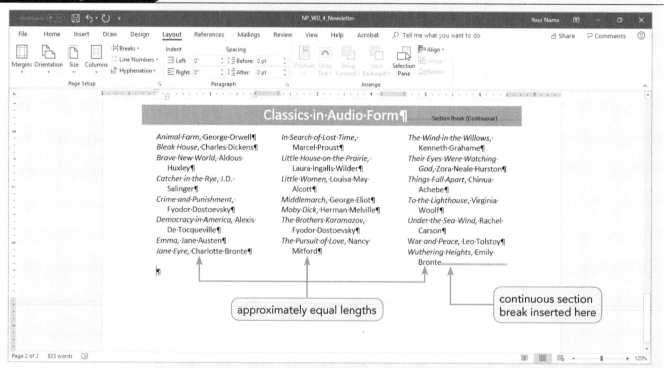

Word balances the text between the three columns, moving some text from the bottom of the left column to the middle column, and from the middle column to the right column, so the three columns are approximately the same length.

Note that you can also adjust the length of a column by inserting a column break using the Breaks button in the Page Setup group on the Layout tab. A column break moves all the text and graphics following it to the next column. Column breaks are useful when you have a multipage document formatted in three or more columns, with only enough text on the last page to fill some of the columns. In that case, balancing columns on the last page won't work. Instead, you can use a column break to distribute an equal amount of text over all the columns on the page. However, as with page breaks, you need to be careful with column breaks because it's easy to forget that you inserted them. Then, if you add or remove text from the document, or change it in some other significant way, you might end up with a page layout you didn't expect.

Enhancing the Newsletter's Formatting

A newsletter is a good opportunity to take advantage of some of Word's flashier formatting options, such as adding a page border and changing the theme colors. Vassily asks you to do both in order to make the newsletter even more eye-catching.

To change the theme colors and insert a border around both pages of the newsletter:

▶ **1.** Change the Zoom level to **Multiple Pages**.

▶ **2.** On the ribbon, click the **Design** tab.

▶ **3.** In the Document Formatting group, click the **Colors** button, scroll down, and then click **Green**. The colors of the various document elements—such as the text boxes, the icon, and headings—change to reflect the new theme colors. See Figure 4–37.

Figure 4–37   **Newsletter with new theme colors**

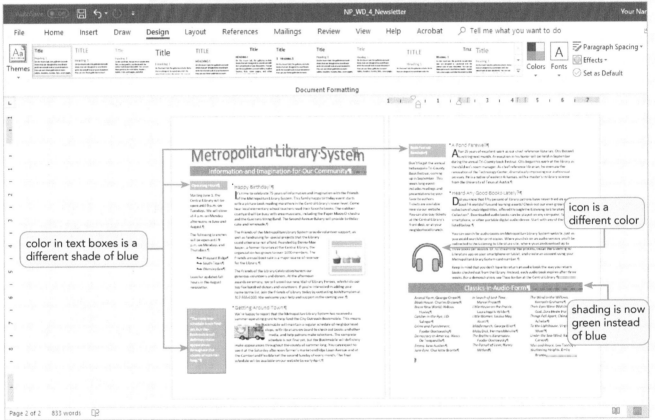

Ruth Black/Shutterstock.com; Mascha Tace/Shutterstock.com

▶ **4.** In the Page Background group, click the **Page Borders** button. The Borders and Shading dialog box opens with the Page Border tab displayed.

▶ **5.** In the Setting section, click the **Box** setting.

Vassily is happy with all the default page border settings, except one; he wants to change the border color to green.

▶ **6.** Click the **Color** arrow to open the Color gallery, and then click the **Green, Accent 1** square, which is the fifth square from the left in the top row of the Theme Colors section. The Color gallery closes, and the Green, Accent 1 color is displayed in the Color box.

▶ **7.** Click **OK**. The newsletter now has a simple, green border, as shown earlier in the Session 4.1 Visual Overview.

8. Compare the newsletter to the Session 4.1 Visual Overview, and adjust the position of the various elements as necessary, to make your newsletter match the Visual Overview as closely as possible. Note that you can click a text box or graphic object to select it, and then use the arrow keys on your keyboard to nudge the item up, down, left, or right. Don't be concerned with trying to get the text to wrap around the bookmobile image exactly as it does in the Session 4.1 Visual Overview. Just make sure at least two lines of text wrap above it, and that the heading "A Fond Farewell" appears at the top of page 2.

9. Save the document. Finally, to get a better sense of how the document with complicated formatting will look when printed, it's a good idea to review it with nonprinting characters turned off.

10. On the ribbon, click the **Home** tab.

11. In the Paragraph group, click the **Show/Hide** button ¶ to turn off nonprinting characters.

12. Change the Zoom level to **120%**, and then scroll to display page 2.

13. On page 2, in the sentence above the heading "Classics in Audio form," replace "Theo Jordan" with your first and last names. If your name is long enough to cause the sentence to flow to a second line, use only your first initial and last name instead.

14. **sam**⬆ Save the document.

Vassily plans to have the newsletter printed by a local printing company. Linda, his contact at the printing company, has asked him to email her the newsletter as a PDF.

Saving a Document as a PDF

A **PDF**, or **Portable Document Format file**, contains an image showing exactly how a document will look when printed. Because a PDF can be opened on any computer, saving a document as a PDF is a good way to ensure that it can be read by anyone. This is especially useful when you need to email a document to people who might not have Word installed on their computers. All PDFs have a file extension of .pdf. By default, PDFs open in Adobe Acrobat Reader, a free program installed on most computers for reading PDFs, or in Adobe Acrobat, a PDF-editing program available for purchase from Adobe.

To save the newsletter document as a PDF:

1. On the ribbon, click the **File** tab to open Backstage view.

TIP

To save a document as a PDF and attach it to an email message in Outlook, click the File tab, click Share in the navigation pane, and in the Attach a copy instead section of the Share dialog box, click PDF.

2. In the navigation pane, click **Export** to display the Export screen with Create PDF/XPS Document selected.

3. Click the **Create PDF/XPS** button. The Publish as PDF or XPS dialog box opens.

4. If necessary, navigate to the location specified by your instructor for saving your files, and then verify that "NP_WD_4_Newsletter" appears in the File name box. Below the Save as type box, verify that the "Open file after publishing" check box is selected. The "Standard (publishing online and printing)" button might be selected by default. This generates a PDF suitable for printing. If you plan to distribute a PDF only via email or over the web, you should select the "Minimum size (publishing online)" button instead. See Figure 4–38.

Figure 4–38   Publish as PDF or XPS dialog box

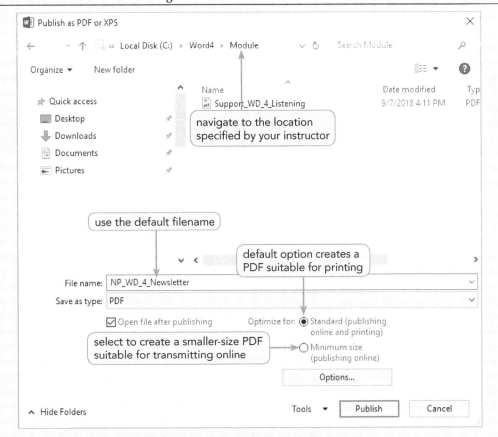

5. Click the **Publish** button. The Publish as PDF or XPS dialog box closes, and, after a pause, Adobe Acrobat Reader, Adobe Acrobat, or Microsoft Edge opens with the NP_WD_4_Newsletter.pdf file displayed.

6. Scroll down and review the PDF, and then close Adobe Acrobat Reader or Adobe Acrobat.

7. In Word, close the document, saving changes if necessary, but keep Word running.

In addition to saving a Word document as a PDF, you can convert a PDF to a Word document.

Converting a PDF to a Word Document

You may sometimes need to use text from a PDF in your own Word documents. Before you can do this, of course, you need to make sure you have permission to do so. Assuming you do, you can open the PDF in Acrobat or Acrobat Reader, drag the pointer to select the text you want to copy, press CTRL+C, return to your Word document, and then press CTRL+V to paste the text into your document. If you need to reuse or edit the entire contents of a PDF, it's easier to convert it to a Word document. This is a very useful option with PDFs that consist mostly of text. For more complicated PDFs, such as the NP_WD_4_Newsletter.pdf file you just created, the results are less predictable.

Vassily has a PDF containing some text about the Listening to Literature app. He asks you to open it in Word and convert it back to a Word document file.

To open the PDF in Word:

▶ 1. On the ribbon, click the **File** tab to open Backstage view.

▶ 2. In the navigation pane, click **Open**, if necessary, to display the Open screen, and then navigate to the **Word4 > Module** folder.

▶ 3. If necessary, click the **arrow** to the right of the File name box, and then click **All Files**.

▶ 4. In the file list, click **Support_WD_4_Listening.pdf**, click the **Open** button, and then, if you see a dialog box explaining that Word is about to convert a PDF to a Word document, click **OK**. The PDF opens in Word, with the name "Support_WD_4_Listening" in the title bar. Now you can save it as a Word document.

▶ 5. Click the **File** tab, click **Save As**, and then navigate to the location specified by your instructor.

▶ 6. Verify that "Word Document" appears in the Save as type box, and then save the document as **NP_WD_4_ListeningRevised**.

▶ 7. Turn on nonprinting characters, set the Zoom level to **120%**, and then review the document, which consists of a WordArt headline and a paragraph of text formatted in the Normal style. If you see one or more extra spaces at the end of the paragraph of text, they were added during the conversion from a PDF to a Word document. In a more complicated document, you might see graphics overlaid on top of text, or columns broken across multiple pages.

▶ 8. Close the **NP_WD_4_ListeningRevised.docx** document.

Session 4.2 Quick Check

REVIEW

1. What term refers to the interior color of the characters in WordArt?

2. Name six types of bitmap files.

3. What kind of laws govern the use of media, including text, line drawings, photographs, and video?

4. When cropping a picture, how can you maintain a specific ratio of width to height?

5. What should you do if you need to ensure that your document can be read on any computer?

PRACTICE

Review Assignments

Data Files needed for the Review Assignments: NP_WD_4-2.docx , Support_WD_4_Island.png, Support_WD_4_Retirement.png, Support_WD_4_Schedule.docx, Support_WD_4_Volunteers.docx,

Vassily is working on another newsletter. This one is for employees of the Indianapolis Public Library system. He has already written the document's text, and he asks you to transform it into a professional-looking newsletter. He also asks you to save the newsletter as a PDF so he can email it to the printer and to edit some text currently available only as a PDF. The finished newsletter should match the one shown in Figure 4–39.

Figure 4–39   Completed employee newsletter

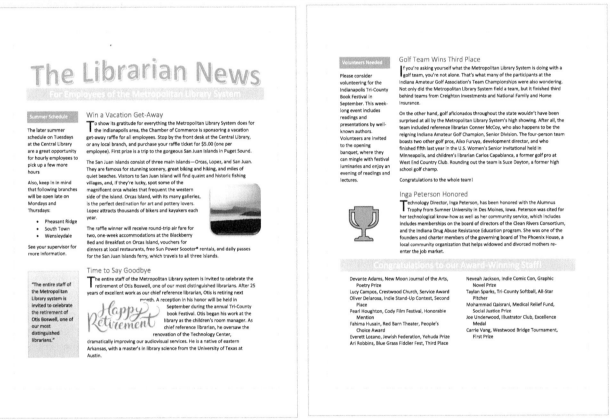

iStock.com/philotera; Alex Gorka/Shutterstock.com

Complete the following steps:

1. Open the file **NP_WD_4-2.docx** from the Word4 > Review folder included with your Data Files, and then save the document as **NP_WD_4_Employees** in the location specified by your instructor.

2. Insert continuous section breaks in the following locations:

   a. On page 1, at the beginning of the "Win a Vacation Getaway" heading, to the left of the "W" in "Win"

   b. On page 2, at the beginning of the shaded heading "Congratulations to our Award-Winning Staff!" to the left of the "C" in "Congratulations"

   c. On page 2, at the beginning of the first name, to the left of the "D" in "Devante"

3. In sections 1 and 3, change the left and right margins to .75 inches. In section 2, change the left margin to 2.5 inches.

4. Format section 4 in two columns of equal width, and then format the entire list of names and awards with a 0.2-inch hanging indent.

5. Search for the term **Sun Power Scooter** in the newsletter, and then add the ® symbol to the right of the final "r."

6. On page 1, click anywhere in the "Win a Vacation Getaway" heading, and then insert a preformatted text box using the Ion Sidebar 1 option.

7. Change the text wrapping setting for the text box to In Front of Text. Change the height of the text box to 4.3 inches and its width to 1.5 inches, and then drag it to position it in the white space in the left margin, with its top edge aligned with the "Win a Vacation Getaway" heading. The left border of the text box should align with the left edge of the shaded paragraph above. Verify that the text box's position is fixed on the page.

8. Change the text box title to **Summer Schedule**. Delete all the placeholder text in the text box, and then insert the text of the Word document **Support_WD_4_Schedule.docx**, which is located in the Word4 > Review folder. Delete any extra paragraph marks at the end of the text, and change the font size for the text and text box title to 11.

9. On the Insert tab, use the Shapes button to draw a rectangular text box that roughly fills the blank space in the lower-left margin of page 1. When you are finished, adjust the height and width as necessary to make the text box 2.5 inches tall and 1.5 inches wide.

10. Make sure the text wrap setting for the text box is set to In Front of Text and that the text box has a fixed position on the page. Drag the text box's anchor up to slightly above the "Time to Say Goodbye" heading to keep the text box from moving to page 2 later, when you add a graphic to page 1.

11. On page 1, in the paragraph below the "Time to Say Goodbye" heading, select the first sentence (which begins "The entire staff of the…"), and then copy it to the Office Clipboard.

12. Paste the copied sentence into the text box at the bottom of page 1, and then add quotation marks at the beginning and end.

13. Use the Align Text button to align the text in the middle of the text box, and then apply the Subtle Effect - Orange, Accent 2 shape style (the light orange style option, the third style from the left in the fourth row of the Shape Styles gallery).

14. On page 2, click in the paragraph that reads "Congratulations to the whole team!" and then insert a preformatted text box using the Ion Sidebar 1 option.

15. Change the text wrapping setting for the text box to In Front of Text. Change the height of the text box to 3.8 inches and its width to 1.5 inches, and then drag it left to position it in the white space in the left margin, with its top edge aligned with the first line of text, and its left edge aligned with the left edge of the shaded heading below. Verify that its position is fixed on the page.

16. Change the text box title to **Volunteers Needed**. Delete all the placeholder text in the text box, and then insert the text of the Word document **Support_WD_4_Volunteers.docx**, which is located in the Word4 > Review folder. Delete any extra paragraph marks at the end of the text, and change the font size for the text and text box title to 11.

17. In the first line of text after each of the four headings formatted with blue font, insert a drop cap that drops two lines.

18. On page 1, select the entire first paragraph, "The Librarian News," including the paragraph mark. Clear the formatting from the paragraph, and then format the text as WordArt, using the Fill: Blue, Accent color 5; Outline: White, Background color 1; Hard Shadow: Blue, Accent color 5 style (the middle option in the bottom row).

19. Change the WordArt text box width to 7 inches, and retain the default height.

20. Retain the Square text wrapping, and make sure the WordArt has a fixed position on the page. Drag the WordArt text box up above the shaded paragraph if necessary, so it appears at the top of the page.

21. Apply the Chevron: Up transform text effect, and then add a shadow using the Offset: Bottom Right style (the first option in the top row of the Outer section).

22. Click at the end of the paragraph below the "Win a Vacation Getaway" heading, and then insert the picture file named **Support_WD_4_Island.png** from the Word4 > Review folder. The alt text is correct, so you don't need to change it.

23. Practice cropping the photo to a shape, and then try cropping it by dragging the cropping handles. Use the Reset Picture button as necessary to restore the picture to its original appearance. When you are finished, crop the picture using a square aspect ratio, and then change its height and width to 1.5 inches. Use the Position button to place the picture in the middle of the right side of page 1 with square text wrapping, and then add the Bevel Rectangle picture style (third row, first style on the right).

24. On page 1, click at the end of the "Time to Say Goodbye" heading, and then insert the picture **Support_WD_4_Retirement.png** from the Word4 > Review folder.

25. Change the alt text to read **The words "Happy Retirement" written in calligraphy** and then rotate the picture so the words are positioned vertically.

26. Change the photo's height to 2.5 inches, and retain the default width. Apply Tight text wrapping, position it in the paragraph below the "Time to Say Goodbye" heading, with two lines of text wrapped above it, fix its position on the page, and then remove the picture's background. Readjust the picture so the paragraph text wraps around it as shown in Figure 4–39. Take care not to let the picture overlap any text.

27. On page 2, click at the end of the paragraph below the "Inga Peterson Honored" heading, and then insert the trophy icon from the Celebration category. The alt text is correct, so you don't need to change it.

28. Apply Tight text wrapping, fix its position on the page, change the icon's height and width to 1.2 inches, drag the icon to center it in the white space below the text box.

29. Apply the Colored Fill – Accent 5, Dark 1 Outline graphics style (third row, second from the right in the Graphics style gallery).

30. Add the Glow: 5 point; Orange, Accent color 2 graphics effect (top row, second from the left in the Glow Variations gallery).

31. Balance the columns at the bottom of page 2.

32. Change the theme colors to Blue Warm.

33. Insert a simple box outline of the default style and width for the entire document. For the border color, use Blue, Accent 2, Lighter 60% (third row, sixth from the left in the Theme Colors palette). Make any additional adjustments necessary to ensure that your newsletter matches the one shown in Figure 4–39. You will probably need to adjust the position of the text boxes on page 1 to ensure that their left edges align with the left edge of the blue-shaded heading above. Likewise, on page 2, you might need to adjust the position of the text box to ensure that its left edge aligns with the left edge of the blue-shaded heading below. Also, on page 1, position the bottom text box so its bottom border aligns with the last line of text on the page.

34. In the second to last line on page 2, replace "Carrie Vang" with your first and last names.

35. Save the document, and then save it again as a PDF named **NP_WD_4_Employees** in the location specified by your instructor. Wait for the PDF to open, review it, and then close the program in which it opened. Close the **NP_WD_4_Employees.docx** document, but leave Word open.

36. In Word, open the **NP_WD_4_Employees.pdf** file, save it as a Word document named **NP_WD_4_EmployeesRevised**, review its appearance, note the problems with the formatting that you would have to correct if you actually wanted to use this new DOCX file, and also note that alt text is no longer associated with the three images. Close the document.

Case Problem 1

Data Files needed for this case Problem: NP_WD_4-3.docx, Support_WD_4_Bins.docx, Support_WD_4_Earth.png, Support_WD_4_Sorting.png

Solana Homes   Malika Foster is the sales manager for Solana Homes, a gated community in suburban Chicago. She wants to emphasize the community's commitment to environmentally friendly practices, such as recycling, so she has written a flyer to include in the packet of information she gives each potential home buyer. Now she needs your help to finish it. The finished flyer should match the one shown in Figure 4–40.

Figure 4-40   Completed recycling flyer

Solana Homes: Creating a Sustainable Community

Recycle, Reuse, Renew

Solana Builds Recycling Pavilion

We're happy to announce that the Solana Homes community will include a recycling pavilion offering state-of-the art collection facilities, with bi-weekly pickups. The pavilion is designed to make recycling easy in all kinds of weather. The Solana architects were motivated by numerous studies demonstrating that community support and accessible facilities greatly increase the number of families committed to recycling.

Recycling Bins

Each household is entitled to one recycling bin for curbside pickup. You can recycle an unlimited amount of materials.

Recycling bins will also be installed throughout the grounds, and residents can schedule curbside pickups at no extra cost. Solana Homes has contracted with Mason Waste Disposal and Recycling to handle trash and recycling pickups. Company owner Ella Fortman has been recognized numerous times as an innovator in co-mingling reuse and recycling.

Hazardous Waste Collection

Many household hazardous wastes can be recycled cleanly and effectively by recycling professionals. Aren't sure what's considered hazardous waste? The labels of most products will provide helpful clues. Look for the following words: caution, danger, toxic, pesticide, keep away from children, flammable, and warning. Acceptable materials include antifreeze, brake fluid, kerosene, oil-based paint, furniture polish, pesticides, herbicides, household batteries, pool chemicals, and fertilizers.

Many hazardous wastes can be recycled

Hazardous waste collection will be handled by the city Sanitation Department, which has a robust hazardous waste treatment program. Sanitation workers will retrieve the items from the curb next to your trash bins on your usual trash pickup day.

Winners of the Solana Green Award

Casey Ann Ramirez-Bosco	Roger Kent Erickson	Haiyan Jiang	Sigrid Del Rio
Michael Paul Berners	Henry Douglas	Tory Jeschke	Harriet Schaefer
Becky Cade	Tomas Carrico	Jacques Lambeau	Jonas Jones
Elina Compere	Clarita Carrico	Tia Morello-Jimenez	Sandra Jane Carmel
Jose Carmela	Kelly Dowell	Mario Ruffolo	Christina
Layla Carrington	Seamus Dante Dolan	Eileen Jasper-Schwartz	Chamberlain
Bruce Butler	Clarissa Fey-Esperanza	Helena Pentakota Smith	Boris Andre Nesaule

Voin_Sveta/Shutterstock.com; lesia_g/Shutterstock.com

Complete the following steps:

1. Open the file **NP_WD_4-3.docx** located in the Word4 > Case1 folder included with your Data Files, and then save it as **NP_WD_4_Flyer** in the location specified by your instructor.

2. Change the document margins to Narrow, and then, where indicated in the document, insert continuous section breaks. Remember to delete each instance of the highlighted text "[Insert SECTION BREAK]" before you insert a section break.

3. In section 2, change the left margin to 3 inches, and then format section 4 in four columns.

4. Format the second paragraph in the document ("Recycle, Reuse, Renew") as WordArt, using the Gradient Fill: Dark Green, Accent color 5; Reflection style (second from the left in the middle row of the WordArt gallery). Change the text box height to 0.7 inches and the width to 7 inches. Change the text wrapping setting to Top and Bottom and fix its position on the page.

If necessary, drag the WordArt down below the first paragraph ("Solana Homes: Creating a Sustainable Community"). Don't be concerned if the WordArt overlaps and is positioned below the section break line.

5. Insert drop caps that drop two lines in the first paragraph after the "Solana Builds Recycling Pavilion" heading and in the first paragraph after the "Hazardous Waste Collection" heading.

6. Click in the fourth paragraph in the document (the one with the drop cap "W"), and then insert a preformatted text box using the Grid Sidebar option. Change the text wrapping setting for the text box to In Front of Text, and then change its height to 2.8 inches and its width to 2.3 inches.

7. Drag the text box to position it in the white space on the left side of the page, and then align its top border with the "Solana Builds Recycling Pavilion" heading.

8. Delete the title placeholder text in the text box, and type **Recycling Bins**. Delete the placeholder paragraphs, and insert the text of the Word document **Support_WD_4_Bins** from the Word4 > Case1 folder. Delete any extra blank paragraphs.

9. In the blank space below the text box, draw a rectangular text box. When you are finished, adjust the height and width to make the text box 1.3 inches tall and 2 inches wide. Apply the Moderate Effect – Turquoise, Accent 1 shape style (second from the left in the second row from the bottom in the Themes Styles section), and then position the text box as shown in Figure 4–40, leaving room for the graphic you will add later.

10. In the text box, type **Many hazardous wastes can be recycled.** Align the text in the middle of the text box, and then use the Center button on the Home tab to center the text between the text box's left and right borders.

11. At the end of the fifth paragraph (which begins "Recycling bins will also be installed..."), insert the picture **Support_WD_4_Earth.png** from the Word4 > Case1 folder.

12. Change the alt text to **Recycle logo** and crop the picture to an oval shape.

13. Apply Square text wrapping, fix its position on the page, and then change its height to 1 inch. Drag the picture to position it so the first line of the fifth paragraph wraps above it, as shown in Figure 4–40.

14. At the end of the first paragraph below the "Hazardous Waste Collection" heading, insert the picture **Support_WD_Sorting.png** from the Word4 > Case1 folder.

15. Change the alt text to **Recycling bins** and then change the picture's height to 1.3 inches.

16. Apply In Front of Text text wrapping, add the Center Shadow Rectangle picture style (second from right in the second row of the Picture Styles gallery), and then position the picture in the left margin, centered between the two text boxes, with a fixed position on the page, as shown in Figure 4–40.

17. Balance the columns at the end of the flyer.

18. In the last line of the document, replace "Boris Andre Nesaule" with your first and last names. Take care not to delete the section break by mistake.

19. Make any adjustments necessary so that your newsletter matches the one shown in Figure 4–40, and then save the document.

20. Save the document as a PDF named **NP_WD_4_FlyerPDF** in the location specified by your instructor. Review the PDF, and then close the program in which it opened.

21. In Word, open the PDF named **NP_WD_4_FlyerPDF.pdf**, save it as **NP_WD_4_FlyerFromPDF**, review its contents, note the corrections you would have to make if you actually wanted to use this document, and also note that alt text is no longer associated with the two images. Close any open documents.

CREATE

Case Problem 2

There are no Data Files needed for this Case Problem.

Ocotillo Health Care   You are a public relations specialist at Ocotillo Health Care in Tempe, Arizona. As part of your training, your supervisor asks you to review online examples of flyers encouraging healthy eating and then re-create the first page of a flyer on healthy eating as a Word document. Instead of writing the complete text of the flyer, you can use placeholder text. Complete the following steps:

1. Open a new, blank document, and then save it as **NP_WD_4_Healthy** in the location specified by your instructor.

2. Open your browser and search online for images of flyers by searching for the keywords **healthy eating flyer image**. Review at least a dozen images of flyers before picking a style that you want to re-create in a Word document. The style you choose should contain at least two pictures. Keep the image of the flyer visible in your browser so you can return to it for reference as you work.

3. In your Word document, create the first page of the flyer. Compose your own WordArt headlines and other headings, or replicate the headlines and headings in the sample flyer. To generate text that you can use to fill the space below the headings, type **=lorem()** and then press ENTER. Change the document theme, theme fonts, and theme colors as necessary to replicate the colors and fonts in the flyer you are trying to copy. Don't worry about the flyer's background color; white is fine.

4. Add at least two pictures, using pictures that you find online. Rotate or flip pictures, and remove their backgrounds as necessary to make them work in the flyer layout. Revise the image's alt text if necessary.

5. Add at least one 3-D model to the flyer. Revise the model's alt text if necessary.

6. Make any other changes necessary so that the layout and style of your document match the flyer example that you found online.

7. Somewhere in the document, attach a comment that reads **I used the following webpage as a model for this flyer design:**, and then include the URL for the flyer image you used as a model. To copy a URL from a browser window, click the URL in the browser's Address bar, and then press CTRL+C.

8. Save the document, close it, and then close your browser.

OBJECTIVES

Session 5.1
- Create a new document from a template
- Move through a document using Go To
- Use the thesaurus to find synonyms
- Customize a document theme
- Save a custom theme
- Select a style set
- Customize a style
- Change character spacing

Session 5.2
- Create a new style
- Inspect styles
- Reveal and compare text formatting details
- Review line and page break settings
- Generate and update a table of contents
- Create and use a template
- Create a Quick Part

Working with Templates, Themes, and Styles

Creating a Summary Report

Case | *Allied Startup Accelerator*

The Allied Center for Business and Technology, in Atlanta, Georgia, is spearheading construction of the Allied Startup Accelerator. The facility will provide guidance to new, technically oriented companies that require the specialized kind of support needed in the fast-moving technology world. Hayden Lazlo, a project manager at the center, is responsible for creating a report designed to help generate interest in the accelerator. Hayden has asked you to help him prepare the report. He's also interested in learning more about Word templates, so he'd like you to do some research by opening a few templates and examining the styles they offer. Next, he wants you to modify the formatting currently applied to his report document, including creating a customized theme, modifying one of the styles, creating a new style, and adding a table of contents. Then he wants you to create a template that can be used for all reports produced by his organization, as well as a reusable text box containing the current mailing address and phone number for the Atlanta Center for Business and Technology, which his coworkers can insert into any Word document via the Quick Parts gallery.

STARTING DATA FILES

Word5 → **Module**

NP_WD_5-1.docx
NP_WD_5-2.docx
Support_WD_5_Diamond.docx
Support_WD_5_Placeholder.docx

Review

NP_WD_5-3.docx
NP_WD_5-4.docx
Support_WD_5_Headings.docx
Support_WD_5_Writers.docx

Case1

NP_WD_5-5.docx

Case2

NP_WD_5-6.docx
NP_WD_5-7.docx

Session 5.1 Visual Overview:

Theme colors, which are one component of a document's theme, are used in the document's styles to format headings, body text, and other elements.

The second component of a document's theme, theme fonts, are used in the document's styles.

Collectively, all the styles available in a document are called a **style set**. This style set, named Word, is applied to all new documents by default.

A third component of a document's theme, **theme effects**, control the look of the reflections, shadows, and other effects that you can add to shapes.

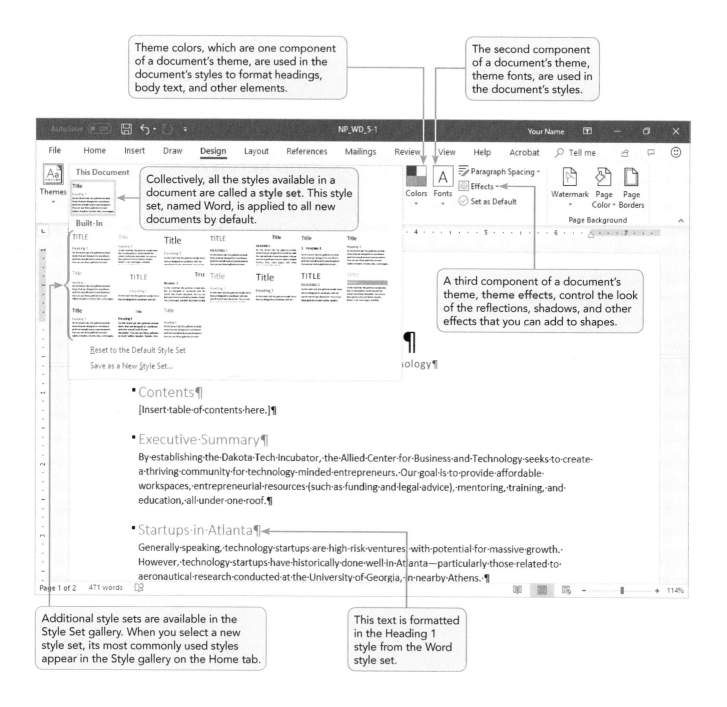

Additional style sets are available in the Style Set gallery. When you select a new style set, its most commonly used styles appear in the Style gallery on the Home tab.

This text is formatted in the Heading 1 style from the Word style set.

Custom Themes and Style Sets

This style set, named Shaded, is applied to the document below. In the Shaded style set, the Heading 1 style formats text with blue paragraph shading and a white font color.

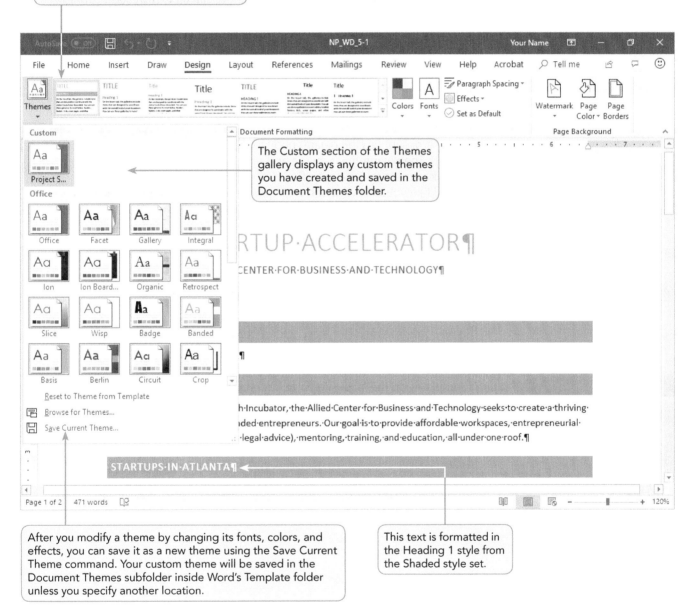

The Custom section of the Themes gallery displays any custom themes you have created and saved in the Document Themes folder.

After you modify a theme by changing its fonts, colors, and effects, you can save it as a new theme using the Save Current Theme command. Your custom theme will be saved in the Document Themes subfolder inside Word's Template folder unless you specify another location.

This text is formatted in the Heading 1 style from the Shaded style set.

Creating a New Document from a Template

A template is a file that you use as a starting point for a series of similar documents so that you don't have to re-create formatting and text for each new document. A template can contain customized styles, text, graphics, or any other element that you want to repeat from one document to another. In this module, you'll customize the styles and themes in a Word document and then save the document as a template to use for future documents. Before you do that, however, you will investigate some of the ready-made templates available at Office.com.

When you first start Word, the Recent screen in Backstage view displays a variety of templates available from Office.com. You can also enter keywords in the Search for online templates box to find templates that match your specific needs. For example, you could search for a calendar template, a birthday card template, or a report template.

Every new, blank document that you open in Word is a copy of the Normal template. Unlike other Word templates, the **Normal template** does not have any text or graphics, but it does include all the default settings that you are accustomed to using in Word. For example, the default theme in the Normal template is the Office theme. The Office theme, in turn, supplies the default body font (Calibri) and the default heading font (Calibri Light). The default line spacing and paragraph spacing you are used to seeing in a new document are also specified in the Normal template.

Hayden would like you to review some templates designed for reports. As you'll see in the following steps, when you open a template, Word actually creates a document that is an exact copy of the template. The template itself remains unaltered, so you can continue to use it as the basis for other documents.

TIP

Templates have the file extension .dotx to differentiate them from regular Word documents, which have the extension .docx.

To review some report templates available on Office.com:

1. On the ribbon, click the **File** tab to open Backstage view, and then click **New** in the navigation pane. The New screen in Backstage view displays thumbnail images of the first page of a variety of templates. See Figure 5–1.

Figure 5–1   Featured templates on the New screen in backstage view

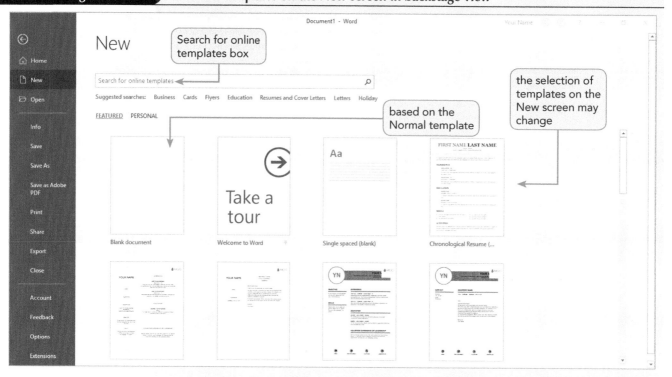

Trouble? If you just started Word, you'll see the list of templates on the Recent screen. You'll be able to complete the next step using the Search for online templates box on the Recent screen.

Below the Search for online templates box are template options available from Office.com. You've already used the Blank document template to open a new, blank document that is based on the Normal template. The list of templates changes as new templates become available, so your screen probably won't match Figure 5–1 exactly.

▶ 2. Click the **Search for online templates** box, type **report**, and then press **ENTER**. The New screen displays thumbnail images for a variety of report templates. If you scroll down to the bottom, you'll see options for searching for templates to use in other Office applications. The Category pane on the right displays a list of report categories. You could click any category to display only the templates in that category.

▶ 3. Click any report template. A window opens with a preview of the template. Note that the template indicates it is provided by Microsoft Corporation. Figure 5–2 shows the Student report with cover photo template.

| Figure 5–2 | Previewing a template |

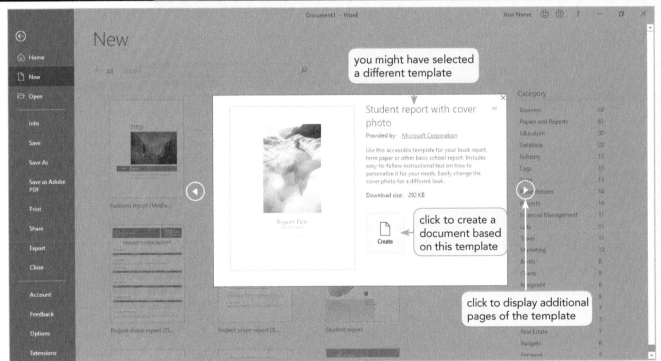

iStock.com/Turnervisual

You could click the Close button ☒ to close the preview window and browse other report templates, but Hayden asks you to continue investigating the current template.

▶ **4.** Click the **Create** button. A new document based on the template opens. Depending on which template you selected, your document might include a cover page, a photo, and a number of content controls designed specifically for the template—similar to the content controls you've seen in other documents. The document also likely contains some placeholder text, a footer, and graphics. You might also see the Researcher pane open on the right side of the Word screen, ready to help you begin researching information for a report.

At this point, you could save the document with a new name and then begin revising it to create an actual report. But since your goal now is to review various templates, you'll close the document.

▶ **5.** Close the document without saving any changes.

▶ **6.** On the ribbon, click the **File** tab, and then click **New** in the navigation pane.

▶ **7.** Search online for newsletter templates, open a document based on one of the templates, and then review the document, noting the various elements it includes.

▶ **8.** Close the newsletter document without saving it.

▶ **9.** Return to the New screen, and search for templates for flyers. Open a new document based on one of the templates, review the document, and then close it without saving it.

PROSKILLS

Decision Making: Using Templates from Other Sources

The Office.com website offers a wide variety of templates that are free to Microsoft Office users. Countless other websites offer templates for free, for individual sale, as part of a subscription service, or a combination of all three. However, you need to be wary when searching for templates online. Keep in mind the following when deciding which sites to use:

- Files downloaded from the Internet can infect your computer with viruses and spyware, so make sure your computer has up-to-date antivirus and anti-malware software before downloading any templates.
- Evaluate a site carefully to verify that it is a reputable source of virus-free templates. Verifying the site's legitimacy is especially important if you intend to pay for a template with a credit card. Search for the website's name and URL using different search engines (such as Bing and Google) to see what other people say about it.
- Some websites claim to offer templates for free, when in fact the offer is primarily a lure to draw visitors to sites that are really just online billboards, with ads for any number of businesses completely unrelated to templates or Word documents. Avoid downloading templates from these websites.
- Many templates available online were created for earlier versions of Word that did not include themes, 3-D models, or other advanced Word design features. Make sure you know what you're getting before you pay for an out-of-date template.

Now that you are finished reviewing report templates, you will open the document containing the report about the Allied Startup Accelerator.

To open Hayden's report document:

▶ **1.**  Open the document **NP_WD_5-1.docx** from the Word5 > Module folder, and then save it as **NP_WD_5_Allied** in the location specified by your instructor.

▶ **2.** Display nonprinting characters and the rulers, switch to Print Layout view if necessary, and then change the Zoom level to **120%**, if necessary. See Figure 5–3.

Figure 5–3   **Report document**

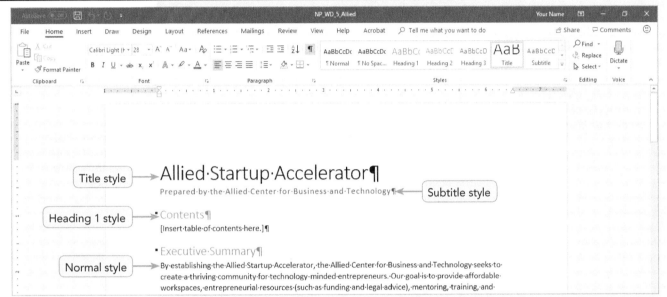

The report is formatted using the default settings of the Normal template, which means its current theme is the Office theme. Text in the report is formatted using the Title, Subtitle, Heading 1, Heading 2, and Normal styles. The document includes a footer containing "Allied Startup Accelerator" and a page number field.

Before you begin revising the document, you should review its contents. To get a quick overview of a document, it's helpful to use the Go To feature.

Using Go To

The Go To tab in the Find and Replace dialog box allows you to move quickly among elements in a document. For example, you can use it to move from heading to heading, from graphic to graphic, or from table to table. In a long document, this is an efficient way to review your work. Although the document is not very long, you can still review its contents using Go To.

To use the Go To feature to review the document:

▶ **1.** If necessary, press **CTRL+HOME** to move the insertion point to the beginning of the document.

▶ **2.** On the ribbon, make sure the Home tab is displayed.

3. In the Editing group, click the **Find arrow** to display the Find menu, and then click **Go To**. The Find and Replace dialog box opens, with the Go To tab displayed. See Figure 5–4.

Figure 5–4   Go To tab in the Find and Replace dialog box

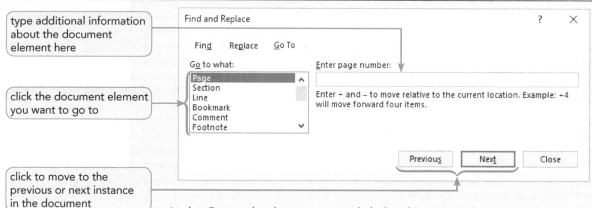

type additional information about the document element here

click the document element you want to go to

click to move to the previous or next instance in the document

In the Go to what box, you can click the document element you want to go to. Then click the Next or Previous buttons to move back and forth among instances of the selected element in the document. You can also enter more specific information in the box on the right. For instance, when Page is selected in the Go to what box, you can type a page number in the box, and then click Next to go directly to that page.

Right now, Hayden would like to review all the headings in the document—that is, all the paragraphs formatted with a heading style.

4. Scroll down to the bottom of the Go to what box, click **Heading**, and then click the **Next** button. The document scrolls down to position the first document heading, "Contents," at the top of the document window.

5. Click the **Next** button again. The document scrolls down to display the "Executive Summary" heading at the top of the document window.

6. Click the **Next** button five more times to display the last heading in the document, "Saturn and Sun Investments," at the top of the document window.

7. Click the **Previous** button to display the "Chandra 3D Printing" heading at the top of the document window, and then close the Find and Replace dialog box.

INSIGHT

Choosing Between Go To and the Navigation Pane

Both the Go To tab in the Find and Replace dialog box and the Navigation pane allow you to move through a document heading by heading. Although you used Go To in the preceding steps, the Navigation pane is usually the better choice for working with headings; it displays a complete list of the headings, which helps you keep an eye on the document's overall organization. However, the Go To tab is more useful when you want to move through a document one graphic at a time or one table at a time. In a document that contains a lot of graphics or tables, it's a good idea to use the Go To feature to make sure you've formatted all the graphics or tables similarly.

Next, before you begin formatting the document, Hayden asks you to help him find a synonym for a word in the text.

Using the Thesaurus to Find Synonyms

In any kind of writing, choosing the right words to convey your meaning is important. If you need help, you can use the thesaurus in Word to look up a list of synonyms, or possible replacements, for a specific word. You can right-click a word to display a shortcut menu with a short list of synonyms or open the Thesaurus pane for a more complete list. Also, this list usually includes at least one antonym—that is, a word with the opposite meaning.

Hayden is not happy with the word "innovators" in the paragraph about Chandra 3D Printing because he thinks it's overused in writing about technical entrepreneurs. He asks you to find a synonym.

To look up a synonym in the thesaurus:

1. In the third to last line on page 1, right-click the word **innovators**. A shortcut menu opens.

2. Point to **Synonyms**. A menu with a list of synonyms for "innovators" is displayed, as shown in Figure 5–5.

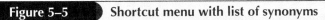

Figure 5–5   Shortcut menu with list of synonyms

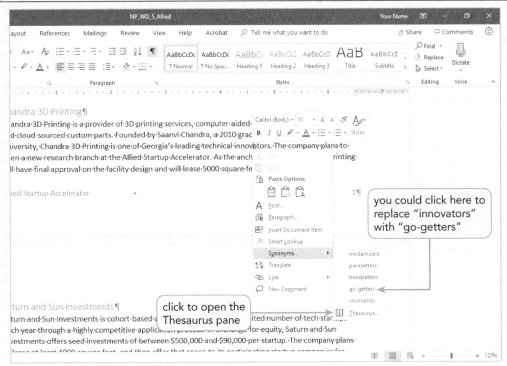

Hayden thinks one word in the list, "go-getters," is a good replacement for "innovators." You could click "go-getters" to insert it in the document in place of "innovators," but Hayden asks you to check the Thesaurus pane to see if it suggests a better option.

▶ **3.** At the bottom of the shortcut menu, click **Thesaurus**. The Thesaurus pane opens on the right side of the document window, with the word "innovators" at the top and a more extensive list of synonyms below. The word "innovators" is also selected in the document, ready to be replaced. See Figure 5–6.

Figure 5–6 | **Thesaurus pane**

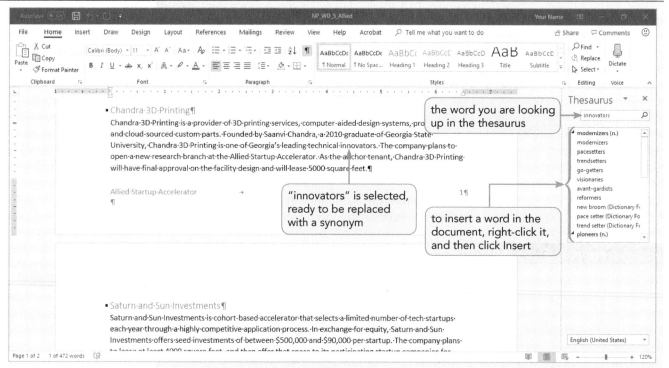

The synonym list is organized by different shades of meaning, with words related to the idea of "modernizers" at the top of the list. You can scroll down the list to see other groups of synonyms, and at least one antonym.

▶ **4.** In the Thesaurus pane, move the pointer over the list of synonyms to display the scroll bar, scroll down to display other synonyms, as well as the antonym at the bottom of the list, and then scroll back up to the top of the list.

▶ **5.** Point to **go-getters**. The word is highlighted in blue, and a down arrow ▼ appears to the right.

▶ **6.** Click the **down arrow** ▼. A menu opens.

Trouble? If the Thesaurus pane changes to display a set of synonyms for the word "go-getters," you clicked the word "go-getters" instead of just pointing at it. Click the Back button ＜ to redisplay the synonyms for "innovators," and then begin again with Step 5.

▶ **7.** Click **Insert** to replace "innovators" with "go-getters" in the document, and then close the Thesaurus pane.

▶ **8.** Save the document.

Now that the document text is finished, you can get to work on the formatting. You'll start by customizing the document theme.

Customizing the Document Theme

A document theme consists of three main components—theme colors, theme fonts, and theme effects. A specific set of colors, fonts, and effects is associated with each theme, but you can mix and match them to create a customized theme for your document. This can be useful in specialized situations, such as when you need to create a series of documents that match an organization's preferred format for reports. After you create a customized theme, you can use it for all new reports that require that particular combination of fonts, colors, and effects.

Recall that the theme fonts are the fonts used in a document's styles. You see them at the top of the font list when you click the Font arrow in the Font group on the Home tab. The theme colors are displayed in the Theme Colors section of any color gallery. The colors used to format headings, body text, and other elements are all drawn from the document's theme colors. Theme effects alter the appearance of shapes. Because they are generally very subtle, theme effects are not a theme element you will typically be concerned with.

When you change the theme colors, fonts, or effects for a document, the changes affect only that document. However, you can also save the changes you make to create a new, custom theme, which you can then use for future documents.

Hayden's report document, which was based on the Normal template, is formatted with the Office theme—which applies a blue font color to the headings by default and formats the headings in the Calibri Light font. Hayden wants to select different theme colors and theme fonts to match the preferred formatting for reports created by the Allied Center for Business and Technology. He doesn't plan to include any graphics, so there's no need to customize the theme effects. You'll start with the theme colors.

Changing the Theme Colors

As you have seen, theme colors, which are designed to coordinate well with each other, are used in the various document styles, including the text styles available on the Home tab. They are also used in shape styles, WordArt styles, and picture styles. So when you want to change the colors in a document, it's always better to change the theme colors rather than selecting individual elements and applying a new color to each element from a color gallery. That way you can be sure colors will be applied consistently throughout the document—for example, the headings will all be shades of the same color.

Reports created by the Allied Center for Business and Technology are typically emailed to many recipients, some of whom might choose to print the reports. To keep printing costs as low as possible for all potential readers of his report, Hayden wants to format his document in black and white. He asks you to apply a set of theme colors consisting of black and shades of gray.

To change the theme colors in the document:

▶ **1.** Press **CTRL+HOME** to display the beginning of the document.

▶ **2.** On the ribbon, click the **Design** tab.

▶ **3.** In the Document Formatting group, move the pointer over the **Colors** button. A ScreenTip is displayed, indicating that the current theme colors are the Office theme colors.

4. Click the **Colors** button. A gallery of theme colors opens, with the Office theme colors selected at the top of the gallery. See Figure 5–7.

Figure 5–7   **Theme Colors gallery**

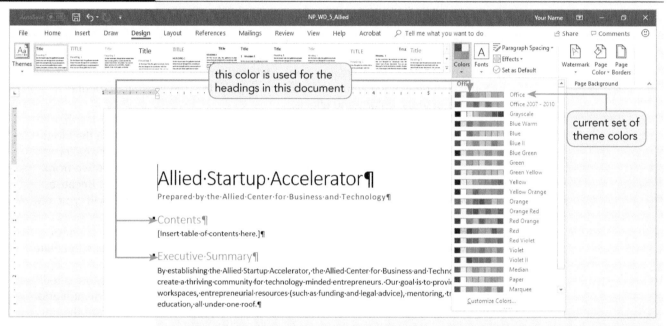

Each set of theme colors contains eight colors, with each assigned to specific elements. For example, the third color from the left is used for headings. The remaining colors are used for other types of elements, such as hyperlinks, page borders, shading, and so on.

Trouble? If you see additional theme colors at the top of the gallery under the "Custom" heading, then custom theme colors have been created and stored on your computer.

5. Move the pointer over the options in the gallery to observe the Live Preview of the colors in the document.

6. Near the top of the gallery, click the **Grayscale** color set, which is the third from the top. The document headings are now formatted in gray.

7. Save the document.

The new colors you selected affect only the report document. Your changes do not affect the Office theme that was installed with Word. Next, Hayden asks you to customize the document theme further by changing the theme fonts.

Changing the Theme Fonts

As with theme colors, you can change the theme fonts in a document to suit your needs. Each theme uses two coordinating fonts—one for the headings and one for the body text. In some themes, the same font is used for the headings and the body text. When changing the theme fonts, you can select from all the font combinations available in any of the themes installed with Word.

To select a different set of theme fonts for the document:

▶ **1.** In the Document Formatting group, move the pointer over the **Fonts** button. A ScreenTip is displayed, indicating that the current fonts are Calibri Light for headings and Calibri for body text.

▶ **2.** Click the **Fonts** button. The Theme Fonts gallery opens, displaying the heading and body font combinations for each theme.

▶ **3.** Scroll down to review the fonts. Hayden prefers the Franklin Gothic set of theme fonts, which includes Franklin Gothic Medium for headings and Franklin Gothic Book for the body text.

▶ **4.** In the Theme Fonts gallery, point to **Franklin Gothic** to display a Live Preview in the document. See Figure 5–8.

| Figure 5–8 | Theme Fonts gallery |

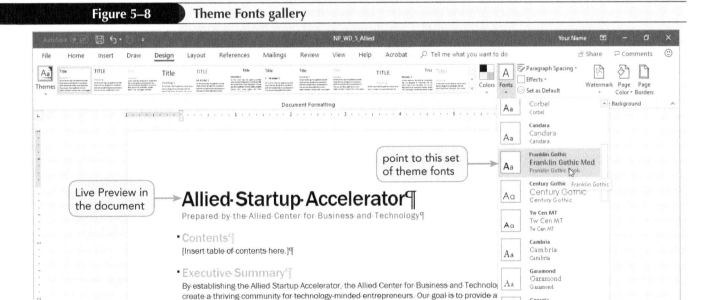

▶ **5.** Click **Franklin Gothic**. The Theme Fonts gallery closes, and the new fonts are applied to the document.

▶ **6.** Save the document.

The changes you have made to the theme fonts for the document do not affect the original Office theme that was installed with Word and that is available to all documents. To make your new combination of theme fonts and theme colors available to other documents, you can save it as a new, custom theme.

Creating Custom Combinations of Theme Colors and Fonts

The theme color and font combinations installed with Word were created by Microsoft designers who are experts in creating harmonious-looking documents. It's usually best to stick with these preset combinations rather than trying to create your own set. However, in some situations you might need to create a customized combination of theme colors or fonts. When you do so, that set is saved as part of Word so that you can use it in other documents.

To create a custom set of theme colors, you click the Colors button in the Document Formatting group on the Design tab and then click Customize Colors to open the Create New Theme Colors dialog box, in which you can select colors for different theme elements and enter a descriptive name for the new set of theme colors. The custom set of theme colors will be displayed as an option in the Theme Colors gallery. To delete a custom set of colors from the Theme Colors gallery, right-click the custom color set in the gallery, click Delete, and then click Yes.

To create a custom set of heading and body fonts, you click the Fonts button in the Document Formatting group on the Design tab, click Customize Fonts, select the heading and body fonts, and then enter a name for the new set of fonts in the Name box. The custom set of theme fonts is displayed as an option in the Theme Fonts gallery. To delete a custom set of fonts from the Theme Fonts gallery, right-click the custom font set in the gallery, click Delete, and then click Yes.

Saving a Custom Theme

You can save a custom theme to any folder, but when you save a custom theme to the default location—the Document Themes subfolder inside the Templates folder—it is displayed as an option in the Themes gallery. To delete a custom theme saved in the Document Themes folder, click the Themes button on the Design tab, right-click the theme, click Delete, and then click Yes.

Hayden asks you to save his combination of theme fonts and theme colors as a new custom theme, using "ACBT," the acronym for "Allied Center for Business and Technology," as part of the file name.

To save the new custom theme:

 ▶ **1.** In the Document Formatting group, click the **Themes** button, and then click **Save Current Theme**. The Save Current Theme dialog box opens. See Figure 5–9.

| Figure 5–9 | Save Current Theme dialog box |

a theme saved to this location appears as an option in the Themes gallery

default theme name

file will be saved as an Office Theme file type

The Document Themes folder is the default location. The default theme name is "Theme1." You can select a different save location and enter a more meaningful theme name.

▶ **2.** Navigate to the save location specified by your instructor.

▶ **3.** Click in the File name box, type **NP_WD_5_Theme** and then click the **Save** button. The Save Current Theme dialog box closes.

Hayden plans to use the new theme to help standardize the look of all documents created in his department. When he is ready to apply it to a document, he can click the Themes button in the Document Formatting group on the Design tab, click Browse for Themes, navigate to the folder containing the custom theme, and then select the theme. If he wants to be able to access his theme from the Themes gallery instead, he will need to save it to the Document Themes folder first.

Hayden likes the document's new look, but he wants to make some additional changes. First, he wants to select a different style set.

Selecting a Style Set

Recall that a style is a set of formatting options that you can apply to a specific text element in a document, such as a document's title, heading, or body text. So far, you have used only the default set of styles available in the Style gallery on the Home tab. You can access 16 additional style sets, or groups of styles, in the Style Set gallery, which is located in the Document Formatting group on the Design tab.

Each style set has a Normal style, a Heading 1 style, a Heading 2 style, and so on, but the formatting settings associated with each style vary from one style set to another. See Figure 5–10.

Figure 5–10 Styles from two different style sets

Default Set	Title Style
	Heading 1 style
	Heading 2 style
	Normal style
Shaded Style Set	TITLE STYLE
	HEADING 1 STYLE
	HEADING 2 STYLE
	Normal style

In the Shaded style set shown in Figure 5–10, the Heading 1 style includes a thick band of color with a contrasting font color. The main feature of the Heading 1 style of the default style set is simply a blue font color. Note that Figure 5–10 shows the styles as they look with the default theme fonts and colors for a new document. The default style set is currently applied to the report document, but because you've changed the theme fonts and colors in the document, the colors and fonts in the document are different from what is shown in Figure 5–10. However, the styles in the report document still have the same basic look as the default styles shown in the figure.

Hayden asks you to select a style set for the report document that makes the Heading 1 text darker, so the headings are easier to read. Before you do that, you'll review the styles currently available in the Style gallery on the Home tab. Then, after you select a new style set, you'll go back to the Style gallery to examine the new styles.

To review the styles in the Style gallery and select a new style set for the document:

▶ **1.** On the ribbon, click the **Home** tab.

▶ **2.** In the Styles group, click the **More** button ⟱, and then review the set of styles currently available in the Style gallery. Note that the icon for the Heading 1 style indicates that it applies a light gray font color.

▶ **3.** On the ribbon, click the **Design** tab.

▶ **4.** In the Document Formatting group, click the **More** button ⟱ to open the Style Set gallery. Move the pointer across the icons in the gallery to display their ScreenTips and to observe the Live Previews in the document.

▶ **5.** Point to the **Lines (Stylish)** style set, which is on the far-right side of the top row. In the Lines (Stylish) style set, the Heading 1 style applies a black font color, with a light gray line that spans the width of the document. See Figure 5–11.

Figure 5–11   Live Preview of the Lines (Stylish) style set

preview of the Title style in the Lines (Stylish) style set

preview of the Heading 1 style in the Lines (Stylish) style set

preview of the Normal style in the Lines (Stylish) style set

Lines (Stylish) style set

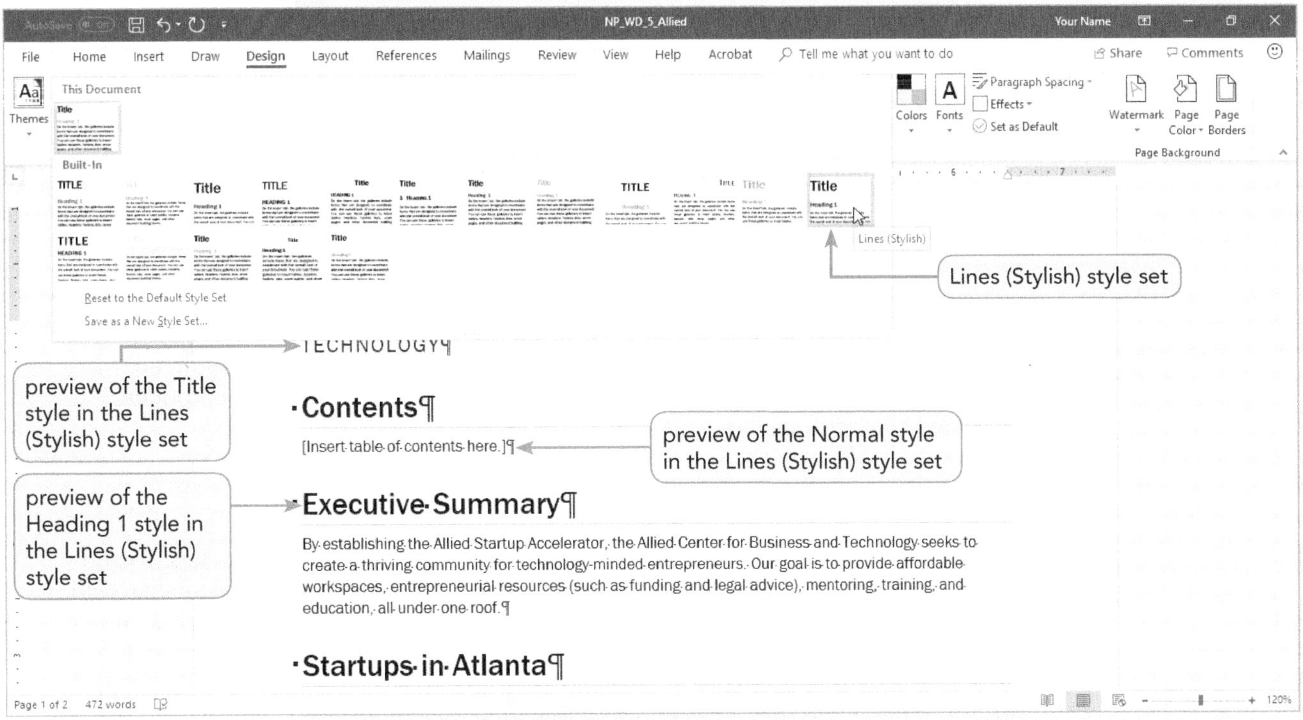

Notice that the theme fonts you specified earlier—Franklin Gothic Medium for headings and Franklin Gothic Book for body text—are still applied, as are the Grayscale theme colors.

6. Click the **Lines (Stylish)** style set. The styles in the document change to reflect the styles in the Lines (Stylish) style set. You can verify this by looking at the Style gallery on the Home tab.

7. On the ribbon, click the **Home** tab.

8. In the Styles group, click the **More** button ⤓ to review the styles available in the Style gallery. The icon for the Heading 1 style indicates that it now applies a black font color. The style also applies a light gray underline, although that is not visible in the Style gallery icon.

9. Click anywhere in the document to close the Style gallery, and then save the document.

The Set as Default Button: A Note of Caution

The Set as Default button in the Document Formatting group on the Design tab saves the document's current formatting settings as the default for any new blank documents you create in Word. In other words, it saves the current formatting settings to the Normal template. You might find this a tempting option, but, as you will learn in Session 5.2, when working with styles, modifying the Normal template is almost never a good idea. Instead, a better option is to save a document with the formatting you like as a new template, which you can then use as the basis for future documents. Exercise similar caution with the Set as Default button in the Font dialog box, which allows you to change the default font for the Normal template.

Customizing Styles

The ability to select a new style set gives you a lot of flexibility when formatting a document. However, sometimes you will want to customize an individual style to better suit your needs. To do so, you can either modify the style or update it. When you modify a style, you open the Modify Style dialog box, where you select formatting attributes to add to the style. When you update a style, you select text in the document that is already formatted with the style, apply new formatting to the text, and then update the style to incorporate the new formatting. Updating a style is usually the better choice because it allows you to see the results of your formatting choices in the document, before you change the style itself.

Hayden asks you to update the Heading 1 style for the report by expanding the character spacing and applying italic formatting. You will begin by applying these changes to a paragraph that is currently formatted with the Heading 1 style. Then you can update the Heading 1 style to match the new formatting. As a result, all the paragraphs formatted with the Heading 1 style will be updated to incorporate expanded character spacing and italic formatting.

Changing Character Spacing

The term **character spacing** refers to the space between individual characters. To add emphasis to text, you can expand or contract the spacing between characters. As with line and paragraph spacing, space between characters is measured in points, with one point equal to 1/72 of an inch. To adjust character spacing for selected text, click the Font Dialog Box Launcher in the Font group on the Home tab, and then click the Advanced tab in the Font dialog box. Of the numerous settings available on this tab, you'll find two especially useful.

First, the Spacing box allows you to choose Normal spacing (which is the default character spacing for the Normal style), Expanded spacing (with the characters farther apart than with the Normal setting), and Condensed spacing (with the characters closer together than with the Normal setting). With both Expanded and Condensed spacing, you can specify the number of points between characters.

Second, the Kerning for fonts check box allows you to adjust the spacing between characters to make them look like they are spaced evenly. Kerning is helpful when you are working with large font sizes, which can sometimes cause evenly spaced characters to appear unevenly spaced. Selecting the Kerning for fonts check box ensures that the spacing is adjusted automatically.

To add expanded character spacing and italic formatting to a paragraph formatted with the Heading 1 style:

▶ **1.** In the document, scroll down if necessary, and select the **Executive Summary** heading, which is formatted with the Heading 1 style.

▶ **2.** Make sure the Home tab is selected on the ribbon.

▶ **3.** In the Font group, click the **Font Dialog Box Launcher**. The Font dialog box opens.

▶ **4.** Click the **Advanced** tab. The Character Spacing settings at the top of this tab reflect the style settings for the currently selected text. The Spacing box is set to Normal. The more advanced options, located in the OpenType Features section, allow you to fine-tune the appearance of characters.

▶ **5.** Click the **Spacing arrow**, and then click **Expanded**. See Figure 5–12.

Figure 5–12   **Changing character spacing in the Font dialog box**

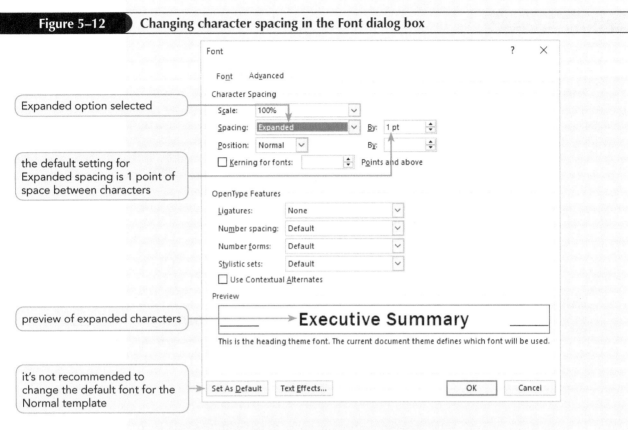

Expanded option selected

the default setting for Expanded spacing is 1 point of space between characters

preview of expanded characters

it's not recommended to change the default font for the Normal template

The By box next to the Spacing box indicates that each character is separated from the other by 1 point of space. You could increase the point setting, but in the current document, 1 point is fine. The Preview section shows a sample of the expanded character spacing.

Next, you need to apply italic formatting, which you could do from the Font group on the Home tab. But since you have the Font dialog box open, you'll do it from the Font tab in the Font dialog box instead.

TIP

Text formatted as hidden is visible only when nonprinting characters are displayed.

6. In the Font dialog box, click the **Font** tab.

   Here you can apply most of the settings available in the Font group on the Home tab and a few that are not available in the Font group—such as colored underlines and small caps (smaller versions of uppercase letters). You can also hide text from view by selecting the Hidden check box.

7. In the Font style box, click **Italic**. The Preview section of the Font tab shows a preview of the italic formatting applied to the "Executive Summary" heading. See Figure 5–13.

Figure 5–13   **Applying italic formatting to text using the Font dialog box**

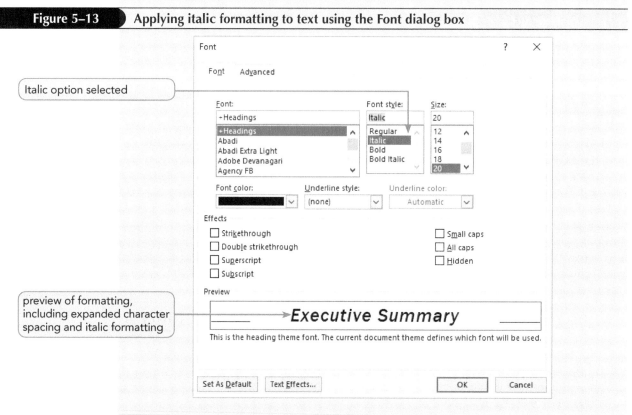

The other font attributes associated with the Heading 1 style are also visible on the Font tab.

▶ **8.** Click **OK** to close the Font dialog box. The selected heading is now italicized, with the individual characters spread slightly farther apart.

▶ **9.** Click anywhere in the "Executive Summary" heading to deselect the text, and then save the document.

Now that the selected heading is formatted the way you want, you can update the Heading 1 style to match it. When working with styles, it's helpful to open the Styles pane to see more information about the styles in the current style set, so you'll do that next.

Displaying the Styles Pane

The Styles pane shows you more styles than are displayed in the Style gallery. You can click a style in the Styles pane to apply it to selected text, just as you would click a style in the Style gallery.

The Styles pane provides detailed information about each style. In particular, it differentiates between character styles, paragraph styles, and linked styles. A **character style** contains formatting options that affect the appearance of individual characters, such as font style, font color, font size, bold, italic, and underline. When you click a character style, it formats the word that contains the insertion point or, if text is selected in the document, any selected characters.

A **paragraph style** contains all the character formatting options as well as formatting options that affect the paragraph's appearance—including line spacing, text alignment, tab stops, and borders. When you click a paragraph style, it formats the entire paragraph that contains the insertion point, or, if text is selected in the document, it formats all selected paragraphs (even paragraphs in which just one character is selected).

A **linked style** contains both character and paragraph formatting options. If you click in a paragraph or select a paragraph and then apply a linked style, both the paragraph styles and character styles are applied to the entire paragraph. If you apply a linked style to a selected word or group of words rather than to an entire paragraph, only the character styles for that linked style are applied to the selected text; the paragraph styles are not applied to the paragraph itself. All of the heading styles in Word are linked styles.

To open the Styles pane to review information about the styles in the current style set:

▶ **1.** Make sure the Home tab is selected on the ribbon.

▶ **2.** In the Styles group, click the **Styles Dialog Box Launcher**. The Styles pane opens on the right side of the document window. See Figure 5–14.

Figure 5–14   Styles pane

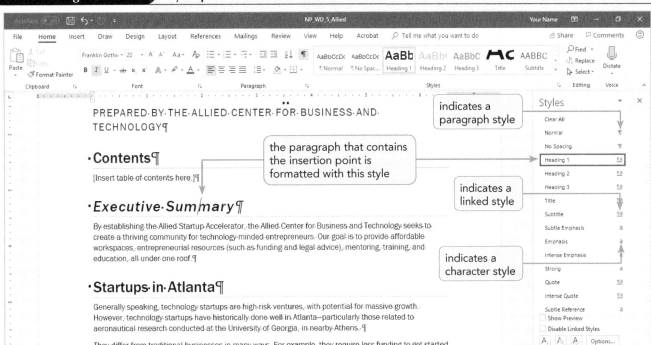

The outline around the Heading 1 style indicates that the insertion point is currently located in a paragraph formatted with that style. A paragraph symbol to the right of a style name indicates a paragraph style, a lowercase letter "a" indicates a character style, and a combination of both indicates a linked style. You can display even more information about a style by moving the pointer over the style name in the Styles pane.

TIP

If the Styles pane is floating over the top of the document window, you can double-click the pane's title bar to dock it on the right side of the document window.

▶ **3.** In the Styles pane, move the pointer over **Heading 1**. An arrow is displayed to the right of the Heading 1 style name, and a ScreenTip with detailed information about the Heading 1 style opens below the style name.

The information in the ScreenTip relates only to the formatting applied by default with the Heading 1 style; it makes no mention of italic formatting or expanded character spacing. Although you applied these formatting changes to the "Executive Summary" heading, they are not yet part of the Heading 1 style.

You'll incorporate the new formatting into the Heading 1 style in the next section, when you update the style.

Updating a Style

Word is set up to save all customized styles to the current document by default. In fact, when you update a style, you don't even have a choice about where to save it—the updated style is automatically saved to the current document, rather than to the current template. If for some reason you needed to save a customized style to the current template instead, you would need to modify the style using the Modify Style dialog box, where you could then select the New documents based on this template button to save the modified style to the current template.

INSIGHT

Preserving the Normal Template

Unless you created a document based on an Office.com template, the current template for any document is probably the Normal template. Any changes you make to the Normal template will affect all new, blank documents that you create in Word in the future, so altering the Normal template is not something you should do casually. This is especially important if you are working on a shared computer at school or work. In that case, you should never change the Normal template unless you have been specifically instructed to do so. Many organizations even take the precaution of configuring their networked computers to make changing the Normal template impossible.

If you want to make customized styles available in other documents, you can always save the current document as a new template. All future documents based on your new template will contain your new styles. Meanwhile, the Normal template will remain unaffected by the new styles.

Next, you'll use the Styles pane to update the Heading 1 style to include italic formatting with expanded character spacing.

REFERENCE

Updating a Style

- On the ribbon, click the Home tab.
- In the Styles group, click the Styles Dialog Box Launcher to display the Styles pane.
- In the document, apply formatting to a paragraph or group of characters.
- Click in the formatted paragraph (if you are updating a paragraph or linked style) or in the formatted group of characters (if you are updating a character style).
- In the Styles pane, right-click the style you want to update to display a shortcut menu.
- Click Update *Style* to Match Selection (where *Style* is the name of the style you want to update).

To update the Heading 1 style:

The insertion point must be located in the "Executive Summary" heading to ensure that you update the Heading 1 style with the correct formatting.

▶ **1.** In the document, make sure the insertion point is located in the paragraph containing the "Executive Summary" heading, which is formatted with the Heading 1 style.

▶ **2.** In the Styles pane, right-click **Heading 1**. A menu opens with options related to working with the Heading 1 style. See Figure 5–15.

Figure 5–15 | **Heading 1 style menu**

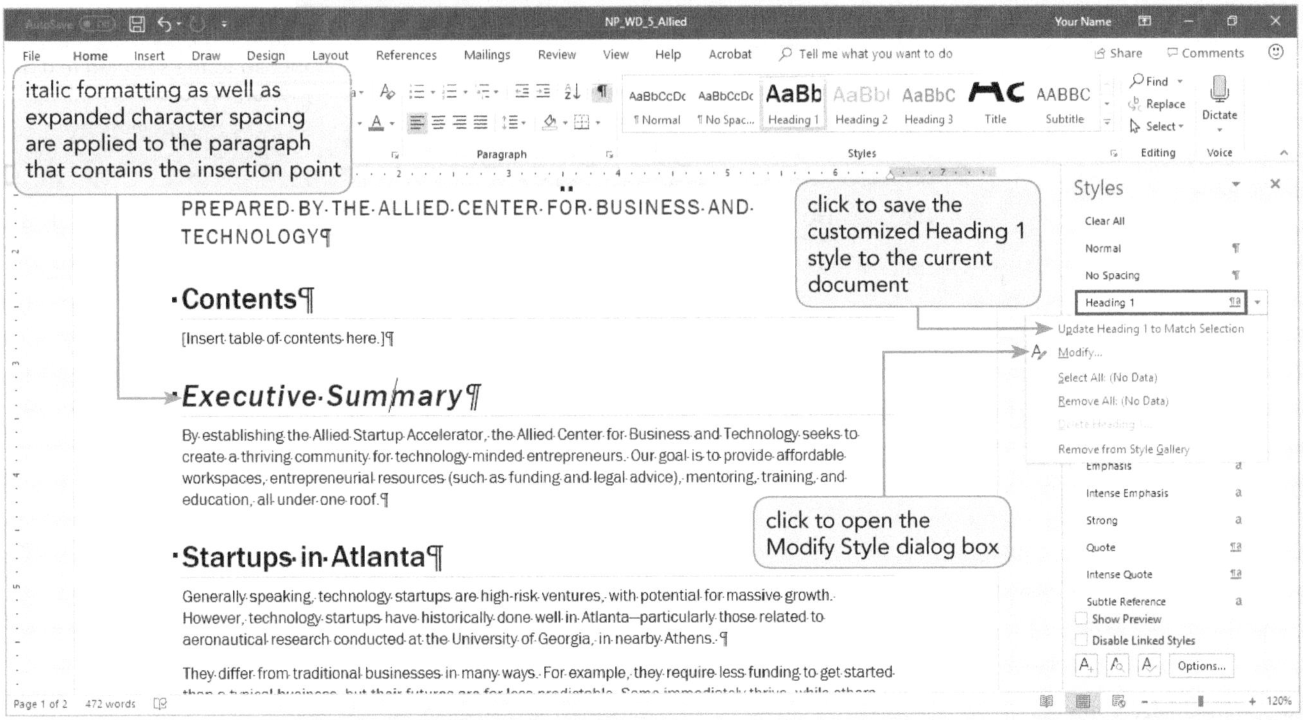

italic formatting as well as expanded character spacing are applied to the paragraph that contains the insertion point

PREPARED·BY·THE·ALLIED·CENTER·FOR·BUSINESS·AND· TECHNOLOGY¶

·**Contents**¶

[Insert·table·of·contents·here.]¶

Executive·Summary¶

By·establishing·the·Allied·Startup·Accelerator,·the·Allied·Center·for·Business·and·Technology·seeks·to· create·a·thriving·community·for·technology-minded·entrepreneurs.·Our·goal·is·to·provide·affordable· workspaces,·entrepreneurial·resources·(such·as·funding·and·legal·advice),·mentoring,·training,·and· education,·all·under·one·roof.¶

·**Startups·in·Atlanta**¶

Generally·speaking,·technology·startups·are·high-risk·ventures,·with·potential·for·massive·growth.· However,·technology·startups·have·historically·done·well·in·Atlanta—particularly·those·related·to· aeronautical·research·conducted·at·the·University·of·Georgia,·in·nearby·Athens.·¶

They·differ·from·traditional·businesses·in·many·ways.·For·example,·they·require·less·funding·to·get·started·

click to save the customized Heading 1 style to the current document

click to open the Modify Style dialog box

3. Click **Update Heading 1 to Match Selection**. The Heading 1 style is updated to reflect the changes you made to the "Executive Summary" heading. As a result, all the headings in the document formatted in the Heading 1 style now have italic formatting with expanded character spacing.

4. Save the document. The updated Heading 1 style is saved along with the document. No other documents are affected by this change to the Heading 1 style.

You can also use the Styles pane to create a new style for a document. You will do that in the next session.

Session 5.1 Quick Check

REVIEW

1. What is a template?

2. Suppose you want to move through a document one graphic at a time. Should you use the Navigation pane or the Go To tab in the Find and Replace dialog box?

3. Explain how to change a document's theme fonts.

4. Explain how to select a new style set.

5. What template is applied to each new document by default?

6. What is the difference between a character style and a paragraph style?

Session 5.2 Visual Overview:

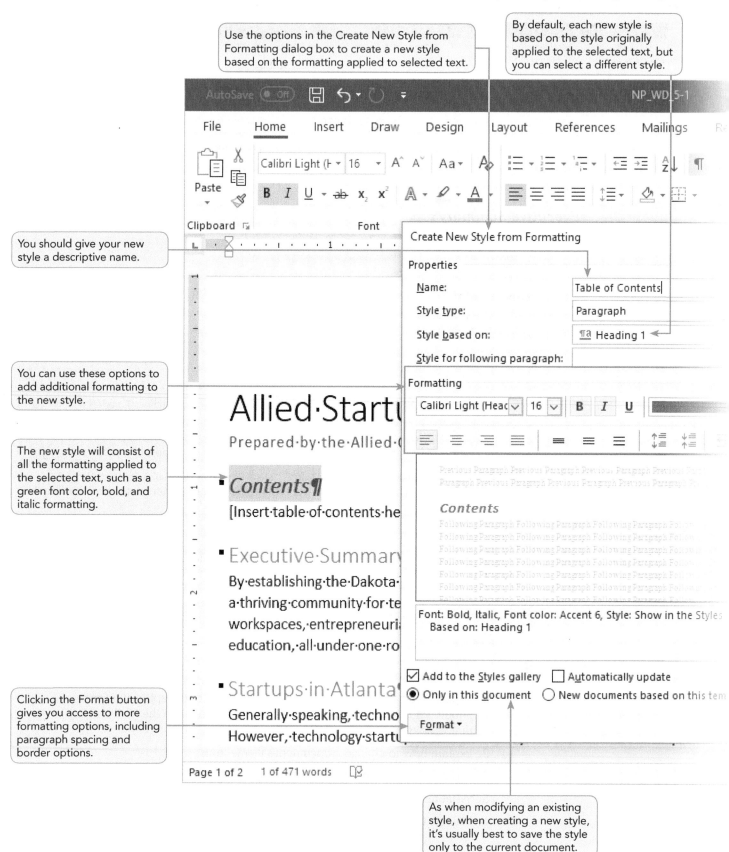

Use the options in the Create New Style from Formatting dialog box to create a new style based on the formatting applied to selected text.

By default, each new style is based on the style originally applied to the selected text, but you can select a different style.

You should give your new style a descriptive name.

You can use these options to add additional formatting to the new style.

The new style will consist of all the formatting applied to the selected text, such as a green font color, bold, and italic formatting.

Clicking the Format button gives you access to more formatting options, including paragraph spacing and border options.

As when modifying an existing style, when creating a new style, it's usually best to save the style only to the current document.

Creating a New Style

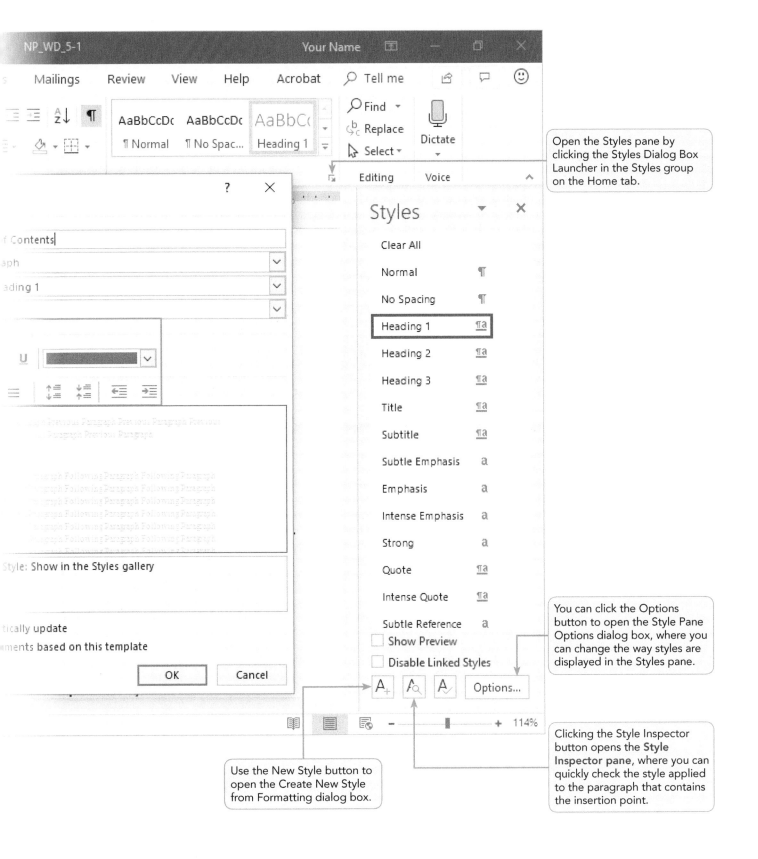

Open the Styles pane by clicking the Styles Dialog Box Launcher in the Styles group on the Home tab.

You can click the Options button to open the Style Pane Options dialog box, where you can change the way styles are displayed in the Styles pane.

Use the New Style button to open the Create New Style from Formatting dialog box.

Clicking the Style Inspector button opens the **Style Inspector pane**, where you can quickly check the style applied to the paragraph that contains the insertion point.

Creating a New Style

Creating a new style is similar to updating a style, except that instead of updating an existing style to match the formatting of selected text, you save the text's formatting as a new style. By default, a new style is saved to the current document. You can choose to save a new style to the current template, but, as explained earlier, that is rarely advisable.

To begin creating a new style, select text with formatting you want to save, and then click the New Style button in the lower-left corner of the Styles pane. This opens the Create New Style from Formatting dialog box, where you can assign the new style a name and adjust other settings.

Remember that all text in your document has a style applied to it, whether it is the default Normal style or a style you applied. When you create a new style based on the formatting of selected text, the new style is based on the style originally applied to the selected text. That means the new style retains a connection to the original style, so that if you make modifications to the original style, these modifications will also be applied to the new style.

For example, suppose you need to create a new style that will be used exclusively for formatting the heading "Budget" in all upcoming reports. You could start by selecting text formatted with the Heading 1 style, then change the font color of the selected text to purple, and then save the formatting of the selected text as a new style named "Budget." Later, if you update the Heading 1 style—perhaps by adding italic formatting—the text in the document that is formatted with the Budget style will also be updated to include italic formatting because it is based on the Heading 1 style. Note that the opposite is not true—changes to the new style do not affect the style on which it is based.

When creating a new style, you must also consider what will happen when the insertion point is in a paragraph formatted with your new style, and you then press ENTER to start a new paragraph. Typically, that new paragraph is formatted in the Normal style, but you can choose to have a different style applied if you prefer. You make this selection using the Style for following paragraph box in the Create New Style from Formatting dialog box.

In most cases, any new styles you create will be paragraph styles. However, you can choose to make your new style a linked style or a character style instead.

> **TIP**
>
> To break the link between a style and the style it is based on, click the Style based on arrow in the Create New Style from Formatting dialog box, and then click (no style).

REFERENCE

Creating a New Style

- Select the text with the formatting you want to save as a new style.
- In the lower-left corner of the Styles pane, click the New Style button to open the Create New Style from Formatting dialog box.
- Type a name for the new style in the Name box.
- Make sure the Style type box contains the correct style type. In most cases, Paragraph style is the best choice.
- Verify that the Style based on box displays the style on which you want to base your new style.
- Click the Style for following paragraph arrow, and then click the style you want to use. Normal is usually the best choice.
- To save the new style to the current document, verify that the Only in this document option button is selected; or to save the style to the current template, click the New documents based on this template option button.
- Click OK.

Hayden wants you to create a new paragraph style for the "Contents" heading. It should look just like the current Heading 1 style, with the addition of small caps formatting. He asks you to base the new style on the Heading 1 style and to select the Normal style as the style to be applied to any paragraph that follows a paragraph formatted with the new style.

To format the "Contents" heading in small caps:

▶ **1.** If you took a break after the last session, make sure the NP_WD_5_Allied. docx document is open in Print Layout view with the nonprinting characters and the ruler displayed. Confirm that the document Zoom level is set at 120% and that the Styles pane is docked on the right side of the document window.

▶ **2.** Make sure the Home tab is selected on the ribbon.

▶ **3.** In the document, select the **Contents** heading.

▶ **4.** In the Font group, click the **Font Dialog Box Launcher**, and then, in the Font dialog box, click the **Font** tab, if necessary.

▶ **5.** In the Effects section, click the **Small caps** check box to select it. See Figure 5–16.

Figure 5–16   **Formatting the "Contents" heading**

▶ **6.** Click **OK**. The Font dialog box closes, and the "Contents" heading is formatted in small caps.

Now that the text is formatted the way you want, you can save its formatting as a new style.

To save the formatting of the "Contents" heading as a new style:

▶ **1.** Verify that the "Contents" heading is still selected.

▶ **2.** In the lower-left corner of the Styles pane, click the **New Style** button ⓐ. The Create New Style from Formatting dialog box opens. A default name for the new style, "Style1," is selected in the Name box. The name "Style1" is also displayed in the Style for following paragraph box.

3. Type **Contents** to replace the default style name with the new one. The Style type box contains Paragraph by default, which is the type of style you want to create. The Style based on box indicates that the new Contents style is based on the Heading 1 style, which is also what you want. Notice that the Style for following paragraph box is now blank. You need to select the Normal style.

4. Click the **Style for following paragraph arrow**, and then click **Normal**. See Figure 5–17.

Figure 5–17   Creating a new style

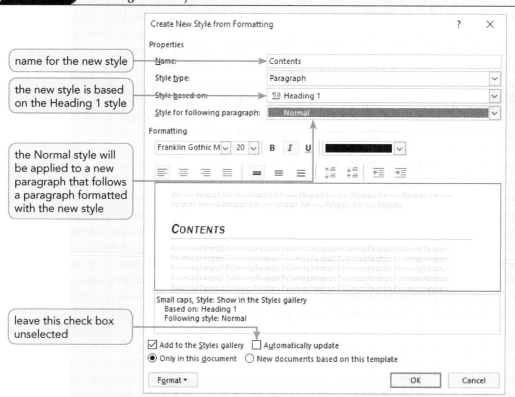

- name for the new style
- the new style is based on the Heading 1 style
- the Normal style will be applied to a new paragraph that follows a paragraph formatted with the new style
- leave this check box unselected

---

5. In the lower-left corner of the dialog box, verify that the Only in this document button is selected.

Note that, by default, the Automatically update check box is not selected. As a general rule, you should not select this check box because it can produce unpredictable results in future documents based on the same template.

If you plan to use a new style frequently, it's helpful to assign a keyboard shortcut to it. Then you can apply the style to selected text simply by pressing the keyboard shortcut.

TIP

To assign a keyboard shortcut to an existing style, right-click the style in the Styles pane, click Modify, click the Format button, and then click Shortcut key.

6. In the lower-left corner of the Create New Style from Formatting dialog box, click the **Format** button, and then click **Shortcut key** to open the Customize Keyboard dialog box. If you wanted to assign a keyboard shortcut to the Contents style, you would click in the Press new shortcut key box, press a combination of keys not assigned to any other function, and then click the Assign button. For now, you can close the Customize Keyboard dialog box without making any changes.

7. Click **Close**. You return to the Create New Style from Formatting dialog box.

8. Click **OK**. The Create New Style from Formatting dialog box closes. The new Contents style is added to the Style gallery and to the Styles pane. See Figure 5–18.

Figure 5–18   Contents style added to Style gallery and Styles pane

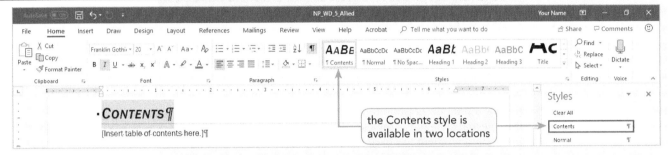

the Contents style is available in two locations

After you update a style or create a new one, you can create a custom style set that contains the new or updated style.

9. On the ribbon, click the **Design** tab.

10. In the Document Formatting group, click the **More** button ⟱, and then click **Save as a New Style Set**. The Save as a New Style Set dialog box opens, with the QuickStyles folder selected as the save location by default. Only style sets saved to the QuickStyles folder will appear in the Style Set gallery.

In this case, you don't actually want to create a new style set, so you can close the Save as a New Style Set dialog box.

11. Click **Cancel**, and then save the document.

Managing Your Styles

If you create a lot of styles, the Style gallery can quickly become overcrowded. To remove a style from the Style gallery without deleting the style itself, right-click the style in the Style gallery, and then click Remove from Style Gallery.

To delete a style entirely, open the Styles pane, and then right-click the style. What happens next depends on the type of style you are trying to delete. If the style was based on the Normal style, you can click Delete *Style* (where *Style* is the name of the style you want to delete), and then click Yes. If the style was based on any other style, you can click Revert to *Style* (where *Style* is the style that the style you want to delete was based on), and then click Yes.

If you create a new style and then paste text formatted with your style in a different document, your new style will be displayed in that document's Style gallery and Styles pane. This means that a document containing text imported from multiple documents can end up with a lot of different styles. In that case, you'll probably reformat the document to use only a few styles of your choosing. But what do you do about the remaining, unused styles? You could delete them, but that can be time-consuming. It's sometimes easier to hide the styles that are not currently in use in the document. At the bottom of the Styles pane, click the Options button to open the Style Pane Options dialog box, click the Select styles to show arrow, and then click In current document.

The styles used in the report document are relatively simple. However, in a long document with many styles, it's easy to lose track of the style applied to each paragraph and the formatting associated with each style. In that case, it's important to know how to display additional information about the document's formatting.

Displaying Information About Styles and Formatting

When you need to learn more about a document's formatting—perhaps because you're revising a document created by someone else—you should start by opening the Styles pane. To quickly determine which style is applied to a paragraph, you can click a paragraph (or select it) and then look to see which style is selected in the Styles pane. To display a brief description of the formatting associated with that style, you can point to the selected style in the Styles pane. However, if you need to check numerous paragraphs in a long document, it's easier to use the Style Inspector pane, which remains open while you scroll through the document and displays only the style for the paragraph that currently contains the insertion point. To see a complete list of all the formatting applied to a paragraph, you can use the **Reveal Formatting pane**. Within the Reveal Formatting pane, you can also choose to compare the formatting applied to two different paragraphs.

Inspecting Styles

You can use the Style Inspector to examine the styles attached to each of the paragraphs in a document. When you are using the Style Inspector, it's also helpful to display the Home tab on the ribbon so the Style gallery is visible.

> **To use the Style Inspector pane to examine the styles in the document:**
>
> ▶ **1.** On the ribbon, click the **Home** tab.
>
> ▶ **2.** On page 1, click anywhere in the **[Insert table of contents here.]** paragraph. The Normal style is selected in both the Style gallery and the Styles pane, indicating that the paragraph is formatted with the Normal style.
>
> ▶ **3.** At the bottom of the Styles pane, click the **Style Inspector** button [icon]. The Style Inspector pane opens and is positioned next to the Styles pane. See Figure 5–19.

Figure 5–19   Style Inspector pane

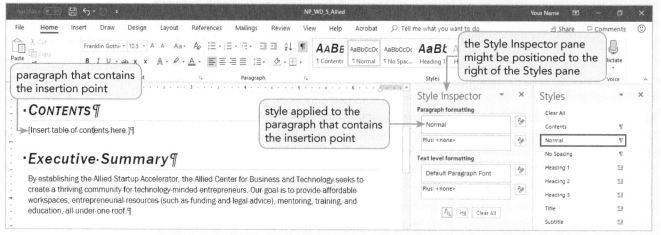

Trouble? If the Style Inspector pane on your computer is floating over the top of the document window, drag it to position it the left of the Styles pane, and then double-click the pane's title bar to dock the Style Inspector pane next to the Styles pane.

In the Style Inspector pane, the top box under "Paragraph formatting" displays the name of the style applied to the paragraph that currently contains the insertion point.

4. Press **CTRL+↓**. The insertion point moves down to the next paragraph, which contains the "Executive Summary" heading. The Style Inspector pane tells you that this paragraph is formatted with the Heading 1 style.

5. Press **CTRL+↓** as necessary to move the insertion point down through the paragraphs of the document, observing the style names displayed in the Style Inspector pane as well as the styles selected in the Styles pane. Note that the bulleted paragraphs below the "Our Board of Directors" heading are formatted with the List Paragraph style. This style is applied automatically when you format paragraphs using the Bullets button in the Paragraph group on the Home tab.

6. Scroll up, and select the paragraph **[Insert table of contents here.]**.

Finding Styles

Suppose you want to find all the paragraphs in a document formatted with a specific style. One option is to right-click the style in the Styles pane, and then click Select All *Number* Instances, where *Number* is the number of paragraphs in the document formatted with the style.

Another way to find paragraphs formatted with a particular style is by using the Find tab in the Find and Replace dialog box. If necessary, click the More button to display the Format button in the lower-left corner of the Find tab. Click the Format button, click Style, select the style you want in the Find Style dialog box, and then click OK. If you want to find specific text formatted with the style you selected, you can type the text in the Find what box on the Find tab, and then click Find Next to find the first instance. If, instead, you want to find any paragraph formatted with the style, leave the Find what box blank.

You can also use the Find and Replace dialog box to find paragraphs formatted with one style and then apply a different style to those paragraphs. On the Replace tab, click in the Find what box and use the Format button to select the style you want to find. Then, click in the Replace with box and use the Format button to select the style you want to use as a replacement. Click Find Next to find the first instance of the style, and then click Replace to apply the replacement style. As you've probably guessed, you can also type text in the Find what and Replace with boxes to find text formatted with a specific style and replace it with text formatted in a different style.

Next, Hayden wants you to use the Reveal Formatting panes to learn more about the formatting applied by the Normal and Heading 2 styles.

Examining and Comparing Formatting in the Reveal Formatting Pane

You access the Reveal Formatting pane by clicking a button in the Style Inspector pane. Because the Reveal Formatting pane describes only formatting details without mentioning styles, it's helpful to keep the Style Inspector pane open while you use the Reveal Formatting pane.

To examine formatting details using the Reveal Formatting pane:

▶ **1.** At the bottom of the Style Inspector pane, click the **Reveal Formatting** button . The Reveal Formatting pane opens, displaying detailed information about the formatting applied to the selected paragraph. It is positioned to the right of the Styles pane in Figure 5–20, but on your computer it might be to the left of the Styles pane or to the left of the Style Inspector.

Figure 5–20	Displaying formatting details in the Reveal Formatting pane

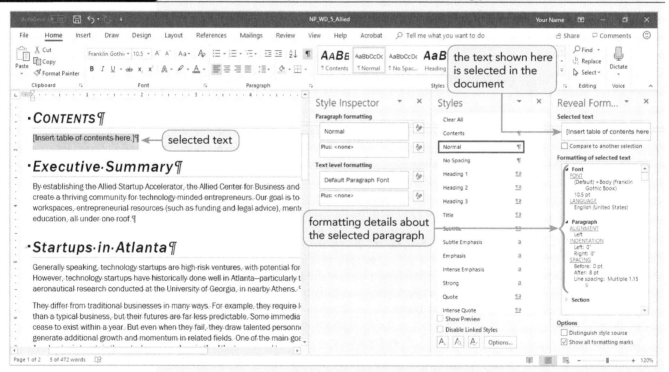

Trouble? If the Reveal Formatting pane on your computer is floating over the top of the document window, double-click the pane's title bar to dock the Reveal Formatting pane next to the other two panes.

The Formatting of selected text box displays information about the formatting applied to the paragraph that contains the insertion point. Note that this information includes no mention of the style used to apply this formatting, but you can still see the style's name, Normal, displayed in the Style Inspector pane.

Now that you have the Reveal Formatting pane open, you can use it to compare the formatting of one paragraph to another paragraph. Hayden asks you to compare text formatted with the Normal style to text formatted with the Heading 2 style.

To compare the formatting of one paragraph to another:

1. In the Reveal Formatting pane, click the **Compare to another selection** check box to select it. The options in the Reveal Formatting pane change to allow you to compare the formatting of one paragraph to that of another. Under Selected text, both text boxes display the selected text, "[Insert table of contents here.]" This tells you that, currently, the formatting applied to the selected text is being compared to itself.

   Now you'll compare this paragraph to one formatted with the Heading 2 style.

2. In the document, scroll down to page 2 and select the heading text **Saturn and Sun Investments**, which is formatted with the Heading 2 style. The text "Saturn and Sun Investments" is displayed in the Reveal Formatting pane, in the text box below "[Insert table of contents here.]" The Formatting differences section displays information about the formatting applied to the two different paragraphs. See Figure 5–21.

Figure 5–21	Comparing one paragraph's formatting with another's

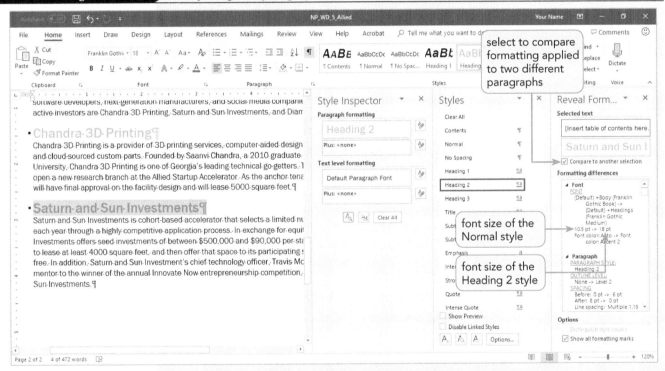

TIP

Text formatted in a white font is not visible in the text boxes at the top of the Reveal Formatting pane. To use the Reveal Formatting pane with white text, temporarily format it in black.

The information in the Reveal Formatting pane is very detailed. But, generally, if you see two settings separated by a hyphen and a greater than symbol, the item on the right relates to the text in the bottom box. For example, in the Font section, you see "10.5 pt -> 18 pt." This tells you that the text in the top text box, "[Insert table of contents here.]," is formatted in a 10.5-point font, whereas the text in the bottom text box, "Saturn and Sun Investments," is formatted in an 18-point font.

The Paragraph section of the Reveal Formatting pane provides some information about two important default settings included with all heading styles in Word—line and page break settings.

Reviewing Line and Page Break Settings

By default, all the heading styles in Word are set up to ensure that a heading is never separated from the paragraph that follows it. For example, suppose you have a one-page document that includes a heading with a single paragraph of body text after it. Then suppose you add text before the heading that causes the heading and its paragraph of body text to flow down the page so that, ultimately, the entire paragraph of body text moves to page 2. Even if there is room for the heading at the bottom of page 1, it will move to page 2, along with its paragraph of body text. The setting that controls this is the **Keep with next** check box on the Line and Page Breaks tab in the Paragraph dialog box. By default, the Keep with next check box is selected for all headings.

A related setting on the same tab is the **Keep lines together** check box, which is also selected by default for all headings. This setting ensures that if a paragraph consists of more than one line of text, the lines of the paragraph will never be separated by a page break. This means that if one line of a paragraph moves from page 1 to page 2, all lines of the paragraph will move to page 2.

A nonprinting character in the shape of a small black square is displayed next to any paragraph for which either the Keep lines together setting or the Keep with next setting is selected. Because both settings are selected by default for all the heading styles (Heading 1 through Heading 9), you always see this nonprinting character next to text formatted with a heading style. By default, the Keep lines together setting and the Keep with next setting are deselected for all other styles. However, if you have a paragraph of body text that you want to prevent from breaking across two pages, you could apply the Keep lines together setting to that paragraph.

One helpful setting related to line and page breaks—Widow/Orphan control—is selected by default for all Word styles. The term **widow** refers to a single line of text alone at the top of a page. The term **orphan** refers to a single line of text at the bottom of a page. When selected, the **Widow/Orphan control** check box, which is also found on the Line and Page Breaks tab of the Paragraph dialog box, ensures that widows and orphans never occur in a document. Instead, at least two lines of a paragraph will appear at the top or bottom of a page.

You can see evidence of the line and page break settings in the formatting information displayed in the Reveal Formatting pane. Hayden asks you to check these settings for the report document. You'll start by displaying information about only the paragraph formatted with the Heading 2 style.

To review line and page break settings in the Reveal Formatting pane:

▶ 1. In the Reveal Formatting pane, click the **Compare to another selection** check box to deselect it. The Reveal Formatting pane changes to display information only about the formatting applied to the text "Saturn and Sun Investments," which is currently selected in the document.

   The Style Inspector pane tells you that "Saturn and Sun Investments" is formatted with the Heading 2 style, so all the information in the Reveal Formatting pane describes the Heading 2 style.

▶ 2. In the Formatting of selected text box, scroll down to display the entire Paragraph section.

▶ 3. Review the information below the blue heading "LINE AND PAGE BREAKS." The text "Keep with next" and "Keep lines together" tells you that these two settings are active for the selected text. The blue headings in the Reveal Formatting pane are actually links that open a dialog box with the relevant formatting settings.

4. In the Formatting of selected text box, click **LINE AND PAGE BREAKS**. The Paragraph dialog box opens, with the Line and Page Breaks tab displayed. See Figure 5–22.

Figure 5–22   Line and Page Breaks tab in the Paragraph dialog box

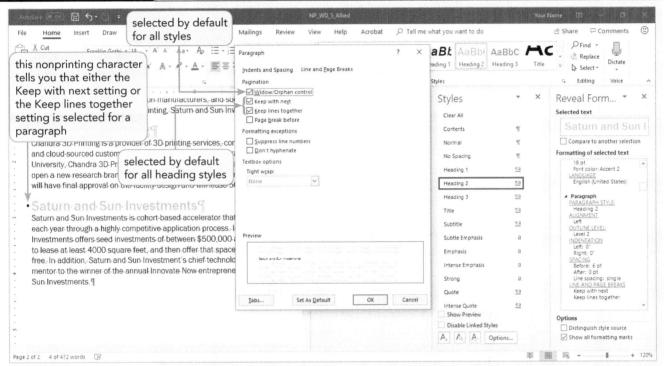

The settings on the tab are the settings for the selected paragraph, which is formatted with the Heading 2 style. The Widow/Orphan control, Keep with next, and Keep lines together check boxes are all selected, as you would expect for a heading style.

You are finished reviewing formatting information, so you can close the Paragraph dialog box and the Reveal Formatting pane.

5. In the Paragraph dialog box, click **Cancel**; and then, in the Reveal Formatting pane, click the **Close** button ⊠.

6. In the Style Inspector pane, click the **Close** button ⊠; and then, in the Styles pane, click the **Close** button ⊠.

7. Click anywhere in the document to deselect the "Saturn and Sun Investments" heading.

You are almost finished working on Hayden's report. Your next task is to add a table of contents.

Generating a Table of Contents

TIP

To delete a table of contents, click the Table of Contents button, and then click Remove Table of Contents.

You can use the Table of Contents button in the Table of Contents group on the References tab to generate a table of contents that includes any text to which you have applied heading styles. A **table of contents** is essentially an outline of the document. By default, in a table of contents, Heading 1 text is aligned on the left, Heading 2 text is indented slightly to the right below the Heading 1 text, Heading 3 text is indented slightly to the right below the Heading 2 text, and so on.

The page numbers and headings in a table of contents in Word are hyperlinks that you can click to jump to a particular part of the document. When inserting a table of contents, you can insert one of several predesigned formats. If you prefer to select from more options, open the Table of Contents dialog box where, among other settings, you can adjust the level assigned to each style within the table of contents.

REFERENCE

Generating a Table of Contents

- Apply heading styles, such as Heading 1, Heading 2, and Heading 3, to the appropriate text in the document.
- Move the insertion point to the location in the document where you want to insert the table of contents.
- On the ribbon, click the References tab.
- In the Table of Contents group, click the Table of Contents button.
- To insert a predesigned table of contents, click one of the Built-In styles in the Table of Contents menu.
- To open a dialog box where you can choose from a variety of table of contents settings, click Custom Table of Contents to open the Table of Contents dialog box. Click the Formats arrow and select a style, change the Show levels setting to the number of heading levels you want to include in the table of contents, verify that the Show page numbers check box is selected, and then click OK.

The current draft of Hayden's report is fairly short, but the final document will be much longer. He asks you to create a table of contents for the report now, just after the "Contents" heading. Then, as Hayden adds sections to the report, he can update the table of contents.

To insert a table of contents into the document:

▶ 1. Scroll up to display the "Contents" heading on page 1.

▶ 2. Below the heading, delete the placeholder text **[Insert table of contents here.]**. Do not delete the paragraph mark after the placeholder text. Your insertion point should now be located in the blank paragraph between the "Contents" heading and the "Executive Summary" heading.

▶ 3. On the ribbon, click the **References** tab.

▶ 4. In the Table of Contents group, click the **Table of Contents** button. The Table of Contents menu opens, displaying a gallery of table of contents formats. See Figure 5–23.

Figure 5–23   Table of Contents menu

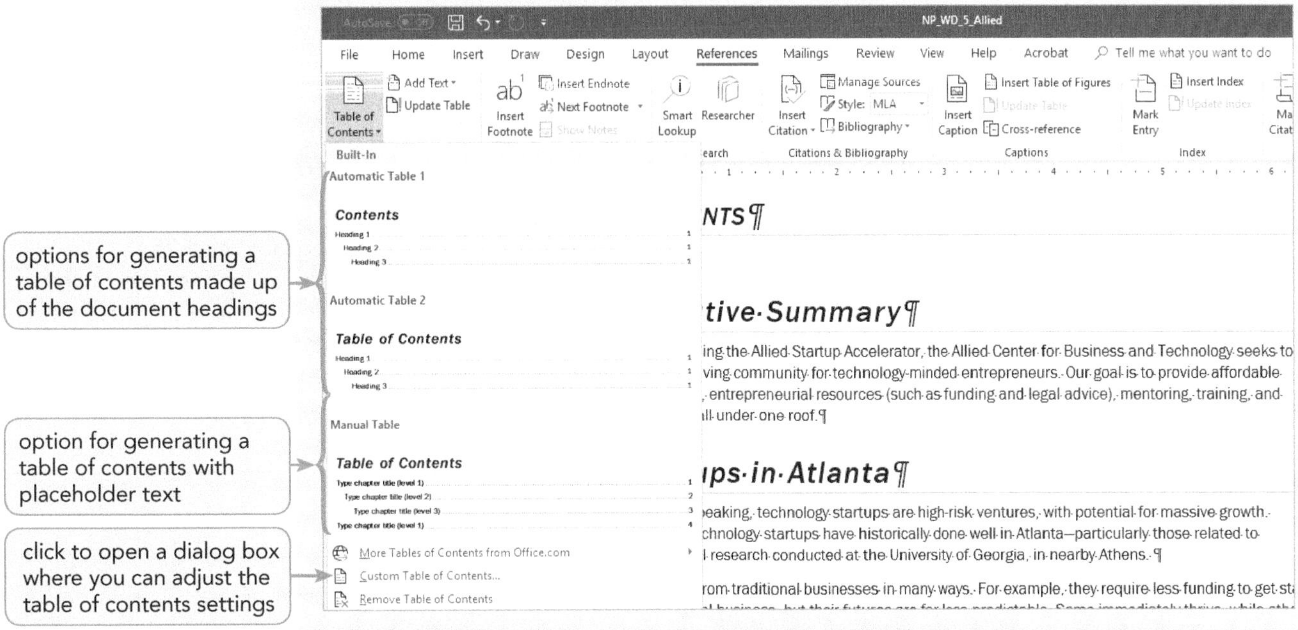

options for generating a table of contents made up of the document headings

option for generating a table of contents with placeholder text

click to open a dialog box where you can adjust the table of contents settings

The Automatic Table 1 and Automatic Table 2 options each insert a table of contents made up of the first three levels of document headings in a predefined format. Each of the Automatic options also includes a heading for the table of contents. Because Hayden's document already contains the heading "Contents," you do not want to use either of these options.

The Manual option is useful only in specialized situations, when you need to type the table of contents yourself—for example, when creating a book manuscript for an academic publisher that requires a specialized format.

You'll use the Custom Table of Contents command to open the Table of Contents dialog box.

▶ **5.** Below the Table of Contents gallery, click **Custom Table of Contents**.

The Table of Contents dialog box opens, with the Table of Contents tab displayed. See Figure 5–24.

Figure 5–24   Table of Contents dialog box

text formatted with the Contents style is included in the table of contents

table of contents format will come from the document's template

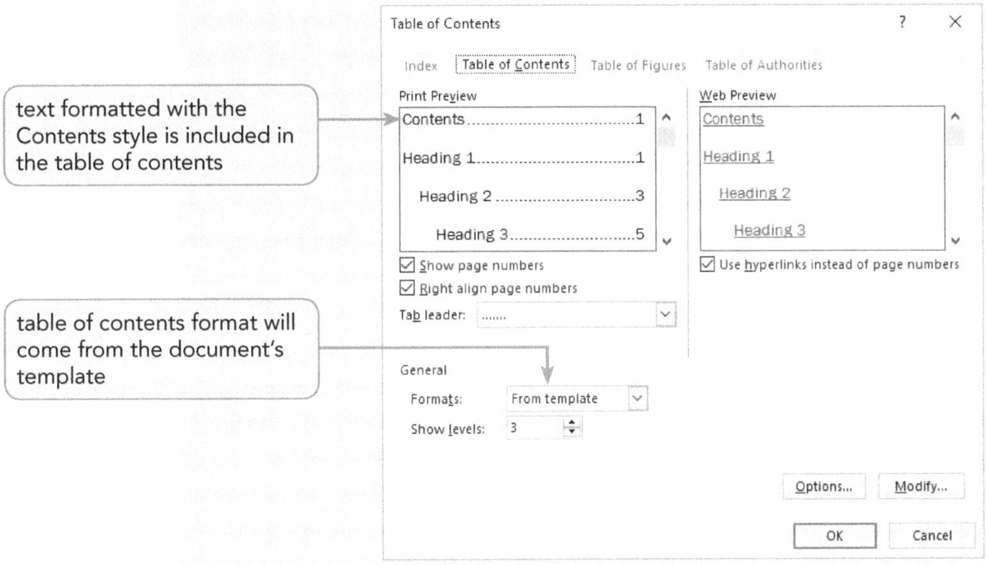

The Print Preview box on the left shows the appearance of the table of contents in Print Layout view, while the Web Preview box on the right shows what the table of contents would look like if you displayed it in Web Layout view. The Formats box shows the default option, From template, which applies the table of contents styles provided by the document's template.

In the Print Preview section, notice that the Contents heading style, which you created in Session 5.1, appears in the table of contents at the same level as the Heading 1 style.

6. In the lower-right corner of the Table of Contents dialog box, click the **Options** button. The Table of Contents Options dialog box opens. The Styles check box is selected, indicating that Word will compile the table of contents based on the styles applied to the document headings.

7. In the TOC level list, review the priority level assigned to the document's styles, using the vertical scroll bar, if necessary. See Figure 5–25.

Figure 5–25 **Checking the styles used in the table of contents**

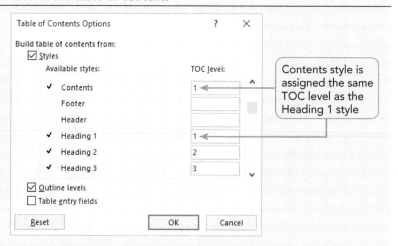

If the box next to a style name is blank, then text formatted with that style does not appear in the table of contents. The numbers next to the Contents, Heading 1, Heading 2, and Heading 3 styles tell you that any text formatted with these styles appears in the table of contents. Heading 1 is assigned to level 1, Heading 2 is assigned to level 2, and Heading 3 is assigned to level 3.

Like Heading 1, the Contents style is assigned to level 1; however, you don't want to include the "Contents" heading in the table of contents itself. To remove any text formatted with the Contents style from the table of contents, you need to delete the Contents style level number.

8. Delete the **1** from the TOC level box for the Contents style, and then click **OK**. "Contents" is no longer displayed in the sample table of contents in the Print Preview and Web Preview sections of the Table of Contents dialog box.

9. Click **OK** to accept the remaining default settings in the Table of Contents dialog box. Word searches for text formatted with the Heading 1, Heading 2, and Heading 3 styles, and then places those headings and their corresponding page numbers in a table of contents. The table of contents is inserted at the insertion point, below the "Contents" heading. See Figure 5–26.

Figure 5–26 | Table of contents inserted into document

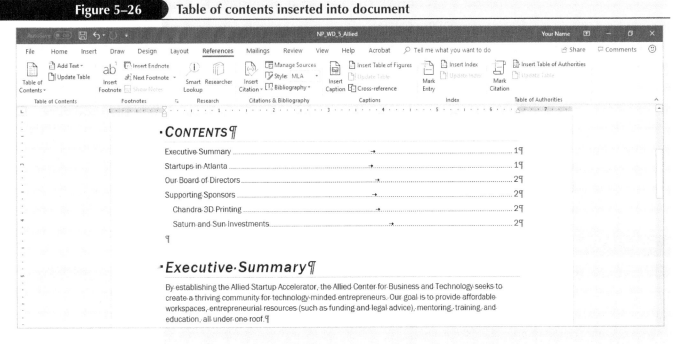

The text in the table of contents is formatted with the TOC styles for the current template. Depending on how your computer is set up, the table of contents might appear on a light gray background.

You can check the hyperlink formatting to make sure the headings really do function as links.

▶ **10.** Press and hold **CTRL** while you click **Saturn and Sun Investments** in the table of contents. The insertion point moves to the beginning of the "Saturn and Sun Investments" heading near the bottom of page 2.

▶ **11.** Save the document.

Updating a Table of Contents

If you add or delete a heading in the document or add body text that causes one or more headings to move to a new page, you can quickly update the table of contents by clicking the Update Table button in the Table of Contents group on the References tab. To add text that is not formatted as a heading to the table of contents, you can select the text, format it as a heading, and then update the table of contents. However, if you already have the References tab displayed, it's more efficient to select the text in the document, use the Add Text button in the Table of Contents group to add a Heading style to the selected text, and then update the table of contents.

Hayden has information on a third participating organization saved as a separate Word file, which he asks you to insert at the end of the document. You will do this next and then add the new heading to the table of contents.

To add a section to the report and update the table of contents:

▶ **1.** Press **CTRL+END** to move the insertion point to the end of the document, and then press **ENTER**.

▶ **2.** On the ribbon, click the **Insert** tab.

▶ **3.** In the Text group, click the **Object arrow** 🔲▾ , and then click **Text from File**.

▶ **4.** Navigate to the **Word5 > Module** folder, click **Support_WD_Diamond.docx**, and then click the **Insert** button.

▶ **5.** Select the paragraph **Diamond X25 Software**.

▶ **6.** On the ribbon, click the **References** tab.

▶ **7.** In the Table of Contents group, click the **Add Text** button. The Add Text menu opens. See Figure 5–27.

| Figure 5–27 | Add Text menu |

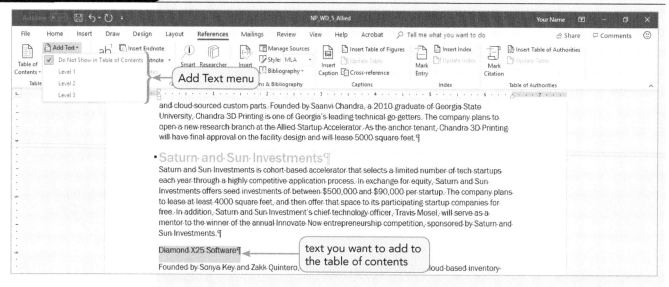

▶ **8.** Click **Level 2**. The text is formatted with the Heading 2 style to match the headings for the sections about the other participating organizations. Now that the text is formatted with a heading style, you can update the table of contents.

▶ **9.** Scroll up so you can see the table of contents, and then, in the Table of Contents group, click the **Update Table** button. The Update Table of Contents dialog box opens.

You can use the Update page numbers only option button if you don't want to update the headings in the table of contents. This option is useful if you add additional content that causes existing headings to move from one page to another. In this case, you want to update the entire table of contents.

▶ **10.** Click the **Update entire table** option button to select it, and then click **OK**. The table of contents is updated to include the "Diamond X25 Software" heading. See Figure 5–28.

Figure 5–28 | **Updated table of contents**

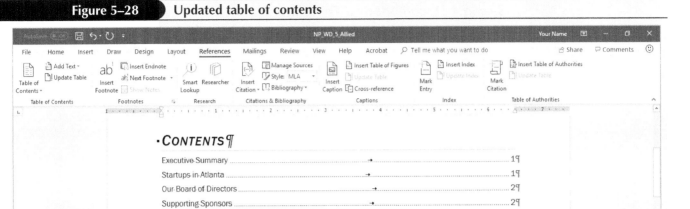

11. In the document, scroll down below the "Our Board of Directors" heading on page 2, and replace "Cordelia May" with your first and last names.

12. Press **CTRL+END** to move the insertion point to the last paragraph in the document, which is blank, and then press **DEL** to delete the blank paragraph.

13. **sam⁺** Save the document.

Now that you are finished working on Hayden's report, he asks you to use the document to create a template that can be used for all reports issued by the Allied Center for Business and Technology.

Saving a Document as a Template

If you frequently need to create a particular type of document, it's a good idea to create your own template for that type of document. Organizations often use templates to ensure that all employees use the same basic format for essential documents. When creating a template, you can save it to any folder on your computer. After you save it, you can open the template to revise it just as you would open any other document. You can also use the Save As option in Backstage view to create a new document based on the template, in which case Word Document will be selected as the file type in the Save As dialog box. If you want to be able to open a new document based on the template from the New screen, you need to save your template to the Custom Office Templates folder that is installed with Word.

Saving a Document as a Template

- On the ribbon, click the File tab, and then click Export in the navigation pane.
- Click Change File Type, click Template, and then click the Save As button to open the Save As dialog box with Word Template selected in the Save as type box.
- Navigate to the folder in which you want to save the template. To save the template to the Custom Office Templates folder that is installed with Word, click the Documents folder in the navigation pane of the Save As dialog box, and then click Custom Office Templates.
- In the File name box, type a name for the template.
- Click Save.

You will save the new Allied Center for Business and Technology template in the location specified by your instructor; however, you'll also save it to the Custom Office Templates folder so you can practice opening a new document based on your template from the New screen in Backstage view.

To save the document as a new template:

▌ **1.** Save the document to ensure that you have saved your most recent work.

TIP

You can also click the File tab, click Save As, and then select Word Template as the file type.

▌ **2.** On the ribbon, click the **File** tab, and then click **Export** in the navigation pane.

▌ **3.** Click **Change File Type**. The Export screen displays options for various file types you can use when saving a file. For example, you could save a Word document as a Plain Text file that contains only text, without any formatting or graphics. See Figure 5–29.

Figure 5–29   **Export screen with Change File Type options in Backstage view**

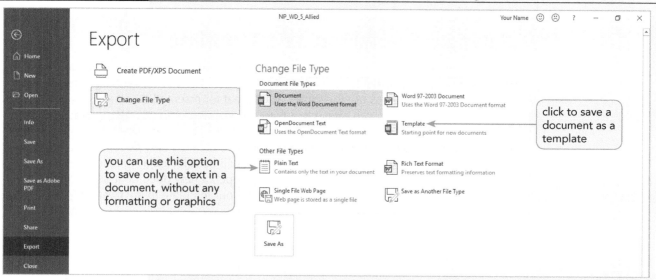

▌ **4.** Under Change File Type, click **Template**, and then click the **Save As** button. The Save As dialog box opens with Word Template selected in the Save as type box.

▌ **5.** If necessary, navigate to the location specified by your instructor. Next, you'll replace the selected, default file name with a new one.

▌ **6.** In the File name box, type **NP_WD_5_Template**. See Figure 5–30.

Figure 5–30   **Saving a document as a template**

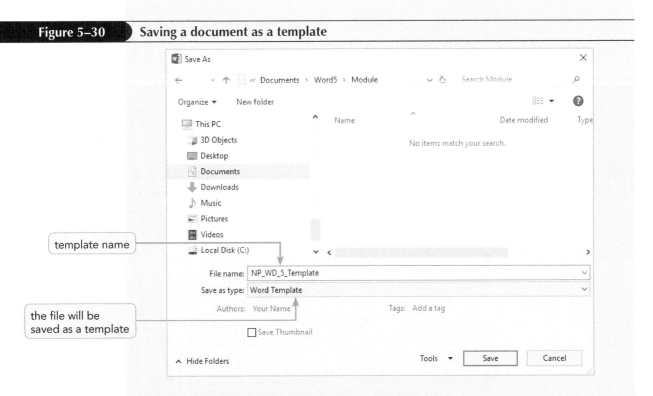

> **7.** Click **Save**. The Save As dialog box closes, and the document, which is now a template with the .dotx file extension, remains open.

Written Communication: Standardizing the Look of Your Documents

Large companies often ask their employees to use a predesigned template for all corporate documents. If you work for an organization that does not require you to use a specific template, consider using one anyway in order to create a standard look for all of your documents. A consistent appearance is especially important if you are responsible for written communication for an entire department because it ensures that colleagues and clients will immediately recognize documents from your department.

Be sure to use a professional-looking template. If you decide to create your own, use document styles that make text easy to read, with colors that are considered appropriate in your workplace. Don't try to dazzle your readers with design elements. In nearly all professional settings, a simple, elegant look is ideal.

To make the new template really useful to Hayden's colleagues, you need to delete the specific information related to the Allied Startup Accelerator and replace it with placeholder text explaining the type of information required in each section. In the following steps, you will delete the body of the report and replace it with some placeholder text. Hayden wants to use the current subtitle, "Prepared by the Allied Center for Business and Technology," as the subtitle in all reports, so there's no need to change it. However, the title will vary from one report to the next, so you need to replace it with a suitable placeholder. You'll retain the table of contents. When Hayden's colleagues use the template to create future reports, they can update the table of contents to include any headings they add to their new documents.

To replace the information about the Allied Startup Accelerator with placeholder text:

▶ **1.** Scroll up to the top of the document, and then replace the report title "Allied Startup Accelerator" with the text **[Insert title here.]**. Be sure to include the brackets so the text will be readily recognizable as placeholder text. To ensure that Hayden's colleagues don't overlook this placeholder, you can also highlight it.

▶ **2.** On the ribbon, click the **Home** tab, if necessary.

▶ **3.** In the Font group, click the **Text Highlight Color** button ✏️⌄, and then click and drag the highlight pointer ⬩ over the text **[Insert title here.]**. The text is highlighted in yellow, which is the default highlight color. Note that you could click the Text Highlight Color arrow and select a different color before using the highlight pointer.

▶ **4.** Press **ESC** to turn off the highlight pointer.

▶ **5.** Scroll down below the table of contents, and then delete everything in the document after the "Executive Summary" heading so all that remains is the "Executive Summary" heading.

▶ **6.** Press **ENTER** to insert a blank paragraph below the heading. Now you can insert a file containing placeholder text for the body of the template.

▶ **7.** In the blank paragraph under the "Executive Summary" heading, insert the **Support_WD_5_Placeholder.docx** file from the Word5 > Module folder included with your Data Files. See Figure 5–31.

| Figure 5–31 | Template with placeholder text |

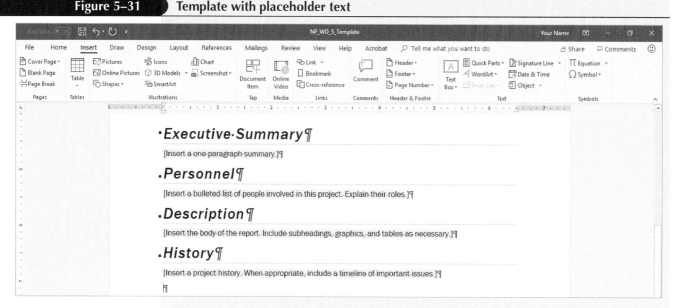

Scroll up to review the document, and notice that the inserted placeholder text is highlighted and the headings are all correctly formatted with the Heading 1 style. When Hayden created the Placeholder document, he formatted the text in the default Heading 1 style provided by the Office theme. But when you inserted the file into the template, Word automatically applied your updated Heading 1 style. Now you can update the table of contents.

▶ **8.** On the ribbon, click the **References** tab.

9. In the Table of Contents group, click the **Update Table** button. The table of contents is updated to include the new headings.

10. On the Quick Access Toolbar, click the **Save** button 🖫 to save your changes to the template just as you would save a document.

At this point, you have a copy of the template stored in the location specified by your instructor. If you closed the template, clicked the File tab, and then opened the template again from the same folder, you would be opening the template itself and not a new document based on the template. If you want to be able to open a new document based on the template from the New screen, you have to save the template to the Custom Office Templates folder. You'll do that next. You can also open a new document based on a template by double-clicking the template file from within File Explorer. You'll have a chance to try that in the Case Problems at the end of this module.

To save the template to the Custom Office Templates folder:

1. On the ribbon, click the **File** tab, and then click **Save As** in the navigation pane.

2. Click **This PC** if necessary, and then click the **Browse** button to open the Save As dialog box.

3. In the navigation pane of the Save As dialog box, click the **Documents** folder, and then, in the folder list on the right, double-click **Custom Office Templates**. See Figure 5–32.

Figure 5–32 **Saving a template in the Custom Office Templates folder**

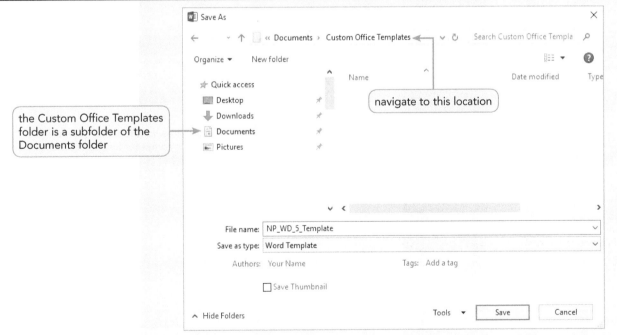

4. Click the **Save** button to save the template to the Custom Office Templates folder and close the Save As dialog box.

5. On the ribbon, click the **File** tab, and then click **Close** in the navigation pane to close the template, just as you would close a document.

The template you just created will simplify the process of creating new reports in Hayden's department.

Opening a New Document Based on Your Template

Documents created using a template contain all the text and formatting included in the template. Changes you make to this new document will not affect the template file, which remains unchanged in the Custom Office Templates folder.

Hayden would like you to use the new template to begin a report on the Allied Center for Business and Technology's annual event promoting the importance of soft skills in technology fields.

To open a new document based on the template you created:

1. On the ribbon, click the **File** tab, and then click **New** in the navigation pane.

2. Note that the New screen in Backstage view includes two links—FEATURED and PERSONAL. The FEATURED link is selected by default, indicating that the templates currently featured by Office.com are displayed. To open the template you just saved to the Custom Office Templates folder, you need to display the personal templates instead.

3. Click **PERSONAL**. The NP_WD_5_Template template is displayed as an option on the New screen. See Figure 5–33.

Figure 5–33	Opening a document based on the template you created

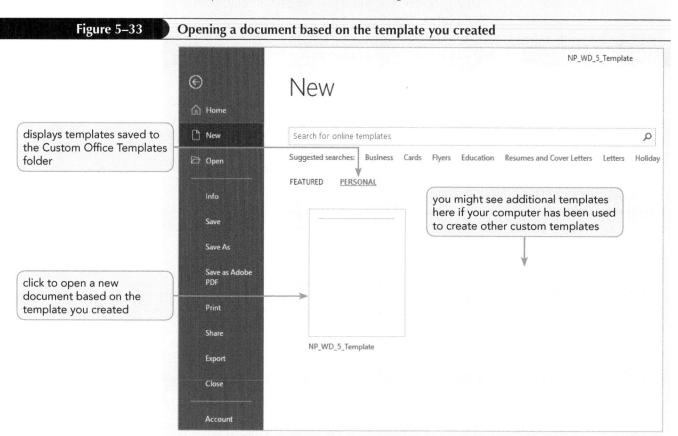

4. Click **NP_WD_5_Template**. A new document opens, containing the text and formatting from the NP_WD_5_Template.dotx template.

▶ **5.** Delete the placeholder **[Insert title here.],** and type **Soft Skills Academy** in its place. If necessary, remove the yellow highlighting.

Hayden and his colleagues will add new material to this report later. For now, you can close it.

▶ **6.** Save the document as **NP_WD_5_SoftSkills** in the location specified by your instructor, and then close the document.

Next, to ensure that you can repeat the steps in this module if you choose to, you will delete the NP_WD_5_Template.dotx file from the Custom Office Templates folder. You can delete it from within the Open dialog box.

▶ **7.** On the ribbon, click the **File** tab, and then click **Open** in the navigation pane.

▶ **8.** Click the **Browse** button.

▶ **9.** In the navigation pane of the Open dialog box, click the **Documents** folder, and then double-click **Custom Office Templates**. The NP_WD_5_Template.dotx template is displayed in the file list.

▶ **10.** Right-click **NP_WD_5_Template.dotx** to display a shortcut menu, click **Delete**, and then click **Yes**.

The template file is removed from the file list.

▶ **11.** Click **Cancel** to close the Open dialog box, and then close Backstage view.

Creating a template makes it easy to create a series of similar documents. But what if you want to insert specific text such as an address or email address or a graphic such as a logo in many different documents? In that case, you can save the item as a Quick Part.

Creating a New Quick Part

A **Quick Part** is reusable content that you create and that you can then insert into any document later with a single click in the Quick Parts gallery. For example, you might create a letterhead with your company's address and logo. To save the letterhead as a Quick Part, you select it and then save it to the Quick Parts gallery. Later, you can insert the letterhead into a document by clicking it in the Quick Parts gallery.

By default, a new Quick Part appears as an option in the Quick Parts gallery. However, you can assign a Quick Part to any gallery you want. For example, you could assign a text box Quick Part to the Text Box gallery so that every time you click the Text Box button on the Insert tab, you see your text box as one of the options in the Text Box gallery.

Quick Parts are just one type of a larger category of reusable content known as **building blocks**. All of the ready-made items that you can insert into a document via a gallery are considered building blocks. For example, preformatted headers, preformatted text boxes, and cover pages are all examples of building blocks. Some reference sources use the terms "building block" and "Quick Part" as if they were synonyms, but in fact a Quick Part is a building block that you create.

When you save a Quick Part, you always save it to a template; you can't save a Quick Part to an individual document. Which template you save it to depends on what you want to do with the Quick Part. If you want the template to be available to all new documents created on your computer, you should save it to the Building Blocks template. The **Building Blocks template** is a special template that contains all the building blocks installed with Word on your computer, as well as any Quick Parts you save to it. If you want to restrict the Quick Part to only documents based on the current template, or if you want to be able to share the Quick Part with someone else, you should save it to the current template. To share the Quick Part, you simply distribute the template to anyone who wants to use the Quick Part.

Creating and Using Quick Parts

- Select the text, text box, header, footer, table, graphic, or other item you want to save as a Quick Part.
- On the ribbon, click the Insert tab.
- In the Text group, click the Quick Parts button, and then click Save Selection to Quick Part Gallery.
- In the Create New Building Block dialog box, replace the text in the Name box with a descriptive name for the Quick Part.
- Click the Gallery arrow, and then choose the gallery to which you want to save the Quick Part.
- To make the Quick Part available to all documents on your computer, select Building Blocks in the Save in box. To restrict the Quick Part to the current template, select the name of the template on which the current document is based.
- Click OK.

Hayden has created a text box containing the address and phone number for the Allied Center for Business and Technology. He asks you to show him how to save the text box as a Quick Part. He wants the Quick Part to be available to all new documents created on his computer, so you'll need to save it to the Building Blocks template.

To save a text box as a Quick Part:

1. Open the document **NP_WD_5-2.docx** from the Word5 > Module folder, and then save it as **NP_WD_5_Address** in the location specified by your instructor.

2. Display nonprinting characters and the rulers, switch to Print Layout view, and then change the Zoom level to **120%**, if necessary.

3. Click the **text box** to select it, taking care to select the entire text box and not the text inside it. When the text box is selected, you'll see the anchor symbol in the left margin.

4. On the ribbon, click the **Insert** tab.

5. In the Text group, click the **Quick Parts** button. If any Quick Parts have been created on your computer, they will be displayed in the gallery at the top of the menu. Otherwise, you will see only the menu shown in Figure 5–34.

Figure 5–34 **Quick Parts menu, with no Quick Parts visible**

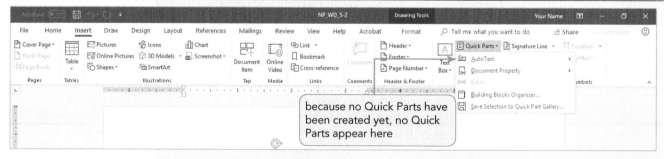

6. At the bottom of the menu, click **Save Selection to Quick Part Gallery**. The Create New Building Block dialog box opens. The name of this dialog box is appropriate because a Quick Part is a type of building block. See Figure 5–35.

Figure 5-35   Create New Building Block dialog box

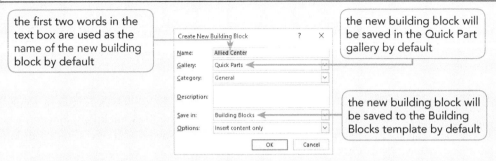

the first two words in the text box are used as the name of the new building block by default

the new building block will be saved in the Quick Part gallery by default

the new building block will be saved to the Building Blocks template by default

By default, the first two words in the text box, "Allied Center," are used as the default name for the new building block. You could type a new name, but Hayden is happy with the default. Also, the default setting in the Gallery box tells you that the new building block will be saved in the Quick Parts gallery. You could change this by selecting a different gallery name. The Save in box indicates that the Quick Part will be saved to the Building Blocks template, which means it will be available to all documents on your computer.

Hayden asks you to accept the default settings.

7. Click **OK** to accept your changes and close the Create New Building Block dialog box.

You've finished creating the new Quick Part. Now you can try inserting it in the current document.

To insert the new Quick Part into the current document:

1. Press **CTRL+END** to move the insertion point to the end of the document.

2. In the Text group, click the **Quick Parts** button. This time, the Quick Parts gallery is displayed at the top of the menu. See Figure 5-36.

Figure 5-36   New Quick Part in the Quick Parts gallery

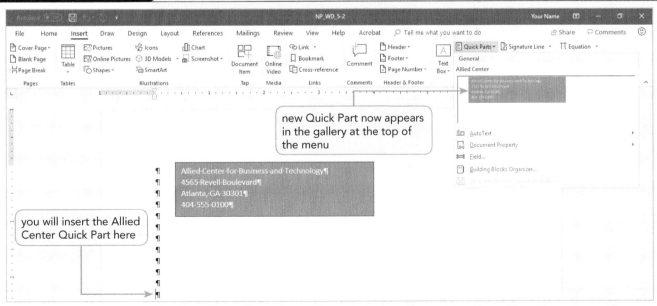

new Quick Part now appears in the gallery at the top of the menu

Allied·Center·for·Business·and·Technology¶
4565·Revell·Boulevard¶
Atlanta,·GA·30301¶
404-555-0100¶

you will insert the Allied Center Quick Part here

3. Click the **Allied Center** Quick Part. A copy of the orange text box is inserted at the end of the document, at the insertion point.

4. In the newly inserted text box, replace the phone number with your first and last names, and then save the document.

TIP

To open the Building Blocks Organizer with a particular Quick Park selected, right-click the Quick Part in the Quick Parts gallery, and then click Organize and Delete.

The new Quick Part is stored in the Quick Parts gallery, ready to be inserted into any document. However, after reviewing the Quick Part, Hayden has decided he wants to reformat the address text box and save it as a new Quick Part later. So you'll delete the Quick Part you just created.

To delete a Quick Part:

1. In the Text group, click the **Quick Parts** button and then click **Building Blocks Organizer** to open the Building Blocks Organizer dialog box. Here you see a list of all the building blocks, including Quick Parts, available in your copy of Word. See Figure 5–37.

Figure 5–37   **Building Blocks Organizer dialog box**

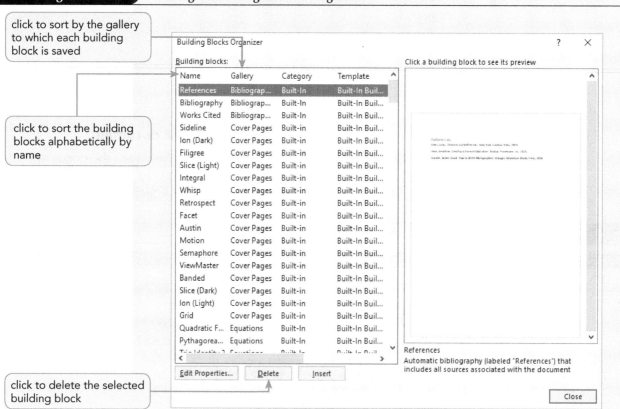

The list on your computer will be somewhat different from the list shown in Figure 5–37.

You can click a building block in the list and then click the Edit Properties button to open a dialog box where you can rename the building block and make other changes. You can also use the Building Blocks Organizer to delete a building block.

▶ **2.** Click the **Name** column header to sort the building blocks alphabetically by name, scroll down and click **Allied Center**, click the **Delete** button, and then click **Yes** in the warning dialog box. The Allied Center Quick Part is deleted from the list in the Building Blocks Organizer.

▶ **3.** Click **Close**.

▶ **4.** In the Text group, click the **Quick Parts** button, and verify that the Allied Center Quick Part is no longer displayed in the Quick Parts gallery.

Finally, to completely delete the Quick Part from the Building Blocks template, you need to save the current document. In the process of saving the document, Word will save your changes to the Building Blocks template, which controls all the building blocks available in your copy of Word. If you don't save the document now, you'll see a warning dialog box later, when you attempt to close the document. It's easy to get confused by the wording of this warning dialog box, and you might end up restoring your Quick Part rather than deleting it.

To avoid seeing this warning dialog box entirely, remember to save the current document after you delete a Quick Part.

▶ **5.** Save the **NP_WD_5_Address.docx** document, and then close it.

Hayden is happy to know how to save Quick Parts to the Building Blocks template. He'll create a new Quick Part later and save it to a custom template so that he can make it available to everyone at the Allied Center for Business and Technology.

REVIEW

Session 5.2 Quick Check

1. By default, is a new style saved to the current document or to the current template?

2. Explain how to create a new style.

3. What pane displays a complete list of the formatting applied to the paragraph that currently contains the insertion point?

4. Which setting on the Line and Page Breaks tab of the Paragraph dialog box ensures that if a paragraph consists of more than one line of text, the lines of the paragraph will never be separated by a page break?

5. What must you do to your document before you can create a table of contents for it?

6. Where should you save a custom template if you want to be able to access it from the New screen in Backstage view?

7. Define "building block" and give some examples.

Review Assignments

Data Files needed for the Review Assignments: NP_WD_5-3.docx, NP_WD_5-4.docx, Support_WD_5_Headings.docx, Support_WD_5_Writers.docx

Hayden's template is now used for all reports created by employees of the Allied Center for Business and Technology. Inspired by Hayden's success with the template, a project manager for the Allied Startup Accelerator Planning Commission, Malisa Kunchai, wants you to help with a report on construction plans for the new facility. After you format the report, she'd like you to save the document as a new template and then create a Quick Part. Complete the following steps:

1. Create a new document based on the Business report (Professional design) template from Office.com. (If you can't find that template, choose another.) Replace the title placeholder in the document with your name, and then save the document as **NP_WD_5_DocumentFromTemplate** in the location specified by your instructor. If you see a dialog box explaining that the document is being upgraded to the newest file format, click OK.

2. Close the document.

3. Open the document **NP_WD_5-3.docx** from the Word5 > Review folder included with your Data Files, and then save it as **NP_WD_5_Construction** in the location specified by your instructor.

4. Use the Go To feature to review all the headings in the document.

5. In the first line of the "History" section, use the Thesaurus pane to replace "excited" with a synonym. Use the third synonym in the list of words related to "happy."

6. Change the theme colors to Green, and then change the theme's fonts to the Franklin Gothic fonts.

7. Save the new colors and fonts as a theme named **NP_WD_5_ConstructionReportTheme** in the location specified by your instructor.

8. Change the style set to Lines (Simple).

9. Change the formatting of the "History" heading by adding italic formatting and by changing the character spacing so that it is expanded by 1 point between characters.

10. Update the Heading 1 style to match the newly formatted "History" heading.

11. Revise the "Scope" heading by changing the font size to 16 points, and then update the Heading 2 style to match the newly formatted "Scope" heading.

12. Create a new paragraph style for the "Contents" heading that is based on the Heading 1 style but that also includes Lime, Accent 3 paragraph shading. Name the new style **Contents**, select Normal as the style for the following paragraph, and then save the new style to the current document.

13. Open the Style Inspector pane, and check the style applied to each paragraph in the document. Then use the Reveal Formatting pane to compare the formatting applied to the "Contents" heading with the formatting applied to the "History" heading.

14. Delete the placeholder text directly below the "Contents" heading, and then insert a custom table of contents that does not include the Contents style. Except for excluding the Contents style, use the default settings in the Table of Contents dialog box.

15. Insert a blank paragraph at the end of the document, and then insert the **Support_WD_5_Writers.docx** file from the Word5 > Review folder. Add the text **Contributing Writers** to the table of contents as a Level 1 heading, and then delete the blank paragraph at the end of the document.

16. At the end of the report, replace "Student Name" with your first and last names.

17. Save your changes to the NP_WD_5_Construction.docx document.

18. Save the document as a Word Template named **NP_WD_5_ConstructionReportTemplate** in the location specified by your instructor.

19. On page 1, replace the title "CONSTRUCTING THE ALLIED STARTUP ACCELERATOR" with the placeholder text **[Insert title here.]**, and then highlight the placeholder in the default yellow color.

20. Delete everything in the report after the blank paragraph after the table of contents.

21. In the blank paragraph below the table of contents, insert the **Support_WD_5_Headings.docx** file from the Word5 > Review folder.

22. In the Contributing Staff Members section, replace "Student Name" with your first and last names, and then update the table of contents.

23. Save the template, save it again to the Custom Office Templates folder, and then close it.

24. From the New screen in Backstage view, open a new document based on the template you just created, enter **Projections for Growth** as the document title, save the new document as **NP_WD_5_Projections** in the location specified by your instructor, and then close it.

25. Delete the **NP_WD_5_ConstructionReportTemplate.dotx** template from the Custom Office Templates folder.

26. Open the document **NP_WD_5-4.docx** from the Word5 > Review folder, and then save it as a Word Template named **NP_WD_5_AcceleratorAddressTemplate** in the location specified by your instructor.

27. Save the blue text box as a Quick Part named **Address**. Save it to the template named **NP_WD_5_AcceleratorAddressTemplate.dotx**, not to the Building Blocks template.

28. Save the template and close it.

Case Problem 1

APPLY

Data File needed for this Case Problem: NP_WD_5-5.docx

Robbins Morrow Aerospace Manufacturing   Laqueta Porter is a project manager for Robbins Morrow Aerospace Manufacturing, a company that produces parts for small aircraft. The manufacturing team often takes on special projects for long-time customers. Management requires a comprehensive status report on each project every month. These reports can be quite long, so it's necessary to include a table of contents on the first page. Your job is to create a template that Laqueta and her fellow project managers can use when compiling their reports.

Complete the following steps:

1. Open the document **NP_WD_5-5.docx** from the Word5 > Case1 folder included with your Data Files, and then save it as **NP_WD_5_Status** in the location specified by your instructor.

2. Use Go To to review all the tables in the document.

3. Change the change the theme colors to Blue II, change the theme fonts to Arial, and then save the current theme as a custom theme named **NP_WD_5_StatusTheme** in the location specified by your instructor

4. Change the style set to Basic (Stylish).

5. Format the "Contents" heading by changing the character spacing to Expanded, with 2 points of space between the expanded characters. Increase the font size to 22 points, add italic formatting, and then change the font color to one shade darker, using the Teal, Accent 6, Darker 50% font color. Update the Heading 1 style for the current document to match the newly formatted heading.

6. Create a new paragraph style for the company name at the top of the document that is based on the Heading 1 style but that also includes Turquoise, Accent 1, Lighter 40% paragraph shading; White, Background 1 font color; 24-point font size; and center alignment. Reduce the points of paragraph spacing before the paragraph to 0, and increase the points after the paragraph to 36. Name the new style **Company**. Select the Normal style as the style for the following paragraph, and save the style to the current document.

7. Remove the Company style from the Style gallery.

8. Below the "Contents" heading, replace the placeholder text with a custom table of contents that does not include the Company style.

9. In the document, delete the paragraph containing the "Contents" heading, and then update the table of contents to remove "Contents" from it.

10. Click in the paragraph before the table of contents, and increase the spacing after it to 24 points.

11. Add the "General Recommendations" heading, in the second to last paragraph of the document, to the table of contents at the same level as the "Project Summary" heading.

12. In the document's last paragraph, replace "ensuring" with a synonym. In the Thesaurus pane, use the second synonym in the list of words related to "safeguarding."

13. Save your changes to the document, and then save it as a template named **NP_WD_5_StatusTemplate** in the location specified by your instructor.

14. On page 3, save the complete "Scope Statement" section (including the heading, and the placeholder text) as a Quick Part named **Scope Statement**. Save the Quick Part to the **NP_WD_5_StatusTemplate.dotx** template.

15. Delete the complete "Scope Statement" section from the body of the template, including the heading and the placeholder text.

16. Update the table of contents to remove the "Scope Statement" heading.

17. Save the template to its current location, and then save the template again to the Custom Office Templates folder. Close the template.

18. Open a document based on your new template, and then save the new document as **NP_WD_5_StatusVectora** in the location specified by your instructor.

19. Replace the first placeholder with the current date, and then replace the second placeholder with **your name**. If necessary, remove the yellow highlighting from the date and your name. In the Project Summary table, replace "[Insert project name.]" with **Vectora 527 Rotor Bar** and then remove the yellow highlighting if necessary.

20. Above the "Progress" heading, insert the Scope Statement Quick Part.

21. Update the table of contents to include the new heading.

22. Save and close the document, and then delete the NP_WD_5_StatusTemplate.dotx file from the Custom Office Templates folder.

Case Problem 2

Data Files needed for this Case Problem: NP_WD_5-6.docx, NP_WD_5-7.docx

Chronos and Mercer Pharmaceuticals   Blake Peralta is a technical writer at Chronos and Mercer Pharmaceuticals. Blake often uses Word styles in the reports and other publications he creates for the company, and he wants to learn more about managing styles. In particular, he wants to learn how to copy styles from one document to another. He's asked you to help him explore the Style Pane Options, Manage Styles, and Organizer dialog boxes. He would also like your help creating a Quick Part for a memo header. Complete the following steps:

1. Open the document **NP_WD_5-6.docx** from the Word5 > Case2 folder included with your Data Files, and then save it as **NP_WD_5_Memo** in the location specified by your instructor. This document contains the text you will eventually save as a Quick Part. It contains all the default styles available in any new Word document, as well as one style, named "Memorandum," which Blake created earlier. In the following steps, you will copy styles from another document to this document. For now, you can close it.

2. Close the NP_WD_5_Memo.docx document.

3. Open the document **NP_WD_5-7.docx** from the Word5 > Case2 folder, and then save it as **NP_WD_5_Styles** in the location specified by your instructor. This document contains styles created by Blake, which you will copy to the NP_WD_5_Memo.docx document. It also includes sample paragraphs formatted with Blake's styles, and one paragraph that you will format with a style later in this Case Problem.

Explore 4. Open the Style Pane Options dialog box, and then change the settings so the Styles pane displays only the styles in the current document, in alphabetical order. Before closing this dialog box, verify that these settings will be applied only to the current document rather than to new documents based on this template.

Explore 5. Open a new, blank document, and then use the Screenshot button in the Illustrations group on the Insert tab to create a screenshot of the NP_WD_5_Styles.docx document.

6. Copy the screenshot to the Clipboard, and then paste it in the blank paragraph at the end of the NP_WD_5_Styles.docx document, just as you would paste text that you had previously copied to the Clipboard. Close the document in which you created the screenshot without saving it.

Explore 7. At the bottom of the Styles pane, click the Manage Styles button, and then click the Import/Export button to open the Organizer dialog box. Close the Normal template, and open the **NP_WD_5_Memo.docx** document instead. (*Hint*: On the right, under the In Normal box, click the Close File button, and then click the Open File button. In the Open dialog box, you'll need to display all files.)

Explore 8. Copy the following styles from the NP_WD_5_Styles.docx document to the NP_WD_5_Memo.docx document: Company Name, Department, Documentation Heading, and Product Description. Then copy the Memorandum style from the NP_WD_5_Memo.docx document to the NP_WD_5_Styles.docx document.

9. Close the Organizer dialog box, and save your changes to the NP_WD_5_Memo.docx document when asked.

10. In the NP_WD_5_Styles.docx document, apply the Memorandum style to the text "Sample of Memorandum style," in the document's third to last paragraph.

11. Save the NP_WD_5_Styles.docx document, and then close it.

12. Open the NP_WD_5_Memo.docx document, and then review the list of styles in the Styles pane to locate the styles you just copied to this document from the NP_WD_5_Styles.docx document.

13. Apply the Company Name style to "Chronos and Mercer Pharmaceuticals" in the second paragraph.

14. Save the NP_WD_5_Memo.docx document, and then save it again as a template named **NP_WD_5_MemoTemplate** in the location specified by your instructor.

15. Select all of the text in the document, and then save it as a Quick Part named **Memo 1**. Save the Quick Part to the current template, not to the Building Blocks template.

16. Change the Paragraph shading for the first paragraph to the Turquoise, Accent 1 color, and then save the document text as a new Quick Part named **Memo 2**. Again, save the Quick Part to the current template.

17. Delete all the text from the template, save the NP_WD_5_MemoTemplate.dotx file, and then close it.

Explore 18. Open a File Explorer window, and then navigate to the location where you saved the NP_WD_5_Memo_Template.dotx file. Open a new document based on the template by double-clicking the template's file name in File Explorer.

19. Save the new document as **NP_WD_5_SampleMemo** in the location specified by your instructor, insert the Memo 2 Quick Part in the document, and then save and close the document.

Using Mail Merge

Creating a Form Letter, Mailing Labels, and a Phone Directory

Case | *Sun and Soul Wellness Resort*

Amalia Ferreira manages the spa at Sun and Soul Wellness Resort, a luxury vacation destination in San Diego, California. The resort has just reopened its newly renovated spa facility. To encourage San Diego residents to patronize the spa, Amalia staffed a booth at several local community events and collected names and addresses of potential clients. Amalia plans to send a form letter to these people announcing the improvements to the spa and offering a free nutrition or fitness counselling appointment to anyone who shows a copy of the letter at the spa's front desk.

The form letter will also contain specific details for individual people, such as name and address. For people who indicated that they prefer yoga classes, the letter will include a sentence about the new yoga studios. For those who prefer weight lifting classes, the letter will include a sentence about the new weight room. Amalia has already written the text of the form letter. She plans to use the mail merge process to add the personal information for each person to the form letter. She asks you to revise the form letter by inserting a Date field in the document that will display the current date. Then she wants you to use the Mail Merge feature in Word to create customized letters. After you create the merged letters, Amalia would like you to create mailing labels for the envelopes and a directory of employee phone numbers. Finally, you'll convert some text to a table so that it can be used in a mail merge.

STARTING DATA FILES

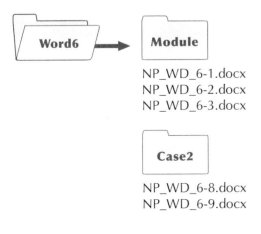

Word6 → **Module**

NP_WD_6-1.docx
NP_WD_6-2.docx
NP_WD_6-3.docx

Review

NP_WD_6-4.docx
NP_WD_6-5.docx
NP_WD_6-6.docx

Case1

NP_WD_6-7.docx

Case2

NP_WD_6-8.docx
NP_WD_6-9.docx

Session 6.1 Visual Overview:

Use the Start Mail Merge button to select the type of main document you are creating. Possible types include letters, envelopes, emails, labels, and directories.

The Select Recipients button allows you to select an existing data source or create a new one in the New Address List dialog box.

The Mailings tab contains four groups of options that, working left to right, walk you through the process of creating a mail merge.

To complete the mail merge, you click the Finish & Merge button. This creates a new document, the **merged document**, which contains a separate copy of the main document for each record in the data source.

The Edit Recipient List button allows you to make changes to a data source.

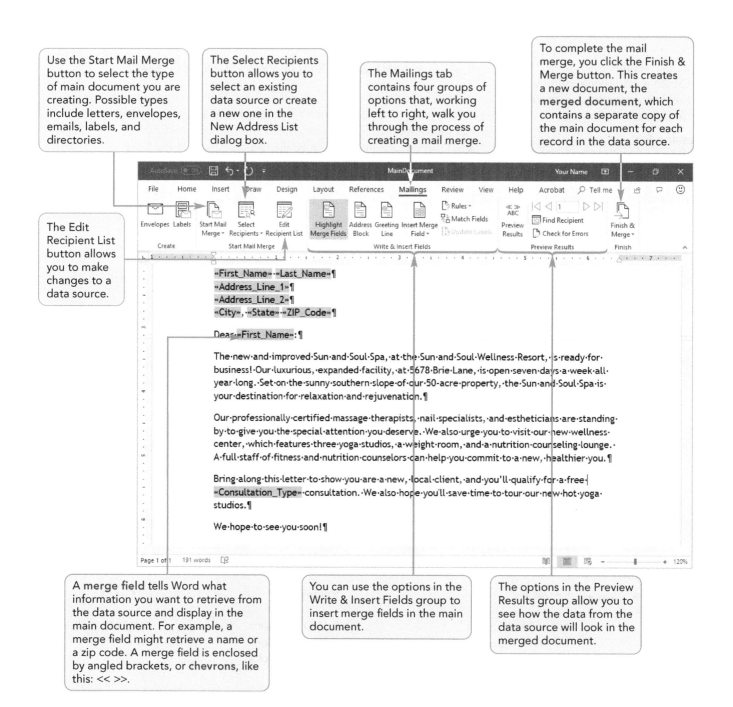

A **merge field** tells Word what information you want to retrieve from the data source and display in the main document. For example, a merge field might retrieve a name or a zip code. A merge field is enclosed by angled brackets, or **chevrons**, like this: << >>.

You can use the options in the Write & Insert Fields group to insert merge fields in the main document.

The options in the Preview Results group allow you to see how the data from the data source will look in the merged document.

Mail Merge

A **data source** is a file that contains information, such as names and addresses, that is organized into fields and records; the merge fields cause the information in the data source to be displayed in the main document. You can use a Word table, an Excel spreadsheet, or other types of files as data sources, or you can create a new data source using the New Address List dialog box.

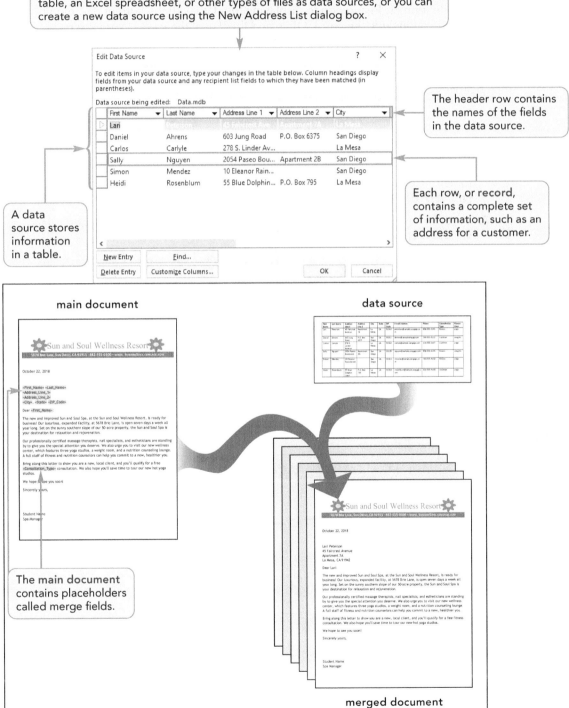

The **header row** contains the names of the fields in the data source.

Each row, or **record**, contains a complete set of information, such as an address for a customer.

A **data source** stores information in a table.

The **main document** contains placeholders called merge fields.

Inserting a Date Field

A **Date field** is an instruction that tells Word to display the current date in a document. Although a Date field is not a merge field, it's common to use Date fields in mail merge documents to ensure that the main document always includes the current date. Every time you open a document containing a Date field, it updates to display the current date. To insert a Date field, you use the Date and Time dialog box to select from a variety of date formats. In addition to displaying the date with the current day, month, and year, you can include the current time and the day of the week. Word inserts a Date field inside a content control; unless the content control is selected, the field looks like ordinary text.

Amalia asks you to insert a Date field in her document before beginning the mail merge process.

To open Amalia's document and insert a Date field:

▶ 1. **sam↓** Open the document **NP_WD_6-1.docx** from the Word6 > Module folder included with your Data Files, and then save it as **NP_WD_6_MainDocument** in the location specified by your instructor.

▶ 2. Display nonprinting characters, switch to Print Layout view, display the rulers, and then set the Zoom level to **120%**.

▶ 3. Review the contents of the letter. Notice that the fourth paragraph includes the placeholder text "[INSERT DATE FIELD]."

▶ 4. Delete the placeholder text **[INSERT DATE FIELD]**, taking care not to delete the paragraph mark after the placeholder text. When you are finished, the insertion point should be located in the second blank paragraph of the document, with two blank paragraphs below it.

▶ 5. On the ribbon, click the **Insert** tab.

▶ 6. In the Text group, click the **Date & Time** button. The Date and Time dialog box opens. See Figure 6–1.

Figure 6–1   Date and Time dialog box

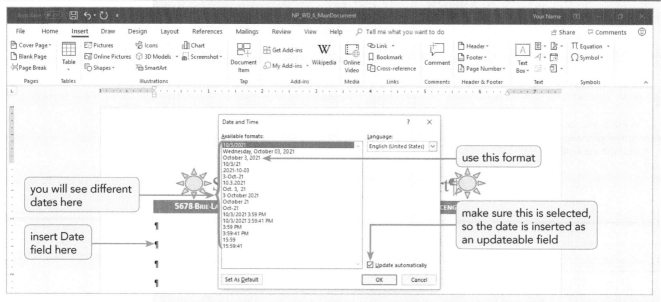

you will see different dates here

insert Date field here

use this format

make sure this is selected, so the date is inserted as an updateable field

The Available formats list provides options for inserting the current date and time. In this case, you want to insert the date as a content control in a format that includes the complete name of the month, the date, and the year (for example, March 11, 2021).

▶ **7.** In the Available formats list, click the third format from the top, which is the month, date, and year format.

▶ **8.** If necessary, select the **Update automatically** check box so the date is inserted as a content control that updates every time you open the document.

▶ **9.** Click **OK**. The current date is inserted in the document. At this point, it looks like ordinary text. To see the content control, you have to click the date.

▶ **10.** Click the date to display the content control. If you closed the document and then opened it a day later, the content control would automatically display the new date. See Figure 6–2.

Figure 6–2   Date field inside content control

current date is displayed inside a content control

▶ **11.** Scroll down to display the letter's closing, change "Amalia Ferreira" to your first and last names, and then scroll back up to the beginning of the letter.

▶ **12.** Save the document.

Now that the document contains the current date, you can begin the mail merge process.

Performing a Mail Merge

When you perform a mail merge, you insert individualized information from a data source into a main document. A main document can be a letter or any other kind of document containing merge fields that tell Word where to insert names, addresses, and other variable information from the data source. A main document can contain photos, shapes, SmartArt, tables, links to online videos, or any other type of non-text element. It can also be formatted with any theme or style set you want, or with any page layout options you want. For example, you could format a main document with custom margins, created by clicking the Margins button on the Layout tab, clicking Custom Margins, and then adjusting the Margins settings on the Margins tab of the Page Setup dialog box. In other words, the overall look of the main document is up to you, but you should take care to make sure it looks professional and is easy to read.

When you **merge** the main document with information from the data source, you produce a new document called a merged document. The Session 6.1 Visual Overview summarizes mail merge concepts.

Amalia's main document is the letter shown in the Session 6.1 Visual Overview. In this session, you will insert the merge fields shown in this letter. You'll also create Amalia's data source, which will include the name and address of each potential client. The data source will also include information about each person's preferred type of consultation (fitness or nutrition) and preferred type of fitness class (yoga or weight lifting).

You can perform a mail merge by using the Mail Merge pane, which walks you through the steps of performing a mail merge. You access the Mail Merge pane by clicking the Start Mail Merge button in the Start Mail Merge group on the Mailings tab and then clicking the Step-by-Step Mail Merge Wizard command on the menu. You can also use the options on the Mailings tab, which streamlines the process and offers more tools. In this module, you'll work with the Mailings tab to complete the mail merge for Amalia. The Mailings tab organizes the steps in the mail merge process so that you can move from left to right across the ribbon using the buttons to complete the merge.

Starting the Mail Merge and Selecting a Main Document

The first step in the mail merge process is selecting the type of main document. Your choice of main document type affects the commands that are available to you later as you continue through the mail merge process, so it's important to make the correct selection at the beginning. In this case, you will use a letter as the main document.

To start the mail merge process and select a main document:

▶ **1.** On the ribbon, click the **Mailings** tab.

Notice that most of the buttons in the groups on the Mailings tab are grayed out, indicating the options are unavailable. These options become available only after you begin the mail merge process and select a data source.

▶ **2.** In the Start Mail Merge group, click the **Start Mail Merge** button. The Start Mail Merge menu opens, as shown in Figure 6–3.

Figure 6–3   **Start Mail Merge menu**

The first five options on the menu allow you to specify the type of main document you will create. Most of the options involve print items, such as labels and letters, but you can also select an email message as the type of main document. In this case, you'll create a letter.

▶ 3. Click **Letters**. The Start Mail Merge menu closes.

Next, you need to select the list of recipients for Amalia's letter; that is, you need to select the data source.

▶ 4. In the Start Mail Merge group, click the **Select Recipients** button. The Select Recipients menu allows you to create a new recipient list, use an existing list, or select from Outlook Contacts (the address book in Outlook).

Because Amalia hasn't had a chance to create a data source yet, she asks you to create one.

▶ 5. Click **Type a New List**. The New Address List dialog box opens, as shown in Figure 6–4.

| Figure 6–4 | New Address List dialog box |

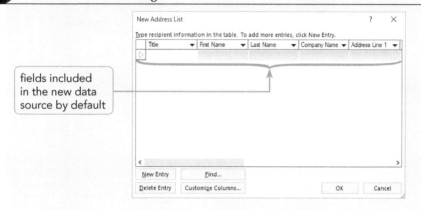

fields included in the new data source by default

The default fields for a data source are displayed in this dialog box. Before you begin creating the data source, you need to identify the fields and records Amalia wants you to include.

Creating a Data Source

As described in the Session 6.1 Visual Overview, a data source is a file that contains information organized into fields and records. Typically, the data source for a mail merge contains a list of names and addresses, but it can also contain email addresses, phone numbers, and other data. Various kinds of files can be used as the data source, including an Excel workbook or an Access database. You can also use a file from another kind of database, such as one created by a company to store its sales information. For a simple mail merge project, such as a phone directory, you can use a table stored in a Word document.

When performing a mail merge, you'll usually select an existing data source file—created in another application—that already contains the necessary information. However, in this module, you'll create a new data source in Word and then enter the data into it so you can familiarize yourself with the basic structure of a data source. After creating the new data source, you'll save the file in its default format as an Access database file, with an .mdb file extension. Microsoft Outlook also uses MDB files to store contact information—in which case they are referred to as Microsoft Office Address Lists files.

When you create a new data source, Word provides a number of default fields, such as First Name, Last Name, and Company Name. You can customize the data source by adding new fields and removing the default fields that you don't plan to use. When creating a data source, keep in mind that each field name must be unique; you can't have two fields with the same name.

The Microsoft Office Address Lists file you will create in this session will contain information about Amalia's potential clients, including each person's name, address, preferred type of consultation (fitness or nutrition), and preferred type of fitness class (yoga or weight lifting). Figure 6–5 shows one of the forms Amalia used to collect the information.

Figure 6–5	New client information card

The information on each form will make up one record in the data source. Each blank on the form translates into one field in the data source, as shown in Figure 6–6.

Figure 6–6	Fields to include in the data source

Field Names	Description
First Name	Client's first name
Last Name	Client's last name
Address Line 1	Client's street address
Address Line 2	Additional address information, such as an apartment number
City	City
State	State
ZIP Code	Zip code
E-mail Address	Email address
Phone	Home or mobile number
Consultation Type	Preferred consultation type
Fitness Class	Preferred fitness class

Even though you won't need email addresses or phone numbers to complete the mail merge, it's a good idea to include them in the data source. That way, Amalia can reuse the data source in future mail merges to send emails or when creating a directory of client phone numbers. When creating a data source, it's always wise to think ahead to possible future uses for it.

REFERENCE

Creating a Data Source for a Mail Merge

- On the ribbon, click the Mailings tab.
- In the Start Mail Merge group, click the Select Recipients button, and then click Type a New List to open the New Address List dialog box.
- To select the fields for your data source, click the Customize Columns button to open the Customize Address List dialog box.
- To delete an unnecessary field, select it, click the Delete button, and then click Yes.
- To add a new field, click the Add button, type the name of the field in the Add Field dialog box, and then click OK.
- To rearrange the order of the field names, click a field name, and then click the Move Up button or the Move Down button.
- To rename a field, click a field name, click the Rename button to open the Rename Field dialog box, type a new field name, and then click OK to close the Rename Field dialog box.
- Click OK to close the Customize Address List dialog box.
- In the New Address List dialog box, enter information for the first record, click the New Entry button, and then enter the information for the next record. Continue until you are finished entering all the information for the data source, and then click OK to open the Save Address List dialog box.
- Type a name for the data source in the File name box. By default, Word will save the file to the My Data Sources folder unless you specify another save location. Click the Save button. The file is saved with the .mdb file extension.

You're ready to create the data source for the form letter using information Amalia has given you for three potential clients. However, before you begin entering information, you need to customize the list of fields to include only the fields Amalia requires.

To customize the list of fields before creating the data source:

▶ **1.** In the New Address List dialog box, click the **Customize Columns** button. The Customize Address List dialog box opens. Here you can delete the fields you don't need, add new ones, and arrange the fields in the order you want. You'll start by deleting some fields.

▶ **2.** In the Field Names box, verify that **Title** is selected, and then click the **Delete** button. A message is displayed, asking you to confirm the deletion.

▶ **3.** Click the **Yes** button. The Title field is deleted from the list of field names.

▶ **4.** Continue using the Delete button to delete the following fields: **Company Name**, **Country or Region**, and **Work Phone**.

Next, you need to add some new fields. When you add a new field, it is inserted below the selected field, so you'll start by selecting the last field in the list.

▶ **5.** In the Field Names box, click **E-mail Address**, and then click the **Add** button. The Add Field dialog box opens, asking you to type a name for your field. See Figure 6–7.

Figure 6–7   Add Field dialog box

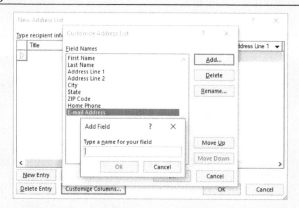

6. Type **Consultation Type** and then click **OK**. The field "Consultation Type" is added to the Field Names list.

7. Use the Add button to add the **Fitness Class** field below the Consultation Type field.

   Next, you need to move the E-mail Address field up above the Home Phone field, so that the fields are in the same order as they appear on the form shown in Figure 6–5.

8. Click **E-mail Address**, and then click the **Move Up** button. The E-mail Address field moves up, so it is now displayed just before the Home Phone field.

   Finally, because Amalia's form asks people to fill in a home or mobile phone number, you need to change "Home Phone" to simply "Phone."

9. Click **Home Phone**, and then click the **Rename** button to open the Rename Field dialog box.

10. In the To box, replace "Home Phone" with **Phone** and then click **OK** to close the Rename Field dialog box and return to the Customize Address List dialog box. See Figure 6–8.

Figure 6–8   Customized list of field names

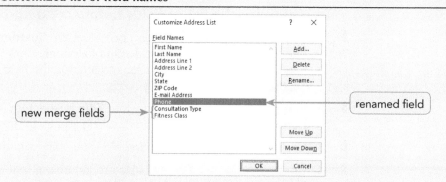

11. Click **OK** in the Customize Address List dialog box to close it and return to the New Address List dialog box. This dialog box reflects the changes you just made. For instance, it no longer includes the Title field. The fields are listed in the same order as they appeared in the Customize Address List dialog box.

12. Use the horizontal scroll bar near the bottom of the New Address List dialog box to scroll to the right to display the Consultation Type and Fitness Class fields. See Figure 6–9.

| Figure 6–9 | Changes made to New Address List dialog box |

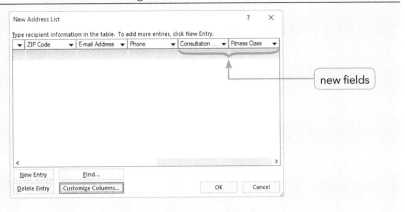

Organizing Field Names

INSIGHT

Although the order of field names in the data source doesn't affect their placement in the main document, it's helpful to arrange field names logically in the data source so you can enter information quickly and efficiently. For example, you'll probably want the First Name field next to the Last Name field. To make it easier to transfer information from a paper form to a data source, it's a good idea to arrange the fields in the same order as on the form, just like you did in the preceding steps. Also, note that if you include spaces in your field names, Word will replace the spaces with underscores when you insert the fields into the main document. For example, Word transforms the field name "First Name" into "First_Name."

Now that you have specified the fields you want to use, you are ready to enter the information into the data source.

Entering Data into a Data Source

Amalia has given you three completed new client information forms and has asked you to enter the information from the forms into the data source. You'll use the New Address List dialog box to enter the information. As you press TAB to move right from one field to the next, the dialog box will scroll to display fields that are not currently visible.

To enter data into a record using the New Address List dialog box:

1. In the New Address List dialog box, scroll to the left to display the First Name field.

2. Click in the **First Name** field, if necessary, and then type **Lari** to enter the first name of the first person.

   Do not press SPACEBAR after you finish typing an entry in the New Address List dialog box.

TIP

You can press SHIFT+TAB to move the insertion point to the previous field.

3. Press **TAB** to move the insertion point to the Last Name field.

4. Type **Peterson** and then press **TAB** to move the insertion point to the Address Line 1 field.

5. Type **45 Faircrest Avenue** and then press **TAB** to move the insertion point to the Address Line 2 field.

6. Type **Apartment 7A** and then press **TAB** to move the insertion point to the City field.

7. Type **La Mesa** and then press **TAB** to move the insertion point to the State field.

8. Type **CA** and then press **TAB** to move the insertion point to the ZIP Code field.

9. Type **91942** and then press **TAB** to move the insertion point to the E-mail Address field.

10. Type **peterson@sample.cengage.com** and then press **TAB** to move the insertion point to the Phone field.

11. Type **858-555-0105** and then press **TAB** to move the insertion point to the Consultation Type field.

12. Type **fitness** and then press **TAB**. The insertion point is now in the Fitness Class field, which is the last field in the data source.

13. Type **yoga** and then stop. Do not press TAB.

14. Use the horizontal scroll bar to scroll to the left, and then review the data in the record. See Figure 6–10.

| Figure 6–10 | Completed record |

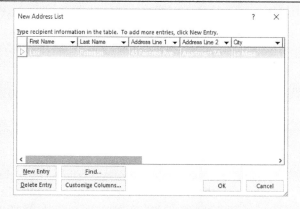

You have finished entering the information for the first record of the data source. Now you're ready to enter information for the next two records. You can create a new record by clicking the New Entry button, or by pressing TAB after you have finished entering information into the last field for a record. Note that within a record, you can leave some fields blank. For example, only two of the three new client forms include information for the Address Line 2 field.

To add additional records to the data source:

▶ **1.** In the New Address List dialog box, click the **New Entry** button. A new, blank record is created.

▶ **2.** Enter the information shown in Figure 6–11 for the next two records. To start the Carlos Carlyle record, press **TAB** after completing the Fitness Class field for the Daniel Ahrens record.

Figure 6–11   Information for records 2 and 3

First Name	Last Name	Address Line 1	Address Line 2	City	State	ZIP Code	E-mail Address	Phone	Consultation Type	Fitness Class
Daniel	Ahrens	603 Jung Road	P.O. Box 6375	San Diego	CA	91911	ahrens@sample.cengage.com	760-555-0112	nutrition	weights
Carlos	Carlyle	278 S. Linder Avenue		La Mesa	CA	91942	carlyle@sample.cengage.com	619-555-0107	nutrition	yoga

Note that the Address Line 2 field should be blank in the Carlos Carlyle record.

Trouble? If you start a fourth record by mistake, click the Delete Entry button to remove the blank fourth record.

You have entered the records for three potential clients. Amalia's data source eventually will contain hundreds of records for spa clients. The current data source, however, contains the records Amalia wants to work with now. Next, you need to save the data source.

Saving a Data Source

TIP

In File Explorer, the file type for a Microsoft Office Address Lists file is "Microsoft Access Database."

After you finish entering data for your new data source, you can close the New Address List dialog box. When you do so, the Save Address List dialog box opens, where you can save the data source using the default file type, Microsoft Office Address Lists.

To save the data source:

▶ **1.** In the New Address List dialog box, click **OK**. The New Address List dialog box closes, and the Save Address List dialog box opens, as shown in Figure 6–12.

Figure 6–12   Saving the data source

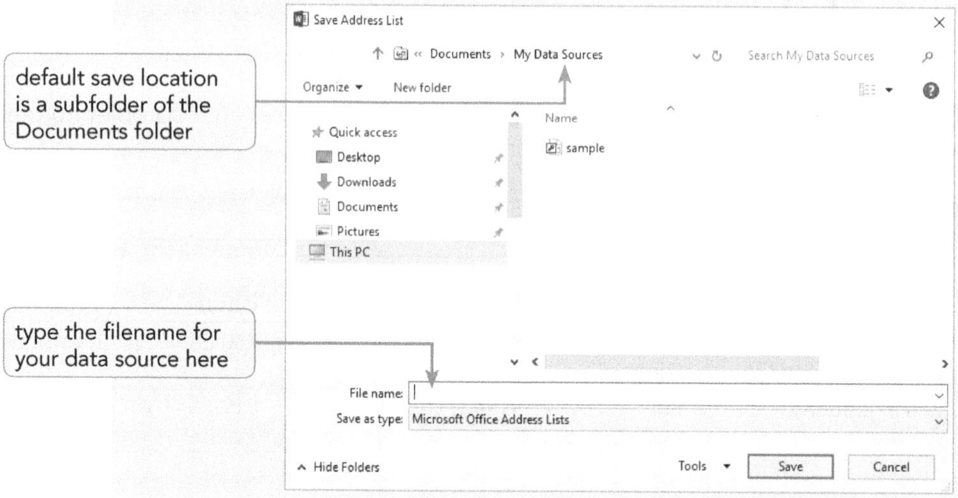

default save location is a subfolder of the Documents folder

type the filename for your data source here

The Save as type box indicates that the data source will be saved as a Microsoft Office Address Lists file. The File name box is empty; you need to name the file before saving it.

2. Click the **File name** box, if necessary, and then type **NP_WD_6_Data**.

   Unless you specify another save location, Word will save the file to the My Data Sources folder, which is a subfolder of the Documents folder.

   In this case, you'll save the data source in the same location in which you saved the main document.

3. Navigate to the location in which you saved the main document, and then click the **Save** button. The Save Address List dialog box closes, and you return to the main document.

The next step in the mail merge process is to add the necessary merge fields to the main document. For Amalia's letter, you need to add merge fields for the inside address, for the salutation, and for each person's preferred consultation type and fitness class.

Decision Making: Planning Your Data Source

When creating a data source, think beyond the current mail merge task to possible future uses for your data source. For example, Amalia's data source includes both an E-mail Address field and a Phone field—not because she wants to use that information in the current mail merge project, but because she can foresee needing these pieces of information at a later date to communicate with her clients. Having all relevant client information in one data source will make it easier to retrieve and use the information effectively.

In some cases, you'll also want to include information that might seem obvious. For example, Amalia's data source includes a State field even though all of her current clients live in or around San Diego, California. However, she included a State field because she knows that her pool of addresses could expand sometime in the future to include residents of other states.

Finally, think about the structure of your data source before you create it. Try to break information down into as many fields as seems reasonable. For example, it's always better to include a First Name field and a Last Name field, rather than simply a Name field, because including two separate fields makes it possible to alphabetize the information in the data source by last name. If you entered first and last names in a single Name field, you could alphabetize only by first name.

If you're working with a very small data source, breaking information down into as many fields as possible is less important. However, it's very common to start with a small data source and then, as time goes on, find that you need to continually add information to the data source, until you have a large file. If you failed to plan the data source adequately at the beginning, the expanded data source could become difficult to manage.

You also need to consider the type of file you use to store your data source. In this session, you created a data source from within Word and saved it as a Microsoft Office Address Lists file. If you wanted, you could edit the file later in Microsoft Access, using its powerful data manipulation features. If you are more comfortable working in Excel, consider creating your data source in Excel instead, so that you can take advantage of its simpler data manipulation options.

Inserting Merge Fields

When inserting merge fields into the main document, you must include proper spacing around the fields so that the information in the merged document will be formatted correctly. To insert a merge field, you move the insertion point to the location where you want to insert the merge field, and then click the Insert Merge Field arrow in the Write & Insert Fields group.

For Amalia's letter, you will build an inside address by inserting individual merge fields for the address elements. The letter is a standard business letter, so you'll place merge fields for the name and address below the date. Note that you could also insert the address as one address block field. But in these steps, you'll insert separate fields for each part of the address, so you can get some practice inserting fields.

To insert a merge field in the main document:

▶ **1.** Click in the second blank paragraph below the date.

▶ **2.** In the Write & Insert Fields group, click the **Insert Merge Field arrow**.
   A menu opens with the names of all the merge fields in the data source.
   Note that the spaces in the merge field names have been replaced with
   underscores. See Figure 6–13.

Figure 6–13 Insert Merge Field menu

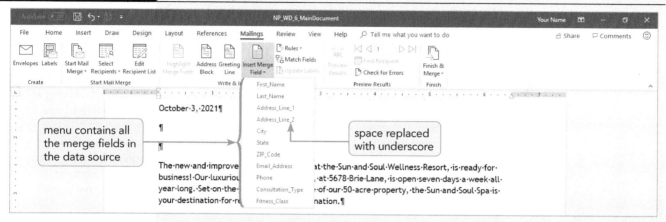

menu contains all the merge fields in the data source

space replaced with underscore

Trouble? If the Insert Merge Field dialog box opens, you clicked the Insert Merge Field button instead of the Insert Merge Field arrow. Close the dialog box and repeat Step 2.

3. Click **First_Name**. The Insert Merge Field menu closes, and the merge field is inserted into the document.

The merge field consists of the field name surrounded by double angled brackets << >>, also called chevrons.

Trouble? If you make a mistake and insert the wrong merge field, click to the left of the merge field, press DEL to select the field, and then press DEL again to delete it.

4. In the Write & Insert Fields group, click the **Highlight Merge Fields** button. The First_Name merge field is displayed on a gray background, making it easier to see in the document. See Figure 6–14.

TIP

You can only insert merge fields into a main document using the tools on the Mailings tab or in the Mail Merge pane. You cannot type merge fields into the main document—even if you type the angled brackets.

Figure 6–14 First_Name merge field highlighted in main document

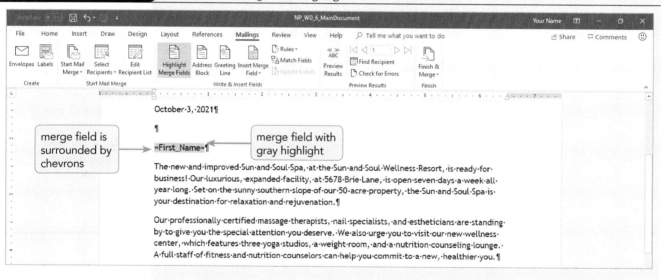

merge field is surrounded by chevrons

merge field with gray highlight

Later, when you merge the main document with the data source, Word will replace the First_Name merge field with information from the First Name field in the data source.

Now you're ready to insert the merge fields for the rest of the inside address. You'll add the necessary spacing and punctuation between the merge fields as well. You might be accustomed to pressing SHIFT+ENTER to start a new line in an inside address without inserting paragraph spacing. However, because your data source includes a record in which one of the fields (the Address Line 2 field) is blank, you need to press ENTER to start each new line. As you will see later in this Module, this ensures that Word hides the Address Line 2 field in the final merged document whenever that field is blank. To maintain the proper spacing in the main document, you'll adjust the paragraph spacing after you insert all the fields.

To insert the remaining merge fields for the inside address:

▶ **1.** Press **SPACEBAR** to insert a space after the First_Name merge field, click the **Insert Merge Field arrow**, and then click **Last_Name**.

▶ **2.** Press **ENTER** to start a new paragraph, click the **Insert Merge Field arrow**, and then click **Address_Line_1**. Word inserts the Address_Line_1 merge field into the form letter.

▶ **3.** Press **ENTER**, click the **Insert Merge Field arrow**, and then click **Address_Line_2**. Word inserts the Address_Line_2 merge field into the form letter.

▶ **4.** Press **ENTER**, insert the **City** merge field, type **,** (a comma), press **SPACEBAR** to insert a space after the comma, and then insert the **State** merge field.

▶ **5.** Press **SPACEBAR**, and then insert the **ZIP_Code** merge field. The inside address now contains all the necessary merge fields. See Figure 6–15.

Figure 6–15   **Main document with merge fields for inside address**

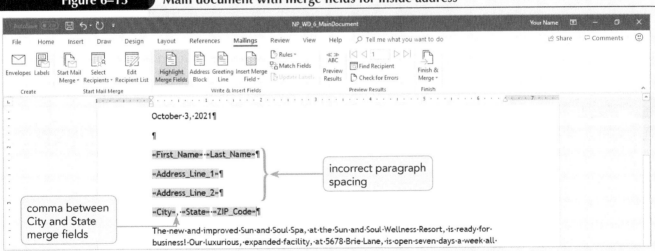

Next, you will adjust the paragraph spacing for the inside address.

▶ **6.** Select the first three paragraphs of the inside address.

▶ **7.** On the ribbon, click the **Home** tab.

▶ **8.** In the Paragraph group, click the **Line and Paragraph Spacing** button ⌶☰⌄, and then click **Remove Space After Paragraph**. The paragraph spacing is removed, so that the paragraphs of the inside address are now correctly spaced.

You can now add the salutation of the letter, which will contain each person's first name. In the following steps, you'll get some practice combining text with merge fields. But keep in mind that you could also insert a greeting line by clicking the Greeting Line button in the Write & Insert Fields group. You could then use the options in the Insert Greeting Line dialog box to create a greeting that makes use of name fields in the data source.

To insert the merge field for the salutation:

▶ 1. Insert a new paragraph after the ZIP_Code field, type **Dear** and then press **SPACEBAR**.

▶ 2. On the ribbon, click the **Mailings** tab.

▶ 3. In the Write & Insert Fields group, click the **Insert Merge Field arrow**, click **First_Name** to insert this field into the document, and then type : (a colon).

▶ 4. Save the document.

You'll further personalize Amalia's letter by including merge fields that will allow you to reference each person's preferred consultation type and fitness class.

To add a merge field for the preferred consultation type:

▶ 1. If necessary, scroll down to display the paragraph that begins "Bring along this letter...."

▶ 2. In the second line of the paragraph that begins "Bring along this letter," select the placeholder text **[CONSULTATION TYPE]**, including the brackets. You'll replace this phrase with a merge field. Don't be concerned if you also select the space following the closing bracket.

▶ 3. Insert the **Consultation_Type** merge field. Word replaces the selected text with the **Consultation_Type** merge field.

▶ 4. Verify that the field has a single space before it (on the preceding line) and after it. Add a space on either side if necessary. See Figure 6-16.

Figure 6-16 Main document after inserting merge fields

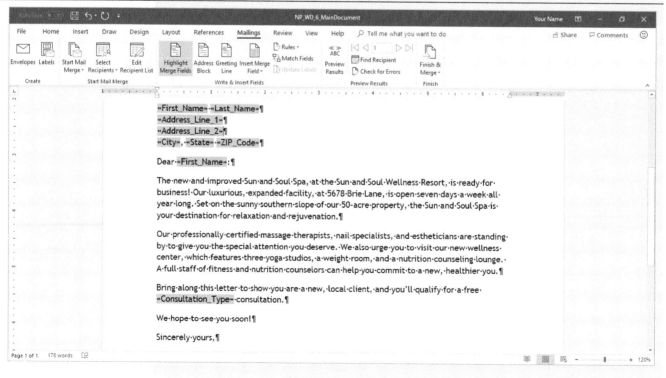

> **Trouble?** The text before and after the inserted merge fields might be marked with a blue underline because Word mistakenly identifies the text as a grammatical error. You can ignore the blue underlines.

▶ **5.** Save the document.

The main document now contains almost all the necessary merge fields. You need to add one more that displays one sentence for records that contain "yoga" in the Fitness Class field, and a different sentence for records that contain "weights" in the Fitness Class field. You can do that by creating a mail merge rule.

Creating a Mail Merge Rule

A **mail merge rule** is an instruction that tells Word to complete a mail merge a certain way depending on whether a specific condition is met. For example, a condition could specify that a particular value must appear in one of the mail merge fields. This would allow you to create a mail merge rule that tells Word to skip a record in the data source if the ZIP Code field contains a particular zip code. Such a rule would be useful if you were creating letters announcing the grand opening of a new car wash and wanted to avoid sending letters to people who live in a distant zip code, because they live too far away to be likely clients.

One of the most useful type of mail merge rules is an **If...Then...Else rule**, which tells Word to choose between two options based on the contents of a particular field. In this case, Amalia wants to create a mail merge rule based on the contents of the Fitness Class field, which contains one of two possibilities: yoga or weights. It's easier to understand how an If...Then...Else rule works if you replace "Else" with "Otherwise." With this in mind, the basic logic of the rule Amalia wants you to create is shown in Figure 6–17. If the Fitness Class field contains the word "yoga" then Word will insert the sentence about the new hot yoga studios. Otherwise (that is, if the Fitness Class field contains "weights" instead of "yoga"), Word will insert the sentence about the new weight rooms. In this case, the line "The Fitness Class field contains the word yoga" is the condition.

Figure 6–17   Amalia's If...Then...Else rule

IF

The Fitness Class field contains the word *yoga*.

THEN

Insert the sentence *We also hope you'll save time to tour our new hot yoga studios.*

ELSE (OTHERWISE)

Insert the sentence *And by the way, feel free to spend an hour trying out our new weight room.*

In the following steps, you'll create a mail merge rule.

To create an If...Then...Else mail merge rule:

▶ **1.** Click at the end of the paragraph that contains the <<Consultation Type>> field, and press **SPACEBAR** to insert a space after the period.

▶ **2.** In the Write & Insert Fields group, click the **Rules** button and then click **If...Then...Else** to open the Insert Word Field: IF dialog box. In the first row of boxes, you need to specify the condition that needs to be met in order for Word to insert the sentence about yoga studios.

▶ **3.** Click the **Field name arrow**, scroll down and then click **Fitness_Class**. By default, the Comparison box contains "Equal to" which is what you want. Now you need to specify what the Fitness Class field must contain in order for Word to display the sentence about hot yoga studios.

▶ **4.** Click the Compare to box and type **yoga**. Next, you need to type the sentence that you want Word to insert when the Fitness Class field contains the word "yoga."

▶ **5.** Click the **Insert this text** box, and then type **We also hope you'll save time to tour our new hot yoga studios.** Finally, you need to type the sentence that you want Word to insert when the Fitness Class field contains the word "weights."

▶ **6.** Click the **Otherwise insert this text** box, and then type **And by the way, feel free to spend an hour trying out our new weight room.** Your Insert Word Field: IF dialog box should match Figure 6–18.

Figure 6–18 **Insert Word Field: IF dialog box**

condition that needs to be met for Word to insert a sentence about yoga studios

sentence Word will insert if the condition is true

sentence Word will insert if the condition is false

Insert Word Field: IF

IF

Field name: Fitness_Class   Comparison: Equal to   Compare to: yoga

Insert this text:
We also hope you'll save time to tour our new hot yoga studios.

Otherwise insert this text:
And by the way, feel free to spend an hour trying out our new weight room.

OK   Cancel

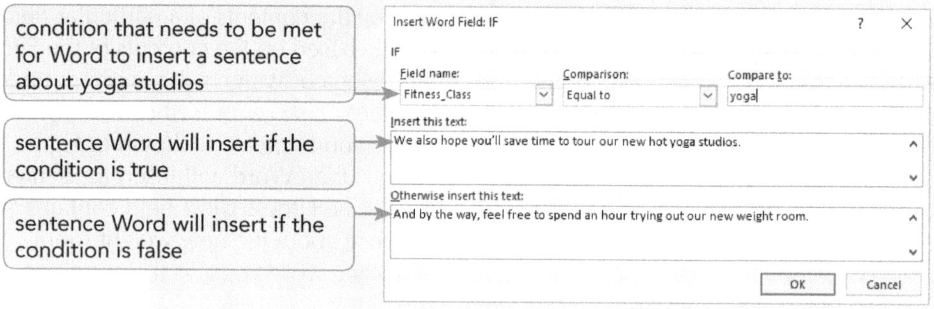

▶ **7.** Click **OK**. The sentence about the yoga studios is inserted into the document as a placeholder. When you complete the mail merge, the sentence included in the letters will vary, depending on the contents of the Fitness Class field. For now, you just need to make sure that the placeholder sentence is formatted to match the rest of the document.

▶ **8.** Triple-click in the paragraph to select the entire paragraph, click the **Home** tab, click the **Font arrow**, click **Trebuchet MS (Body)**, and then save the document. Now the entire paragraph is formatted in the same font.

▶ **9.** Click anywhere in the document. See Figure 6–19.

Figure 6-19   Placeholder sentence formatted to match the rest of the paragraph

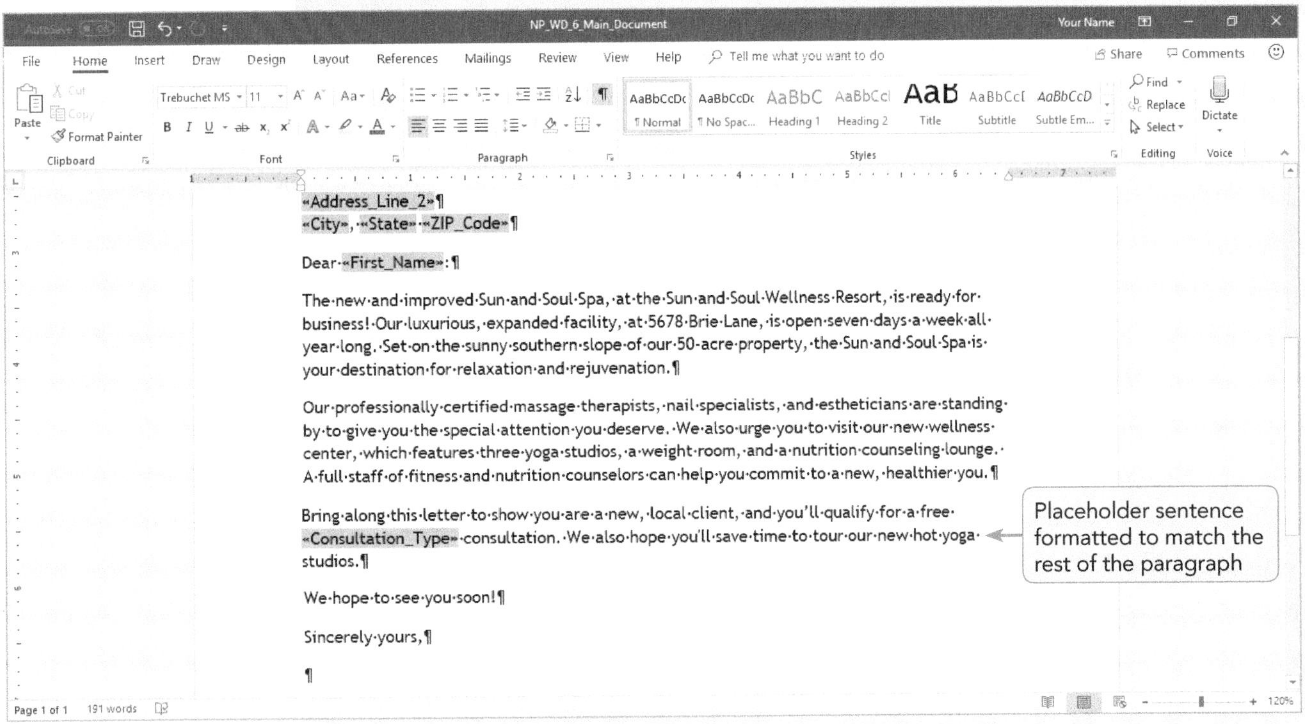

You've finished creating the mail merge rule. Your next step is to preview the merged document to see how the letter will look after Word inserts the information for each potential client.

Previewing the Merged Document

When you preview the merged document, you can check one last time for any missing spaces between the merge fields and the surrounding text. You can also look for any other formatting problems, and, if necessary, make final changes to the data source.

To preview the merged document:

▶ 1. Click the **Mailings** tab.

▶ 2. In the Preview Results group, click the **Preview Results** button, and then scroll up to display the inside address. The data for the first record (Lari Peterson) replaces the merge fields in the form letter. On the ribbon, the Go to Record box in the Preview Results group shows which record is currently displayed in the document. See Figure 6–20.

Figure 6–20   **Letter with merged data for first record**

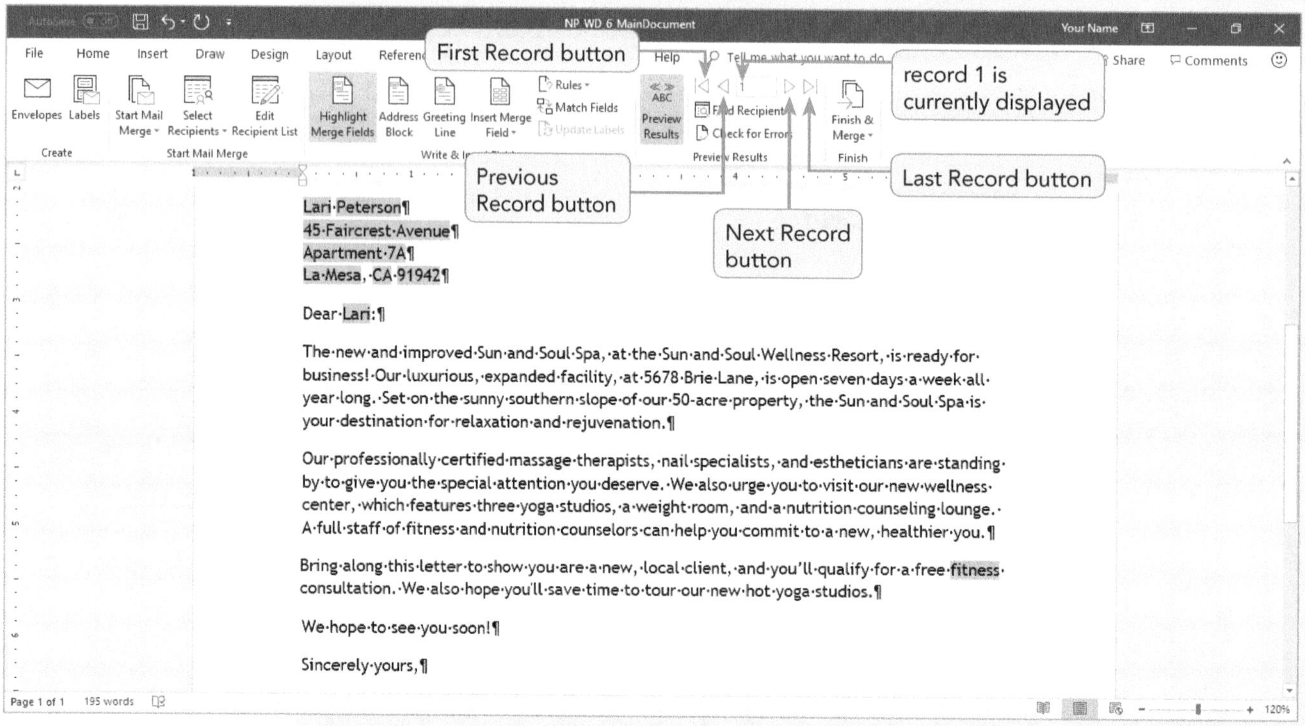

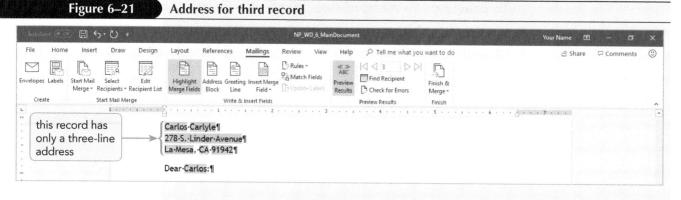

Note that the inside address, which includes information from the Address Line 2 field, contains a total of four lines.

▶ 3. Carefully check the Lari Peterson letter to make sure the text and formatting are correct, and make any necessary corrections. In particular, make sure that the spacing before and after the merged data is correct; it is easy to accidentally omit spaces or add extra spaces around merge fields.

▶ 4. In the Preview Results group, click the **Next Record** ▷ button. The data for Daniel Ahrens is displayed in the letter. As with the preceding record, the inside address for this record includes four lines of information.

▶ 5. Click the **Next Record** button ▷ again to display the data for Carlos Carlyle in the letter. In this case, the inside address includes only three lines of information. See Figure 6–21.

Figure 6–21   **Address for third record**

▶ 6. In the Preview Results group, click the **First Record** button ◁ to redisplay the first record in the letter (with data for Lari Peterson).

The main document of the mail merge is complete. Now that you have previewed the merged documents, you can finish the merge.

Merging the Main Document and the Data Source

When you finish a merge, you can choose to merge directly to the printer. In other words, you can choose to have Word print the merged document immediately without saving it as a separate file. Alternatively, you can merge to a new document, which you can save using a new file name. If your data source includes an E-mail Address field, you can also create a mail merge in email format, generating one email for every email address in the data source.

Amalia wants to save an electronic copy of the merged document for her records, so you'll merge the data source and main document into a new document.

To complete the mail merge:

▶ 1. In the Finish group, click the **Finish & Merge** button. The Finish & Merge menu displays the three merge options. See Figure 6–22.

| Figure 6–22 | Finishing the merge |

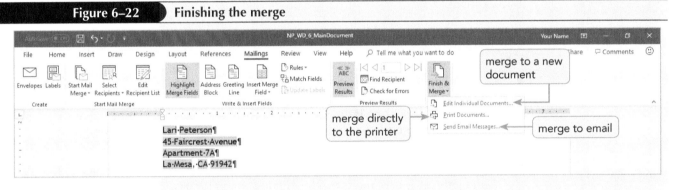

▶ 2. In the Finish & Merge menu, click **Edit Individual Documents**. The Merge to New Document dialog box opens. Here, you need to specify which records to include in the merge. You want to include all three records from the data source.

▶ 3. Verify that the **All** option button is selected, and then click **OK**. Word creates a new document named Letters1, which contains three pages—one for each record in the data source. See Figure 6–23.

Figure 6–23   Merged document

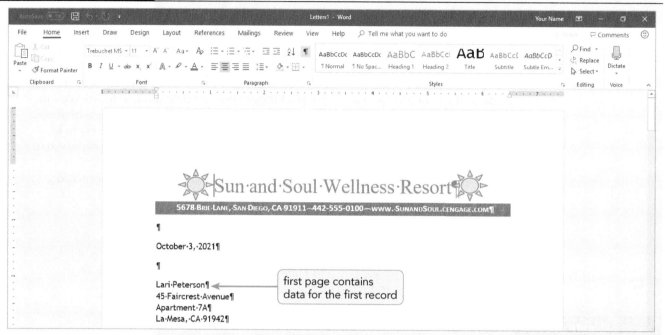

In this new document, the merge fields have been replaced by the specific names, addresses, and so on from the data source.

4. Scroll down and review the contents of the document. Note that each letter is addressed to a different person, and that the preferred consultation type varies from one letter to the next. Also, each letter contains either the sentence about the new yoga studios or the sentence about the weight room.

5. Scroll back to the first page of the document, and as you scroll, notice that the letters are separated by Next Page section breaks.

6. Save the merged document in the location specified by your instructor, using the file name **NP_WD_6_MergedLetters**.

7. **sam** Close the **NP_WD_6_MergedLetters.docx** document. The document named "**NP_WD_6_MainDocument.docx**" is now the active document.

After completing a merge, you need to save the main document. This ensures that any changes you might have made to the data source during the course of the mail merge are saved along with the main document.

8. **sam** Save and close the **NP_WD_6_MainDocument.docx** file.

Note that if you need to take a break while working on a mail merge, you can save the main document and close it. The data source and field information are saved along with the document. When you're ready to work on the merge again, you can open the main document and update the connection to the data source. You'll see how this works at the beginning of the next session, when you will learn how to use additional mail merge features.

REVIEW

Session 6.1 Quick Check

1. Explain how to insert a Date field that updates automatically every time the document is opened.

2. Define the following:
   a. merge field
   b. record
   c. main document
   d. data source

3. List at least three types of files that you can use as data sources in a mail merge.

4. What is the first step in performing a mail merge?

5. Explain how to use the options on the Mailings tab to insert a merge field into a main document.

6. What button do you click to begin creating a mail merge rule?

Session 6.2 Visual Overview:

The Edit Recipient List button opens the Mail Merge Recipients dialog box.

In the Mail Merge Recipients dialog box, you can make changes that affect individual records or the structure and organization of the data source itself.

To sort a data source according to the contents of a particular field, click that field's column header. To sort in ascending order, click the field header once. To sort in descending order, click it twice.

A checkmark indicates that a record will be included in the merge. By default, all records are checked. To omit a record from the merge, click its check box to delete the checkmark.

To make changes to the contents of individual records, select the data source in the Data Source box, and then click the Edit button to open the Edit Data Source dialog box.

AutoSave ● Off ⊟ ↶ ⟳ ⤓   MainDocument

File   Home   Insert   Draw   Design   Layout   References   **Mailings**

Envelopes   Labels   Start Mail Merge ▾   Select Recipients ▾   Edit Recipient List   Highlight Merge Fields   Address Block   Greeting Line   Insert Merge Field ▾

Create | Start Mail Merge | Write & Insert Fields

Mail Merge Recipients   ?

This is the list of recipients that will be used in your merge. Use the options below to add to or change yo
Use the checkboxes to add or remove recipients from the merge. When your list is ready, click OK.

Data Source	✔	Last Name ▾	First Name ▾	Address Line 1 ▾	Address L
Data.mdb	✔	Peterson	Lari	45 Faircrest Avenue	Apartme
Data.mdb	✔	Ahrens	Daniel	603 Jung Road	P.O. Box
Data.mdb	✔	Carlyle	Carlos	278 S. Linder Avenue	
Data.mdb	✔	Nguyen	Sally	2054 Paseo Boulevard	Apartme
Data.mdb	✔	Mendez	Simon	10 Eleanor Rains Street	
Data.mdb	✔	Rosenblum	Heidi	55 Blue Dolphin Crest	P.O. Box

‹

Data Source

Data.mdb

Edit...   Refresh

Refine recipient list

A↓Z Sort...
▥ Filter...
⊠↓ Find duplicates...
🔎 Find recipient...
☑ Validate addresses...

To sort by more than one field, click the Sort command.

You can click the Filter command to further customize a data source. When you filter data, you temporarily display only records that contain a particular value in a particular field.

195 words

you deserve. We al
studios, a weight ro
counselors can help

Bring along this letter to show you are a new, local clie
consultation. We also hope you'll save time to tour our

Editing a Data source

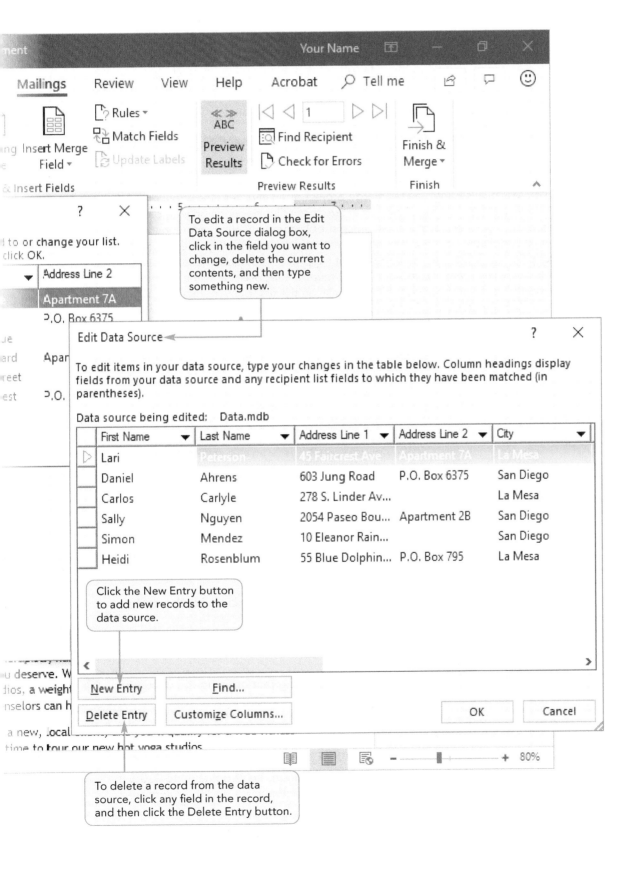

To edit a record in the Edit Data Source dialog box, click in the field you want to change, delete the current contents, and then type something new.

Edit Data Source

To edit items in your data source, type your changes in the table below. Column headings display fields from your data source and any recipient list fields to which they have been matched (in parentheses).

Data source being edited: Data.mdb

First Name	Last Name	Address Line 1	Address Line 2	City
Lari	Peterson	45 Faircrest Ave	Apartment 7A	La Mesa
Daniel	Ahrens	603 Jung Road	P.O. Box 6375	San Diego
Carlos	Carlyle	278 S. Linder Av...		La Mesa
Sally	Nguyen	2054 Paseo Bou...	Apartment 2B	San Diego
Simon	Mendez	10 Eleanor Rain...		San Diego
Heidi	Rosenblum	55 Blue Dolphin...	P.O. Box 795	La Mesa

Click the New Entry button to add new records to the data source.

New Entry   Find...

Delete Entry   Customize Columns...   OK   Cancel

To delete a record from the data source, click any field in the record, and then click the Delete Entry button.

Reopening a Main Document

Performing a mail merge creates a connection between the main document file and the data source file. This connection persists even after you close the main document and exit Word. The connection is maintained as long as you keep both files in their original locations. The two files don't have to be in the same folder; each file just has to remain in the folder it was in when you first performed the mail merge.

When you reopen a main document, you see a warning dialog box explaining that data from a database (that is, the data source) will be placed in the document you are about to open. You can click Yes to open the document with its connection to the data source intact.

PROSKILLS

Teamwork: Sharing Main Documents and Data Sources

In professional settings, a mail merge project often involves files originating from multiple people. The best way to manage these files depends on your particular situation. For instance, at a small office supply company, the marketing manager might supply the text of a main document introducing monthly sales on printer supplies, while the sales manager might supply an updated list of names and addresses of potential customers every month. Suppose that you are the person responsible for performing the mail merge on the first of every month. You'll be able to work more efficiently if you, the marketing manager, and the sales manager agree ahead of time on one storage location for the project. For example, you might set up a special folder on the company network for storing these files.

In large companies that maintain massive databases of customer information, a data source is typically stored at a fixed network location. In those situations, you'll probably need to work with the technical staff who manage the databases to gain access to the data sources you need for your mail merge projects. Maintaining the security of such data sources is extremely important, and you usually can't access them without a password and the appropriate encryption software.

Amalia has information about some additional potential clients. She wants you to add this information to the data source that you used in the previous mail merge, and she wants you to perform another merge with the new data. To add the new client information, you will start by opening the NP_WD_6_MainDocument.docx file, which is linked to the data source.

To reopen the main document with its connection to the data source intact:

▸ 1. Open the document **NP_WD_6_MainDocument.docx** from the location in which you stored it in Session 6.1.

Word displays a warning message indicating that opening the document will run a SQL command. SQL (usually pronounced *sequel*) is the database programming language that controls the connection between the main document and the data source.

▸ 2. Click **Yes** to open the main document with its link to the data source intact.

▸ 3. On the ribbon, click the **Mailings** tab, change the Zoom level to 120% if necessary, and make sure the nonprinting characters and the rulers are displayed.

The main document displays the data for the last record you examined when you previewed the merged document (Lari Peterson). You can alternate between displaying the merge fields and the information from the data file by toggling the Preview Results button on the Mailings tab.

Trouble? If you see the merge fields instead of the data for one of the records, skip to Step 5.

▶ **4.** In the Preview Results group, click the **Preview Results** button to deselect it. The merge fields are displayed in the main document. At the beginning of the letter, the Date field, which is not a merge field, continues to display the current date.

▶ **5.** If necessary, highlight the merge fields by clicking the **Highlight Merge Fields** button in the Write & Insert Fields group.

INSIGHT

Maintaining, Breaking, and Reestablishing the Connection to a Data Source

As you have seen, when you reopen a main document, Word displays a warning dialog box, where you can click Yes to open the document with its connection to the data source intact. But what if you want to break the connection between the main document and the data source? One option is to click No in the warning dialog box. In that case, the main document opens with no connection to the data source. If the main document is currently open and already connected to the data source, you can break the connection by clicking Normal Word Document on the Start Mail Merge menu. You can reestablish the connection at any time by starting the mail merge over again and using the Select Recipients button to select the data source.

Keep in mind that you could also break the connection between a main document and its data source if you move one or both of the files to a different folder. Exactly what happens in this case depends on how your computer is set up and where you move the files. In the case of a broken connection, when you open the main document, you'll see a series of message boxes informing you that the connection to the data source has been broken. Eventually, you will see a Microsoft Word dialog box with a button labelled Find Data Source, which you can click, and then use the Select Data Source dialog box to locate and select your data source.

If you are creating mail merges for personal use, it's a good idea to either store the data source in the default My Data Sources folder or store the data source and the main document together—in a folder other than the My Data Sources folder. The latter option is best if you think you might need to move the files to a different computer. That way, if you do need to move them, you can move the entire folder.

Editing a Data Source

After you complete a mail merge, you might need to make some changes to the data source and redo the merge. You can edit a data source in two ways—from within the program used to create the data source, or via the Mail Merge Recipients dialog box in Word. If you are familiar with the program used to create the data source, the simplest approach is to edit the file from within that program. For example, if you were using an Excel worksheet as your data source, you could open the file in Excel, edit it (perhaps by adding new records), save it, and then reselect the file as your data source. To edit the Microsoft Office Address Lists file that you created as a data source for this project, you can use the Mail Merge Recipients dialog box.

REFERENCE

Editing a Microsoft Office Address Lists Data Source in Word

- Open the main document for the data source you want to edit.
- On the ribbon, click the Mailings tab.
- In the Start Mail Merge group, click the Edit Recipient List button.
- In the Data Source box in the Mail Merge Recipients dialog box, select the data source you want to edit, and then click the Edit button to open the Edit Data Source dialog box.
- To add a record, click the New Entry button, and then enter the data for the new record.
- To delete a record, click any field in the record, and then click the Delete Entry button.
- To add or remove fields from the data source, click the Customize Columns button, click Yes in the warning dialog box, make any changes, and then click OK. Remember that if you remove a field, you will delete any data entered into that field for all records in the data source.
- Click OK in the Edit Data Source dialog box, click Yes in the Microsoft Office Word dialog box, and then click OK in the Mail Merge Recipients dialog box.

Amalia would like you to add information for three new clients to the data source.

To edit the data source by adding records:

1. In the Start Mail Merge group, click the **Edit Recipient List** button.

   The Mail Merge Recipients dialog box opens, displaying the contents of the data source that is currently connected to the main document—the NP_WD_6_Data.mdb file.

   This dialog box is designed to let you edit any data source, not just the one currently connected to the main document. To edit the NP_WD_6_Data.mdb file, you first need to select it in the Data Source box in the lower-left corner of the dialog box. If you had multiple data sources stored in the same folder as the NP_WD_6_Data.mdb file, you would see them all in this list box.

2. In the Data Source box, click **NP_WD_6_Data.mdb**. The file name is selected.

   Note that the file has the extension .mdb, which is the file extension for an Access database file—the default format for a data source created in Word. See Figure 6-24.

| Figure 6–24 | NP_WD_6_Data.mdb file selected in the Data Source box of the Mail Merge Recipients dialog box |

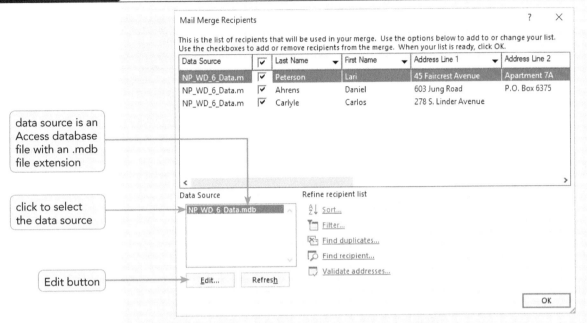

3. Click the **Edit** button. The Edit Data Source dialog box opens.

4. Click the **New Entry** button, and then enter the information for the three new records shown in Figure 6–25.

| Figure 6–25 | New client data |

First Name	Last Name	Address Line 1	Address Line 2	City	State	ZIP Code	E-Mail Address	Phone	Consultation Type	Fitness Class
Sally	Nguyen	2054 Paseo Boulevard	Apartment 2B	San Diego	CA	92199	nguyen@ sample. cengage.com	858-555-0135	fitness	weights
Simon	Mendez	10 Eleanor Rains Street		San Diego	CA	91911	mendez@ sample. cengage.com	760-555-0102	fitness	yoga
Heidi	Rosenblum	55 Blue Dolphin Crest	P.O. Box 795	La Mesa	CA	91942	rosenblum@ sample. cengage.com	619-555-0199	nutrition	yoga

When you are finished, you will have a total of six records in the data source. Notice that the record for Simon Mendez contains no data in the Address Line 2 field.

5. Click **OK**, and then click the **Yes** button in the message box that asks if you want to update the NP_WD_6_Data.mdb file. (Note, you might have to wait a moment for the message box to appear.) You return to the Mail Merge Recipients dialog box, as shown in Figure 6–26.

Figure 6–26 **New records added to data source**

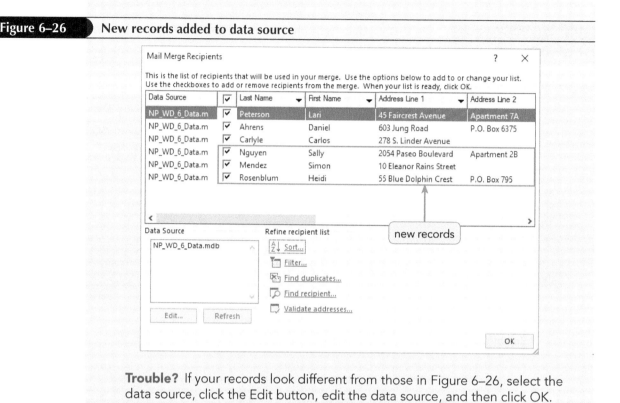

Trouble? If your records look different from those in Figure 6–26, select the data source, click the Edit button, edit the data source, and then click OK.

You'll leave the Mail Merge Recipients dialog box open so you can use it to make other changes to the data source.

Sorting Records

You can sort, or rearrange, information in a data source table just as you can sort information in any other table. To quickly sort information in ascending order (*A* to *Z*, lowest to highest, or earliest to latest) or in descending order (*Z* to *A*, highest to lowest, or latest to earliest), click a field's heading in the Mail Merge Recipients dialog box. The first time you click the heading, the records are sorted in ascending order. If you click it a second time, the records are sorted in descending order.

To perform a more complicated sort, you can click the Sort command in the Mail Merge Recipients dialog box to open the Filter and Sort dialog box, where you can choose to sort by more than one field. For example, you could sort records in ascending order by last name, and then in ascending order by first name. In that case, the records would be organized alphabetically by last name, and then, in cases where multiple records contained the same last name, those records would be sorted by first name.

Sorting a Data Source by Multiple Fields

- On the ribbon, click the Mailings tab.
- In the Start Mail Merge group, click the Edit Recipient List button to open the Mail Merge Recipients dialog box.
- Click Sort to open the Sort Records tab in the Filter and Sort dialog box.
- Click the Sort by arrow, select the first field you want to sort by, and then select either the Ascending option button or the Descending option button.
- Click the Then by arrow, select the second field you want to sort by, and then select either the Ascending option button or the Descending option button.
- If necessary, click the Then by arrow, select the third field you want to sort by, and then select either the Ascending option button or the Descending option button.
- Click OK to close the Filter and Sort dialog box.
- Click OK to close the Mail Merge Recipients dialog box.

As Amalia looks through the letters to the potential clients in the merged document, she notices one problem—the letters are not grouped by zip codes. Currently, the letters are in the order in which people were added to the data source file. Amalia plans to use business mail (also known as bulk mail) to send her letters, and the U.S. Postal Service offers lower rates for mailings that are separated into groups according to zip code. She asks you to sort the data file by zip code and then by last name, and then merge the main document with the sorted data source.

To sort the data source by zip code:

▶ 1. In the Mail Merge Recipients dialog box, click **Sort**. The Filter and Sort dialog box opens, with the Sort Records tab displayed.

▶ 2. Click the **Sort by arrow** to display a menu, scroll down in the menu, and then click **ZIP Code**. The Ascending button is selected by default, which is what you want.

▶ 3. In the Then by box, directly below the Sort by box, click the **Then by arrow**, and then click **Last Name**. See Figure 6–27.

Figure 6–27   Sorting by zip code and by last name

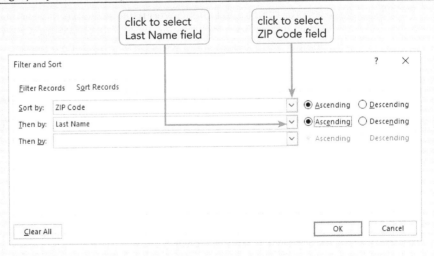

▶ **4.** Click **OK**. Word sorts the records from lowest zip code number to highest, and then, within each zip code, it sorts the records by last name.

In the Mail Merge Recipients dialog box, the record for Daniel Ahrens, with zip code 91911, is now at the top of the data source list. The record for Simon Mendez, which also has a zip code of 91911, comes second. The remaining records are sorted similarly, with the record for Sally Nguyen the last in the list. When you merge the data source with the form letter, the letters will appear in the merged document in this order.

▶ **5.** Click **OK**. The Mail Merge Recipients dialog box closes.

▶ **6.** On the Mailings tab, in the Preview Results group, click the **Preview Results** button. The data for Daniel Ahrens is displayed in the main document.

▶ **7.** In the Finish group, click the **Finish & Merge** button, and then click **Edit Individual Documents**.

▶ **8.** In the Merge to New Document dialog box, verify that the **All** option button is selected, and then click **OK**. Word generates the new merged document with six letters—one letter per page as before, but this time the first letter is addressed to Daniel Ahrens.

▶ **9.** Scroll down and verify that the letters in the newly merged document are arranged in ascending order by zip code and then in ascending order by last name.

▶ **10.** Save the new merged document in the location specified by your instructor, using the file name **NP_WD_6_MergedLetters2**, and then close it. You return to the NP_WD_6_MainDocument.docx file. Save the **NP_WD_6_ MainDocument.docx** file, and keep it open for the next set of steps.

TIP

To omit an individual record from a merge, you can deselect the corresponding check box in the Mail Merge Recipients dialog box rather than using a filter.

Next, Amalia would like you to create a set of letters to send to potential clients who listed "nutrition" as their preferred type of consultation.

Filtering Records

Amalia wants to inform potential clients that nutrition consultations are now available seven days a week. She asks you to modify the form letter and then merge it with the records of potential clients who have indicated that nutrition is their preferred type of consultation. To select specific records in a data source, you filter the data source to temporarily display only the records containing a particular value in a particular field.

To filter the data source to select specific records for the merge:

▶ **1.** In the Preview Results group, click the **Preview Results** button to deselect it and display the merge fields in the NP_WD_6_MainDocument.docx file instead of the data from the data source.

▶ **2.** Save the NP_WD_6_MainDocument.docx with the new name **NP_WD_6_MainDocument2** in the location specified by your instructor.

▶ **3.** In the document, scroll down to the second paragraph in the body of the letter, and then, at the end of the third line of that paragraph, click to the right of the word "lounge" and press **SPACEBAR** to insert a space between the "e" and the period.

4. Type **(with nutrition counselors available seven days a week)** and then verify that the sentence reads "…and a nutrition counseling lounge (with nutrition counselors available seven days a week)."

5. Save the document.

6. In the Start Mail Merge group, click the **Edit Recipient List** button to open the Mail Merge Recipients dialog box, and then scroll to the right so you can see the Consultation Type field.

7. In the header row, click the **Consultation Type arrow**. A menu opens, listing all the entries in the Consultation Type field, as well as a few other options. See Figure 6–28.

| Figure 6–28 | Filtering records in a data source |

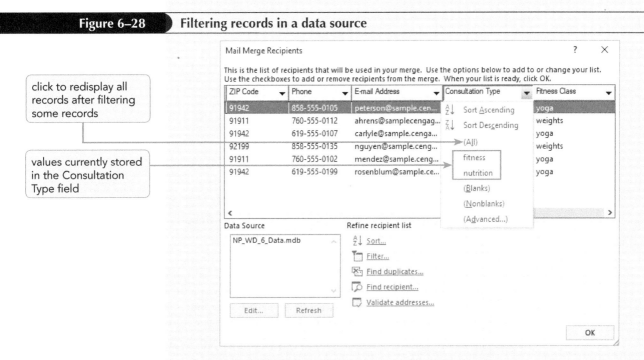

click to redisplay all records after filtering some records

values currently stored in the Consultation Type field

Trouble? If the records sort by Consultation Type, with the records for fitness at the top, you clicked the Consultation Type column header instead of the arrow. That's not a problem; you don't need to undo the sort. Repeat Step 6, taking care to click the arrow.

You can use the "(All)" option to redisplay all records after previously filtering a data source. The "(Advanced)" option takes you to the Filter Records tab in the Filter and Sort dialog box, where you can perform complex filter operations that involve comparing the contents of one or more fields to a particular value to determine whether a record should be displayed. In this case, however, you can use an option in this menu.

8. Click **nutrition**. Word temporarily hides all the records in the data source except those that contain "nutrition" in the Consultation Type field. See Figure 6–29.

| Figure 6–29 | Filtered data source |

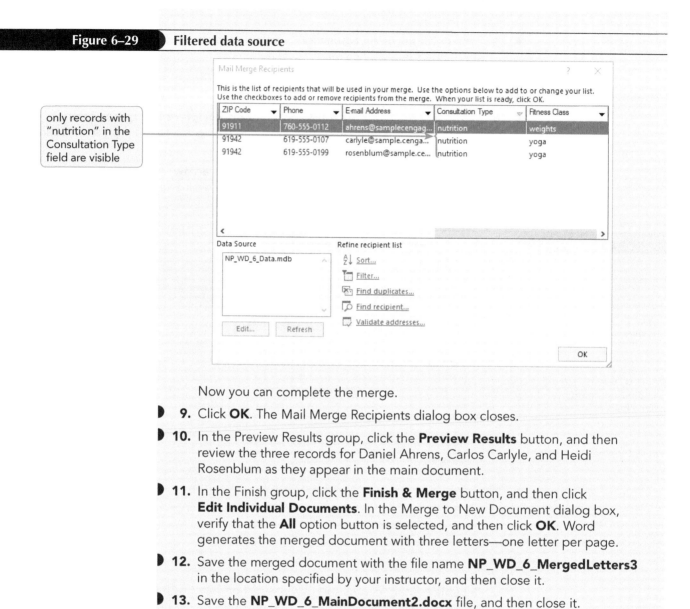

Now you can complete the merge.

▶ **9.** Click **OK**. The Mail Merge Recipients dialog box closes.

▶ **10.** In the Preview Results group, click the **Preview Results** button, and then review the three records for Daniel Ahrens, Carlos Carlyle, and Heidi Rosenblum as they appear in the main document.

▶ **11.** In the Finish group, click the **Finish & Merge** button, and then click **Edit Individual Documents**. In the Merge to New Document dialog box, verify that the **All** option button is selected, and then click **OK**. Word generates the merged document with three letters—one letter per page.

▶ **12.** Save the merged document with the file name **NP_WD_6_MergedLetters3** in the location specified by your instructor, and then close it.

▶ **13.** Save the **NP_WD_6_MainDocument2.docx** file, and then close it.

Next, you'll create and print mailing labels for the form letters.

Creating Mailing Labels

Amalia could print the names and addresses for the letters directly on envelopes, or she could perform a mail merge to create mailing labels. The latter method is easier because she can print 14 labels at once rather than printing one envelope at a time.

Amalia has purchased Avery® Laser Printer labels, which are available in most office-supply stores. Word supports most of the Avery label formats, allowing you to choose the layout that works best for you. Amalia purchased Avery 5162 Address Labels in 8 1/2 × 11-inch sheets that are designed to feed through a printer. Each label measures 4 × 1.33 inches. Each sheet contains seven rows of labels, with two labels in each row, for a total of 14 labels. See Figure 6–30.

TIP

It is a good idea to print one page of a label document on regular paper so you can check your work before printing on the more expensive sheets of adhesive labels.

Figure 6–30   Layout of a sheet of Avery® 5162 Address Labels

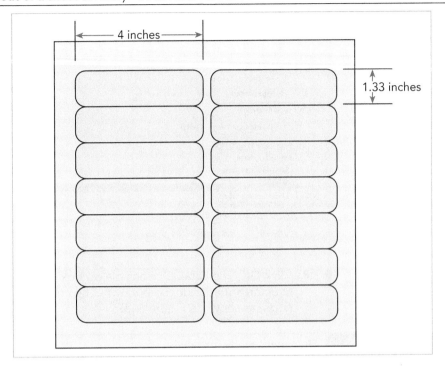

Performing a mail merge to create mailing labels is similar to performing a mail merge to create a form letter. You begin by selecting Labels as the type of main document and then you specify the brand and product number for the labels you are using. You will also need to specify a data source file. In this case, you'll use the Microsoft Office Address Lists data source file, NP_WD_6_Data.mdb, which you created and used in the form letter mail merges.

To specify the main document for creating mailing labels:

▶ **1.** Open a new, blank document, and then save the document as **NP_WD_6_MainDocument3** in the location specified by your instructor.

▶ **2.** Make sure the rulers and nonprinting characters are displayed, and zoom out so you can see the whole page.

▶ **3.** On the ribbon, click the **Mailings** tab.

▶ **4.** In the Start Mail Merge group, click the **Start Mail Merge** button.

At this point, if you wanted to merge to envelopes instead of labels, you could click Envelopes to open the Envelope Options dialog box, where you could select the envelope size you wanted to use. In this case, however, you want to merge to labels.

▶ **5.** Click **Labels**. The Label Options dialog box opens.

▶ **6.** Click the **Label vendors arrow** to display a list of vendors, scroll down, and then click **Avery US Letter**.

▶ **7.** Scroll down the Product number box, and then click **5162 Address Labels**. See Figure 6–31.

Figure 6–31 Label Options dialog box

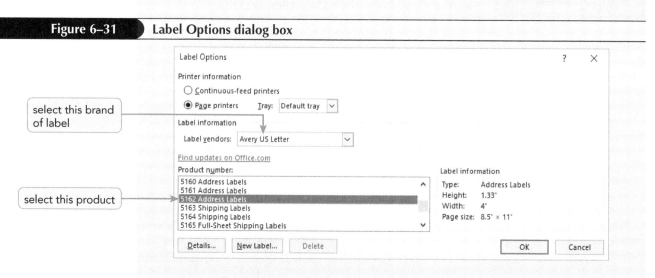

select this brand
of label

select this product

8. Click **OK**. The Label Options dialog box closes, and Word inserts a table structure into the document, with one cell for each of the 14 labels on the page, as shown in Figure 6–32.

Figure 6–32 Document ready for labels

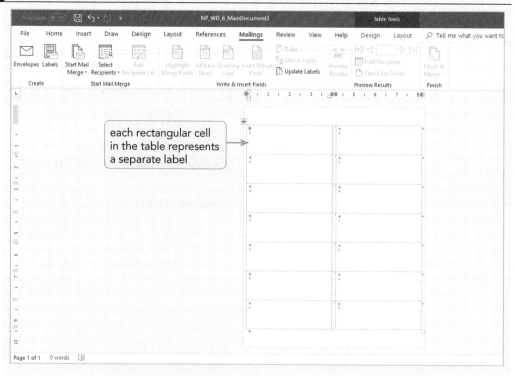

each rectangular cell in the table represents a separate label

As with all table gridlines, these gridlines are visible only on the screen; they will not be visible on the printed labels.

Trouble? If you don't see the table gridlines, click the Table Tools Layout tab, and then, in the Table group, click the View Gridlines button to select it.

You have finished setting up the document. Next, you need to select the data source you created earlier. Note that the changes you made to the data source as a whole earlier in this session (sorting the records and selecting only some records) have no effect on the data source in this new mail merge. However, the changes you made to individual records (such as editing individual records or adding new records) are retained.

To continue the mail merge for the labels:

1. In the Start Mail Merge group, click the **Select Recipients** button, and then click **Use an Existing List**. The Select Data Source dialog box opens.

2. Navigate to the location where you stored the NP_WD_6_Data.mdb file, select the **NP_WD_6_Data.mdb** file, and then click the **Open** button. The Select Data Source dialog box closes, and you return to the main document.

3. Change the Zoom level to **120%** so you can read the document. In each label except the first one, the code <<Next Record>> is displayed. This code tells Word to retrieve the next record from the data source for each label.

4. Verify that the insertion point is located in the upper-left label, and make sure the Mailings tab is still selected on the ribbon.

TIP

You can only use the Address Block merge field if you include a State field in your data source.

5. In the Write & Insert Fields group, click the **Address Block** button. The Insert Address Block dialog box opens. The left pane displays possible formats for the name in the address block. The default format, "Joshua Randall Jr.," inserts first and last names, along with the other address information, which is what Amalia wants. The Preview pane on the right currently shows the first address in the data source, which is the address for Lari Peterson.

6. In the Preview section of the Insert Address Block dialog box, click the **Next** button ▷. The record for Daniel Ahrens is displayed in the Preview pane, as shown in Figure 6–33. Note that you could also use the Insert Address Block dialog box to insert an inside address in a letter.

| Figure 6–33 | Previewing addresses in the Insert Address Block dialog box |

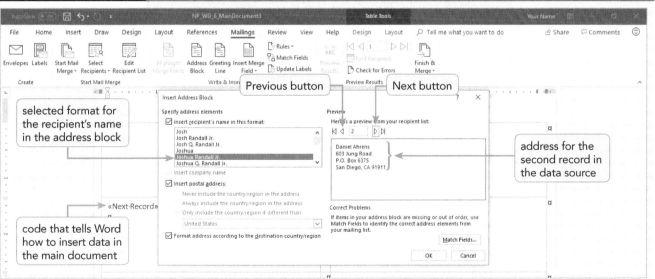

7. Click **OK**. The Insert Address Block dialog box closes, and an AddressBlock merge field is displayed in the upper-left label on the page. Next, you need to update the remaining labels to match the one containing the AddressBlock merge field.

8. In the Write & Insert Fields group, click the **Update Labels** button. The AddressBlock merge field is inserted into all the labels in the document, as shown in Figure 6–34.

Figure 6–34   Field codes inserted into document

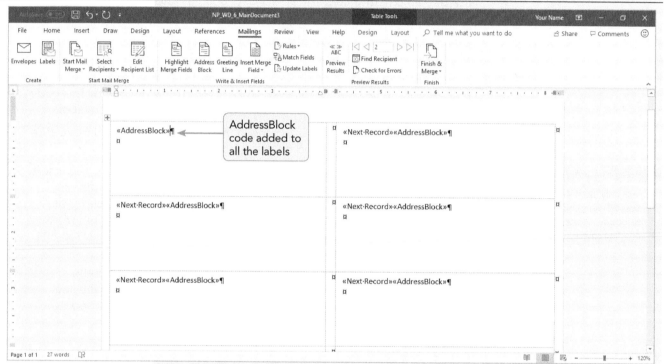

In all except the upper-left label, the Next Record code is displayed to the left of the AddressBlock merge field.

You are ready to preview the labels and complete the merge. To ensure that you see all the labels in the preview, you need to make sure the Go to Record box in the Preview Results group displays the number "1".

To preview the labels and complete the merge:

1. If necessary, click the **First Record** button ⊲ in the Preview Results group to display "1" in the Go to Record box.

2. In the Preview Results group, click the **Preview Results** button. The addresses for Amalia's six potential clients are displayed in the main document. See Figure 6–35.

Figure 6–35 | **Previewing addresses in labels**

3. In the Finish group, click the **Finish & Merge** button, and then click **Edit Individual Documents**.

4. In the Merge to New Document dialog box, verify that the **All** option button is selected, and then click **OK**. The finished labels are inserted into a new document named Labels1.

5. Scroll through the document. The document contains space for 14 labels, but because the data source contains only six records, the new document only contains addresses for six labels.

6. In the upper-left label, change "Lari Peterson" to your first and last names, and then save the merged document as **NP_WD_6_MergedLabels** in the location specified by your instructor.

7. Close the **NP_WD_6_MergedLabels.docx** document, and then save and close the **NP_WD_6_MainDocument3.docx** file.

Creating a Phone Directory

Next, Amalia wants you to create a phone directory for all spa employees. She has already created a Word document containing the phone numbers; you will use that document as the data source for the merge. You'll set up a mail merge as before, except this time you will select Directory as the main document type. Keep in mind that you should use a Word document as a data source only for a simple project like a directory. For letters, it's better to use an Access database, an Excel workbook, or a Microsoft Office Address Lists file. You'll start by examining the Word document that Amalia wants you to use as the data source, and then you'll create the main document.

To review the data source and create the main document for the directory:

▶ 1. Open the document **NP_WD_6-2.docx** from the Word6 > Module folder, and then save it as **NP_WD_6_PhoneData** in the location specified by your instructor. The information in this document is arranged in a table with three column headings—"First Name," "Last Name," and "Phone." The information in the table has already been sorted in alphabetical order by last name.

The Mail Merge Recipients dialog box does not display data from a Word document data source in the same way that it displays other types of data. Also, sorting and filtering does not work the same for Word document data sources as it does for other types of files. To avoid problems, it's easier to edit a Word document data source by opening the document separately, making any necessary changes, and then saving and closing the document.

▶ 2. Replace "Kiley Bradoff" with your first and last names, and then save and close the **NP_WD_6_PhoneData.docx** file.

▶ 3. Open a new, blank document, display nonprinting characters and the rulers, if necessary, and then change the Zoom level to **120%**.

▶ 4. Save the main document as **NP_WD_6_MainDocument4** in the location in which you saved the **NP_WD_6_PhoneData.docx** document.

▶ 5. On the ribbon, click the **Mailings** tab.

▶ 6. In the Start Mail Merge group, click the **Start Mail Merge** button, and then click **Directory**.

▶ 7. In the Start Mail Merge group, click the **Select Recipients** button, and then click **Use an Existing List** to open the Select Data Source dialog box.

▶ 8. In the dialog box, navigate to and select the Word document named **NP_WD_6_PhoneData.docx**, and then click the **Open** button.

You're ready to insert the fields in the main document. Amalia wants the directory to include the names at the left margin of the page and the phone numbers at the right margin, with a dot leader in between. Recall that a dot leader is a dotted line that extends from the last letter of text on the left margin to the beginning of the nearest text aligned at a tab stop.

To set up the directory main document with dot leaders:

▶ 1. With the insertion point in the first line of the document, insert the **First_Name** merge field, press **SPACEBAR**, and then insert the **Last_Name** merge field.

▶ 2. In the Write & Insert Fields group, click the **Highlight Merge Fields** button. The First_Name and Last_Name merge fields are displayed on a gray background. Now you'll set a tab stop at the right margin (at the 5.5-inch mark on the horizontal ruler) with a dot leader.

▶ 3. On the ribbon, click the **Home** tab.

TIP
You can click the Clear All button in the Tabs dialog box to delete all the tab stops in the document.

▶ 4. In the Paragraph group, click the **Paragraph Dialog Box Launcher** to open the Paragraph dialog box, and then in the lower-left corner of the Indents and Spacing tab, click the **Tabs** button. The Tabs dialog box opens.

5. In the Tab stop position box, type **5.5** and then click the **Right** option button in the Alignment section.

6. Click the **2 ....** option button in the Leader section. See Figure 6–36.

Figure 6–36	Creating a tab with a dot leader

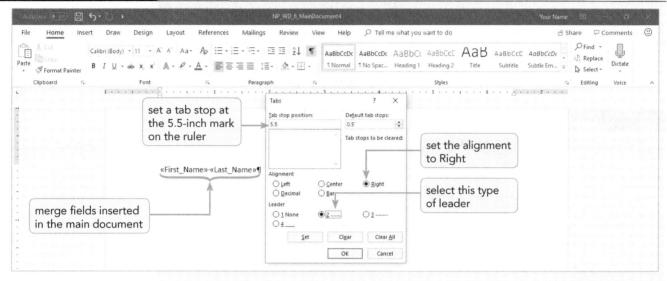

7. Click **OK**. Word clears the current tab stops and inserts a right-aligned tab stop at the 5.5-inch mark on the horizontal ruler.

8. Press **TAB** to move the insertion point to the new tab stop. A dotted line stretches from the Last_Name merge field to the right side of the page.

9. On the ribbon, click the **Mailings** tab.

Be sure to press ENTER here to ensure that each name and phone number is displayed on a separate line.

10. Insert the **Phone** merge field at the insertion point. The dot leader shortens to accommodate the inserted merge fields.

11. Press **ENTER**. The completed main document should look like the one shown in Figure 6–37.

Figure 6–37	Completed main document for the phone directory

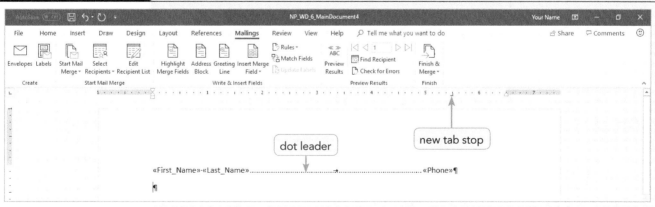

You are now ready to merge this file with the data source.

To finish the merge for the phone directory:

▶ **1.** In the Preview Results group, click the **Preview Results** button, and then review the data for the first record in the document.

▶ **2.** In the Finish group, click the **Finish & Merge** button, and then click **Edit Individual Documents**. In the Merge to New Document dialog box, verify that the **All** option button is selected, and then click **OK**. Word creates a new document that contains the completed phone list.

▶ **3.** Press **ENTER** to insert a new paragraph at the beginning of the document.

▶ **4.** Click in the new paragraph, type **Employee Directory** and then format the new text using the **Heading 1** style. See Figure 6–38.

Figure 6–38 Completed phone directory

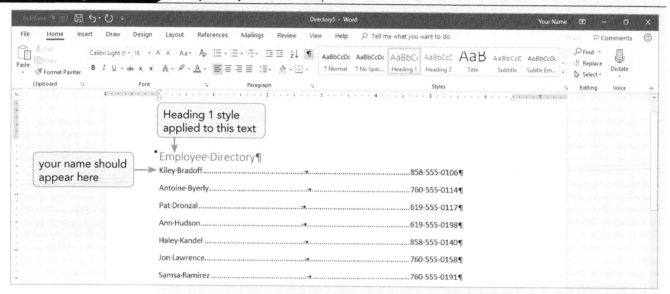

▶ **5.** Save the document as **NP_WD_6_MergedDirectory** in the location in which you saved the main document, and then close it.

▶ **6.** Save and close the **NP_WD_6_MainDocument4.docx** file.

Amalia needs your help with one other task related to managing information about the spa's clients and employees.

Converting Text to a Table

TIP

To convert a table to text, click in the table, click the Table Tools Layout tab, click Convert to Text in the Data group, click the separator you prefer, and then click OK.

To be completely proficient in mail merges, you should be able to take information from a variety of sources and set it up for use as a data source. In particular, it's helpful to be able to convert text to a table. For example, address information exported from email and contact management programs often takes the form of a **comma-separated values (CSV) file**, a text file in which each paragraph contains one record, with the fields separated by commas. CSV files can have a .txt or .csv file extension. The commas in a CSV file are known as **separator characters**, or sometimes delimiters.

You can use the Convert Text to Table command on the Table menu to transform text from a Word document or a CSV file into a table. But first you need to make sure the text is set up correctly; that is, you need to make sure that separator characters are used consistently to divide the text into individual fields. In a CSV file, commas are used as separator characters, but you might encounter a Word document that uses tab characters, or other characters, as separator characters. After you verify that separator characters are used consistently within a document, you need to make sure each paragraph in the document contains the same number of fields.

Upon conversion, each field is formatted as a separate cell in a column, and each paragraph mark starts a new row, or record. Sometimes a conversion might not turn out the way you expect. In that case, undo it, and then review the text to make sure each paragraph contains the same number of data items, with the items divided by the same separator character.

Amalia's assistant, who isn't familiar with Word tables, typed some information about new clients as text in a Word document. He forgot to include an email address and phone number for each client. Amalia wants to convert the text to a table and then add columns for the missing information. The next time the clients visit the spa, one of the assistants can ask for the missing information and then add it to the table.

To convert text into a table:

▶ **1.** Open the document named **NP_WD_6-3.docx** from the Word6 > Module folder, and then save it as **NP_WD_6_Table** in the location specified by your instructor.

▶ **2.** Display nonprinting characters, if necessary, and then change the Zoom level to **120%**. See Figure 6–39.

Figure 6–39	Text with inconsistent separator characters

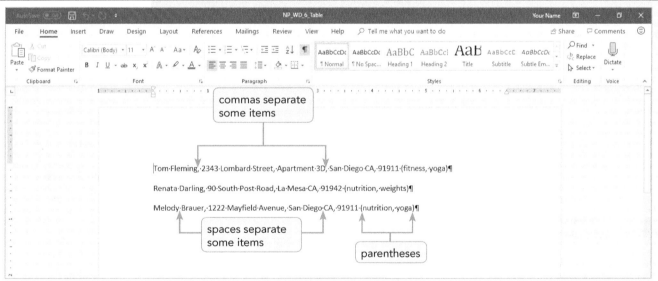

The document consists of three paragraphs, each of which contains a client's name, address, city, state, zip code, preferred consultation type, and preferred fitness class. Some of the fields are separated by commas and spaces (for example, the address and the city), but some are separated only by spaces, with no punctuation character (for example, the first and last names). Also, the preferred consultation type and fitness class are enclosed in parentheses. You need to edit this information so that fields are separated by commas, with no parentheses enclosing the last two items.

▶ **3.** Edit the document to insert a comma after each first name, city, and zip code, and then delete the parentheses in each paragraph.

Before you can convert the text into a table, you also need to make sure each paragraph includes the same fields. Currently, the first paragraph includes two pieces of address information—a street address and an apartment number, which is equivalent to an Address Line 1 field and an Address Line 2 field. However, the other paragraphs only include an Address Line 1 field.

▶ **4.** In the second paragraph, click to the right of the comma after "Road," press **SPACEBAR**, and then type **,** (a comma).

▶ **5.** In the third paragraph, click to the right of the comma after "Avenue," press **SPACEBAR**, and then type **,** (a comma). Now the second and third paragraphs each contain a blank field. See Figure 6–40.

Figure 6–40 **Text set up for conversion to a table**

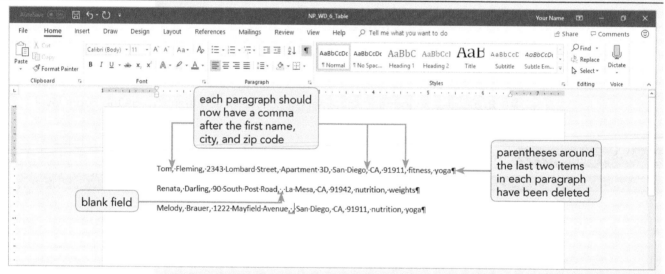

each paragraph should now have a comma after the first name, city, and zip code

parentheses around the last two items in each paragraph have been deleted

blank field

Tom, Fleming, 2343 Lombard Street, Apartment 3D, San Diego, CA, 91911, fitness, yoga¶

Renata, Darling, 90 South Post Road, , La Mesa, CA, 91942, nutrition, weights¶

Melody, Brauer, 1222 Mayfield Avenue, , San Diego, CA, 91911, nutrition, yoga¶

▶ **6.** Press **CTRL+A** to select the entire document.

▶ **7.** On the ribbon, click the **Insert** tab.

▶ **8.** In the Tables group, click the **Table** button, and then click **Convert Text to Table**. The Convert Text to Table dialog box opens. See Figure 6–41.

Figure 6–41 **Converting text to a table**

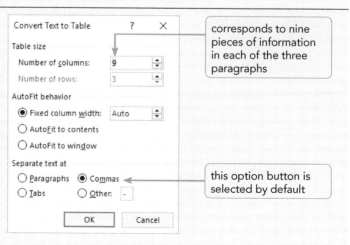

corresponds to nine pieces of information in each of the three paragraphs

this option button is selected by default

Note that the Number of columns setting is 9, and the Number of rows setting is 3. This corresponds to the nine fields in each of the three paragraphs.

In the Separate text at section of the dialog box, you can choose from three possible separator characters—paragraphs, commas, and tabs. If the text in your document was separated by a character other than paragraphs, commas, or tabs, you could type the character in the box to the right of the Other button. In this case, though, the default option, Commas, is the correct choice because the information in each paragraph is separated by commas.

▶ **9.** Click **OK**. The Convert Text to Table dialog box closes, and the text in the document is converted into a table consisting of nine columns and three rows.

▶ **10.** Save the document.

Now that you have converted the text to a table, you need to finish the table by adding the columns for the phone numbers and email addresses and adding a header row to identify the field names.

To finish the table by adding columns and a header row:

▶ **1.** Switch to Landscape orientation, and then select the column containing the zip codes.

▶ **2.** On the ribbon, click the **Table Tools Layout** tab.

▶ **3.** In the Rows & Columns group, click the **Insert Right** button twice to add two blank columns to the right of the column containing zip codes.

▶ **4.** Select the table's top row, and then in the Rows & Columns group, click the **Insert Above** button.

▶ **5.** Enter the column headings shown in Figure 6–42, and format the column headings in bold.

| Figure 6–42 | Table with new columns and column headings |

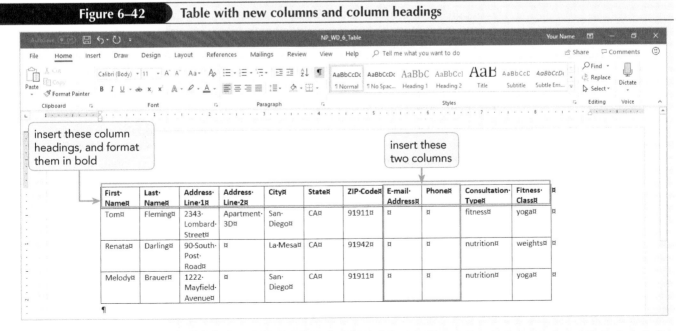

▶ **6.** Save the **NP_WD_6_Table.docx** file, and then close it.

You have finished converting text into a table. Amalia can use the table later as the data source for another mail merge. As her business expands, she plans to continue to use the mail merge feature in Word to inform her clients about new offerings at the spa.

Combining Data with a Microsoft Office Address Lists File

If you have data in a Word file that you want to combine with data in a Microsoft Office Address Lists file, or any other Microsoft Access file, start by setting up the Word document as a table. That way, you can be sure that each record includes the same fields. You can also review the table quickly to confirm that you have entered data in the various fields in a consistent format. Once you are confident that you have set up the table correctly, you can begin the process of combining it with the Microsoft Office Address Lists file.

First, delete the heading row, and then convert the table back to text by clicking the Table Tools Layout tab, clicking Convert to Text in the Data group, clicking the Commas button, and then clicking OK. Next, save the Word file as a Plain Text file with the .txt file extension, and then close it. Finally, open the Microsoft Office Address Lists file in Access, click the External Data tab, click the New Data Source in the Import & Link group, click From File, and then click Text File. In the Get External Data – Text File dialog box, click the Append a copy of the records to the table button, click the Browse button to select the plain text file you created, click Open, click OK, click Finish, and then click Close. To display the expanded address list, double-click Office_Address_List in the All Access Objects pane.

Session 6.2 Quick Check

1. Does the connection between a main document and its data source persist after you close the main document, if you keep both files in their original locations?

2. What are two ways to edit a data source?

3. Suppose you want to edit a Microsoft Office Address Lists data source named Employees, and the Mail Merge Recipients dialog box is open. What must you do to begin editing the data source?

4. Suppose the Edit Data Source dialog box is open. What button should you click to add a new entry to the data source?

5. Explain how to filter a data source.

6. Suppose you are creating a phone directory and have inserted the necessary merge fields in the first paragraph of the document. What do you need to do to ensure that each name and phone number is displayed on a separate line?

PRACTICE

Review Assignments

Data Files needed for the Review Assignments: NP_WD_6-4.docx, NP_WD_6-5.docx, NP_WD_6-6.docx

The renovated spa at Sun and Soul Wellness Resort is a big hit with local residents as well as resort guests. Amalia has greatly expanded her local client base, and now she is adding a full schedule of fitness classes. Anyone who signs up for two months of classes also receives a wellness consultation. On the class sign-up form, clients can choose between a nutrition or fitness consultation. Now Amalia wants to send a letter inviting clients to reserve a time for their consultation. At the end of the letter, she wants to include one sentence promoting the spa's massage services, and another sentence promoting the spa's facial services, depending on which spa service the client prefers. She also needs to create an email directory of suppliers she deals with regularly. Finally, she needs to convert some additional client information into a table that she can use as a data source.

Complete the following steps:

1. Open the document **NP_WD_6-4.docx** from the Word6 > Review folder included with your Data Files, and then save the document as **NP_WD_6_ConsultationMainDocument** in the location specified by your instructor.
2. In the first paragraph, replace the placeholder text "[INSERT DATE FIELD]" with a Date field that displays the current month, day, and year—in the format March 11, 2021.
3. Begin the mail merge by selecting Letters as the type of main document.
4. Create a data source with the following fields in the following order: First Name, Last Name, Address Line 1, Address Line 2, City, State, ZIP Code, E-mail Address, Phone, Consultation Type, and Favorite Service. Remove any extra fields, and rename fields as necessary.
5. Create four records using the information shown in Figure 6–43.

Figure 6–43   Information for new data source

First Name	Last Name	Address Line 1	Address Line 2	City	State	ZIP Code	E-mail Address	Phone	Consultation Type	Favorite Service
Calista	Cutler	299 Eastley Avenue	Apartment 4A	La Mesa	CA	91942	calista@sample.cengage.com	619-555-0176	fitness	massage
Ruby	Pushkin	821 Emerald Lane		San Diego	CA	31035	ruby@sample.cengage.com	760-555-0123	nutrition	massage
Lupita	Morelo	52 Red Earth Road	P.O. Box 2233	La Mesa	CA	91942	lupita@sample.cengage.com	619-555-0143	fitness	facial
Marcus	Hesse	933 Nakoma Way		San Diego	CA	31028	marcus@sample.cengage.com	760-555-0190	nutrition	facial

6. Save the data source as **NP_WD_6_ConsultationData** in the location in which you saved the main document.
7. Edit the data source to replace "Marcus Hesse" with your first and last names.
8. Sort the data source in ascending order by zip code and then by last name.
9. Replace the placeholder text "[INSERT INSIDE ADDRESS]" with an inside address consisting of the necessary separate merge fields. Adjust the paragraph spacing in the inside address as necessary.
10. In the salutation, replace the placeholder text "[INSERT FIRST NAME]" with the First_Name merge field.
11. In the body of the letter, replace the placeholder text "[INSERT CONSULTATION TYPE]" with the Consultation Type merge field.

12. At the end of the paragraph that begins "If you haven't sampled..." create an If...Then...Else mail merge rule that inserts one of two sentences as follows:
    - If the Favorite Service field contains "massage," then insert **Keep in mind our award-winning massage services are available at a 20% discount on Tuesdays and Thursdays.**
    - If the Favorite Service field contains "facial," then insert **Don't forget that your first facial is free as long as you sign up for three facials within two months.**

13. Adjust the formatting and spacing of the placeholder text inserted by the mail merge rule, as necessary.

14. Save your changes to the main document, and then preview the merged document. Correct any formatting or spacing problems.

15. Merge to a new document, save the merged document as **NP_WD_6_ ConsultationMergedLetters** in the location in which you saved the main document, and then close the file.

16. Filter the data source to display only records for clients who requested a nutrition consultation, and then complete a second merge. Save the new merged document as **NP_WD_6_ ConsultationMergedLetters2** in the location in which you saved the main document. Close all documents, saving all changes.

17. Open a new, blank document, and create a set of mailing labels using the vendor Avery US Letters and product number 5162. Save the main document as **NP_WD_6_ SpaLabelsMainDocument** in the location in which you saved the **NP_WD_6_ConsultationData** file.

18. Select the **NP_WD_6_ConsultationData.mdb** file you created earlier in this assignment as the data source.

19. Insert an AddressBlock merge field in the "Joshua Randall Jr." format, and then update the labels.

20. Preview the merged labels, merge to a new document, and then save the new document as **NP_WD 6_MergedSpaLabels** in the location in which you saved the main document. Save and close all open documents.

21. Open the document **NP_WD_6-5**, and then save it as **NP_WD_6_SupplierData** in the location specified by your instructor. Change "Harvey Siska" to your first and last names, save the document, and close it.

22. Open a new, blank document, and then save it as **NP_WD_6_SupplierDirectory** in the location in which you saved the **NP_WD_6_SupplierData.docx** file. Create a directory main document. Select the **NP_WD_6_SupplierData.docx** file as the data source.

23. Set a right tab at 4 inches with a dot leader, and insert the necessary merge fields so that the directory shows a contact followed by a comma, followed by the company name and, on the right side of the page, the email address for each company. Merge to a new document, and then, at the top of the merged document, insert the heading **Vendor Contacts** formatted with the Heading 1 style. Save the merged document as **NP_WD_6_MergedSuppliers** in the location in which you saved the main document. Save and close all open documents.

24. Open the document **NP_WD_6-6.docx** from the Word6 > Review folder, and then save it as **NP_WD_6_ClientData** in the location specified by your instructor. Convert the data in the document to a table with eight columns. Insert a header row with the following column headers formatted in bold—**First Name**, **Last Name**, **Address Line 1**, **Address Line 2**, **City**, **State**, **ZIP code**, and **Consultation Type**. Replace "Tai Chen" with your first and last names. Save and close the document.

Case Problem 1

Data File needed for this Case Problem: NP_WD_6-7.docx

Great West Coding Academy   Deandre Baird is the executive director of Great West Coding Academy, a nonprofit institution in Las Vegas, Nevada, devoted to helping non-native English speakers learn to write programming code. As part of a new fund-raising campaign for the school, Deandre plans to send out customized letters to last year's donors, asking them to consider donating the same amount or more this year. He asks you to help him create the letters and the envelopes for the campaign.

Complete the following steps:

1. Open the document **NP_WD_6-7.docx** from the Word6 > Case1 folder, and then save it as **NP_WD_6_GWCAMainDocument** in the location specified by your instructor. In the closing, replace "Deandre Baird" with your first and last names.
2. In the first paragraph, replace the placeholder text "[INSERT DATE FIELD]" with a Date field that displays the current month, day, and year—in the format March 11, 2021.
3. Begin the mail merge by selecting Letters as the type of main document.
4. Create a data source with the following field names, in the following order—**Title**, **First Name**, **Last Name**, **Address Line 1**, **Address Line 2**, **City**, **State**, **ZIP code**, **E-mail Address**, and **Donation Amount**.
5. Enter the four records shown in Figure 6–44.

Figure 6–44   Four records for new data source

Title	First Name	Last Name	Address Line 1	Address Line 2	City	State	ZIP Code	E-mail Address	Donation Amount
Mr.	Tenzen	Sung	844 Sumerdale Way	Unit 6	Las Vegas	NV	88901	sung@sample.cengage.com	$2,500
Mr.	Darryl	Fuhrman	1577 Shanley Boulevard	Apartment 4C	Las Vegas	NV	88105	fuhrman@sample.cengage.com	$700
Ms.	Susannah	Wilder	4424 Rue Paris Avenue		New Mesa	NV	88133	wilder@sample.cengage.com	$250
Ms.	Cynthia	Borrego	633 Hempstead Springs Road		Las Vegas	NV	89124	borrego@sample.cengage.com	$300

6. Save the data source as **NP_WD_6_GWCAData** in the location in which you saved the main document.
7. Edit the data source to replace "Tenzen Sung" with your first and last names. Change the title to **Ms.** if necessary.
8. Sort the data source alphabetically by last name.
9. Build an inside address using separate merge fields. Remember to include the Title field. Adjust paragraph spacing as necessary.
10. Add a salutation using a Greeting Line field with the default settings on the appropriate line in the document. Verify that you deleted all placeholder text in the date paragraph, inside address, and the salutation.
11. In the paragraph that begins "In order to continue…," insert the Donation_Amount merge field where indicated. Delete the placeholder text.
12. Save your changes to the NP_WD_6_GWCAMainDocument.docx file. Preview the merged document, and then merge to a new document.
13. Save the merged letters document as **NP_WD_6_GWCAMergedLetters** in the location in which you saved the main document, and then close it.

14. Save the NP_WD_6_GWCAMainDocument.docx file, and then close it.

15. Open a new, blank document, and then save it as **NP_WD_6_GWCAEnvelopes** in the location in which you saved the main document. The school has envelopes with a preprinted return address, so you don't need to type a return address. Begin the mail merge by selecting Envelopes as the type of main document, and then select Size 10 (4 1/8 × 9 1/2 in) as the envelope size in the Envelope Options dialog box.

16. For the data source, use the **NP_WD_6_GWCAData.mdb** file that you saved in Step 6. In the recipient address area of the envelope, insert an AddressBlock merge field in the format "Mr. Joshua Randall Jr.".

17. Filter the records in the NP_WD_6_GWCAData.mdb file so that only records with Las Vegas addresses are included in the merge.

18. Merge to a new document.

19. Save the merged document as **NP_WD_6_GWCAMergedEnvelopes** in the location in which you saved the main document, and then close it. Save the main document and close it.

Case Problem 2

Data Files needed for this Case Problem: NP_WD_6-8.docx, NP_WD_6-9.docx

4SaleByMe Real Estate   You have offered to help an elderly friend sell the home she has owned for thirty years. Instead of contracting with a real estate agent, you and your friend have decided to sell the house using the online listing service 4SaleByMe. For a small fee, the company will host a page on its website describing the home. It's up to you and your friend to generate interest by hosting open-house events, promoting the house's webpage through social media, and using mail merge to send out letters to members of a boating club who might be interested in the easy lake access the home provides, and also to members of a local biking club, who might be interested in the home's easy access to bike trails. To complete the mail merge tasks, you need to create a data source, write a letter, add merge fields, and create mailing labels. Finally, you need to diagnose some problems with a directory containing names of people who will be helpful to you while selling the house, and also create some labels that you want to use to send letters to the people in the directory.

Complete the following steps:

1. Open a new document and save it as **NP_WD_6_HouseData**.

2. Change the orientation to Landscape, and then create the table shown in Figure 6–45 and then enter data for four people. Use fictitious names and addresses from your area. For the Club field, enter **Boating** for two records and **Biking** for two records.

Figure 6–45   **Table structure with field names for data source**

First Name	Last Name	Address Line 1	Address Line 2	City	State	ZIP Code	Club

3. Save the **NP_WD_6_HouseData.docx** document in the location specified by your instructor, and then close it.

4. Open a new blank document, and then save it as **NP_WD_6_HouseMainDocument** in the same location you saved the data file.

5. Begin the mail merge by selecting Letters as the type of main document.

6. Select the **NP_WD_6_HouseData.docx** file as the data source.

7. In the main document, change the top margin to 2.5 inches, to leave room for the 4SaleByMe Real Estate letterhead.

8. Write a letter to potential buyers that includes a date field. Also include an Address Block field and a Greeting Line field that are suitable for your data file. Assume that you will be using 4SaleByMe Real Estate letterhead, so there's no need to include a return address.

9. Include one paragraph explaining why you are writing the letter, and a second paragraph describing the house. Somewhere in the description, create a mail merge rule that displays the following text depending on the contents of the Club field:

   - If the Club field contains "Biking," insert the following in the document: **You are probably already familiar with the extensive bike trails in the area. The Seven Springs trail, which connects to four other trails, is only two minutes away by bike.**

   - If the Club field contains "Boating," insert the following in the document: **The popular Blue Ribbon boat ramp, on the shores of Lake Mendota, is a mere five minutes away by car. The ramp is free to state residents, so there's no need to rent a slip at a commercial marina.**

10. Include a complimentary close and a signature line, leaving space for your signature.

11. Sort the records in the data source in ascending order by last name.

12. Preview the merged document, and note that the lines of the inside address (inserted by the AddressBlock merge field) are spaced too far apart. Make any changes necessary so the inside address and the salutation include the appropriate amount of paragraph and line spacing.

13. Preview all the records in the document.

14. Merge to a new document. Save the merged document as **NP_WD_6_MergedHouseLetters** in the location in which you saved the main document.

15. Close all open documents, saving all changes.

16. Open the document **NP_WD_6-8.docx** from the Word6 > Case2 folder, and save it as **NP_WD_6_IncompleteLabels** in the location specified by your instructor. Attach a comment to the zip code in the first label that explains what error in the main document would result in a set of labels that includes information for only one record.

17. Change "Tony Flores" to your first and last name.

18. Save and close the document.

19. Open the document **NP_WD_6-9.docx** from the Word6 > Case2 folder, and save it as **NP_WD_6_IncompleteDirectory** in the location specified by your instructor. This merged directory will list people you'll need to contact at some point while trying to sell the house, along with each person's profession. The data source for this merged document included the following fields: First Name, Last Name, and Profession. Attach a comment to the name "Tony" that explains what error in the main document would result in a directory formatted like the one in the NP_WD_6_Directory.docx file.

20. Replace **Student Name** with your name, then save and close the document.

21. Save and close the document.

Collaborating with Others and Integrating Data

Preparing an Information Sheet

OBJECTIVES

Session 7.1
- Track changes in a document
- Compare and combine documents
- Accept and reject tracked changes
- Embed an Excel worksheet
- Modify an embedded Excel worksheet

Session 7.2
- Link an Excel chart
- Modify and update a linked Excel chart
- Create bookmarks
- Insert and edit hyperlinks
- Optimize a document for online viewing
- Create and publish a blog post

Case | *Movie Time Trivia*

Rima Khouri is the marketing director for PYRAMID Games. The company is currently developing a new board game called Movie Time Trivia. Like many game companies, PYRAMID Games plans to use a crowdfunding website to raise the money required to finish developing and marketing its latest product. As part of her marketing effort, Rima also plans to email an information sheet about the fund-raising campaign to interested gamers she met at a recent gaming convention. Rima has asked James Benner, the company's development manager, to review a draft of the information sheet. While James is revising the document, Rima has asked you to work on another copy, making additional changes. When you are finished with your review, Rima wants you to merge James's edited version of the document with your most recent draft.

After you create a new version of the document for Rima, she wants you to add some fund-raising data from an Excel workbook. She also needs you to add a pie chart James created and optimize the information sheet for online viewing. Finally, Rima wants you to help her create a blog post in Word discussing the crowdfunding campaign.

STARTING DATA FILES

Word7 → **Module**

NP_WD_7-1.docx
NP_WD_7-2.xlsx
NP_WD_7-3.docx
NP_WD_7-4.docx
Support_WD_7_Goals.xlsx
Support_WD_7_James.docx

Review

NP_WD_7-5.docx
NP_WD_7-6.xlsx
NP_WD_7-7.docx
Support_WD_7_Funding.xlsx
Support_WD_7_SportsJames.docx

Case1

NP_WD_7-8.docx
NP_WD_7-9.xlsx

Case2

NP_WD_7-10.docx
Support_WD_7_Aziz.docx
Support_WD_7_Tommy.docx

Session 7.1 Visual Overview:

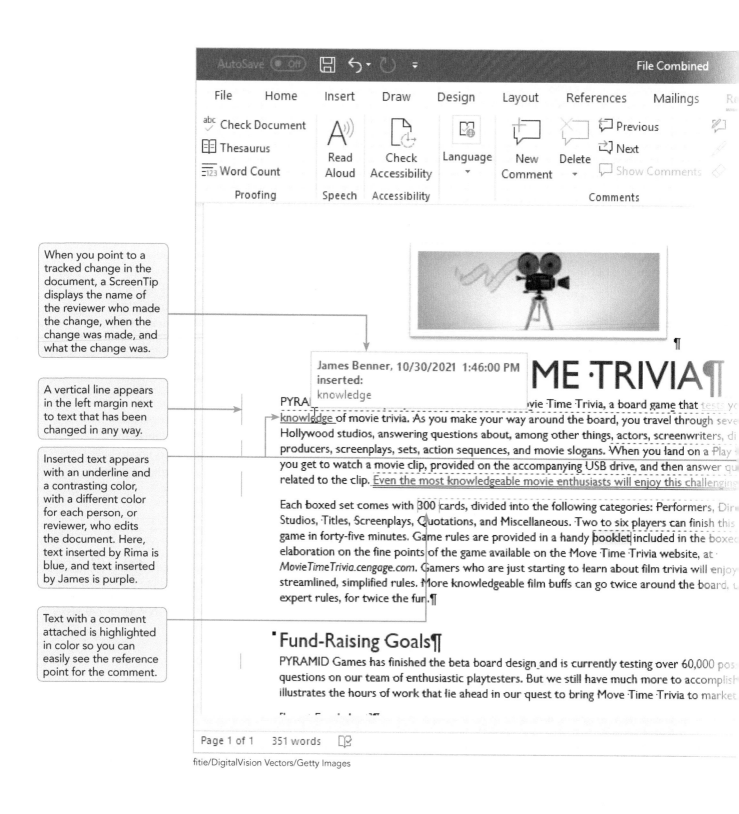

When you point to a tracked change in the document, a ScreenTip displays the name of the reviewer who made the change, when the change was made, and what the change was.

A vertical line appears in the left margin next to text that has been changed in any way.

Inserted text appears with an underline and a contrasting color, with a different color for each person, or reviewer, who edits the document. Here, text inserted by Rima is blue, and text inserted by James is purple.

Text with a comment attached is highlighted in color so you can easily see the reference point for the comment.

James Benner, 10/30/2021 1:46:00 PM inserted:
knowledge

ME TRIVIA¶

PYRA[...] [...]vie Time Trivia, a board game that [...] [...]knowledge of movie trivia. As you make your way around the board, you travel through seve[...] Hollywood studios, answering questions about, among other things, actors, screenwriters, di[...] producers, screenplays, sets, action sequences, and movie slogans. When you land on a Play [...] you get to watch a movie clip, provided on the accompanying USB drive, and then answer qu[...] related to the clip. Even the most knowledgeable movie enthusiasts will enjoy this challengin[...]

Each boxed set comes with 300 cards, divided into the following categories: Performers, Dir[...] Studios, Titles, Screenplays, Quotations, and Miscellaneous. Two to six players can finish this [...] game in forty-five minutes. Game rules are provided in a handy booklet included in the boxe[...] elaboration on the fine points of the game available on the Move Time Trivia website, at [...] MovieTimeTrivia.cengage.com. Gamers who are just starting to learn about film trivia will enjoy[...] streamlined, simplified rules. More knowledgeable film buffs can go twice around the board, u[...] expert rules, for twice the fun.¶

Fund-Raising Goals¶

PYRAMID Games has finished the beta board design and is currently testing over 60,000 pos[...] questions on our team of enthusiastic playtesters. But we still have much more to accomplish[...] illustrates the hours of work that lie ahead in our quest to bring Move Time Trivia to market[...]

Page 1 of 1   351 words

fitie/DigitalVision Vectors/Getty Images

Tracking Changes

The Review tab contains all the options you need for editing a document using tracked changes and comments.

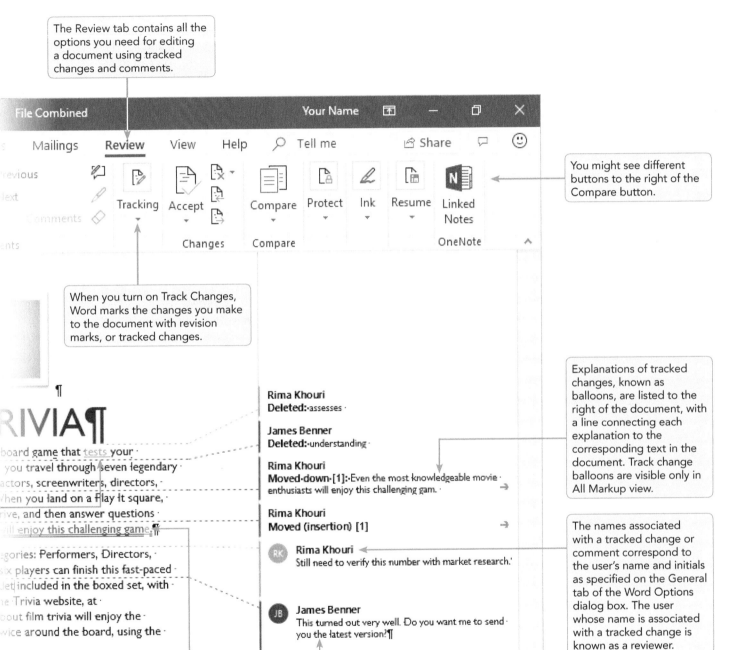

When you turn on Track Changes, Word marks the changes you make to the document with revision marks, or tracked changes.

You might see different buttons to the right of the Compare button.

Explanations of tracked changes, known as balloons, are listed to the right of the document, with a line connecting each explanation to the corresponding text in the document. Track change balloons are visible only in All Markup view.

The names associated with a tracked change or comment correspond to the user's name and initials as specified on the General tab of the Word Options dialog box. The user whose name is associated with a tracked change is known as a reviewer.

Comments are often used along with Track Changes.

Green font and a green double underline indicate that this text was moved from one location in the document and inserted in this new location.

Editing a Document with Tracked Changes

The Track Changes feature in Word simulates the process of marking up a hard copy of a document with a colored pen, but offers many more advantages. Word keeps track of who makes each change, assigning a different color to each reviewer and providing ScreenTips indicating details of the change, such as the reviewer's name and the date and time the change was made. Using the buttons on the Review tab, you can move through the document quickly, accepting or rejecting changes with a click of the mouse.

Rima is ready to revise her first draft of the document. She asks you to turn on Track Changes before you make the edits for her. To ensure that her name is displayed for each tracked change, and that your screens match the figures in this module, you will temporarily change the username on the General tab of the Word Options dialog box to "Rima Khouri." You'll also change the user initials to "RK."

To change the username and turn on Track Changes:

▶ **1. sam** ⬇ Open the document **NP_WD_7-1.docx** located in the Word7 > Module folder included with your Data Files, and then save the document as **NP_WD_7_Rima** in the location specified by your instructor.

▶ **2.** Switch to Print Layout view if necessary, display the rulers and nonprinting characters, and change the document Zoom level to **110%**. You'll use this Zoom setting for the first part of this module to ensure that you can see all the tracked changes in the document.

▶ **3.** On the ribbon, click the **Review** tab.

▶ **4.** In the Tracking group, click the **Dialog Box Launcher** to open the Track Changes Options dialog box, and then click **Change User Name**. The Word Options dialog box opens, with the General tab displayed.

▶ **5.** On a piece of paper, write down the current username and initials, if they are not your own, so you can refer to it when you need to restore the original username and initials later in this module. Although the user initials do not appear on the Word screen, in a printed document the username is replaced with the user initials to save space. Therefore, you should always change the user initials whenever you change the username.

▶ **6.** Click in the **User name** box, delete the current username, and then type **Rima Khouri**.

▶ **7.** Click in the Initials box, delete the current initials, and then type **RK**.

▶ **8.** Click the **Always use these values regardless of sign in to Office** check box to insert a checkmark, if necessary. If you don't check this box, the name of the person currently signed into Office.com will appear in the document's tracked changes, no matter what username is entered in the User name box.

▶ **9.** Click **OK**. The Word Options dialog box closes, and you return to the Track Changes Options dialog box.

▶ **10.** Click **OK** to close the Track Changes Options dialog box.

TIP

To prevent collaborators from turning off Track Changes, click the Track Changes arrow, click Lock Tracking, create a password if you want to use one, and then click OK.

▶ **11.** In the Tracking group, click the **Track Changes** button. The gray highlighting on the Track Changes button tells you that it is selected, indicating that the Track Changes feature is turned on.

Trouble? If you see a menu, you clicked the Track Changes arrow rather than the button itself. Press ESC to close the menu, and then click the Track Changes button to turn on Track Changes.

12. In the Tracking group, verify that the Display for Review box displays "All Markup." This setting ensures that tracked changes are displayed in the document as you edit it.

> **Trouble?** If the Display for Review box does not display "All Markup," click the Display for Review arrow, and then click All Markup.

13. In the Tracking group, click the **Show Markup** button, and then point to **Balloons**. See Figure 7–1.

Figure 7–1   Track Changes turned on

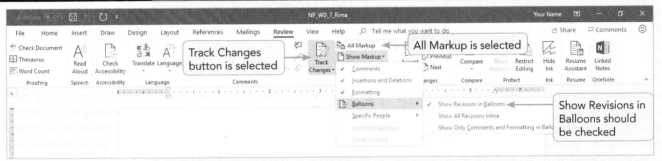

14. If you do not see a checkmark next to Show Revisions in Balloons, click **Show Revisions in Balloons** now to select it and close the menu. Otherwise, click anywhere in the document to close the menu.

Now that Track Changes is turned on, you can begin editing Rima's document. First, Rima needs to change the word "assesses" in the first sentence to "tests."

To edit Rima's document and view the tracked changes:

1. In the line below the "Movie Time Trivia" heading, select the word **assesses** and then type **tests**. The new word, "tests," is displayed in color, with an underline. A vertical line is displayed in the left margin, drawing attention to the change. To the right of the document, the username associated with the change (Rima Khouri) is displayed, along with an explanation of the change. See Figure 7–2.

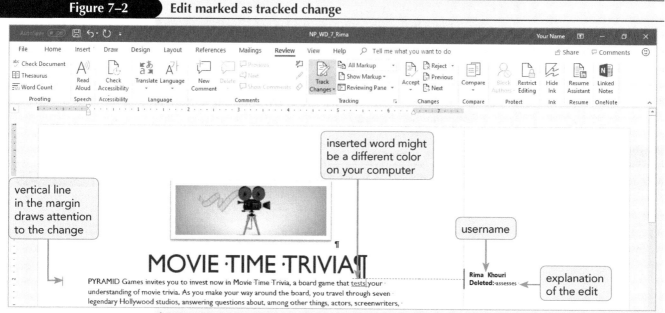

Figure 7–2 Edit marked as tracked change

inserted word might be a different color on your computer

vertical line in the margin draws attention to the change

username

explanation of the edit

MOVIE·TIME·TRIVIA¶

PYRAMID Games invites you to invest now in Movie Time Trivia, a board game that tests your understanding of movie trivia. As you make your way around the board, you travel through seven legendary Hollywood studios, answering questions about, among other things, actors, screenwriters,

Rima Khouri
Deleted: assesses

fitie/DigitalVision Vectors/Getty Images

2. Move the pointer over the newly inserted word "tests." A ScreenTip displays information about the edit, along with the date and time the edit was made.

3. Move the pointer over the explanation of the change to the right of the document. The explanation is highlighted, and the dotted line connecting the change in the document to the explanation turns solid. In a document with many tracked changes, this makes it easier to see which explanation is associated with which tracked change.

Next, Rima wants you to move the second-to-last sentence in this paragraph to the end of the paragraph.

4. Press **CTRL**, and then click in the sentence that begins "Even the most knowledgeable…." The entire sentence is selected. Don't be concerned that the word "game," at the end of the sentence is misspelled. You'll correct that error shortly.

5. Drag the sentence to insert it at the end of the paragraph, and then click anywhere in the document to deselect it. See Figure 7–3.

Figure 7–3   Tracked changes showing text moved to a new location

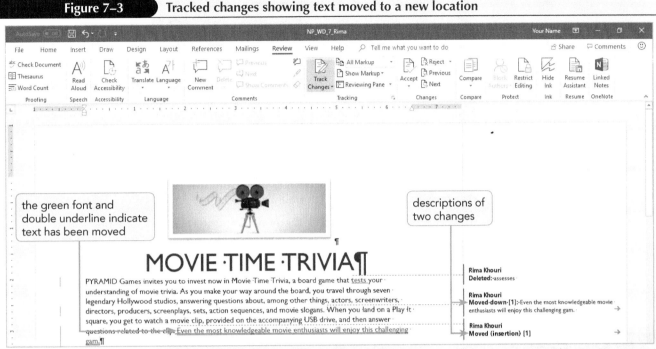

the green font and double underline indicate text has been moved

descriptions of two changes

fitie/DigitalVision Vectors/Getty Images

The sentence is inserted with a double underline in green, which is the color Word uses to denote moved text. Word also inserts a space before the inserted sentence and marks the nonprinting space character as a tracked change. A vertical bar in the left margin draws attention to the moved text.

To the right of the document, descriptions of two new changes are displayed. The "Moved down [1]" change shows the text of the sentence that was moved. The "Moved (insertion) [1]" change draws attention to the sentence in its new location at the end of the paragraph.

A blue, right-facing arrow next to a tracked change explanation indicates that the change is related to another change. You can click the arrow to select the related change.

▶ **6.** Next to the "Moved (insertion) [1]" change, click the blue, right-facing arrow ➡️ to select the moved sentence in the "Moved down [1]" balloon. See Figure 7–4.

Figure 7–4   Selecting a related change

clicking this arrow selects the related change

related change

fitie/DigitalVision Vectors/Getty Images

After reviewing the sentence in its new location at the end of the paragraph, Rima notices that she needs to add an "e" to the last word in the sentence so that it reads "…this challenging game."

▶ 7. In the sentence you moved in Step 5, click to the right of the "m" in "gam," and then type the letter **e**. The newly inserted letter is displayed in the same color as the word "tests" at the beginning of the paragraph.

Finally, Rima asks you to insert a comment reminding her that the number of cards in each boxed set might change. Comments are commonly used with tracked changes. In All Markup view, they are displayed, along with other edits, to the right of the document.

▶ 8. In the first line of the second main paragraph (which begins "Each boxed set comes with 300…"), select the number **300**.

▶ 9. In the Comments group, click the **New Comment** button. The number "300" is highlighted in the same color used for the word "tests," and the insertion point moves to the right of the document, ready for you to type the comment text.

▶ 10. Type **I still need to verify this number with market research.** See Figure 7–5.

Figure 7–5 **Comment added to document**

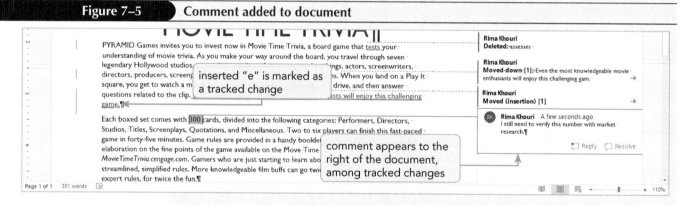

▶ 11. Save your document.

Adjusting Track Changes Options

The default settings for Track Changes worked well as you edited Rima's document. However, you can change these settings if you prefer. For instance, you could choose not to display formatting changes as tracked changes, or you could select a different color for inserted text. To get a more streamlined view of the document, you can switch from All Markup view to Simple Markup view.

To view Track Changes options:

▶ 1. In the Tracking group, click the **Dialog Box Launcher**. The Track Changes Options dialog box opens. See Figure 7–6.

Figure 7–6   Track Changes Options dialog box

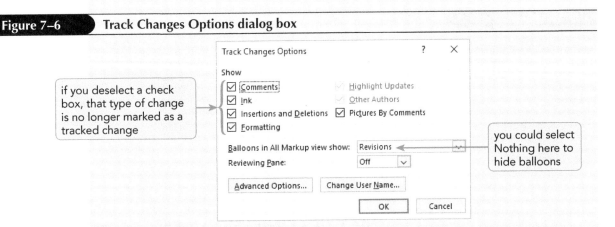

The check boxes in the Show section control which types of edits are marked as tracked changes. For example, the Formatting check box is currently selected. If you didn't want formatting changes to be marked as tracked changes, you could deselect the Formatting check box. Note that Revisions is currently selected in the "Balloons in All Markup view show" box. To turn off the balloon feature, so that no track changes or comment balloons are displayed to the right of the document in All Markup view, you could select Nothing instead.

2. Click **Advanced Options**. The Advanced Track Changes Options dialog box opens.

The options in this dialog box allow you to select the colors you want to use for various types of edits. For example, you can use the Color box next to the Insertions box to select a color to use for inserted text. Note that the default setting for Insertions, Deletions, Comments, and Formatting is By author. This means that Word assigns one color to each person who edits the document. When you are working with multiple reviewers, you should always retain the By author settings to ensure that you can easily distinguish the edits made by each reviewer.

3. Click **Cancel** to close the Advanced Track Changes Options dialog box, and then click **Cancel** to close the Track Changes Options dialog box.

After reviewing the tracked changes with you, Rima decides the number of details shown in All Markup view makes the document too difficult to read. She wants you to switch to Simple Markup view instead.

To switch to Simple Markup view:

1. In the Tracking group, click the **Display for Review arrow**, and then click **Simple Markup**. See Figure 7–7.

Figure 7–7 Simple Markup view

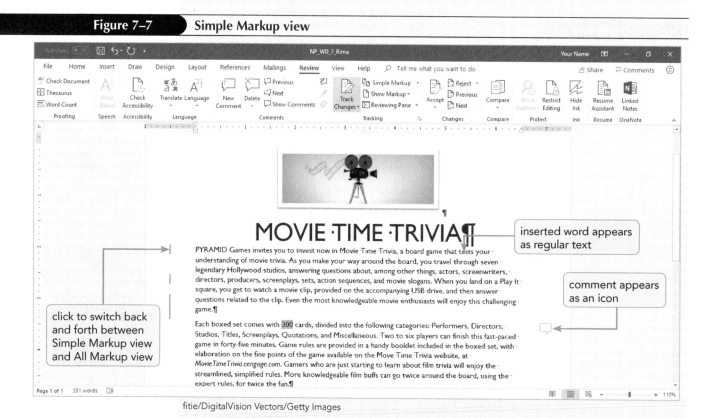

fitie/DigitalVision Vectors/Getty Images

Trouble? If the comment balloon is still visible on your screen, click the Show Comments button in the Comments group on the Review tab to deselect it.

All of the tracked changes in the document are now hidden, and the comment balloon is replaced with an icon in the right margin. The inserted word "tests" is in black font, like the surrounding text, as is the sentence you moved to the end of the paragraph. The only sign that the document contains tracked changes is the red vertical bar in the left margin. You can click a vertical bar to switch back and forth between Simple Markup view and All Markup view.

2. Click the red vertical bar to the left of the paragraph that begins "PYRAMID Games hopes…." The document switches to All Markup view, with all the tracked changes and the comment visible. The vertical bar in the left margin changes from red to gray.

3. Click the gray vertical bar to the left of the paragraph that begins "PYRAMID Games hopes…." The document switches back to Simple Markup view.

Rima has received James's edited copy of the first draft via email, and now she'd like your help in combining her edited copy of the NP_WD_7_Rima.docx document with James's copy.

Comparing and Combining Documents

When you work in a collaborative environment with multiple people contributing to the same document, the Compare and Combine features in Word are essential tools. They allow you to see the difference between multiple versions of a document, with tracked changes highlighting the differences. The Compare and Combine features are similar, but they have different purposes.

The **Compare** feature, which is designed to help you quickly spot the differences between two copies of a document, is intended for documents that *do not* contain tracked changes. After it compares the two documents, Word notes the differences between the revised document and the original document with tracked changes, with all the tracked changes assigned to the username associated with the revised document.

The **Combine** feature, which is designed for documents that *do* contain tracked changes, allows you to see which reviewers made which changes. In a combined document, each reviewer's tracked changes are displayed, with each tracked change assigned to the reviewer who made that change. The Combine feature works well when you want to combine, or merge, two documents to create a third document. You can then combine additional reviewed versions of the document into this new document, until you have incorporated all the tracked changes from all your reviewers. Because the Combine feature allows you to incorporate more than two documents into one, it's the option you'll use most when collaborating with a group.

When you compare or combine documents, you select one document as the original and one as the revised document. Together, these two documents are known as the **source documents**. By default, Word then creates a new, third document, which consists of the original document's text edited with tracked changes to show how the revised document differs. The source documents themselves are left unchanged. If Word detects a formatting conflict—that is, if identical text is formatted differently in the source documents—Word displays a dialog box allowing you to choose which formatting you want to keep. You can choose to keep the formatting of the original document or the revised document, but not both. Occasionally, Word will display this formatting conflict dialog box even if both source documents are formatted exactly the same. If so, keep the formatting for the original document, and continue with the process of combining the documents.

REFERENCE

Comparing and Combining Documents

- On the ribbon, click the Review tab.
- In the Compare group, click the Compare button.
- Click Compare to open the Compare Documents dialog box, or click Combine to open the Combine Documents dialog box.
- Next to the Original document box, click the Browse button, navigate to the location of the document, select the document, and then click the Open button.
- Next to the Revised document box, click the Browse button, navigate to the location of the document, select the document, and then click the Open button.
- Click the More button, if necessary, to display options that allow you to select which items you want marked with tracked changes, and then make any necessary changes.
- Click OK.

When you start combining or comparing documents, it's not necessary to have either the original document or the revised document open. In this case, however, the NP_WD_7_Rima.docx document, which you will use as the original document, is open. You'll combine this document with James's edited copy.

To combine Rima's document with James's document:

▶ **1.** Make sure you have saved your changes to the NP_WD_7_Rima.docx document.

▶ **2.** In the Compare group, click the **Compare** button. A menu opens with options for comparing or combining two versions of a document.

▶ **3.** Click **Combine**. The Combine Documents dialog box opens.

▶ **4.** Click the **More** button. The dialog box expands to display check boxes, which you can use to specify the items you want marked with tracked changes.

Trouble? If the dialog box has a Less button instead of a More button, the dialog box is already expanded to show the check boxes for selecting additional options. In this case, skip Step 4.

In the Show changes section at the bottom of the dialog box, the New document option button is selected by default, indicating that Word will create a new, combined document rather than importing the tracked changes from the original document into the revised document, or vice versa.

Now you need to specify the NP_WD_7_Rima.docx document as the original document. Even though this document is currently open, you still need to select it.

▶ **5.** Next to the Original document box, click the **Browse** button ▭ to open the Open dialog box.

▶ **6.** If necessary, navigate to the location where you saved the NP_WD_7_Rima document, click **NP_WD_7_Rima.docx** in the file list, and then click the **Open** button. You return to the Combine Documents dialog box, where the file name "NP_WD_7_Rima" is displayed in the Original document box.

Next, you need to select the document you want to use as the revised document.

▶ **7.** Next to the Revised document box, click the **Browse** button ▭, navigate to the **Word7 > Module** folder included with your Data Files if necessary, select the document **Support_WD_7_James.docx**, and then click the **Open** button. The file name "Support_WD_7_James" is displayed in the Revised document box. See Figure 7–8.

Figure 7–8   **Selecting the original and revised documents**

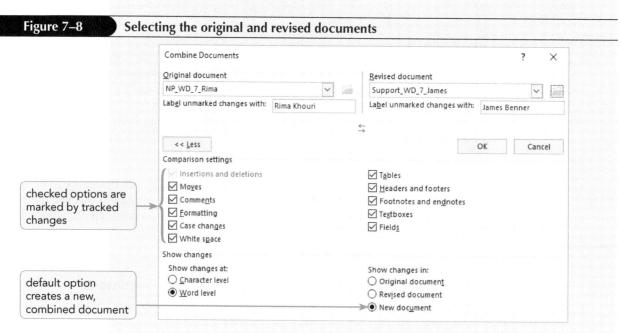

TIP

If you need to compare or combine a series of documents, use the Editor pane afterwards to look for errors resulting from missing spaces or misplaced letters in the final document.

8. Click **OK**. The Combine Documents dialog box closes.

A new document opens. It contains the tracked changes from both the original document and the revised document.

At this point, depending on the previous settings on your computer, you might see only the new, combined document, or you might also see the original and revised documents open in separate windows. You might also see the Reviewing pane, with a list of all the changes, as shown in Figure 7–9.

Figure 7–9   **Two documents combined**

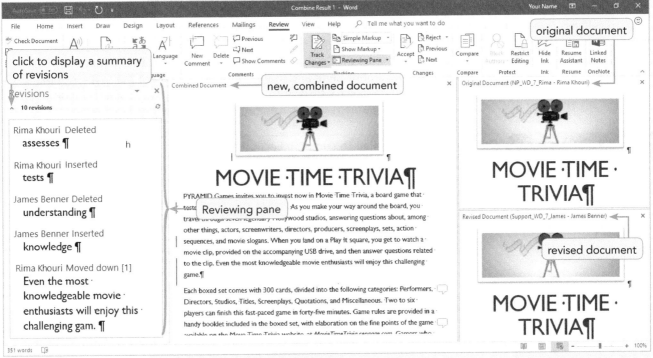

fitie/DigitalVision Vectors/Getty Images

Note that your combined document might have a different name than the one shown in Figure 7–9. For instance, it might be named "Document 1," instead of "Combine Result 1." Also, if you do see the Reviewing pane, don't be concerned if it is displayed at a different Zoom level than what you see in Figure 7–9. If you prefer, you can click in the Reviewing pane, and then change the Zoom setting on the status bar to make the revisions easier to read.

9. In the Compare group, click the **Compare** button, and then point to **Show Source Documents**.

10. If a checkmark appears next to Show Both, press ESC twice to close both menus; otherwise, click **Show Both**. Your screen should now match Figure 7–9.

Trouble? If the Reviewing pane is still not displayed, click the Reviewing Pane button in the Tracking group to display the Reviewing pane.

Trouble? If your Reviewing pane is displayed horizontally rather than vertically, as shown in Figure 7–9, click the Reviewing Pane arrow in the Tracking group, and then click Reviewing Pane Vertical.

Note that the combined document and the two source documents are all displayed in Simple Markup. Also, instead of Print Layout view, which you typically use when working on documents, the three documents are displayed in Web Layout view. You'll learn more about Web Layout view later in this module. For now, all you need to know is that in Web Layout view, the line breaks change to suit the size of the document window, making it easier to read text in the small windows.

It's helpful to have the source documents displayed when you want to quickly compare the two documents. For example, right now Rima wants to scroll down the documents to see how they differ. When you scroll up or down in the Revised Document pane, the other documents scroll as well.

To scroll the document panes simultaneously:

▌ **1.** Move the pointer over the Revised Document (Support_WD_7_James – James Benner) pane to display its scroll bar, and then drag the scroll bar down to display the "Fund-Raising Goals" heading. The text in the Combined Document pane and in the Original Document (NP_WD_7_Rima - Rima Khouri) pane scrolls down to match the text in the Revised Document (Support_WD_7_James - James Benner) pane. See Figure 7–10.

Figure 7–10 | **Document panes scrolled to compare versions**

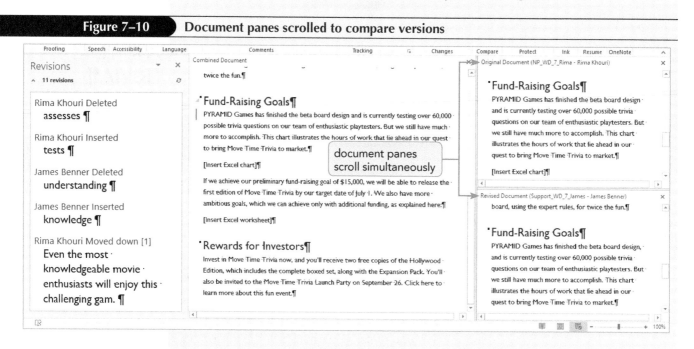

Now that you've reviewed both documents, you can hide the source documents to make the combined document easier to read. After you hide the source documents, you can review the edits in the Reviewing pane.

To hide the source documents and review the edits in the Reviewing pane:

▌ **1.** In the Compare group, click the **Compare** button, point to the **Show Source Documents** button, and then click **Hide Source Documents**. The panes displaying the original and revised documents close, and the combined document window switches to Print Layout view.

Trouble? If the combined window does not switch to Print Layout view, click the Print Layout view button 📃 on the status bar.

TIP

To hide a reviewer's edits, click the Show Markup button in the Tracking group, point to Specific People, and then click the person's name.

2. Move the pointer over the list of edits in the Reviewing pane to display the vertical scroll bar, and then scroll down and review the list of edits. Notice that the document contains the edits you made earlier (under Rima's name) as well as edits made by James Benner.

Rima prefers to review changes using All Markup view instead of the Reviewing pane.

3. In the Tracking group, click the **Reviewing Pane** button to deselect it. The Reviewing pane closes.

4. In the Tracking group, click the **Display for Review arrow**, and then click **All Markup**.

5. In the Tracking group, click the **Show Markup** button, point to Balloons, and then make sure **Show Revisions in Balloons** is selected.

6. Save the document as **NP_WD_7_Combined** in the location specified by your instructor.

7. In the Tracking group, click the **Track Changes** button to turn off Track Changes. This ensures that you won't accidentally add any additional edit marks as you review the document.

8. Change the Zoom level to **120%**.

INSIGHT

Using Real-Time Co-Authoring to Collaborate with Others

Combining documents is a powerful way to incorporate the work of multiple people in one document. The only drawback to combining documents is that, typically, one person is charged with combining the documents, reviewing the tracked changes, and then making decisions about what to keep and what to delete. In some situations, it's more effective to give all team members the freedom to edit a document at the same time, with every person's changes showing up on everyone else's screen. You can accomplish this by saving a document to OneDrive and then sharing it using the co-authoring feature in Word.

To get started, click Share in the upper-right corner of the Word window to open the Share pane, and then save the document to OneDrive. Next, use the options in the Share pane to either: 1) enter the email addresses for the people you want to share the document with, as well as a message inviting them to work on the document; or 2) create a sharing link, which you can then email to your collaborators, and which they can then click to open the document in Office 365, the online version of Microsoft Office. After a delay of a few minutes or less, you and all of your collaborators can begin editing the document, while being able to see everyone else's changes to the document in real time.

Next, you will review the edits in the NP_WD_7_Combined.docx document to accept and reject the changes as appropriate.

Accepting and Rejecting Changes

The document you just created contains all the edits from two different reviewers—Rima's changes made in the original document and James's changes as they appeared in the revised document. In the combined document, each reviewer's edits are displayed in a different color, making it easy to see which reviewer made each change.

When you review tracked changes in a document, the best approach is to move the insertion point to the beginning of the document, and then navigate through the document one change at a time using the Next and Previous buttons in the Changes group on the Review tab. This ensures you won't miss any edits. As you review a tracked change, you can either accept the change or reject it.

REFERENCE

Accepting and Rejecting Changes

- Move the insertion point to the beginning of the document.
- On the ribbon, click the Review tab.
- In the Changes group, click the Next button to select the first edit or comment in the document.
- To accept a selected change, click the Accept button in the Changes group.
- To reject a selected change, click the Reject button in the Changes group.
- To accept all the changes in the document, click the Accept arrow, and then click Accept All Changes.
- To reject all the changes in the document, click the Reject arrow, and then click Reject All Changes.

To accept and reject changes in the NP_WD_7_Combined.docx document:

1. Press **CTRL+HOME** to move the insertion point to the beginning of the document.

2. In the Changes group, click the **Next** button. To the right of the document, in a tracked change balloon, the deleted word "assesses" is selected, as shown in Figure 7–11.

Figure 7–11 | **First change in document selected**

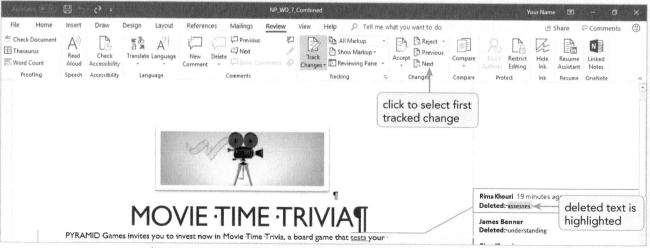

fitie/DigitalVision Vectors/Getty Images

Trouble? If the insertion point moves to Rima's comment, you clicked the Next button in the Comments group instead of the Next button in the Changes group. Repeat Steps 1 and 2.

3. In the Changes group, click the **Accept** button. The tracked change balloon is no longer displayed, indicating that the change has been accepted. The inserted word "tests" is now selected in the document.

   Trouble? If you see a menu below the Accept button, you clicked the Accept arrow by mistake. Press ESC to close the menu, and then click the Accept button.

4. Click the **Accept** button. In a tracked change balloon to the right of the document, James's deletion of the word "understanding" is selected. See Figure 7-12.

Figure 7–12	Reviewing James's changes

James deleted the word "understanding" and replaced it with the word "knowledge," which is displayed in the document as a tracked change. The inserted word, the tracked change balloon for the deleted word, and the icon in James's comment further down in the document are all the same color.

Because the word "knowledgeable" is used later in this same paragraph, Rima prefers to keep the original word, "understanding," so you need to reject James's change.

5. In the Changes group, click the **Reject** button to reject the deletion of the word "understanding." The tracked change balloon is no longer displayed, and the word "understanding" is restored in the document, to the left of the inserted word "knowledge," which is now selected. See Figure 7–13.

Figure 7–13	Document after rejecting change

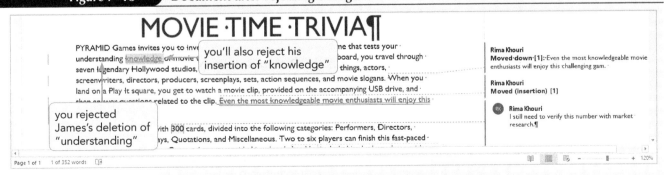

6. Click the **Reject** button. The inserted word "knowledge" is removed from the document. To the right of the document, in a tracked change balloon, the sentence that you moved is now selected.

7. Click the **Accept** button. The tracked change balloon containing the moved sentence and the related "Moved (insertion) [1]" tracked change balloon are no longer displayed. In the document, the sentence itself is displayed in black, like the surrounding text, indicating that the change has been accepted. Now the space before the moved sentence, which Word automatically inserted when you moved the sentence, is selected.

8. Click the **Accept** button to accept the insertion of the space, and then click the **Accept** button again to accept the insertion of the letter "e" at the end of "gam."

   The insertion point moves to the beginning of Rima's comment. Rima has received final confirmation that 300 is indeed the correct number of cards, so you can delete the comment.

9. In the Comments group, click the **Delete** button to delete the comment.

10. In the Changes group, click the **Next** button. (You could also click the Next button in the Comments group since the next item is a comment.)

    The insertion point moves to the beginning of James's comment, although you might need to scroll down to see it. Rima has already seen a draft of the rules booklet, so you can delete the comment.

11. In the Comments group, click the **Delete** button to delete the comment.

12. In the Changes group, click the **Next** button. A Microsoft Word dialog box opens with a message indicating that there are no more comments or tracked changes in the document.

13. Click **OK** to close the dialog box.

14. At the end of the last paragraph in the document, click to the left of the period, and type **or contact *your name***, where *your name* is your first and last name. When you are finished, the text should read "about this fun event, or contact *your name*."

Now that you have finished editing and reviewing the document with tracked changes, you need to restore the original username and initials settings. Then you can close Rima's original document, which you no longer need.

To restore the original username and initials settings and close Rima's original document:

1. In the Tracking group, click the **Dialog Box Launcher** to open the Track Changes Options dialog box.

2. Click the **Change User Name** button, and then change the username and initials back to their original settings on the General tab of the Word Options dialog box.

3. Click **OK** to close the Word Options dialog box, and then click **OK** again to close the Track Changes Options dialog box.

4. On the taskbar, click the **Word** button, and then click the **NP_WD_7_Rima - Word** thumbnail to display the document.

▶ **5.** Close the **NP_WD_7_Rima.docx** document.

▶ **6.** Save the **NP_WD_7_Combined.docx** document, and then display the rulers.

▶ **7.** On the ribbon, click the **Home** tab.

INSIGHT

Checking for Tracked Changes

Once a document is finished, you should make sure it does not contain any tracked changes or comments. This is especially important in situations where comments or tracked changes might reveal sensitive information that could jeopardize your privacy or the privacy of the organization you work for.

You can't always tell if a document contains comments or tracked changes just by looking at it because the comments or changes for some or all of the reviewers might be hidden. Also, the Display for Review box in the Tracking group on the Review tab might be set to No Markup, in which case all tracked changes would be hidden. To determine whether a document contains any tracked changes or comments, open the Reviewing pane and verify that the number of revisions for each type is 0. You can also use the Document Inspector to check for a variety of issues, including leftover comments and tracked changes. To use the Document Inspector, click the File tab to display the Info tab, click Check for Issues, click Inspect Document, and then click the Inspect button.

Now that you have combined James's edits with Rima's, you are ready to add the Excel worksheet data and the pie chart to the document.

Embedding and Linking Objects from Other Programs

The programs in Office 2019 are designed to accomplish specific tasks. As you've seen with Word, you can use a word-processing program to create, edit, and format documents such as letters, reports, newsletters, and proposals. On the other hand, Microsoft Excel, a **spreadsheet program**, allows you to organize, calculate, and analyze numerical data in a grid of rows and columns and to illustrate data in the form of charts. A spreadsheet created in Microsoft Excel is known as a **worksheet**. Each Excel file— called a **workbook**—can contain multiple worksheets. Throughout this module, a portion of an Excel worksheet is referred to as a **worksheet object**, and a chart is referred to as a **chart object**.

Sometimes it is useful to combine information created in the different Office programs into one file. For her document, Rima wants to use fund-raising goals from an Excel worksheet. She also wants to include an Excel chart that shows the hours of work remaining on the project. You can incorporate the Excel data and chart into Rima's Word document by taking advantage of **object linking and embedding**, or **OLE**, a technology that allows you to share information among the Office programs. This process is commonly referred to as **integration**.

Before you start using OLE, you need to understand some important terms. Recall that in Word, an object is anything that can be selected and modified as a whole, such as a table, picture, or block of text. Another important term, **source program**, refers to the program used to create the original version of an object. The program into which the object is integrated is called the **destination program**. Similarly, the original file that contains the object you are integrating is called the **source file**, and the file into which you integrate the object is called the **destination file**.

You can integrate objects by either embedding or linking. **Embedding** is a technique that allows you to insert a copy of an object into a destination document. You can double-click an embedded object in the destination document to access the tools of the source program, allowing you to edit the object within the destination document using the source program's tools. Because the embedded object is a copy, any changes you make to it are not reflected in the original source file and vice versa. For instance, you could embed data from a worksheet named Itemized Expenses into a Word document named Travel Report. Later, if you change the Itemized Expenses file, those revisions would not be reflected in the Travel Report document. The opposite is also true; if you edit the embedded object from within the Travel Report file, those changes will not be reflected in the source file Itemized Expenses. The embedded object retains no connection to the source file.

Figure 7–14 illustrates the relationship between an embedded Excel worksheet object in Rima's Word document and the source file.

Figure 7–14 **Embedding an Excel worksheet object in a Word document**

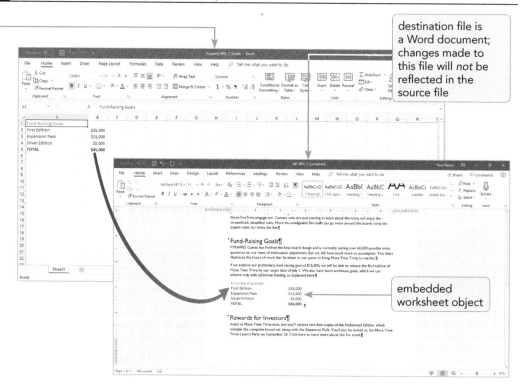

source file is an Excel workbook; changes made to this file will *not* be reflected in the destination file

destination file is a Word document; changes made to this file will *not* be reflected in the source file

embedded worksheet object

Linking is similar to embedding, except that the object inserted into the destination file maintains a connection to the source file. Just as with an embedded object, you can double-click a linked object to access the tools of the source program. However, unlike with an embedded object, changes to a linked object show up in both the destination file and the source file. The linked object in the destination document is not a copy; it is a shortcut to the original object in the source file.

Figure 7–15 illustrates the relationship between the data in James's Excel chart and the linked object in Rima's Word document.

Figure 7–15   Linking an Excel chart object to a Word document

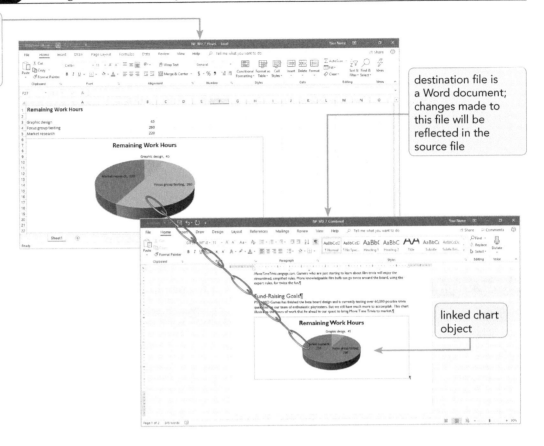

source file is an Excel workbook; changes made to this file will be reflected in the destination file

destination file is a Word document; changes made to this file will be reflected in the source file

linked chart object

Decision Making: Choosing Between Embedding and Linking

Embedding and linking are both useful when you know you'll want to edit an object after inserting it into Word. But how do you decide whether to embed or link the object? Create an embedded object if you won't have access to the original source file in the future, or if you don't need (or want) to maintain the connection between the source file and the document containing the linked object. Two advantages of embedding are that the source file is unaffected by any editing in the destination document, and the two files can be stored separately. You could even delete the source file from your disk without affecting the copy embedded in your Word document. A disadvantage is that the file size of a Word document containing an embedded object will be larger than the file size of a document containing a linked object.

Create a linked object whenever you have data that is likely to change over time and when you want to keep the object in your document up to date. In addition to the advantage of a smaller destination file size, both the source file and the destination file can reflect recent revisions when the files are linked. A disadvantage to linking is that you have to keep track of two files (the source file and the destination file) rather than just one.

Embedding an Excel Worksheet Object

To embed an object from an Excel worksheet into a Word document, you start by opening the Excel worksheet (the source file) and copying the Excel object to the Office Clipboard. Then, in the Word document (the destination file), you open the Paste Special dialog box. In this dialog box, you can choose to paste the copied Excel object in a number of different forms. To embed it, you select Microsoft Excel Worksheet Object.

Rima wants to include the company's fund-raising goals in her document. If she needs to adjust numbers in the fund-raising goals later, she will need access to the Excel tools for recalculating the data. Therefore, you'll embed the Excel object in the Word document. Then you can use Excel commands to modify the embedded object from within Word.

To embed the Excel data in the Word document:

▶ **1.** Scroll down to the paragraph above the "Rewards for Investors" heading, and then delete the placeholder text [**Insert Excel worksheet**], taking care not to delete the paragraph mark after it. The insertion point should now be located in a blank paragraph above the "Rewards for Investors" heading.

Now you need to open James's Excel file and copy the fund-raising data.

▶ **2.** Start Microsoft Excel 2019, open the file **Support_WD_7_Goals.xlsx** located in the Word7 > Module folder included with your Data Files, and then maximize the Excel program window if necessary. See Figure 7–16.

Figure 7–16   **Support_WD_7_Goals.xlsx file open in Excel**

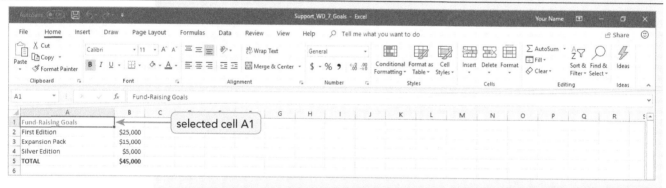

An Excel worksheet is arranged in rows and columns, just like a Word table. The intersection between a row and a column is called a **cell**; an individual cell takes its name from its column letter and row number. For example, the intersection of column A and row 1 in the upper-left corner of the worksheet is referred to as cell A1. Currently, cell A1 is selected, as indicated by its dark outline.

To copy the fund-raising data to the Office Clipboard, you need to select the entire block of cells containing the fund-raising data.

▶ **3.** Click cell **A1** (the cell containing the text "Fund-Raising Goals"), if necessary, press and hold **SHIFT**, and then click cell **B5** (the cell containing "$45,000"). See Figure 7–17.

Figure 7–17   **Fund-raising data selected in worksheet**

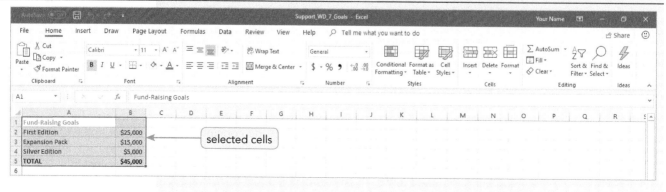

Now that the data is selected, you can copy it to the Office Clipboard.

Be sure to keep Excel open; otherwise, you won't have access to the commands for embedding the data in Word.

▶ 4. Press **CTRL+C**. The border around the selected cells has a moving, marquee effect, indicating that you have copied the data in these cells to the Office Clipboard. Next, you will switch to Word without closing Excel.

▶ 5. On the taskbar, click the **Word** button 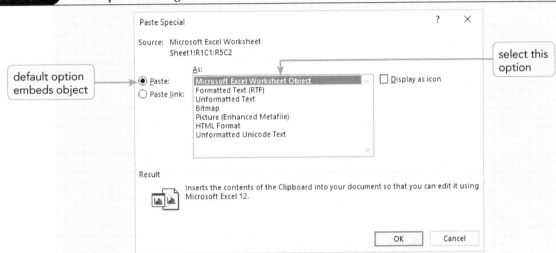 to return to the NP_WD_7_Combined.docx document. The insertion point is still located in the blank paragraph above the "Rewards for Investors" heading.

▶ 6. On the ribbon, click the **Home** tab, if necessary.

▶ 7. In the Clipboard group, click the **Paste arrow**, and then click **Paste Special** to open the Paste Special dialog box.

▶ 8. In the As list, click **Microsoft Excel Worksheet Object**. See Figure 7–18.

Figure 7–18	**Paste Special dialog box**

Next, you can choose to embed the Excel object or link it, depending on whether you select the Paste button (for embedding) or the Paste link button (for linking). The Paste button is selected by default, which is what you want in this case.

▶ 9. Click **OK**. The Excel worksheet object is inserted in the Word document, as shown in Figure 7–19.

Figure 7–19	**Excel worksheet object embedded in Word document**

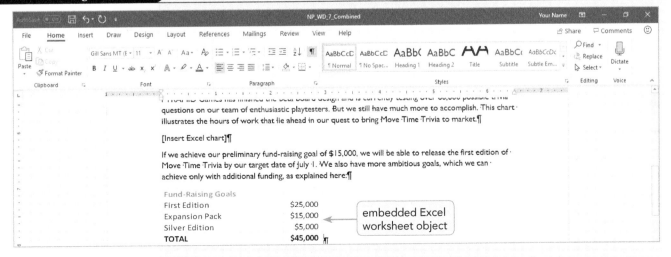

Trouble? If you don't see the top or bottom horizontal gridline in the embedded Excel object, don't be concerned. It won't affect the rest of the steps.

At this point, the Excel data looks like an ordinary table. But because you embedded it as an Excel worksheet object, you can modify it from within Word, using Excel tools and commands.

Modifying an Embedded Worksheet Object

After you embed an object in Word, you can modify it in two different ways. First, you can click the object to select it, and then move or resize it just as you would a graphic object. Second, you can double-click the object to display the tools of the source program on the Word ribbon and then edit the contents of the object. After you modify the embedded object using the source program tools, you can click anywhere else in the Word document to deselect the embedded object and redisplay the usual Word tools on the ribbon.

Rima would like to center the Excel object on the page. Also, the value for the First Edition is incorrect, so she asks you to update the fund-raising goals with the new data.

To modify the embedded Excel object:

1. Click anywhere in the Excel object. Selection handles and a dotted outline are displayed around the Excel object, indicating that it is selected. With the object selected, you can center it as you would center any other selected item.

2. Make sure the **Home** tab is selected on the ribbon.

3. In the Paragraph group, click the **Center** button 	≡. The Excel object is centered between the left and right margins of the document.

4. Double-click anywhere inside the Excel object. The object's border changes to resemble the borders of an Excel worksheet, with horizontal and vertical scroll bars, row numbers, and column letters. The Word tabs on the ribbon are replaced with Excel tabs.

   Trouble? If you don't see the Excel borders around the worksheet object, click outside the worksheet object to deselect it, and then repeat Step 4. If you still don't see the Excel borders, save the document, close it, reopen it, and then repeat Step 4.

   You need to change the value for the First Edition from $25,000 to $30,000. Although you can't see it, a formula automatically calculates and displays the total in cell B5. After you increase the value for the First Edition, the formula will increase the total in cell B5 by $5,000.

5. Click cell **B2**, which contains the value $25,000, and then type **30,000**.

6. Press **ENTER**. The new value "$30,000" is displayed in cell B2. The total in cell B5 increases from $45,000 to $50,000. See Figure 7–20.

Figure 7–20   **Revised data in embedded Excel object**

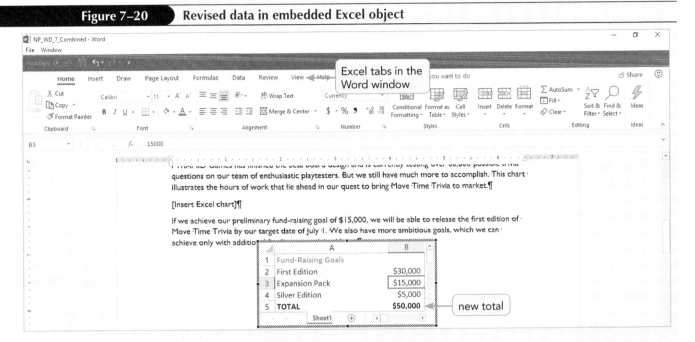

> **7.** In the document, click outside the borders of the Excel object to deselect it. The Word tabs are now visible on the ribbon again.

> **8.** On the taskbar, click the **Microsoft Excel** button to display the Excel window.
>
>   Because you embedded the Excel object rather than linking it, the First Edition value of $25,000 and the Total of $45,000 remain unchanged.

> **9.** On the ribbon, click the **File** tab, and then click **Close** in the navigation pane without saving any changes. The Support_WD_7_Goals.xlsx workbook closes, but Excel remains open.

In this session, you worked with tracked changes in a document. You learned how to combine and compare documents, and you accepted and rejected tracked changes in a combined document. You also embedded an Excel Worksheet object in a Word document and modified the embedded worksheet object from within Word. In the next session, you'll learn how to link an object instead of embedding it. You'll also create bookmarks, insert and edit hyperlinks in a document, and optimize the document for online viewing. Finally, you'll learn how to create and publish a blog post.

REVIEW

Session 7.1 Quick Check

1. How can you ensure that your name is displayed for each tracked change?

2. Explain how to turn on Track Changes.

3. Which provides a more streamlined view of a document's tracked changes, All Markup view or Simple Markup view?

4. What should you do before using the Next and Previous buttons to review the tracked changes in a document?

5. Explain the difference between a linked object and an embedded object.

6. How do you start editing an embedded Excel object in Word?

Session 7.2 Visual Overview:

To link an Excel chart object to a Word document, you first need to open the Excel workbook that contains the chart.

The Paste Options menu offers different ways to paste text, a chart, or other items from a source file. You can choose between keeping the formatting of the source file or using the formatting of the destination file. Here, the Excel file is the source file, and the Word file is the destination file.

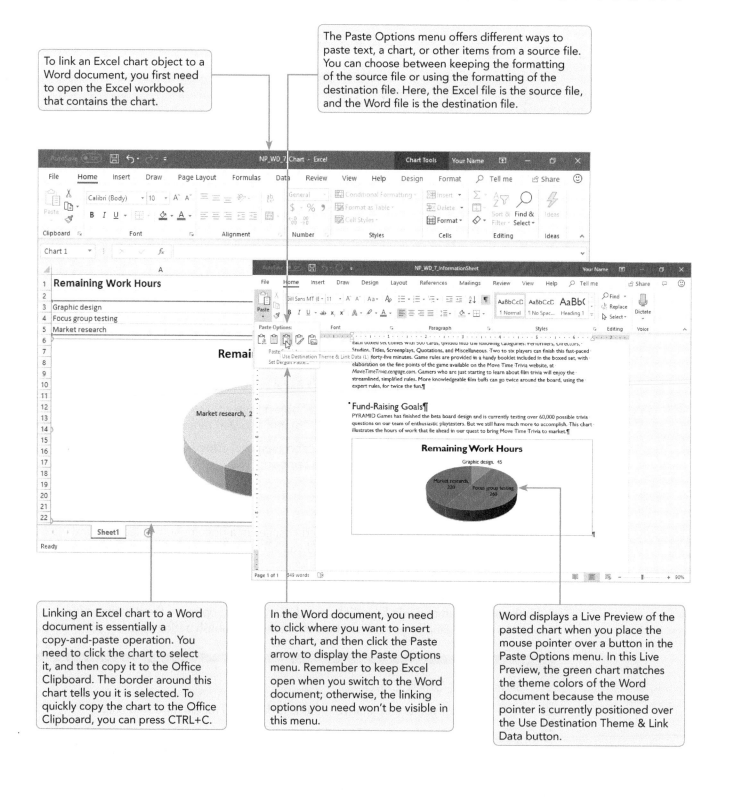

Linking an Excel chart to a Word document is essentially a copy-and-paste operation. You need to click the chart to select it, and then copy it to the Office Clipboard. The border around this chart tells you it is selected. To quickly copy the chart to the Office Clipboard, you can press CTRL+C.

In the Word document, you need to click where you want to insert the chart, and then click the Paste arrow to display the Paste Options menu. Remember to keep Excel open when you switch to the Word document; otherwise, the linking options you need won't be visible in this menu.

Word displays a Live Preview of the pasted chart when you place the mouse pointer over a button in the Paste Options menu. In this Live Preview, the green chart matches the theme colors of the Word document because the mouse pointer is currently positioned over the Use Destination Theme & Link Data button.

Linking an Excel Chart Object

You can edit a linked chart object from within the Word document.

After you select the chart in the Word document, you click the Edit Data button on the Chart Tools Design tab. This opens a spreadsheet window with the Excel source file displayed.

If the chart in the Word window does not change to reflect changes made to data in the spreadsheet window, you can click the Refresh Data button to update the chart in the Word window.

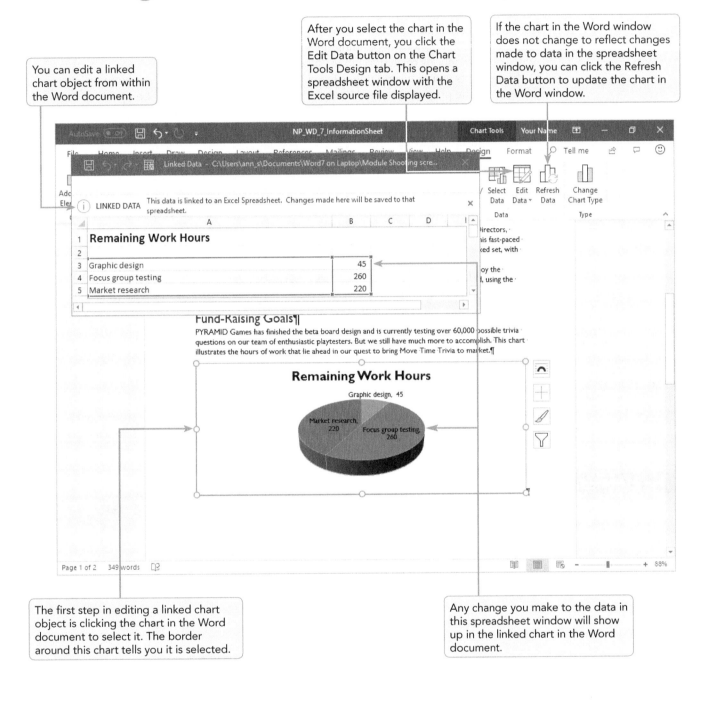

The first step in editing a linked chart object is clicking the chart in the Word document to select it. The border around this chart tells you it is selected.

Any change you make to the data in this spreadsheet window will show up in the linked chart in the Word document.

Linking an Excel Chart Object

When you link an object to a Word document, you start by selecting the object in the source program and copying it to the Office Clipboard. Then you return to Word and select one of the linking options from the Paste Options menu. The Paste Options menu displays different options depending on what you have copied to the Office Clipboard, with specific options related to tables, pictures, and other elements.

Rima wants you to insert James's Excel chart, which illustrates the remaining hours of work on the project, into her Word document. Because James will be updating numbers in the chart soon, she decides to link the chart rather than embed it. That way, once the chart is updated in the source file, the new data will be displayed in Rima's Word document as well.

The chart Rima wants to use is stored in a workbook. Because you'll make changes to the chart after you link it, you will start by saving the workbook with a new name before you link it. This leaves the original workbook file unchanged in case you want to repeat the module steps later. Normally, you don't need to save a file with a new name before you link it to a Word document.

To link the Excel chart to Rima's document:

TIP

To link a Word file to the current document: on the Insert tab, click the Object button, click the Create from File tab, select the Link to file check box, click the Browse button, and select the file.

1. If you took a break after the previous session, make sure the **NP_WD_7_Combined.docx** document is open in Print Layout view and that Excel is open.

2. In Excel, open the file named **NP_WD_7-2.xlsx** from the Word7 > Module folder included with your Data Files, and then save it with the name **NP_WD_7_Hours** in the location specified by your instructor.

   The worksheet includes data and a pie chart illustrating the data.

3. Click the rectangular chart border. Do not click any part of the chart itself. Selection handles appear on the chart border. The worksheet data used to create the chart is also highlighted in purple and blue. See Figure 7–21.

Figure 7–21   Pie chart selected in worksheet

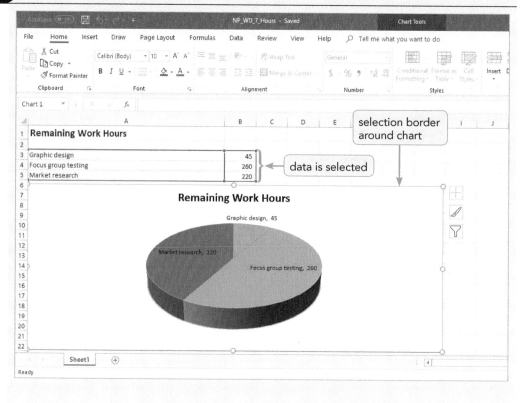

Trouble? If you see borders or handles around individual elements of the pie chart, you clicked the chart itself rather than the border. Click in the worksheet outside the chart border, and then repeat Step 3.

4. Press **CTRL+C** to copy the pie chart to the Office Clipboard.

5. On the taskbar, click the **Word button** 📧 to display the Word window with the NP_WD_7_Combined.docx document.

6. On the ribbon, make sure the Home tab is selected.

7. In the second paragraph after the "Fund-Raising Goals" heading, delete the placeholder text **[Insert Excel chart]** but not the paragraph symbol after it, and then verify that the insertion point is located in a blank paragraph between two paragraphs of text.

8. In the Clipboard group, click the **Paste arrow** to display the Paste Options menu.

9. Move the pointer over the icons on the Paste Options menu, and notice the changing appearance of the chart's Live Preview, depending on which Paste Option you are previewing.

For linking, you can choose between the Use Destination Theme & Link Data option, which formats the chart with the teal, purple, and blue colors of the Word document's current theme, and the Keep Source Formatting & Link Data option, which retains the purple, blue, and orange colors of the Excel workbook. See Figure 7–22.

| Figure 7–22 | Linking options on the Paste Options menu |

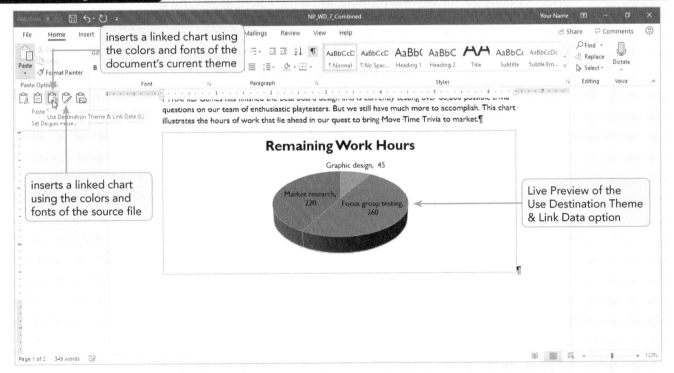

Use the button's ScreenTip to verify you are about to click the Use Destination Theme & Link Data button. It's easy to click the wrong button on the Paste Options menu.

10. On the Paste Options menu, click the **Use Destination Theme & Link Data** button 🗐. The chart is inserted in the document. It is formatted with the teal, purple, and blue colors and font of the Gallery theme used in the Word document.

Storing Linked Files

When linking objects, it is important to keep the source and destination files in their original storage locations. If you move the files or the folders in which they are stored, you will disrupt the connection between the source file and the document containing the linked object because the shortcut in the destination file will no longer have a valid path to the source file.

For example, suppose you insert a linked Excel file into a Word document, and then later a colleague moves the Excel file to a different folder. The next time you open the Word document and try to update the linked object, you will see a dialog box explaining that the linked file is not available. At that point, you can make the link functional again by updating the path to the linked objects. To do so, click the File tab on the ribbon, and then click Info in the navigation pane, if necessary. On the Info screen, click Edit Links to Files. In the Links dialog box, click the link whose location has changed, click the Change Source button, and then navigate to the new location of the source file.

Modifying the Linked Chart Object

The advantage of linking compared to embedding is that you can change the data in the source file, and those changes will automatically be reflected in the destination file as well.

Rima has received James's updated data about the total hours remaining on the project, and she wants the chart in her document to reflect this new information. You will update the data in the source file. You'll start by closing Excel so you can clearly see the advantages of working with a linked object.

To modify the chart in the source file:

▶ 1. On the taskbar, click the **Microsoft Excel** button 🔳 to display the Excel window, and then close Excel.

▶ 2. On the taskbar, click the **Word** button 🔳, if necessary, to display the Word window.

▶ 3. Click anywhere in the white area inside the chart border. Selection handles appear on the chart border, and the two Chart Tools contextual tabs are displayed on the ribbon.

   Trouble? If you see a selection border around the pie chart itself, in addition to the selection border around the chart and the title, you can ignore it.

▶ 4. On the ribbon, click the **Chart Tools Design** tab. See Figure 7–23.

Figure 7–23   **Chart selected in Word**

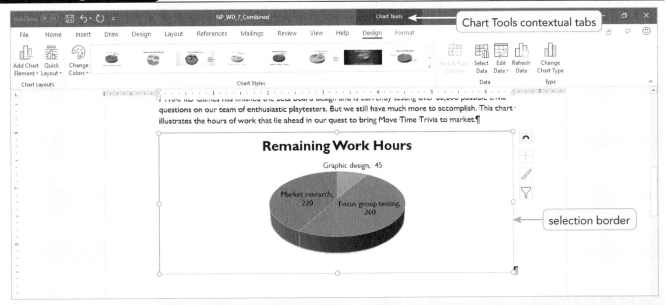

TIP

To edit the source file directly in Excel, click the Edit Data arrow to display a menu, and then click Edit Data in Excel.

5. In the Data group, click the **Edit Data** button. A spreadsheet that contains the chart data opens on top of the Word document.

Your spreadsheet might be larger or smaller than the one shown in Figure 7–24.

Figure 7–24   **Spreadsheet window with chart data**

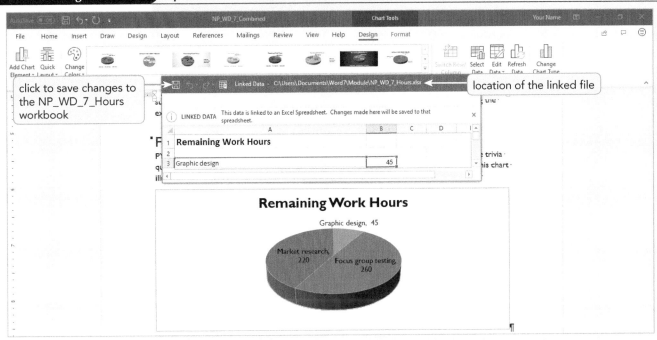

The file path at the top of the spreadsheet window shows the location of the linked file you are about to edit.

▶ **6.** In the Excel window, click cell **B3**, which contains the value "45," and then type **75**.

▶ **7.** Press **ENTER**. The new value is entered in cell B3, and the label in the "Graphic design" section of the pie chart changes from 45 to 75 in the linked chart in the Word document. Although you can't see the pie chart in the Excel spreadsheet window, it has also been updated to display the new value.

Trouble? If the chart in the Word document does not change to show the new value, click anywhere in the white area inside the chart border, and then click the Refresh Data button in the Data group on the Chart Tools Design tab in the Word window. Then, click cell B4 in the spreadsheet window.

▶ **8.** In the Excel window, type **300** in cell B4, and then press **ENTER**. The new number is entered in cell B4, and the value in the "Focus group testing" section of the pie charts in both the Excel and Word windows changes to match. See Figure 7–25.

Figure 7–25   Modifying the linked chart data

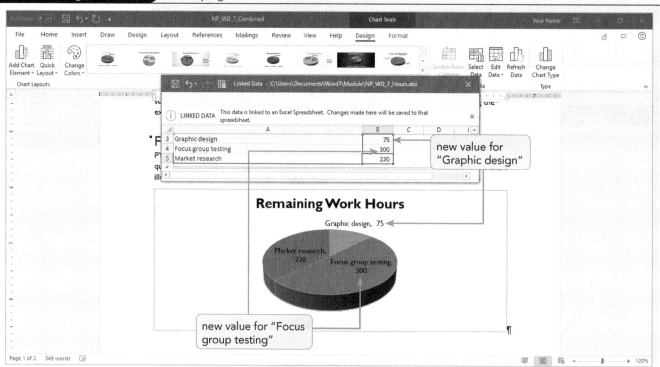

▶ **9.** At the top of the spreadsheet window, click the **Save** button 🖫, and then click the **Close** button ✕ to close the spreadsheet window.

▶ **10.** In the Word document, click anywhere outside the chart to deselect it, and then save the NP_WD_7_Combined.docx document.

When you edited the data in the spreadsheet window, you were actually editing the NP_WD_7_Hours.xlsx workbook. If you wanted, you could start Excel and open the NP_WD_7_Hours.xlsx workbook to verify that it contains the new values.

INSIGHT

Editing a Linked Worksheet Object

The steps for editing a linked worksheet object are slightly different from the steps for editing a linked chart object. Start by right-clicking the linked worksheet object in Word, and then point to Linked Worksheet Object on the shortcut menu, and click Edit Link. This opens the workbook in Excel, where you can edit the data and save your changes. When you are finished, close the workbook, and then return to the Word document. If the data is not immediately updated within the Word document, right-click the linked worksheet object in the Word document to open a shortcut menu, and then click Update Link. When you open a Word document containing a linked worksheet object, you might see a dialog box asking if you want to update the document with the data from the linked files. Click Yes to continue.

Note that linked worksheet objects don't offer the formatting options of a Word table. To improve the appearance of a worksheet object, you can transform it into a regular Word table by breaking the link, as described later in this module. After you break the link, you can format the new table just as you would format any table.

Rima is finished with her work on the chart. She does not expect the data in it to change, so she wants to break the link between the Excel workbook and the Word document.

Breaking Links

If you no longer need a link between files, you can break it. When you break a link, the source file and the destination file no longer have any connection to each other, and changes made in the source file do not affect the destination file. After breaking the link to the source file, you can change the formatting of a chart object from within the Word document, using the Chart Tools contextual tabs, but you can't make any changes related to the data shown in the chart. In the case of an Excel worksheet, after you break the link to the source file, the worksheet turns into a Word table.

REFERENCE

Breaking a Link to a Source File

- On the ribbon, click the File tab.
- On the Info screen, scroll down if necessary, and then click Edit Links to Files to open the Links dialog box.
- In the list of links in the document, click the link that you want to break.
- Click the Break Link button.
- Click Yes in the dialog box that opens, asking you to confirm that you want to break the link.
- Click OK to close the Links dialog box.

Now, you will break the link between Rima's document and the NP_WD_7_Hours workbook.

To break the link between the Word document and the Excel workbook:

▶ **1.** On the ribbon, click the **File** tab. Backstage view opens with the Info screen displayed.

▶ **2.** Scroll down to display the lower-right corner of the Info screen, and then click **Edit Links to Files**. The Links dialog box opens with the only link in the document (the link to the NP_WD_7_Hours workbook) selected. See Figure 7–26.

Figure 7-26   **The Links dialog box**

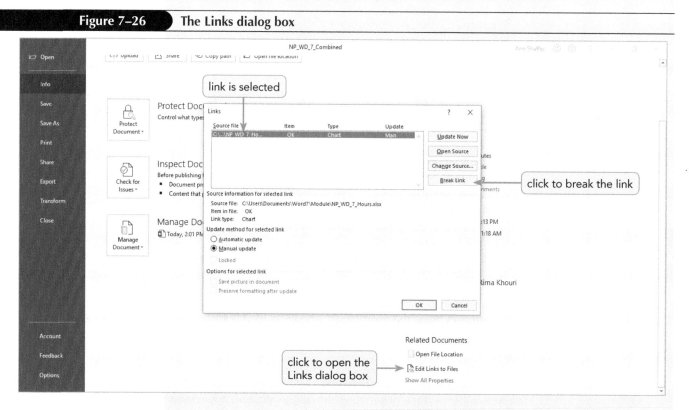

> 3. In the Links dialog box, click the **Break Link** button, and then click **Yes** in the dialog box that opens, asking if you are sure you want to break the link. The word "NULL" now appears under the heading Source file in the Links dialog box, indicating there is no source file for the chart in the document.

> 4. Click **OK** to close the dialog box. You return to the Info screen in Backstage view.

> With the link broken, you can no longer edit the Excel data from within Word. You can verify this by looking at the Chart Tools Design tab.

> 5. At the top of the navigation bar, click the **Back** button ⊖ to close Backstage view and return to the document.

> 6. Click anywhere inside the chart border to select the chart.

> 7. On the ribbon, click the **Chart Tools Design** tab, if necessary. Notice that the Edit Data button in the Data group is grayed out, indicating this option is no longer available.

> 8. Click anywhere outside the chart border to deselect it, and then save the document.

INSIGHT

Using the Chart Tool in Word

The Chart tool in Word offers a simplified way to insert a chart in a document that does not involve opening Excel. To get started, click where you want to insert the chart, and then follow these steps:

1. Click the Chart button in the Illustrations group on the Insert tab.
2. In the left-hand pane of the Insert Chart dialog box, click the type of chart you want to create.
3. On the right side of the Insert Chart dialog box, select a chart style. For example, if you selected Column in step 2, you could choose a Stacked Column chart, a 3-D Stacked Column chart, or one of several other options.
4. Click OK to close the Insert Chart dialog box. The chart is added to the document, and a worksheet window opens above the chart.
5. In the worksheet window, enter row and column headings, and then enter data for your chart. The information you enter in the worksheet automatically appears in the chart window.
6. In the Word window, click the default chart title to select it, delete the text inside the title box, and replace it with an appropriate title.
7. Use the Chart Tools Design tab to change the look of your chart. To change the chart colors, use the Change Colors button in the Chart Styles group. You can also select a new style in the Chart Styles group. Use the Add Chart Element button on the Chart Tools Design tab to add, remove, or reposition a title, data labels, a legend, axes, gridlines, or other chart element. To add an outline to a chart element, right-click the element to display two shortcut menus, click the Outline button, and then click a color in the color palette.
8. Click outside the chart border to deselect the chart, close the worksheet window, and then close any extra formatting panes that might have opened while you were working on the chart.
9. To revise a chart, click it to select it, click the Chart Tools Design tab, and then click the Edit Data button in the Data group to open a worksheet window containing the chart data.
10. To resize a chart to specific dimensions, select it, and then use the Size options on the Chart Tools Format tab.

Using Hyperlinks in Word

TIP

Hyperlinks are commonly referred to as "links," but take care not to confuse them with the OLE links you worked with earlier in this module.

A hyperlink is a word, phrase, or graphic that you can click to jump to another part of the same document, to a separate Word document, to a file created in another program, or to a webpage. When used thoughtfully, hyperlinks make it possible to navigate a complicated document or a set of files quickly and easily. And as you know, you can also include email links in documents, which you can click to create email messages.

Rima wants you to add two hyperlinks to the document—one that jumps to a location within the document, and one that opens a different document.

Inserting a Hyperlink to a Bookmark in the Same Document

Creating a hyperlink within a document is actually a two-part process. First, you need to mark the text you want the link to jump to—either by formatting the text with a heading style or by inserting a bookmark. A **bookmark** is an electronic marker that refers to specific text, a picture, or another object in a document. Second, you need to select the text that you want users to click, format it as a hyperlink, and specify the bookmark or heading as the target of the hyperlink. The **target** is the place in the document to which the link connects. In this case, Rima wants to create a hyperlink at the beginning of the document that targets the embedded Fund-Raising Goals Excel worksheet object near the end of the document. Figure 7–27 illustrates this process.

Figure 7–27 **Hyperlink that targets a bookmark**

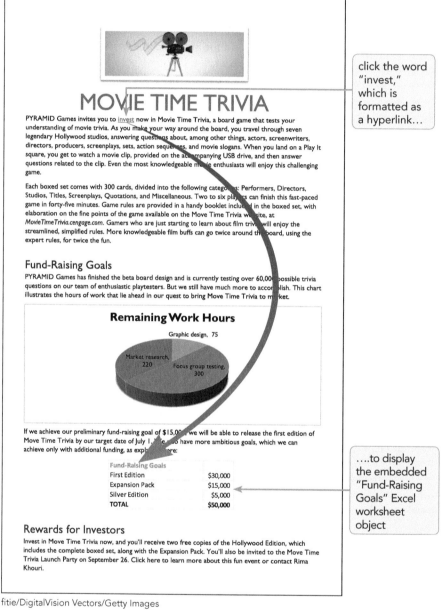

fitie/DigitalVision Vectors/Getty Images

To create a hyperlink in Rima's document, you'll first need to designate the worksheet object as a bookmark.

To insert a bookmark:

1. Scroll down and click the "Fund-Raising Goals" worksheet object, on page 2. A dotted outline and handles are displayed around the worksheet object, indicating that it is selected.

2. On the ribbon, click the **Insert** tab.

3. In the Links group, click the **Bookmark** button. The Bookmark dialog box opens. You can now type the bookmark name, which cannot contain spaces.

4. In the Bookmark name box, type **Goals**. See Figure 7–28.

| Figure 7–28 | Creating a bookmark |

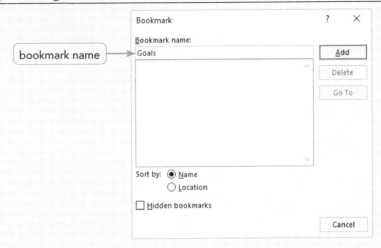

TIP

To delete a bookmark, click it in the Bookmark dialog box, and then click the Delete button.

5. Click the **Add** button. The Bookmark dialog box closes. Although you can't see any change in the document, the "Fund-Raising Goals" worksheet object has been designated as a bookmark.

The bookmark you just created will be the target of a hyperlink, which you will create next.

REFERENCE

Creating a Hyperlink to a Location in the Same Document

- Select the text, graphic, or other object that you want to format as a hyperlink.
- On the ribbon, click the Insert tab.
- In the Links group, click the Link button to open the Insert Hyperlink dialog box.
- In the Link to pane, click Place in This Document.
- In the Select a place in this document list, click the bookmark or heading you want to link to, and then click OK.

Rima wants you to format the word "invest" at the beginning of the document as a hyperlink that will target the bookmark you just created.

To create and test a hyperlink to the bookmark:

1. Scroll up to page 1, and then, in the first line under the "Movie Time Trivia" heading, select the word **invest**.

2. In the Links group on the Insert tab, click the **Link** button. The Insert Hyperlink dialog box opens.

3. In the Link to pane, click **Place in This Document** to select it, if necessary. The "Select a place in this document" list shows the headings and

TIP

If you are storing your documents on OneDrive, then clicking the Links arrow displays a list of recent OneDrive documents. Click a document name to insert a link to it in the current document.

bookmarks in the document. Here you can click the bookmark or heading you want as the target for the hyperlink.

4. Under Bookmarks, click **Goals**. See Figure 7–29.

Figure 7–29   **Inserting a hyperlink to a location in the same document**

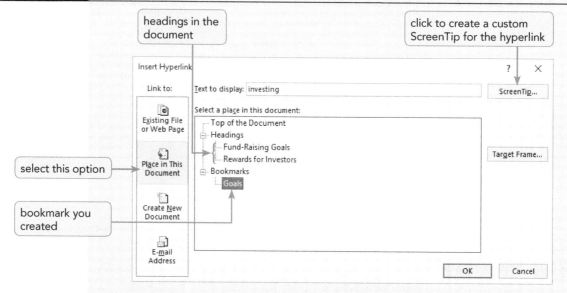

You can click the ScreenTip button to open the Set Hyperlink ScreenTip dialog box and type custom text for the hyperlink's ScreenTip, which appears when you place the pointer over the hyperlink in the document. In this case, however, Rima prefers to use the default ScreenTip.

TIP

To change a hyperlink's font color, open the Styles pane and modify the Hyperlink style.

5. Click **OK**. The word "invest" is now formatted in the hyperlink style for the Gallery theme, which applies a red font color with an underline. The hyperlink targets the Goals bookmark that you created in the last set of steps. You can verify this by clicking the hyperlink.

6. Move the pointer over the hyperlink **invest**. The default ScreenTip displays the name of the bookmark and instructions for following the link. See Figure 7–30.

Figure 7–30   **Displaying the ScreenTip for a hyperlink**

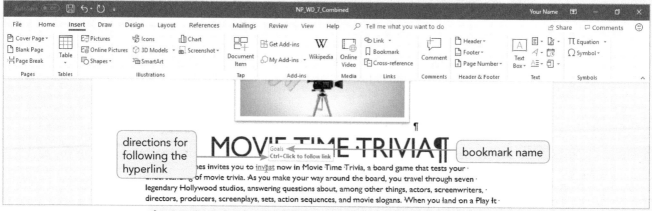

fitie/DigitalVision Vectors/Getty Images

7. Press and hold **CTRL**, and then click the **invest** hyperlink. The insertion point jumps to the "Fund-Raising Goals" worksheet object on page 2.

▶ **8.** Scroll up to review the "invest" hyperlink. It is now purple, which is the color for clicked links in the Gallery theme.

▶ **9.** Save your document.

Next, you will create a hyperlink that jumps to a different document.

Creating Hyperlinks to Other Documents

When you create a hyperlink to another document, you need to specify the document's file name and storage location as the hyperlink's target. The document can be stored on your computer or on a network; it can even be a webpage stored somewhere on the web. In that case, you need to specify the webpage's URL (web address) as the target. When you click a hyperlink to another document, the document opens on your computer, with the beginning of the document displayed. Keep in mind that if you move the document containing the hyperlink, or if you move the target document, the hyperlink will no longer work. However, if you create a hyperlink to a webpage on the Internet, the link will continue to work no matter where you store the document containing the hyperlink.

REFERENCE

Creating a Hyperlink to Another Document

- Select the text, graphic, or other object you want to format as a hyperlink.
- On the ribbon, click the Insert tab.
- In the Links group, click the Link button to open the Insert Hyperlink dialog box.
- In the Link to pane, click Existing File or Web Page.
- To target a specific file on your computer or network, click the Look in arrow, navigate to the folder containing the file, and then click the file in the file list.
- To target a webpage, type its URL in the Address box.
- Click OK.

Rima wants to insert a hyperlink that, when clicked, will open a Word document containing details about the Movie Time Trivia Launch Party. You'll start by opening the document containing the party details and saving it with a new name.

To create a hyperlink to a document with details about the Movie Time Trivia Launch Party:

▶ **1.** Open the document **NP_WD_7-3.docx** located in the Word7 > Module folder included with your Data Files, save it as **NP_WD_7_Party** in the location specified by your instructor, and then close it.

▶ **2.** In the NP_WD_7_Combined.docx document, scroll down to the end of the document, and then select the word **here** in the last sentence.

▶ **3.** On the ribbon, click the **Insert** tab, if necessary.

▶ **4.** In the Links group, click the **Link** button. The Insert Hyperlink dialog box opens.

▶ **5.** In the Link to pane, click **Existing File or Web Page**. The dialog box displays options related to selecting a file or a webpage.

▶ **6.** Click the **Look in arrow**, navigate to the location where you stored the NP_WD_7_Party.docx file, if necessary, and then click **NP_WD_7_Party** in the file list. See Figure 7–31.

Figure 7-31   **Inserting a hyperlink to a different document**

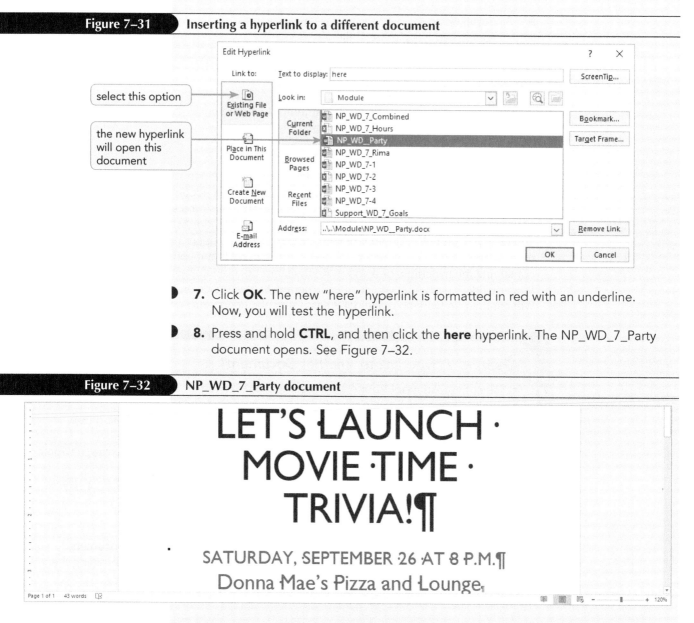

7. Click **OK**. The new "here" hyperlink is formatted in red with an underline. Now, you will test the hyperlink.

8. Press and hold **CTRL**, and then click the **here** hyperlink. The NP_WD_7_Party document opens. See Figure 7-32.

Figure 7-32   **NP_WD_7_Party document**

> # LET'S LAUNCH · MOVIE ·TIME · TRIVIA!¶
>
> SATURDAY, SEPTEMBER 26 AT 8 P.M.¶
> Donna Mae's Pizza and Lounge¶

9. Close the NP_WD_7_Party.docx document, and then return to the NP_WD_7_Combined.docx document. The link is now purple because you clicked it.

10. Save your document.

Now that you have finalized the document and added the necessary hyperlinks, you will optimize the document for online viewing by switching to Web Layout view and adding some formatting that is useful for documents that will be viewed online.

Optimize a Document for Online Viewing

When preparing a document intended solely for online distribution, you can focus on how the page will look on the screen, without having to consider how it will look when printed. This means you can take advantage of some formatting options that are visible only on the screen, such as a background page color or a background fill effect. You can also switch to **Web Layout view**, which displays a document as it would look in a web browser.

In Web Layout view, the text spans the width of the screen, with no page breaks and without any margins or headers and footers. The advantage of Web Layout view is that it allows you to zoom in on the document text as close as you want, with the text rewrapping to accommodate the new Zoom setting. By contrast, in Print Layout view, if you increase the Zoom setting too far, you end up having to scroll from side-to-side to read an entire line of text. The only downside to Web Layout view is that graphics may shift position as the text wrapping changes. However, these changes are only visible in Web Layout view. When you switch back to Print Layout view, you will see the original page layout.

Rima wants to switch to Web Layout view before she continues formatting the document.

TIP

Zooming in on text in Web Layout View is helpful when you have multiple panes open; the text wraps for easy reading.

To switch to Web Layout view:

▶ **1.** On the status bar, click the **Web Layout** button. The document text expands to span the entire Word screen.

▶ **2.** Use the Zoom slider on the status bar to increase the Zoom setting to **160%**. The text rewraps to accommodate the new setting.

▶ **3.** Scroll down and review the entire document, which no longer has any page breaks. See Figure 7–33.

Figure 7–33   **Document displayed in Web Layout view, zoomed to 160%**

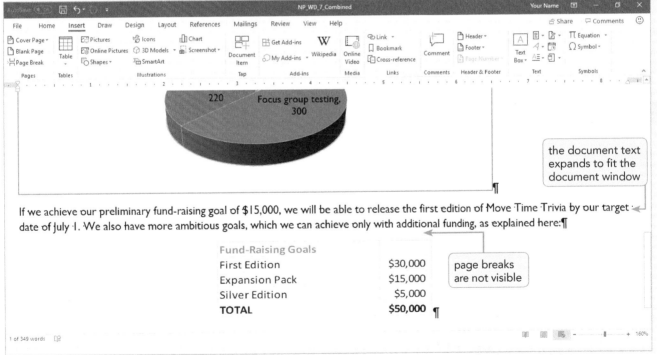

Applying a Background Fill Effect

To make the document more eye-catching when it's displayed on a screen, Rima wants to add a background fill effect. A **background fill effect** is a repeating graphic element, such as a texture, a photo, or a color gradient, that is visible only when a document is displayed online. It's essential to use fill effects judiciously. In the hands of a trained graphic designer, they can be striking; if used carelessly, they can be garish and distracting. As a general rule, you should avoid using photos and textures and instead stick with simple colors or color gradients.

Rima decides to use a gradient background in shades of blue.

To apply a background fill effect to the document:

▶ **1.** On the ribbon, click the **Design** tab.

▶ **2.** In the Page Background group, click the **Page Color** button. The Page Color gallery opens, with a menu at the bottom. You could click a color in the gallery to select it as a background color for the page. To select another type of background effect, you need to click Fill Effects.

▶ **3.** Click **Fill Effects** to open the Fill Effects dialog box, and then click the **Gradient** tab, if necessary. Note that you could use other tabs in this dialog box to add a textured, patterned, or picture background.

▶ **4.** In the Colors section, click the **Two colors** button. The Color 1 and Color 2 boxes and arrows are displayed.

▶ **5.** Click the **Color 1 arrow**, and then click **Indigo, Accent 5, Lighter 80%**, the second color from the right in the second row of the Theme Colors section.

▶ **6.** Click the **Color 2 arrow**, and then click **White, Background 1**, the first color on the left in the top row of the Theme Colors section.

▶ **7.** In the Shading styles section, click the **Vertical** option button to change the gradient pattern so it stretches vertically up and down the page. Compare your dialog box to Figure 7-34.

Figure 7-34   Selecting a gradient background

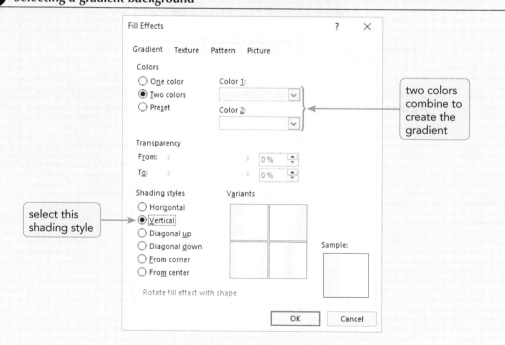

▶ 8. Click **OK**. The document's background is now a gradient that varies between white and light blue.

▶ 9. Scroll down, if necessary, so you can see the Fund-Raising Goals worksheet object.

The gradient background is light enough to make the document text easy to read. However, to make the gridlines of the worksheet object easier to see, you can change the object's background color.

To change the background for the Fund-Raising Goals worksheet object:

▶ 1. Right-click the worksheet object to display a shortcut menu, and then click **Picture**. The Format Object dialog box opens, with the Picture tab displayed.

▶ 2. Click the **Colors and Lines** tab to display settings related to the colors used in the worksheet object. In the Fill section, the Color box currently displays "No Color," indicating that the object's background is the same as the document's background.

▶ 3. In the Fill section, click the **Color arrow**, and then click **White, Background 1**, the first color in the top row of the Theme Colors section.

▶ 4. Click **OK** to close the Format Object dialog box. The worksheet object now has a white background, which makes the gridlines easier to see.

▶ 5. Click outside the worksheet object to deselect it, and then save the document.

Next, you will add horizontal lines to separate the various sections of the document.

Inserting Horizontal Lines

Horizontal lines allow you to see at a glance where one part of a document ends and another begins. Unlike background colors and fill effects, horizontal lines do appear in printed documents, along with the document text. However, they are commonly used in documents that are meant to be viewed only online.

Rima wants you to add a horizontal line before the "Fund-Raising Goals" heading and before the "Rewards for Investors" heading.

To insert horizontal lines into the document:

▶ 1. Scroll up and click at the beginning of the "Fund-Raising Goals" heading.

▶ 2. On the ribbon, click the **Home** tab.

▶ 3. In the Paragraph group, click the **Borders arrow** ⊞ ˅ to open the Borders gallery, and then click **Horizontal Line** to insert a default gray line.

Rima wants to change the line's color. She also wants to make the line shorter, so it doesn't span the full page.

▶ 4. Right-click the horizontal line to display a shortcut menu, and then click **Picture**. The Format Horizontal Line dialog box opens, with settings for changing the line's width, height, color, and alignment. The current Width setting is 100%, meaning that the line spans the entire page from left to right. To leave a little space on each side, you need to lower the percentage.

5. Triple-click the **Width** box, and then type **75**. Because the Center alignment option at the bottom of the dialog box is selected by default, the shorter line will be centered on the page, with space to its left and its right.

6. Click the **Color arrow**, and then click **Indigo, Accent 5, Darker 50%**, the second color from the right in the bottom row of the Theme Colors section. The Color gallery closes, and the Use solid color (no shade) check box is now selected. See Figure 7–35.

Figure 7–35 Format Horizontal Line dialog box

Format Horizontal Line
?
Horizontal Line
Width
75%
Measure in:
Percent
Height
1.5 pt
Color
Use solid color (no shade)
Alignment
Left
Center
Right
OK
Cancel
this setting leaves space on both sides of the line
selected by default

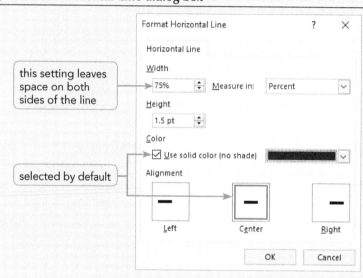

7. Click **OK**, and then click anywhere in the document to deselect the horizontal line. Your document should look similar to Figure 7–36.

Figure 7–36 Newly inserted horizontal line

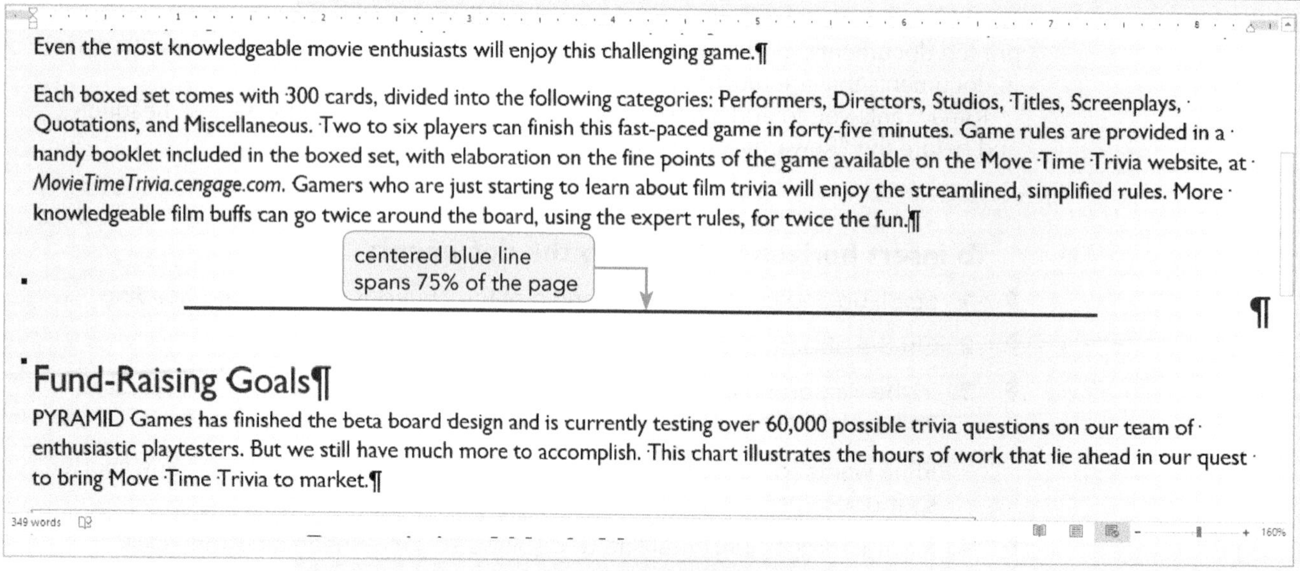

Even the most knowledgeable movie enthusiasts will enjoy this challenging game.¶
Each boxed set comes with 300 cards, divided into the following categories: Performers, Directors, Studios, Titles, Screenplays, Quotations, and Miscellaneous. Two to six players can finish this fast-paced game in forty-five minutes. Game rules are provided in a handy booklet included in the boxed set, with elaboration on the fine points of the game available on the Move Time Trivia website, at MovieTimeTrivia.cengage.com. Gamers who are just starting to learn about film trivia will enjoy the streamlined, simplified rules. More knowledgeable film buffs can go twice around the board, using the expert rules, for twice the fun.¶
centered blue line spans 75% of the page
¶
Fund-Raising Goals¶
PYRAMID Games has finished the beta board design and is currently testing over 60,000 possible trivia questions on our team of enthusiastic playtesters. But we still have much more to accomplish. This chart illustrates the hours of work that lie ahead in our quest to bring Move Time Trivia to market.¶
349 words
160%

Now, you can copy the line, and then insert it before the other heading.

TIP

To remove a horizontal line, click the line to select it, and then press DEL.

8. Click the horizontal line to select it, and then press **CTRL+C** to copy it to the Clipboard.

9. Scroll down, click to the left of the "R" in the "Rewards for Investors" heading, insert a new paragraph, format the new blank paragraph with the Normal style, and then press **CTRL+V** to insert the horizontal line before the heading.

10. Save the document.

You've finished formatting the NP_WD_7_Combined.docx document. Next, Rima needs to edit the hyperlink that opens the document with information about the launch party.

INSIGHT

Saving a Word Document as a Webpage

Webpages are special documents designed to be viewed in a program called a **browser**. The browser included in Windows 10 is Microsoft Edge. Because webpages include code written in Hypertext Markup Language, or **HTML**, they are often referred to as HTML documents.

To create sophisticated webpages, you'll probably want to use a dedicated HTML editor, such as Adobe Dreamweaver. However, in Word you can create a simple webpage from an existing document by saving it as a webpage. When you do so, Word inserts HTML codes that tell the browser how to format and display the text and graphics. Fortunately, you don't have to learn HTML to create webpages with Word. When you save the document as a webpage, Word creates all the necessary HTML codes (called tags); however, you won't actually see the HTML codes in your webpage.

You can choose from several different webpage file types in Word. The Single File Web Page file type is a good choice when you plan to share your webpage only over a small network and not over the Internet. When you want to share your files over the Internet, it's better to use the Web Page, Filtered option, which breaks a webpage into multiple smaller files, for easier transmittal.

To save a document as a webpage, follow these steps:

1. Click the File tab, click Save as, and then click Browse to open the Save As dialog box.
2. Navigate to the location where you want to save the webpage.
3. If desired, type a new file name in the File name box.
4. Click the Save as type arrow, and then click one of the webpage file types.
5. Click the Save button. If you saved the document using the Web Page, Filtered option, click Yes in the warning dialog box.

Note that after you save a document as a webpage, Word displays it in Web Layout view.

Editing Hyperlinks

Rima's document contains two hyperlinks—the "invest" link, which jumps to the Fund-Raising Goals worksheet object, and the "here" link, which jumps to the NP_WD_7_Party.docx document. To give all the Movie Time Trivia documents a coherent look, Rima saved a new version of the party invitation that is formatted with a fill effect. Now she wants you to edit the "here" hyperlink, so it opens this new version of the document. To make it possible to repeat these steps later if you want, you'll start by saving the formatted document with a new name.

To edit the "here" hyperlink:

▶ **1.** Open the document **NP_WD_7-4.docx** located in the Word7 > Module folder included with your Data Files, and then switch to Web Layout view, if necessary, so you can see the two-color gradient background.

▶ **2.** Save the document as **NP_WD_7_FormattedParty** in the location specified by your instructor, and then close it.

▶ **3.** In the NP_WD_7_Combined.docx document, scroll down to the end of the document, and then position the pointer over the **here** hyperlink near the end of the document to display a ScreenTip, which indicates that the link will jump to a document named NP_WD_7_Party.docx.

Trouble? If you also see a ScreenTip that reads "Chart Area" you can ignore it.

▶ **4.** Right-click the **here** hyperlink to open a shortcut menu, and then click **Edit Hyperlink**. The Edit Hyperlink dialog box opens. It looks just like the Insert Hyperlink dialog box, which you have already used. To edit the hyperlink, you simply select a different target file.

▶ **5.** In the Link to pane, verify that the Existing File or Web Page option is selected.

▶ **6.** Navigate to the location where you saved the NP_WD_7_FormattedParty document, if necessary, and then click **NP_WD_7_FormattedParty** in the file list.

▶ **7.** Click **OK**. You return to the NP_WD_7_Combined.docx document.

▶ **8.** Place the pointer over the hyperlink to display a ScreenTip, which indicates that the link will now jump to a document named NP_WD_7_FormattedParty.

▶ **9.** Press and hold **CTRL**, and then click the **here** hyperlink. The NP_WD_7_FormattedParty.docx document opens.

▶ **10.** sam⬆ Close the **NP_WD_7_FormattedParty.docx** document, and then save and close the **NP_WD_7_Combined.docx** document.

PROSKILLS

Teamwork: Emailing Word Documents

After you optimize a document for online viewing, you can share it with colleagues via email. To get started emailing a document, first make sure you have set up Microsoft Outlook as your email program. Then, in Word, open the document you want to email. On the ribbon, click the File tab, and then click Share in the navigation bar. On the Share screen, click either Word Document or PDF. This opens a new email message in Outlook, with the file attached.

When you email documents, keep in mind the following:

- Many email services have difficulty handling attachments larger than 4 MB. Consider storing large files in a compressed (or zipped) folder to reduce their size before emailing them.

- Other word-processing programs and early versions of Word might not be able to open files created in the latest version of Word. To avoid problems with conflicting versions, you have two options. You can save the Word document as a rich text file (using the Rich Text File document type in the Save As dialog box) before emailing it; all versions of Word can open rich text files. Another option is to save the document as a PDF.

- If you plan to email a document that contains links to other files, remember to email all the linked files.

- Attachments, including Word documents, are sometimes used maliciously to spread computer viruses. Remember to include an explanatory note with any email attachment so that the recipient can be certain the attachment is legitimate. Also, it's important to have a reliable virus checker program installed if you plan to receive and open email attachments.

The new documents are just one way to share information about Movie Time Trivia. Rima also wants to write a blog post discussing the game's development. She asks you to help her create a blog post in Word.

Creating and Publishing a Blog Post

Creating a blog post in Word is similar to creating a new Word document except that instead of clicking Blank document on the New screen in Backstage view, you click Blog post. Note that before you can publish your blog post using Word, you need to register a blog account with an Internet blog provider that is compatible with Microsoft Word.

Rima asks you to help her create a blog post about the development of the Movie Time Trivia game.

To create and publish a blog post:

▶ **1.** On the ribbon, click the **File** tab, and then click **New** in the navigation bar to display the icons for the various document templates.

▶ **2.** Scroll down if necessary, and then click **Blog post**.

▶ **3.** In the Blog post window, click the **Create** button, if necessary. A blank blog post opens. Assuming you have not previously registered for a blog account, you also see the Register a Blog Account dialog box.

To register a blog account, you could click the Register Now button to open the New Blog Account dialog box. From there, you could follow the prompts to register your blog account. Rima will register her blog account later, so you can skip the registration step for now.

4. Click the **Register Later** button to close the dialog box.

5. At the top of the blog post, click the **[Enter Post Title Here]** placeholder, and then type **Movie Time Trivia**.

6. Click in the blank paragraph below the blog title, and then type **Movie Time Trivia is a board game that tests your knowledge of film trivia**. See Figure 7–37.

| Figure 7–37 | Blog post |

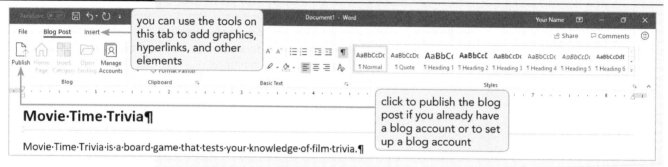

At this point, you could use the tools on the Insert tab to add hyperlinks, graphics, and other items to your blog post. Rima plans to add more text and some graphics to her blog post later. For now, you can save the post, and then explore options for publishing it.

7. Save the blog post as **NP_WD_7_Blog** in the location specified by your instructor. Note that a blog post is a regular Word document file, with a .docx extension.

8. On the Blog Post tab, in the Blog group, click the **Publish** button.

Assuming you have not previously registered for a blog account, you see the Register a Blog Account dialog box again. At this point, you could click the Register an Account button and then follow the on-screen instructions to register a blog account and publish your blog. Because Rima plans to do that later, you can close the blog post for now.

Trouble? If you see a menu below the Publish button, you clicked the Publish arrow instead of the Publish button. Press ESC, and then click the Publish button.

9. Click **Cancel** to close the Register a Blog Account dialog box, and then click **OK** in the Microsoft Word dialog box.

10. Close the blog post.

TIP

To add, remove, or change blog accounts, click the Manage Accounts button in the Blog group on the Blog Post tab.

Rima plans to write weekly blog posts describing the company's progress with the new game. Combined with the fact sheet, they will help generate interest in the company's crowd-sourcing effort.

INSIGHT

Working with Saved and Unsaved Document Versions

By default, as you work on a document, versions of it are automatically saved every ten minutes. To change how often a version is saved, click the File tab, click Options in the navigation bar, click Save in the navigation bar in the Word Options dialog box, and then change the number of minutes in the Save AutoRecover information every box.

If you want to open an autosaved version of the current document, click the File tab to display the Info screen. If autosaved versions of the document are available, they are listed in the Manage Document section, along with the date and time each version was saved. Click a version to open it in Read Mode as a read-only document with "(Autorecovered Version)" in the title bar. At this point, you can save the document with a new name if you want. To compare an autosaved version with the current version of the document, right-click the version in the Manage Document section of the Info screen, and then click Compare with Current. To delete an autosaved version of a document, right-click the version in the Manage Document section of the Info screen, and then click Delete This Version.

If your computer shuts down unexpectedly with unsaved changes while a document is open, you might see a Recovered section in the Recent screen the next time you start Word. To recover an unsaved version of a document, click Show Recovered Files in the Recovered section to create a new, blank document with the Document Recovery pane open. In the pane, click the unsaved version of the document that you want to open. You can also click the Manage Document button on the Info Screen, and then click Recover Unsaved Documents to display the Open dialog box with the folder that contains unsaved versions of files selected.

REVIEW

Session 7.2 Quick Check

1. Describe two options on the Paste Options menu that allow you to control the formatting applied to a linked Excel chart.

2. What is the first step in creating a hyperlink to a location in the same document?

3. Are horizontal lines displayed on a printed page?

4. What is the difference between the way text is displayed in Web Layout view and the way it is displayed in Print Layout view?

5. Explain how to edit a hyperlink.

6. What do you need to do before you can publish a blog post?

Review Assignments

Data Files needed for the Review Assignments: NP_WD_7-5.docx, NP_WD_7-6.xlsx, NP_WD_7-7.docx, Support_WD_7_Funding.xlsx, Support_WD_7_SportsJames.docx

Rima is working on a document about a new game. She has written a draft of the document and has emailed it to James. While he reviews it, Rima asks you to turn on Track Changes and continue working on the document. Then, she can combine her edited version of the document with James's, accepting or rejecting changes as necessary. She also needs you to insert some data from an Excel worksheet as an embedded object and insert an Excel chart as a linked object. She then wants you to create a version of the document with hyperlinks, optimize the document for online viewing, and create a blog post. Complete the following steps:

1. Open the document **NP_WD_7-5.docx** located in the Word7 > Review folder included with your Data Files. Save the file as **NP_WD_7_SportsRima** in the location specified by your instructor.

2. Change the username to **Rima Khouri** and the user initials to **RK**, and then turn on Track Changes.

3. In the second paragraph, move the sentence that begins "When you land on a Ref It square..." to the end of the paragraph, and then add an **s** to the word "drive" in that sentence so the text reads "...USB drives...."

4. In the third paragraph, in the first line, attach a comment to the number "300" that reads **Should this be 325?**

5. Just before the period at the end of the document, add **or contact *your name*** (replacing *your name* with your first and last name) so that the sentence reads "Click here to learn more about this fun event or contact *your name*."

6. Save your changes to the NP_WD_7_SportsRima.docx document.

7. Combine the NP_WD_7_SportsRima.docx document with James's edited version, which is named **Support_WD_7_SportsJames.docx**. Use the NP_WD_7_SportsRima.docx document as the original document.

8. Save the combined document as **NP_WD_7_SportsCombined** in the location specified by your instructor.

9. Turn off Track Changes, and then reject James's deletion of "chart" and his insertion of "graph." Accept all the other changes in the document. Delete all comments.

10. Change the username and initials back to their original settings, and then save the NP_WD_7_SportsCombined.docx document. Close the NP_WD_7_SportsRima.docx document, saving changes if you didn't save them earlier.

11. In the NP_WD_7_SportsCombined.docx document, replace the placeholder "[Insert Excel worksheet]" with the funding goals in the **Support_WD_7_Funding.xlsx** file. Include everything from cell A1 through cell B5. Insert the worksheet as an embedded object, and then close the Support_WD_7_Funding.xlsx file.

12. Center the embedded object, and then change the "Complete and Release Expansion Pack" value in the embedded worksheet object from $8,500 to **$7,500**.

13. Open the workbook **NP_WD_7-6.xlsx**, and then save it as **NP_WD_7_WorkHours** in the location specified by your instructor. Copy the pie chart to the Office Clipboard.

14. Return to the NP_WD_7_SportsCombined.docx document, and then replace the placeholder "[Insert Excel chart]" with a linked copy of the chart using the destination theme.

15. Save the NP_WD_7_SportsCombined.docx document, and then close it.

16. Return to the NP_WD_7_WorkHours.xlsx workbook in Excel. Edit the data in the workbook by changing the hours for focus group testing to **125**, and the hours for Research and question development to **300**. Save the workbook, and then close Excel.

17. Open the **NP_WD_7_SportsCombined.docx** document and review the chart. If it doesn't contain the new numbers, click the chart, and use the Refresh Data button to update the chart.

18. Save the NP_WD_7_SportsCombined.docx document, and then save the document with the new name **NP_WD_7_NoExcelLinks** in the location specified by your instructor.

19. Break the link to the Excel workbook, and then save the document.

20. Format the Excel worksheet object as a bookmark named **Funding**. In the first line of the third paragraph below the page title, format the phrase "Stadium Time Trivia Expansion Pack" as a hyperlink that targets the "Funding" bookmark. Test the hyperlink to make sure it works. Save the document.

21. Open the document **NP_WD_7-7.docx** from the Word7 > Review folder included with your Data Files, and then save the file as **NP_WD_7_ReleaseParty** in the location specified by your instructor. Close the NP_WD_7_ReleaseParty.docx document, and return to the NP_WD_7_NoExcelLinks.docx document.

22. In the last line of the document, format the word "here" as a hyperlink that targets the NP_WD_7_ReleaseParty.docx document. Test the hyperlink to make sure it works, and then close the NP_WD_7_ReleaseParty.docx document. Save the NP_WD_7_NoExcelLinks.docx document.

23. Switch to Web Layout view, and add a two-color gradient page color using Dark Teal, Text 2, Lighter 80% as Color 1 and White, Background 1 as Color 2—with the shading style set to Diagonal up.

24. Change the background color for the worksheet object to White, Background Color 1.

25. Insert a horizontal line in a new paragraph, formatted in the Normal style, before the "Our Goals" heading. Keep the default width, but change the color to Dark Teal, Text 2. Insert an identical horizontal line before the "Your Reward for Investing" heading.

26. Save and close the NP_WD_7_NoExcelLinks.docx document.

27. Create a new blog post without attempting to register a blog account. Save the blog post as **NP_WD_7_DevelopmentBlog** in the location specified by your instructor. Insert **Plans for New Games** as the post title, and then type the following as the text of the blog post: **PYRAMID Games is developing several new games focused on baseball and soccer**.

28. Save and close the NP_WD_7_DevelopmentBlog.docx file.

Case Problem 1

Data Files needed for this Case Problem: NP_WD_7-8.docx, NP_WD_7-9.xlsx

Streamers Celebrations, LLC   You recently started working as an event planner at Streamers Celebrations, LLC. You need to write a letter to a client that includes the budget for a corporate picnic. The budget is stored in an Excel workbook, and you want to embed the budget in the letter as an Excel worksheet object. After you embed the worksheet object, you need to make some edits to the document using Track Changes. Finally, the company owner is considering using Word to create posts for the company's events blog, so she asks you to create a sample blog post.

Complete the following steps:

1. Open the document **NP_WD_7-8.docx** from the Word7 > Case1 folder included with your Data Files. Save the file as **NP_WD_7_Picnic** in the location specified by your instructor.

2. In the signature line, replace "Student Name" with your name.

3. Delete the placeholder "[Insert Excel worksheet]" but not the paragraph symbol after it. When you are finished, there should be one blank paragraph before the paragraph that begins "Next week I suggest…."

4. Start Excel, open the workbook **NP_WD_7-9.xlsx** from the Word7 > Case1 folder included with your Data Files, and then save it as **NP_WD_7_PicnicBudget** in the location specified by your instructor.

5. Select the two-column list of items and amounts, from cell A6 through cell B10, and then copy the selection to the Clipboard.

6. Insert the worksheet data into the Word document in the blank paragraph that previously contained the placeholder text. Insert the data as a linked object that uses the destination styles.

7. Save the Word document, and then return to the NP_WD_7_PicnicBudget.xlsx workbook and close Excel.

8. Starting from within the Word window, edit the linked worksheet object to change the amount for food and beverages to **3,250**. (*Hint*: Remember that the steps for editing a linked worksheet object are different from the steps for editing a linked chart. Also, note that you don't need to type the dollar sign. Excel adds that automatically.) Save the workbook, close Excel, and then update the link in Word.

9. Save the NP_WD_7_Picnic.docx document, and then save it again as **NP_WD_7_PicnicNoLinks** in the location specified by your instructor.

10. Break the link in the **NP_WD_7_PicnicNoLinks.docx** document.

11. Format the budget table using the Grid Table 4 – Accent 5 table style.

12. If necessary, change the username to your first and last names, change the initials to your initials, and then turn on Track Changes.

13. At the beginning of the letter, replace "3/1/2021" with the current date using the format March 1, 2021.

14. In the inside address, change "Lane" to **Avenue**.

15. At the end of the paragraph that begins "Next week I suggest we visit…" add the sentence **In the meantime, please call if you have any questions.**

16. Save your changes to the NP_WD_7_PicnicNoLinks.docx document, and then save it with the new name **NP_WD_7_PicnicChangesAccepted** in the location specified by your instructor.

17. Turn off Track Changes, close the Reviewing pane if necessary, and then reject the replacement of "Avenue" for "Lane." Accept all the other changes in the document.

18. Return the username and initials to their original settings.

19. Save the NP_WD_7_PicnicChangesAccepted.docx document, and then close it.

20. Create a new blog post without attempting to register a blog account. Save the blog post as **NP_WD_7_InvitationsBlog** in the location specified by your instructor. Insert **Invitation Tips from Streamers Celebrations, LLC** as the post title, and then type the following as the text of the blog post: **You can use Word's 3-D models to add a little excitement to your event invitations. Here's just one example**.

21. Insert a 3-D model of your choosing in a new paragraph below the sentence you typed in Step 20, and then select a different view of the model in the 3D Model Views group on the 3D Model Tools format tab.

22. Save and close the blog post.

Case Problem 2

Data Files needed for this Case Problem: NP_WD_7-10.docx, Support_WD_7_Aziz.docx, Support_WD_7_Tommy.docx

123 Project Management   Kendall Aihara is the marketing manager for 123 Project Management, a consulting company that specializes in weekend project management seminars and week-long classes on specific topics. She is creating a series of fact sheets that she can email to potential students. The fact sheets will summarize course offerings at the school. Each fact sheet will also include a link to an Internet video about project management. Kendall has already emailed a draft of her first fact sheet to her two colleagues, Aziz and Tommy, and she now needs to combine their versions with hers to create a final draft. However, because Aziz forgot to turn on Track Changes before he edited the document, Kendall will need to compare her draft with his so that she can see his changes marked as tracked changes.

After she finishes accepting and rejecting changes, Kendall wants you to show her how to add a video to the document. A video production company is preparing a series of videos that she will eventually incorporate into her fact sheets before distributing them; but for now, she asks you to show her how to insert any video from the Internet. Finally, after the fact sheet is finished, Kendall would like you to help her create a chart that illustrates the average distance each client travels to 123 Project Management.

Complete the following steps:

1. Open the document **NP_WD_7-10**.docx from the Word7 > Case2 folder included with your Data Files, save it as **NP_WD_7_Kendall** in the location specified by your instructor, review the document to familiarize yourself with its contents, and then close it.

2. Open the document **Support_WD_7_Aziz**.docx from the Word7 > Case2 folder, review its contents, and then close it.

⊕ **Explore** 3. Compare the NP_WD_7_Kendall.docx document with the Support_WD_7_Aziz.docx document, using NP_WD_7_Kendall.docx as the original document, and show the changes in a new document.

4. Review the new document to verify that Aziz's changes to Kendall's draft are now displayed as tracked changes, and then save the document as NP_WD_7_AzizTrackedChanges.docx in the location specified by your instructor.

5. Open the document **Support_WD_7_Tommy.docx** from the Word7 > Case2 folder, review its contents, and then close it.

6. Combine the document Support_WD_7_Tommy with the NP_WD_7_AzizTrackedChanges document, using the Support_WD_7_Tommy file as the original document.

7. Save the new document as **NP_WD_7_FactSheet** in the location specified by your instructor.

8. Accept all changes in the document, turn off Track Changes, if necessary, and then use the Editor pane to correct any errors caused by missing spaces.

⊕ **Explore** 9. Use Word Help to learn how to insert an Internet video in a document. Insert a blank paragraph at the end of the document, and then insert a video of a project management lecture. Take care to choose a video that is appropriate for a professional setting. After you insert the video in the document, click the Play button on the video image to test it. Press the Esc button to close the video window when you are finished watching it.

⊕ **Explore** 10. In the Word document, size the video image just as you would an ordinary picture so that it fits on the first page.

11. Save the Coding Academy Fact Sheet document, and close it and any other open documents.

12. Open a new, blank document, and then save it as **NP_WD_7_CommuteChart** in the location specified by your instructor.

13. Use the Chart tool in Word to create a bar chart. Select the 3-D Stacked Bar type. For the chart title, use **Student Commute Mileage**.

14. Include the data shown in Figure 7–38. To delete the default items in Column D, right-click the gray column D header and then click Delete.

Figure 7–38 Data for bar chart

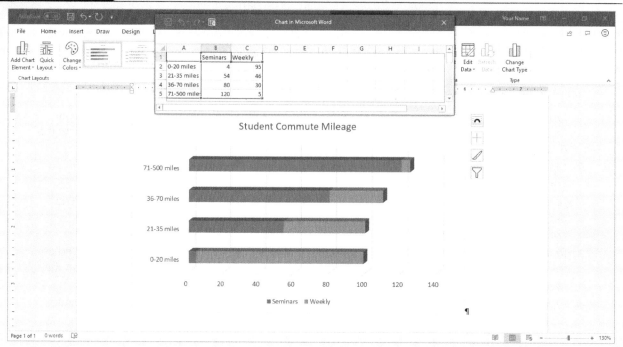

Explore 15. Close the spreadsheet window, and then format the chart with the Style 8 chart style.

16. Save and close all documents.

Customizing Word and Automating Your Work

Automating a Document for a Rock Climbing Gym

OBJECTIVES

Session 8.1
- Insert a shape
- Add text to a shape
- Apply ligatures and stylistic sets to text
- Compress photos
- Translate text
- Add a custom paragraph border
- Create a watermark

Session 8.2
- Edit building block properties
- Copy a building block to another document or template
- Copy a style to another document or template
- Add properties to a document
- Insert document properties into the document content
- Insert and customize fields

Session 8.3
- Learn about Trust Center settings
- Record and run macros
- Edit macros using Visual Basic
- Copy macros to another document or template
- Record an AutoMacro

Case | *Alexander Griffin Rock Gym*

Sam Nguyen manages Alexander Griffin Rock Gym, an indoor rock climbing gym in the student fitness center at Elliot Bay College in Seattle, Washington. All students and alumni who want to use the gym must sign a waiver acknowledging that they understand the potential risks. Sam has asked you to help him create the waiver as a Word template, which he'll place on the desktop of the computer at the front counter. Employees will be able to double-click the file to create new Word documents based on the template.

Sam wants you to add some additional content to the template, including the company name on a photo background; placeholders in Spanish, Chinese, and Vietnamese for the legal text; and a watermark and header indicating the template is a draft. He wants you to use a Quick Part and a style stored in another template and insert document properties in the template. He also wants you to add dialog boxes that will pop up, requesting the information that needs to be filled in when each new waiver document is created. In addition, Sam wants you to create a macro to insert the company slogan in a footer. Finally, he wants you to create an AutoMacro to highlight a reminder to request proof of age from each customer.

STARTING DATA FILES

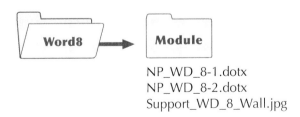

Module
NP_WD_8-1.dotx
NP_WD_8-2.dotx
Support_WD_8_Wall.jpg

Review
NP_WD_8-3.dotx
Support_WD_8_NewStyles.dotx
Support_WD_8_People.jpg

Case1
NP_WD_8-4.dotx
Support_WD_8_RealtyStyles.dotx

Case2
NP_WD_8-5.dotx
Support_WD_8_Planting.jpg
Support_WD_8_Potomac.dotx

Session 8.1 Visual Overview:

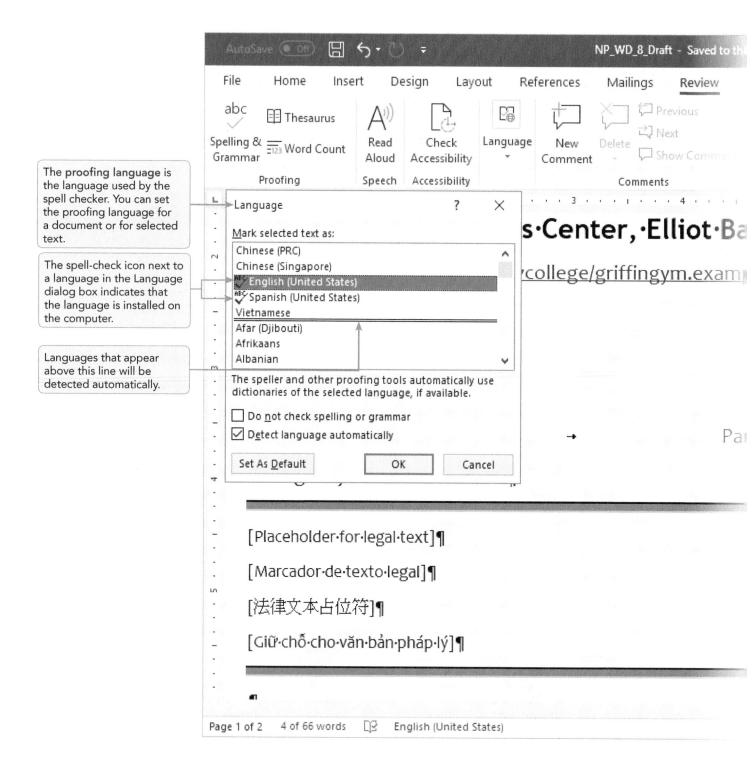

The **proofing language** is the language used by the spell checker. You can set the proofing language for a document or for selected text.

The spell-check icon next to a language in the Language dialog box indicates that the language is installed on the computer.

Languages that appear above this line will be detected automatically.

Translating Text

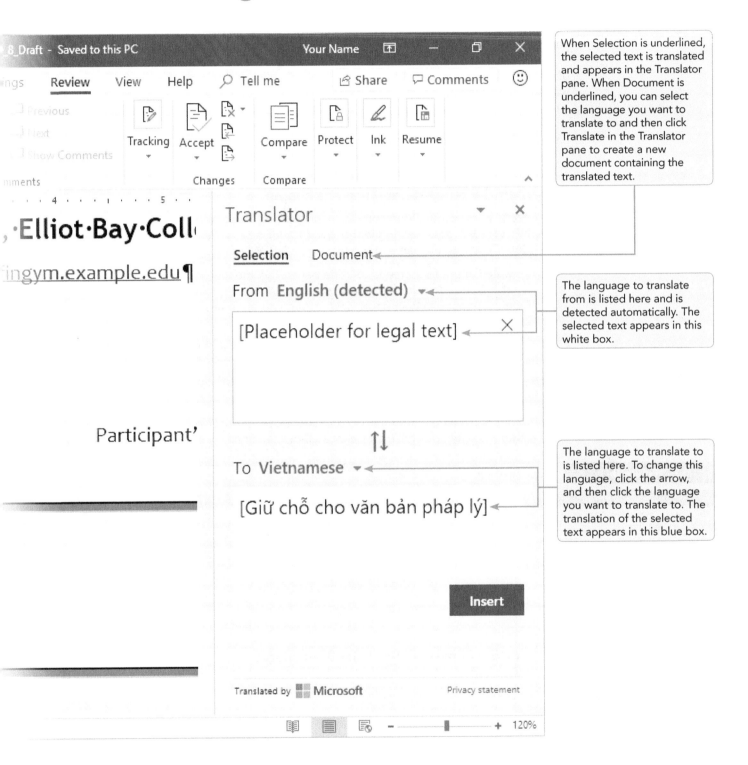

When Selection is underlined, the selected text is translated and appears in the Translator pane. When Document is underlined, you can select the language you want to translate to and then click Translate in the Translator pane to create a new document containing the translated text.

The language to translate from is listed here and is detected automatically. The selected text appears in this white box.

The language to translate to is listed here. To change this language, click the arrow, and then click the language you want to translate to. The translation of the selected text appears in this blue box.

Inserting a Shape

You can add a variety of shapes to a document, such as lines, rectangles, stars, and more. To draw a shape, click the Shapes button in the Illustrations group on the Insert tab, click a shape in the gallery, and then click and drag to draw the shape in the size you want. Like any object, you can resize a shape after you insert it.

Sam wants you to add a rectangle shape that contains the company name at the top of the template. He has already created a draft of the template with most of the text he wants to include, so you'll open that template and then add the shape to it. To modify a template, you must open it using the Open screen in Backstage view. If you double-click a file in a File Explorer window or open it via the New screen, a new document based on the template will be created.

To open the template and insert a shape:

▶ 1. **sam** ⬇ Using the Open command in Backstage view, open the template **NP_WD_8-1.dotx** located in the Word8 > Module folder included with your Data Files. The file name in the title bar is NP_WD_8-1.

   Trouble? If the file name in the title bar is Document1 (or some other number), close the document and then repeat Step 1, taking care to use the Open command in Backstage view so that you open the template rather than create a new document based on the template.

▶ 2. Save the file as a template named **NP_WD_8_Draft** in the location specified by your instructor.

▶ 3. If necessary, change the Zoom level to **120%**, and then display the rulers and nonprinting characters.

▶ 4. Click the **Insert** tab, and then in the Illustrations group, click the **Shapes** button. The Shapes gallery opens, as shown in Figure 8–1.

> Be sure to save the file as a template and not as a document, and verify that you are saving the template to the correct folder.

Figure 8–1   Shapes gallery

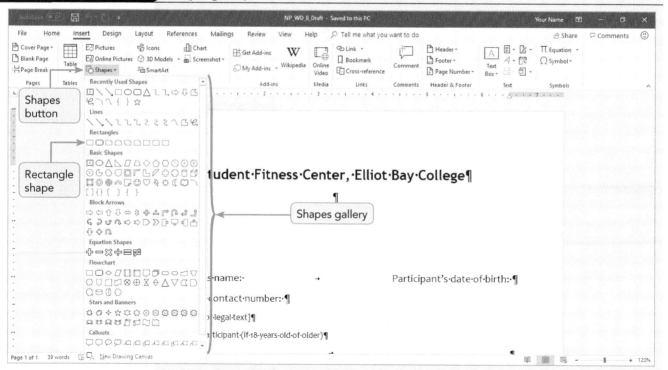

5. Under Rectangles, click the **Rectangle** shape. (Use the ScreenTip to identify the shape.) The gallery closes, and the pointer changes to the thin cross pointer ╋.

6. At the top of the document, click to insert a rectangle that is one-inch square. The Drawing Tools Format tab appears on the ribbon.

7. Click the **Drawing Tools Format** tab. The measurements of the shape appear in the Shape Height and Shape Width boxes in the Size group.

8. Click in the **Shape Height** box to select the value in it, type **1.5**, and then press **ENTER**. The height of the shape changes to 1.5 inches. Unlike pictures, the aspect ratio for shapes is not locked, so the width of the shape doesn't change.

9. Click in the **Shape Width** box, type **8.5**, and then press **ENTER**. The rectangle is now the same width as the page.

10. In the Arrange group, click the **Align** button, and then click **Align Center**. The center of the shape aligns with the center of the page.

11. Click the **Align** button again, and then click **Align Top**. The top of the rectangle aligns with the top margin on the page. The rectangle is on top of the first three paragraphs in the document. You will fix this later.

You've already had a little experience with one type of shape—a text box is a shape specifically designed to contain text. However, you can add text to any shape you draw—just start typing while the shape is selected.

To add text to a shape and format it:

1. With the shape selected, type **Alexander Griffin Rock Gym**. (Do not type the period.) The text appears in the shape, centered horizontally.

2. On the Drawing Tools Format tab, in the Text group, click the **Align Text** button. On the menu, Middle is selected. Although the vertical alignment of the text in the shape is set to Middle, the text itself is not centered vertically because like a regular paragraph in a document, the paragraph in the shape has eight points of space below it. See Figure 8–2.

Figure 8–2   **Paragraph center-aligned horizontally and vertically, with space after the paragraph**

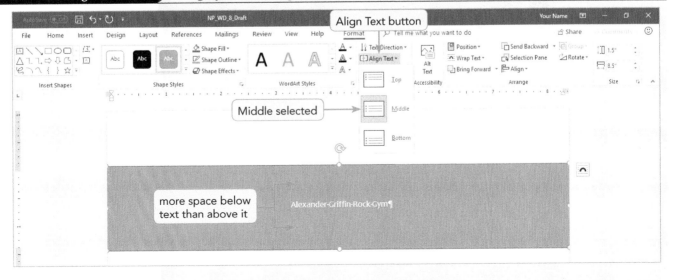

TIP

You can change the indent of text in a shape by clicking the Increase Indent or Decrease Indent button in the Paragraph group on the Home tab or by dragging the Left Indent marker on the ruler.

3. Click the **Layout** tab, and then in the Paragraph group, change the value in the After box to **0 pt**. The text in the shape moves down a little and is now centered vertically. If you wanted to change the horizontal alignment of text in a shape, you would use the alignment buttons in the Paragraph group on the Home tab.

4. Point to the rectangle border so that the pointer changes to the move pointer ⁺⥁, and then click the border. The entire shape is selected. When you select the entire shape, text formatting is applied to all the text in the shape.

5. On the ribbon, click the **Home** tab.

6. In the Font group, click the **Font arrow**, scroll down the list, and then click **Trebuchet MS**.

7. In the Font group, click the **Font Size arrow**, and then click **28**.

8. In the Font group, click the **Bold** button ⌷B⌷. The text in the shape is now 28-point, bold Trebuchet MS.

Next, you need to change the shape's fill. When you draw a shape, it is filled with the Accent 1 color from the Theme Colors set. You can modify the fill of a shape by changing its color; by adding a gradient (shading in which one color blends into another or varies from one shade to another), a textured pattern, or a picture; or by removing it completely.

You can also modify the outline of a shape. The default outline is a darker shade of the Accent 1 theme color. You can change the outline by changing its color, width, and style, or you can remove it completely.

To change the shape's fill and remove the outline:

1. Click the **Drawing Tools Format** tab, and then in the Shape Styles group, click the **Shape Fill arrow**. The Shape Fill gallery opens. On the color palette, the Orange, Accent 1 color is selected. The default shape fill is the theme's Accent 1 color. See Figure 8–3.

Figure 8–3 Shape Fill menu

2. Click the **Brown, Accent 5** color. The shape fill changes to a shade of brown.

3. In the Shape Styles group, click the **Shape Fill arrow**, and then point to **Gradient**. A submenu opens. See Figure 8–4.

| **Figure 8–4** | Gradient gallery on the Shape Fill menu |

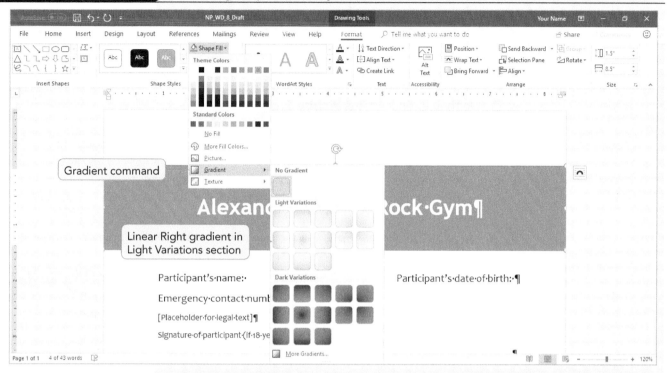

4. In the Light Variations section, click the **Linear Right** gradient (the first gradient in the second row in the Light Variations section). The shape fill changes to a gradient in shades of brown, with the darker shade on the left fading to a lighter shade on the right. Now you'll remove the outline.

5. In the Shape Styles group, click the **Shape Outline arrow**, and then click **No Outline**. The outline is removed.

Sam has decided he wants you to fill the shape with a photo to make it more dramatic. When a shape filled with a picture is selected, both the Picture Tools Format tab and the Drawing Tools Format tab appear on the ribbon.

To fill a shape with a picture:

1. On the Drawing Tools Format tab, in the Shape Styles group, click the **Shape Fill arrow**, and then click **Picture**. The Insert Pictures dialog box opens.

2. Click **From a file**. The Insert Picture dialog box opens.

3. Navigate to the **Word8 > Module** folder, click **Support_WD_8_Wall.jpg**, and then click **Insert**. The shape is filled with the photo.

When you fill a shape with a photo whose dimensions are different from the shape's dimensions, the photo is distorted to force it to fill the shape. In this case, the photo was distorted because it was stretched horizontally to fill the width of the shape and shrunk vertically to fit inside the shape.

You can fix this by using the Fill or Fit commands on the Crop menu. The Fill command matches the picture's height or width to the shape's height or width (whichever is longer) and crops the rest of picture. The Fit command fits the picture completely inside the shape while maintaining the aspect ratio of the picture. This means there will likely be empty space around the picture inside the shape.

To adjust the picture inside the shape:

▶ **1.** On the ribbon, click the **Picture Tools Format** tab.

▶ **2.** In the Size group, click the **Crop arrow**, and then click **Fit**. The proportions of the picture are reset and the entire picture fits inside the rectangle. This leaves empty space in the shape on either side of the picture.

▶ **3.** In the Size group, click the **Crop arrow**, and then click **Fill**. The picture is enlarged to completely fill the width of the shape, and the top and bottom of the picture are cropped off. In the Size group, the Crop button is selected.

▶ **4.** Move the pointer on top of the picture inside the shape. The pointer changes to the four-headed arrow pointer ✛.

▶ **5.** Press and hold the mouse button, and then drag the picture down until the top of the picture is aligned with the top of the shape. The Crop button is still selected.

▶ **6.** In the Size group, click the **Crop** button. The Crop button is no longer selected, and the crop handles are removed from the shape.

The text on top of the picture is a little hard to read. To make the text more readable, you will change the transparency of the picture and change the color of the text.

To change the transparency of the picture and the color of the text:

▶ **1.** On the Picture Tools Format tab, in the Adjust group, click the **Transparency** button. A gallery of transparency percentages opens. If you wanted to customize the transparency, you could click Picture Transparency Options to open the Format Picture pane, where you could enter a custom transparency percentage. See Figure 8–5.

Figure 8–5   **Transparency gallery**

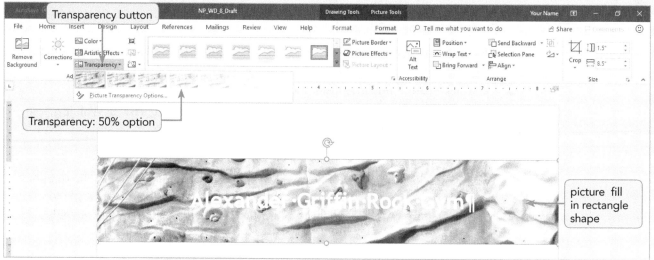

Sorbis/Shutterstock.com

▶ **2.** In the gallery, click the **Transparency: 50%** option. The picture inside the shape is 50 percent more transparent, and you can now see the text in the first paragraph behind the rectangle.

▶ **3.** Click the **Home** tab.

▶ **4.** In the Font group, click the **Font color arrow** ⬚, and then click the **Brown, Text 2, Darker 50%** color.

Next, you need to move all the text in the document down so that the first line of text in the document is not underneath the rectangle.

▶ **5.** Click anywhere in the paragraph that begins with "Participant's name," and then press the ↑ key three times. The insertion point is in the first paragraph behind the rectangle.

▶ **6.** On the ribbon, click the **Layout** tab, and then in the Paragraph group, change the value in the Before box to **114 pt**. The first paragraph now has 114 points of space before it, shifting it below the rectangle.

▶ **7.** Save the changes to the template.

Applying Advanced Text Formatting

As with regular text, you can apply a variety of text effects and formatting to text that you add to a shape. In addition to the basic formatting options—such as font size, font color, and italic formatting—Word offers more advanced text formatting options, including ligatures and stylistic sets. A **ligature** is a connection between two characters. In some fonts, you can apply ligatures to visually connect characters such as the letter "f" and the letter "i." Some font designers also provide additional styles—called stylistic sets—for the characters within a font. Some of the style changes are obvious; others are very subtle. Ligatures and stylistic sets are not available for all fonts.

Sam wants you to use ligatures in the company name in the rectangle shape to connect the second "f" and "i" in "Griffin." He also wants you to see if there are any stylistic sets available that will change the shape of any of the letters.

To change the ligature setting and stylistic set of the text in the shape:

▶ **1.** Click the rectangle shape's border to select the entire shape, and then on the ribbon, click the **Home** tab.

▶ **2.** In the Font group, click the **Text Effects and Typography** button ⬚, and then point to **Ligatures**. The Ligatures submenu opens. See Figure 8–6.

Figure 8–6   Ligatures submenu

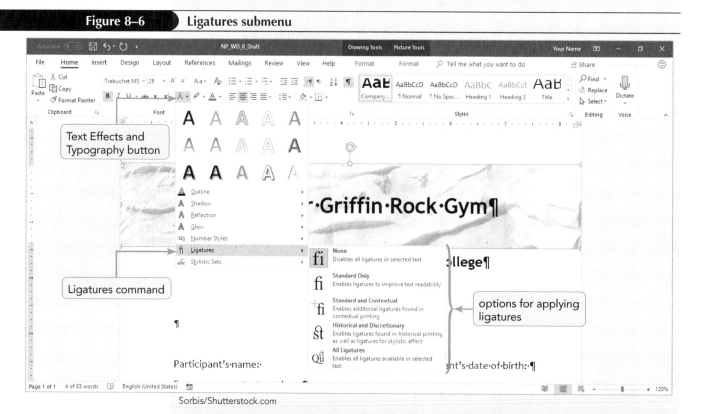

Sorbis/Shutterstock.com

3. Click **Historical and Discretionary**. The second "f" and "i" in "Griffin" are now joined.

4. In the Font group, click the **Text Effects and Typography** button Ⓐⱽ , and then point to **Stylistic Sets**. The Stylistic Sets submenu opens. The default set is displayed at the top, with alternate sets provided by the font designer below. In the second stylistic set in the "Individual" section, the "A" has a crossbar that is lower than the default version, and the round part of the "R" is slightly larger. See Figure 8–7.

| Figure 8–7 | Stylistic Sets submenu |

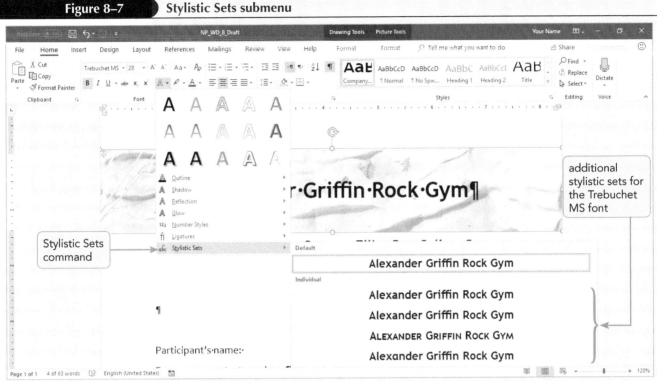

Sorbis/Shutterstock.com

▶ **5.** Click the second style below "Individual." The style of the font changes, and the letters "A" and "R" change shape. You can see the change if you undo the action and then redo it.

▶ **6.** On the Quick Access Toolbar, click the **Undo** button ↶. The action of changing the stylistic set is undone, and the letter "A" is changed back to its original style.

▶ **7.** On the Quick Access Toolbar, click the **Redo** button ↷. The stylistic set is reapplied, and the letters "A" and "R" are again changed.

▶ **8.** Save the changes to the template.

Compressing Pictures in a Document

Pictures added to Word documents are compressed by default to 220 pixels per inch (ppi). This setting, which can be changed in the Word Options dialog box, is applied automatically to all pictures in the document. You can change the default setting to High fidelity or to 330, 220, 150, or 96 ppi, or you can turn off the automatic compression feature. For some pictures, you can choose to compress them further after you insert them. See Figure 8–8 for a description of the compression options available.

Figure 8–8	Photo compression settings

Compression Setting	Compression Value	When to Use
High fidelity	Photos are compressed very minimally.	Use when a picture in a document will be viewed on a high-definition (HD) display, when photograph quality is of the highest concern, and when file size is not an issue.
HD (330 ppi)	Photos are compressed to 330 pixels per inch.	Use when the quality of the photograph needs to be maintained on HD displays and file size is of some concern.
Print (220 ppi)	Photos are compressed to 220 pixels per inch.	Use when the quality of the photograph needs to be maintained when printed. This is the default resolution.
Web (150 ppi)	Photos are compressed to 150 pixels per inch.	Use when a picture in a document will be viewed on a low-definition display or uploaded to a webpage.
E-mail (96 ppi)	Photos are compressed to 96 pixels per inch.	Use when it is important to keep the overall file size small, such as for documents that need to be emailed.
Use default resolution	Photos are compressed to the resolution specified on the Advanced tab in the Word Options dialog box. (The default setting is 220 ppi.)	Use when file size is not an issue, or when the quality of the photo display is more important than file size.
Do not compress images in file	Photos are not compressed at all.	Use when it is critical that photos remain at their original resolution.

Compressing photos reduces the size of the file, but it also reduces the quality of the photos. When you compress pictures, you remove pixels. If the picture is small, some compression won't matter; but if the picture is large or if you remove too many pixels, the difference in quality will be noticeable.

Before you change the compression of the photo in the shape, you'll verify the current default compression setting.

To check the picture compression setting for the NP_WD_8_Draft template:

1. On the ribbon, click the **File** tab, scroll down, and then in the navigation pane, click **Options**. The Word Options dialog box opens.

2. In the navigation pane, click **Advanced** to display the Advanced options, and then scroll down until you can see the Image Size and Quality section. See Figure 8–9.

Figure 8–9   Advanced options in the Word Options dialog box

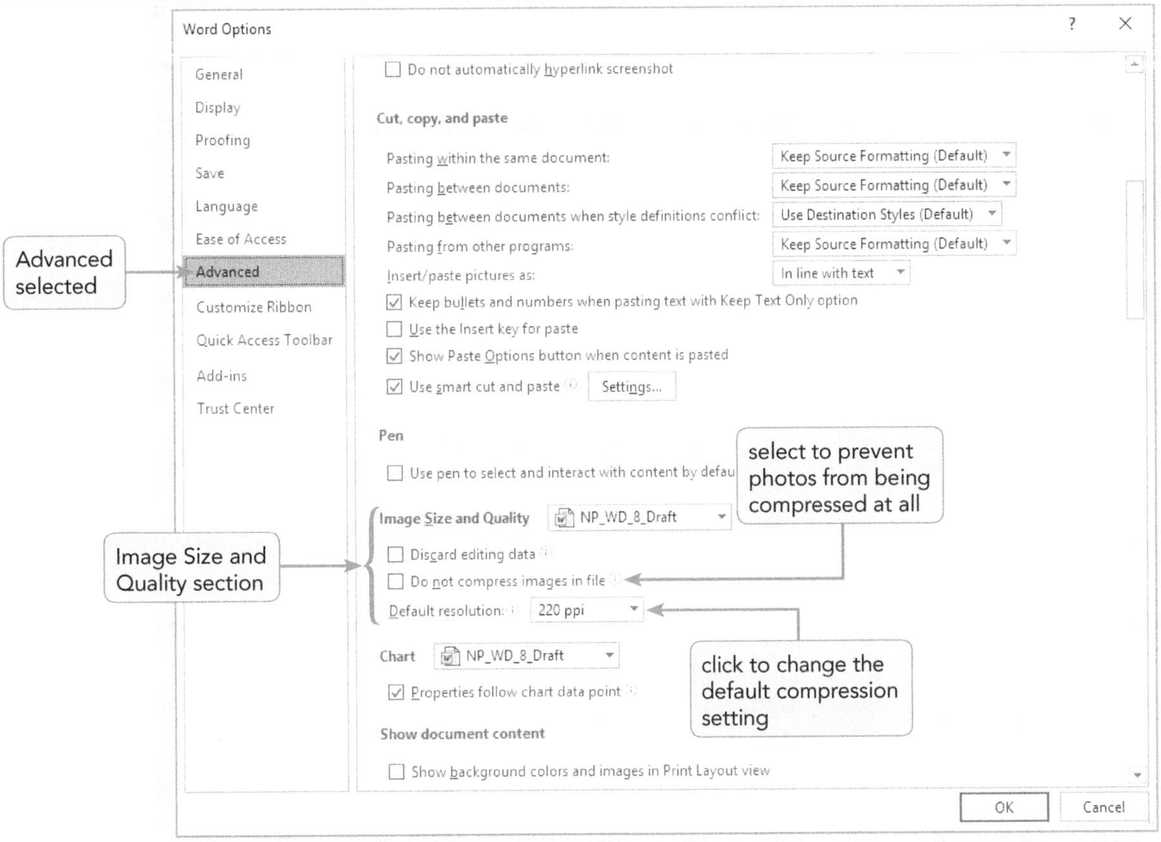

- Advanced selected
- Image Size and Quality section
- select to prevent photos from being compressed at all
- click to change the default compression setting

> **3.** In the Image Size and Quality section, verify that the box next to "Default resolution" contains 220 ppi.

> **4.** Click **Cancel** to close the dialog box without making any changes.

The waiver form will not be distributed for customers to take home—they will simply sign it and give it back to the employee who checks them in. However, Sam wants to be able to send the template via email to various people in the company for their approval. He also wants to be able to email the final form to customers so they can print and sign the form ahead of time. Therefore, he wants you to compress the photo to the smallest size possible.

REFERENCE

Modifying Photo Compression Settings

- Click a photo to select it.
- On the ribbon, click the Picture Tools Format tab.
- In the Adjust group, click the Compress Pictures button to open the Compress Pictures dialog box.
- Click the option button next to the resolution you want to use.
- To apply the new compression settings to all the photos in the file, click the Apply only to this picture check box to deselect it.
- To keep cropped areas of photos, click the Delete cropped areas of pictures check box to deselect it.
- Click OK.

To compress the photo further:

▶ **1.** With the entire shape selected, click the **Picture Tools Format** tab.

▶ **2.** In the Adjust group, click the **Compress Pictures** button ⊡ . The Compress Pictures dialog box opens. Under Resolution, the Use default resolution option button is selected. See Figure 8–10.

Figure 8–10   **Compress Pictures dialog box**

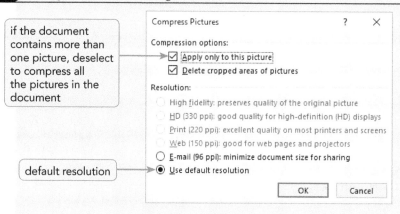

if the document contains more than one picture, deselect to compress all the pictures in the document

default resolution

▶ **3.** Click the **E-mail (96 ppi)** option button. This setting compresses the photos to the smallest possible size.

At the top of the dialog box, under Compression options, the Apply only to this picture check box is selected. This is the only photo in the document, so changing this setting will have no effect. The Delete cropped areas of pictures check box is also selected. To make the file size as small as possible, you will leave this check box selected as well.

▶ **4.** Click **OK**. The photo is compressed to 96 ppi, and the cropped areas are removed. You can verify this using the Crop button.

▶ **5.** In the Size group, click the **Crop** button. The crop handles appear around the picture, and the cropped portion of the picture below the shape is gone.

▶ **6.** In the Size group, click the **Crop** button to turn that option off.

Translating Text

You can use tools in Word to translate text into other languages. Keep in mind, however, that the translations generated by Word are not always perfect. After you translate all or part of a document, have an expert in the language review the translation and make any necessary corrections. See the Session 8.1 Visual Overview for more information about translating text.

Selecting an Option for Translating Text

You can use the Translate button in the Language group on the Review tab to translate selected text in a document or to translate the entire document. If you translate the entire document, a new document containing the translated text is created.

At Elliot Bay College, many students and alumni speak English as a second language. The first language for some students is Spanish, while other students speak Chinese or Vietnamese as a first language. Sam wants to provide the legal disclaimers in the waiver in Spanish, Chinese, and Vietnamese as well as in English. He has placeholder text in the document to indicate where the legal text of the waiver will be added. He wants you to add this same placeholder text in Spanish, Chinese, and Vietnamese to remind him to have the legal text translated after it is provided.

To translate selected text:

▶ **1.** Scroll down to position the paragraph that begins with "Participant's name" at the top of the document window.

▶ **2.** Select the entire line containing the text "[Placeholder for legal text]."

▶ **3.** Click the **Review** tab.

▶ **4.** In the Language group, click the **Translate** button, and then click **Translate Selection**. The Translator pane opens on the right. See Figure 8–11.

| Figure 8–11 | Translator pane |

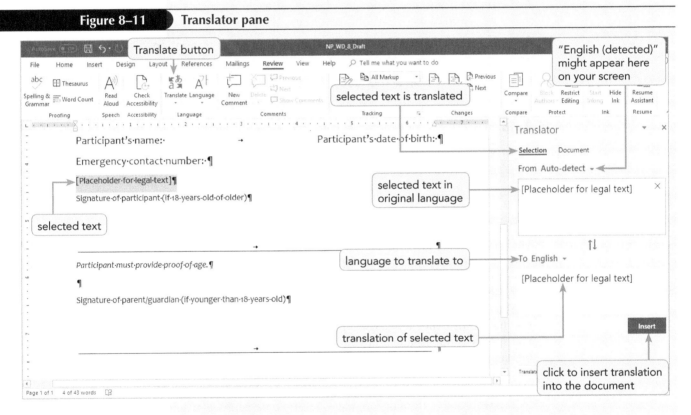

Trouble? If the Use Intelligent Services? dialog box appears, click Turn on.

At the top of the pane, Selection is underlined, which means only the selected text will be translated. You could click Document to translate the entire document instead. The selected text appears in the top white box, and the label above it identifies the language of the text you want to translate, in this case, English. The label above the bottom blue box identifies the language you want to translate the selected text to, in this case, English. The text in the blue box is the translation of the selected text.

Trouble? If English does not appear after "To" above the blue box, don't worry about it. Continue with Step 5.

▶ **5.** In the Translator pane, next to "To English," click the **arrow** ▼. An alphabetical list of languages appears. The bottom of the list is hidden.

▶ **6.** In the Translator pane, drag the scroll box down to the bottom of the scroll bar.

▶ **7.** Scroll the alphabetical list of languages, and then click **Spanish**. The Spanish translation of the selected text appears in the blue box.

▶ **8.** In the document, click at the end of the line "[Placeholder for legal text]," and then press **ENTER**.

▶ **9.** In the Translator pane, click **Insert**. The Spanish translation is pasted at the location of the insertion point.

▶ **10.** In the document, click at the end of the line that contains the Spanish translation, and then press **ENTER** to insert a new blank paragraph. In the Translator pane, the text you originally selected still appears in the white From box.

▶ **11.** In the Translator pane, next to "To Spanish," click the **arrow** ▼, scroll the list up, and then click **Chinese Simplified**. The Chinese translation of the selected text appears in the blue box.

▶ **12.** In the Translator pane, click **Insert**. The Chinese translation is pasted at the location of the insertion point in the document.

▶ **13.** Click in the blank paragraph below the Chinese translation.

▶ **14.** In the Translator pane, change the translation language to **Vietnamese**, and then click **Insert**. The Vietnamese translation appears in the document.

▶ **15.** At the top of the Translator pane, click the **Close** button ✕.

▶ **16.** If you turned intelligent services on, click the **File** tab, scroll down and click **Options**, click the **Enable services** check box to remove the checkmark, and then click **OK**.

Changing the Proofing Language of Specific Words

The spell checker in Word can be very helpful, but when it flags words that are spelled correctly, the wavy red lines under the words can be distracting. In the waiver template, words in the two foreign phrases are flagged as misspelled. This is because the proofing language for the template is set to English.

You can change the proofing language for an entire document or template or for only specific words to any language supported by Microsoft Office. If the proofing language you specify is not installed on your computer, the words in that language will no longer be flagged as misspelled, but Word will not be able to determine if the foreign language words are spelled correctly. However, if you open the file on a computer that has that language installed, you can use the spell checker to check the words.

You will set the proofing languages for the paragraphs containing the three foreign phrases to the specific languages used.

To set the proofing language for the paragraphs containing text in other languages:

▶ **1.** Select the entire paragraph containing the Spanish translation of "Placeholder for legal text." The wavy red lines that indicate misspelled words appear below the words.

Trouble? If there are no wavy red lines below the Spanish words, continue with Step 2, but note that you will not see any differences after completing Step 5.

▶ **2.** On the Review tab, in the Language group, click the **Language** button, and then click **Set Proofing Language**. The Language dialog box opens. See Figure 8–12.

Figure 8–12   Language dialog box

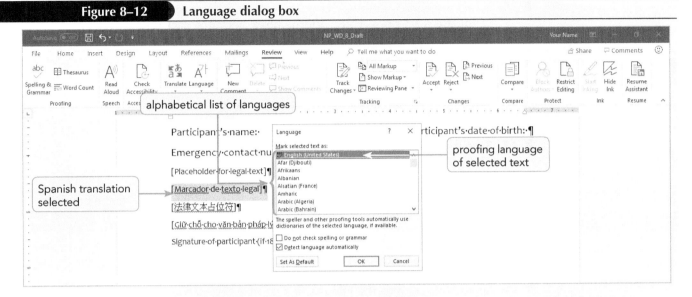

By default, the selected text is marked as English. The spell check icon next to English (United States) indicates that this language is installed. If there are any other languages above the line, it means that words typed in those languages should be detected automatically as long as the Detect language automatically check box is selected.

3. Make a note of any other languages that are listed below English on your screen and above the line. You will need to reset this list later.

4. Scroll down the alphabetical list until you see Spanish (United States). Notice that all the variations of Spanish have a spell-check icon next to them. Microsoft Office sold in English-speaking countries comes with the English, Spanish, and French languages installed.

   Trouble? If there is no spell-check icon next to Spanish (United States), then that language is not installed on your computer. The proofing language will still be changed for the selected words; continue with Step 5.

5. Click **Spanish (United States)**, and then click **OK**. The wavy red lines under the selected words disappear.

   Trouble? If a yellow bar appears at the top of the document below the ribbon telling you that you are missing proofing tools, click the Close button ☒ at the right end of the yellow bar.

6. Select the entire paragraph containing the Chinese translation, click the **Language** button in the Language group, and then click **Set Proofing Language**. At the top of the list, "Spanish (United States)" now appears above the line with English.

7. Scroll the list until you can see Chinese (Singapore). The spell-check icon does not appear next to this language. This means the language is not installed on your computer.

8. Click **Chinese (Singapore)**, and then click **OK**. The dialog box closes and the wavy red lines are removed from below the Chinese translation.

▶ **9.** Select the entire paragraph containing the Vietnamese translation, open the Language dialog box, select **Vietnamese**, and then click **OK**. The wavy red lines are removed from below the Vietnamese translation, and the yellow MISSING PROOFING TOOLS bar appears at the top of the document below the ribbon. The yellow bar tells you that Vietnamese is not being checked and asks if you want to download proofing tools. Sam will install the language later, so you will close the message bar.

▶ **10.** At the right end of the yellow bar, click the **Close** button ✕ .

▶ **11.** Save the changes to the template.

Now you will reset the languages list to the state it was in before you set the proofing languages for the foreign phrases.

To reset the proofing languages list:

▶ **1.** On the ribbon, click the **File** tab, and then in the navigation pane, click **Options**. The Word Options dialog box opens.

▶ **2.** In the navigation pane, click **Language**. Language options appear in the dialog box. See Figure 8–13.

| **Figure 8–13** | **Language options in the Word Options dialog box** |

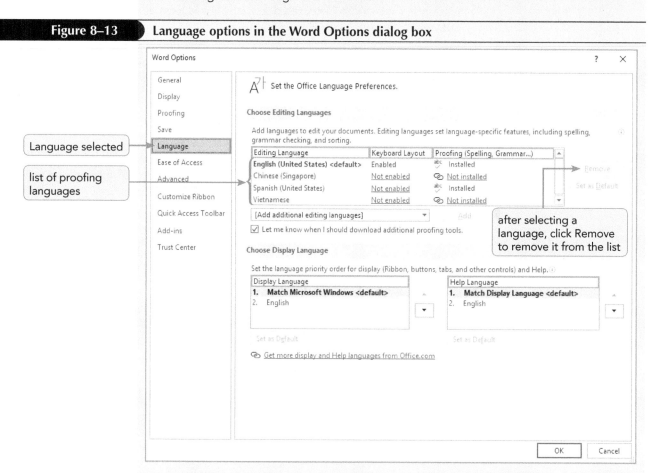

3. In the Choose Editing Languages section, click **Chinese (Singapore)** in the list. The buttons to the right of the list become available.

4. If Chinese (Singapore) was not listed in the Language dialog box (shown in Figure 8–12) before you set the proofing languages, click **Remove** to remove Chinese (Singapore) from the list; if Chinese (Singapore) was listed in the Language dialog box, do not click Remove.

5. If Spanish (United States) and Vietnamese were not listed in the Language dialog box before you set the proofing languages, remove them.

TIP

You can also open the Language tab in the Word Options dialog box by clicking the Language button in the Language group on the Review tab, and then clicking Language Preferences.

6. Click **OK**. The Word Options dialog box closes. If you removed any languages, the Microsoft Office Language Preferences Change dialog box opens with a message indicating you need to restart Office for your language changes to take effect. You don't need to restart Word right now. The change will take effect the next time you close and restart Word.

   Trouble? If you did not remove any of the three languages, the dialog box does not appear. Click anywhere in the document to deselect the text, and skip Step 7.

7. Click **OK**, and then click anywhere in the document to deselect the text.

8. Save the changes to the template.

PROSKILLS

Written Communication: Utilizing Global Content Standards

The world is smaller than it ever has been. Many companies do business with companies in other countries or have international customers. If you work for a company that has international ties, you should evaluate the documents you create to make sure they contain information that is appropriate for and clear to an international audience. For example, when a date is written using numbers in the United States, the first number is the month and the second is the day of the month. In Europe, the order is reversed—the first number is the day of the month and the second is the month. It is important to know how your audience will interpret a date written as numbers. For example, August 12, 2021 would be written as 8/12/2021 in the United States, and as 12/8/2021 in Europe. A European reading the United States format and someone from the United States reading the European format could interpret the date as December 8, 2021. Customers and foreign companies with whom your company does business will appreciate your efforts to consider their needs.

Adding a Custom Paragraph Border

Borders can be used not only to draw attention to text but also to separate parts of a document so it is easier to read. You already know how to add a basic border around a paragraph. You can also create a custom border by changing the style, line weight (thickness), and color.

Adding a Custom Border

- Position the insertion point in the paragraph to which you want to add a custom border.
- On the ribbon, click the Home tab.
- In the Paragraph group, click the Borders arrow, and then click Borders and Shading to open the Borders tab in the Borders and Shading dialog box.
- In the Setting list, click the Custom button.
- In the Style list, click a border style.
- Click the Color arrow, and then click a border color.
- Click the Width arrow, and then click a border width.
- In the Preview area, click the sides of the paragraph around which you want the border to appear.
- Click OK.

Sam wants you to add a border to separate the top part of the waiver, which contains the customer data, and the part of the waiver that will contain the legal language cautioning climbers that they potentially could be injured.

To insert a custom border in the template:

1. Click anywhere in the paragraph containing "Emergency contact number." This is the last line of customer information. The next line will contain the legal paragraphs that need to be added to the waiver.

2. Click the **Home** tab.

3. In the Paragraph group, click the **Borders arrow** ⊞ ˅ , and then click **Borders and Shading**. The Borders and Shading dialog box opens with the Borders tab selected.

4. In the Style list, scroll to the bottom of the list, and then click the third style from the bottom. In the Preview area on the right, the border encompasses the entire paragraph. You need to change this using the Custom setting on the left side of the dialog box.

5. In the Setting list on the left, click the **Custom** button. Now you need to remove the borders from the top and sides of the paragraph.

6. In the Preview area, click the left border. The border you clicked is removed from the preview.

7. Click the top and right borders of the paragraph in the Preview area to remove those borders. Now you will change the thickness of the border.

8. Click the **Width** arrow, and then click **4 ½ pt**. The border at the bottom of the paragraph in the Preview area is still three points. You need to reapply it with the new width selected.

9. In the Preview area, click the border at the bottom of the paragraph. The border is now 4½ points wide. See Figure 8–14.

Figure 8–14   Borders tab in the Borders and Shading dialog box

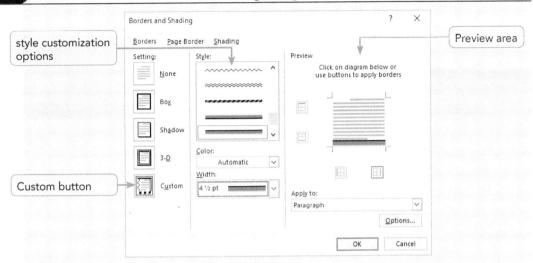

style customization options

Custom button

Preview area

▶ **10.** Click **OK**. The custom border you created appears below the "Emergency contact number" paragraph.

The border is closer to the paragraph above it than to the paragraph below it. You will adjust the space between the border and the paragraph you applied it to so that it appears centered between the two paragraphs.

To change the space between the border line and the text:

▶ **1.** Make sure the insertion point is still in the paragraph containing "Emergency contact number."

▶ **2.** On the Home tab, in the Paragraph group, click the **Borders arrow** ⊞ ▾, and then click **Borders and Shading**. The Borders and Shading dialog box opens.

▶ **3.** In the dialog box, click **Options**. The Border and Shading Options dialog box opens. See Figure 8–15.

Figure 8–15   Border and Shading Options dialog box

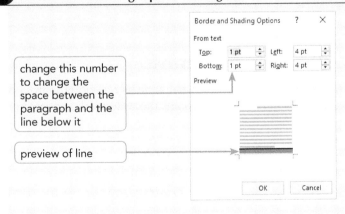

change this number to change the space between the paragraph and the line below it

preview of line

▶ **4.** Click in the **Bottom** box, and then change the value to **8 pt**.

▶ **5.** Click **OK**, and then click **OK** in the Borders and Shading dialog box. The border you added shifts eight points below the paragraph containing "Emergency contact number" and the line you inserted. See Figure 8–16.

Figure 8–16	Paragraph with eight points of space between it and the custom border

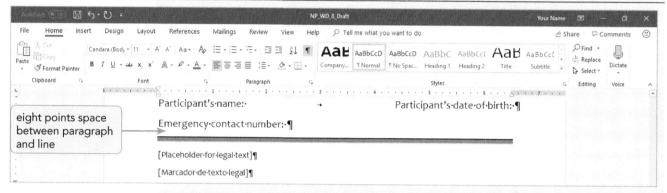

Sam tells you that he also wants the border to appear between the legal text and the section that will contain the signature of the participant. The border is part of the paragraph formatting, so you can use the Format Painter to copy it.

To use the Format Painter to copy the paragraph border:

▶ **1.** Select the paragraph containing "Emergency contact number."

▶ **2.** On the Home tab, in the Clipboard group, click the **Format Painter** button, and then click anywhere on the Vietnamese translation you inserted. The font and paragraph formatting of the "Emergency contact number" paragraph is applied to the paragraph containing the Vietnamese translation.

   Trouble? If the font size of the Vietnamese translation changed to 14 points, select the entire paragraph containing the Vietnamese translation, click the Font size arrow in the Font group on the Home tab, and then click 11.

▶ **3.** Click a blank area of the document, and then save the changes to the template.

Creating a Watermark

A **watermark** is text or a graphic that appears behind or in front of existing text on the printed pages of a document. Usually, the watermark appears in a light shade in the background of each printed page.

REFERENCE

Creating a Custom Text Watermark

- On the ribbon, click the Design tab.
- In the Page Background group, click the Watermark button, and then click Custom Watermark to open the Printed Watermark dialog box.
- Click the Text watermark option button.
- Click the Text arrow, and then click an option in the list; or delete the text in the Text box, and then type the text you want to use as the watermark.
- If desired, click the Font arrow, and then click a font; click the Size arrow, and then click a font size; and click the Color arrow, and then click a color.
- If desired, deselect the Semitransparent check box to make the text darker.
- If desired, click the Horizontal option button to lay out the text horizontally rather than diagonally.
- Click OK.

Sam wants you to add a watermark identifying the waiver as a draft document. You'll do this next.

To add a watermark:

1. On the ribbon, click the **Design** tab, and then in the Page Background group, click the **Watermark** button. The Watermark gallery opens. The gallery is divided into sections: Confidential, Disclaimers, and Urgent. See Figure 8–17.

Figure 8–17	Watermark gallery and menu

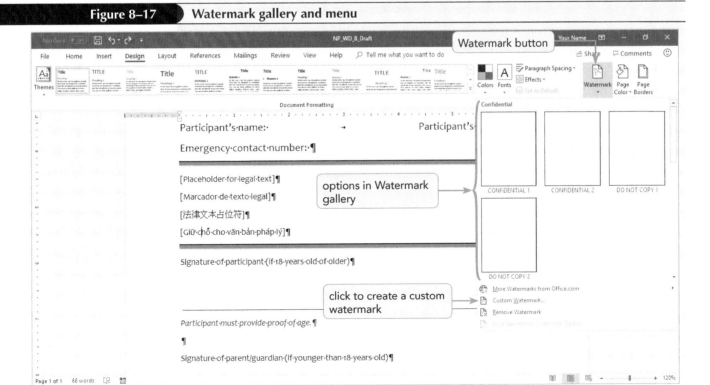

Although Draft is in the gallery both as a horizontal and a diagonal watermark, you will see what other options are available.

▶ **2.** Scroll to the bottom of the gallery to see the rest of the choices, and then below the gallery, click **Custom Watermark**. The Printed Watermark dialog box opens. The No watermark option button is selected, so none of the commands except the three option buttons are available to be selected. See Figure 8–18.

Figure 8–18   **Printed Watermark dialog box**

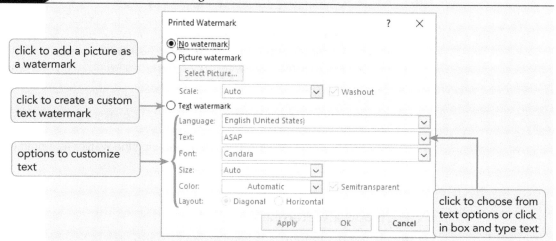

click to add a picture as a watermark

click to create a custom text watermark

options to customize text

click to choose from text options or click in box and type text

▶ **3.** Click the **Text watermark** option button. The commands below that option button become available.

▶ **4.** Click the **Text arrow** to open a list of text watermarks. There are more options in this list than there were in the gallery. You can select one of these or type your own in the Text box.

▶ **5.** Click **DRAFT**. You can customize text watermarks by changing the language, font, font size, font color, and transparency of the text. You can also change the direction of the text. With the default options, the text will be semitransparent, light gray, and slanted in a diagonal direction.

▶ **6.** Click **OK**. "DRAFT" appears in light gray, arranged horizontally, as a watermark in the template.

▶ **7.** Save the changes to the template.

In this session, you added a shape with formatted text, inserted a photo as the shape fill, compressed the photo, applied ligatures and stylistic sets to the text in the shape, translated text, and added a custom border and a watermark. In the next session, you'll edit the properties of a building block, copy a Quick Part and a style from one template to another, and add properties and fields to the template.

Customizing the Ribbon, Quick Access Toolbar, and Status Bar

You can modify the ribbon, the Quick Access Toolbar, and the status bar to suit your working style. To customize the ribbon and the Quick Access Toolbar, click the File tab on the ribbon, and then in the navigation pane, click Options to open the Word Options dialog box. Click Customize Ribbon or click Quick Access Toolbar in the navigation pane on the left. The dialog box changes to show two lists. The list on the left contains the commands available to either the ribbon or the Quick Access Toolbar. The list on the right contains the tabs on the ribbon or the buttons on the Quick Access Toolbar. By default, the list on the left displays the most popular commands. To see all the available commands, click the Choose commands from arrow above the list of commands on the left, and then click All Commands. To see all available macros, click the Choose commands from arrow, and then click Macros.

To add a button to the Quick Access Toolbar, click a command in the list on the left, and then click Add; to remove a button, click it in the Customize Quick Access Toolbar list on the right, and then click Remove. The process of customizing the ribbon is a little more complex. You cannot delete any buttons, groups, or tabs that are on the ribbon by default. To add a button, you need to create a new group on an existing tab or create a new tab and then create a group on that tab. To create a new tab, in the Customize the Ribbon list on the right, click the tab after which you want the new tab to appear, and then click New Tab. To create a new group, click the tab on which you want the group to appear, and then click New Group. With the new group selected, click commands in the list on the left, and then click Add. Rename the new tab or group by selecting it in the Customize the Ribbon list and then clicking Rename. If you want to reset the ribbon or the Quick Access Toolbar, click Reset in the dialog box, and then click Reset all customizations.

To customize the status bar, right-click a blank area of the status bar to open a menu of buttons you can add. Buttons with a checkmark next to them are already on the status bar. Click a button that does not have a checkmark next to it to add it to the status bar. Click a button that has a checkmark next to it to remove it from the status bar.

Sam is pleased with the final template. He thinks it will help his employees work more efficiently.

Session 8.1 Quick Check

1. How do you add text to a shape that you draw?
2. What is a ligature?
3. What is the default compression for photos in a Word document?
4. What properties of a paragraph border can you change?
5. What is the proofing language?
6. What is a watermark?

Session 8.2 Visual Overview:

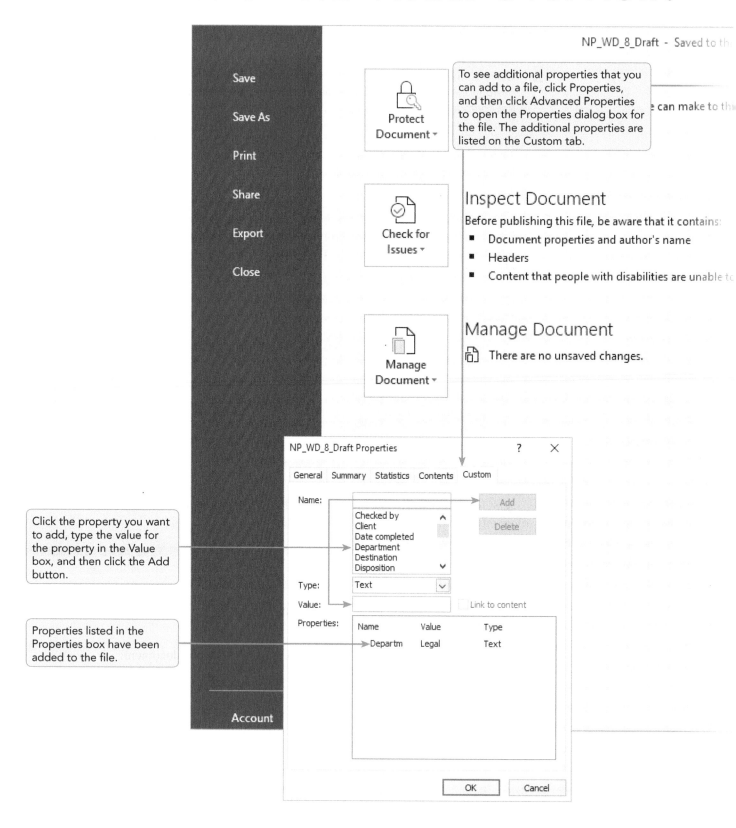

NP_WD_8_Draft - Saved to th

Save

Save As

Print

Share

Export

Close

Account

Protect Document ▾

To see additional properties that you can add to a file, click Properties, and then click Advanced Properties to open the Properties dialog box for the file. The additional properties are listed on the Custom tab.

e can make to th

Inspect Document

Before publishing this file, be aware that it contains:

- Document properties and author's name
- Headers
- Content that people with disabilities are unable to

Check for Issues ▾

Manage Document

There are no unsaved changes.

Manage Document ▾

Click the property you want to add, type the value for the property in the Value box, and then click the Add button.

Properties listed in the Properties box have been added to the file.

NP_WD_8_Draft Properties ? ✕

General Summary Statistics Contents **Custom**

Name:

| Checked by |
| Client |
| Date completed |
| Department |
| Destination |
| Disposition |

Add

Delete

Type: Text ▾

Value: ☐ Link to content

Properties:

Name	Value	Type
Departm	Legal	Text

OK   Cancel

File Properties

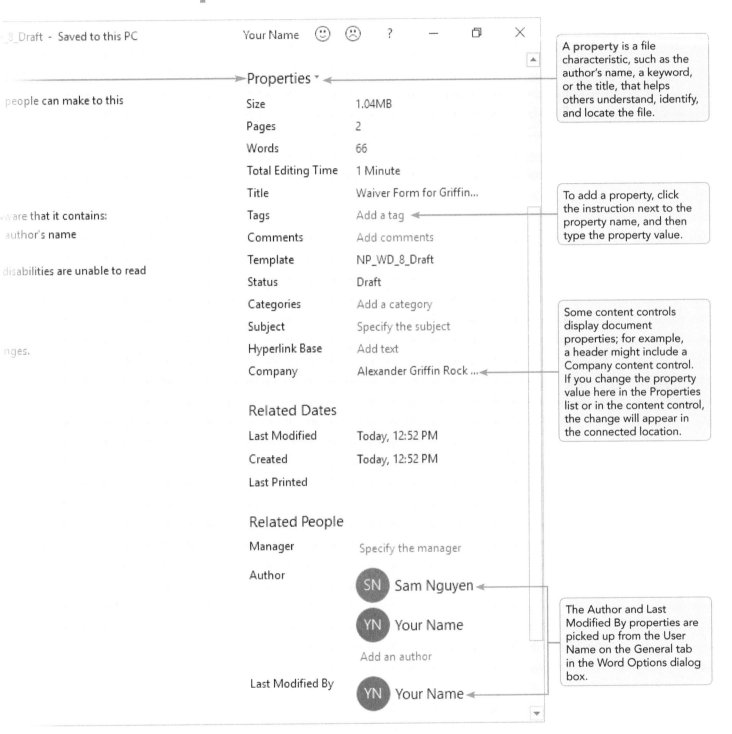

_8_Draft - Saved to this PC

people can make to this

...ware that it contains:

author's name

disabilities are unable to read

...nges.

Your Name   😊 ☹ ?   —   ⬜   ✕

Properties ▾

Size	1.04MB
Pages	2
Words	66
Total Editing Time	1 Minute
Title	Waiver Form for Griffin...
Tags	Add a tag
Comments	Add comments
Template	NP_WD_8_Draft
Status	Draft
Categories	Add a category
Subject	Specify the subject
Hyperlink Base	Add text
Company	Alexander Griffin Rock ...

Related Dates

Last Modified	Today, 12:52 PM
Created	Today, 12:52 PM
Last Printed	

Related People

Manager	Specify the manager
Author	SN Sam Nguyen
	YN Your Name
	Add an author
Last Modified By	YN Your Name

A **property** is a file characteristic, such as the author's name, a keyword, or the title, that helps others understand, identify, and locate the file.

To add a property, click the instruction next to the property name, and then type the property value.

Some content controls display document properties; for example, a header might include a Company content control. If you change the property value here in the Properties list or in the content control, the change will appear in the connected location.

The Author and Last Modified By properties are picked up from the User Name on the General tab in the Word Options dialog box.

Editing Building Block Properties

Building blocks, which are all of the preformatted content—including Quick Parts—that you can insert into a document via a Word gallery, are stored in templates. They can be stored in the Building Blocks template on a computer so that they are available to all documents on that computer, or they can be stored in a document template so that they are always available to people who use the template, no matter what computer they work on.

Previously, Sam created a template in which he stores styles and building blocks that are used frequently in company documents. He did this so he can keep all of this information in one place. One of the items in that template is a formatted Quick Part that contains the webpage address of the Rock Gym. Sam wants you to copy that Quick Part from his template to the NP_WD_8_Draft template, but first, you'll look at the Quick Parts gallery in the NP_WD_8_Draft template to confirm that the gallery currently does not contain any Quick Parts.

To examine the Quick Parts gallery in the NP_WD_8_Draft template:

▶ **1.** If you took a break after the last session, use the Open command in Backstage view to open the **NP_WD_8_Draft** template. First, you'll examine the Quick Parts gallery in this template.

▶ **2.** On the ribbon, click the **Insert** tab.

▶ **3.** In the Text group, click the **Explore Quick Parts** button. If any Quick Parts were stored in this template, they would appear at the top of the Quick Parts menu; however, no Quick Parts are currently stored in the NP_WD_8_Draft template.

> **Trouble?** If you see Quick Parts on the menu, they are stored in the Normal template or in the Building Blocks template, both of which are stored on your computer. You can ignore those Quick Parts.

▶ **4.** Press **ESC** to close the Explore Quick Parts menu.

Like files, building blocks have properties. In Sam's template, the Rock Gym Webpage Address Quick Part is missing a Description property. You'll open the template Sam created and save a copy in the location where you are saving your files. Then you'll edit the Rock Gym Webpage Address Quick Part by adding a description so that the user understands what the Quick Part contains.

To edit the properties for the Quick Part:

▶ **1.** Use the Open command in Backstage view to open the template **NP_WD_8-2.dotx** located in the Word8 > Module folder, and then save it as a template named **NP_WD_8_Styles** in the location specified by your instructor. This file appears to be empty.

▶ **2.** On the ribbon, click the **Insert** tab, and then in the Text group, click the **Explore Quick Parts** button. A Quick Part containing the formatted web address of the Rock Gym webpage appears in the gallery above the Quick Parts menu.

▶ **3.** Point to the **Rock Gym Webpage Address** Quick Part. Note that no ScreenTip appears.

▶ **4.** Right-click the **Rock Gym Webpage Address** Quick Part, and then on the shortcut menu, click **Edit Properties**. The Modify Building Block dialog box opens. See Figure 8–19.

Figure 8-19   Modify Building Block dialog box

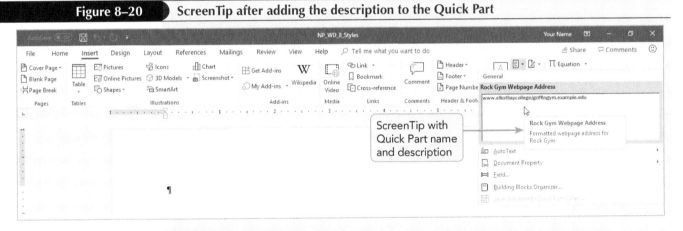

type a description of the Quick Part here

click to move the Quick Part to another gallery

click to move the Quick Part to another template

▶ **5.** Click in the **Description** box, type **Formatted webpage address for Rock Gym**, and then click **OK**. A dialog box opens, asking if you want to redefine the building block entry.

▶ **6.** Click **Yes**. Now you'll examine the description in the ScreenTip.

▶ **7.** In the Text group, click the **Explore Quick Parts** button 📄▾, and then point to the **Rock Gym Webpage Address** Quick Part. A ScreenTip now appears containing the Quick Part name as well as the description you added. See Figure 8-20.

Figure 8-20   ScreenTip after adding the description to the Quick Part

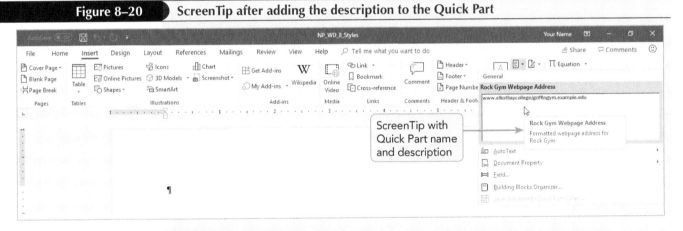

ScreenTip with Quick Part name and description

▶ **8.** Save the changes to the template.

Copying a Building Block to Another Document or Template

Now that you've edited the Rock Gym Webpage Address Quick Part stored in the NP_WD_8_Styles template, you'll copy it to the NP_WD_8_Draft template. To copy a building block from one custom template to another, you first change the location in which the building block is saved from the custom template to the Normal template or to the Building Blocks template. The Normal template is the template on which new, blank documents are based, and the Building Blocks template contains all the building blocks, such as the headers available on the Header button, that are available to all Word documents. From within the custom template, you edit the Save in property of the building block so it is saved to the custom template.

REFERENCE

Copy a Quick Part to Another Template

- In the template containing the Quick Part you want to copy, click the Insert tab on the ribbon.
- In the Text group, click the Explore Quick Parts button to open the Quick Parts gallery.
- Right-click the Quick Part you want to copy, and then click Edit Properties to open the Modify Building Block dialog box.
- Click the Save in arrow, and then click Normal or Building Blocks.
- Click OK.
- In the template to which you want to copy the Quick Part, click the Insert tab, and then in the Text group, click the Explore Quick Parts button.
- Right-click the Quick Part you are copying, and then click Edit Properties to open the Modify Building Block dialog box.
- Click the Save in arrow, and then click the current template name.
- To keep a copy of the Quick Part in the original template, close that template without saving changes.

To copy a Quick Part between templates:

▶ 1. In the NP_WD_8_Styles template, open the Modify Building Block dialog box for the Rock Gym Webpage Address Quick Part again.

▶ 2. In the dialog box, click the **Save in arrow**. The list that opens contains the current template, NP_WD_8_Styles, and the Normal and Building Blocks templates. It does not include the NP_WD_8_Draft template even though that template is open. You'll store the Rock Gym Webpage Address Quick Part in the Building Blocks template.

▶ 3. Click **Building Blocks**, click **OK**, and then click **Yes** to confirm that you want to redefine the entry. Now you can access the Quick Part from within the NP_WD_8_Draft template.

   Next, you'll switch to the NP_WD_8_Draft template. Do not save the changes made to the NP_WD_8_Styles template.

▶ 4. On the ribbon, click the **View** tab.

▶ 5. In the Window group, click the **Switch Windows** button, and then click **NP_WD_8_Draft** to make it the active template.

▶ 6. Click the **Insert** tab if necessary, and then in the Text group, click the **Explore Quick Parts** button 📄▾. The Rock Gym Webpage Address Quick Part now appears in the gallery because it was stored in the Building Blocks template.

▶ 7. Right-click the **Rock Gym Webpage Address** Quick Part, and then click **Edit Properties**. The Modify Building Block dialog box opens with Building Blocks listed in the Save in box. You need to change the Save in location to the NP_WD_8_Draft template.

▶ 8. Click the **Save in arrow**, click **NP_WD_8_Draft**, click **OK**, and then click **Yes** to confirm the change.

▶ 9. Switch back to the NP_WD_8_Styles template, and then open the Quick Parts gallery. The Rock Gym Webpage Address Quick Part no longer appears in the gallery. To keep the Rock Gym Webpage Address Quick Part in the NP_WD_8_Styles template, you will close the template without saving the changes to it.

▶ 10. In the title bar, click the **Close** button ❌. A dialog box opens asking if you want to save the changes to NP_WD_8_Styles.

▶ **11.** Click **Don't Save**. The NP_WD_8_Styles template closes, and the NP_WD_8_ Draft template is the active template. Because you did not save the change you made to the template, the Rock Gym Webpage Address Quick Part is still stored in the NP_WD_8_Styles template.

▶ **12.** Save the changes to the NP_WD_8_Draft template. Now the Rock Gym Webpage Address Quick Part is also saved with the NP_WD_8_Draft template.

Finally, you'll insert the Rock Gym Webpage Address Quick Part in the NP_WD_8_Draft template.

▶ **13.** At the top of the document, click in the empty paragraph below "Student Fitness Center, Elliot Bay College."

▶ **14.** On the Insert tab, in the Text group, click the **Explore Quick Parts** button ▣▾, and then click the **Rock Gym Webpage Address** Quick Part to insert it into the template. See Figure 8–21.

| Figure 8–21 | Rock Gym Webpage Address Quick Part inserted in NP_WD_8_Draft template |

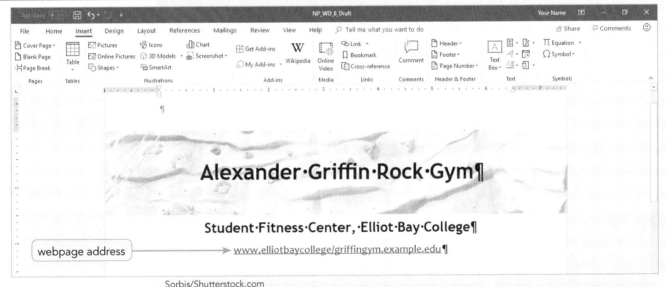

Sorbis/Shutterstock.com

▶ **15.** Save the changes to the template.

INSIGHT

Creating Building Blocks in Other Galleries

Word has many predesigned building blocks for a wide variety of items, including cover pages, calendars, numbering, and text boxes. For example, when you click the Header or Footer button on the Insert tab, the preformatted options in the gallery are building blocks.

In addition to creating Quick Parts—building blocks stored in the Quick Parts gallery— you can create custom building blocks in any of the galleries that contain building blocks. For example, if you create a custom header, you can use the Save Selection to Quick Part Gallery command on the Quick Parts menu to open the Create New Building Block dialog box. In that dialog box, click the Gallery arrow and then click Headers to store the custom header in the Headers gallery instead of in the Quick Parts gallery.

Copying a Style to Another Document or Template

You can also copy styles from one document or template to another. To do this, you open the Styles pane, click the Manage Styles button to open the Manage Styles dialog box, and then click the Import/Export button to open the Organizer dialog box. In this dialog box, you can copy specific styles from one document or template to another.

REFERENCE

Copying a Style to Another Document or Template

- On the ribbon, click the Home tab.
- In the Styles group, click the Styles Dialog Box Launcher.
- In the Styles pane, click the Manage Styles button to open the Edit tab in the Manage Styles dialog box.
- Click the Import/Export button to open the Styles tab in the Organizer dialog box.
- Below the In Normal list on the right, click Close File.
- Below the empty box on the right, click Open File, navigate to the location of the document or template to which or from which you want to copy a style, click the file, and then click Open.
- In the list containing the style you want to copy, click the style name.
- Click Copy.
- Click Close.

Sam wants you to create a new style from the formatted company name in the rectangle shape at the top of the NP_WD_8_Draft template. Then he would like you to copy this style to the NP_WD_8_Styles template.

To create a new style:

TIP

To change attributes of the Body and Heading fonts, open the Manage Styles dialog box, click +Body or +Headings in the Font list, and change the desired attributes.

1. In the rectangle at the top of the NP_WD_8_Draft template, select **Alexander Griffin Rock Gym**.

2. On the ribbon, click the **Home** tab.

3. In the Styles group, click the **More** button ⏷, and then click **Create a Style**. The Create New Style from Formatting dialog box opens. The default style name is selected in the Name box. See Figure 8–22.

Figure 8–22 **Create New Style from Formatting dialog box**

4. In the Name box, type **Company Name** and then click **OK**. The style is added to the template and to the Style gallery.

5. Save the changes to the template.

Now that you've created the Company Name style, you can copy it to the NP_WD_8_Styles template.

To copy a style from one template to another:

▶ **1.** On the Home tab, in the Styles group, click the **Styles Dialog Box Launcher**. The Styles pane opens.

▶ **2.** At the bottom of the Styles pane, click the **Manage Styles** button A . The Manage Styles dialog box opens with the Edit tab selected. This dialog box lists all the styles available to the document. See Figure 8–23.

Figure 8–23   **Edit tab in the Manage Styles dialog box**

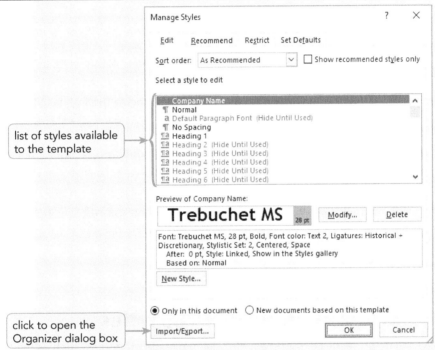

list of styles available to the template

click to open the Organizer dialog box

▶ **3.** At the bottom of the Manage Styles dialog box, click **Import/Export**. The Organizer dialog box opens with the Styles tab selected. See Figure 8–24.

Figure 8–24   **Styles tab in the Organizer dialog box**

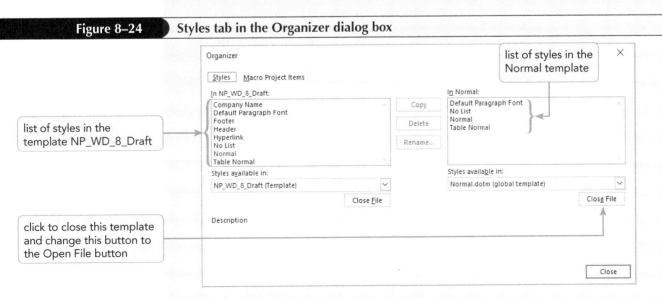

list of styles in the Normal template

list of styles in the template NP_WD_8_Draft

click to close this template and change this button to the Open File button

The "In NP_WD_8_Draft" list on the left contains the list of styles stored in the NP_WD_8_Draft template. The "In Normal" list on the right contains the list of styles stored in the Normal template. You want to copy a style from the NP_WD_8_Draft template to the NP_WD_8_Styles template.

▶ **4.** Below the In Normal list, click **Close File**. The list of styles in the Normal template is removed, and the Close File command button changes to the Open File command button.

▶ **5.** Click **Open File** to open the Open dialog box.

▶ **6.** Navigate to the location where you are storing your files, click the **NP_WD_8_Styles** template, and then click **Open**. The list of styles stored in the NP_WD_8_Styles template appears in the list on the right side of the Organizer dialog box.

TIP

To change the list in the Open dialog box to include documents as well as templates, click All Word Templates next to File name in the dialog box, and then click All Word Documents.

You can copy from either list to the other list. If you select a style in the list on the right, the Copy command button changes to point to the list on the left. You need to copy the selected Company Name style in the In NP_WD_8_Draft list on the left to the In NP_WD_8_Styles list on the right.

▶ **7.** With the Company Name style selected in the In NP_WD_8_Draft list on the left, click **Copy**. The Company Name style is copied to the list of styles stored in the NP_WD_8_Styles template.

▶ **8.** Click **Close**. A dialog box opens telling you that you have modified content in NP_WD_8_Styles and asking if you want to save the changes to that template.

▶ **9.** Click **Save**. The copied style is saved to the NP_WD_8_Styles template even though that template is not currently open.

▶ **10.** In the Styles pane, click the **Close** button ☒.

Working with File Properties

File properties describe a file. You can use file properties, such as the file size, the number of pages, or the title, to organize documents or to search for files that have specific properties. See the Session 8.2 Visual Overview for more information about file properties.

Some content controls are linked to document properties so that the controls "pick up" and display the property information. For example, if you insert a header that includes a Title content control, that control is tied to the Title document property, and if you specified a Title document property for the document, it will be displayed in the Title content control in the header. The connection works both ways, so that if you change the title in a Title content control, the Title document property will be changed as well.

Adding Document Properties

To add properties, you need to display the Info screen in Backstage view. Sam wants you to add several properties. First, he wants you to add yourself as a document author. He also wants you to add a descriptive Title property, Status property, and Company property.

To add document properties:

▶ **1.** On the ribbon, click the **File** tab, and then scroll to the bottom of the screen. The Info screen in Backstage view is displayed. The document properties are listed on the right side of the screen. See Figure 8–25.

Figure 8–25   **Document properties on the Info screen**

When a document is created, if you are signed in to your Microsoft account, the Author and Last Modified By properties are picked up from your Microsoft account username; if you are not signed in to your Microsoft account, the Author property is picked up from the User name box in the Word Options dialog box. Because Sam created the original document, his name is listed as the Author. You'll add yourself as an author.

▶ **2.** In the Related People section, click **Add an author**, type your name in the box that appears, and then click a blank area of the screen.

Trouble? If you pressed ENTER after typing your name and a dialog box opens, click a blank area of the screen.

▶ **3.** In the Properties section at the top of the right pane, next to Title, click **Add a title**, type **Waiver Form for Griffin Rock Gym** in the box that appears, and then click a blank area of the screen. The Title property is not the same as the file name. The Title property appears in any Title content controls in the template, such as in a header or footer that contains a Title content control.

Now you need to add the Status and Company properties. These properties are not currently visible.

▶ **4.** Scroll to display the bottom of the Info screen, and then click **Show All Properties**. The Properties list expands to include all of the common document properties, and you can now see the Status and Company properties.

▶ **5.** Next to Status, click **Add text**, and then type **Draft**.

▶ **6.** Next to Company, click **Specify the company**, type **Alexander Griffin Rock Gym**, and then click a blank area of the screen.

Trouble? If a company name appears in the box next to Company, delete it, and then type Alexander Griffin Rock Gym.

Sam also wants you to add a Department property identifying the Legal department as the department that will ultimately store the master version of the template. The Department property is not listed on the Info screen. To add this property, you need to open the Properties dialog box for the template and then add the property on the Custom tab.

To add a custom document property:

▶ **1.** At the top of the list of document properties, click the **Properties** button, and then click **Advanced Properties**. The NP_WD_8_Draft Properties dialog box opens with the Summary tab selected. The Title, Author, and Company boxes reflect the changes you made on the Info screen.

Trouble? If the Summary tab is not selected, click the Summary tab.

▶ **2.** Click the **Custom** tab. This tab lists additional properties you can add.

▶ **3.** In the Name list near the top of the dialog box, click **Department**. "Department" appears in the Name box above the list.

▶ **4.** Click in the **Value** box, type **Legal** and then click **Add**. "Department" and the value you gave it appear in the Properties list below the Value box.

▶ **5.** Click **OK**.

▶ **6.** On the Info screen, in the navigation pane, click **Save**. The changes to the template are saved, and Backstage view closes.

The properties you added will make it easy for Sam to organize and locate files based on these properties, and he won't have to insert text into content controls that are linked to these properties.

Inserting Document Properties into the Template

Sam wants you to add a header that contains the Status property. The watermark that identifies the document as a draft will remain in the template until it is finalized by the Legal department. He will update the Status property as he makes changes to the template before it is finalized.

Many of the standard document file properties are listed in a submenu on the Quick Parts menu, so you can insert them from there. When you insert a document property from the Quick Parts menu, you insert it as a content control.

To insert a document property as a content control into the template:

▶ **1.** On the ribbon, click the **Insert** tab.

▶ **2.** In the Header & Footer group, click the **Header** button, and then click **Edit Header**. The header area in the document becomes active, and the Header & Footer Tools Design tab is the active tab.

▶ **3.** Click the **Insert** tab.

4. In the Text group, click the **Explore Quick Parts** button, and then point to **Document Property**. A submenu listing some of the document properties opens. See Figure 8–26.

Figure 8–26 Document Property submenu on the Quick Parts menu

Sorbis/Shutterstock.com

5. Click **Status**. A content control labeled Status appears in the header with "Draft" in it.

Now you will make sure that the property in the content control changes if you change it on the Info screen, and vice versa.

To update the Status property:

1. On the ribbon, click the **File** tab, scroll down, and then click **Show All Properties**. The Status property is "Draft."

2. Next to Status, click **Draft** to select the word, and then type **First Revision**.

3. Scroll up if necessary, and then at the top of the navigation pane, click the **Back** button. In the header, the Status property in the content control is updated with the new property value.

4. In the header, select **First Revision**, type **Draft**, and then double-click in the document. Header & Footer view closes.

5. On the ribbon, click the **File** tab, scroll down, and then click **Show All Properties**. In the Properties list, examine the Status property. It should be "Draft," but the change to the property may not appear until you close and reopen the file. You'll do that next.

6. In the navigation pane, click **Save**, and then close the **NP_WD_8_Draft** file without closing Word.

Trouble? If you clicked the Close button to close the document, a dialog box opens, asking if you want to save changes to "Building Blocks." Click Cancel.

▶ 7. Use the Open command in Backstage view to open the **NP_WD_8_Draft** file, click the **File** tab, scroll down, click the **Show All Properties** link, and confirm that the Status property is "Draft."

▶ 8. Scroll up if necessary, and then at the top of the navigation pane, click the **Back** button ⊖ to close Backstage view.

Sam also wants you to insert the Department property in the header, but that property does not appear on the Document Property submenu on the Quick Parts menu. To insert this custom property, you'll need to insert it as a field.

Automating Documents Using Fields

Using fields is a powerful method for automating a document. Recall that a field is a code that instructs Word to insert information that can change in a document. For example, when you insert the current date using the Insert Date and Time button in the Text group on the Insert tab and keep the Update automatically check box selected, you actually insert a field. Word provides many fields that you can include in documents. Figure 8–27 lists some of the most common fields.

Figure 8–27   Common fields

Field	Code (Example)	Action
Date	{DATE \@ "MMMM d, yyyy"}	Inserts the current date/time
Fill-in	{FILLIN "Your name?" * MERGEFORMAT}	Inserts information filled in by the user
NumPages	{NUMPAGES}	Inserts the total number of pages in the document
Page	{PAGES}	Inserts the current page number
Ref	{REF BookmarkName}	Inserts the contents of the specified bookmark

When you insert a field into a document, the corresponding field code includes the name of the field and an optional instruction, prompt, and switches, which are enclosed in braces { } (also called French brackets or curly brackets). An **instruction** is a word or phrase that specifies what the field should do, such as display a **prompt**, which is a phrase that tells the user how to proceed. A **switch** is a command that follows *, \#, \@, or \! and turns on or off certain features of the field. For example, a switch can specify how the result of the field is formatted. Figure 8–28 shows a field code that contains a field name, instructions, and a switch.

Figure 8–28   Components of a field code

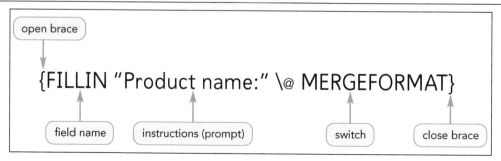

The field name, FILLIN, specifies that this field asks the user to supply (fill in) some information. The instruction is a prompt (Product name:) that tells the user what to type. The switch (\@ MERGEFORMAT) specifies that the field's result (the user fill-in information) should retain any formatting applied to the field even if the user fills in new information. All field codes must include braces and a field name, but not all field codes include instructions and switches.

Inserting a Custom Property Using the Field Dialog Box

One of the things you can insert as a field is a custom file property. The Department property is a custom property, so to insert it in the header, you need to use the Field dialog box. You'll do this now.

To insert a custom property as a field:

▶ **1.** Double-click in the header area. The header becomes active, and the insertion point is before the word "Draft."

▶ **2.** Press **TAB** twice to move the Draft property to the right margin in the header, and then press the ← key twice to move the insertion point back to the left margin.

▶ **3.** On the ribbon, click the **Insert** tab.

▶ **4.** In the Text group, click the **Explore Quick Parts** button 🗐 ▾ , and then click **Field**. The Field dialog box opens.

▶ **5.** In the Please choose a field section, click the **Categories arrow**, and then click **Document Information**. The Field names list is filtered to include only fields in the Document Information category.

▶ **6.** In the Field names list, click **DocProperty**. The middle section of the dialog box changes to display options for the DocProperty field. See Figure 8–29.

| Figure 8–29 | Field dialog box with the DocProperty field selected |

properties for selected field

click to filter the list to fields in a specific category

selected field

click to see the code for the selected field, including instructions and switches

▶ **7.** In the Property list, click **Department**, and then click **OK**. "Legal," the Department property for the document, appears in the header.

Trouble? If the field code is displayed in the header instead of the word "Legal," press ALT+F9.

Now that you've inserted a field, you can examine its field code. You'll do this now.

To examine the field code:

▶ **1.** In the header, right-click **Legal**, and then on the shortcut menu, click **Toggle Field Codes**. The field code for the field you right-clicked appears instead of the content. The field code for the Department document property is { DOCPROPERTY Department * MERGEFORMAT }.

▶ **2.** Right-click **Draft**. The Toggle Field Codes command is not on this shortcut menu because this is a content control, not a field. (Although some content controls contain fields, this one does not.) Notice that this shortcut menu includes the command Remove Content Control.

▶ **3.** Right-click the Department field code at the left margin in the header, and then click **Toggle Field Codes**. The field code is hidden again, and only the contents of the field are displayed.

▶ **4.** Double-click anywhere in the document except in the header to close the header area.

PROSKILLS

Teamwork: Using Properties and Fields

Templates are helpful when you work with a team of people who all need to create similar documents. If you want all users to insert specific document properties in the documents created from the template, displaying the properties in content controls or as fields in the template helps ensure that the needed information is not overlooked and is always inserted in each document. Keep this in mind if you need to create a template for use by a group.

Customizing the Date Field

You're already familiar with the Date field, which inserts the current date and time or inserts parts of the date and time in the format you select, such as the full name for the current month (for example, February) and the day, but not the year or any part of the time.

Fields are updated when you open a document, but sometimes they must be updated while you are working on a document to ensure they contain the most recent information. For example, if you insert the NumPages field, which identifies the total number of pages in a document, and then create additional pages in the document, you need to update the field. This is important if you plan to print the document before closing it.

Sam wants the NP_WD_8_Draft template to be updated with the current date whenever it is opened. You'll insert the Date field using the Insert Date and Time button on the ribbon, and then you'll examine the field codes for the Date field.

To insert the Date field and view the field codes:

▶ **1.** Click in the empty paragraph below the webpage address.

▶ **2.** On the ribbon, click the **Insert** tab, if necessary, and then in the Text group, click the **Insert Date and Time** button 🗓 to open the Date and Time dialog box.

▶ **3.** In the Available formats list, click the format located fifth from the bottom (the format in the style 5/25/2021 3:21:42 PM). You want the date to be inserted as a field that will be updated every time the template is opened.

▶ **4.** If the Update automatically check box is not selected, click the **Update automatically** check box to select it.

▶ **5.** Click **OK**. The current date and time to the second are inserted in the document.

▶ **6.** Click the date. Although this is a field, the borders of a content control appear around the date, and the title tab includes an Update command button.

TIP

You can also press F9 to update the selected field.

▶ **7.** On the title tab of the content control, click **Update**. The time is updated to a few seconds later than when you inserted it.

▶ **8.** Right-click the date, and then click **Toggle Field Codes** on the shortcut menu. The field codes for the field you right-clicked are displayed instead of the content. The field code for the format you chose is { DATE \@ "M/d/ yyyy h:mm:ss am/pm" }.

The field code for the date specifies how the date is formatted. You could change the format of the date by editing the field code, or you could select another format in the Field dialog box.

The part of the field code that specifies how the date will appear consists of a string of letters. Most of it is easily decipherable. For example, if you look at the field code for the date currently displayed in the document, it is apparent that "d" (or "D") indicates the date, "y" (or "Y") indicates the year, and "s" indicates seconds. You also should be able to figure out that an uppercase "M" indicates the month, while a lowercase "m" indicates minutes. What is not obvious from this example is that an uppercase "H" and a lowercase "h" indicate different things. A lowercase "h" indicates the hour using the 12-hour format, and this format needs "am/pm" as part of the field code. An uppercase "H" indicates the hour using the 24-hour standard; this format does not need "am/pm" as part of the format.

Date field codes also indicate the number of digits used or whether the month is displayed as letters or numbers. The letters "yy" will display the year as two digits, while "yyyy" will display the year as four digits. Months are displayed as follows:

- "M" displays the month as a single digit for January through September, and two digits for October through December.
- "MM" displays the month as two digits for all months.
- "MMM" displays the month using its three-letter abbreviation.
- "MMMM" displays the month using the full word.

REFERENCE

Editing a Field Code

- Right-click the field, click Toggle Field Codes, and then edit the field code.

or

- Right-click the field, and then click Edit Field on the shortcut menu to open the Field dialog box with the field selected in the Field names list.
- Click Field Codes.
- Edit the code in the Field codes box.
- Click OK.

Sam wants you to change the format of the Date field so it does not include the seconds and so that it displays the time using the 24-hour format rather than the 12-hour format and am/pm.

To edit the Date field format:

▶ **1.** Right-click the date field code, and then click **Edit Field** on the shortcut menu. The Field dialog box opens. Date is selected in the Field names list on the left, and the format you chose is selected in the Date formats list in the middle.

▶ **2.** At the bottom of the dialog box, click **Field Codes**. The right side of the dialog box changes to display the Advanced field properties section with the field code for the selected format listed in the Field codes box. The general format for the syntax of the Date field appears under the Field codes box. See Figure 8–30.

Figure 8–30 | **Field dialog box with the Date field codes displayed**

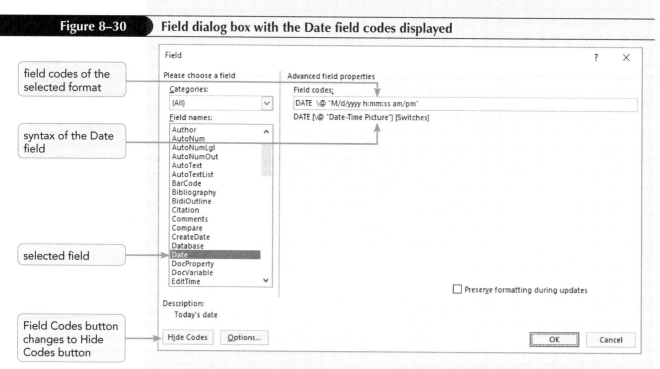

field codes of the selected format

syntax of the Date field

selected field

Field Codes button changes to Hide Codes button

▶ **3.** In the Field codes box, click between "pm" and the double quotation marks, and press **BACKSPACE** nine times to delete ":ss am/pm".

▶ **4.** Press the ← key three times to move the insertion point to between "h" and the colon, press **BACKSPACE** to delete the "h," and then type **H**.

5. Click **OK**. The Field dialog box closes, and the date appears in the new format. Note that the field codes automatically toggled off.

6. Right-click the date, and then click **Toggle Field Codes** on the shortcut menu. The field code is now { DATE \@ "M/d/yyyy H:mm" }.

7. Toggle the field codes off, and then save the changes to the template.

Inserting a Fill-In Field

A Fill-in field is a field that causes a dialog box to open, prompting the user to enter information when a document is created from a template. When you insert a Fill-in field, you need to type the text that will prompt the user for the required information.

Inserting a Fill-In Field

- On the ribbon, click the Insert tab.
- In the Text group, click the Explore Quick Parts button, and then click Field.
- In the Field names list, click Fill-in.
- In the Field properties section, click in the Prompt box, and then type the text you want to appear in the dialog box that opens.
- Click the Preserve formatting during updates check box to deselect it.
- Click OK.
- Click Cancel in the dialog box that opens containing the prompt.

For each customer, Sam's employees will double-click the waiver template on the desktop to create a new document based on the template. To make sure all the information is entered in the template, Sam wants a dialog box to open requesting each piece of information. You'll add Fill-in fields to do this.

To insert a Fill-in field:

1. Position the insertion point after the space following "Participant's name:".

2. On the Insert tab, in the Text group, click the **Explore Quick Parts** button, and then click **Field**. The Field dialog box opens.

3. In the Please choose a field section, scroll the alphabetical Field names list, and then click **Fill-in**. The middle part of the dialog box changes to display a Prompt box, where you will type the text that will appear as an instruction in the dialog box that opens when the document is opened. See Figure 8–31.

Figure 8-31 Field dialog box with the Fill-in field selected

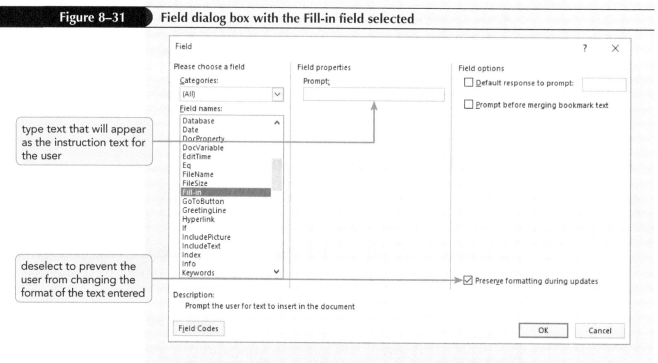

type text that will appear as the instruction text for the user

deselect to prevent the user from changing the format of the text entered

Trouble? If you don't see the Fill-in option in the list, click the Categories arrow, and then click (All).

4. In the Field properties section, click in the **Prompt** box, and then type **Enter participant's name:** (with a colon at the end).

5. Click the **Preserve formatting during** updates check box to deselect it. When this check box is checked, Word preserves any formatting that the user applies to the field. For example, if you change the format to bold, red formatting, and this check box is selected, the bold, red formatting will appear when you update the field. If you clear this check box, Word will update the field information but retain the original formatting.

6. Click **OK**. A Microsoft Word dialog box appears with the prompt you typed, "Enter participant's name:". See Figure 8-32.

Figure 8-32 Prompt box for the Fill-in field

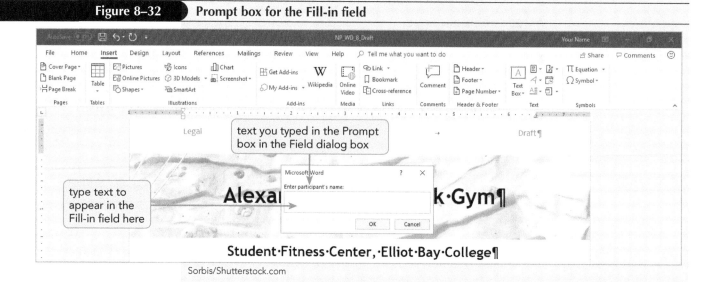

text you typed in the Prompt box in the Field dialog box

type text to appear in the Fill-in field here

Sorbis/Shutterstock.com

This is the dialog box that will appear when a document based on this template is first opened. Anything the user types in the box will appear at the location of the Fill-in field in the document. You want the field to be empty in the template so that the user can enter the climber's name each time a new document is created from the template, so you will close this dialog box without entering any text.

▶ **7.** Click **Cancel** to close the dialog box. It looks as if there is no change in the document. The insertion point is blinking after the space to the right of "Participant's name:".

▶ **8.** Right-click the space to the right of "Participant's name:", and then click **Toggle Field Codes** on the shortcut menu. The Fill-in field code is displayed. The Fill-in field code has no switch, but it does include the text you specified for the prompt. You can click anywhere in the field code to modify the prompt or to add a switch.

▶ **9.** Right-click the Fill-in field code, and then click **Toggle Field Codes** to hide the field codes.

Next, you'll insert Fill-in fields for the participant's date of birth and for an emergency contact number.

To create the Fill-in fields for the participant's date of birth and an emergency contact number:

▶ **1.** Position the insertion point after the space following "Participant's date of birth:".

▶ **2.** On the Insert tab, in the Text group, click the **Explore Quick Parts** button ▣▾, and then click **Field** to open the Field dialog box.

▶ **3.** Scroll down the Field names list, and then click **Fill-in**.

▶ **4.** In the Field properties section, click in the **Prompt** box, and then type **Enter participant's date of birth:** (including the colon).

▶ **5.** Click the **Preserve formatting during updates** check box to deselect it, and then click **OK**. The Field dialog box closes, and a dialog box opens containing the prompt to enter the participant's date of birth.

▶ **6.** Click **Cancel**.

▶ **7.** Position the insertion point after the space following "Emergency contact number:" and then insert a Fill-in field with the prompt text **Enter participant's emergency contact number:** (including the colon). (Do not preserve formatting during updates.)

▶ **8.** Save the changes to the template.

Make sure you save the changes to the template because you will be creating a document based on this template in the next set of steps.

Now that you've added the Fill-in fields, you need to test them to make sure they work as you expect when you open a document based on the NP_WD_8_Draft template. Recall that if you save a template to the Custom Office Templates folder, you can open a new document based on that template directly from the New screen in Backstage view. If a template is stored in a folder other than the Custom Office Templates folder, you need to double-click the document in the File Explorer folder window to create a new document based on that template.

To create a new document based on the template and add text to the Fill-in field:

1. On the taskbar, click the **File Explorer** button [ ]. The File Explorer window opens.

2. Navigate to the drive and folder where you are saving your files. The blue bar at the top of the NP_WD_8_Draft icon indicates that it is a template file.

3. Point to the **NP_WD_8_Draft** template. The ScreenTip that appears indicates that the file is a Microsoft Word template.

   Trouble? If no ScreenTip appears, the folder is in Content view. Click the View tab on the ribbon, and then in the Layout group, click any view except Content.

4. Double-click the **NP_WD_8_Draft** template. A new document based on the template is created, and the prompt for the first Fill-in field appears, asking for the participant's name. The insertion point is in the prompt dialog box.

   Trouble? If the prompt dialog box does not appear, close the document, save the changes to the NP_WD_8_Draft template, and then repeat Step 4.

5. In the Enter participant's name box, type **John Doe** and then click **OK**. The dialog box closes, and the second Fill-in field prompt box appears, asking for the participant's date of birth.

6. Type **8/22/2002**, and then click **OK**. The third Fill-in field prompt dialog box opens asking for the participant's emergency contact number. You will close this dialog box without entering any data.

7. Click **OK**. The contents of the template appear in a new document with the information you typed in the prompt boxes after Participant's name and Participant's date of birth. You need to add the phone number.

8. To the right of "Emergency contact number:", right-click after the space following the colon, and then on the shortcut menu, click **Update Field**. The dialog box requesting the contact number appears again.

9. Type **(206) 555-0125**, and then click **OK**. The phone number appears in the document. Notice that the current date and time appear below the webpage address near the top of the document.

10. Close the document without saving it. The NP_WD_8_Draft template is the active template again.

    Trouble? If you are taking a break and closing Word, a dialog box appears asking if you want to save changes to "Building Blocks." Click Don't Save.

In addition to the fields you used, there are a few other fields, for which there are no content controls to insert the equivalent information, that are useful to know about. These fields are described in Figure 8–33. These fields are all available in the Field dialog box.

Figure 8–33   Useful fields

Field	Description of Inserted Text
FileName	Name of the saved file
FileSize	Size of the file on disk
NumPages	Total number of pages
SaveDate	Date the document was last saved
UserInitials	User initials on the General page in the Word Options dialog box
UserName	User name on the General page in the Word Options dialog box

In this session, you've edited the properties for building blocks, copied building blocks and styles, added and updated file properties, and inserted properties as a content control and as a field. You also created Fill-in fields to request information from the user. In the next session, you'll record and edit a macro, save the document in which the macro is stored, and then copy a macro from one template to another. You'll also record an AutoMacro that will run every time a document is created based on the template.

REVIEW

Session 8.2 Quick Check

1. What is a property?

2. How do you copy a building block from one template to another?

3. How do you access document properties?

4. What are the two ways you can insert a document property?

5. How do you update a field?

6. What is a Fill-in field?

Session 8.3 Visual Overview:

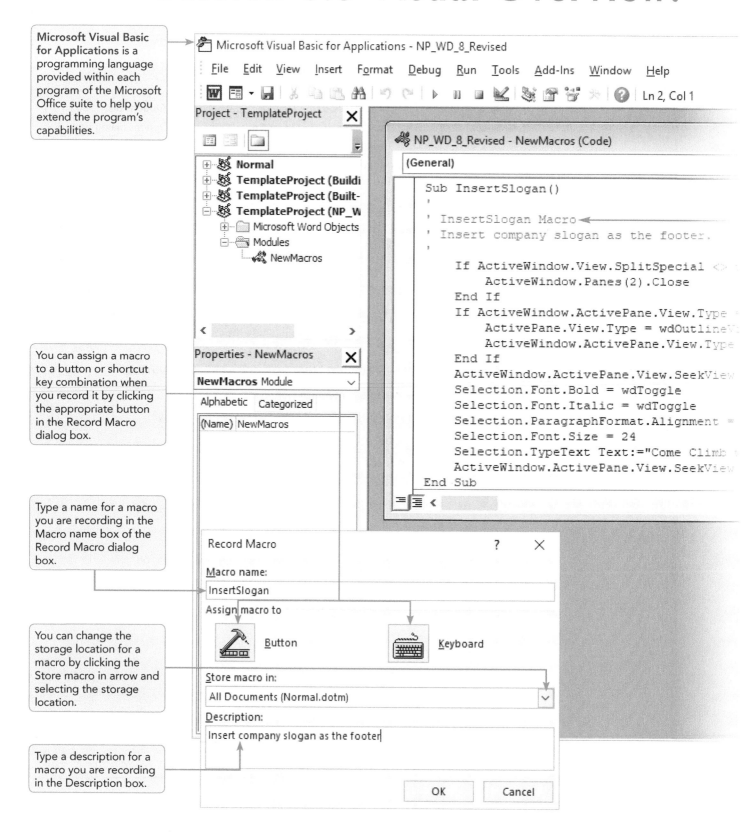

Microsoft Visual Basic for Applications is a programming language provided within each program of the Microsoft Office suite to help you extend the program's capabilities.

You can assign a macro to a button or shortcut key combination when you record it by clicking the appropriate button in the Record Macro dialog box.

Type a name for a macro you are recording in the Macro name box of the Record Macro dialog box.

You can change the storage location for a macro by clicking the Store macro in arrow and selecting the storage location.

Type a description for a macro you are recording in the Description box.

Microsoft Visual Basic for Applications - NP_WD_8_Revised

File   Edit   View   Insert   Format   Debug   Run   Tools   Add-Ins   Window   Help

Ln 2, Col 1

Project - TemplateProject

- Normal
- TemplateProject (Buildi
- TemplateProject (Built-
- TemplateProject (NP_W
  - Microsoft Word Objects
  - Modules
    - NewMacros

Properties - NewMacros

NewMacros Module

Alphabetic   Categorized

(Name) NewMacros

NP_WD_8_Revised - NewMacros (Code)

(General)

```
Sub InsertSlogan()
'
' InsertSlogan Macro
' Insert company slogan as the footer.
'
    If ActiveWindow.View.SplitSpecial <>
        ActiveWindow.Panes(2).Close
    End If
    If ActiveWindow.ActivePane.View.Type
        ActivePane.View.Type = wdOutlineV
        ActiveWindow.ActivePane.View.Type
    End If
    ActiveWindow.ActivePane.View.SeekView
    Selection.Font.Bold = wdToggle
    Selection.Font.Italic = wdToggle
    Selection.ParagraphFormat.Alignment =
    Selection.Font.Size = 24
    Selection.TypeText Text:="Come Climb
    ActiveWindow.ActivePane.View.SeekView
End Sub
```

Record Macro   ?   ✕

Macro name:

InsertSlogan

Assign macro to

[Button]   Button   [Keyboard]   Keyboard

Store macro in:

All Documents (Normal.dotm)

Description:

Insert company slogan as the footer

OK   Cancel

Working with Macros

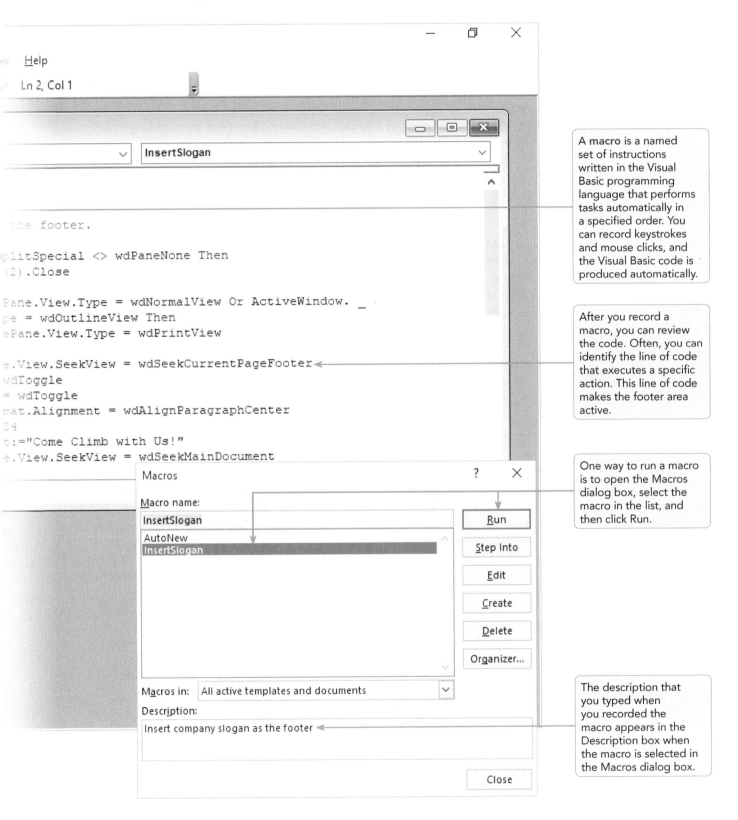

A **macro** is a named set of instructions written in the Visual Basic programming language that performs tasks automatically in a specified order. You can record keystrokes and mouse clicks, and the Visual Basic code is produced automatically.

After you record a macro, you can review the code. Often, you can identify the line of code that executes a specific action. This line of code makes the footer area active.

One way to run a macro is to open the Macros dialog box, select the macro in the list, and then click Run.

The description that you typed when you recorded the macro appears in the Description box when the macro is selected in the Macros dialog box.

Planning a Macro

Macros can help automate repetitive tasks. See the Session 8.3 Visual Overview for more information about macros. Using macros to run frequently executed commands has two main advantages. Combining a number of keystrokes and mouse clicks into a macro saves time and helps you complete your work faster. Also, assuming you record a macro accurately—without typos or other mistakes—the keystrokes and mouse clicks will always play back error-free. A macro that inserts text or performs formatting operations will consistently insert the same text and perform the same formatting operations.

Before you record the steps of a macro, you should plan the macro carefully to help you avoid making errors when you record it. Sam wants you to create a macro that will insert the formatted company slogan into the footer of the document. To insert formatted text in the footer, you need to:

- Activate the footer area—To accomplish this, you'll click the Insert tab on the ribbon, click the Footer button in the Header & Footer group, and then click Edit Footer on the menu.

- Turn on bold formatting—To accomplish this, you'll click the Home tab, and then click the Bold button in the Font group. By turning on the character formatting before you type the text, you save yourself the step of selecting the text after you type it.

- Right-align the text—To accomplish this, you'll click the Align Right button in the Paragraph group on the Home tab. Because this is a paragraph formatting command and you don't need to do anything in order to select the current paragraph, you could perform this step before or after you type the text.

- Change the font size to 24 points—To accomplish this, you'll click the Font Size arrow in the Font group on the Home tab, and then click 24.

- Type the text—You'll type the slogan for the Rock Gym ("Come Climb with Us!").

- Close the footer area—To accomplish this, you'll click the Header & Footer Tools Design tab, and then click the Close Header and Footer button in the Close group. You want to add this as part of the macro because after you insert the text in the footer, you're finished working in the footer area.

Now that you have a plan, you can set up the recording in the Macros dialog box. In the Macros dialog box, you need to do the following:

- Name the macro—A macro name must begin with a letter and can contain a maximum of 80 letters and numbers; the name can't contain spaces, periods, or other punctuation (although you can use the underscore character). The macro name should summarize its function. For example, if you record a macro to resize a picture, you could name the macro ResizePic.

- Describe the macro (optional)—A detailed description of a macro helps you recall its exact function. This is especially important if a macro performs a complex series of operations that can't be summarized in the macro name. For example, a simple macro name, such as PositionPicLeft, doesn't describe the picture features, such as borders and text wrapping. You could include that type of information in the description.

- Attach the macro to a template or document—Unless you specify otherwise, macros you create are attached to the global template, Normal.dotx, and are available in every Word document created on that computer. You can choose instead to attach a macro to another open template. When you do this, the macro is available whenever that template is open or when a new document is created based on that template, even if the template or new document is opened on another computer.

- Assign the macro to a toolbar button, menu, or keyboard shortcut (optional)—To make it a little easier to run a macro, you can assign a macro to a button that you add to the Quick Access Toolbar or to a keyboard shortcut.

One potential disadvantage to working with macros is that they are sometimes used to spread computer viruses. Therefore, on most computers, Word is set to prevent macros from running without your knowledge. However, the settings can be changed so that macros are prevented from running at all. You need to make sure that you will be able to run the macro that you are going to record. You'll do that next.

Examining Trust Center Settings

A macro virus is a virus written into a macro code. Because you can't tell if a macro has a virus when you open a document, Word has built-in security settings to protect your computer. The default setting is for macros to be disabled and for a yellow Security Warning bar to be displayed at the top of the document with a message stating this. See Figure 8–34. In this case, you can click the Enable Content button if you are sure the macros in the document are safe to run. If you enable content in a document and then save it, the document becomes a trusted document on your computer and the Security Warning bar will not appear the next time you open that document.

| Figure 8–34 | Security warning stating that macros have been disabled |

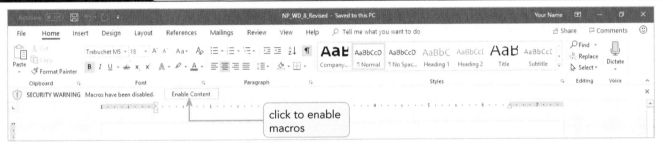

click to enable macros

Another setting completely disables macros. When you try to run one, a dialog box appears, stating that macros are disabled and that you do not have the option to override this setting.

You'll check your macro security settings now.

To check macro security settings:

▶ 1. On the ribbon, click the **File** tab, scroll down, and then in the navigation pane, click **Options**. The Word Options dialog box opens.

▶ 2. In the navigation pane, click **Trust Center**. The dialog box changes to display links to articles about security and privacy on the Internet and the Trust Center Settings button.

▶ 3. Click **Trust Center Settings**. The Trust Center dialog box opens.

▶ 4. In the navigation pane, click **Macro Settings**, if necessary. The Trust Center shows the current macro settings. See Figure 8–35.

| Figure 8–35 | Trust Center dialog box displaying macro settings |

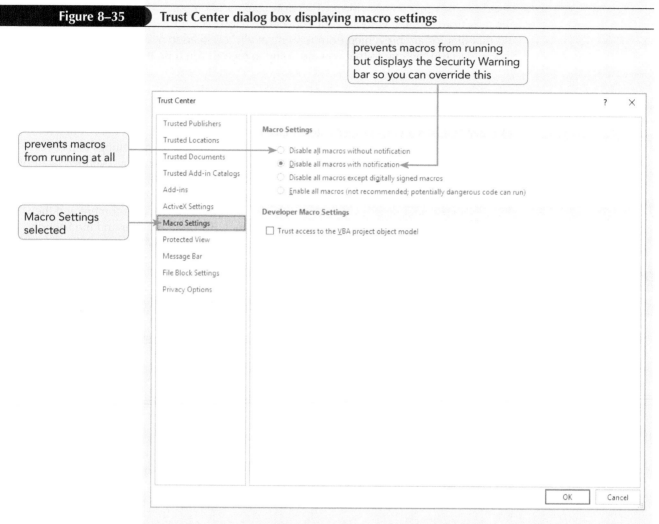

5. If the Disable all macros with notification option button is not selected, note which option is selected so you can reset this setting at the end of the module, and then click the **Disable all macros with notification** option button.

6. Click **OK**, and then click **OK** in the Word Options dialog box.

Recording a Macro

To record a macro, you turn on the macro recorder, perform keystrokes and mouse operations, and then turn off the macro recorder. When you play back the macro, Word performs the same sequence of keystrokes and mouse clicks. Note that you can't record mouse operations within the document window while you record a macro—for example, you can't select text with the mouse or drag and drop text—but you can use the mouse to select buttons and options on the ribbon.

You are ready to record the macro that inserts the slogan for the Rock Gym as a right-aligned footer.

Recording a Macro

- On the ribbon, click the View tab.
- In the Macros group, click the Macros arrow, and then click Record Macro; or on the status bar, click the Start Recording button.
- In the Record Macro dialog box, type a name for the macro in the Macro name box and type a description for the macro in the Description box.
- To save the macro in the current document or template, click the Store macro in arrow, and then select the document or template name.
- Use the Button or Keyboard button to assign the macro to a button or assign a shortcut key combination, respectively.
- Click OK to start recording the macro.
- Perform the mouse actions and keystrokes you want to record.
- On the ribbon, click the View tab. In the Macros group, click the Macros arrow, and then click Stop Recording; or on the status bar, click the Stop Recording button.

Before you record the macro, you'll name the macro, attach it to the template, add a description of the macro, and assign it to a shortcut key combination.

To prepare to record the InsertSlogan macro:

▶ **1.** If you took a break after the last session, use the Open command in Backstage view to open the **NP_WD_8_Draft.dotx** template.

▶ **2.** On the ribbon, click the **View** tab.

▶ **3.** In the Macros group, click the **Macros arrow**, and then click **Record Macro**. The Record Macro dialog box opens. The temporary name Macro1 is selected in the Macro name box. See Figure 8–36.

Figure 8–36   **Record Macro dialog box**

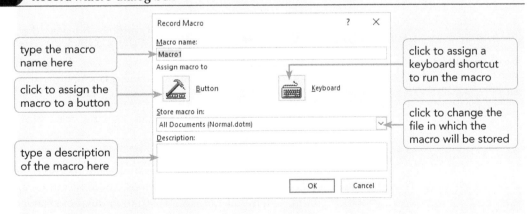

▶ **4.** In the Macro name box, type **InsertSlogan**.

You want to attach the macro to the current template, not to the Normal template.

▶ **5.** Click the **Store macro in arrow**, and then click **Documents Based On NP_WD_8_Draft**.

▶ **6.** Click in the **Description** box, and then type **Insert company slogan as the footer** in the box. Next, you'll assign the macro to a shortcut key combination so you don't need to open the Macros dialog box to run it.

Be sure to switch the macro location to the template. Otherwise, the macro will be stored on your computer and will not be in your final template file.

▶ **7.** Click the **Keyboard** button. The Customize Keyboard dialog box opens. The macro is selected in the Commands list, and the insertion point is blinking in the Press new shortcut key box. See Figure 8–37.

Figure 8–37	Customize Keyboard dialog box

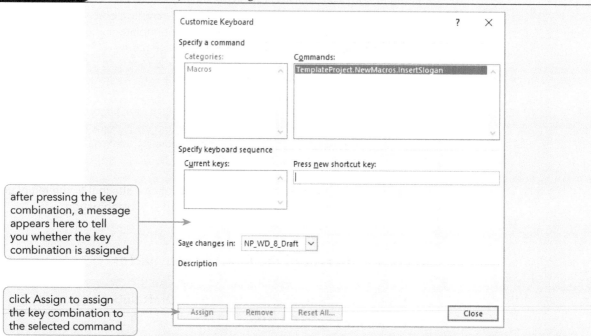

after pressing the key combination, a message appears here to tell you whether the key combination is assigned

click Assign to assign the key combination to the selected command

▶ **8.** Press **ALT+CTRL+SHIFT+A**. A message appears below the Current keys box stating that this key combination is unassigned.

▶ **9.** Click **Assign**. The key combination you chose appears in the Current keys list. Now when you press ALT+CTRL+SHIFT+A, the macro you are about to record will run.

▶ **10.** Click **Close** in the Customize Keyboard dialog box. The dialog boxes close, and the pointer changes to the macro recording pointer ▯, indicating that you are recording a macro. On the status bar, the Stop Recording button ▮ appears (in place of the Start Recording button ▯).

     Trouble? If the Start Recording button was not on the status bar in the place where the Stop Recording button is now, it is not a problem.

From this point, Word records every keystroke and mouse operation you make until you stop the recording, so perform these steps carefully and complete them exactly as shown. If you make a mistake, you can stop recording and start over. It does not matter how long you take to perform the steps. When the macro is run, the steps will execute very quickly.

When you finished with all the steps, click the Stop Recording button ▮ on the status bar, or on the View tab, in the Macros group, click the Macros arrow, and then click Stop Recording.

To record the InsertSlogan macro:

TIP

You can pause the recording by clicking the Macros arrow in the Macros group on the View tab, and then clicking Pause Recording.

▶ **1.** On the ribbon, click the **Insert** tab.

Trouble? If you make a mistake while recording the macro, stop recording, and then repeat the "To prepare to record the InsertSlogan macro" steps. Click Yes when you are asked if you want to replace the existing macro, and then repeat this set of steps.

▶ **2.** In the Header & Footer group, click the **Footer** button, and then click **Edit Footer**. The footer becomes active. The slogan needs to be formatted in bold.

▶ **3.** On the ribbon, click the **Home** tab, and then in the Font group, click the **Bold** button B . Sam wants the slogan right-aligned.

▶ **4.** In the Paragraph group, click the **Align Right** button ☰ . The font size of the slogan needs to be 24 points.

▶ **5.** In the Font group, click the **Font Size arrow**, and then click **24**.

▶ **6.** Type **Come Climb with Us!**. After the text is inserted in the footer, you want the footer area to be inactive.

▶ **7.** Click the **Header & Footer Tools Design** tab, and then in the Close group, click the **Close Header and Footer** button. You are finished recording the steps of the macro.

▶ **8.** On the ribbon, click the **View** tab.

▶ **9.** In the Macros group, click the **Macros arrow**, and then click **Stop Recording**. The pointer changes back to the normal pointer, and the button on the status bar changes back to the Start Recording button 📑 .

Now that you've recorded a macro, you're ready to run it.

Running Macros

To **run** a macro means to cause the recorded or programmed steps of the macro to be executed. To run a macro, you can open the Macros dialog box, select the macro in the list, and then click Run. To open the Macros dialog box, you click the Macros button in the Macros group on the View tab. If you assigned the macro to a button when you recorded it, you can click the button to run the macro. Finally, if you assigned a keyboard shortcut to the macro when you recorded it, as you did when you recorded the InsertSlogan macro, you can press the shortcut keys you assigned.

To test the macro you created, you need to remove the footer and the formatting that was inserted when you recorded the macro. Note that you can't do this with the Remove Footer command on the Footer menu because that command deletes only the text; it does not remove the formatting. If you ran the macro with the formatting still applied in the footer, it would toggle the bold formatting command off. Instead, you will make the footer area active, remove the formatting, and then delete the footer text. After completing those steps, you can run the macro.

To run the InsertSlogan macro:

▶ **1.** Double-click in the footer area, and then select the entire line and the paragraph mark.

▶ **2.** Click the **Home** tab, and then in the Font group, click the **Clear All Formatting** button [A◊]. The formatting is removed, and the text is left-aligned.

▶ **3.** Press **DEL** to delete the text in the footer, and then double-click anywhere in the document to make the footer inactive.

▶ **4.** Press **ALT+CTRL+SHIFT+A**. The formatted footer is entered in the footer area, and the footer area becomes inactive. The macro works as it should. You can use the Undo button to see the list of tasks the macro performed.

▶ **5.** On the Quick Access Toolbar, click the **Undo arrow** [⤺▾]. Notice that the top several actions all begin with "VBA-" ("VBA" refers to the Visual Basic programming language). These are the recorded actions that the macro performed. See Figure 8–38.

| **Figure 8–38** | **Undo list after running the macro** |

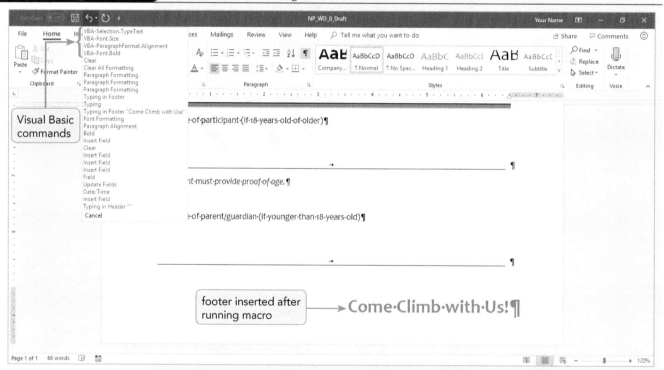

footer inserted after running macro → Come·Climb·with·Us!¶

▶ **6.** Press **ESC** to close the Undo menu without selecting anything.

Sam decides he wants the slogan to be italicized and centered in the footer. You could record a new macro, but it's easier to edit the one you already recorded.

Editing a Macro Using the Visual Basic Window

When you record a macro, you are actually creating a Visual Basic program. Each action you performed while recording the macro created a line of code in Visual Basic. You can see the code by opening the Visual Basic window. You can usually examine the code and identify specific actions even if you don't have a thorough understanding of Visual Basic.

You'll open the Visual Basic window and examine it.

To open the Visual Basic window and examine the code for the InsertSlogan macro:

▶ **1.** On the ribbon, click the **View** tab, and then in the Macros group, click the **Macros** button. The Macros dialog box opens, listing the macro you recorded.

> **Trouble?** If you see other macros listed in the Macros dialog box, they are probably stored in the Normal template on your computer. Continue with the next step.

▶ **2.** In the list of macros, click **InsertSlogan**, if necessary, and then click **Edit**. The Microsoft Visual Basic for Applications window opens with an open Code window displaying the InsertSlogan macro commands. See Figure 8–39.

Figure 8–39	Visual Basic window with the code for the InsertSlogan macro

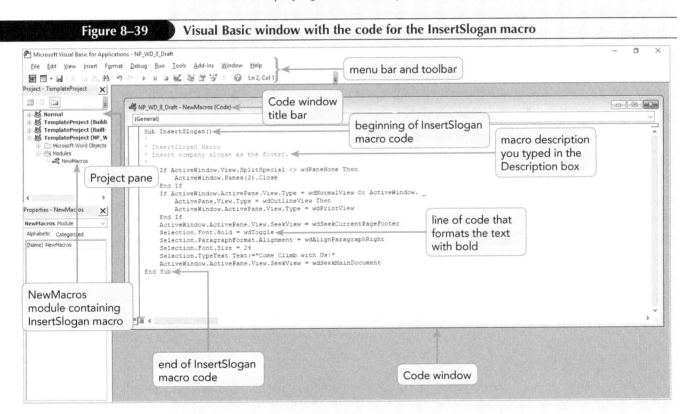

In addition to the Code window, the Visual Basic window includes a Project pane, which displays a list of all templates saved on the computer you are working on. Instead of a ribbon with tabs and buttons, the Visual Basic window contains a menu bar and a toolbar with buttons.

> **Trouble?** If the Code window is not open, click View on the Visual Basic menu bar, and then click Code.

When you record a macro, it is stored in something called a module. Notice that the title bar of the Code window does not contain the macro name; it contains NewMacros—the name of the module—instead. As you can see in the first line in the Code window, the macro starts with "Sub" followed by the macro name, and the last line contains "End Sub." If you recorded a second macro in this template, the commands for that macro would be listed below the "End Sub" line, and the second macro would be enclosed between its own "Sub" and "End Sub" lines.

The line of code "Selection.Font.Bold = wdToggle" is the line that was recorded with you clicked the Bold button. The line "Selection.ParagraphFormat.Alignment = wdAlignParagraphRight" is the line that was recorded when you clicked the Align Right button. You'll edit the macro by adding a line of code similar to the line that formats the text as bold to format the slogan so it is also italicized. Then you will modify the line of code that contains the paragraph alignment instruction so that the text is centered.

To edit the InsertSlogan macro and test the revised macro:

1. In the Code window, click at the end of the line "Selection.Font.Bold = wdToggle." To add the command to italicize the text, you type the same code on a new line, except you will replace the word "Bold" with "Italic."

2. Press **ENTER**, type **Selection.Font.Italic = wdToggle** (do not type a period). Next, you will modify the line of code that right-aligns the text so that the text will be centered instead of right-aligned.

3. Click at the end of the line "Selection.ParagraphFormat.Alignment = wdAlignParagraphRight."

4. Press **BACKSPACE** five times, and then type **Center**. The line now reads "Selection.ParagraphFormat.Alignment = wdAlignParagraphCenter".

5. In the title bar of the Visual Basic window, click the **Close** button ☒. The Visual Basic window closes, and the NP_WD_8_Draft template is the active window. Changes you have made to the code are saved automatically with your Word document. Now you'll test the revised macro.

   Trouble? If the Visual Basic window is still open, you clicked the Close button in the Code window. Click the Close button in the title bar of the Visual Basic window.

6. Clear the formatting from the footer text, delete the footer text, and then close the footer area. This time, you'll run the macro from the Macros dialog box.

7. Click the **View** tab, and then in the Macros group, click the **Macros** button. The Macros dialog box opens with InsertSlogan listed.

8. If necessary, click **InsertSlogan** to select it, and then click **Run**. The edited macro runs, and the footer is now centered and italicized as well as bold.

Now that you've recorded and tested the macro, you need to save the template with the macro.

Saving a Document with Macros

In order to save macros in a document, the document must be saved as a Macro-Enabled Document or a Macro-Enabled Template. If you try to save a document or a template that contains macros in the ordinary Word Document or Template file format, a warning dialog box appears, asking if you want to save the document as a "macro-free" document—in other words, without the macros. If you click Yes, the macro is not saved when you save the changes. If you click No, the Save As dialog box opens so that you can change the file type to one that is macro-enabled.

To save the template with the macro:

▶ **1.** On the Quick Access Toolbar, click the **Save** button 🖫. A dialog box opens, warning that the macro cannot be saved in a macro-free document and asking if you want to continue saving as a macro-free document. This is not what you want.

▶ **2.** Click **No**. The dialog box closes, and the Save As dialog box appears.

▶ **3.** Click the **Save as type arrow**. Notice that two file types are macro-enabled—a Word document and a Word template. You want to save this as a macro-enabled template.

▶ **4.** Click **Word Macro-Enabled Template**. The current folder, which is listed in the Address bar at the top of the dialog box, changes to the Custom Office Templates folder.

▶ **5.** Navigate to the location where you are storing your files.

▶ **6.** **sam**🔼 In the File name box, replace "Draft" with **Revised** so that the file name is NP_WD_8_Revised, and then click **Save**. The template is saved as a macro-enabled template.

Be sure to navigate to the folder where you are storing your files. Otherwise, the template will be stored in the Custom Office Templates folder on your hard drive.

Copying Macros to Another Document or Template

You can copy macros from one document or template to another. To do this, you open the same Organizer dialog box you used when you copied the Company Name style to the NP_WD_8_Styles template. In this case, you'll use the Macros tab instead of the Styles tab.

When you copy recorded macros that are stored in the NewMacros module of a particular document or template, you actually copy the entire module. If a document or template contains multiple macros and you want to copy only one of them, first copy the NewMacros module. Then, in the document or template to which you copied the macro, open the Visual Basic window and delete the code for the macros you don't want; or open the Macros dialog box, select each macro that you don't want, and then click Delete.

REFERENCE

Copying Macros to Another Document or Template

- On the ribbon, click the View tab.
- In the Macros group, click the Macros button to open the Macros dialog box.
- Click Organizer to open the Macro Project Items tab in the Organizer dialog box.
- Below the In Normal list on the right, click Close File.
- Below the empty box on the right, click Open File, navigate to the location of the document or template you want to copy macros to or from, click the file, and then click Open.
- In the list containing the macro you want to copy, click NewMacros.
- Click Copy.
- Click Close.

Sam wants you to copy the macro you recorded to the NP_WD_8_Styles template. You'll do this now.

To copy macros from the template to another template:

▶ **1.** On the ribbon, click the **View** tab, if necessary, and then in the Macros group, click the **Macros** button. The Macros dialog box opens.

▶ **2.** Click **Organizer**. The Organizer dialog box opens with the Macro Project Items tab selected. See Figure 8–40.

| Figure 8–40 | Macro Project Items tab in the Organizer dialog box |

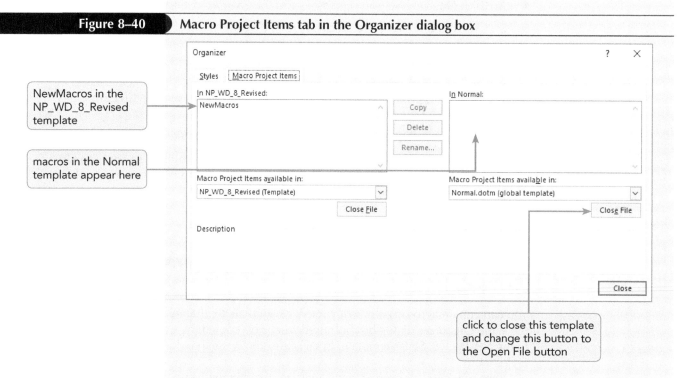

NewMacros in the NP_WD_8_Revised template

macros in the Normal template appear here

click to close this template and change this button to the Open File button

▶ **3.** Below the In Normal list on the right, click **Close File**. The command button changes to Open File.

▶ **4.** Click **Open File**, navigate to the location where you are storing your files, click the **NP_WD_8_Styles** template, and then click **Open**. In the Organizer dialog box, "To NP_WD_8_Styles" appears above the box on the right. The box is empty because that template does not contain any macros. In the In NP_WD_8_Revised list on the left, NewMacros is selected.

▶ **5.** Click **Copy**. NewMacros is copied to the To NP_WD_8_Styles list.

▶ **6.** Click **Close**. A dialog box opens, asking if you want to save the changes to "NP_WD_8_Styles."

▶ **7.** Click **Save**. A dialog box opens, asking if you want to continue saving the document as a macro-free document.

▶ **8.** Click **No**. The Save As dialog box opens.

▶ **9.** Click the **Save as type arrow**, and then click **Word Macro-Enabled Template**. The current folder changes to the Custom Office Templates folder.

▶ **10.** Navigate to the location where you are storing your files, change the file name to **NP_WD_8_StylesWithMacros**, and then click **Save**. The template is saved as a macro-enabled template named NP_WD_8_StylesWithMacros. Note that the NP_WD_8_Revised template is still the active template.

INSIGHT

Copying Macros When the Destination File Already Contains a NewMacros Module

If you want to copy a macro or macros contained in a NewMacros module from one template to another template that already contains a NewMacros module, you need to copy the code in the Visual Basic window. To do this, open both the template containing the macro you want to copy and the destination template, and then open the Visual Basic window in either template. In the Project pane on the left, one of the projects listed includes the name of the template containing the macro, and one includes the name of the template to which you want to copy the macro. Under the Project whose name includes the current template's name, NewMacros is selected. Next to the Project whose name includes the other open document's name, click the plus sign to expand the list. In the expanded list, click the plus sign next to Modules so you can see NewMacros in that document. Right-click that instance of NewMacros, and then click View Code to open the NewMacros Code window for that document. In the Code window that contains the code you want to copy, drag to select all of the code from the Sub line through the End Sub line, click Edit on the menu bar, and then click Copy. Make the other Code window active, click below the last End Sub line in that window, click Edit on the menu bar, and then click Paste. Then you can close the Visual Basic window and save the template that contains the pasted code.

Recording an AutoMacro

An **AutoMacro** is a macro that runs automatically when you perform certain basic operations, including starting Word, creating a document, opening a document, closing a document, and closing Word. AutoMacros have special reserved names so that when you create a macro using one of them, the macro runs at the point determined by the code built into that AutoMacro. For example, if you use the reserved name AutoNew to create a macro and save it in a template, the macro will run automatically when you create a new document based on that template. Figure 8–41 lists the AutoMacros and describes when each runs.

Figure 8–41   AutoMacros available in Word

AutoMacro Name	When the AutoMacro Runs
AutoExec	Runs each time you start Word
AutoNew	Runs when you start a new document
AutoOpen	Runs each time you open an existing document
AutoClose	Runs each time you close a document
AutoExit	Runs each time you exit Word

Sam wants to remind his employees that they must ask for identification that proves the age of each customer. He asks you to record an AutoNew macro in the NP_WD_8_ Revised template so that whenever a new document is created from the template, the document will scroll to display the line "Participant must provide proof of age." in the window and highlight it in yellow. Although the line is easy to see in the document now, after the legal text is added, it will be either at the bottom of the first page or on the second page.

To create the AutoNew macro:

▶ **1.** On the ribbon, click the **View** tab, if necessary.

▶ **2.** In the Macros group, click the **Macros arrow**, and then click **Record Macro**. The Record Macro dialog box opens.

▶ **3.** In the Macro name box, type **AutoNew**. This macro name tells Word to run the macro when you begin a new document based on this template.

▶ **4.** Click the **Store macro in arrow**, and then click **Documents Based On NP_WD_8_Revised** so the macro runs only if a new document is opened from the NP_WD_8_Revised template.

▶ **5.** Click in the **Description** box, and then type **Highlight line stating that participant must provide proof of age** in the box. You won't assign this macro to a toolbar or a keyboard shortcut because it will run automatically when the new document is opened.

▶ **6.** Click **OK**.

You're now ready to record the commands of the AutoNew macro. The first thing you need to do is scroll to display "Participant must provide proof of age." in the window and select the text. If the template was finished—that is, if the legal language was already added—you could use the arrow keys to move the insertion point down, and then select the text. Because adding the legal text will change the number of lines and paragraphs between the beginning of the document and the phrase, you need to use the Find command instead.

▶ **7.** On the ribbon, click the **Home** tab.

TIP

Click Special in the expanded Find and Replace dialog box to add special characters to the Find what box or the Replace with box.

▶ **8.** In the Editing group, click the **Find arrow**, and then click **Advanced Find**. The Find and Replace dialog box opens with the Find tab selected. You're using the Advanced Find box because when you click Find Next, the text is selected, not just highlighted as it is when you use the Navigation pane.

▶ **9.** In the Find what box, type **Participant must provide proof of age.**, and then click **Find Next**. The phrase is highlighted in the document.

▶ **10.** Click **Cancel** to close the Find and Replace dialog box.

▶ **11.** In the Font group, click the **Text Highlight Color** button 🖍 to highlight the selected text with yellow, and then press the ← key to deselect the highlighted text. This completes the operations for the AutoNew macro.

▶ **12.** On the status bar, click the **Stop Recording** button ▪. You don't want to save the template with the highlighting, so you'll remove the highlighting before saving the template again.

▶ **13.** Select the yellow highlighted text "Participant must provide proof of age."

▶ **14.** In the Font group, click the **Text Highlight Color arrow** 🖍⌄ then click **No Color**.

▶ **15.** Save the changes to the template.

Now you need to test your template. Remember, to create a new document based on a template, you need to double-click it in a File Explorer window.

When you create a document based on a macro-enabled template, the macros are not saved in the new document even if you save the new document as a macro-enabled document. However, the macros will still be available from within the document if the template and the document remain in their original folders. If you move the document to another computer, the macros will no longer be available to the document.

To test the AutoNew macro in a new document based on the NP_WD_8_Revised template:

1. On the taskbar, click the **File Explorer** button [icon]. The File Explorer window opens.

2. Navigate to the drive and folder where you are saving your files. Double-click the **NP_WD_8_Revised** template. A new document based on the template is created, and the prompt for the first Fill-in field appears, asking for the participant's name.

3. Type your name, and then click **OK**. The dialog box asking for the participant's date of birth opens.

4. Type **8/22/2002** and then click **OK**. The dialog box asking for the contact number opens.

5. Type **(206) 555-0125** and then click **OK**. The dialog box closes and the content of the document is displayed. The AutoNew macro runs and the phrase "Participant must provide proof of age." is highlighted.

   Trouble? If a dialog box opens warning you that macros in this project are disabled, you closed Word since you created the AutoNew macro. Click OK in the dialog box, and then click the Enable Content button in the Security Warning bar at the top of the document.

6. Save the document as a regular Word document—that is, not macro-enabled—named **NP_WD_8_Test** in the location specified by your instructor, and then close the document.

7. If you needed to change the Macro Settings in the Trust Center dialog box, open the Word Options dialog box, click **Trust Center** in the navigation pane, click **Trust Center Settings**, click the option button next to the setting originally applied on your computer, and then click **OK** twice.

8. Close the **NP_WD_8_Revised** template and close Word. A dialog box opens, asking if you want to save changes to "Building Blocks." This appears because when you copied the Quick Part from the NP_WD_8_Styles template to the NP_WD_8_Draft template, you first copied it to the Building Blocks template and then removed it from the Building Blocks template. Because you did not actually change the Building Blocks template, it does not matter if you save the changes.

   Trouble? If you took a break after the previous session, this dialog box already appeared and will not appear again. Skip Step 9.

9. Click **Don't Save**. Word closes.

Session 8.3 Quick Check

REVIEW

1. What is a macro?

2. What are two advantages of using a macro?

3. Briefly describe how to record a macro.

4. Why would you need to edit a macro?

5. How do you run a macro named MyMacro if it's not assigned to a button on the Quick Access Toolbar or to a shortcut key combination?

6. What are AutoMacros?

Review Assignments

Data Files needed for the Review Assignments: NP_WD_8-3.dotx, Support_WD_8_NewStyles.dotx, Support_WD_8_People.jpg

Students and alumni of Elliot Bay College can reserve the Rock Gym for special events, such as a birthday or graduation party. Sam Nguyen created another template that employees of the Rock Gym can use when they schedule an event. He wants you to add graphic elements and other elements, including file properties, and record macros to make filling out the form easier. Complete the following steps:

1. Open the template **NP_WD_8-3.dotx** located in the Word8 > Review folder included with your Data Files. Save the template as a macro-enabled template named **NP_WD_8_Form** in the location specified by your instructor. (*Hint*: After changing the file type to a macro-enabled template, make sure you navigate to the location where you are saving your files.)

2. Insert a rectangle shape that is the width of the document (8.5 inches wide) and 1.5 inches high. In the shape, type **Alexander Griffin Rock Gym**, press ENTER, and then type **Student/Alumni Event Registration**. Position the shape so it is aligned with the center of the page and with the top of the page.

3. Change the fill color of the shape to Brown, Accent 5, and then fill the shape with the Linear Down gradient in the Dark Variations section of the Gradient gallery. Remove the shape outline.

4. Copy the style named Company Name from the template **Support_WD_8_NewStyles.dotx**, located in the Word8 > Review folder, to the NP_WD_8_Form template, and then apply it to all of the text in the rectangle.

5. Change the text color of the text "Student/Alumni Event Registration" to Light Yellow, Background 2, and then change the stylistic set to the third set in the Individual list.

6. Add a custom paragraph border below the paragraph containing "Contact Number." Select the style that uses dashes separated by dots (the last style in the Styles list when you first open the Borders and Shading dialog box). Change the weight of the line to 1½ points. Increase the space between the bottom of the paragraph and the border to 8 points.

7. Insert another rectangle shape 2 inches high and 8.5 inches wide. Align the rectangle vertically with the bottom of the page and horizontally with the center of the page.

8. Remove the shape outline, and then fill the shape with the picture in the file **Support_WD_8_People.jpg**, located in the Word8 > Review folder. Adjust the picture so it is not distorted and so that the top of the picture aligns with the top of the rectangle.

9. Compress the photo in the rectangle to E-mail (96 ppi) and remove cropped areas.

10. Copy the Rock Gym Webpage Address Quick Part from the template named **Support_WD_8_NewStyles.dotx** located in the Word8 > Review folder to the NP_WD_8_Form template. Close the Support_WD_8_NewStyles template without saving changes.

11. Show all properties on the Info screen, and then add **Sam Nguyen** as the Manager property and **Events** as the Categories property.

12. Add the custom document property "Checked by" with your name as the value.

13. In the footer, type **Checked by**, press SPACEBAR, and then insert the custom property Checked by as a field. Press ENTER, type **Approved by**, press SPACEBAR, and then insert the Manager property as a content control.

14. In the paragraph containing "Current Date," after the Tab character, insert the Date field set to update automatically, and then edit the field codes so that the date and time appear in the format June 25, 2021 3:10 PM. (*Hint*: Update the field after you edit the field code.)

15. Add the following Fill-in fields, remembering to deselect the Preserve formatting during updates check box for each Fill-in field you create.

    a. After the Tab character next to "Event Date:" insert a Fill-in field with the prompt **Enter event date:**

    b. After the Tab character next to "Student/Alumnus Name:" insert a Fill-in field with the prompt **Enter student/alumnus name:**

    c. After the Tab character next to "Contact Number:" insert a Fill-in field with the prompt **Enter contact number:**

16. Translate the placeholder text "[Information about required deposit]" into Spanish, and then place the translation between square brackets in a paragraph below the English placeholder text. Translate the same text again into Chinese Simplified and Vietnamese, and place each translation in paragraphs below the Spanish translation.

17. Change the proofing language of the paragraphs in Spanish, Chinese, and Vietnamese to Spanish (United States), Chinese (Singapore), and Vietnamese, respectively. Then remove Spanish, Chinese (Singapore), and Vietnamese as proofing languages if they were not set as proofing languages before you did this step.

18. Add the text watermark SAMPLE arranged diagonally across the page.

19. Change your macro security settings, if necessary, so that macros are disabled with notification.

20. Record a macro named **InsertWebPageAddress** stored in documents based on NP_WD_8_Form. Type **Insert Rock Gym webpage address in header** as the Description. Assign the keyboard shortcut **ALT+CTRL+SHIFT+B** to the macro. When the macro starts recording, do the following:

    a. Click the Insert tab, click the Header button in the Header & Footer group, and then click Edit Header.

    b. Click the Insert tab. In the Text group, click the Explore Quick Parts button, and then click the Rock Gym Webpage Address Quick Part.

    c. Click the Home tab, and then in the Paragraph group, click the Align Right button.

    d. Click the Header & Footer Tools tab, and then in the Close group, click the Close Header and Footer button.

    e. Stop recording.

21. Edit the InsertWebPageAddress macro so that the header is center-aligned. In the header, remove the formatting, delete the text, and then close the Header area. Test the macro by running it.

22. Create an **AutoNew** macro stored in the NP_WD_8_Form template with **Highlight deposit percentage** as the description. The steps for this macro are:

    a. Use the Advanced Find box to find 10%.

    b. In the Font group on the Home tab, click the Text Highlight Color button.

    c. Press the ↓ key.

    d. Stop recording.

23. Remove the highlight you added while recording the AutoNew macro, and save the changes to the template.

24. Open a File Explorer window, navigate to the location where you are saving your files, and then double-click the NP_WD_8_Form template. Add **June 4, 2021** as the date of the event, your name as the student/alumnus name, and **(206) 555-0103** as the contact number.

25. Save the document as a regular Word document—that is, not macro-enabled—named **NP_WD_8_FormTest** in the location specified by your instructor, and then close the document.

26. If you changed the security settings for macros, reset the security to its original level. Close the NP_WD_8_Form template, saving changes if prompted, and close Word. Do not save the changes to the Building Blocks template.

APPLY

Case Problem 1

Data Files needed for this Case Problem: NP_WD_8-4.dotx, Support_WD_8_RealtyStyles.dotx

Franklin Realty Group Deb Surma owns Franklin Realty in Franklin, Massachusetts. When clients interested in purchasing a home first contact the agency, agents fill out a Housing Preferences sheet. Deb created a template to collect this information, and she asks you to complete it by adding Fill-in fields and formatting. Complete the following steps:

1. Open the template **NP_WD_8-4.dotx** from the Word8 > Case1 folder included with your Data Files, and then save it as a macro-enabled template named **NP_WD_8_Realty** in the location specified by your instructor. (Make sure you navigate to the correct folder after changing the file type.) Change your macro security settings, if necessary, so that macros are disabled with notification.

2. Copy the Franklin Realty and Web Address Quick Parts from the template **Support_WD_8_RealtyStyles.dotx**, located in the Word8 > Case1 folder to the NP_WD_8_Realty template. Edit the properties of the Franklin Realty Quick Part to include **Letterhead** as the description. Edit the properties of the Web Address Quick Part to include **Website** as the description.

3. Insert the Franklin Realty Quick Part at the beginning of the document. Click after the phone number, press ENTER, and then insert the Web Address Quick Part. If there is a blank paragraph below the website address, delete it.

4. Insert a rectangle that is 1.3 inches high and 6.5 inches wide. Remove the fill from the rectangle. Change the color of the shape outline to White, Background 1, Darker 50%. Change the weight of the shape outline to 6 points. Apply the Round bevel effect to the shape (using the Shape Effects menu).

5. Align the rectangle with the center and the top of the page. Change the left indent of the paragraphs inserted with the Franklin Realty and Web Address Quick Parts to 0.25 inches, and then change the space before the paragraph containing "Franklin Realty Group" to 18 points.

6. Copy the style Form Heading from the template **Support_WD_8_RealtyStyles.dotx**, located in the Word8 > Case1 folder to the NP_WD_8_Realty template. Apply the style to the text Housing Preferences.

7. Add your name as an Author property. On the Info screen in Backstage view, right-click the Author property Deb Surma, and then click Remove Person. Insert the Author property as a content control next to "Agent."

8. In the blank paragraph above "Name," insert the current date as a field that gets updated automatically, and then modify the field as needed so the date appears in the format 3 Mar 2021.

9. Below the paragraph containing "Phone," add a double-line border that is 1½ points wide. Change the space between the line and the paragraph to 12 points.

10. Next to each of the paragraphs below the date, add the following Fill-in fields. Do not preserve formatting for any of them.
    a. Name: **Client name**
    b. Address: **Client address**
    c. Phone: **Client phone**
    d. Type: **House or Condo?**
    e. Number of bedrooms: **# of bedrooms**
    f. Garage: **Garage required?**
    g. Central air: **Central air required?**
    h. Finished basement: **Finished basement required?**
    i. Fireplace: **Fireplace required?**

11. Add the custom text watermark ORIGINAL diagonally on the page.

12. Record a macro named **InsertFooter** stored in documents based on NP_WD_8_Realty to insert **Franklin Realty Group** as a footer. Add **Insert Franklin Realty Group as a footer** as the description. Assign the keyboard shortcut **ALT+CTRL+SHIFT+C** to the macro. As part of the macro, center the footer, format the text as Arial, and apply the middle stylistic set in the Individual section. (*Hint*: You need to press and hold SHIFT, and then press an arrow key to select the text to format it.)

13. Save the template, and then create a new document based on the NP_WD_8_Realty template. Enter your name in the Client name Fill-in field, 123 Main St., Franklin, MA 02038 as the address, (508) 555-0198 as the phone number, and reasonable responses in the rest of the prompt boxes. Save the document as a document named **NP_WD_8_RealtyTest** in the location specified by your instructor.

14. Change the macro security settings back to the original setting, if necessary, and then close all open documents. Do not save changes to the Building Blocks template, and do not save changes to the Support_WD_RealtyStyles template.

Case Problem 2

CHALLENGE

Data Files needed for this Case Problem: NP_WD_8-5.dotx, Support_WD_8_Planting.jpg, Support_WD_8_Potomac.dotx

Potomac Pro Groundskeeping   Scott Rivera is the owner of Potomac Pro Groundskeeping, a commercial landscaping company in Alexandria, Virginia. Scott wants to create a form listing the services his company offers for new customers. He wants to be able to give it to new customers so they can check off the services they want. Scott started creating the form, and he asked you to use the document he created to create a template for collecting customers' information. Complete the following steps:

1. Open the document **NP_WD_8-5.dotx**, located in the Word8 > Case2 folder included with your Data Files, and then save it as a macro-enabled template named **NP_WD_8_Landscaping** in the location specified by your instructor. Make sure you navigate to the correct folder after changing the file type.

2. Change the macro security settings, if necessary.

3. Copy the Quick Part named **Company Name** from the **Support_WD_8_Potomac.dotx** template to the NP_WD_8_Landscaping template. Close the Support_WD_8_Potomac template without saving changes. Insert the Company Name Quick Part in the first paragraph in the document.

4. Insert the Flowchart: Preparation shape (in the Flowchart section of the Shapes gallery), and then resize it so that it is 6.5 inches wide and 0.5 inch high. Align its center with the center of the page, and then position it so the green alignment guide indicates that the top of the shape aligns with the bottom of the paragraph containing the company name.

5. Apply the Subtle Effect – Blue, Accent 1 shape style in the second column of the Theme Styles section of the Shape Styles gallery, and then remove the shape outline.

6. In the shape, type **1430 Lincoln Avenue, Alexandria, VA 22314**. Change the font size to 12 points. Remove the space below this paragraph.

⊕ **Explore** 7. Display the Fill-in field code after "Company or Office Park." (*Hint*: Right-click to the right of the paragraph mark after the space following "Company or Office Park," and then click Toggle Field Codes.) Copy the field code, and then paste the copied code after the space following "Contact Name:" and after the space following "Street Address:". Edit the prompts in the pasted codes to match the text in each line.

⊕ **Explore** 8. Insert a Fill-in field after "City, State, Zip" with the prompt **City, State, Zip**, setting the default response to **Alexandria, VA 22314**. (*Hint*: Select the appropriate check box in the Field options section of the Field dialog box.)

9. Add a border above the paragraph containing "Services." Use the triple-line border that is just above the wavy line in the Style list and change its color to the Blue, Accent 1, Darker 25% color. Adjust the spacing between "Services" and the line to 8 points.

10. Select the "Sign a three-year contract for a 10% discount!" paragraph, and apply the second stylistic set in the Individual section.

✦ **Explore** 11. Insert the picture **Support_WD_8_Planting.jpg**, located in the Word8 > Case2 folder, as a picture watermark with the Washout effect.

12. Create an AutoNew macro that moves the insertion point to the end of the document by pressing CTRL+END, and then moves the insertion point up one line so that it is positioned after the space after "Lead Tech." Store the macro in the NP_WD_8_Landscaping template, and type **Position the insertion point after Lead Tech** as the Description.

13. Save the changes to the template.

✦ **Explore** 14. Translate the entire document into Spanish. Save the Spanish version as a macro-enabled template named **NP_WD_8_Spanish** in the location where you are saving your files. (Note that the Fill-in field prompts and the text in the shape will not be translated.)

15. Copy the macro you recorded from the NP_WD_8_Landscaping template to the NP_WD_8_Spanish template. Save the changes to the NP_WD_8_Spanish template.

16. Create a new document based on the NP_WD_8_Landscaping template. Enter **Riverside Industrial Park** as the office park name, your name as the customer name, enter **123 Main St.** as the street address, and then accept the default text for the city, state, and zip code. After the AutoNew macro runs, type **Scott** as the landscaper's name. Save the document as **NP_WD_8_LandscapingTest** in the location specified by your instructor.

17. Change the macro security settings back to the original setting, if necessary. Close all open documents. Do not save changes to the Building Blocks template.

OBJECTIVES

Session 9.1
- Plan and design an online form
- Split cells
- Rotate and align text
- Move gridlines
- Modify borders
- Change cell margins

Session 9.2
- Learn about content controls
- Insert content controls
- Modify the properties of content controls
- Modify placeholder text in content controls
- Test content controls

Session 9.3
- Learn about cell referencing in formulas
- Use a formula in a table
- Group content controls
- Restrict document editing for a form
- Fill in an online form

Creating Online Forms Using Advanced Table Techniques

Developing an Order Form

Case | *SS Mississippi Star*

Emi Nakata is the activities director on the SS *Mississippi Star*, a steamboat cruise ship that cruises the Mississippi River between Memphis, Tennessee and New Orleans, Louisiana. Several times a year, she plans themed cruises, such as cruises that provide a focus on art, dance, bird watching, genealogy, or cooking. She is currently planning a crafts cruise, and one of the activities that will be offered is painting pottery. Passengers who participate in this activity can pick up their finished pieces after they are dry, have them delivered to their cabins, or pay a fee to have the pieces shipped home. Emi asks you to create an online form to collect each participant's name and contact information as well as their preference for collecting the finished pottery pieces.

You'll start with a partially completed Word table that Emi created. First, you'll modify the structure and the format of the table. Next, you'll add different types of content controls and special fields to accept specific types of information, and you'll customize the placeholder text to help the user fill out the form. You'll also add a formula that will calculate the shipping fee if a passenger wants to ship their painted piece home. When the form is complete, you'll add a password to protect the form from being changed accidentally, and then you'll test the form by filling in sample information.

STARTING DATA FILES

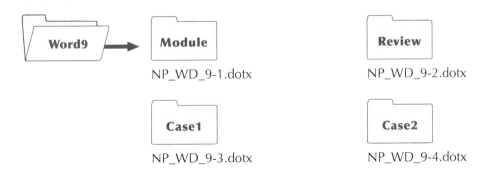

Word9 → Module
NP_WD_9-1.dotx

Review
NP_WD_9-2.dotx

Case1
NP_WD_9-3.dotx

Case2
NP_WD_9-4.dotx

Session 9.1 Visual Overview:

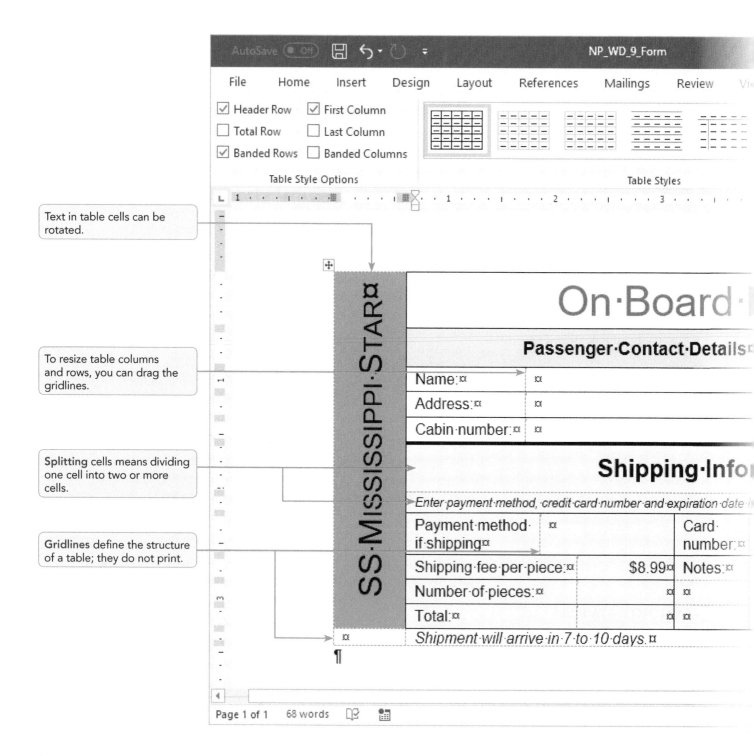

Text in table cells can be rotated.

To resize table columns and rows, you can drag the gridlines.

Splitting cells means dividing one cell into two or more cells.

Gridlines define the structure of a table; they do not print.

Custom Table

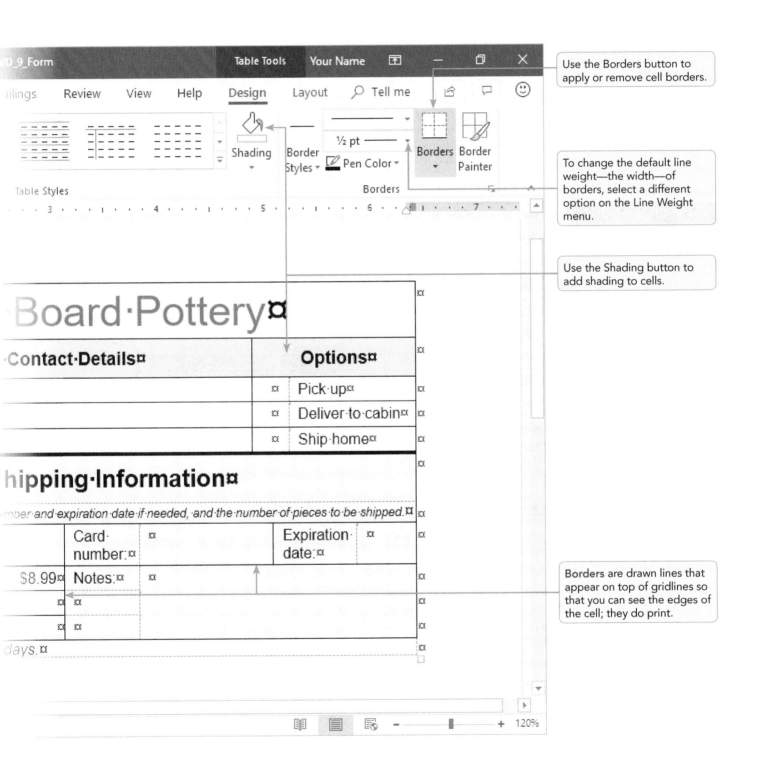

Use the Borders button to apply or remove cell borders.

To change the default line weight—the width—of borders, select a different option on the Line Weight menu.

Use the Shading button to add shading to cells.

Borders are drawn lines that appear on top of gridlines so that you can see the edges of the cell; they do print.

Creating and Using Online Forms

An online form is a document that contains labels and corresponding blank areas in which a user enters the information requested. When you create an online form using Word, it's a good idea to use a template file rather than a regular Word file so that users can't change the form itself when entering their information.

To create an online form, you need to add content controls. You have used content controls that display information about a document, such as the document title or the author name. When a content control is linked to information in a document, such as the document title, that information is inserted in the document wherever that control appears. When you insert a content control in a form, you create an area that can contain only the type of information that you specify, such as text or a date. You can also specify a format for the information stored in a control and create rules that determine what kind of information the control will accept. For example, Figure 9–1 shows a form with different types of information, including text, a date, and a value selected from a list.

| Figure 9–1 | Portion of an online form |

The fact that you can specify the type of information that appears in a control, thereby allowing only certain types of data, helps prevent users from entering incorrect information. Placeholder text in each control tells the user what information is required for that particular part of the form.

Planning and Designing the Form

The online form you'll create for Emi will consist of a Word table that will contain space for the following:

• The passenger's contact information and cabin number

• A section that lists the passenger's choice for getting the pottery home (pick up, deliver to the passenger's cabin, or ship to their home)

• A section that lists the shipping fee per piece and calculates the total and lists the passenger's payment choice

• A notes area

Figure 9–2 shows Emi's sketch for the online form. She wants you to use a table structure to keep the elements organized.

Figure 9–2   Sketch of the structure of the online form

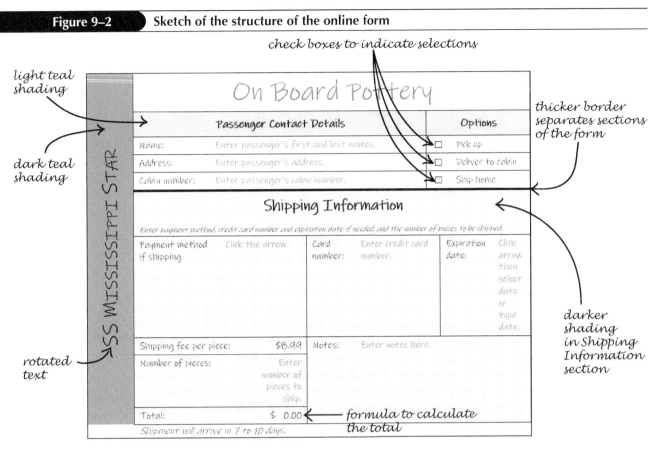

One advantage of online forms is that programmers can extract the data that users enter and export it to a database. If you need to design a form whose information will be extracted and exported to a database, include only one piece of data or information in each cell or content control. For example, the type of credit card, the credit card number, and the credit card expiration date would need to be stored in three separate content controls. This also applies to names and addresses. First and last names should be in separate content controls, and each part of an address—the street address, city, state, and zip code—should be in separate content controls.

The form in this module has been formatted so you can focus on all the components you can use to create a form without spending too much time executing the same skills. Therefore, in this form there is only one container for the passenger's first and last names, and only one container for the passenger's address. Also note that most people have an email address and more than one phone number. Normally, containers for these pieces of information would need to be included in a form. Again, to keep the form simple for this module, this information is not collected.

PROSKILLS

Decision Making: Using a Table as the Structure for a Form

Planning the layout of a form is important. If you skip this step, you could end up with a form that is so confusing that users miss important sections. You want the labels and areas in which the user enters the data to be clear and easy to understand. A table is an easy way to organize a form in a logical way. The rows and columns provide a natural organization for labels and areas where the user fills in information. You can add shading and formatting to specific cells to make certain parts of the table stand out or to divide the form into sections. Taking the time to plan and make decisions about how data should appear in a form will result in a form that is easy to build and easy for someone to fill out, and one that collects data that is useful and accurate.

Creating a Custom Table for a Form

Emi created the table for the form and saved it as a template. You'll customize the table based on Emi's design shown earlier in Figure 9–2.

To open the template and save it with a new name:

▶ 1. **sam** ↓ Use the Open command in Backstage view to open the template **NP_WD_9-1.dotx**, which is located in the Word9 > Module folder included with your Data Files.

▶ 2. Save the file as a Word template named **NP_WD_9_Form** in the location specified by your instructor. You will not be including any macros in this template.

▶ 3. If necessary, change the Zoom level to **120%**, and then display the rulers and nonprinting characters.

To format the table to match Emi's sketch, you'll start by merging some cells and then inserting a new column on the left side of the table for the name of the form.

Merging and Splitting Cells

As you have seen, you can merge cells in the same row, the same column, or the same rectangular block of rows and columns. To begin formatting the form, you need to merge some of the cells that contain headings so that they more clearly label the sections of the form.

To merge cells in the table:

▶ 1. In the first row, click in the cell containing "On Board Pottery," and then drag across the three blank cells to the right of that cell. The four cells in the first row are selected.

TIP

You can also click the Eraser button in the Draw group on the Table Tools Layout tab, and then click a gridline between cells to merge the two cells.

▶ 2. On the ribbon, click the **Table Tools Layout** tab, and then in the Merge group, click the **Merge Cells** button. The four cells are merged into one cell.

▶ 3. In the second row, merge the cells containing "Passenger Contact Details" and the blank cell to its right, and then merge the cells containing "Options" and the blank cell to its right. The second row in the table now contains two merged cells.

▶ 4. In the last column, merge the empty cell to the right of the cell containing "Notes" with the two cells beneath it. Compare your screen to Figure 9–3.

Figure 9–3   **Merged cells in the table**

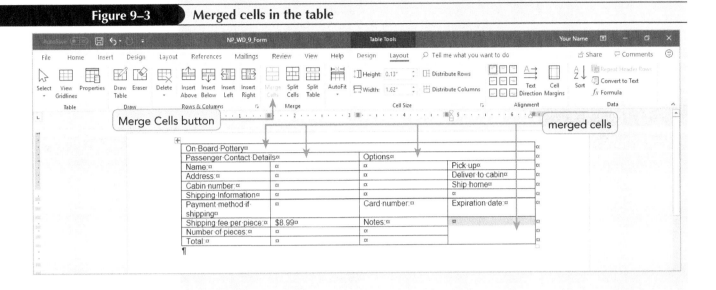

Emi's sketch shows the ship name to the left of the table, rotated so it reads from bottom to top on a shaded background without any borders. To add this to the form, you will insert a new blank column as the first column in the table, then you will merge the cells of the new column to form one long cell.

To insert a new column and merge the cells:

▶ **1.** In the first row, click in the "On Board Pottery" cell.

▶ **2.** On the Table Tools Layout tab, in the Rows & Columns group, click the **Insert Left** button. A new column is inserted to the left of the current column, and all the cells in the new column are selected.

▶ **3.** In the Merge group, click the **Merge Cells** button. The new column now contains one merged cell.

▶ **4.** Type **SS Mississippi Star**.

In Emi's sketch, there is a note below the table. You need to add a new row at the bottom of the table to contain this note.

To add a new bottom row and merge the cells:

▶ **1.** Click in the first column in the cell containing "SS Mississippi Star," if necessary.

▶ **2.** On the Table Tools Layout tab, in the Rows & Columns group, click the **Insert Below** button. A new second row is inserted. This is because the merged cell in the first column is considered to be in the first row.

▶ **3.** On the Quick Access Toolbar, click the **Undo** button ⤺. The new second row is removed.

▶ **4.** In the last row, click the "Total" cell, and then in the Rows & Columns group, click the **Insert Below** button. A new bottom row is added to the table.

▸ **5.** In the new bottom row, click in the second cell, and then type the following: **Shipment will arrive in 7 to 10 days.** (including the period).

▸ **6.** In the last row, merge the cells in the second, third, fourth, and fifth columns. The last row now contains two cells—one in the first column, and one merged cell that spans the second through fifth columns. See Figure 9–4.

Figure 9–4 Table with new column and row

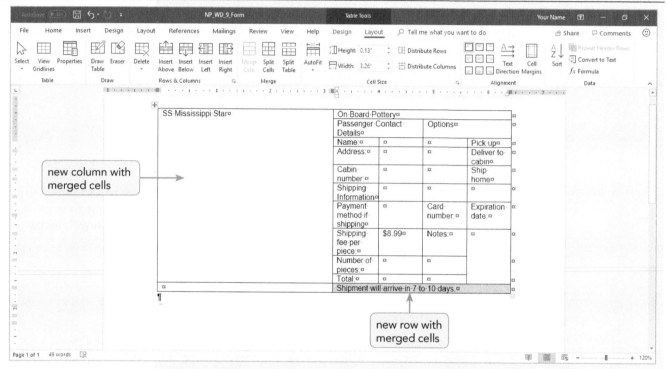

new column with merged cells

new row with merged cells

▸ **7.** Save the template.

You can also split cells. If you split cells vertically, you increase the number of columns in a row. If you split cells horizontally, you increase the number of rows in a column. If you select multiple adjacent cells, when you split them, you can specify whether you want to first merge the selected cells into one cell before the split, or whether you want each cell split individually.

Splitting Cells

- Select the cell or cells that you want to split.
- On the ribbon, click the Table Tools Layout tab, and then in the Merge group, click the Split Cells button.
- In the Split Cells dialog box, check the Merge cells before split check box if you want the cell contents to merge into one cell before they split into more columns or rows; or uncheck the Merge cells before split check box if you want the cell contents to split into columns and rows without merging first.
- Set the number of columns and rows into which you want to split the current cell or cells.
- Click OK.

In Emi's sketch, there is a cell to the right of the cell containing "Card number," and there is a cell to the right of the cell containing "Expiration date." To create these cells, you will split each of those cells into two columns.

To split cells into two columns:

▶ **1.** In the seventh row in the table, select the last two cells in the row (the cells containing "Card number" and "Expiration date").

▶ **2.** On the Table Tools Layout tab, in the Merge group, click the **Split Cells** button. The Split Cells dialog box opens. See Figure 9–5.

| Figure 9–5 | Split Cells dialog box |

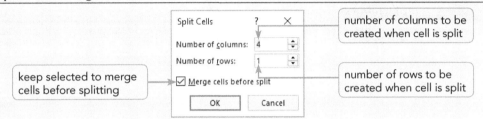

The values in the Number of columns and Number of rows boxes are based on the number of cells selected. Also, the Merge cells before split check box is selected. With these options, the two selected cells will be merged into one cell, and all of the text in the two cells will be combined into that one merged cell. Then the merged cell will be split into four columns, and the text in the selected cells will be distributed in the new cells. In this case, it would place the text in the first two cells created by the split. This is not what you want. Instead, you want each individual cell to split so that the text from each of the original selected cells appears in the left cell in each pair and a new cell is created to the right of each of the original two cells.

▶ **3.** In the Split Cells dialog box, click the **Merge cells before split** check box to deselect it. The value in the Number of columns box changes to 2. Now each of the selected cells will be split into two columns and one row.

▶ **4.** Click **OK**. Each selected cell is split into two columns, with the text from each of the original selected cells appearing in the left cell in each pair.

In Emi's sketch, there is a row below the row containing "Shipping Information," but this row is not included in the Word table she created. You could insert a row using one of the Insert commands in the Rows & Columns group on the Table Tools Layout tab. But because you need to merge the cell containing "Shaded Area for Office Use Only" with the cells to its right, you'll use the Split Cells button to merge the cells in this row into one cell, and then split the merged row into two rows.

To split the "Shipping Information" cell into two rows:

▶ **1.** Select the cell containing "Shipping Information" and the three blank cells to its right.

TIP

To split a table into two or more tables, click in the row that you want to be the first row in the new table, and then on the Table Tools Layout tab, in the Merge group, click the Split Table button.

▶ **2.** On the Table Tools Layout tab, in the Merge group, click the **Split Cells** button. This time, you will keep the Merge cells before split check box selected because you want the cells in the row to merge into one cell before splitting into two rows so that each row contains only one wide cell.

▶ **3.** In the Number of columns box, type **1**, press **TAB** to move to the Number of rows box, type **2**, and then click **OK**. The selected cells merge into one cell, and then that cell is split into two rows.

▶ **4.** Click in the new blank cell below "Shipping Information," and then type **Enter payment method, credit card number and expiration date if needed, and the number of pieces to be shipped.** (including the period). See Figure 9–6.

| Figure 9–6 | Form after splitting cells |

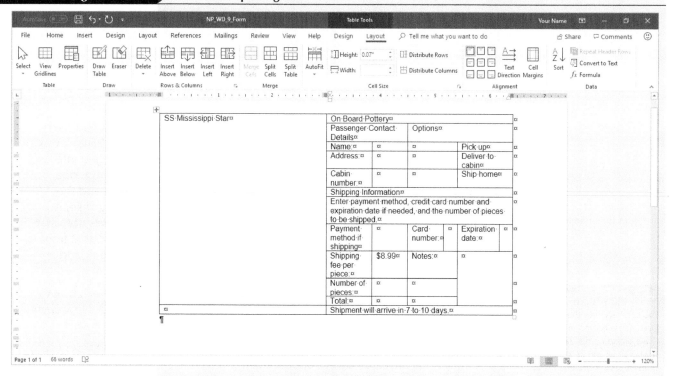

▶ **5.** Save the template.

Rotating Text in a Cell

You can rotate text in a cell to read from the top to the bottom or from the bottom to the top. In Emi's sketch, the ship name in the first column reads from the bottom of the column up to the top. You'll do this next.

To rotate the text in the first column:

▶ **1.** Click in the merged cell in the first column. You don't need to select any text because the command to rotate the text in the cell applies to all the text in the cell.

2. On the Table Tools Layout tab, in the Alignment group, click the **Text Direction** button. The text in the first column rotates so that it reads from top to bottom. Note that the icon on the Text Direction button changed to reflect this.

3. Click the **Text Direction** button again. The text in the cell and the arrows on the button change to show the text reading from bottom to top. See Figure 9–7. If you clicked the button again, the text would read from left to right again.

Figure 9–7   **Cell with rotated text**

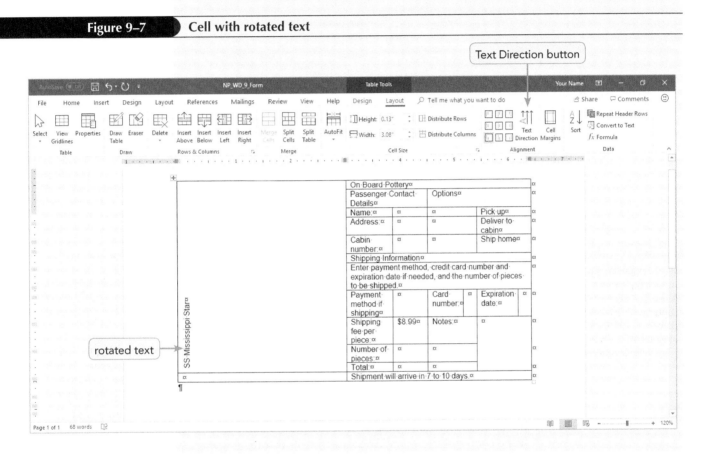

Moving Gridlines to Change Column Widths and Row Heights

Next, you need to adjust the cell sizes in the table. To match Emi's sketch, you need to format individual cells within a column to be different widths. The default setting for tables in Word is for the columns to automatically resize larger if needed to accommodate long text strings. For many tables, this works well. For this form, however, you need to be able to control the column widths. Therefore, before you change the column widths and row heights in the table, you need to change the table property that causes the columns to automatically resize to fit the text. After you do that, if you set column widths, they will stay the width you specify.

To turn off automatic resizing in the table's properties:

1. On the Table Tools Layout tab, in the Table group, click the **Properties** button. The Table Properties dialog box opens with the Table tab selected.

2. Click **Options**. The Table Options dialog box opens. See Figure 9–8.

Figure 9–8   **Table Properties and Table Options dialog boxes**

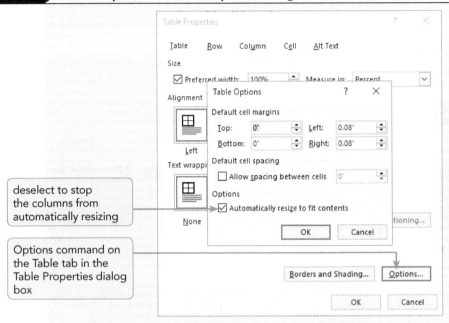

deselect to stop
the columns from
automatically resizing

Options command on
the Table tab in the
Table Properties dialog
box

TIP

You can also click the
AutoFit button in the Cell
Size group on the Table
Tools Layout tab, and then
click Fixed Column Width
to stop columns from
automatically resizing.

▶ **3.** Click the **Automatically resize to fit contents** check box to deselect it. This will stop the columns from automatically resizing.

▶ **4.** Click **OK**, and then click **OK** in the Table Properties dialog box.

You can resize columns and rows by specifying column widths and row heights in the boxes in the Cell Size group on the Table Tools Layout tab; by changing the measurements on the Row and Column tabs in the Table Properties dialog box; or by dragging the gridlines in the table. To resize the width of individual cells, you first select the cell, and then type a measurement in the Width box in the Cell Size group on the Table Tools Layout tab or drag the left or right gridline.

When you resize columns, rows, and cells by dragging the gridlines, you can see how the change in size affects the contents of the cells. Also, when you drag gridlines, the columns, rows, or cells on either side of the gridline you are dragging adjust so that the overall table width is not affected. If you change sizes by entering new values in the Height and Width boxes in the Cell Size group on the Table Tools Layout tab, only the column or row whose measurement you changed is affected. This means that the table width or height changes because none of the other columns or rows adjust.

Now that you have created the basic table structure, you will adjust cell widths and heights to match Emi's sketch.

To change the width of columns:

▶ **1.** Click in the first column, if necessary. On the ruler, the Move Table Column marker ⊞ between the first two columns is positioned at the 3-inch mark.

▶ **2.** On the Table Tools Layout tab, in the Cell Size group, click in the **Width** box, type **0.7**, and then press **ENTER**. The first column is now only 0.7 inches wide, and the table no longer stretches horizontally from margin to margin. This is because only the width of the first column changed.

3. On the Quick Access Toolbar, click the **Undo** button ↺. The width of the first column changes back to its original width of 3.08 inches.

4. Position the pointer on top of the gridline between the first two columns so that the pointer changes to the column resize pointer ◄║►.

5. Press and hold the mouse button, drag the gridline to the left until the Move Table Column marker ▦ is just to the right of the 0.5-inch mark on the ruler, and then release the mouse button. The measurement in the Width box in the Cell Size group on the Table Tools Layout tab should be 0.69". As the width of the first column changed, the width of the second column adjusted so that the overall width of the table stayed the same. See Figure 9–9.

| Figure 9–9 | **Resized columns** |

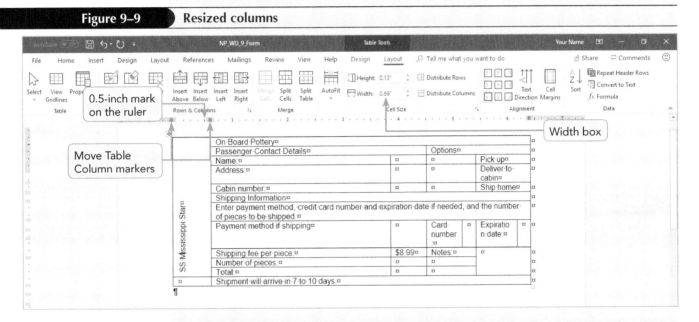

Trouble? If the measurement in the Width box in the Cell Size group on the Table Tools Layout tab is not exactly 0.69", don't worry about it.

In Emi's sketch, the width of the cells in the Passenger Contact Details section is different than the width of the cells in the rows beneath it. To change the width of some of the cells in a column, you need to select those cells first. Then you can drag the gridline to the right of the selected cells.

To change the width of selected cells:

1. Click in the cell containing "Name," and then drag down through the next two cells below it. The three cells from the cell containing "Name" through the cell containing "Cabin number" are selected.

2. Position the pointer on top of the gridline to the right of the selected cells so that the pointer changes to the column resize pointer ◄║►.

3. Press and hold the mouse button, drag the gridline to the left until the gridline is just to the right of the cell marker in the "Cabin number" cell, and then release the mouse button. The Move Table Column marker ▦ is just to the left of the 1.625-inch mark on the ruler (the 1⅝-inch mark), and the measurement in the Width box in the Cell Size group on the Table Tools Layout tab should be 1.12".

Trouble? If the measurement in the Width box in the Cell Size group on the Table Tools Layout tab is not exactly 1.12", don't worry about it.

If you press and hold ALT while you are dragging a gridline, the measurement between gridlines in the table appears on the ruler between the Move Table Column markers. You need to make several more adjustments to cell widths in the table so that the form will match Emi's sketch. You will press ALT while you are dragging so that your screen matches the figures in this text as closely as possible.

To change the width of selected cells to exact measurements:

1. Select the three cells to the right of the "Name," "Address," and "Cabin number" cells.

2. Press and hold **ALT**, position the pointer over the gridline on the right side of the selected cells so that it changes to ‹‖›, press and hold the mouse button, and then drag the pointer to the right slightly. The ruler changes to indicate the exact widths between the Move Table Column markers. (Note that these widths are a little narrower than the cell width.) See Figure 9–10.

| Figure 9–10 | Moving a gridline while pressing ALT |

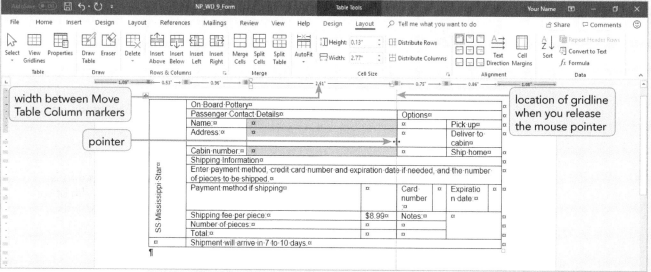

Trouble? When you press ALT, Key Tips—labels identifying the letter you can press on the keyboard to select a command on the ribbon—appear on the ribbon. You can ignore them while you are resizing the column.

Trouble? The exact measurement between the second and third Move Table Column markers on your screen might not match the measurement shown in Figure 9–10. Do not be concerned about this.

3. Using the measurements on the ruler as a guide and keeping **ALT** pressed, drag the gridline to the right until the distance between the Move Table Column markers marking the borders of the selected cells is about 3", and

then release the mouse button and **ALT**. The width of the selected cells and the cells to the right of the selected cells changes.

4. Select the three empty cells to the left of the cells containing "Pick up," "Deliver to cabin," and "Ship home," press and hold **ALT**, and then drag the gridline on the right side of the selected cells to the left until the distance between the Move Table Column markers marking the borders of the selected cells is about 0.2" and the width of the cells to the right of the selected cells is about 1". (Make sure "Deliver to cabin" stays on one line.)

5. Click in the cell containing "Passenger Contact Details."

6. On the Table Tools Layout tab, in the Table group, click the Select button, and then click Select Cell. The cell containing "Passenger Contact Details" is selected.

7. Drag the gridline on the right side of the selected cell to the right so that it aligns with the gridline on the right of the three empty cells below it. If you press ALT while you are dragging, the measurement between the two Move Table Column markers marking the borders of the selected cell is about 4.11".

   Trouble? If you have trouble aligning the gridlines, press ALT while you drag.

   Trouble? If the widths of other cells below the "Passenger Contact Details" cell also change, you clicked in the "Passenger Contact Details" cell instead of selecting it. Undo the width change, and then repeat Steps 5 through 7, taking care to select the entire cell in Step 6 before dragging the gridline in Step 7.

8. Select the cell containing "Payment method if shipping," resize it so the measurement between the two Move Table Column markers marking the left and right edges of the selected cell is about 1.1", and then resize the cell to its right so the measurement between the two Move Table Column markers marking the gridlines of the selected cell is also about 1.1".

9. Resize the cell containing "Card number" so the measurement between the two Move Table Column markers marking the left and right edges of the selected cell is about 0.55", resize the cell to its right so the measurement between the two Move Table Column markers marking the left and right edges of the selected cell is about 1.1", and then resize the cell containing "Expiration date" so the measurement between the two Move Table Column markers marking the left and right edges of the selected cell is about 0.63".

10. Select the cell containing "Shipping fee per piece" and the two cells below it, and then resize the selected cells so the measurement between the two Move Table Column markers marking the left and right edges of the selected cells is about 1.45".

11. Select the three cells to the right of the cells containing "Shipping fee per piece," "Number of pieces," and "Total," and then resize the selected cells so the measurement between the two Move Table Column markers marking the left and right edges of the selected cells is about 0.75" and the right gridline of the selected cells aligns with the left gridline of the "Card number" cell in the row above the selected cells.

12. Select the cell containing "Notes" and the two empty cells below it, and then resize the selected cells so that the distance between the Move Table Column markers marking the left and right edges of the selected cells is about 0.55" and the right gridline aligns with the right gridline of the "Card number" cell. Compare your table to the one shown in Figure 9–11.

Figure 9–11	Table with resized columns

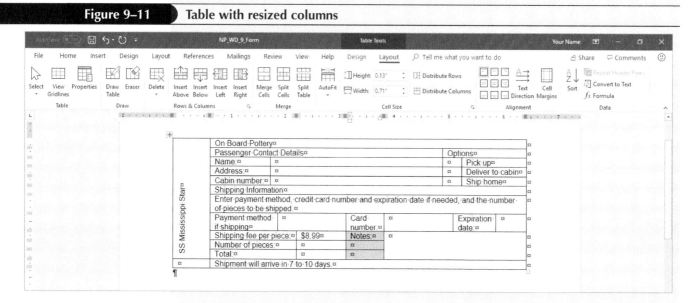

Trouble? If the measurement in the Width box in the Cell Size group on the Table Tools Layout tab is not 0.69" for the first column, resize the first column so that the distance between the Move Table Column markers is 0.53". If the measurement in the Width box is not 1.12" for the cells containing "Name," "Address," and "Cabin number," select those three cells and resize them so that the measurement between the Move Table Column markers is 0.97".

You can also adjust the height of rows in a table. To visually separate the various sections of the form, you'll increase the height of the section heading rows.

To change the height of the section heading rows by moving the gridlines:

1. Click anywhere in the table, making sure that no text is selected, and then position the pointer over the bottom gridline of the row containing "Passenger Contact Details" and "Options" so that it changes to the row resize pointer ⬍.

2. Press and hold **ALT**, and then drag the bottom gridline down until the distance between the Adjust Table Row markers on the vertical ruler that mark the top and bottom edges of the row is about 0.3".

3. Drag the bottom gridline of the row containing "Shipping Information" down until the distance between the Adjust Table Row markers on the vertical ruler that mark the top and bottom edges of the row is about 0.4" and the row is approximately double its original height. See Figure 9–12.

Figure 9–12 **Rows resized in table**

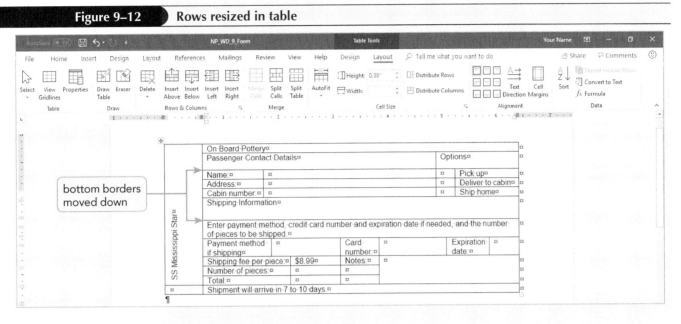

▶ **4.** Save the template.

Using the AutoFit Command

The AutoFit button in the Cell Size group on the Table Tools Layout tab offers some additional options for changing the width of table columns. When you first create a table, its columns are all the same width, and the table stretches from the left to the right margin. If you enter data that is wider than the cell you are typing in, the data wraps in the cell to the next line. (Note that if the word you type is long and does not contain any spaces, the column will widen as much as needed to fit the word until the columns to its right are 0.15 inches wide, at which point the text will wrap in the cell.) If you want the columns to resize wider to accommodate data, you can select the table, click the AutoFit button, and then click AutoFit Contents. When you do this, columns that contain data that is longer than the width of the column will resize wider, if possible, to accommodate the widest entry. If the widest entry in a column is narrower than the column, the AutoFit Contents command will resize that column narrower to just fit that data. If you have adjusted column widths, either manually or by using the AutoFit Contents command, so that the table no longer stretches from the left to the right margin, you can click the AutoFit button and then click AutoFit Window. This will resize all the columns proportionally so that the table stretches from the left to the right margin. This command is useful if you paste a table copied from another file and it is too wide to fit on the page.

Aligning Cell Content

Now that you've sized the rows and columns appropriately, you can align the text within cells. The text in the cells of a table is, by default, left-aligned and positioned at the top of the cell. On the Table Tools Layout tab, in the Alignment group, there are nine buttons you can use to align text in a cell. You can align text at the left and right edges of a cell, and you can center-align it. You can also change the vertical alignment to position the text at the top, middle, or bottom of a cell.

To make the form more attractive and easier to read, you'll center the text for the section headings and change the alignment of the text in the first column.

To change the alignment of text in cells:

1. In the first row, click in the "On Board Pottery" cell. On the Table Tools Layout tab, in the Alignment group, the Align Top Left button ⊟ is selected. Because this row is only tall enough to fit one line of text, you don't need to change the vertical alignment, but you do need to center it horizontally.

2. In the Alignment group, click the **Align Top Center** button ⊟.

3. Select the cells containing "Passenger Contact Details" and "Options." The text in these cells needs to be centered both horizontally and vertically.

4. In the Alignment group, click the **Align Center** button ⊟.

5. Align the text in the cell containing "Shipping Information" both horizontally and vertically.

   The empty cells in the Options section will contain check boxes. The check boxes will look better if they are centered horizontally and vertically. And the labels in the cells next to them would look better if they were center-aligned vertically.

6. Click in the cell to the left of the "Pick up" cell, drag down to the cell to the left of the "Ship home" cell, and then in the Alignment group, click the **Align Center** button ⊟.

7. Click in the "Pick up" cell, drag down to the "Ship home" cell, and then in the Alignment group, click the **Align Center Left** button ⊟.

8. Select the cell containing "$8.99" and the two cells below it, and then in the Alignment group, click the **Align Top Right** button ⊟.

9. In the first column, click in the cell containing the rotated text. The nine alignment buttons in the Alignment group change so the lines are vertical instead of horizontal.

10. In the Alignment group, click the **Align Center** button ⊡. The text in the first column is center-aligned. See Figure 9–13.

Figure 9–13 **Table after changing the alignment of text in cells**

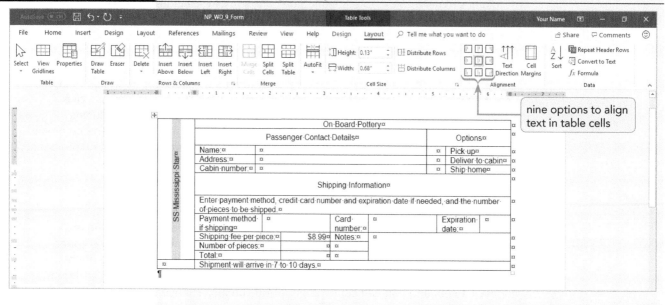

11. Save the template.

Removing Borders

A table is defined by its gridlines; borders are lines that appear on top of gridlines. Gridlines do not print, but borders do. You can display or hide gridlines while you are working; but even when hidden, the gridlines still define the table's structure. When you create a table, ½-point borders appear along all the gridlines by default.

To match Emi's sketch, you'll remove the borders between all the labels and the empty cells next to them. You'll begin by removing the right border of cells that contain the labels for the passenger information. You will do this by deselecting commands on the Borders menu.

To remove borders from cells using the commands on the Borders menu:

▸ **1.** Under "Passenger Contact Details," select the cells containing "Name," "Address," and "Cabin number."

▸ **2.** On the ribbon, click the **Table Tools Design** tab.

▸ **3.** In the Borders group, click the **Borders arrow** ▦ ▾. The Borders menu opens. All of the border options in the Borders menu are selected except No Border and the two diagonal borders. See Figure 9–14.

| Figure 9–14 | Borders menu |

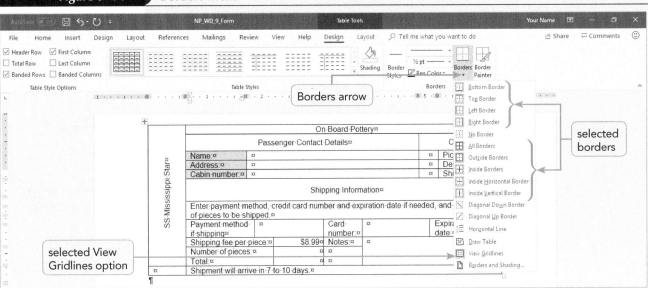

Trouble? If the Borders menu did not open, you clicked the Borders button instead of the arrow beneath it. Undo the change, and then repeat Step 3.

▸ **4.** Click **Right Border**. The menu closes, and the right border is removed from the selected cells.

▸ **5.** Deselect the cells. If gridlines are visible, a dotted line appears where the right border was; if gridlines are not visible, you don't see anything where the right border was.

▸ **6.** Click in one of the cells whose right border you removed, and then click the **Borders arrow** ▦ ▾ again. Note that now, not only is the Right Border option deselected, but all of the Borders options below it are deselected as well.

TIP

You can also click the View Gridlines button in the Table group on the Table Tools Layout tab to display or hide gridlines.

7. If the View Gridlines command at the bottom of the Borders button menu is not selected, click **View Gridlines**; if it is selected, click a blank area of the document to close the Borders button menu without making any changes. Even though you removed the right border from these cells, the gridline that defines the structure of these cells is still there. See Figure 9–15.

Figure 9–15 | **Table after a border between columns is removed**

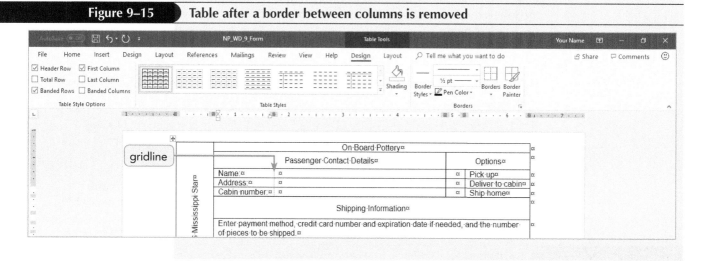

Sometimes it's hard to figure out exactly which commands on the Borders menu should be selected or deselected, so you might find it easier to use the Borders and Shading dialog box to modify or remove borders. You'll use this method to remove the borders to the left of the labels in the Options section.

To remove borders using the Borders and Shading dialog box:

1. Select the three cells containing labels under "Options" (from the cell containing "Pick up" through the cell containing "Ship home").

2. On the Table Tools Design tab, in the Borders group, click the **Borders arrow** ⊞, and then click **Borders and Shading**. The Borders and Shading dialog box opens with the Borders tab on top. See Figure 9–16.

Figure 9–16   Borders tab in the Borders and Shading dialog box

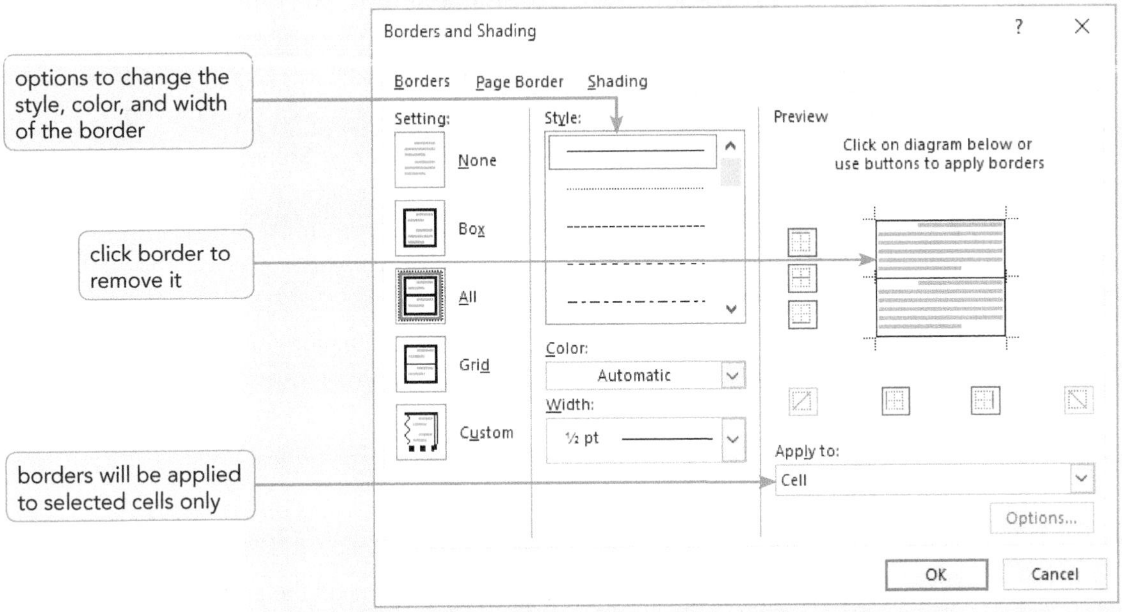

options to change the style, color, and width of the border

click border to remove it

borders will be applied to selected cells only

In the Apply to box at the bottom of the Preview section, note that "Cell" is selected. This means any changes you make will be applied to each of the selected cells. The Preview section illustrates the borders on the selected cells. In the Setting list, the All button is selected.

3. In the Preview section, click the left border. The border disappears. Notice that in the Setting list, the All button is deselected, and the Custom button is now selected.

   Trouble? If one of the other borders disappeared or if you added a vertical border, click that border to make it reappear or disappear, and then click the left border in the Preview section again.

4. Click **OK**, and then click a blank area of the table to deselect the cells. The left border of the cells you had selected is removed.

Next, you need to remove the borders between the cells containing "Payment method if shipping," "Card number," and "Expiration date" and the empty cells to the left of each of those cells. You also need to remove the borders between the cells containing the labels related to shipping fees and the empty cells to the right. You'll also remove all the borders in the Notes section so it looks like one large section. Finally, you will remove the borders around the sentence in the last row and around the form name in the first column.

To remove additional borders:

1. Remove the right border of the cells containing "Payment method if shipping," "Card number," and "Expiration date."

2. Remove the right border of the cells containing "Shipping fee per piece," "Number of pieces," and "Total."

3. Select the cell containing "Notes" and the two cells below it.

4. On the Table Tools Design tab, in the Borders group, click the **Borders arrow** ⊞ ⌄, and then click **Inside Horizontal Border**. The borders between the three selected cells are removed. Keep the three cells selected.

5. In the Borders group, click the **Borders arrow** ⊞ ⌄, and then click **Right Border**. The right borders of the selected cells are removed.

6. Remove the border between the cell containing "Shipping Information" and the cell beneath it.

7. In the last row, select the two cells, remove the left, right, and bottom borders, and the border between the empty first cell and the cell containing "Shipment will arrive in 7 to 10 days."

8. In the top cell in the first column (the cell containing the rotated text), remove the top, bottom, and left borders.

9. Save the template.

Changing the Width of Borders

When you create a table, ½-point borders appear along all the gridlines by default. You can modify the borders so they are different widths, or line weights. You'll make the top border of the "Shipping Information" cell thicker than the rest of the borders in the table. To do this, you can use the Borders and Shading dialog box, or you can use the Border Painter button in the Borders group on the Table Tools Design tab.

To draw a thicker border to separate the top of the form and the shipping information section:

1. On the Table Tools Design tab, click the **Line Weight arrow** ½ pt ——— ⌄ and then click **3 pt**. Now, any borders you insert will be 3 points thick rather than the default ½ point. Notice that the Border Painter button in the Borders group is now selected, and the pointer is now the paintbrush pointer 🖌.

2. Drag the pointer along the top border of the cell containing "Shipping Information." The top border is now 3 points wide. See Figure 9–17.

Figure 9–17   3-point border separates table sections

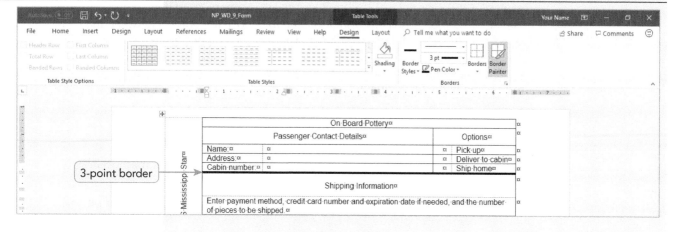

Trouble? If only part of the line above the cell containing "Shipping Information" is thicker, you clicked instead of dragging along the border. Drag along the remaining part of the border to finish drawing the thicker border.

▶ **3.** In the Borders group, click the **Border Painter** button. The button is deselected and the pointer changes back to its usual shape.

Changing Cell Margins

Cell margins are the distance between the contents of cells and the cells' gridlines. When you create a new table, the default top and bottom cell margins for all the cells are zero inches, and the default left and right cell margins are 0.08 inches.

The table for the form is very compact and seems a little tight. To fix this, you'll first change the top and bottom margins of all the cells in the table to 0.03 inches.

To change the cell margins for all the cells in the table:

▶ **1.** On the ribbon, click the **Table Tools Layout** tab.

▶ **2.** In the Table group, click the **Properties** button. The Table Properties dialog box opens with the Table tab selected.

▶ **3.** Click **Options**. The Table Options dialog box opens. The default cell margins for the cells in the table are at the top of the dialog box. See Figure 9–18.

Figure 9–18 ▶ **Table Options dialog box**

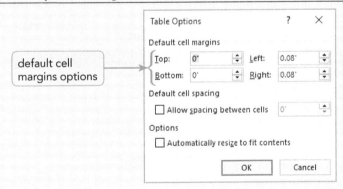

default cell margins options

▶ **4.** In the Default cell margins section, click the **Top** box up arrow three times. The value in the Top box changes to 0.03".

▶ **5.** Use the same method to change the value in the **Bottom** box to 0.03".

▶ **6.** Click **OK**, and then click **OK** in the Table Properties dialog box. The margins above and below each cell entry increase to 0.03".

TIP

To change the space between cells in a table, select the Allow spacing between cells check box, and change the value in the box.

Most of the table looks fine, but the cell containing "Shipping Information" and the cell below it don't need the wider top and bottom margins, nor do the cells in the bottom row. You'll change the top and bottom margins for those cells now.

To change cell margins for specific cells:

TIP

To change a table to a floating object and wrap text around it, click the Properties button in the Table group on the Table Tools Layout tab, and then in the Text wrapping section, click the Around button.

▶ **1.** Select the cell containing "Shipping Information" and the cell below it.

▶ **2.** On the Table Tools Layout tab, in the Table group, click the **Properties** button. The Table Properties dialog box opens.

▶ **3.** Click the **Cell** tab, and then click **Options**. The Cell Options dialog box opens. It is similar to the Table Options dialog box. Because the Same as the whole table check box is selected, the margin boxes in the Cell margins section are not available.

▶ **4.** Click the **Same as the whole table** check box to deselect it. Now the margin boxes are available.

▶ **5.** Click the **Top** box down arrow three times to change the value to 0", and then click the **Bottom** box down arrow three times to change the value in that box to 0" as well.

▶ **6.** Click **OK**, and then click **OK** in the Table Properties dialog box. The top and bottom margins in the "Shipping Information" cell and the cell below it are changed back to 0 inches.

You also need to change the top and bottom margins in the cells in the last row back to 0 inches.

▶ **7.** Select the two cells in the last row in the table (the cell containing "Shipment will arrive in 7 to 10 days." and the cell to its left), and then in the Table group, click the **Properties** button. The Table Properties dialog box opens with the Cell tab selected.

▶ **8.** Click **Options**, click the **Same as the whole table** check box to deselect it, change the values in the Top and Bottom boxes to **0"**, and then click **OK** twice. Compare your screen to Figure 9–19.

Figure 9–19	Table after changing the cell margins

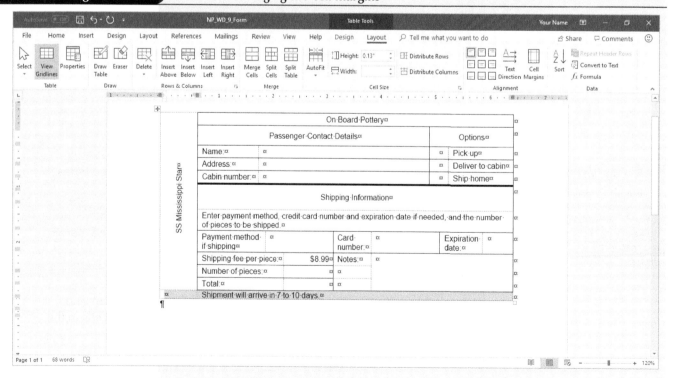

▶ **9.** Save the template.

Applying Custom Formatting to Text and Cells

To finish the form, you will add formatting to the table. First, you will change the font, font size, and font style of some of the text.

To change the font, font size, and font style of text in cells:

1. In the first column, select **SS Mississippi Star**, and then on the ribbon, click the **Home** tab.

2. In the Font group, click the **Font Size arrow**, and then click **22**.

3. In the Font group, click the **Font Dialog Box Launcher**. The Font dialog box opens with the Font tab selected.

4. In the Effects section, click the **Small caps** check box, and then click **OK**. The lowercase letters in the selected text are now small uppercase letters.

5. In the first row, select **On Board Pottery**.

6. In the Font group, click the **Font Size arrow**, and then click **28**.

7. In the Font group, click the **Font Color arrow** $\boxed{A\;\vee}$, and then click the **Teal, Accent 5, Darker 25%** color.

8. In the second row, select the cells containing "Passenger Contact Details" and "Options," change the font size of the text in the selected cells to **12** points, and then in the Font group, click the **Bold** button $\boxed{B}$.

9. Select the text **Shipping Information**, change the font size to **16** points, and then in the Font group, click the **Bold** $\boxed{B}$ button.

10. In the cell below the "Shipping Information" cell, select all of the text, change the font size to **8** points, and then in the Font group, click the **Italic** button $\boxed{I}$.

11. In the last row, select **Shipment will arrive in 7 to 10 days.**, and then in the Font group, click the **Italic** button $\boxed{I}$.

Now you will add colored shading to the cells containing "Passenger Contact Details" and "Options," and gray shading to the Shipping Information section.

To shade cells in the table:

1. Select the cells containing "Passenger Contact Details" and "Options."

2. On the Home tab, in the Paragraph group, click the **Shading arrow** $\boxed{\diamond\;\vee}$ and then click the **Teal, Accent 5, Lighter 60%** color.

3. In the cell containing "Shipping Information," click between the words "Shipping" and "Information," and then drag down to the second to last row. All the cells below the thick border are selected except the cells to the right of the "Card number," "Expiration date," and "Notes" cells and the cells in the bottom row.

4. Press and hold **CTRL**, click in the empty cell to the right of the "Card number" cell, drag down to the merged cell to the right of the "Notes" cell, and then release **CTRL**. Now all the cells below the thick border are selected except the cells in the last row.

TIP

To change the font of text in a table cell, select the text or the cell, click the Font arrow in the Font group on the Home tab, and then click the font you want to use.

TIP

You can also use the Shading button in the Table Styles group on the Table Tools Design tab.

5. In the Paragraph group, click the **Shading arrow** [⬧ ▾], and then click the **Gray, Accent 6, Lighter 80%** color. The selected cells are filled with the color you selected.

6. Click in the merged cell in the first column (the cell containing "SS Mississippi Star"), and then change the shading color to the **Teal, Accent 5** color.

Now you will see what the table looks like without the gridlines being visible and without the hidden formatting marks.

7. In the Paragraph group, click the **Show/Hide ¶** button [¶] to deselect it.

8. On the ribbon, click the **Table Tools Layout** tab, and then in the Table group, click the **View Gridlines** button to deselect it. See Figure 9–20.

Figure 9–20 | **Final structure and design of the table**

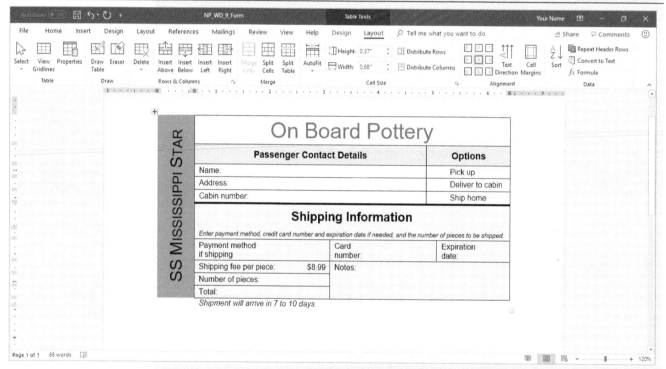

9. In the Table group, click the **View Gridlines** button. The gridlines are again displayed.

10. Click the **Home** tab, and then in the Paragraph group, click the **Show/Hide ¶** button [¶] to select it.

11. Save the template.

You have created and formatted a custom table. In the next session, you will add content controls that passengers will use to enter their information.

REVIEW

Session 9.1 Quick Check

1. What does it mean to split cells in a table?
2. How do you rotate text in a table cell?
3. What happens when you select a cell and then change its dimensions in the Height and Width boxes in the Cell Size group on the Table Tools Layout tab?
4. What appears below the horizontal ruler when you press and hold ALT as you drag a column gridline?
5. How do you align text in a cell?
6. What are cell margins?

Session 9.2 Visual Overview:

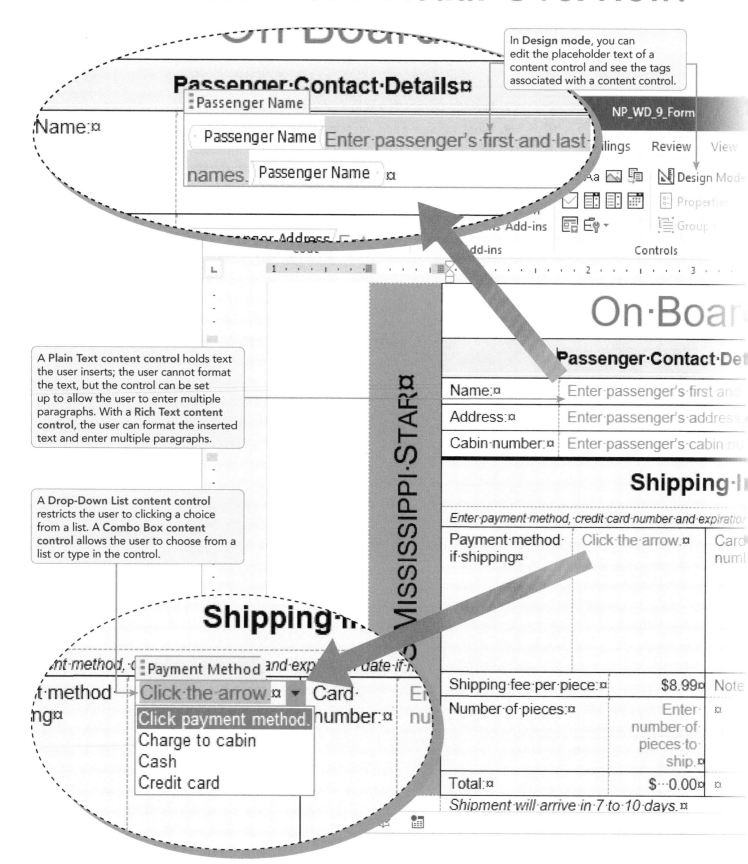

In **Design mode**, you can edit the placeholder text of a content control and see the tags associated with a content control.

A **Plain Text content control** holds text the user inserts; the user cannot format the text, but the control can be set up to allow the user to enter multiple paragraphs. With a **Rich Text content control**, the user can format the inserted text and enter multiple paragraphs.

A **Drop-Down List content control** restricts the user to clicking a choice from a list. A **Combo Box content control** allows the user to choose from a list or type in the control.

Content Controls

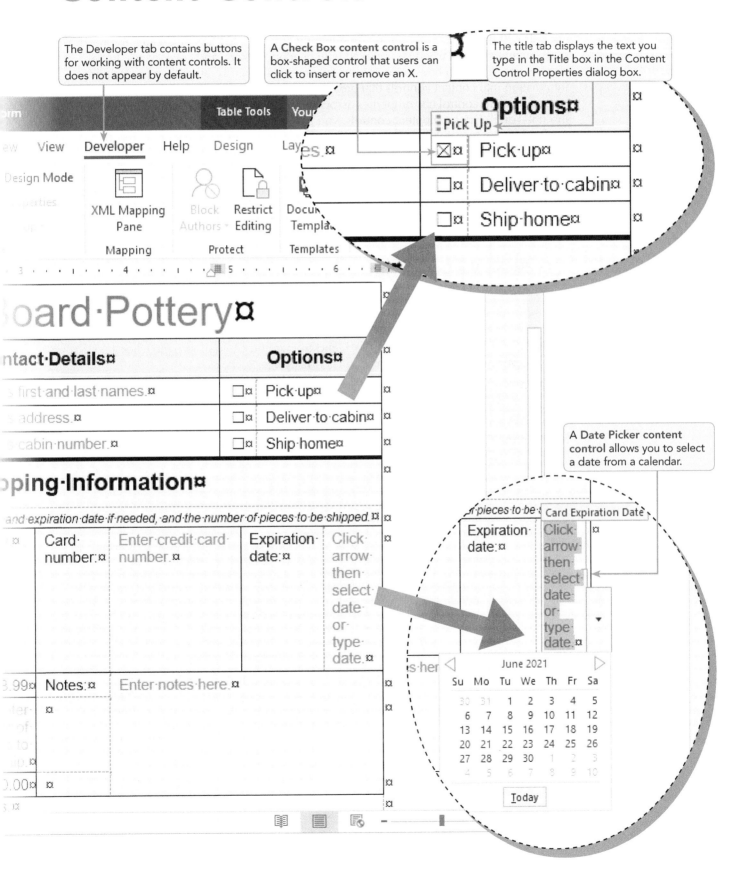

The Developer tab contains buttons for working with content controls. It does not appear by default.

A **Check Box** content control is a box-shaped control that users can click to insert or remove an X.

The title tab displays the text you type in the Title box in the Content Control Properties dialog box.

A **Date Picker** content control allows you to select a date from a calendar.

Understanding Content Controls

You have formatted the table to make it attractive and easy to read. Now you need to insert the most important elements of an online form—content controls. The content controls will help users enter information into the form quickly and efficiently. You have used content controls when you worked with headers, footers, and cover pages. In this session, you will learn how to insert your own content controls rather than just entering information into content controls that are already there.

Each content control has properties associated with it that you specify when you insert it. For all types of content controls, you can specify a title, which is displayed in a title tab at the top of the content control. You can also choose whether to allow the content control to be deleted and whether to allow users to edit the contents of the control after they have entered information. In addition, each type of content control has other properties that you can adjust that are specific to that control.

The options for inserting content controls are located on the Developer tab. You'll display the Developer tab now.

To display the Developer tab on the ribbon:

▶ **1.** If you took a break after the last session, use the Open command in Backstage view to open the file **NP_WD_9_Form.dotx** from the location where you are saving your files.

▶ **2.** On the ribbon, click the **File** tab, and then in the navigation pane, click **Options**. The Word Options dialog box opens.

▶ **3.** In the navigation pane, click **Customize Ribbon**. The right pane of the dialog box changes to show two lists—one labeled Choose commands from, and one labeled Customize the Ribbon.

▶ **4.** In the Customize the Ribbon list, click the **Developer** check box to select it, if necessary. See Figure 9–21.

TIP

You can also right-click a tab on the ribbon, and then click Customize the Ribbon on the shortcut menu.

Figure 9–21	Word Options dialog box with Customize Ribbon selected

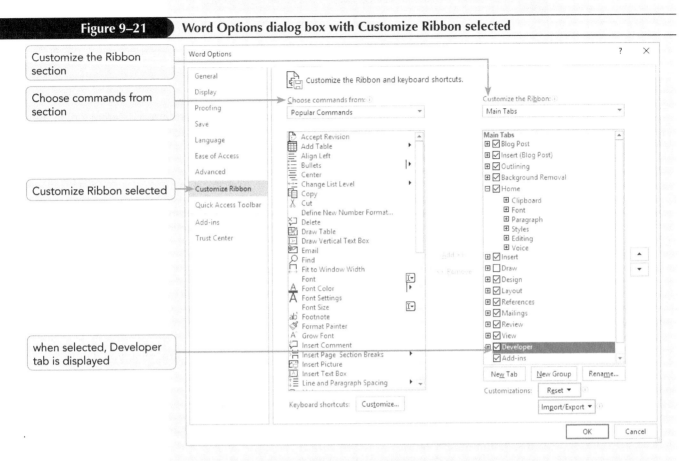

5. Click **OK**. The dialog box closes, and the Developer tab is displayed on the ribbon to the right of the View tab.

Inserting Text Content Controls

To allow a user to input text in a form, you insert Plain Text or Rich Text content controls. Rich Text content controls allow the user to add multiple paragraphs of text and to format some or all of the text. Plain Text content controls are restricted to single paragraphs, although you can specifically allow users to insert manual line breaks. In addition, in a Plain Text content control, all of the text must be formatted identically; for example, if the user formats one word with bold, all of the text will be formatted with bold.

Inserting a Plain Text or a Rich Text Content Control

- On the ribbon, click the Developer tab, and then in the Controls group, click the Plain Text Content Control or the Rich Text Content Control button.
- In the Controls group, click the Properties button.
- In the Title box, type a control title.
- If you want the text entered in the content control to be formatted differently than the default format, click the Use a style to format text typed into the empty control check box, and then click the Style arrow and select a style, or click New Style to define a new style.
- Click the Content control cannot be deleted check box if you want to prevent users from deleting the content control.
- For a Plain Text content control, click the Allow carriage returns (multiple paragraphs) check box to allow the user to insert more than one paragraph.
- Click the Remove content control when contents are edited check box to delete the content control and leave only the text the user inserts.
- Click OK.
- If desired, switch to Design mode, and then replace the default placeholder text with specific instructions to the user.

You need to enter several Plain Text content controls in the form. First, you'll enter one in the cell to the right of the "Name" cell.

To insert a Plain Text content control and set its properties:

▶ **1.** In the "Passenger Contact Details" section, click in the cell to the right of the cell containing "Name," and then on the ribbon, click the **Developer** tab.

▶ **2.** In the Controls group, click the **Plain Text Content Control** button Aa. A Plain Text content control is inserted in the cell. See Figure 9–22.

Figure 9–22   **Plain Text content control inserted**

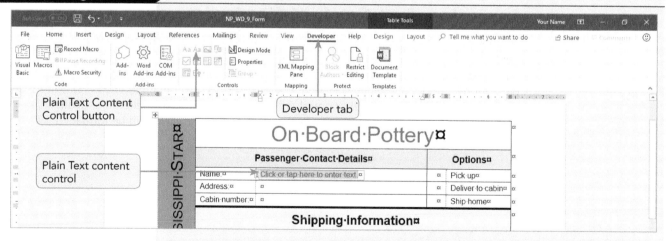

▶ **3.** In the Controls group, click the **Properties** button. The Content Control Properties dialog box opens. The Title property identifies the content control. See Figure 9–23.

Figure 9–23 | Content Control Properties dialog box for a Plain Text content control

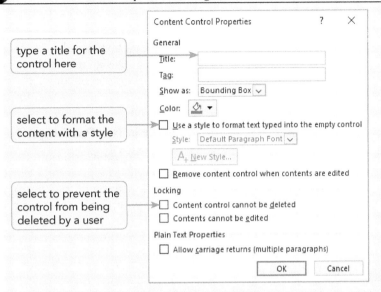

type a title for the control here

select to format the content with a style

select to prevent the control from being deleted by a user

If the user will need to enter multiple paragraphs in a Plain Text control, click the Allow carriage returns (multiple paragraphs) check box in the Content Control Properties dialog box.

4. Click in the Title box, and then type **Passenger Name**. This text will be displayed in the tab at the top of the control in the form. To make the passenger's name stand out, you will format it with the Strong style, which formats it as bold.

5. Click the **Use a style to format text typed into the empty control** check box, click the **Style arrow**, and then click **Strong**.

Next, you'll set a property in the control so users won't be able to delete the content control.

6. Click the **Content control cannot be deleted** check box, and then click **OK**. The title "Passenger Name" now appears on the title tab of the content control. See Figure 9–24.

Figure 9–24 | Title tab on a content control after adding a Title property

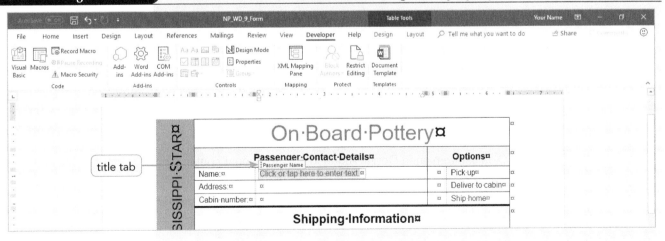

title tab

7. Click a blank area of the table to deselect the content control.

Usually, the user knows what information to enter into a control just by looking at the title. However, someone using the form for the first time might need instructions, and both new and experienced users sometimes need clarification regarding how to enter information. To assist the user, you can customize the placeholder text to provide specific instructions for each control.

Emi wants you to modify the placeholder text to make the form more clear. To change the placeholder text, you need to switch to Design mode. If you are not in Design mode, you will enter information into the control instead of editing the placeholder text.

To change the placeholder text in the Passenger Name content control:

▶ **1.** In the Controls group, click the **Design Mode** button. The button is selected, and tags appear at the beginning and end of the Plain Text content control that you inserted. Tags mark the location of the control in the document and are useful when you plan to use your form in another program. Because you didn't type anything in the Tag box in the Content Control Properties dialog box, the tag is the same as the Title property. See Figure 9–25.

Figure 9–25	Form in Design mode

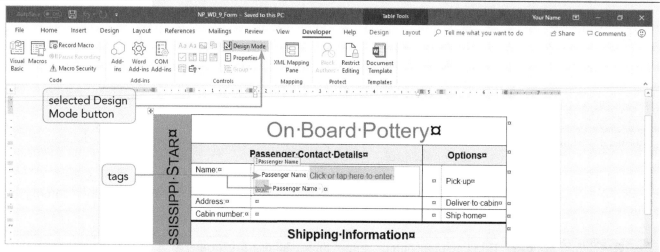

▶ **2.** Select the placeholder text **Click or tap here to enter text** (but do not select the period), and then type **Enter passenger's first and last names**. The text you typed replaces the default placeholder text.

Trouble? If any of the text you type is black instead of gray, undo your change, carefully select just the current placeholder text without selecting the period, and then type the new placeholder text in Step 2.

You can remain in Design mode to add additional content controls. You need to add Plain Text content controls in the cells to the right of "Address," "Cabin number," "Card number," "Number of pieces," and "Notes."

To enter additional Plain Text content controls:

▶ **1.** Click in the cell to the right of the cell containing "Address," insert a Plain Text content control, and then in the Controls group, click the **Properties** button.

2. In the Title box, type **Passenger Address**.

3. Click the **Content control cannot be deleted** check box, and then click **OK**.

4. Select the placeholder text **Click or tap here to enter text** (but do not select the period), and then type **Enter passenger's address**.

> **Trouble?** If the replacement placeholder text that you type is black instead of gray, and if you don't see the Passenger Address tags, click the Undo button ↺ to undo the change you made. Click the Design Mode button in the Controls group to select it, and then repeat Step 4.

5. Click in the cell to the right of the "Cabin number" cell, insert a Plain Text content control, and then open the Content Control Properties dialog box.

6. Enter **Cabin Number** as the Title property, click the **Content control cannot be deleted** check box, click **OK**, and then replace the placeholder text with **Enter passenger's cabin number**.

7. In the cell to the right of the "Card number" cell, insert a Plain Text content control that cannot be deleted, add **Credit Card Number** as the Title property, and then replace the placeholder text with **Enter credit card number**.

8. In the cell to the right of the "Number of pieces" cell, insert a Plain Text content control that cannot be deleted, add **No. of Pieces** as the Title property, and then replace the placeholder text with **Enter number of pieces to ship**.

9. In the cell to the right of the "Notes" cell, insert a Plain Text content control that cannot be deleted, add **Notes** as the Title property, and then replace the placeholder text with **Enter notes here**.

10. Save the changes to the template.

> **TIP**
>
> To delete a control, make sure the form is in Design mode, right-click the control, and then click Remove Content Control on the shortcut menu.

All the text content controls are now inserted in the form. It's a good idea to test content controls after you insert them. First, you need to turn Design mode off.

To turn off Design mode and test two of the Plain Text content controls:

1. In the Controls group, click the **Design Mode** button to deselect it.

2. Click in the cell containing the Passenger Name content control (the cell to the right of the cell containing "Name" in the "Passenger Contact Details" section). The content control is selected, and you see the title tab with the name of the content control on it.

3. Type **Jane Doe**. The text you typed replaces the placeholder text, and it is formatted with the Strong style as you specified in the Properties dialog box when you inserted this content control.

4. Click in the cell to the right of the cell containing "Address." The placeholder text in this cell is selected, and the title tab containing "Passenger Address" is displayed.

5. Type **123 Main Street**. The name replaces the placeholder text. This text is not formatted with a style.

> Now that you have tested the two content controls, you need to delete the text you typed to reset the content controls so they display the placeholder text.

▶ **6.** On the Quick Access Toolbar, click the **Undo** button 🔄. The text you typed in the Address content control is removed. You can also use the BACKSPACE and DEL keys to delete text in content controls.

   Trouble? If all the text in the Passenger Address content control was not removed, click the Undo button 🔄 as many times as needed to delete all of the address you typed.

▶ **7.** Click in the cell containing "Jane Doe," and then press **BACKSPACE** and **DEL** as needed to delete the name.

▶ **8.** Click in any other cell in the table. The placeholder text reappears in the Passenger Name content control.

Inserting Date Picker Content Controls

To create a content control that contains a date, you use the Date Picker content control. When you insert a Date Picker content control, you can specify what the date will look like in the completed form. To do this, you select a format from a list or create your own format using the same pattern of letters you used when you modified the Date field. For example, the format d-MMM-yy displays the date January 7, 2021, as 7-Jan-21, and the format dddd, MMMM dd, yyyy displays the date as Wednesday, January 07, 2021.

REFERENCE

Inserting a Date Picker Content Control

- On the ribbon, click the Developer tab, and then in the Controls group, click the Date Picker Content Control button.
- In the Controls group, click the Properties button.
- In the Title box, type the control title.
- Click the Content control cannot be deleted check box if you want to prevent the user from deleting the content control.
- In the Display the date like this list, click a format for the date, or replace the letters that indicate the format in the box as needed.
- Click OK.
- If desired, switch to Design mode, and then replace the default placeholder text with specific instructions to the user.

For the cell that will contain the expiration date for the passenger's credit card, Emi wants you to insert a content control that allows only a date to be entered. To do this, you will use a Date Picker content control.

To insert a Date Picker content control in the form:

TIP

To allow a user to insert a picture in a form, use a Picture content control.

▶ **1.** Click in the cell to the right of the cell containing "Expiration date," and then in the Controls group, click the **Date Picker Content Control** button 📅. A Date Picker content control is entered in the cell.

▶ **2.** In the Controls group, click the **Properties** button. The Content Control Properties dialog box for a Date Picker control opens. The top of this dialog box is the same as the Content Control Properties dialog box for a Text control. See Figure 9–26.

Figure 9–26   **Content Control Properties dialog box for a Date Picker content control**

3. In the Title box, type **Card Expiration Date**, and then click the **Content control cannot be deleted** check box.

   Now you need to select the format of the date. Credit card expiration dates include only the month and year; for example, if a card expires in June 2023, it would appear as 06/2023. In the list in the Date Picker Properties section of the dialog box, the first date format is selected, and in the "Display the date like this" box, the format is M/d/yyyy.

4. Click in the **Display the date like this** box, press ← if necessary to position the insertion point before "M," and then type **M**. Now months that are expressed with a single digit will have a zero before the month number.

5. Press → once to position the insertion point before the first forward slash, and then press **DEL** twice to delete "/d". The format is now MM/yyyy.

6. Click **OK**. Now you need to change the placeholder text.

7. In the Controls group, click the **Design Mode** button to switch to Design mode, and then replace the placeholder text with **Click arrow then select date or type date**.

8. Save the template.

Now you will test the Date Picker content control that you entered. First, you must turn off Design mode.

To test the Card Expiration Date content control:

▶ **1.** In the Controls group, click the **Design Mode** button to exit Design mode. The content control in the cell containing the Card Expiration Date content control is still selected, but now an arrow appears at the right edge of the control.

▶ **2.** On the Card Expiration Date content control, click the **arrow**. A calendar appears showing the current month with a blue box around the current date. To change the date, you click the forward or backward arrows next to the month name. The Today button at the bottom inserts the current date and closes the calendar. See Figure 9–27.

Figure 9–27	Using the Date Picker content control to select a date

▶ **3.** At the top of the calendar, click ▷ several times to scroll to any month in the future, and then click **1**. The calendar closes, and the month and the year you chose appear in the cell in the format you specified when you inserted the content control—in this case, a two-digit number for the month and a four-digit number for the year. For example, if you clicked a date in February 2022, it will appear as 02/2022. Because this format shows only the month and year, you can click any date in the month.

▶ **4.** On the Quick Access Toolbar, click the **Undo** button 🔄. The date you selected is removed from the content control.

▶ **5.** Type **Feb 2022**, and then click any other cell in the table. The date you typed appears as 02/2022.

▶ **6.** On the Quick Access Toolbar, click the **Undo** button 🔄. The date you typed is removed from the content control.

Inserting List Content Controls

When the information required in a form is limited to specific entries, you can use content controls that offer the user a list of choices. You create the list, and the user clicks one of the choices in the list. This type of content control makes it possible for the user to complete a form faster and without making any spelling errors. Word offers three types of list content controls—Drop-Down List, Combo Box, and Building Block Gallery.

Drop-Down List content controls restrict the user to clicking a choice from a list. When you insert the control, you add items to the list and arrange them in an order that suits you. When users complete the form, they are allowed to choose only one item from the list. They cannot type anything else in the control.

REFERENCE

Inserting a Drop-Down List or Combo Box Content Control

- On the ribbon, click the Developer tab, and then in the Controls group, click the Drop-Down List Content Control or the Combo Box Content Control button.
- In the Controls group, click the Properties button.
- In the Title box, type the control title.
- Click the Content control cannot be deleted check box if you want to prevent the user from deleting the content control.
- Click Add to open the Add Choice dialog box. In the Display Name box, type an entry for the list, and then click OK. Repeat for each entry you want to include in the list.
- To change the wording of an entry, click the entry in the list, and then click the Modify button. In the Modify Choice dialog box, edit the text in the Display Name box, and then click OK.
- To move an entry up or down in the list, click it, and then click Move Up or Move Down.
- To remove an entry from the list, click it, and then click the Remove button.
- Click OK.
- If desired, switch to Design mode, and then replace the default placeholder text with specific instructions to the user.

If a passenger wants to ship their painted piece home, they need to pay the shipping fee. They can have it charged to their cabin, pay in cash, or use a credit card. You need to insert a Drop-Down List content control that includes these choices in the drop-down list.

To insert a Drop-Down List content control for the payment method:

▶ **1.** Click in the blank cell to the right of "Payment method if shipping."

▶ **2.** In the Controls group, click the **Drop-Down List Content Control** button ▦ and then click the **Properties** button. The Content Control Properties dialog box for a Drop-Down List appears. See Figure 9–28.

Figure 9–28 Content Control Properties dialog box for a Drop-Down List content control

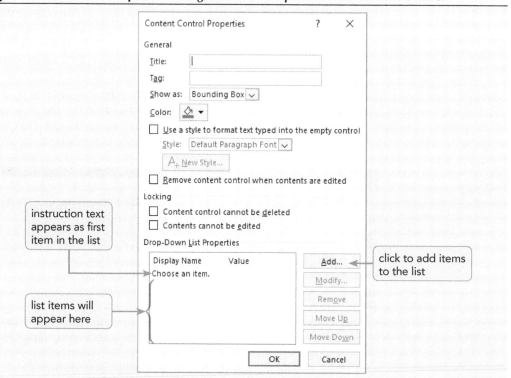

3. In the Title box, type **Payment Method**, and then click the **Content control cannot be deleted** check box. Now you need to add the items that will appear in the drop-down list below the instruction text.

4. Click **Add**. The Add Choice dialog box opens. The insertion point is in the Display Name box.

5. Type **Cash**. As you typed in the Display Name box, the same text appeared in the Value box. You can connect a form to an Access database; and if you do, the contents of the Value field are entered into the database. You can ignore this for now.

6. Click **OK**. The Add Choice dialog box closes, and "Cash" appears as the first item in the list below "Choose an item."

7. Add **Charge to cabin** and **Credit card** to the list. You want to move "Charge to cabin" up so it is the first item in the list below the "Choose an item" instruction text.

8. In the list, click **Charge to cabin**, and then click **Move Up**. "Charge to cabin" is now the first item in the list below the instruction text. Now you need to modify the instruction text.

9. In the list, click **Choose an item.**, and then click **Modify**. The Modify Choice dialog box opens. It's identical to the Add Choice dialog box.

10. Replace the text in the Display Name box with **Click payment method.** and then click **OK**. See Figure 9–29.

Figure 9–29   List items added and reordered

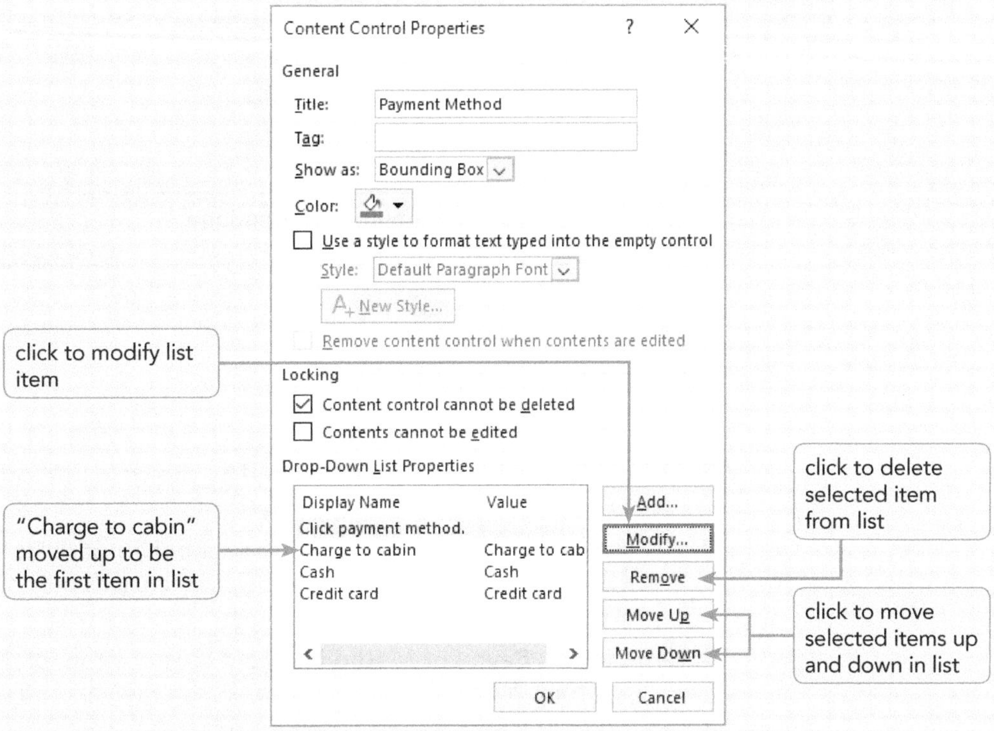

click to modify list item

"Charge to cabin" moved up to be the first item in list

click to delete selected item from list

click to move selected items up and down in list

▶ **11.** Click **OK** to close the Content Control Properties dialog box.

▶ **12.** Turn on Design mode, and then replace the placeholder text in the Payment Method content control with **Click the arrow**.

▶ **13.** Save the changes to the template.

Now you'll test the Drop-Down List content control. Remember, you need to turn Design mode off before you can use the content controls.

To test the Drop-Down List content control:

▶ **1.** Turn off Design mode, and then click the **Payment Method** content control arrow. The list of choices you typed in the Content Control Properties dialog box appears. See Figure 9–30.

Figure 9–30 **Drop-Down List content control list displayed**

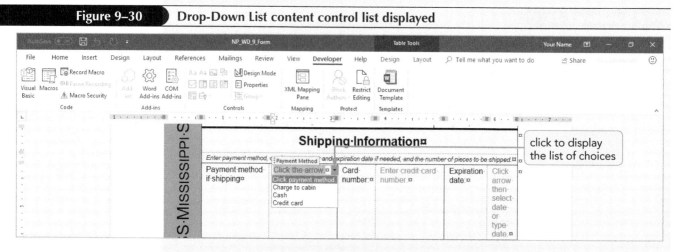

> **2.** In the list, click **Charge to cabin**. The choice you selected appears in the content control.

> **3.** Press **DEL**. The text in the content control is not deleted. This is because it is a Drop-Down List content control and the user's only option is to choose an item in the list.

> **4.** Click the **Payment Method** content control arrow, and then click **Click payment method.** The instructional text appears in the control again.

> **5.** Type any letter or number. Nothing happens for the same reason nothing happened when you tried to delete your choice.

A Combo Box content control is similar to a Drop-Down List content control in that it offers the user a list of choices. But a Combo Box content control also allows users to type their own response if it doesn't appear in the list provided. For example, if a business created an online form for their customers, the list for the Combo Box content control that contains the customer's city could include the city the business is in as well as a few neighboring cities and towns. If most of the business's customers live in one of the cities in the list, this would make it easier and quicker for those customers to select their city names. However, occasionally customers from other cities may want to purchase something. Unlike a Drop-Down List content control, the Combo Box content control would allow those customers to type the name of their city in the control.

Building Block Gallery content controls are also similar to Drop-Down List content controls. However, instead of creating the list of choices a user can click, you select AutoText, Equations, Tables, Quick Parts, or a custom gallery of building blocks. When the user clicks the arrow on the content control, they can select an item in the gallery you chose.

Inserting Check Box Content Controls

Many of the dialog boxes you have used in Word and in other programs include check boxes that you click to select and deselect items. Similarly, a Check Box content control is a box-shaped control that users can click to insert or remove an "X." You might include check box content controls in an online survey form for questions such as, "Which of the following items do you plan to purchase in the next six months?"

Inserting a Check Box Content Control

- On the ribbon, click the Developer tab, and then in the Controls group, click the Check Box Content Control button.
- In the Controls group, click the Properties button.
- In the Title box, type the control title.
- Click the Content control cannot be deleted check box if you want to prevent users from deleting the content control.
- Click OK.

You need to add Check Box content controls in the three empty cells in the Options section.

To insert Check Box content controls:

1. Click in the cell to the left of the "Pick up" cell, and then on the ribbon, click the **Developer** tab, if necessary.

2. In the Controls group, click the **Check Box Content Control** button . A Check Box content control is inserted in the cell. See Figure 9–31.

Figure 9–31   **Check Box content control inserted in the form**

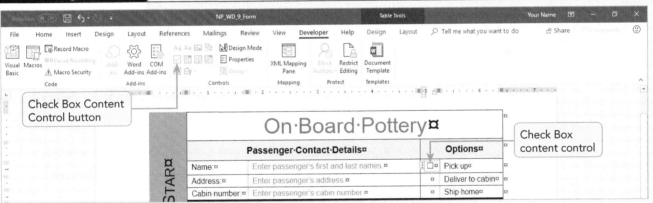

3. In the Controls group, click the **Properties** button to open the Content Control Properties dialog box for a Check Box content control. See Figure 9–32.

Figure 9–32 Content Control Properties dialog box for a Check Box content control

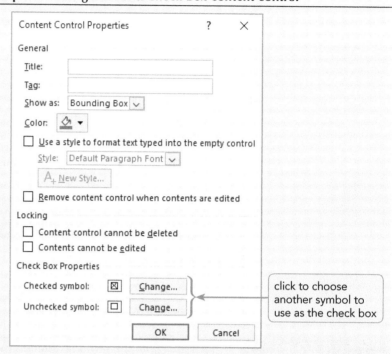

4. In the Title box, type **Pick Up**, click the **Content control cannot be deleted** check box to select it, and then click **OK**.

5. Click in the cell to the left of the "Deliver to cabin" cell, insert a Check Box content control, and then open the Content Control Properties dialog box.

6. In the Title box, type **Deliver**, click the **Content control cannot be deleted** check box to select it, and then click **OK**.

7. Click in the cell to the left of the "Ship home" cell, insert a Check Box content control, and then open the Content Control Properties dialog box.

8. In the Title box, type **Ship**, click the **Content control cannot be deleted** check box to select it, and then click **OK**.

9. Save the changes to the template.

Make sure you save the changes to the template so that you have a final version of the template before continuing with the next section.

Now you need to test the Check Box content controls. To select (place an "X" in) or deselect (remove the "X" from) a Check Box content control, you can click it, or while the content control is active, press SPACEBAR.

To test the Check Box content controls:

1. Make sure Design mode is turned off.

2. Click the **Pick Up** check box. The box is selected, as indicated by the "X" inside it.

3. Press **TAB** twice. The Deliver Check Box content control is selected.

4. Press **SPACEBAR**. The check box is selected.

5. Click the **Pick Up** check box to remove the "X," and then click the **Deliver** check box to remove the "X."

INSIGHT

Repeating Section Content Controls

A Repeating Section content control is a content control that allows you to duplicate the contents of the content control by clicking a plus sign that is displayed when the content control is active. For example, suppose you create a table to list your home inventory for insurance purposes. You could add a Text content control in the first column to name the item, a Picture content control in the second column so you can add a picture of the item, and a Date Picker content control in the third column to indicate when the item was purchased. You select all three content controls, and then insert a Repeating Section content control. When you click the plus sign button displayed below and to the right of the active Repeating Section content control, another row is created in the table containing the same content controls as in the first row. Note that if you use the Group command, you can no longer click the plus sign button to duplicate the content of a Repeating Section content control; however, if you use the Restrict Editing command, you can. You'll learn about the Group and Restrict Editing commands in Session 9.3.

The form is almost complete. In the next session, you'll finish the form by inserting a formula in the cell next to "Total" to calculate the total fee, and then you will restrict editing in the form so that users can enter information only in the appropriate cells.

REVIEW

Session 9.2 Quick Check

1. What tab must be displayed on the ribbon in order to access content controls?

2. What is the difference between a Rich Text content control and a Plain Text content control?

3. How do you provide the user with instructions for using a content control?

4. What button must be selected in the Controls group on the Developer tab in order to edit the placeholder text of a content control?

5. What is the difference between a Combo Box content control and a Drop-Down List content control?

6. What is a Check Box content control?

Session 9.3 Visual Overview:

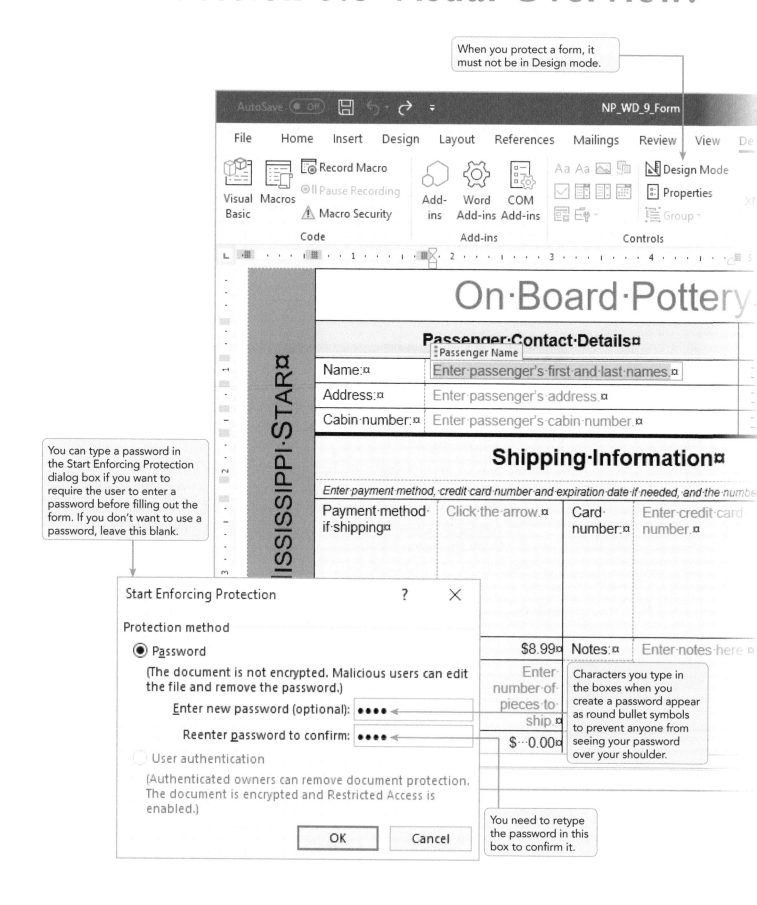

When you protect a form, it must not be in Design mode.

You can type a password in the Start Enforcing Protection dialog box if you want to require the user to enter a password before filling out the form. If you don't want to use a password, leave this blank.

Characters you type in the boxes when you create a password appear as round bullet symbols to prevent anyone from seeing your password over your shoulder.

You need to retype the password in this box to confirm it.

Protecting a Document

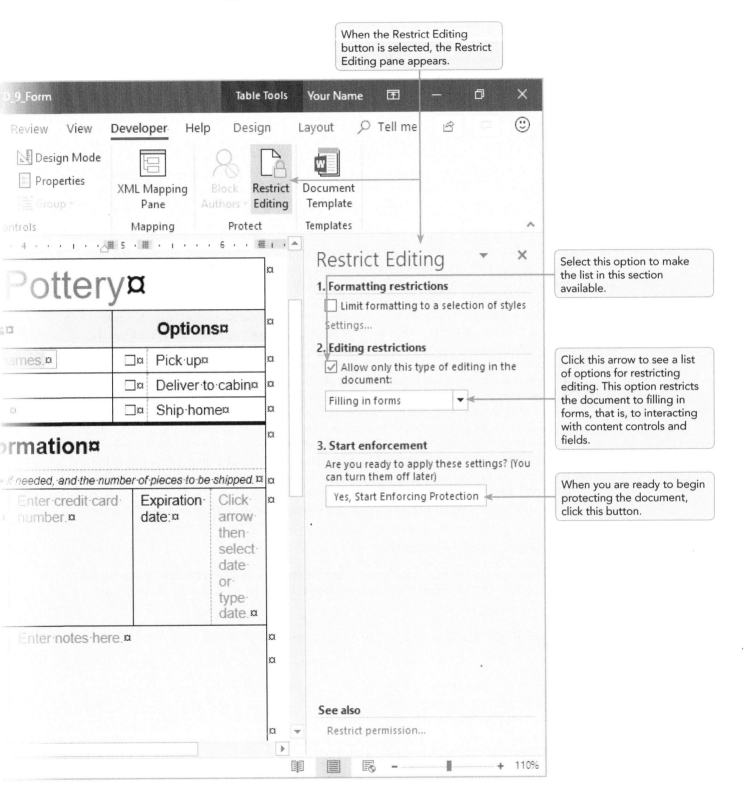

When the Restrict Editing button is selected, the Restrict Editing pane appears.

Select this option to make the list in this section available.

Click this arrow to see a list of options for restricting editing. This option restricts the document to filling in forms, that is, to interacting with content controls and fields.

When you are ready to begin protecting the document, click this button.

Using Formulas in a Table

A **formula** is a mathematical statement that calculates a value. You can add formulas to cells in tables to calculate values based on the values in other cells in the table. For example, in the form you are creating, the cell to the right of the "Total" cell needs to contain a formula that multiplies the shipping fee per piece by the number of pieces to be shipped. Before you insert a formula in a table, you need to understand how cells are referenced in a table.

Referencing Table Cells

In order to use a formula in a cell, you need to refer to specific cells in the table. As you have seen when working with embedded Excel worksheet objects, cells in a table are referenced by a letter that corresponds to the column and a number that corresponds to the row. The first column is column A, the second column is column B, and so on; likewise, the first row is row 1, the second row is row 2, and so on. This means the cell in the first column and the first row is cell A1, the cell in the first column and the second row is cell A2, and the cell in the second column and the first row is cell B1.

It can be difficult to identify a cell's reference in a table containing merged and split cells because each row might have a different number of columns and each column might have a different number of rows. To identify the column letter in any row, count from the left to the right in each row. In the table you created, row 1 contains two columns—columns A and B—with the ship name "SS Mississippi Star" in column A and the "On Board Pottery" in column B. Row 2 contains three columns. As in row 1, column A contains the ship name, but column B contains "Passenger Contact Details," and column C contains "Options." This is because although the merged cell containing the ship name is cell A1, it is also the first cell in all of the rows it is next to, making the column containing the cell with "Passenger Contact Details" column B.

Counting rows in a table with merged and split cells is a little trickier. In all of the columns in the table you created, even column A, there are 12 rows—the total number of rows in the table. This means that even though it appears as if there are only two rows in column A, the cell without borders in the last row in column A (the cell to the left of the cell containing the footnote) is cell A12 because there are 12 rows in the table and this cell appears next to the other cells in row 12.

Now that you understand how to reference cells, you need to understand formulas.

Understanding Formulas

When you insert a formula in a table, you use the Formula button in the Data group on the Table Tools Layout tab. Formulas in a table always start with an equal sign. For example,

$$= 1 + 2$$

is a formula that calculates the sum of 1 plus 2, which is 3. The formula

$$= 2 * 3$$

multiplies 2 by 3 to produce a result of 6. In this formula, the numbers 2 and 3 are **constants**—values that don't change.

Formulas can also include **variables**, which are symbols for values that can change. For example, if you want to add the values that appear in cells A1 and A2 in a Word table, you could write the formula as follows:

$$= A1 + A2$$

This formula looks in the referenced cells (cells A1 and A2) and uses the contents to calculate the result of the formula. So if cell A1 contains 1 and cell A2 contains 2, the result of adding these two numbers—3—is displayed. If you change the values in the referenced cells—for example, if you change the value in cell A1 to 4—then the result of the formula will change without you needing to modify the formula, in this example, to 6.

Formulas can also contain functions. A **function** is a named operation that replaces the action of an arithmetic expression; basically, it's a shorthand way of writing a formula. Word provides 18 functions that you can use in tables. One of the most commonly used functions is the SUM function, which adds numbers. Most functions have **arguments**, which are values that the function needs in order to calculate its result. Arguments appear between parentheses immediately after the name of the function. For example, the SUM function to add the values in cells A1 and A2 would be written as follows:

$$= SUM(A1,A2)$$

In this example, cells A1 and A2 are the arguments. Because tables are grids, and functions such as SUM are frequently used at the bottom of a column or the end of a row, you can use LEFT, RIGHT, ABOVE, and BELOW as the argument, and SUM will add the contents of all the cells in the specified direction.

Inserting a Formula in a Table Cell

A formula in a table cell is a field that can be updated when you change the data used in the formula calculation. Like any field, when you insert a formula in a table cell, you can specify how the result will be formatted in the document. To do this, you choose a pattern of digits and symbols, such as $#,###,### or 00.00, that describes how the number will look. Figure 9–33 lists the most commonly used symbols for describing a number format.

Figure 9–33 **Symbols that describe number formats**

Symbol	Purpose	Example
0 (Zero)	Displays a digit in place of the zero in the field result. If the result doesn't include a digit in that place, the field displays a zero.	"00.0" displays "05.0" "0" displays an integer of any number of digits
#	Displays a digit in place of the # only if the result requires it. If the result doesn't include a digit in that place, the field displays a space.	"$##.00"displays "$ 5.00"
. (decimal point)	Determines the decimal point position.	See examples above.
, (comma)	Separates a series of three digits.	"$#,###,###" displays "$3,450,000"
- (hyphen)	Includes a minus sign if the number is negative or a space if the number is positive.	"-0" displays an integer as " 5" or "-5"
; (semicolon)	Separates the format of positive and negative numbers.	"$##0.00;-$##0.00" displays "$ 55.50" if positive, "-$ 55.50" if negative
(parentheses around negative number)	Puts parentheses around a negative result.	"$##0.00;($##0.00)" displays "$ 55.50" if positive, "($ 55.50)" if negative
$, %, etc.	Displays a special character in the result.	"0.0%" displays "5.0%"

You need to insert a formula in the cell to the right of the cell containing "Total" to multiply the shipping fee per piece by the number of pieces. This cell is in the third column—column C—and is in the second-to-last row of the table, row 11. To calculate the total, you will multiply the value in the cell to the right of the "Shipping fee per piece" cell—cell C9—and the value in the cell to the right of the "Number of pieces" cell—cell C10.

You will insert the formula now.

To insert a formula for the total fee:

▶ **1.** If you took a break after the last session, use the Open command in Backstage view to open the file **NP_WD_9_Form.dotx** from the location where you are saving your files.

▶ **2.** Click in the cell to the right of the cell containing "Total." This is the cell that will contain the formula to multiply the shipping fee per piece by the number of pieces being shipped.

▶ **3.** On the ribbon, click the **Table Tools Layout** tab, and then in the Data group, click the **Formula** button. The Formula dialog box opens. The SUM function appears in the Formula box with the argument ABOVE, and the insertion point is blinking after "ABOVE." See Figure 9–34.

Figure 9–34	**Formula dialog box**

▶ **4.** Press **BACKSPACE** as many times as needed to delete SUM(ABOVE), but do not delete the equal sign.

Trouble? If you deleted the equal sign, type =.

▶ **5.** Click the **Paste function arrow**. The list that appears contains the functions available to use in Word documents. You need the function that multiplies values.

▶ **6.** Scroll down the alphabetical list, and then click **PRODUCT**. In the Formula box, =PRODUCT() appears with the insertion point between the parentheses. You need to insert the arguments so that the function multiplies the value in cell C9 by the value in cell C10.

▶ **7.** Type **C9,C10**. The function is now =PRODUCT(C9,C10).

▶ **8.** Click the **Number format** arrow, and then click **$#,##0.00;($#,##0.00)** to set the number format as a dollar amount. This style formats positive numbers so the dollar sign appears before the number, a comma is used to separate thousands, and two decimal places are used to show cents. Negative numbers are formatted the same way except they will appear between parentheses. If you wanted to, you could edit the format. For example, you could delete ".00" so that the result appears as a whole dollar amount.

▶ **9.** Click **OK**. The dialog box closes. The result of the calculation—"$ 0.00"— appears in the cell to the right of the "Total" cell. The result is $0 because there is no value in the cell that is supposed to contain the number of pieces so the formula is multiplying 8.99 by zero.

▶ **10.** Change the Zoom level to **100%**, and then compare your screen to the final form shown in Figure 9–35.

| Figure 9–35 | Final form |

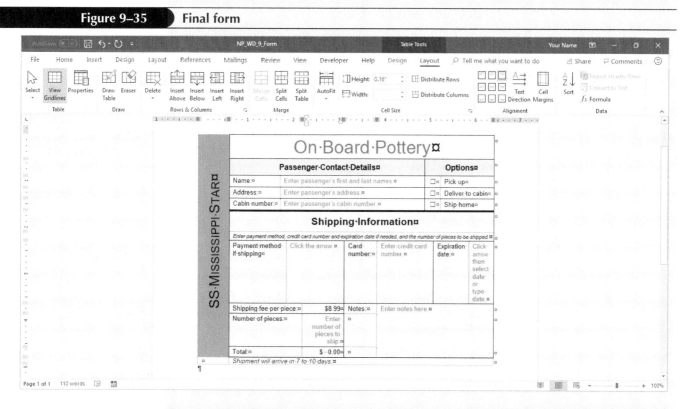

> **11.** Change the Zoom level back to **120%**, and then save the changes to the template.

Now you need to test the formula. Recall that fields update when the document is opened, when you click the Update Field command on the shortcut menu, or when you press F9.

To test the formula:

> **1.** Click the **No. of Pieces** content control, and then type **3**. Now you need to update the formula field.

> **2.** Right-click the field in the cell to the right of the "Total" cell, and then on the shortcut menu, click **Update Field**. The value in the field updates to $ 26.97. The formula works correctly.

> **3.** On the Quick Access Toolbar, click the **Undo** button 🔄 twice to remove the 3 in the cell to the right of the "Number of pieces" cell. The actions you took while testing the formula are undone.

Grouping Content Controls

When you create an online form, you need to prevent users from modifying the form except for being able to enter values in content controls. To do this, select the labels and content controls to which you want to apply the command, and then use the Group command in the Controls group on the Developer tab. You will do this now.

To group content controls:

▶ **1.** Press **CTRL+A**. All of the template content is selected.

▶ **2.** On the ribbon, click the **Developer** tab.

▶ **3.** In the Controls group, click the **Group** button, and then click **Group**. Now nothing in the form can be modified except the content controls.

Now you'll test some of the content controls in the protected form to make sure they still work as expected.

To test the form:

▶ **1.** Click in the cell containing "On Board Pottery," and then type any character. Nothing happens because the Group command prevents any part of the form from being modified except content controls.

▶ **2.** Click the **Passenger Name** content control, type your name, and then press **TAB**. The next content control to the right is selected—the Pick Up Check Box content control.

▶ **3.** Click the **Pick Up** check box to select it.

▶ **4.** Click the **No. of Pieces** content control, and then type **2**. Now you need to update the field containing the formula.

▶ **5.** Right-click the field to the right of the cell containing "Total." The Update Field command is on the shortcut menu, but it is not available to be clicked— it is grayed out.

▶ **6.** On the Quick Access Toolbar, click the **Undo arrow** ⟲ , and then in the menu, click the entry **Typing** followed by your name. All the changes you made to the form while testing it are undone.

Trouble? If all the changes to the form are not undone, click the Undo button ⟲ again.

Because the Group command prevents anything in the form from being changed except for content controls, the Update field command is not available on the shortcut form. Therefore, you need to use another method to protect the content that you don't want users to be able to change. First, you'll ungroup the form.

To ungroup the content controls:

▶ **1.** Click anywhere in the table.

▶ **2.** On the Developer tab, in the Controls group, click the **Group** button.

▶ **3.** Click **Ungroup**.

Restricting Document Editing

As you have seen, the Group command applies restrictions for editing the document so that users can enter data only in content controls and are prevented from making changes to the text or structure of the form. However, because the form you are working on includes a formula field that needs to be updated after you enter values in content controls, you need to set editing restrictions by using the Restrict Editing command.

When you use the Restrict Editing command, you can specify that the document is read-only, meaning a user can open and view it but cannot make any changes to it. You can also give restricted access to users for either making tracked changes or adding comments. Finally, for a form, you want users to be able to enter content in the content controls and to update fields, so you can give them limited access to fill in the form. Refer to the Session 9.3 Visual Overview for more information about setting editing restrictions.

One advantage to using the Restrict Editing command instead of the Group command is that you can set a password to prevent users from turning the restriction off. When you create a password, you should create one that you can easily remember but that others cannot easily guess. If you forget the password, there is no way to recover it and you will not be able to remove the editing restriction.

Because a form that has editing restrictions allows the user to enter data only in content controls, make sure you do not select the "Remove content control when contents are edited" property for content controls you insert. If you do, as soon as the user types one character in a control, the control will be deleted, and the user will not be able to enter any more data.

REFERENCE

Restricting Editing for Filling in a Form

- On the ribbon, click the Developer tab, and then in the Protect group, click the Restrict Editing button.
- In the Restrict Editing pane, click the "Allow only this type of editing in the document" check box to select it, click the arrow, and then click Filling in forms.
- Click Yes, Start Enforcing Protection. If the button is grayed out (not available), click the Design Mode button in the Controls group on the Developer tab to turn off Design mode.
- In the Start Enforcing Protection dialog box, type a password in the Enter new password (optional) box, type the same password in the Reenter password to confirm box, and then click OK; or, if you do not want to use a password, just click OK.
- To turn off protection, click Stop Protection at the bottom of the pane.
- If you used a password, type it in the Password box in the Unprotect Document dialog box, and then click OK.

You'll restrict editing in the form so that the only thing users can do is enter data in the content controls.

To restrict editing for filling in a form:

▶ **1.** On the ribbon, click the **Developer** tab, and then make sure Design mode is turned off. You cannot restrict editing when the form is in Design mode.

▶ **2.** In the Protect group, click the **Restrict Editing** button. The Restrict Editing pane opens to the right of the document window. See Figure 9–36.

Figure 9–36   Restrict Editing pane

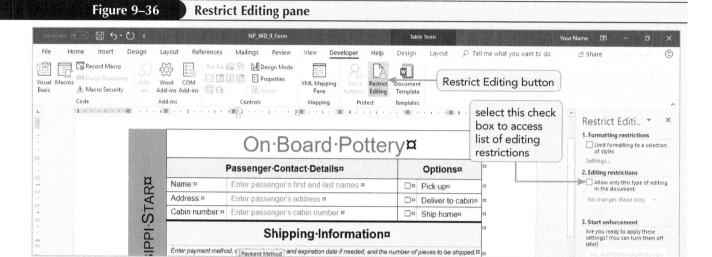

3. In the "2. Editing restrictions" section, click the **Allow only this type of editing in the document** check box to select it. The box below that check box becomes available and displays "No changes (Read only)."

4. Click the section 2 **arrow** to display a list of ways you can choose to restrict editing, and then click **Filling in forms**.

5. In the "3. Start enforcement" section, click **Yes, Start Enforcing Protection**. The Start Enforcing Protection dialog box opens.

   In the next steps, be very careful to type the password exactly as shown or you will not be able to open it later.

TIP

To protect the form without setting a password, click OK in the Start Enforcing Protection dialog box without typing anything.

6. Click in the **Enter new password (optional)** box, and then type **Form** as the password. The characters you type appear as round bullet symbols. Passwords are case sensitive, so "Form" is not the same as "form." Note that this password is not a strong password—it would be easy for someone to guess, and it does not contain numbers or symbols in addition to letters. However, for the purposes of testing the form, it's fine.

7. Press **TAB** to move the insertion point to the Reenter password to confirm box, type **Form**, and then click **OK**. The Restrict Editing pane changes to inform you that the document is protected from unintentional editing, and the Stop Protection command button appears at the bottom of the pane. Because you can't edit the form now, most of the buttons on the ribbon are unavailable (grayed out). See Figure 9–37.

| Figure 9–37 | Form after restricting editing |

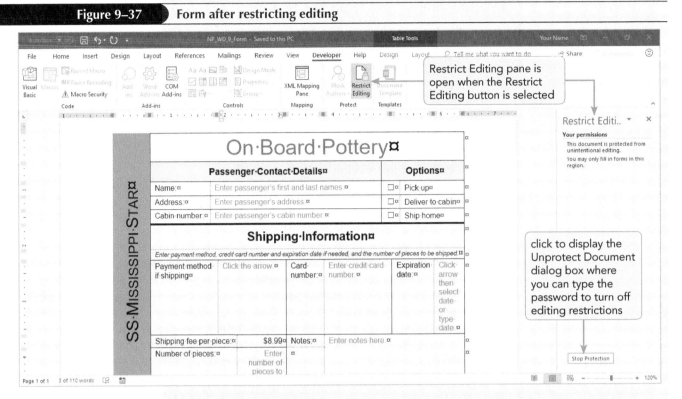

Trouble? If a dialog box appears telling you that the passwords don't match, click OK, delete the dots in both password boxes, and then repeat Steps 6 and 7.

▶ **8. sam'**⬆ Save the changes to the template.

Make sure you save the changes so that when you create a new document based on this template, the new document will be based on the most recent version.

If you ever want to remove the password, display the Restrict Editing pane, and then click Stop Protection. If a password is set, the Unprotect Document dialog box opens with a Password box. Type the password in the Password box, and then click OK. The Restrict Editing pane changes to display the options for setting restrictions again.

Filling in the Online Form

So far, you have been acting as the form designer and creator. Now it's time to try out the form from the user's point of view to make sure there are no unexpected glitches. You can do this by filling in the form just as a user would.

Because the form template is not saved in the Custom Office Templates folder, you need to double-click the form template in a File Explorer window.

To open a new form from the template:

▶ **1.** On the taskbar, click the **File Explorer** button 🔲 . The File Explorer window opens.

▶ **2.** Navigate to the drive and folder where you are saving your files, and then double-click the **NP_WD_9_Form** template. A new document based on the template is created, and the first content control—the Passenger Name content control—is selected.

Now you will enter information in the form.

To enter information in the form:

▶ **1.** With the Passenger Name content control selected, type your first and last names, and then press **TAB**. The text you typed appears in the cell and is formatted in bold because of the Properties settings you entered earlier, and the Passenger Address content control is now selected. This is an example of why you should always test the final form. When you were creating the form and you pressed TAB after entering data in the Passenger Name content control, the Pick Up Check Box content control was selected. By testing the form in a new document, you will have the same experience as a person using the form will have.

▶ **2.** In the Passenger Address content control, type **123 Main St., Natchez, MS 39120**, and then press **TAB**. The Cabin Number content control is selected.

▶ **3.** In the Cabin Number content control, type **401**, and then press **TAB**. The Payment Method content control is selected.

▶ **4.** Click the **Payment Method** content control arrow, click **Credit card**, and then press **TAB**. The Credit Card Number content control is selected.

▶ **5.** In the Credit Card Number content control, type **1234 5678 9012**, and then press **TAB**. The Card Expiration Date content control is selected.

▶ **6.** Click the Card Expiration Date **arrow**, scroll to June of the current year, and then click any date. The calendar closes, the date is displayed in the format 06/2021, and the insertion point is before "06" in the date.

▶ **7.** Press → seven times to position the insertion point after the year, press **BACKSPACE** twice, and then type **22**. The expiration date is now 06/2022.

▶ **8.** Press **TAB**. The Notes content control is selected.

▶ **9.** Type **Leave on back porch.** and then press **TAB**. The No. of Pieces content control is selected.

▶ **10.** In the No. of Pieces content control, type **4**. Now you need to update the field containing the formula.

▶ **11.** Right-click the field in the cell to the right of the "Total" cell to open the shortcut menu. The Update Field command is again on this menu, and because the form is restricted, it is the only command available.

▶ **12.** Click **Update Field**. "$ 35.96"—the result of multiplying the shipping fee by the number of pieces—is displayed in the cell.

The check boxes in the Options section were never selected as you pressed TAB to move around the form.

13. To the left of the "Ship home" cell, click the check box. An "X" appears in the check box. After you click the check box, the Payment Method content control becomes selected. Compare your screen to Figure 9–38.

Figure 9–38   **Form completed in a new document**

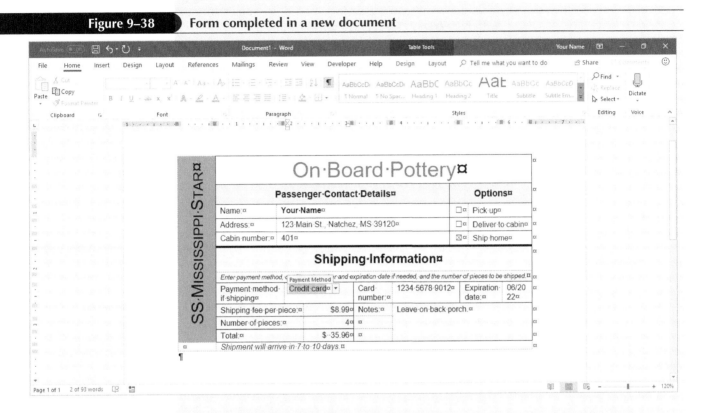

As you saw, pressing TAB to move from one content control to another did not work as expected. There is no way to fix this when a protected form contains content controls unless you create fairly complex macros in the Visual Basic window. If the online form will be filled out by employees, you can train them in the best way to fill out the form. If the online form will be filled out by new users each time, such as by new customers, you should take the order in which the content controls are selected when you press TAB into consideration when you create the form. For example, in the NP_WD_9_Form template, you could move the Options section so it is between the Passenger Contact Details and Shipping Information sections. Then the user's eye will be drawn to the check boxes even if they press TAB after entering the cabin number. Likewise, the Notes section could be placed below the rows that contain the fees and total calculation. You could also add an instruction reminding the user to right-click the Total field to update the result.

To save the test form and remove the Developer tab from the ribbon:

▶ **1.** On the Quick Access Toolbar, click the **Save** button , navigate to the location where you are saving your files, replace the text in the File name box with **NP_WD_9_Test**, and then click **Save**.

You're ready to show the completed template and test form to Emi. Before you do, you'll remove the Developer tab from the ribbon.

▶ **2.** If the Developer tab was not displayed when you started working with content controls, hide it by right-clicking any tab on the ribbon, clicking **Customize the Ribbon**, clicking the **Developer** check box in the Customize the Ribbon list, and then clicking **OK**.

▶ **3.** Close the **NP_WD_9_Test** document.

▶ **4.** Close the **NP_WD_9_Form** template.

PROSKILLS

Problem Solving: Organizing a Form

The form you created in this module contains information organized in a logical way for the person who needs to create and store the form. However, as you saw when you entered the information in the form, it is not set up in the most logical way for a user who presses TAB to move from one control or field to the next. When you design a form, keep TAB behavior in mind and try to come up with a design that works for both the person entering the data and the person reading the form. For example, for this form, you could fill all the cells that the user needs to fill out with a color to draw the user's attention to those cells. You could also consider redesigning the table so that pressing TAB moves the user through the form in a more logical order—such as taking the user through the personal contact information fields before moving on to the credit card information fields. If you keep the end user—the person who will be filling out the form—in mind, you will be able to create a form that is easy to fill out without missing any of the content controls.

Emi is pleased with the appearance of the form you created and with how well it works. She's sure it will make the process of gathering information from passengers more efficient.

Session 9.3 Quick Check

REVIEW

1. In a table, how do you reference the cell in the third column and the first row?
2. What is a formula?
3. What is always the first character in a formula in a Word table?
4. What is a variable?
5. What is an argument?
6. How does the number 34 appear if the format is specified as $##0;($##0)?
7. What happens when you use the Group command on a form that contains content controls?

PRACTICE

Review Assignments

Data Files needed for the Review Assignments: NP_WD_9-2.dotx

For theme cruises for people interested in writing, Emi Nakata arranges for successful published authors to give lectures. She also schedules a private reception after the lecture for interested passengers. Although the cost of the lecture is included in the cruise fee, passengers who want to attend the private reception need to register and pay a $75 fee. Emi asked you to create an online form that she can use to register passengers for the reception. She added most of the information she wants to include in a table. You need to format the table, insert content controls and a formula, and test the form. Complete the following steps:

1. Open the template **NP_WD_9-2.dotx** from the Word9 > Review folder included with your Data Files, and then save it in the location specified by your instructor as a template named **NP_WD_9_Reception**.

2. In the first row, select all five cells, and then split the selected cells into one column and two rows, merging the cells before you split them. Move the text "Private Reception" into the cell in the new second row.

3. Select all the cells to the right of the cells containing "Name," "Address," "Phone," and "Email." (A total of 12 cells should be selected.) Split the selected cells into one column and four rows, merging the cells before you split them.

4. Merge the following cells:
   a. in the last row, the cell containing text and the next two cells to its right (The cell in the last column of that row should not be merged.)
   b. in the first column, the cell containing "Contact Info" and the three cells below it
   c. in the first column, the cell containing "Reception Details" and the next two cells below it (The cell in the bottom row of the first column should not be merged with the "Reception Details" cell.)

5. Select the cells containing "Reception Date," Author Name," and "Reception Location," and then split each cell into two cells in the same row. (*Hint*: Do not merge the cells before splitting.) There should be an empty cell to the right of each of the cells you selected.

6. Split the cell containing "Food Allergies" into one column and two rows. Then split the cell in the new row below the "Food Allergies" cell into four columns.

7. Select the empty cell above the "Allergy notes" cell, and then split that cell into four columns and two rows.

8. Select the "Allergy notes" cell and the cell below it, and then split those cells into two columns and one row. (Merge the cells before splitting so that the result is two cells.)

9. Rotate the text in the merged cells containing "Contact Info" and "Reception Details" so the text reads up from the bottom.

10. In the first row, change the size of "SS Mississippi Star" to 28 points and change the font color to Teal, Accent 5, Darker 25%.

11. In the second row, shade the cell containing "Private Reception" with the Teal, Accent 5, Darker 25% color, and change the font color to White, Background 1. Change the font size to 28 points, and then add bold and small caps formatting.

12. In the first column, change the size of the text in the two merged cells to 10 points, change the font color to Teal, Accent 5, Darker 50%, and format it as bold.

13. Format the text in the cells containing "Name," "Address," "Phone," "Email," "Reception Date," "Author Name," "Reception Location," "Reception Fee," "No. of Tickets," "Total," "Food Allergies," and "Allergy notes" as bold. Then change the size of the text "Allergy notes" to 10 points.

14. Shade the cell containing "Food Allergies" and all of the cells below it with the Dark Purple, Text 2, Lighter 80% color.

15. In the last row, italicize the text "Tickets will not be issued until payment is processed."

16. In the Food Allergies section, in the three cells in column G below the cell containing "Food Allergies," enter the following: **Peanuts**, **Tree nuts**, and **Dairy**. In the three cells in column I (the last column), enter the following: **Shellfish**, **Gluten**, and **Other**.

17. Center the content of the cells containing "SS Mississippi Star," "Private Reception," "Contact Info," "Reception Details," and "Food Allergies" both horizontally and vertically.

18. Center the content of the cells containing "Reception Date," "Author Name," and "Reception Location" and the empty cells to their right vertically (but leave these cells left-aligned horizontally.)

19. Center the content of the cells containing "Reception Fee," "No. of Tickets," and "Total" vertically (but leave these cells left-aligned horizontally). Then center the content of the cells to the right of each of these cells vertically, and change the horizontal alignment of those cells so the contents are right-aligned.

20. Center the content of the cells containing the types of food allergies vertically, but leave them left-aligned horizontally. Center the content of the cells to the left of the six types of food allergies both vertically and horizontally.

21. Turn off the option to automatically resize the table to fit its contents, and then change the top and bottom cell margins for all the cells in the table to **0.02"**. Change the top and bottom cell margins for the cells in the first and second rows back to **0"**.

22. Resize the columns so the distance between the Move Table Column markers matches the measurements shown in Figure 9–39. Make sure you resize the columns in the order they are listed. (*Hint*: Note that the table has nine columns—column A through column I—and 12 rows. The cell containing "Reception Date" is in cell B7, and the cell containing "Author Name" is in cell B9 because in the "Food Allergies" section, there are extra rows.)

Figure 9–39   Column measurements for the table in the NP_WD_9_Reception form

Cells	Measurement
"Contact Info," "Reception Details," and the blank cell below them (cells A3, A7, and A12)	0.3"
Cells in column B from the cell containing "Name" through the cell containing "Reception Location" (cells B3 through B11)	0.8"
Cells to the right of the cells containing "Reception Date," "Author Name," and "Reception Location" (cells C7, C9, and C11)	2.3"
"Reception Fee," "No. of Tickets," and "Total" (cells D7, D9, and D11)	0.8"
Cells to the right of the cells containing "Reception Fee," "No. of Tickets," and "Total" (cells E7, E9, and E11)	0.4"
Cell containing "Tickets will not be issued until payment is processed" (cell B12)—make sure the right border of this cell aligns with the right border of cells E7, E9, and E11	4.75"
Three cells in the first column below "Food Allergies" (cells F8, F9, and F10)	0.5"
Three cells in the second column below "Food Allergies" (cells G8, G9, and G10)	1"
Three cells in the third column below "Food Allergies" (cells H8, H9, and H10)	0.5"
"Allergy Notes" (cell F11)	0.5"

23. Add a 3-point border between row 6 and row 7.

24. Change the Line Weight box in the Borders group on the Table Tools Design tab back to ½ point, and then remove the borders from the right side of the following cells:
    - B3 ("Name") through B11 ("Reception Location")
    - D7 ("Reception Fee") through D11 ("Total")
    - F11 ("Allergy notes")

25. Remove the border from the left side of the cells containing "Peanuts," "Tree nuts," "Dairy," "Shellfish," "Gluten," and "Other."

26. Remove the top, left, and right borders from cell A1 (the cell containing "SS Mississippi Star").

27. In the last row, remove the border between the first and second cells.

28. Display the Developer tab, if necessary, and then insert Plain Text content controls in the cells to the right of the cells listed in Figure 9–40. Use the contents of the cell to the left of the content control as the title of the control. Do not allow the controls to be deleted. Revise the placeholder text as indicated in Figure 9–40.

Figure 9–40   **Placeholder text for the Plain Text content controls in the NP_WD_9_Reception form**

Cell	Placeholder Text
Name	**Enter passenger name.**
Address	**Enter passenger address.**
Phone	**Enter passenger phone number.**
Email	**Enter passenger email address.**
Author Name	**Enter author name.**
No. of Tickets	**Enter number of tickets.**
Allergy notes	**Enter additional information about food allergies.**

29. Change the properties of the Name content control (cell C3) so that it uses the Strong style.

30. Insert a Date Picker content control in the cell to the right of "Reception Date" (cell C7) with the title of **Reception Date**. Do not allow the control to be deleted, and use M/d/yy as the date format. Change the placeholder text to **Click arrow, scroll to month, and click date.** (including the period).

31. Insert a Drop-Down List content control in the cell to the right of "Reception Location" (cell C11). Use **Reception Location** as the title, do not allow the control to be deleted, and add **Mark Twain Lounge**, **Ragtime Club**, and **Delta Grille** as the choices. Reorder these options so that they are in alphabetical order. Change the instruction text at the top of the list and the placeholder text to **Select reception location.** (including the period).

32. Insert a Check Box content control in each of the cells to the left of the six types of food allergies. Use the text in the cell to the right of each check box as the title, and do not allow them to be deleted.

33. Insert a formula in cell E11 (the cell to the right of the cell containing "Total") to multiply the contents of the cell to the right of "Reception Fee" by the contents of the cell to the right of "No. of Tickets." Change the format to show currency with no decimal places. (*Hint*: Remove the decimal point and the two zeros after the decimal point both inside and outside the parentheses.)

34. Restrict editing in the template for filling in a form with the password **Reception**.

35. Save the changes to the template. Hide the Developer tab if it was hidden at the beginning of the Review Assignments.

36. Open a new document based on the NP_WD_9_Reception template. (*Hint*: Remember to double-click the template in a File Explorer window.) Fill in the form using the passenger data **John Doe**, **123 Main St.**, **Hannibal**, **MO 63401**, **(573) 555-0188** as the phone number, **j.doe@ example.com** as the email address, **August 15, 2021** as the reception date, **Jane Smith** as the author name, Mark Twain Lounge as the reception location, **3** as the number of tickets, and select Tree nuts as a food allergy. Insert your name in the cell to the right of "Notes." Remember to update the formula field in the cell that calculates the total fee.

37. Save the completed form as **NP_WD_9_ReceptionTest** in the location specified by your instructor. Close all open documents.

Case Problem 1

Data File needed for this Case Problem: NP_WD_9-3.dotx

Las Cruces College   Incoming freshmen at Las Cruces College in Las Cruces, New Mexico, fill out dorm preference forms that indicate their preference for a room style (single, double, and so on) and their personal living style (messy/neat, early riser/late bedtime, and so on). Maura Sheehan, the college's director of admissions, has asked you to create an online form that incoming freshmen can fill out when they attend orientation in the late spring. Complete the following steps:

1. Open the file **NP_WD_9-3.dotx**, located in the Word9 > Case1 folder. Save the file as a template named **NP_WD_9_Dorm** in the location specified by your instructor.

2. Select the table and then change the option so that the table does not automatically resize to fit contents.

3. Select all of the cells in the first row, and then split them into one column and two rows. Move "Dorm Preferences" into the second row. Format the text in the first row with 24-point Copperplate Gothic Bold. Change the size of the text in the second row to 16 points. Change the alignment of the text in the first and second rows to Top Center.

4. Remove all the borders around the merged cell in the first row. Remove all the borders around the merged cell in the second row except for the bottom border.

5. In the fourth and sixth rows, merge all the cells. Shade the merged cells in the fourth and sixth rows with the Black, Text 1 color, and then change the alignment of the text in each row to Top Center.

6. In the fifth row (which contains cells with the text "First Choice," "Second Choice," "Third Choice," and "Fourth Choice"), select all four cells, and then split the cells into two rows, keeping the text in the fifth row (the cells in the new sixth row will be empty). Center-align the contents of all of the cells in the fifth row and in the new sixth row both horizontally and vertically. Remove the border between rows 5 and 6. If necessary, change the height of rows 5 and 6 to 0.32" in the Height box in the Cell Size group on the Table Tools Layout tab.

7. Merge cells A8 through A11, and then shade the merged cell with the Light Gray, Accent 2, Lighter 80% color. Merge cells C8 through C11, and then shade the merged cell with the Light Gray, Accent 1, Darker 25% color.

8. In merged cell A8, type **Sleep Habits**. In merged cell C8, type **Neatness**. Change the font size of the text in cell A8 and cell C8 to 16 points. Rotate the text in merged cell A8 and in merged cell C8 so it reads from the bottom up, and then center the text in both cells horizontally and vertically.

9. Shade cell B8 (the cell containing "Select all that apply.") with the Light Gray, Accent 2, Lighter 80% color. Shade cell D8 (the cell containing "How neat are you? Select only one.") with the Light Gray, Accent 1, Darker 25% color.

10. Split cells B9 (the cell containing "Bed before 11 p.m."), B10 (the cell containing "Early riser"), B11 (the cell containing "Late riser"), and B12 (the empty cell in the last row) into two columns so that the text is in column B and there is an empty cell to the right of each of those cells (cell B12 will not contain any text). Center the contents of cells B9, B10, and B11 vertically and keep them left-aligned. Center the contents of the empty cells C9, C10, and C11 both horizontally and vertically.

11. Split cells E9 (the cell containing "Very neat"), E10 (the cell containing "Somewhat neat"), E11 (the cell containing "Not neat"), and E12 (the empty cell in the last row) into two columns so that the text is in column E and there is an empty cell to the right of each of those cells (cell E12 will not contain any text). Center the contents of cells E9, E10, and E11 vertically and keep them left-aligned. Center the contents of the empty cells F9, F10, and F11 both horizontally and vertically.

12. Remove all the borders around cells A8, B8, D8, E8, and all the cells in row 12. Select cells B9 through C11, and then remove all the borders except for the inside horizontal borders. Select cells E9 through F11, and then remove all the borders except for the inside horizontal borders and the right border.

13. The distances between the Move Table Column markers of the cells in the table are listed in Figure 9–41. Remember to adjust the widths from left to right. The widths of the cells in your table should be adjusted to be as close as possible to the widths listed in Figure 9–41.

Figure 9–41   **Column measurements for the table in the NP_WD_9_Dorm form**

Cell	Measurement
A3 (the cell containing "Name")	0.5"
B3 (the cell to the right of the cell containing "Name")	2.9"
C3 (the cell containing "Student ID Number") (*Hint*: Make sure "Student ID Number" fits on one line.)	1.3"
A8 and A12 (the cell containing "Sleep Habits" and the empty cell below it)	0.3"
B9 through B12 (the cell containing "Bed before 11 p.m." through the empty cell below the cell containing "Late riser")	1.5"
B8 (the cell containing "Select all that apply") and C8 through C12 (the cell to the right of the cell containing "Bed before 11 p.m." through the empty cell in the last row in column C) (*Hint*: Click in cell B8 to the right of "Select all that apply." and then drag straight down to cell C12. Note that cell B8 will be wider than cells C8 through C12 even after you make this adjustment.)	0.25"
D8 and D12 (the cell containing "Neatness" and the empty cell below it)	0.3"
E9 through E12 (the cell containing "Very neat" through the empty below the cell containing "Not neat")	2.9"

14. Merge cells A12 through C12 (the first three cells in the last row), and then shade the merged cell with the Light Gray, Accent 2, Lighter 80% color. Merge cells D12 through F12 (the last three cells in the last row), and then shade the merged cell with the Light Gray, Accent 1, Darker 25% color.

15. In cells B10, B11, E9, E10, and E11, select the text below the first line, italicize it, and then change the font size of the italicized text to nine points.

16. Insert a Plain Text content control in cell B3 (the cell to the right of the cell containing "Name") with the title **Student Name** and formatted with the Strong style. Do not allow the control to be deleted. Change the placeholder text to **Enter your name.** (including the period).

17. Insert a Plain Text content control in cell D3 (the cell to the right of the cell containing "Student ID Number") with the title **Student ID**. Do not allow the control to be deleted. Change the placeholder text to **Enter your student ID number.** (including the period).

18. Insert a Drop-Down List content control in cell A6 (the cell below the cell containing "First Choice"). The Title property is **Room Style**. The choices in the list are **Single**, **Double**, **Triple**, and **Suite (6 to 8 people)**. Change the first option in the list (the instruction text) to **Select a dorm room style.** (including the period). Change the placeholder text to **Click arrow.** (including the period). Insert this same content control in cells B6, C6, and D6.

19. Insert Check Box content controls in cells C9, C10, C11, F9, F10, and F11. Do not add a Title property to these controls. Do not allow the controls to be deleted.

20. Turn on Design mode, group all of the content to protect the form's structure, and then turn off Design mode.

21. Save the changes to the form.

22. Create a new document based on the NP_WD_9_Dorm template. Add your name as the student name, type **12-3456** as the Student ID number, select a different option in each of the dorm style choice lists, and then follow the instructions to select options in the bottom section.

23. Save the new document as **NP_WD_9_DormTest** in the location specified by your instructor. Close all open documents.

CHALLENGE

Case Problem 2

Data File needed for this Case Problem: NP_WD_9-4.dotx

Charleston Office Supply Center   Carlos Gomez is the senior manager at Charleston Office Supply Center in Charleston, South Carolina. The store sells office supplies to businesses in and around Charleston. They offer same-day delivery on most items. The store was established less than a year ago, and the owners have asked Carlos to try to streamline their ordering system. Carlos asks you to help him create an online form, which will need to contain several formulas. Carlos realizes that Excel would be a better tool to use; however, Excel is not installed on the computers his staff will be using to input the orders, so for now, the staff will use a Word form. Complete the following steps:

1. Open the template **NP_WD_9-4.dotx** from the Word9 > Case2 folder included with your Data Files, and then save it as a template to the location specified by your instructor with the name **NP_WD_9_Order**.

2. Merge the four cells in the first row, and then split the merged cell into two rows. Move the text "Order Form" to the cell in the second row, and then remove the blank paragraph below "Charleston Office Supply Center," if necessary.

3. In the first row, format the text as 28-point Franklin Gothic Demi Condensed, and change its color to Brown, Accent 3, Darker 50%. Center the text horizontally, and then remove all the cell borders.

4. In the second row, shade the cell with the Brown, Accent 3, Darker 25% color, change the size of the text to 20 points, and change the text color to White, Background 1. Center the text horizontally.

5. In the third row, shade the cells with the Brown, Accent 3, Lighter 80% color.

6. Select cells D3 through D9 (the cell in row 3 containing "Total" through the last cell in column D), and then drag the left border to change the width of these cells so that the distance between the Move Table Column markers on the ruler is about 1".

7. Select cells C3 through C9 (the cell containing "Price" through the last cell in column C), and then drag the left border to change the width of these cells so that the distance between the Move Table Column markers on the ruler is about 0.9".

8. Select cells B3 and B4 (the cell containing "Quantity" and the blank cell below it), and then drag the left border to change the width of these cells so that the distance between the Move Table Column markers on the ruler is about 0.8".

9. Merge cells A6 and B6 (the cell containing "Notes" and the cell to its right). Then merge the six cells below this merged cell. Remove the border between the "Notes" cell and the merged cell below it. (*Hint*: If you can't remove the border between the cells, try removing the border below the "Notes" cell or the border above the blank cell below the "Notes" cell.)

10. Shade cells B6 through C8 (the block of six cells from the cell containing "Subtotal" to the cell to the right of the cell containing "Tax") with the Brown, Accent 3, Lighter 60% color.

11. Shade cells B9 and C9 (the cells in the bottom row containing "Total" and the cell to its right) with the Black, Text 1 color. (Note that the text changes to white automatically.) Apply bold formatting to these cells.

12. In the fourth row, right-align cell D4 (the cell below the "Total" cell in column D), and then right-align cell C4 (the cell below the cell containing "Price"). Right-align cells C6 (the cells to the right of "Subtotal") through C9 (the cell to the right of "Total").

13. Format the border to the left of the cells containing "Subtotal," "Delivery," "Tax," and the "Total" cell in the last row so it is 3 points wide.

14. Select the four cells in row 5, and then shade the cells with the Black, Text 1 color. Then, with the four cells still selected, change the font size of these cells to 2 points.

15. Insert Plain Text content controls in the cells listed in Figure 9–42. Do not allow the controls to be deleted.

Figure 9–42   **Plain Text content controls for the NP_WD_9_Order form**

Cell	Title	Placeholder Text
A4 (the cell below the cell containing "Item")	Item	Type item name.
B4 (the cell below the cell containing "Quantity")	Quantity	Enter quantity.
C4 (the cell below the cell containing "Price")	Price per Item	Enter price per item.
A7 (the merged cell below the cell containing "Notes"	Notes	Enter notes if needed.
C7 (the cell to the right of the cell containing "Delivery")	Delivery	Refer to delivery fee chart.

16. In cell D4 (the cell below the cell containing "Total"), insert a formula that multiplies the value in cell B4 (the cell below "Quantity") by the value in cell C4 (the cell below "Price"). Format the number using the format that shows a dollar sign.

✦ **Explore** 17. Select the entire fourth row in the table (the row containing the content controls and the formula), and then add a Repeating Section Content Control.

18. In the cell to the right of the cell containing "Subtotal," insert a formula that uses the SUM function to add the values in the cells above the cell using "ABOVE" as the argument. Format the number using the format that shows a dollar sign.

✦ **Explore** 19. Select the cell containing the formula field to the right of the cell containing "Subtotal," and then create a bookmark named **Subtotal**. Then, in the cell to the right of the cell containing "Tax," insert a formula that multiplies the sales tax in Charleston, South Carolina (9%) by the value stored in the field bookmarked by the Subtotal bookmark. (*Hint*: To calculate the sales tax, you need to multiply by 0.09.) Format the number using the format that shows a dollar sign.

Explore 20. Select the cell to the right of the cell containing "Delivery," and then create a bookmark named **Delivery**. Select the cell containing the formula field to the right of the cell containing "Tax," and then create a bookmark named **Tax**.

Explore 21. In the last row, in the cell to the right of the cell containing "Total," insert a formula using the SUM function to add the values stored in the locations bookmarked by the Subtotal, Delivery, and Tax bookmarks. (*Hint*: Use the bookmark names as the arguments for the SUM function.) Format the number using the format that shows a dollar sign. (Note that the empty row with the font size of 2 points is required to prevent the bookmarks from changing when you use the Repeating Section Content Control in Step 24.)

22. Save the changes to the template, and then create a new document based on the template. Save the new document as a document named **NP_WD_9_OrderTest** in the location specified by your instructor.

Explore 23. Add the data listed in Figure 9–43. (*Hint*: Click the Plus Sign button to the right of the row to use the Repeating Section content control to create a new row with the same content controls.)

Figure 9–43   Data for the NP_WD_9_OrderTest document

Item	Quantity	Price per Item
Metal 5-shelf bookcase	5	$275.45
24 × 42 cubicle panels	20	$145.25
Heavy-duty cross-cut shredder	10	$120.00

24. Change the alignment of the entries in the Price cells in the two new rows so that it matches the formatting in the original row.

25. Update the fields in the Total column for the three items. Note that the total price is correct only in the first row.

Explore 26. Edit the formulas in the Total column in the two new rows so that they correctly use the values in their rows to calculate the total. (*Hint*: Toggle the field codes on, and then edit the row references in the field codes.) If necessary, update the fields to recalculate the totals.

27. In the cell to the right of the "Delivery" cell, enter **$50.00**.

28. Update the fields in the cells to the right of "Subtotal" and "Tax" and in the black-shaded cell to the right of "Total."

29. Add your name in the Notes content control, save the NP_WD_9_OrderTest document and close it, and then close the NP_WD_9_Order template.

Managing Long Documents

Creating a Survey Report for a Personal Chef Association

OBJECTIVES

Session 10.1
- Work in Outline view
- Create a master document
- Insert and create subdocuments
- Unlink a subdocument
- Reopen a master document

Session 10.2
- Add numbers to headings
- Add numbered captions
- Create cross-references
- Insert an endnote
- Create a chart in a document
- Restrict editing in a document
- Check for hidden data
- Check for accessibility

Session 10.3
- Evaluate section and page breaks
- Apply different page number formats in document sections
- Create odd and even pages
- Insert a style reference
- Insert nonbreaking hyphens and spaces
- Create and update an index
- Create a table of figures
- Update fields before printing
- Check compatibility with earlier versions of Word
- Encrypt and mark a document as final

Case | *World Association of Personal Chefs*

The World Association of Personal Chefs (WAPC), an organization with headquarters in New York City, provides networking opportunities and educational services for professional personal chefs. Every year, the WAPC holds a meeting that includes seminars, a vendor showcase for new products in an exposition hall, and networking opportunities in the evenings. The Annual Meeting Committee hired Marketfield Research Associates to conduct a survey of the meeting participants, presenters, and corporate patrons to find out if they were satisfied with the meeting this year and to collect suggestions for next year's meeting. Bailey Lawrence, chair of the Annual Meeting Committee, has asked for your help creating a report on the survey results. The report will include front matter (title page, table of contents, and list of figures) and an index as well as numbered figures and cross-references. The report must be set up to print on both sides of the paper, and it will require different formats and footers for even and odd pages. When you are finished with the report, you will safeguard it against unauthorized edits by encrypting it, and then you will mark the report as final.

STARTING DATA FILES

Word10 ➔ **Module**

NP_WD_10-1.docx
Support_WD_10_Patrons.docx
Support_WD_10_Presenters.docx

Review

NP_WD_10-2.docx
Support_WD_10_Alonzo.docx
Support_WD_10_Marie.docx

Case1

NP_WD_10-3.docx
Support_WD_10_Background.docx
Support_WD_10_Market.docx
Support_WD_10_Summary.docx

Case2

(none)

Session 10.1 Visual Overview:

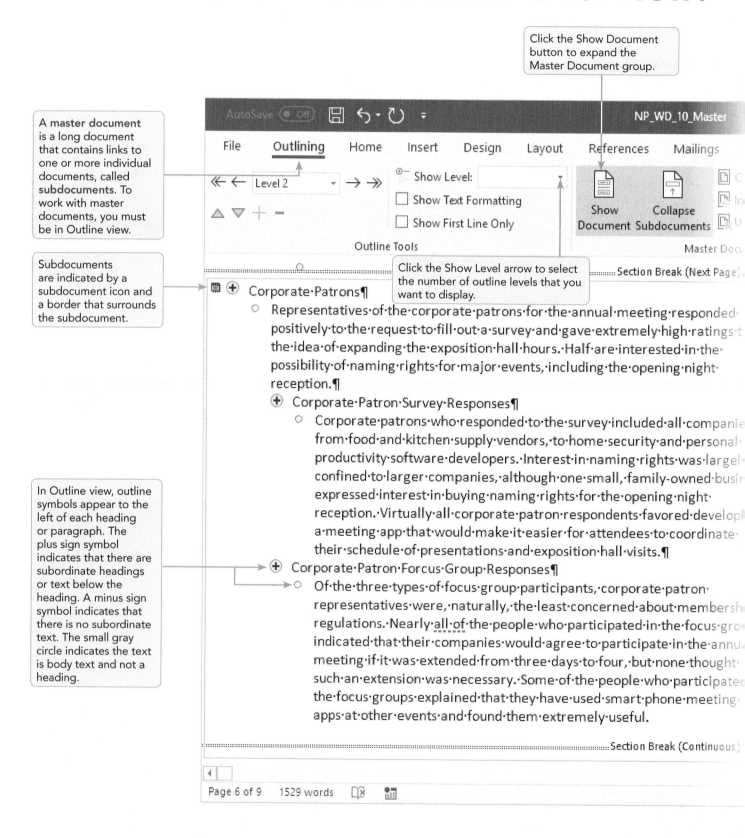

Click the Show Document button to expand the Master Document group.

A master document is a long document that contains links to one or more individual documents, called **subdocuments**. To work with master documents, you must be in Outline view.

Subdocuments are indicated by a subdocument icon and a border that surrounds the subdocument.

Click the Show Level arrow to select the number of outline levels that you want to display.

In Outline view, outline symbols appear to the left of each heading or paragraph. The plus sign symbol indicates that there are subordinate headings or text below the heading. A minus sign symbol indicates that there is no subordinate text. The small gray circle indicates the text is body text and not a heading.

Master Documents

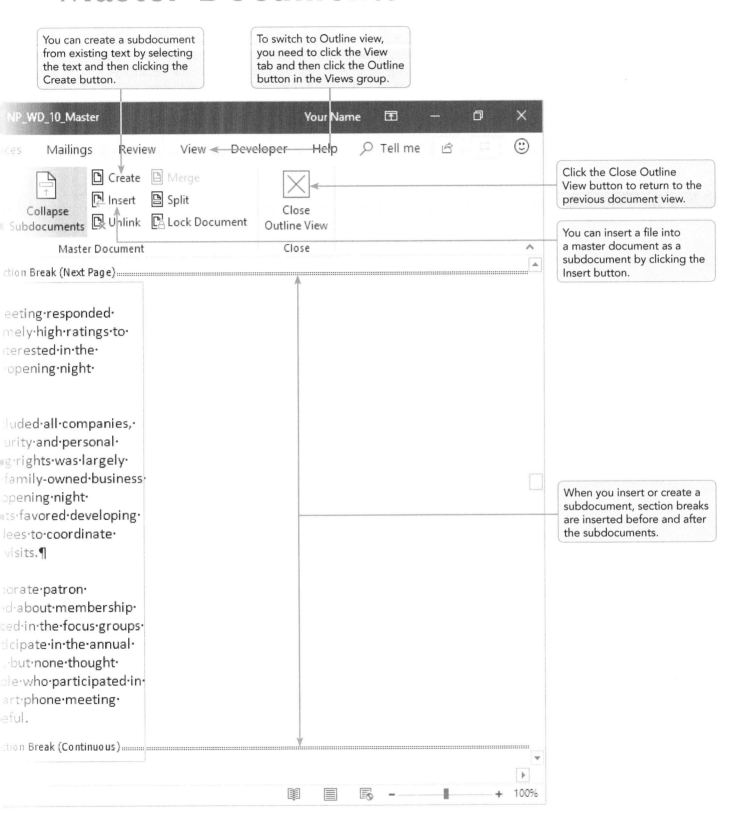

You can create a subdocument from existing text by selecting the text and then clicking the Create button.

To switch to Outline view, you need to click the View tab and then click the Outline button in the Views group.

Click the Close Outline View button to return to the previous document view.

You can insert a file into a master document as a subdocument by clicking the Insert button.

When you insert or create a subdocument, section breaks are inserted before and after the subdocuments.

Working with Master Documents

Manipulating pages in a long document can be cumbersome and time consuming. On the other hand, splitting a long document into several shorter documents makes it hard to maintain consistent formatting and to ensure that section and page numbering are always correct. To avoid these problems, you can use a master document, which combines the benefits of splitting documents into separate files with the advantages of working with a single document. A master document is also helpful when several people are simultaneously working on different parts of the same document. Each team member can submit a separate document; you can then quickly organize these individual documents into a single, complete document by creating a master document. Figure 10–1 illustrates the relationship between master documents and subdocuments.

Figure 10–1	Master document and subdocument

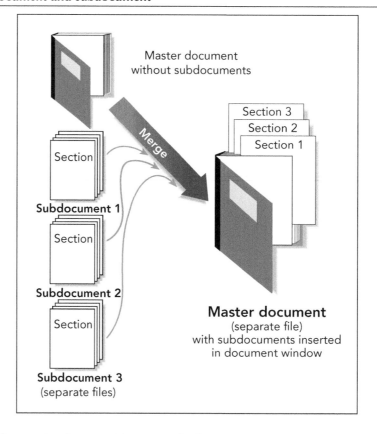

Working with a master document has several advantages:

- **Consistent formatting across elements**—You can set up styles, headers, footers, and other formatting elements in only the master document; any subdocuments you create or insert will have the same formatting.
- **Accurate numbering**—You can number the master document, including all subdocuments, with consecutive page numbers, heading numbers, and figure numbers. If you rearrange, delete, or add material, Word updates the numbers to reflect your changes.
- **Accurate cross-referencing**—You can refer to figures or tables in subdocuments, and Word will keep the cross-references updated.
- **Complete table of contents and index**—You can easily compile a table of contents and create an index for a master document.
- **Faster editing**—You can edit the master document all at once, or you can edit each subdocument individually. Any changes in the master document automatically take effect and are saved in the subdocument files and vice versa.

Working in Outline View

To create a master document, you need to work in Outline view. When you apply a heading style to a paragraph, you also apply an outline level that matches the heading level. The top-level heading (the Heading 1 style) is Level 1, with subheadings (Heading 2, Heading 3, etc.) labeled as Level 2, Level 3, and so on. Paragraphs that are not formatted as headings have Body Text as the outline level.

Creating an Outline in Outline View

The document outline is created when you apply the built-in heading styles to paragraphs. You can also create an outline in Outline view by applying outline levels to paragraphs.

REFERENCE

Creating an Outline in Outline View

- On the View tab, in the Views group, click the Outline button.
- Type the first Level 1 heading, and then press ENTER.
- To demote a heading, click the Demote button in the Outline Tools group on the Outlining tab, or press TAB.
- To promote a heading, click the Promote button in the Outline Tools group on the Outlining tab, or press SHIFT+TAB.
- To change text to body text, click the Demote to Body Text button in the Outline Tools group on the Outlining tab.

Bailey asks you to create the outline for her report. You'll start working on this in Outline view.

To create an outline in Outline view:

1. Start Word, create a new, blank document, and then save it as **NP_WD_10_Draft** in the location specified by your instructor.

2. Display nonprinting characters.

3. On the ribbon, click the **View** tab, and then in the Views group, click the **Outline** button. The document switches to Outline view, and a new tab, Outlining, appears on the ribbon and is selected. The outline level of the current paragraph is Level 1. See Figure 10–2.

Figure 10–2   Outline view

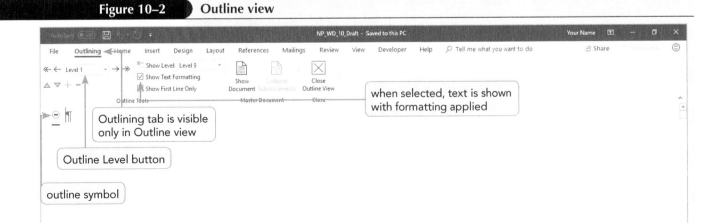

▶ **4.** Change the Zoom level to **120%**.

▶ **5.** Type **Overview** and then press **ENTER**. The text you typed is formatted with the Heading 1 style.

▶ **6.** Type **Corporate Patrons** and then press **ENTER**. You want the next two headings to be Level 2 headings.

▶ **7.** In the Outline Tools group, click the **Demote** button →. The second paragraph indents, the outline symbol next to the second line changes to a plus sign, and the Outline Level button in the Outline Tools group changes to indicate that this paragraph is now Level 2.

▶ **8.** Type **Corporate Patron Survey Responses**, press **ENTER**, type **Corporate Patron Focus Groups**, and then press **ENTER** again. The next heading will be a Level 1 heading.

▶ **9.** In the Outline Tools group, click the **Promote** button ←, and then type **Participants**.

Next, Bailey wants you to add body text under the "Overview" heading. To do this, you'll need to add a new paragraph and then demote it to body text.

To add body text to an outline:

▶ **1.** In the first line of the outline, click after "Overview," and then press **ENTER**. A new paragraph is created at Level 1.

▶ **2.** In the Outline Tools group, click the **Demote to Body Text** button ⇒. The paragraph is indented, and the outline symbol changes to a small gray circle, which indicates body text. The outline symbol next to the first line changes to a plus sign.

▶ **3.** Type **Report on the survey conducted by Marketfield Research Associates** (do not type a period). See Figure 10–3.

Figure 10–3 **Text in Outline view**

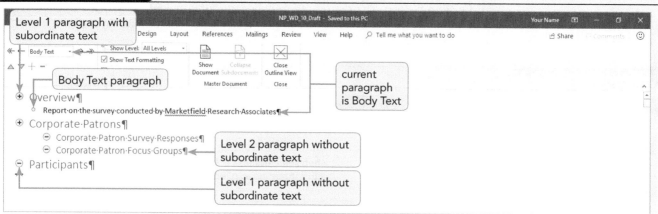

Trouble? If the text on your screen is all black and the same size, click the Show Text Formatting check box in the Outline Tools group to select it.

▶ **4.** Save your changes, and then close the document (but do not close Word).

Changing the Outline Level of a Heading

Bailey added new content to the document, created a custom style for headings in the front and end matter, and added a table of contents. She asks you to continue editing it.

To open the report and view the headings with the custom styles:

▶ 1. **sam**⬇ Open the document **NP_WD_10-1.docx**, located in the Word10 > Module folder included with your Data Files, type your name on the title page in the blank paragraph below "Marie Choi," and then save it as **NP_WD_10_Master** in the location specified by your instructor.

▶ 2. If necessary, change the Zoom level to **120%**.

▶ 3. Scroll down to page 3, and then select **List of Figures**. On the Home tab, in the Styles group, the custom Front/End Matter Heading style is selected. (It appears as "Front/End…" in the Style gallery.)

▶ 4. Scroll up to page 2, and then select **Contents** in the paragraph with the red shading. This paragraph also has the Front/End Matter Heading style applied.

When you use the Table of Contents command to create a table of contents, the outline level of each heading determines whether the heading is included. Paragraphs that have an outline level of Body Text are not included in the table of contents. In the NP_WD_10_Master document, the heading "Contents" is included as the first entry in the table of contents, but it shouldn't be. The "Contents" heading is formatted with the custom Front/End Matter Heading style that Bailey created. To prevent the "Contents" heading from being included in the table of contents, you need to create a new style with an outline level of Body Text.

To create a style based on a heading with the Body Text outline level:

▶ 1. On the Home tab, in the Styles group, click the **More** button ⏷, and then click **Create a Style**. The small Create New Style from Formatting dialog box opens with the text in the Name box selected.

▶ 2. Type **Contents Heading** in the Name box, and then click **Modify**. The large Create New Style from Formatting dialog box opens. You need to change the outline level.

▶ 3. At the bottom of the dialog box, click **Format**, and then click **Paragraph**. The Paragraph dialog box opens with the Indents and Spacing tab selected. In the General section, Level 1 appears in the Outline level box. You need to change the outline level to Body Text.

▶ 4. Click the **Outline level** arrow, click **Body Text**, and then click **OK** in each open dialog box. The new Contents Heading style appears as the first style in the Style gallery. Because you changed the outline level to Body Text, the heading formatted with the Contents Heading style will not be included in the table of contents. You need to update the table of contents to see this change.

▶ 5. Click anywhere in the table of contents below the "Contents" heading, click the **References** tab, and then in the Table of Contents group, click the **Update Table** button. The Update Table of Contents dialog box opens.

▶ 6. Click the **Update entire table** option button, and then click **OK**. The table of contents is updated, and the "Contents" heading is no longer included as an entry in it.

Reorganizing a Document in Outline View

Outline view has several symbols and buttons that you use when viewing and reorganizing your document. Refer to the Session 10.1 Visual Overview for information on these symbols and buttons. To select an entire section, you click the outline symbol next to that section's heading. To move a section after you select it, you can drag it or click the Move Up or Move Down button on the Outlining tab, which is visible only in Outline view. You can also use buttons on the Outlining tab to change the level of a heading. For instance, you might want to change a Level 1 heading to a Level 2 heading or change a Level 3 heading to a Level 1 heading.

Bailey wants you to reorganize the document somewhat. You will do this in Outline view. First, you need to examine the document in Outline view.

To view the document in Outline view:

▶ **1.** Switch to Outline view, and then change the Zoom level to **120%**, if necessary. The entire document is displayed. However, you cannot see the Level 1 headings, including the "List of Figures" heading, and you cannot see the "Contents" heading. This is because the text color of these headings is White, Background 1 and the Show Text Formatting check box in the Outline Tools group is selected.

Trouble? If the Show Text Formatting check box in the Outline Tools group on the Outlining tab is not selected, skip Step 2.

▶ **2.** In the Outline Tools group, click the **Show Text Formatting** check box to deselect it. The Level 1 headings and the "Contents" heading are now visible.

▶ **3.** In the Outline Tools group, click the **Show Level** arrow, and then click **Level 2**. The document changes to hide all the text at the Body Text level and display only the headings at Level 1 and Level 2. There are no Level 3 headings in the document. Note that the first heading in the document is the "List of Figures" heading. This is because the "Contents" heading has the outline level of Body Text.

▶ **4.** Click anywhere in the **Overview** heading, and then in the Outline Tools group, click the **Expand** button ⊞. The "Overview" heading expands to show the next available level. In this case, because there are no Level 3 headings, the body text is displayed.

▶ **5.** In the Outline Tools group, click the **Collapse** button ⊟ to collapse the "Overview" heading and show only Level 1 and Level 2 headings.

You can easily move sections in the document while working in Outline view. When you move a heading in Outline view, you also move the entire section; that is, you move the heading and its subordinate text. Note that it is customary to refer to a part of a document that begins with a heading as a "section." Don't confuse this use of the word "section" with a Word section—as in a part of a document that is identified by section breaks.

Bailey wants the Survey Overview section to be the first section in the Overview section. She also wants the Executive Summary section to appear before the Participants section. You'll move these sections next.

To move sections in the outline:

▶ **1.** Next to the Level 2 heading "Survey Overview," click the **plus sign** outline symbol ⊕. The heading is selected.

2. Position the pointer over the Survey Overview **plus sign** outline symbol ⊕, press and hold the mouse button, and then drag up without releasing the mouse button. As you drag, a horizontal line appears, indicating the position of the heading as you drag. See Figure 10–4.

Figure 10–4   Moving a heading to a new location in the outline

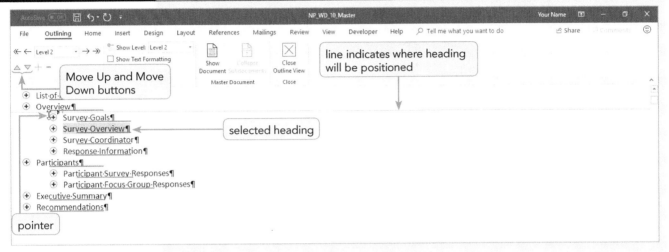

3. When the horizontal line is above the "Survey Goals" heading, release the mouse button. "Survey Overview" now appears above "Survey Goals" and is the first Level 2 heading below the Level 1 heading "Overview."

4. Next to "Participants," click the **plus sign** outline symbol ⊕. The heading next to the symbol that you clicked as well as its subordinate headings are selected.

5. Drag the "Participants" heading and its subordinate headings down below the "Executive Summary" heading.

6. Drag the "Executive Summary" heading above the "Overview" heading.

7. On the Outlining tab, in the Outline Tools group, click the **Show Level** arrow, and then click **All Levels**. The headings expand to display the body text beneath them.

8. Scroll so that the "Executive Summary" heading is at the top of the window. See Figure 10–5.

TIP

You can also click the Move Up and Move Down buttons in the Outline Tools group to move selected headings in an outline.

Figure 10–5   Headings expanded in Outline view

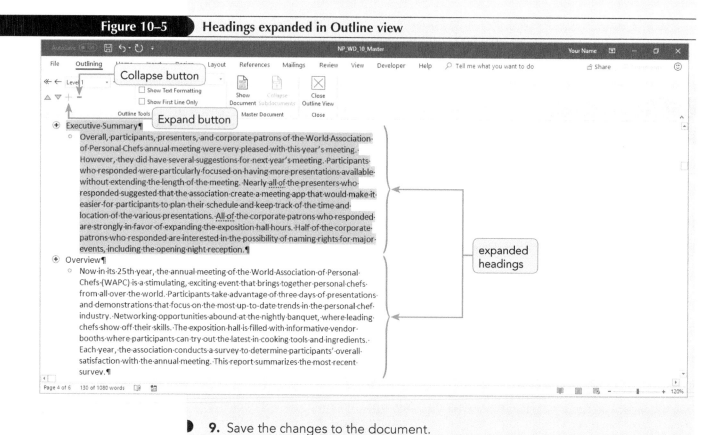

> **9.** Save the changes to the document.

Creating a Master Document

To create a master document, you can convert parts of the document into subdocuments or you can insert existing files as subdocuments. As soon as a document contains subdocuments, it becomes a master document. You can open, edit, and print subdocuments individually; or you can open, edit, and print the entire master document as a single unit. When you save a master document, Word saves each subdocument as a separate file. A master document contains links to its subdocuments rather than the text of the subdocuments themselves. You can display the content of subdocuments in the master document, however, and edit them from within the master document if you want.

To convert part of a document into a subdocument, you need to select the text you want to convert into the subdocument in Outline view. The first paragraph selected must have an outline level (in other words, it cannot be Body Text). To create a master document by using existing files as subdocuments, you insert the files as subdocuments, which creates a link between the master document and the inserted files. Inserting subdocuments into a master document is different from inserting Word files into a document. Inserted Word files become part of the document in which they're inserted, whereas subdocument files remain separate from the master document in which they're inserted.

Sometimes a lock icon 🔒 appears near the subdocument icon 🗐 to indicate that the subdocument is locked. You can't edit locked subdocuments, and commands on the ribbon are unavailable when the insertion point is positioned in a locked subdocument. The lock feature is important when more than one person is working on a master document because it allows only one person at a time to edit a subdocument.

Bailey's master document is the file NP_WD_10_Master. She wants you to create subdocuments from two of the sections currently in the NP_WD_10_Master document, and she wants you to insert two subdocuments created by colleagues.

Module 10 Managing Long Documents | Word   **WD 10–11**

PROSKILLS

Teamwork: Leading a Workgroup

In networking terminology, a group of colleagues who have access to the same network server and work together on a common project is called a **workgroup**. The person who oversees a workgroup must build trust among the team members, figure out how best to facilitate communication among the team members, and give the team members a chance to get to know one another. Often a workgroup is charged with creating a document, and each member is responsible for writing at least one part of the document. If you are the leader of this type of workgroup, it's your job to make sure that each team member has the correct document templates and access to the same styles so that when you combine the subdocuments to create the final master document, it will have a consistent style and formatting.

Creating a Subdocument

When you create a subdocument from text in a master document, a new file containing the text of the subdocument is created in the same folder that contains the master document. The name of the new file is the first paragraph formatted with a heading style. The text of the new subdocument is no longer saved in the master document file; instead a link to the subdocument is added to the master document. As shown in the Session 10.1 Visual Overview, the subdocument appears in a box marked with a subdocument icon.

Bailey wants you to convert the "Participants" and "Recommendations" sections into subdocuments.

To create a subdocument by converting text in the master document:

▶ **1.** Scroll down until you can see the "Participants" heading, and then click the Participants **plus sign** outline symbol. The "Participants" heading and its subordinate text and headings are selected. This is the text you will convert to a subdocument.

▶ **2.** On the Outlining tab, in the Master Document group, click the **Show Document** button to select it. The Master Document group expands to display six additional buttons that you can use to create and work with master documents. See Figure 10–6.

Figure 10–6	Master Document group expanded on Outlining tab

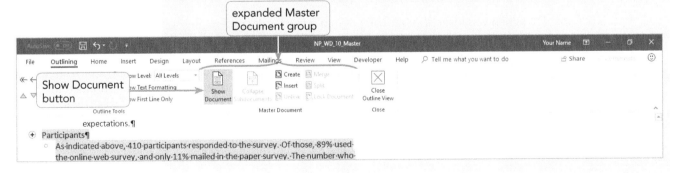

▶ **3.** On the Outlining tab, in the Master Document group, click the **Create** button. A border appears around the "Participants" section, continuous section breaks appear before and after the section, and the Subdocument icon appears to the left of the "Participants" heading.

▶ 4. Scroll down, and then next to the "Recommendations" heading, click the **plus sign** outline symbol ⊕.

▶ 5. In the Master Document group, click the **Create** button. The Recommendations section is now a subdocument.

▶ 6. Save the NP_WD_10_Master file with the new subdocuments. When you save your changes, new files named "Participants" and "Recommendations" are created. You can see this in the Open dialog box.

▶ 7. Click the **File** tab, and then in the navigation pane, click **Open**.

▶ 8. Click **Browse**, and then navigate to the location where you are storing your files, if necessary. You see the two subdocuments that you created from within the master document—Participants and Recommendations. See Figure 10–7.

| Figure 10–7 | Subdocuments in the master document listed in the Open dialog box |

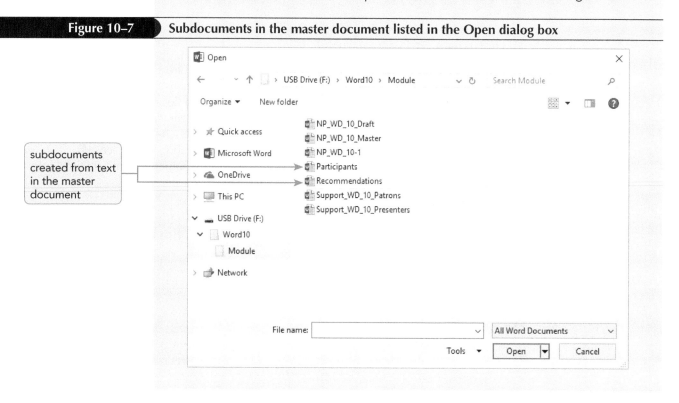

subdocuments created from text in the master document

Inserting Subdocuments

When you insert a subdocument into a master document, the subdocument appears in the master document at the location of the insertion point. Similar to a subdocument created from text in a master document, the inserted subdocument is stored in the subdocument file, and a link is created in the master document to the subdocument.

Alonzo Garza created a document describing corporate patrons who responded to the survey, and Marie Choi created a document about presenters. Bailey asks you to insert these documents into the master document. Before you do this, however, you'll make a backup copy of each of these files.

To make a backup copy of the subdocuments:

▶ 1. Make sure the Open dialog box is still open, navigate to the **Word10 > Module** folder if necessary, and then open the file **Support_WD_10_Presenters.docx**.

▶ 2. Save the file Support_WD_10_Presenters as **NP_WD_10_Presenters** in the location specified by your instructor, and then close this file.

3. Open the file **Support_WD_10_Patrons.docx**, located in the Word10 > Module folder, save it as **NP_WD_10_Patrons** in the location specified by your instructor, and then close this file. The master document NP_WD_10_Master appears in the window in Outline view.

Now you can insert the copies of the two subdocuments into the master document. You'll start with Alonzo's document, which is the NP_WD_10_Patrons document.

To insert subdocuments into the master document:

1. Scroll so you can see the Level 1 heading "Participants," and then click in the empty Body Text paragraph above the section break. This is where you'll insert the first subdocument.

   Trouble? If you can't click in the blank Body Text paragraph, click in the "Participants" paragraph, and then press the ↑ key.

2. In the expanded Master Document group, click the **Insert** button. The Insert Subdocument dialog box, which is similar to the Open dialog box, opens.

3. If necessary, navigate to the location where you are storing your files.

4. Click the file **NP_WD_10_Patrons.docx**, and then click **Open**. The file is inserted as a subdocument at the location of the insertion point (just above the section break above the heading "Participants"). Note that like the created subdocuments, the inserted subdocument has a Continuous section break after it. However, it has a Next Page section break before it.

5. Change the Zoom level to **90%**, scroll so that you can see the entire Corporate Patrons section and the beginning of the Participants section, and then compare your screen to Figure 10–8.

Figure 10–8   **Inserted subdocument**

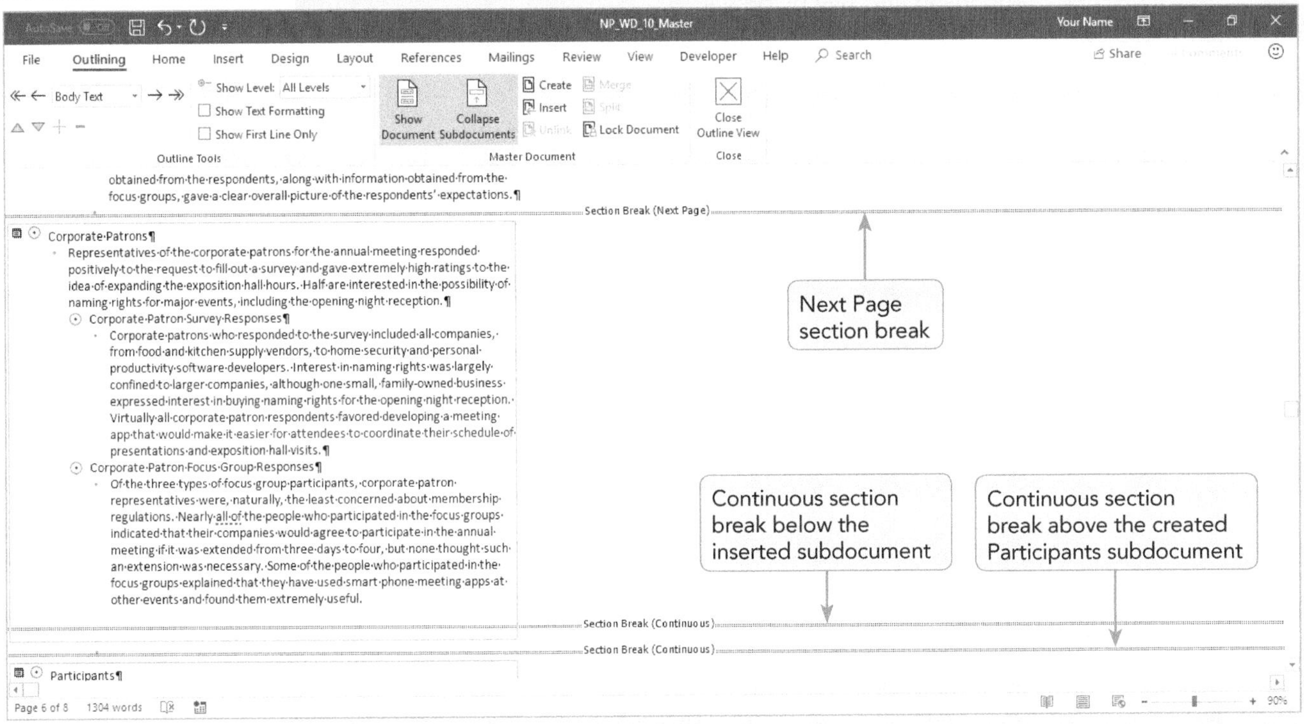

Inserted subdocument

> **Trouble?** If there is only one Continuous section break below the inserted subdocument, click the Undo button ↻ on the Quick Access Toolbar, and then repeat Steps 1 through 4, making sure in Step 1 to click in the empty blank Body Text paragraph above the section break.

▶ **6.** Change the Zoom level back to **120%**, and then scroll down so you can see the "Recommendations" heading.

▶ **7.** Click in the blank Body Text paragraph above the "Recommendations" heading. This is where you'll insert the document created by Marie Choi, NP_WD_10_Presenters, as a subdocument.

▶ **8.** At the insertion point, insert the document **NP_WD_10_Presenters** as a subdocument. The document is inserted as a subdocument with a Next Page section break before it and a Continuous section break after it.

Next, you will save the master document with the subdocuments.

▶ **9.** On the Quick Access Toolbar, click the **Save** button 💾. The NP_WD_10_ Master file is now saved as a master document with four subdocuments.

Examining Subdocument Links

The master document NP_WD_10_Master now contains four subdocuments—or, more precisely, links to four subdocuments. Even though you can manipulate the subdocuments in the master document, the text of these subdocuments is stored in the NP_WD_10_Patrons, Participants, NP_WD_10_Presenters, and Recommendations files, and not in the NP_WD_10_Master file. When the subdocuments are displayed or expanded, you can see the text of the subdocuments. When the subdocuments are collapsed, you see only the hyperlink to the subdocuments. When the link to a subdocument is displayed, the lock icon 🔒 appears next to the subdocument icon 📑. This means you cannot modify the link text.

Note that because the subdocuments are linked to the master document, you should not rename or move the subdocument files. If you do, the link between the master and subdocuments will be broken.

You will examine the links now.

To view the subdocument links:

▶ **1.** In the Master Document group, click the **Collapse Subdocuments** button. The button you clicked changes to the Expand Subdocuments button, and the document scrolls to the beginning.

▶ **2.** Scroll down until you see the links at the end of the document. See Figure 10–9.

Figure 10–9	Links to subdocuments

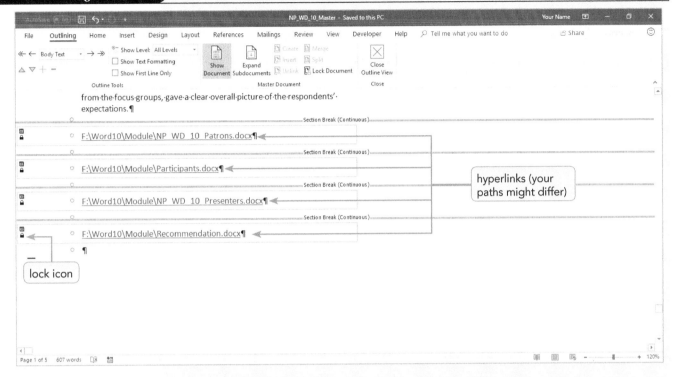

3. In the Master Document group, click the **Expand Subdocuments** button. The button changes back to the Collapse Subdocuments button, and the document scrolls back to the beginning.

4. Scroll down so that you can see that the text of the subdocuments appears in the master document again.

INSIGHT

Splitting and Merging Subdocuments

If one subdocument becomes too long and unwieldy, or if you want two people to work on what is currently one subdocument, you can split the subdocument by dividing it into two subdocument files. On the other hand, if your master document contains adjacent subdocuments that are fairly short and simple with few graphics or tables, it's sometimes helpful to merge the subdocuments. When you merge subdocuments, Word inserts the contents of the second subdocument into the first one. Then when you save the master document, the first subdocument file contains the contents of both subdocuments. The second subdocument file remains on your disk but is no longer used by the master document. You could delete this file without affecting your master document.

To split a subdocument, select the heading you want to split into its own subdocument by clicking the plus sign next to the heading, and then in the Master Document group on the Outlining tab, click the Split button. To merge two adjacent subdocuments, click the subdocument icon next to the first subdocument, press and hold SHIFT, click the subdocument icon next to the second subdocument, and then release SHIFT. Then, in the Master Document group on the Outlining tab, click the Merge button.

Unlinking a Subdocument

You can unlink a subdocument and incorporate the content into the master document. This decreases the number of subdocuments but increases the size of the master document. The removed subdocument file still exists, but the master document file can no longer access it. You can delete this unused subdocument file without affecting the master document.

Bailey decides that the short Recommendations subdocument doesn't need to be a subdocument. She asks you to unlink this content so it is stored in the master document rather than in the subdocument.

To unlink the Recommendations subdocument:

▶ **1.** Next to the Level 1 heading "Recommendations," click the **subdocument** icon 🖹 to select the entire Recommendations subdocument.

▶ **2.** On the Outlining tab, in the Master Document group, click the **Unlink** button. The Recommendations subdocument is unlinked from the master document, and the text of the subdocument becomes part of the master document again.

▶ **3.** Save the changes to the master document.

▶ **4.** Close the NP_WD_10_Master document, but do not close Word.

Reopening a Master Document

When you open a master document that has one or more subdocuments, Word doesn't open the subdocuments or display their text in the master document. Instead, the hyperlinks to the subdocuments appear in the master document. In order to see the text of the subdocuments in the master document, you must expand them in Outline view.

You'll reopen the master document and expand the subdocuments now.

To reopen the NP_WD_10_Master master document and expand the subdocuments:

▶ **1.** Open the **NP_WD_10_Master** document.

▶ **2.** Scroll to page 5. The master document opened with the three subdocuments collapsed to their links. Notice on the status bar that the document is currently six pages long.

Trouble? If, instead of dark orange underlined hyperlinks, you see code that begins with "{HYPERLINK . . .," press ALT+F9 to hide the field codes and display the actual hyperlinks.

Now that you have opened the master document, you need to expand the subdocuments. As with all the master document commands, you must be in Outline view to expand subdocuments.

To expand subdocuments:

▶ **1.** Switch to Outline view.

▶ **2.** On the Outlining tab, in the Master Document group, click the **Show Document** button, and then, if necessary, scroll down so that you can see the three subdocument links above the "Recommendations" heading. Notice that the lock icon 🔒 appears next to each subdocument link. Collapsed subdocuments are always locked.

▶ **3.** In the Master Document group, click the **Expand Subdocuments** button, and then scroll down until you can see that the text of the subdocuments replaced the links.

You have learned how to manipulate subdocuments within a master document. In the next session, you'll add numbers to the headings in the document, add numbered captions to objects in the document, and add cross-references to those captions. Then you will insert an endnote, create a chart in the document, restrict editing so that all changes are tracked with the Track Changes feature, check the document for hidden information, and check the document for accessibility.

INSIGHT

Splitting a Window

To examine two sections of a document at the same time, you can use the Split Window command or the New Window command. To split a window, click the View tab, and then in the Window group, click the Split button. This adds a double horizontal line across the screen, splitting the screen into two windows. You can then scroll in either window to view any part of the document. The other window will not scroll, allowing you to view a different part of the document in the second window. In the Window group on the View tab, the Split button changes to the Remove Split button. To remove the split, you click the Remove Split button.

When you split a window, there is still only one ribbon at the top of the screen. Another way to examine two parts of a document at once is to click the New Window button in the Window group on the View tab. When you do this, a second copy of the document is opened in a new window. The ribbon is displayed at the top of both windows. To view the open Word windows one on top of another, click the Arrange All button in the Window group on the View tab.

REVIEW

Session 10.1 Quick Check

1. What is a master document?

2. What is a subdocument?

3. What are three advantages of using a master document to manage long documents, rather than working with separate, smaller documents?

4. Describe the two ways to create a master document.

5. What happens after you create a subdocument from text in a master document and you save the new master document?

6. Is the text of a subdocument stored in the master document?

7. Describe how to remove a subdocument from a master document.

Session 10.2 Visual Overview:

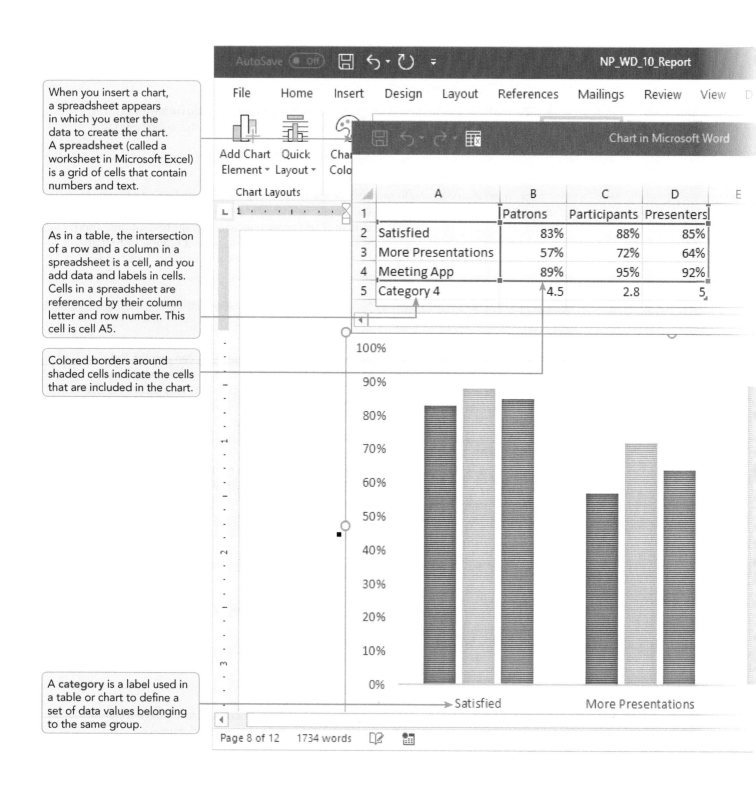

When you insert a chart, a spreadsheet appears in which you enter the data to create the chart. A **spreadsheet** (called a worksheet in Microsoft Excel) is a grid of cells that contain numbers and text.

As in a table, the intersection of a row and a column in a spreadsheet is a cell, and you add data and labels in cells. Cells in a spreadsheet are referenced by their column letter and row number. This cell is cell A5.

Colored borders around shaded cells indicate the cells that are included in the chart.

A **category** is a label used in a table or chart to define a set of data values belonging to the same group.

	A	B	C	D	E
1		Patrons	Participants	Presenters	
2	Satisfied	83%	88%	85%	
3	More Presentations	57%	72%	64%	
4	Meeting App	89%	95%	92%	
5	Category 4	4.5	2.8	5	

NP_WD_10_Report

Chart in Microsoft Word

Add Chart Element ▾   Quick Layout ▾   Cha... Colo...

Chart Layouts

Page 8 of 12   1734 words

Creating a Chart

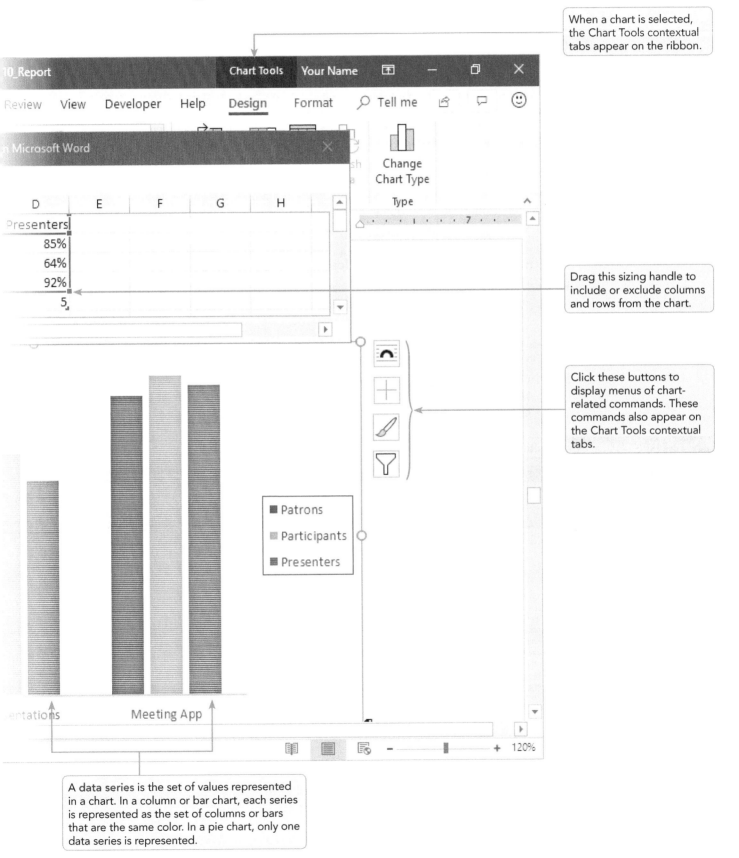

When a chart is selected, the Chart Tools contextual tabs appear on the ribbon.

Drag this sizing handle to include or exclude columns and rows from the chart.

Click these buttons to display menus of chart-related commands. These commands also appear on the Chart Tools contextual tabs.

A **data series** is the set of values represented in a chart. In a column or bar chart, each series is represented as the set of columns or bars that are the same color. In a pie chart, only one data series is represented.

Adding Numbers to Headings

Bailey wants you to give each heading a number—for example, "1. Executive Summary" and "2. Overview." You could manually insert the numbers before each heading, but if you had to add, reorder, or delete a heading, you would need to manually change all the numbers. Instead, you can number the parts of a document by automatically numbering the paragraphs that have an outline level. This feature has several advantages:

- **Automatic sequential numbering**—The heading numbers are maintained in consecutive order, even if you add, delete, or move a section.
- **Numbering across subdocuments**—The same-level headings in subdocuments in the master document are numbered consecutively.
- **Consistent style**—The heading numbers in subdocuments have the number style specified in the master document.

Note that when you use automatic numbering in a master document, the subdocuments must be expanded in order for the headings to be numbered properly.

To number headings automatically in the master document:

▶ 1. If you took a break after the previous session, open the **NP_WD_10_Master** document from the folder where you are saving your files, switch to Outline view, and then expand the subdocuments.

▶ 2. Scroll so that the heading "List of Figures" is at the top of the window, and then click anywhere in the heading "Executive Summary."

▶ 3. On the ribbon, click the **Home** tab, and then in the Paragraph group, click the **Multilevel List** button. The Multilevel List menu opens. The List Library contains four list styles that can be used with headings. See Figure 10–10.

Figure 10–10   **Multilevel list styles**

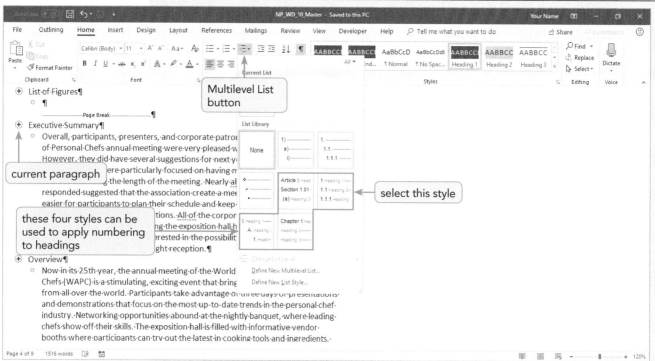

Bailey wants to use the numbering style that shows a number followed by "Heading 1." This style is sometimes called the legal paragraph numbering style.

▶ **4.** Click the last style in the second row of the List Library. The numbers are applied to the document headings, and a sample of the numbering style is now included as part of the heading styles in the Style gallery.

Each Level 1 heading from the insertion point to the end of the document (that is, each heading formatted in the Heading 1 style) has a single number. The numbers assigned to the Level 2 headings consist of the number of the Level 1 heading just above it, followed by a period, and then a sequential number. The "List of Figures" heading does not have numbers next to the headings. This is because the "List of Figures" heading is formatted with a custom style named Front/End Matter Heading, and it is before the "Executive Summary" heading in the document. See Figure 10–11.

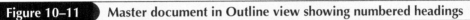

Figure 10–11   **Master document in Outline view showing numbered headings**

Bailey wants you to customize the numbering format so that each number is followed by a period.

▶ **5.** Click the **Multilevel List** button, and then click **Define New Multilevel List**. The Define new Multilevel list dialog box opens. See Figure 10–12.

Figure 10–12 **Define new Multilevel list dialog box**

Level 1 heading selected

type new format here

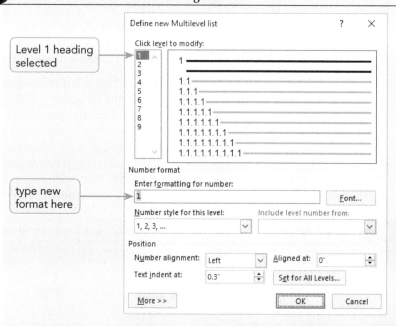

You want to change the default setting "1" for Heading 1 styles to "1." (with a period following the number) and change the default setting for Heading 2 styles to "1.1." (with a period following the second number).

6. In the Click level to modify list, make sure 1 is selected. In the Enter formatting for number box, the number 1 appears because the current paragraph in the document is numbered 1.

7. In the Enter formatting for number box, click to the right of the number 1, and then type a period.

8. In the Click level to modify list, click **2**.

9. In the Enter formatting for number box, click to the right of 1.1, and then type a period after the second 1.

10. Click **OK**. The numbers next to the headings change to include periods after each number. Notice the Heading 1 and Heading 2 styles in the Style gallery in the Styles group on the Home tab have been updated to reflect the new number style.

After you closed the Define new Multilevel list dialog box, the numbering was applied to the "Contents" and the "List of Figures" headings as well. This is because the custom Front/End Matter Heading style that Bailey created for the "List of Figures" heading is based on the Heading 1 style, and the Contents Heading style that you created is based on the "List of Figures" style.

Bailey does not want either the "Contents" or "List of Figures" headings to be numbered with the rest of the headings in the document because they are not really part of the document outline; they are part of the front matter. To fix this, you will modify the style definition of the Front/End Matter Heading and the Contents Heading styles to remove the numbering from these headings.

To modify the style definitions:

▶ **1.** On the Home tab, in the Styles group, right-click the **Contents Heading** style (it appears as Contents… in the Style gallery), and then click **Modify** on the shortcut menu. The Modify Style dialog box opens.

▶ **2.** Click the **Format** button, and then click **Numbering**. The Numbering and Bullets dialog box opens with the Numbering tab selected.

▶ **3.** Click the **None** style to select it, if necessary.

▶ **4.** Click **OK**, and then click **OK** in the Modify Style dialog box. The Contents Heading style has been modified so that it does not include a number. You can see this in the Style gallery on the Home tab.

▶ **5.** Repeat Steps 1 through 4 for the Front/End Matter Heading style (it appears as Front/End… in the Style gallery). In the gallery, the Front/End Matter Heading style no longer has a number before the style name.

▶ **6.** Click the **Outlining** tab.

▶ **7.** In the Outline Tools group, click the **Show Level** arrow, click **Level 2**, and then scroll to see the top of the document. The "List of Figures" heading is no longer numbered. See Figure 10–13.

| Figure 10–13 | Numbering removed from the contents and List of Figures headings |

Make sure you save the changes so you have a final version of the master document.

▶ **8.** Save the changes to the document.

Note that as you edit a document that contains numbered headings, heading numbers might sometimes disappear from some headings. If that happens, select the affected heading, and then apply the correct heading style from the Style gallery.

You can continue to work with the master document, but Bailey tells you that she has all the updated documents from her team members, so you will unlink all of the subdocuments.

To unlink all of the subdocuments:

▶ **1.** Save the document as **NP_WD_10_Report** in the location specified by your instructor.

▶ **2.** Next to the heading "3. Corporate Patrons," click the **subdocument** icon 🖳.

▶ **3.** In the Master Document group, click the **Unlink** button. The subdocument is unlinked from the master document, and the text of the subdocument becomes part of the master document.

▶ **4.** Unlink the subdocument whose first heading is "4. Participants," and then unlink the subdocument whose first heading is "5. Presenters."

▶ **5.** On the Outlining tab, in the Close group, click the **Close Outline View** button.

▶ **6.** Save the changes to the document.

Inserting Numbered Captions

A figure is any kind of illustration, such as a photograph, chart, map, or graph. You can add captions below figures using automatic figure numbering. A **caption** consists of a label, such as "Figure," "Fig.," or "Table," and a number, and usually a description of the figure. When you create captions using the Insert Caption command, the caption is numbered automatically using the Seq field, which inserts an automatic sequence number. For example, the first figure is numbered Figure 1, the second is numbered Figure 2, and so on. If you later insert a figure before an existing figure, move a figure, or reorder the parts of the document, the figure numbers in the captions renumber automatically.

When you add a caption to an inline object, the caption is inserted as text in a new paragraph. When you add a caption to a floating object, it is created inside a text box without a border, and the text wrap on the text box containing the caption is the same as text wrap on the figure it is connected to; that is, if the text wrap on a floating object is Square, the text wrap on the text box containing the caption will be Square as well.

When creating a caption, you can choose to number the captions sequentially as they appear in the document (1, 2, 3, etc.), or you can include the number of the first heading above the caption that is formatted with the Heading 1 style. For example, you could use 1-1 for the first caption under the heading "1. Executive Summary," 1-2 for the second caption under the heading "1. Executive Summary," and so on. The captions for figures in the "2. Overview" section would then be numbered 2-1, 2-2, and so on. This type of numbering is sometimes called double-numbering.

REFERENCE

Creating Captions

- Select the table or figure to which you want to apply a caption.
- On the References tab, in the Captions group, click the Insert Caption button.
- Click the Label arrow, and then click the type of object to which you're applying the caption (for example, figure or table), or click the New Label button, type a new label, and then click OK.
- Click the Position arrow, and then click the option to specify whether you want the caption to appear above or below the figure.
- To use double-numbering that includes the number of the preceding Heading 1 heading, click the Numbering button, select the Include chapter number check box in the Caption Numbering dialog box, and then click OK.
- Click after the number in the Caption box, and then type a caption.
- Click OK.

Bailey included figures to illustrate key points in the report. In section "2.3. Survey Coordinator," she inserted a picture of Anthony Santana, the president of Marketfield Research Associates. Also, in section "6. Recommendations," she added a SmartArt graphic illustrating the survey's conclusions. Bailey wants to include captions for each figure so that she can refer to them in the text.

To create a numbered caption:

▶ **1.** Scroll until you can see the heading "2.3. Survey Coordinator" and the photo of Anthony Santana on page 5. The picture is below the heading "2.3. Survey Coordinator."

▶ **2.** Click the photo of Anthony to select it. This photo is a floating object with Square text wrapping.

▶ **3.** On the ribbon, click the **References** tab, and then in the Captions group, click the **Insert Caption** button. The Caption dialog box opens. The insertion point is blinking to the right of "Figure 1" in the Caption box. See Figure 10–14.

Figure 10–14   Caption dialog box

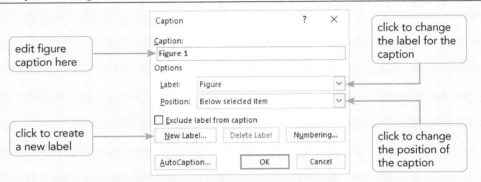

▶ **4.** In the Caption box, type **:** (a colon), press **SPACEBAR**, and then type **Anthony Santana**.

TIP

To change the format of the caption number, such as to Figure 1-1, click the Numbering button in the Caption dialog box.

▶ **5.** In the Caption dialog box, click the **New Label** button. The New Label dialog box opens with the insertion point in the Label box.

▶ **6.** Type **Fig.** (including the period), and then click **OK**. The label in the Caption and Label boxes changes to "Fig."

▶ **7.** Click **OK**. The numbered caption is inserted below the figure as a floating text box without a border and with Square text wrapping. See Figure 10–15.

Figure 10–15   Photo with a caption in a floating text box

Rido/Shutterstock.com

You can see that the figure number in the caption is a field by displaying the field code.

▶ 8. In the figure caption, right-click **1**, and then click **Toggle Field Codes** on the shortcut menu. The field code for the number 1 in the caption appears.

▶ 9. Right-click the field code, and then click **Toggle Field Codes** to display the number instead of the field code.

Now, using the same procedure, you'll insert another numbered caption under the SmartArt graphic illustrating the survey's conclusions.

To insert a numbered caption under the SmartArt graphic:

▶ 1. Scroll so that you can see the SmartArt graphic at the top of page 9.

▶ 2. Click the SmartArt graphic to select it. The SmartArt graphic is an inline object.

▶ 3. On the References tab, in the Captions group, click the **Insert Caption** button. The Caption dialog box opens with Fig. 2 in the Caption box because this will be the second object in the document identified with the label "Fig."

▶ 4. Change the caption in the Caption box to read **Fig. 2: Survey conclusions** and then click **OK**. The caption is inserted below the SmartArt graphic in a new paragraph. Compare your screen to Figure 10–16.

Figure 10–16   SmartArt graphic with a caption in a new paragraph

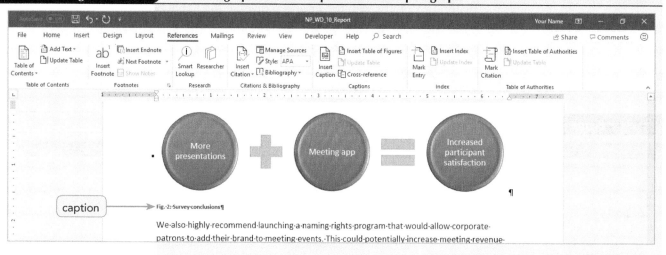

▶ 5. Save the changes to the document.

If you need to modify a caption after it has been inserted, you can edit it as you would any other text in the document.

When you insert a caption for a floating object, the caption is anchored to the same paragraph as the object. This means that if that paragraph moves, both the object and the caption move with it. When you insert a caption for an inline object, the formatting of the paragraph that contains the object changes so that the Keep with next option on the Line and Page Breaks tab in the Paragraph dialog box becomes selected.

Now that you have inserted figure captions for each illustration in the document, you will refer to each of them in the text. For that, you'll use cross-references.

Creating Cross-References

A **cross-reference** is a notation within a document that refers to a figure or table caption, to a heading, or to a footnote or an endnote. If you use the Cross-reference command to insert the reference to a caption and then the figures or tables are reordered, the cross-references will update also. This is because when you insert a cross-reference using the Cross-reference command in Word, a hidden bookmark is created to the item you are referencing and the Ref field is inserted to display the bookmarked item.

REFERENCE

Creating Cross-References

- Move the insertion point to the location where you want to insert the cross-reference.
- Type the text preceding the cross-reference, such as "See" and a space.
- On the References tab, in the Captions group, click the Cross-reference button.
- In the Cross-reference dialog box, click the Reference type arrow, and then select the type of item you want to reference.
- Click the Insert reference to arrow, and then select the amount of information from the reference to be displayed in the cross-reference.
- In the For which list, click the item you want to reference.
- Click Insert to insert the cross-reference.
- Click Close to close the dialog box.

Bailey wants the figures in the report referenced within the text, so you'll insert cross-references to the two figures.

To insert a cross-reference to Figure 1:

▶ 1. Scroll to page 5 so that you can see the heading "2.3. Survey Coordinator."

▶ 2. In the paragraph below the "2.3. Survey Coordinator" heading, in the first line, click between "Santana" and the comma. This is where you will insert the first cross-reference.

▶ 3. Press **SPACEBAR**, type **(see** and then press **SPACEBAR** again. The beginning of the edited sentence is now "Anthony Santana (see , president of…". Now you're ready to insert the automatically numbered cross-reference.

▶ 4. On the References tab, in the Captions group, click the **Cross-reference** button. The Cross-reference dialog box opens. See Figure 10–17.

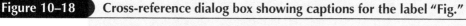

Figure 10–17   **Cross-reference dialog box showing numbered items**

numbered items (headings) in document displayed because Numbered item is selected as the Reference type

click to change the type of item to be referenced

5. Click the **Reference type** arrow, scroll down, and then click **Fig**. The bottom part of the dialog box changes to display the two figure captions in the document, and the Insert reference to box changes to Entire caption. The Insert as hyperlink check box is selected by default. This means you can press and hold CTRL, and then click the cross-reference in the document to jump to the item referenced. See Figure 10–18.

Figure 10–18   **Cross-reference dialog box showing captions for the label "Fig."**

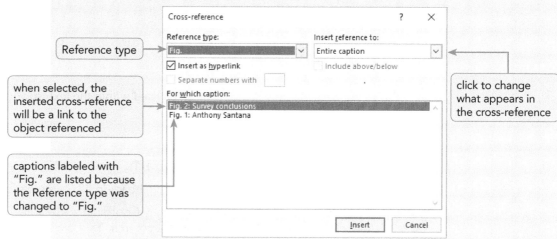

Reference type

when selected, the inserted cross-reference will be a link to the object referenced

captions labeled with "Fig." are listed because the Reference type was changed to "Fig."

click to change what appears in the cross-reference

You want the reference to the figure to list only the label "Fig." and the figure number, not the entire caption.

6. Click the **Insert reference to** arrow, and then click **Only label and number**.

7. In the For which caption list, click **Fig. 1: Anthony Santana**, and then click **Insert**. The cross-reference is inserted in the document. In the dialog box, Cancel changes to Close.

8. Click **Close**, and then type **)** after the cross-reference in the document to close the parentheses. The phrase "(see Fig. 1)" appears in the report, so that the beginning of the sentence is "Anthony Santana (see Fig. 1), president of...."

Trouble? If "Fig. 2" appears as the reference instead of "Fig. 1," you clicked the wrong item in the For which caption list in the Cross-reference dialog box. Delete the reference, and then repeat Steps 4 through 7, taking care to click Fig. 1: Anthony Santana in the list.

▶ **9.** In the first line below the heading "2.3. Survey Coordinator," point to **Fig. 1**. A ScreenTip appears telling you that you can press CTRL and click to use the link.

▶ **10.** Press and hold **CTRL**, and then click. The Fig. 1 label and figure number under the photo of Anthony Santana is selected.

The power of all automatic numbering features in Word—heading numbering, caption numbering, and cross-references—becomes evident when you edit a long document with many figures. Now you'll add cross-references to the other figure.

To insert another cross-reference:

TIP

To move SmartArt shapes, select a shape and then use one of the buttons in the Create Graphic group on the SmartArt Tools Design tab or open the text pane, and move the items in the bulleted list.

▶ **1.** Scroll to the bottom of page 8, and in the last paragraph on the page (the paragraph below the "Recommendations" heading), click after the last sentence.

▶ **2.** Press **SPACEBAR**, type **(See** and then press **SPACEBAR**.

▶ **3.** In the Captions group, click the **Cross-reference** button. The Cross-reference dialog box opens, displaying the settings you used last. Fig. is selected in the Reference type box, and Only label and number is selected in the Insert reference to box. Fig. 2 is selected in the For which caption list because it is the first option in the list.

▶ **4.** Click **Insert**, and then click **Close**. The cross-reference to Fig. 2 is inserted.

▶ **5.** Type **.)** (a period followed by a closing parenthesis).

▶ **6.** Save the changes to the document.

Inserting an Endnote

As you know, an endnote is an explanatory comment or reference that appears at the end of a document. You know to look for an endnote if a reference marker appears next to text.

Bailey needs you to insert two endnotes in the report.

To insert endnotes:

▶ **1.** On page 8, in the last paragraph, position the insertion point after the period at the end of the second to last sentence (after "Therefore, we strongly recommend investigating vendors for such an app.").

TIP

To see the "i" more clearly, increase the Zoom level.

▶ **2.** On the References tab, in the Footnotes group, click the **Insert Endnote** button. The document scrolls to the end, and the insertion point appears next to "i" below a horizontal line at the end of the document. The "i" is inside a dotted-line rectangle and is hard to see.

▶ **3.** Type **The Committee recommends hiring First Labs to develop the app.** (including the period). See Figure 10–19.

Figure 10–19   **Endnote inserted at the end of the document**

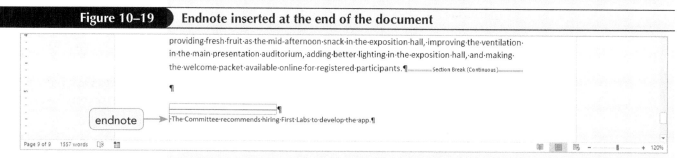

4. Double-click the endnote number **i**. The document scrolls to page 8 and the endnote reference mark is selected.

Trouble? If you have difficulty double-clicking the endnote number, scroll to page 8 so that you can see the endnote reference mark, and then continue with Step 5.

5. Move the pointer on top of the endnote reference mark on page 8. The pointer changes to the reference mark pointer ▯, and the text of the endnote you typed appears in a ScreenTip above the reference mark.

6. Go to page 5, and then in the paragraph below the "2.3. Survey Coordinator" heading, place the insertion point after the period after the second to last sentence (after "The group created three questionnaires—one for participants, one for presenters, and one for corporate patrons.").

7. In the Footnotes group, click the **Insert Endnote** button. The document scrolls to the end, and a new endnote numbered "i" is inserted above the existing endnote. The new endnote appears first because its reference appears earlier in the document. The existing endnote was renumbered "ii".

8. Type **The questionnaires are available online at www.wapc.example. com/questionnaires.** and then press **SPACEBAR**. The webpage address you typed changes to a link after you press SPACEBAR.

Inserting a Chart

The terms "chart" and "graph" often are used interchangeably; however, they have distinct meanings. A **chart** is a graphic that represents data using bars, columns, dots, lines, or other symbols to make the data easier to understand and to make it easier to see the relationships among the data. A **graph** shows the relationship between variables along two axes or reference lines. Although charts show relationships, they don't use a coordinate system like graphs do.

Despite these differences in the definitions, in Word, a chart is any visual depiction of data in a spreadsheet, even if the result is more properly referred to as a graph (such as a line graph). Refer to the Session 10.2 Visual Overview for more information about creating charts in Word.

As you know, you can insert a chart created in Microsoft Excel into any Word document. However, you can also create a chart from within a Word document by clicking the Chart button in the Illustrations group on the Insert tab. Doing so will open a window containing a spreadsheet with sample data, and a sample chart will appear in the document. You can then edit the sample data in the spreadsheet so that your data will be represented in the chart in the document.

Creating a Chart

- On the Insert tab, in the Illustrations group, click the Chart button to open the Insert Chart dialog box.
- In the list on the left, click the desired chart type.
- In the row of styles, click the desired chart style.
- Click OK.
- In the spreadsheet that opens, enter the data that you want to plot.
- In the spreadsheet window, click the Close button.

Bailey would like you to add a chart in section "2.1. Survey Overview" to illustrate some of the survey responses.

To create a chart in the survey document:

1. Scroll to the middle of page 5 so that the last line of the paragraph above the yellow highlighted placeholder text [INSERT CHART] is at the top of the document window, and then delete [**INSERT CHART**] (but do not delete the paragraph mark).

2. On the ribbon, click the **Insert** tab, and then in the Illustrations group, click the **Chart** button. The Insert Chart dialog box opens. See Figure 10–20.

Figure 10–20   **Insert chart dialog box**

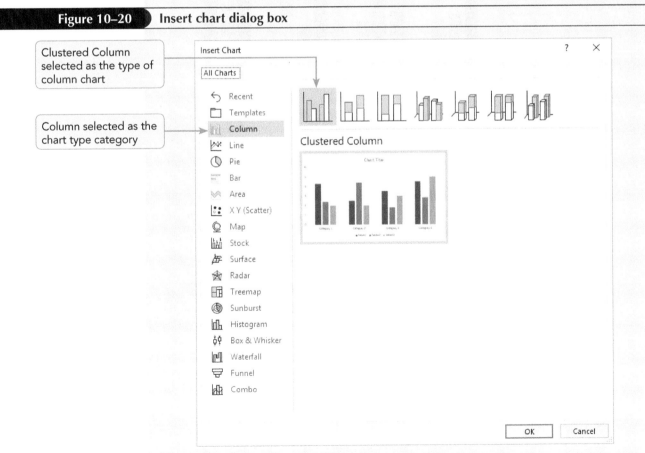

Clustered Column selected as the type of column chart

Column selected as the chart type category

Column is selected in the list of chart type categories on the left, and Clustered Column is selected in the row of column chart types at the top and is shown in the preview area. You want to create a column chart, so you do not need to make any changes.

▶ 3. Click **OK**. A sample column chart is inserted in the document, and a small spreadsheet (sometimes called a datasheet) opens above the chart. The colored borders around the cells in the spreadsheet indicate which cells of data are included in the chart. See Figure 10–21.

Figure 10–21   Spreadsheet containing sample data for a column chart

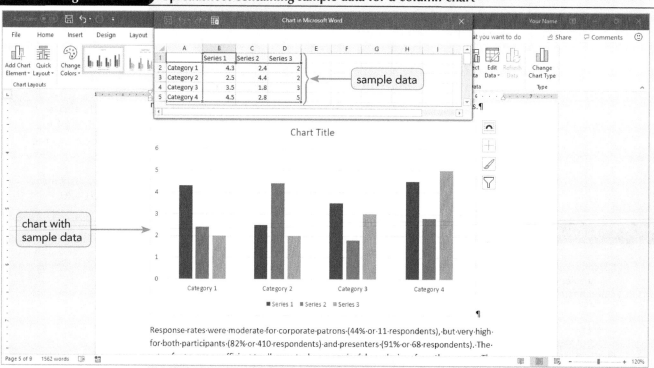

To create the chart for Bailey's report, you must edit the sample data in the spreadsheet. When you work with a worksheet, the selected cell is the **active cell**. Data you enter appears in the active cell. The active cell has a green border around it.

To enter row and column labels in the chart:

▶ 1. In the spreadsheet, click cell **A2**. This is now the active cell. The first category will show the percentage of respondents who answered yes, they were satisfied with this year's meeting.

▶ 2. Type **Satisfied**, and then press **ENTER**. The name of the first category in the chart changes to reflect the new row label that you just typed, and cell A3 is now the active cell.

▶ 3. In cell A3, type **More Presentations**, and then press **ENTER**. This category will show the percentage of respondents who answered yes, they would like more presentations next year. The name of the second category in the chart changes to reflect the new row label that you just typed, and cell A4 is now the active cell. In cell A3, you can no longer see all of the text that you typed.

The column is not wide enough to display all of the text when the cells to its right contain data.

▶ **4.** In cell A4, type **Meeting App**, and then press **ENTER**. This category will show the percentage of respondents who answered yes, they would like a meeting app to make it easier for participants to plan their schedule and keep track of the time and location of the presentations.

▶ **5.** Click cell **B1**, type **Patrons**, and then press **TAB**. The active cell is now cell C1, and the chart legend changes to reflect the new column label.

▶ **6.** In cell C1, type **Participants**, and then press **TAB**.

▶ **7.** In cell D1, type **Presenters**, and then press **ENTER**. Cell B2 is the active cell.

Next, you will widen columns A and C so that you can see the row and column labels.

▶ **8.** Move the pointer on top of the column border between the column A and column B headings—that is, between the boxes containing the column headings A and B—so that the pointer changes to the resize column width pointer **✛**, and then double-click. Column A widens to fit the widest entry in the column—the text in cell A3.

▶ **9.** Move the pointer on top of the column border between the column C and column D headings, and then double-click. Column C widens to fit the widest entry in the column—the text in cell C1. See Figure 10–22.

Figure 10–22   **Row and column labels replaced**

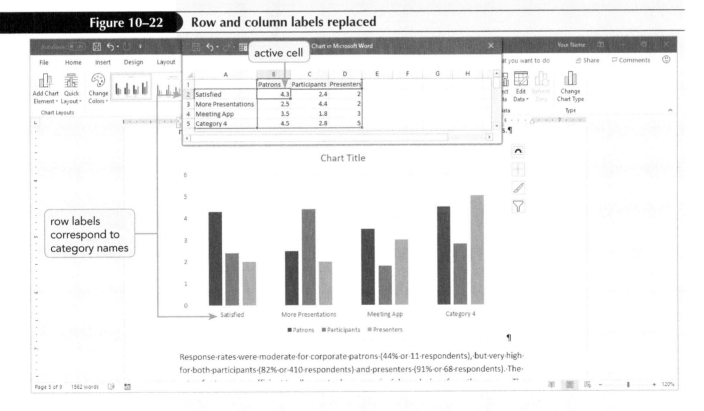

Now you need to enter the data for your chart. You will enter data in cells B2 through D4.

To enter data in the spreadsheet:

▶ **1.** In cell B2, type **83%**, press **ENTER**, type **57%** in cell B3, press **ENTER**, type **89%** in cell B4, and then press **ENTER**. The column chart in the document changes to reflect the new data.

▶ **2.** Click cell **C2**, type **88%**, press **ENTER**, type **72%**, press **ENTER**, type **95%**, and then press **ENTER**.

▶ **3.** Click cell **D2**, type **85%**, press **ENTER**, type **64%**, press **ENTER**, type **92%**, and then press **ENTER**. Compare your screen to Figure 10–23.

Figure 10–23   **Data entered into the spreadsheet**

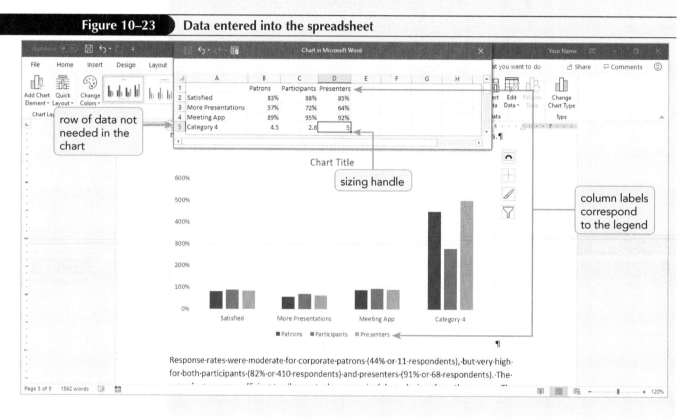

You have entered all the data for the chart. However, the chart still includes a category titled Category 4. There are only three categories in this chart, so you need to exclude the last row of data in the spreadsheet. When you remove it, the largest value on the vertical axis will be 100%, and the chart will be much clearer.

To remove the data in row 5 from the chart:

▶ **1.** Move the pointer on top of the small blue sizing handle at the lower-right corner of cell D5 so that the pointer changes to ⬉.

▶ **2.** Drag the sizing handle up to the bottom of cell D4. The colored border shading indicating which cells will be included in the chart changes to show that row 5 is no longer included. The column chart now includes only three categories, and the highest value on the vertical axis is 100%. See Figure 10–24.

| Figure 10–24 | Chart after excluding row 5 |

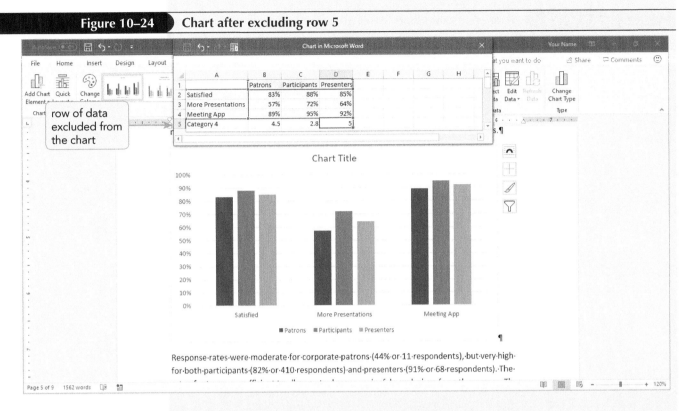

row of data excluded from the chart

	A	B	C	D
1		Patrons	Participants	Presenters
2	Satisfied	83%	88%	85%
3	More Presentations	57%	72%	64%
4	Meeting App	89%	95%	92%
5	Category 4	4.5	2.8	5

Response·rates·were·moderate·for·corporate·patrons·(44%·or·11·respondents),·but·very·high·
for·both·participants·(82%·or·410·respondents)·and·presenters·(91%·or·68·respondents).·The·

Page 5 of 9   1562 words

3. In the spreadsheet title bar, click the **Close** button ☒ to close the spreadsheet. The new chart is selected in the document, and two Chart Tools contextual tabs appear on the ribbon.

Once the chart is in the document, you can modify it by changing or formatting the various elements of the chart. For example, you can apply a chart style to your chart to change its look. You can also edit or remove the title of a chart. Bailey wants you to modify the chart by applying a style, deleting the title, and repositioning the legend.

To change the chart style:

1. To the right of the chart, click the **Chart Styles** button ✐. In the menu that opens, the Style tab is selected. This tab lists the same chart styles that appear in the Chart Styles group on the Chart Tools Design tab on the ribbon. See Figure 10–25.

Figure 10–25 Style tab on the Chart Styles menu

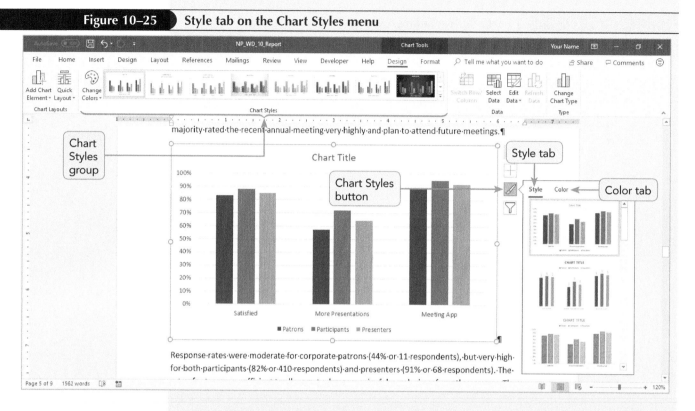

2. On the menu, click the **Style 3** style. The columns in the chart now have faint horizontal stripes, and the legend appears at the top of the chart.

3. On the menu, click the **Color** tab. A list of color palettes for the chart appears.

4. Click the **Colorful Palette 2** palette. The third column in each category changes to gray.

You don't need a chart title because this chart will have a numbered figure caption, so you will remove it. You will also reposition the legend so it appears on the right side of the chart rather than above it.

To remove the chart title and reposition the legend:

1. To the right of the chart, click the **Chart Elements** button ⊞. The Chart Elements menu opens to the left of the chart. See Figure 10–26.

Figure 10–26   Chart Elements menu

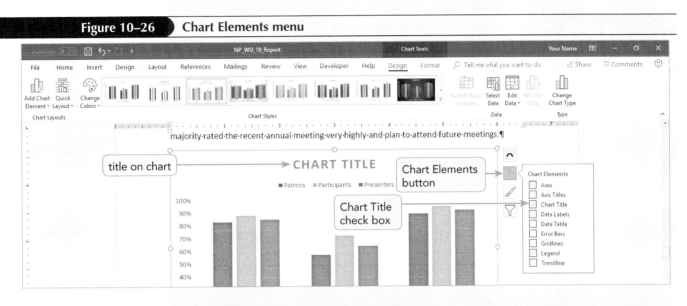

2. On the menu, click the **Chart Title** check box to remove the checkmark. The chart title is removed from the chart.

3. On the menu, point to **Legend**. A small arrow ▶ appears.

4. Click the **arrow** ▶ to open the Legend submenu. See Figure 10–27.

Figure 10–27   Legend submenu on the Chart Elements menu

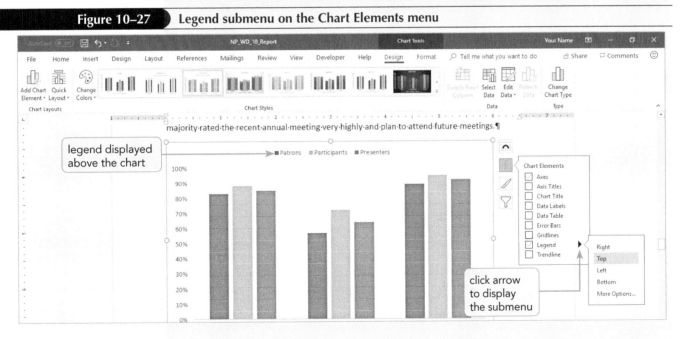

5. In the submenu, click **Right**. The legend now appears to the right of the chart.

6. At the bottom of the Legend submenu, click **More Options**. The Format Legend pane opens with the Legend Options button ⑪ selected on the Legend Options tab.

7. Click the **Fill & Line** button ⬦, and then click **Border** to expand the list of border options. See Figure 10–28.

Figure 10–28 **Format Legend pane with the Fill & Line button selected on the Legend Options tab**

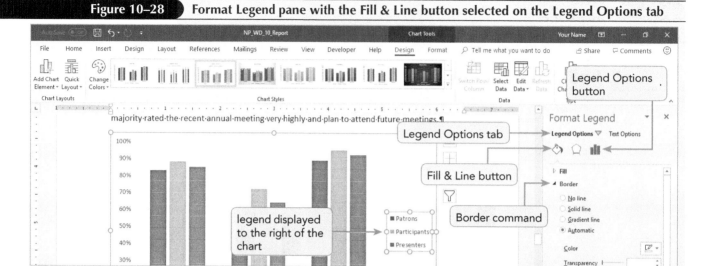

8. Click the **Solid line** option button. A solid line border is added around the legend in the chart.

9. At the top of the Format Legend pane, click the **Close** button ✕, and then click a blank area of the chart to deselect the legend, but keep the chart selected. Now you can see the border that you added around the legend.

Finally, you need to insert a caption under the chart. Recall that this chart was inserted between the photo of Anthony Santana and the SmartArt graphic.

To insert a figure caption under the chart:

1. On the ribbon, click the **References** tab, and then in the Captions group, click the **Insert Caption** button. The Caption dialog box opens, and Fig. 2 appears in the Caption box. This is because you are inserting this caption before the previously numbered Fig. 2. The old Fig. 2 is renumbered as Fig. 3.

   Trouble? If Figure 2 appears in the Caption box, click the Label arrow, and then click Fig.

2. Change the figure caption to **Fig. 2: Chart showing percentage of respondents who said "yes" to questions** and then click **OK**. Because the chart is an inline object, the caption appears in a new paragraph below the chart.

3. Scroll to page 9 to see that the caption under the SmartArt graphic has been renumbered as Fig. 3.

4. Scroll up to see the last sentence on page 8. The cross-reference to Fig. 3 did not update.

5. In the last sentence on page 8, right-click the cross-reference, and then on the shortcut menu, click **Update Field**. The cross-reference is updated so it is "(See Fig. 3.)."

The cross-reference fields in a document update automatically when you close and then reopen the file. You could also press CTRL+A to select all of the text in the document, and then press F9 to update all fields in the selected text.

Now you need to insert a cross-reference to the chart.

To insert a cross-reference to the chart:

▶ **1.** Scroll so that the "2.4. Response Information" heading on page 5 is at the top of the document window, and then click after the last sentence in the paragraph below the heading (which ends with "…and plan to attend future meetings.").

▶ **2.** Press **SPACEBAR**, type **The chart shown in** and then press **SPACEBAR**.

▶ **3.** On the References tab, in the Captions group, click the **Cross-reference** button. The Cross-reference dialog box opens. Fig. is selected as the Reference type, Only label and number appears in the Insert reference to box, and Fig. 2 is selected in the For which caption list.

▶ **4.** Click **Insert**, and then click **Close**. The cross-reference to Fig. 2 is inserted.

▶ **5.** Press **SPACEBAR**, and then type **illustrates the percentage of respondents who responded "yes" to the questions asking if they were satisfied with this year's meeting, if they want more presentations offered next year, and if they want a meeting app.** (including the period).

▶ **6.** Save the changes to the document.

Next, you'll help Bailey control the kinds of changes the other members of the board of directors can make to the report.

INSIGHT

Inserting Equations

If you need to add a complex mathematical equation to a document, you can use the Equation button in the Symbols group on the Insert tab. Click the Equation arrow, and then click one of the common equations on the menu to insert that equation. If the equation you want to enter is not listed in the menu, click the Equation button to insert an equation text box, and then type the equation, using the buttons in the Symbols group on the Equation Tools Design tab to insert mathematical symbols, such as the square root sign ($\sqrt{}$). You can also click buttons in the Structures group on the Equation Tools Design tab to insert mathematical structures such as fractions ($\frac{3}{4}$ or ¾) or the integral sign, which is used in calculus ($\int$).

You can also click the Ink Equation button in the Tools group on the Equation Tools Design tab to open the Math Input Control window. Using a stylus or your finger if you have a touchscreen device or using the pointer, drag to write the equation in the window. When you are finished, click Insert to close the window and insert the equation you drew in the equation text box in the document.

Restricting Editing to Allow Only Tracked Changes or Comments

Because Bailey has already done a fair amount of work on the document, she'd like to retain some control over the kinds of changes the other writers make to it. Therefore, she decides to restrict editing in the document. As you know, you can set editing restrictions for a document. In addition to restricting users to only filling in content controls and form fields, you can prevent users from making formatting changes. When specifying formatting restrictions, you can limit formatting changes in the document to a specific list of styles. You can also prevent users from changing the theme or changing the Quick Style Set. You can force all changes to be tracked, or you can restrict users so that the only type of change they can make is to add comments.

When specifying editing restrictions, you can choose from the following options:

- **Tracked changes**—Allows users to make any editing changes as well as any of the formatting changes allowed by the formatting restrictions, but all changes are marked with revision marks
- **Comments**—Allows users to insert comments, but not to make any other changes
- **Filling in forms**—Allows users to fill in forms only
- **No changes (Read only)**—Allows users to read the document but not to make changes

You can also allow people you specify to edit parts or all of a document. After you select the check box to allow only a specific type of editing in the document, an Exceptions section appears in the Restrict Editing pane. Here, you can click the More users link and then select users who are allowed to edit the document.

When you apply editing restrictions to a document, you can choose to require a password in order to turn off the editing restrictions. If you are restricting editing in a document because you are concerned that someone might make unauthorized changes to the document, then you should definitely use a password. However, if you are restricting editing in a document that will be shared among a small group of colleagues, and you are using the feature simply to ensure that all changes are tracked with revision marks, then a password typically isn't necessary.

It is important that you create passwords you can remember or record them in a secure location. If you protect a document with a password and then forget the password, there is no way to retrieve it.

REFERENCE

Restricting Editing in a Document

- On the Review tab, in the Protect group, click the Restrict Editing button to open the Restrict Editing pane.
- To restrict formatting changes to text formatted with specific styles, select the Limit formatting to a selection of styles check box in the Formatting restrictions section, click Settings to open the Formatting Restrictions dialog box, deselect any style you want to prevent users from changing, and then click OK.
- To prevent users from changing the theme, click Settings in the Formatting restrictions section, select the Block Theme or Scheme switching check box, and then click OK.
- To prevent users from changing the style set, click Settings in the Formatting restrictions section, select the Block Quick Style Set switching check box, and then click OK.
- To specify editing restrictions, select the Allow only this type of editing in the document check box in the Editing restrictions section, click the arrow, and then click the editing restriction you want to apply.
- To allow specific people to edit part of the document, select the Allow only this type of editing in the document check box in the Editing restrictions section, select the part you want to allow them to edit, click the More users link in the Editing restrictions section, type the user's email address, click OK, and then select the check box next to the user's email address.
- In the Start enforcement section, click the Yes, Start Enforcing Protection button.
- If desired, in the Start Enforcing Protection dialog box, type a password in the Enter new password (optional) box and in the Reenter password to confirm box.
- Click OK.

Because Bailey wants to be able to see exactly what changes the other team members make to the report, she decides to protect the document by applying the Tracked changes editing restriction. You already have some experience working with the Track Changes feature, which marks additions, deletions, moved text, and formatting changes with revision marks.

Note that if you apply editing restrictions to a master document, those restrictions are not applied to the separate subdocument files. For example, if you restrict editing in a master document so that all changes are tracked, revision marks will appear in any expanded subdocuments. However, if you open the subdocuments in separate document windows, you can edit the subdocuments without tracking the revisions.

In addition to protecting the document using tracked changes, Bailey wants to apply one formatting restriction—in particular, she wants to block any user from changing the document theme. You're ready to protect the NP_WD_10_Report document.

To apply formatting and editing restrictions to the document:

▶ **1.** On the ribbon, click the **Review** tab, and then in the Protect group, click the **Restrict Editing** button. The Restrict Editing pane opens. Bailey wants to block users from changing the document theme.

▶ **2.** In the 1. Formatting restrictions section, click the **Settings** link to open the Formatting Restrictions dialog box. See Figure 10–29.

Figure 10–29	Restrict Editing pane and the Formatting Restrictions dialog box

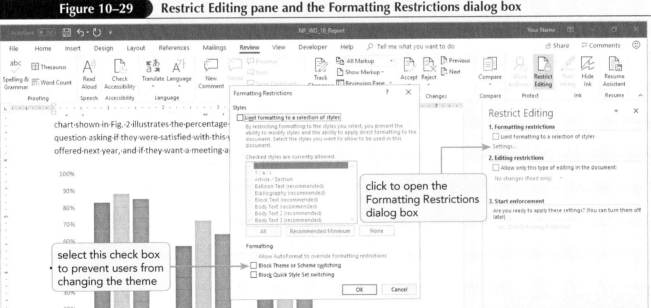

If you wanted to prevent others from modifying styles or applying direct formatting to the document, you would select the "Limit formatting to a selection of styles" check box, and then modify the Checked styles are currently allowed list so that only the styles users may modify are selected.

▶ **3.** Near the bottom of the dialog box, click the **Block Theme or Scheme switching** check box to select it, and then click **OK**. The Formatting Restrictions dialog box closes.

▶ **4.** In the Editing restrictions section of the Restrict Editing pane, click the **Allow only this type of editing in the document** check box.

TIP

To allow people you specify to edit parts or all of a document, select the Allow only this type of editing in the document check box, select the text they will be allowed to edit, select the check box below 2. Editing restrictions, click More users, type the person's email address in the dialog box, and then select that person's email address in the pane.

▶ **5.** In the Editing restrictions section, click the **arrow**—which, by default, is set to No changes (Read only). In addition to the Filling in forms command that you used when you restricted an online form so that users could change only content controls, Tracked changes and Comments appear as options.

▶ **6.** Click **Tracked changes**.

▶ **7.** In the Start enforcement section, click the **Yes, Start Enforcing Protection** button. The Start Enforcing Protection dialog box opens. You will not set a password.

▶ **8.** Click **OK**. The Restrict Editing pane changes to include the Stop Protection button.

▶ **9.** In the Restrict Editing pane, click the **Close** button ☒.

Bailey asks you to revise the Executive Summary section. Because you restricted editing, your changes will be tracked.

To edit the document with restrictions:

▶ **1.** On the Review tab, in the Tracking group, click the **Display for Review** arrow, and then click **All Markup**, if necessary.

▶ **2.** Scroll to the top of page 4 so that you can see the heading "1. Executive Summary" and the paragraph below it. Bailey wants you to edit the beginning of the second sentence in the paragraph so it starts with "They did, however, have several suggestions...."

▶ **3.** In the second sentence below the heading "1. Executive Summary," select **However**, the comma after it, and the space after the comma, and then press **DEL** twice. Because the document is protected for tracked changes, Word marks the selected text and the first character of the next word—the "t" in "they"—for deletion and adds a revision line in the margin.

▶ **4.** Type **T**, click after "did" in the second line, type **,** (a comma), press **SPACEBAR**, and then type **however,** (including the comma).

▶ **5.** On the ribbon, click the **Design** tab. In the Document Formatting group, the Themes button as well as the Colors, Fonts, and Effects buttons are unavailable because you blocked users from changing the document theme. See Figure 10–30.

Figure 10–30   **Restricted document after deleting text**

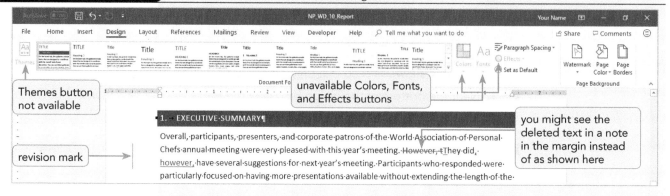

You'll now see what the document would look like if you accepted the revision—that is, if no revision marks appeared in the document.

To review the document with the revision accepted:

▶ **1.** On the ribbon, click the **Review** tab.

▶ **2.** In the Tracking group, click the **Display for Review** arrow, and then click **No Markup**. The revision marks are removed, and the document appears as it would if you had accepted the revisions.

It's helpful to use the No Markup setting to display the document as if all the revision marks have been accepted or rejected, without actually accepting or rejecting the revision marks. However, after you review the document using the No Markup setting, it's easy to forget to go back and accept or reject the revision marks. If you do forget, you might then accidentally send out a document that contains revision marks. Such a mistake could make you look unprofessional, or, even worse—depending on the nature of your revisions—inadvertently reveal sensitive information. To make sure a document doesn't contain any revision marks, or any other types of information that you don't want to reveal to readers of your document, you can use the Document Inspector. Before you do, you'll turn off the editing restrictions.

To turn off the editing and formatting restrictions:

▶ **1.** On the Review tab, in the Protect group, click the **Restrict Editing** button. The Restrict Editing pane opens.

▶ **2.** At the bottom of the pane, click the **Stop Protection** button. Because there is no password assigned, the Restrict Editing pane changes to show the restriction options, and the restrictions are immediately turned off. However, you still need to remove the formatting restrictions.

▶ **3.** In the 1. Formatting restrictions section, click the **Settings** link to open the Formatting Restrictions dialog box, click the **Block Theme or Scheme switching** check box to deselect it, and then click **OK** to close the dialog box.

▶ **4.** Close the Restrict Editing pane, and then save the changes to the document.

Decision Making: Choosing When to Restrict Editing in a Document

It's not convenient or useful to restrict editing in every document you create. But if you plan to send a document to colleagues for their comments, you should take the time to restrict editing in the document first so that your colleagues' changes are tracked with revision marks. Otherwise, you might encounter surprises in documents after they are published, mailed, or emailed. For example, a colleague might introduce an error by changing an important sales figure using outdated sales information, and then forget to tell you about the change. You can prevent this by protecting your shared documents using tracked changes.

Checking a Document with the Document Inspector

The **Document Inspector** examines a document for hidden properties, personal information, and comments and revision marks. If it finds any, it gives you the opportunity to remove them. When you remove revision marks with the Document Inspector, all changes are accepted as if you had used the Accept button in the Changes group on the Review tab.

You can also use the Document Inspector to check a document for personal information stored in the document properties, headers, or footers. In addition, it can search for hidden text (text that is hidden from display using the Hidden check box on the Font tab of the Font dialog box) and for special types of data that can be stored along with the document.

At this point, the document still contains your marked edit to the second sentence in the paragraph below the Executive Summary heading, although you can't see the revision marks. You'll use the Document Inspector now to check for revision marks and other hidden information. To access the Document Inspector, you need to display the Info screen in Backstage view.

To check the document using the Document Inspector:

1. On the ribbon, click the **File** tab to display the Info screen in Backstage view.

2. Click the **Check for Issues** button, and then click **Inspect Document**. The Document Inspector dialog box opens. See Figure 10–31.

Figure 10–31 Document Inspector dialog box

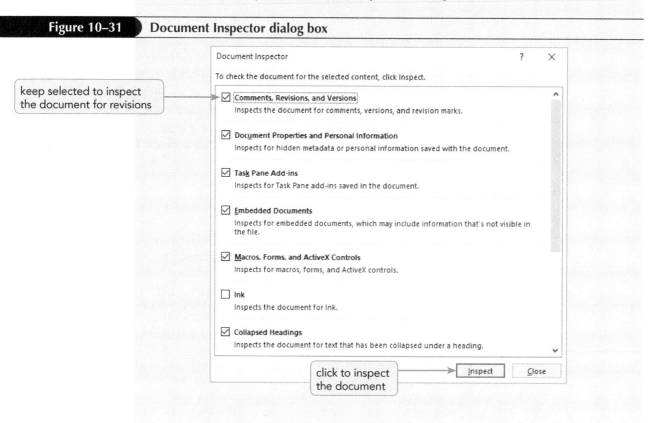

keep selected to inspect the document for revisions

Document Inspector ? ✕

To check the document for the selected content, click Inspect.

☑ Comments, Revisions, and Versions
Inspects the document for comments, versions, and revision marks.

☑ Document Properties and Personal Information
Inspects for hidden metadata or personal information saved with the document.

☑ Task Pane Add-ins
Inspects for Task Pane add-ins saved in the document.

☑ Embedded Documents
Inspects for embedded documents, which may include information that's not visible in the file.

☑ Macros, Forms, and ActiveX Controls
Inspects for macros, forms, and ActiveX controls.

☐ Ink
Inspects the document for Ink.

☑ Collapsed Headings
Inspects the document for text that has been collapsed under a heading.

click to inspect the document

Inspect   Close

Trouble? If a dialog box opens indicating that the file has not been saved, click Yes.

3. Click **Inspect**. The Document Inspector dialog box changes to indicate that revision marks, document properties, embedded documents, and custom XML data were found in the document. See Figure 10–32.

Figure 10–32 | Document Inspector dialog box after inspecting the document

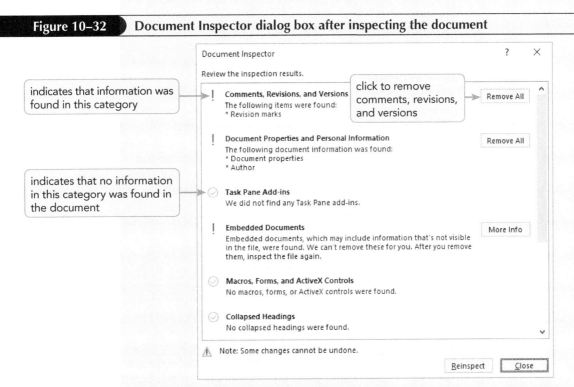

You need to remove the revision marks.

4. In the Comments, Revisions, and Versions section at the top of the dialog box, click **Remove All**. The top section changes to show that all items in that category were successfully removed.

5. Click **Close**. The Document Inspector dialog box closes.

6. At the top of the navigation pane, click the **Back** button ⊖ to close Backstage view. Next, you'll verify that the revision marks were removed.

Trouble? If Backstage view is already closed, skip Step 6.

7. On the Review tab, in the Tracking group, click the **Display for Review** arrow (which currently displays "No Markup"), and then click **All Markup**. If the document contained the revision marks to mark the changes you made to the paragraph below the "1. Executive Summary" heading on page 4, you would see them now. Because you used the Document Inspector to remove all revision marks, the changes you made have been accepted.

8. Save the changes to the document.

Using Synchronous Scrolling

One of the difficult aspects of collaborating on a document with other people is keeping track of which copy of the file is the correct one, and making sure that all the intended edits are entered into the correct file. If confusion arises, you can open up both documents, display them side by side, and then scroll through both documents at the same time. Scrolling through two documents at once—a process known as **synchronous scrolling**—allows you to quickly assess the overall structure of two documents. If this side-by-side comparison suggests numerous differences between the documents, you can then use the Compare feature to examine, in detail, the differences between the two documents.

To use the synchronous scrolling feature, open both documents, and then display the original document in the window. On the ribbon, click the View tab, and then in the Window group, click the View Side by Side button. If three or more documents are open, a dialog box opens so that you can choose the document you want to display next to the original document. If only two documents are open, the second document appears next to the original document. In both windows, the Synchronous Scrolling button is selected in the Window group on the View tab. As you scroll in either document, the other document scrolls at the same pace.

Checking Documents for Accessibility

People with certain physical impairments or disabilities are able to use computers because of technology that makes them accessible. For example, assistive technology can allow people who cannot use their arms or hands to use foot, head, or eye movements to control the pointer. One of the most common assistive technologies is the screen reader, which identifies objects on the screen and produces audio output of the text.

Graphics and tables cause problems for users of screen readers unless they have alt text. When a screen reader encounters an object in a Word document that has alt text, it announces that an object is on the page, and then it reads the alt text. You already know how to add alt text to pictures. Other types of graphics, such as shapes, SmartArt graphics, and charts need alt text as well. You can add alt text to shapes or a SmartArt graphic by clicking the Alt Text button in the Accessibility group on the Drawing Tools or SmartArt Tools Format tab. To add alt text to objects that do not have an Alt Text button on their contextual Format tab, you can right-click the object, and then on the shortcut menu, click Edit Alt Text.

To help you to identify parts of the document that might be problematic for people who must use assistive technologies such as a screen reader, you can use the Accessibility Checker. The Accessibility Checker classifies potential problems into three categories—errors, warnings, and tips. Content flagged as an error is content that is difficult or impossible for people with disabilities to access. Content flagged with a warning is content that is difficult for many people with disabilities to access. Content flagged with a tip isn't necessarily impossible for people with disabilities to access, but it could possibly be reorganized in a way that would make it easier to access.

You will use the Accessibility Checker to see what adjustments you should consider in order to make the document accessible.

To check the document for accessibility issues:

▶ **1.** On the ribbon, click the **File** tab to display the Info screen in Backstage view.

▶ **2.** Click the **Check for Issues** button, and then click **Check Accessibility**. Backstage view closes, and the Accessibility Checker pane is displayed to the right of the document window. Two objects are listed in the Missing alternative text section, and two objects are listed in the Image or objects not inline section.

▶ **3.** In the Accessibility Checker pane, click the object that starts with **Chart**. A number follows "Chart" in the item name in the pane. The document scrolls to the column chart that you inserted. See Figure 10–33.

Figure 10–33 **Chart selected in the Errors section of the Accessibility Checker pane**

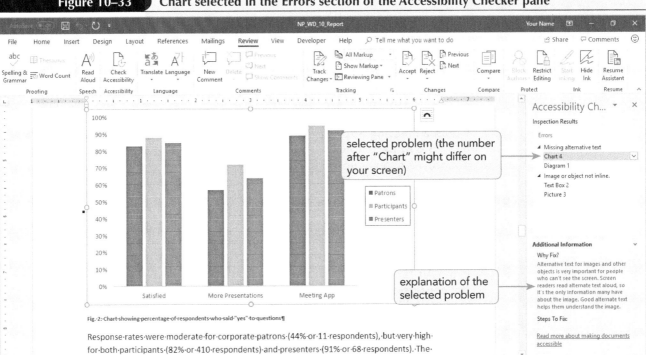

At the bottom of the Accessibility Checker pane, an explanation of the problem and suggestions for how to fix it are displayed. In this case, you can add alt text to the chart to describe it.

▶ **4.** In the document, point to a blank area of the chart so that the "Chart Area" ScreenTip appears, right-click the chart, and then on the shortcut menu, click **Edit Alt Text**. The Alt Text pane opens. You can either add text in the white box that describes the object or click the Mark as decorative check box to indicate to screen readers that this object should be ignored. See Figure 10–34.

Figure 10–34   Alt text options in the Alt Text pane

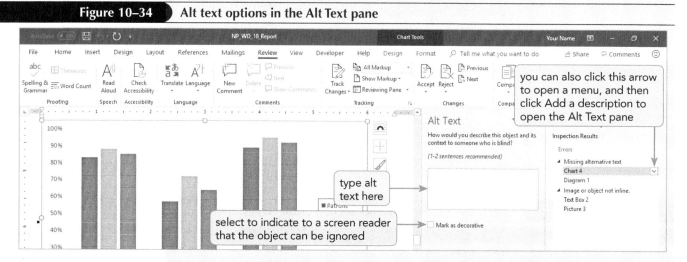

5. Click in the white box, and then type the following: **Column chart showing that over 80% of all respondents were satisfied with this year's meeting; 72% of participants and approximately 60% of corporate patrons and presenters want more presentations next year; and almost everyone wants a meeting app with 89% of corporate patrons, 92% of presenters, and 95% of participants responding "yes" to that question.** (including the period). As soon as you start typing in the Description box, the Chart object is removed from the Errors list in the Accessibility Checker pane.

6. In the Accessibility Checker pane, in the Missing alternative text section, click the **Diagram** item. The document scrolls, and the SmartArt diagram appears. The white box in the Alt Text pane is empty because the selected object does not have any alt text yet.

7. In the Alt Text pane, click in the white box, and then type **Diagram illustrating the conclusion that more presentations coupled with a meeting app should yield increased participant satisfaction.** (including the period).

8. In the Accessibility Checker pane, in the Missing alternative text section, click the **Picture** object. The document scrolls to display the photo of Anthony. In the Alt Text pane, the white box contains the description that was automatically generated when the picture was inserted. Although the description is correct, a more specific description would be more helpful.

9. In the Alt Text pane, select all of the text in the white box, and then type **Photo of Anthony Santana**. (Do not type the period.) The text you typed replaces the selected text.

10. Close the Alt Text pane. In the Accessibility Checker pane, the Missing alternative text section no longer appears.

    Floating objects in a document might not be accessible to people with vision disabilities. To address this concern, you could change floating objects to inline objects. In the Accessibility Checker pane, the Picture object is selected. The photo of Anthony Santana is a floating object.

11. In the Accessibility Checker pane, click the **Text Box** object. The caption under the photo of Anthony is selected. Bailey tells you that it is fine to leave these two objects as floating objects because they are not critical to understanding the document contents.

12. Close the Accessibility Checker pane, and then save the document.

In this session, you added advanced elements to a document, including automatically numbered headings, figure captions, cross-references, and endnotes. You also created a chart from within the document, and then you applied editing restrictions to the document. Finally, you checked the document for hidden information using the Document Inspector and checked it to make sure it is accessible to all readers. In the next session, you'll add different footers on odd and even pages and insert a reference to text formatted with a style on a page in a footer. You will also create an index and a table of figures. Finally, you will check the document for compatibility with earlier versions of Word, encrypt it, and mark it as final.

Session 10.2 Quick Check

REVIEW

1. Explain how to add automatic numbering to section titles in a master document.
2. What button do you use to insert a figure caption?
3. Suppose you want to include the text "(See Figure 3)" in a report, and you want to make sure the figure number is automatically renumbered, if necessary, to reflect additions or deletions of figures in the document. What should you do?
4. What happens when you insert a chart using the Chart button in the Illustrations group on the Insert tab?
5. What kind of editing restrictions can you specify when protecting a document?
6. What types of formatting restrictions can you specify?
7. What does the Document Inspector find?
8. What is alt text?

Session 10.3 Visual Overview:

An **index** is an alphabetical list of entries—that is, words, phrases, and categories (or subjects)—accompanied by the page numbers on which they appear in a printed document. Click the References tab to access the commands for creating an index.

AutoSave ● Off   NP_WD_10_Report

File   Home   Insert   Design   Layout   **References**   Mailings   Review   View

Table of Contents ▾ | Add Text ▾   Update Table | Insert Footnote   Insert Endnote   Next Footnote ▾   Show Notes | Smart Lookup   Researcher | Insert Citation ▾   Manage Style Bibli...

Footnotes   Research   Citations & Bibli...

Mark Index Entry   ?   ✕

Index

Main entry: overview

Subentry:

Options

○ Cross-reference: See

○ Current page

◉ Page range

Bookmark: OverviewBookmark

Page number format

To mark a range of pages as an index entry, select the text, create a bookmark for the selected text, and then select the bookmark in the Page range section as the item to be marked.

Mark Index Entry   ?   ✕

Index

Main entry: WAPC

Subentry:

Options

○ Cross-reference: See

◉ Current page

○ Page range

Bookmark:

Page number format

☐ Bold
☐ Italic

The default is for the Current page option button to be selected.

To mark all instances of a word for the index, click the Mark All button.

This dialog box stays open so that you can mark multiple index entries.

[Mark]   [Mark All]   [Cancel]

1. → EXECUTIVE·SUMMARY¶

Overall,·participants[XE·"respondents:participan... "respondents:presenters"·]·and·corporate·patro... patrons"·]·of·the·World·Association·of·Personal·C... ting,·annual"·\t·"See·annual·... y·did,·however,·have·several·... ponded·were·particularly·fo... tending·the·length·of·the·me... "respondents:presenters"·]·who·responded·sugg... meeting·app·that·would·make·it·easier·for·partic... to·plan·their·schedule·and·keep·track·of·the·time... presentations.·All·... responded·are·strongly·in·favor·of·expanding·the... hours.·Half·of·the·corporate·patrons[XE·"respon... responded·are·interested·in·the·possibility·of·nam... the·opening·night·reception.¶

When you mark an index entry, an XE field code is inserted.

2. → OVERVIEW¶

Now·in·its·25th·year,·the·annual·meeting[XE·"ann... Association·of·Personal·Chefs·(WAPC[XE·"WAPC"...

English (United States)

Indexing a Document

To mark text for inclusion in the index, click the Mark Entry button on the References tab or press ALT+SHIFT+X. The Mark Index Entry dialog box can stay open while you continue to select text and mark index entries.

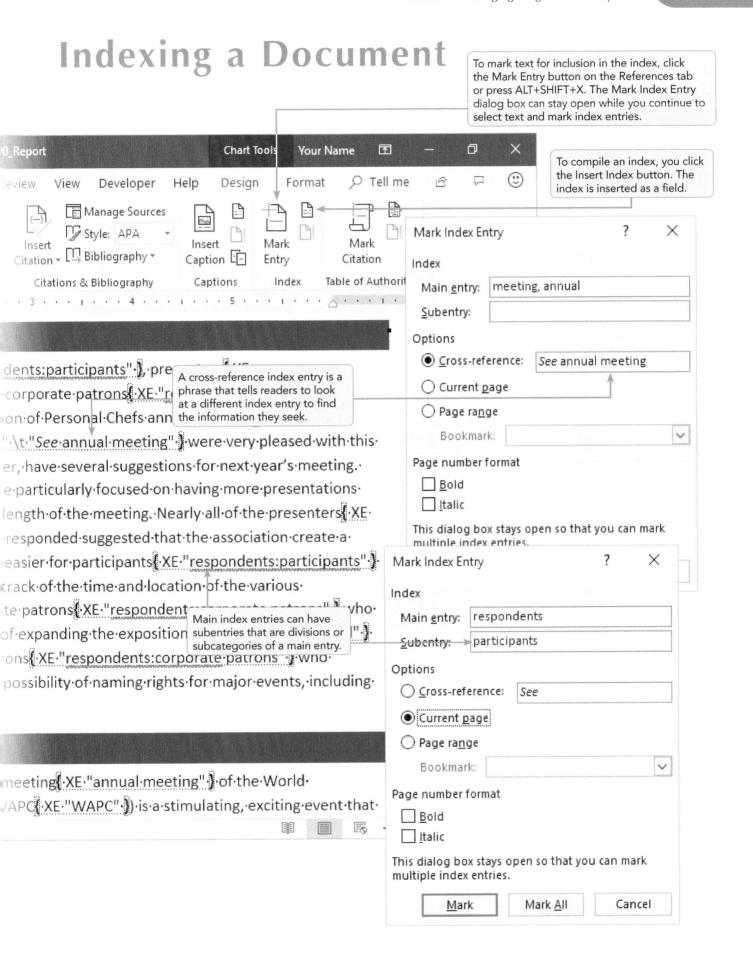

To compile an index, you click the Insert Index button. The index is inserted as a field.

A cross-reference index entry is a phrase that tells readers to look at a different index entry to find the information they seek.

Main index entries can have subentries that are divisions or subcategories of a main entry.

Mark Index Entry

Index

Main entry: meeting, annual

Subentry:

Options

⦿ Cross-reference: _See_ annual meeting
◯ Current page
◯ Page range
   Bookmark:

Page number format
☐ Bold
☐ Italic

This dialog box stays open so that you can mark multiple index entries.

Mark Index Entry

Index

Main entry: respondents

Subentry: participants

Options

◯ Cross-reference: _See_
⦿ Current page
◯ Page range
   Bookmark:

Page number format
☐ Bold
☐ Italic

This dialog box stays open so that you can mark multiple index entries.

[Mark] [Mark All] [Cancel]

Evaluating Section and Page Breaks in a Document

TIP

If you need to add line numbers to a document, on the Layout tab, in the Page Setup group, click the Line Numbers button, and then select an option on the menu.

When you inserted subdocuments in the master document, section breaks were also inserted. Formatting instructions are embedded in a section break. Therefore, if the subdocuments contain formatting that conflicts with formatting in the master document, the entire master document could become corrupt. Also, the Next Page section breaks sometimes create a page break where you don't want one. To avoid bad page breaks and sections with conflicting formatting, you will delete the section breaks now.

To view the page and section breaks in the report:

▶ **1.** If you took a break after the previous session, open the document **NP_WD_10_Report**.

TIP

If you want to scroll from side to side instead of vertically, click the Side to Side button in the Page Movement group on the View tab.

▶ **2.** Press **CTRL+HOME** to move the insertion point to the beginning of the document, if necessary, and then scroll through the document, noting the manual page breaks after the text on page 1, after the table of contents on page 2, and after the empty paragraph below "List of Figures" on page 3. Then note the Next Page section breaks on pages 5 and 7, the two Continuous section breaks on page 6, the Continuous section break just before the Next Page section break on page 7, the two Continuous section breaks on page 8, and the Continuous section break on page 9. (The label for the Continuous section break on page 7 is hidden, and you can see only the dashed lines that represent the break at the end of the paragraph above the Next Page section break.)

You need to remove the unnecessary section breaks so that the page breaks are in the correct locations and so you do not get any unexpected results from formatting instructions that are embedded in the continuous section breaks. When you remove a section break, the section following that break assumes the formatting of the section before it. Therefore, you should remove section breaks starting from the end of a document.

To remove section breaks in the document:

▶ **1.** On page 9, click between the paragraph mark and the Continuous section break, and then press **DEL**. The section break is deleted.

▶ **2.** Scroll up to the middle of page 8.

▶ **3.** Above the "6. Recommendations" heading, click in the Continuous section break that spans the width of the page, and then press **DEL**.

▶ **4.** At the end of the paragraph above the heading "6. Recommendations," click between the period and the Continuous section break, press **ENTER** to insert a paragraph mark, and then press **DEL**.

▶ **5.** Scroll up to the middle of page 7.

▶ **6.** Above the "5. Presenters" heading, click in the Continuous section break that spans the width of the page, and then press **DEL**.

▶ **7.** At the end of the paragraph above the heading "5. Presenters," click between the paragraph mark and the Continuous section break, and then press **DEL**.

▶ **8.** Scroll up to the middle of page 6, and then delete the section break above the heading "4. Participants."

▶ **9.** At the end of the paragraph above the heading "4. Participants," click between the period and the Continuous section break, press **ENTER** to insert a paragraph mark, and then delete the section break at the end of the paragraph above the heading "4. Participants."

▶ **10.** Scroll up to the bottom of page 5, and then delete the section break at the end of the last paragraph. All of the section breaks have been deleted.

▶ **11.** Save the changes to the document.

Applying Different Page Number Formats in Sections

Most books, reports, and other long documents use a different page-numbering scheme for the front matter—the pages preceding the main document, including material such as the title page and table of contents—than for the body of the report. Front matter is usually numbered with lowercase Roman numerals (i, ii, iii, etc.), whereas the pages in the body of the report are numbered with Arabic numerals (1, 2, 3, etc.).

Creating Sections for Different Page-Numbering Schemes

Bailey wants to use a different page-numbering scheme for the front matter of the NP_WD_10_Report document. She also wants to add footers to the document that include the page numbers. You need to create three sections in the document so that you can start the page numbering in the front matter at page i, and start the page numbering in the body of the report at page 1.

To create three sections in the document:

▶ **1.** Scroll to display page 1, and then click the manual page break. You will delete the page break, and then insert a Next Page section break so that the title page is in section 1 and the rest of the report is in section 2.

▶ **2.** Press **DEL**. The manual page break is deleted, and the heading "Contents" and the entire table of contents move up to the current page.

▶ **3.** On the ribbon, click the **Layout** tab.

▶ **4.** In the Page Setup group, click the **Breaks** button, and then under Section Breaks, click **Next Page**. A new page following a section break is created. The insertion point is in a blank paragraph on page 2. You need to delete this blank paragraph.

▶ **5.** Press **DEL**. The blank paragraph is deleted.

▶ **6.** Scroll up to see the list of names on page 1. It doesn't look like there is a section break after your name. You can verify that the section break is there by switching to Draft view.

▶ **7.** On the ribbon, click the **View** tab, and then in the Views group, click the **Draft** button. The document is displayed in Draft view, and you can see the Next Page section break below your name and above the "Contents" heading.

▶ **8.** In the Views group, click the **Print Layout** button.

Now you need to change the page break after the "List of Figures" heading on page 3 to a Next Page section break.

▶ **9.** Scroll to page 3, click the manual page break, and then press **DEL**. The manual page break is deleted, and the "1. Executive Summary" heading and the text that follows it moves up to the current page.

▶ **10.** Position the insertion point in front of "Executive." You will not be able to click in front of the "1" because it is formatted as a numbered list.

▶ **11.** Insert a Next Page section break. Now the title page is in section 1, the front matter is in section 2, and the body of the report is in section 3.

Centering Text Vertically on a Page

Next, you'll format the title page so that the text is centered vertically on the page, and then you'll set up the page numbers for the front matter.

To center the title page text vertically on the page:

▶ **1.** Press **CTRL+HOME** to position the insertion point on page 1 (the title page).

▶ **2.** On the Layout tab, in the Page Setup group, click the **Page Setup Dialog Box Launcher** 🔽. The Page Setup dialog box opens.

▶ **3.** Click the **Layout** tab. Notice that "This section" appears in the Apply to box in the Preview section of the dialog box. This means that the options you select on this tab will affect only the text in this section (which consists only of the title page). See Figure 10–35.

Figure 10–35 **Layout tab in the Page Setup dialog box**

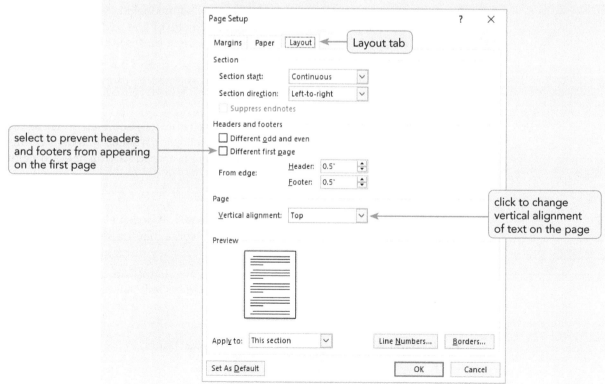

4. Click the **Vertical alignment** arrow, and then click **Center**. This specifies that the text on the title page—the only page in this section—will be centered vertically on the page.

5. Click **OK** to close the dialog box.

6. On the ribbon, click the **View** tab, and then in the Zoom group, click the **One Page** button. You can see that the text on the title page is centered vertically on the page.

7. Switch the Zoom level back to **120%**.

Setting Up Page Numbers in Different Sections

Now you're ready to set up the page numbering for the document. First, you will add page numbers to the front matter. You'll start by inserting a page number using one of the default page number styles. Then you will format the page numbers as lowercase Roman numerals (i, ii, iii, etc.). The title page typically is not counted as a page in the front matter, so you will also specify that the page number on the first page of the front matter—the page containing the table of contents—starts at page i.

To set up page numbers for the front matter:

1. Scroll to page 2, and then position the insertion point to the left of the "Contents" heading.

2. On the ribbon, click the **Insert** tab.

3. In the Header & Footer group, click the **Page Number** button, point to **Bottom of Page**, and then click **Plain Number 3**. The document switches to Header and Footer view, the Header & Footer Tools Design tab is displayed, and a page number field is inserted in the footer at the right margin on page 2. This page number was inserted in the footer on all the pages in the document—in other words, in all three sections.

4. In the Header & Footer group, click the **Page Number** button, and then click **Format Page Numbers**. The Page Number Format dialog box opens. See Figure 10–36.

Figure 10–36   Page Number Format dialog box

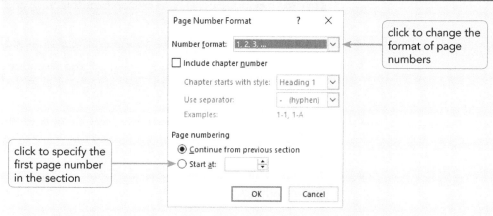

You need to change the format of the page numbers in this section to lowercase Roman numerals.

> **5.** Click the **Number format** arrow, scroll down, and then click **i, ii, iii, ...** .

> **6.** In the Page numbering section, click the **Start at** option button. The Roman numeral one (i) is displayed in the Start at box.

> **7.** Click **OK** to close the Page Number Format dialog box. The page number field in the footer on the Contents page displays the page number "i." Note on the status bar that this is still considered to be page 2 in the document. See Figure 10–37.

Figure 10–37 Page numbered i on page 2 of the document

Callouts on figure: "page number 2 of 8 on the status bar", "Footer -Section 2-", "page number i", "Same as Previous". Status bar: "Page 2 of 8   1615 words   120%"

> **8.** Scroll up so that you can see the footer on page 1 (the title page). The page number in this footer is 1. That's because the options in the Page Number Format dialog box are applied to only the current section, and the insertion point was in the footer in section 2 (the section containing the front matter) when you opened the Page Number Format dialog box.

Bailey does not want a page number to appear on the title page. Recall that when you add information in a header or footer in a document with sections, the headers and footers are linked between sections. You can break this link to enable the creation of a different header or footer in different sections.

To break the link between footers in different sections and remove the footer from the title page:

> **1.** Make sure the insertion point is still in the footer on page 2 (numbered page i in the footer).

> **2.** On the Header & Footer Tools Design tab, in the Navigation group, click the **Link to Previous** button. The button is deselected, and the link between the footers in sections 1 and 2 is removed.

> **3.** Scroll up, and then click in the footer on page 1 (the title page).

> **4.** In the Header & Footer group, click the **Page Number** button, and then click **Remove Page Numbers**. The page number in the footer on page 1 is removed.

> **5.** Scroll down so that you can see the page number on the page containing the table of contents. Because you removed the link between the sections, this page number is still there.

> **6.** Scroll down so that you can see the footer on page 4 (as indicated on the status bar) in the document. This page is numbered 3 in the footer.

Page 4 in the document is numbered page 3 because the footer in this section—section 3—is still linked to the footer in section 2, and you started the page numbering at i (1) in that section. You do want the page numbers in the body of the report to use Arabic numerals (1, 2, 3), but you need to change the formatting so that the numbering in this section starts at page 1. To do this, you'll unlink the sections, and then start the numbering in section 3 with 1.

To set up the page numbers for section 3 to begin with 1:

▶ **1.** Click in the footer on page 4 of the document (currently numbered 3). This is the first page of the body of the report.

▶ **2.** On the Header & Footer Tools Design tab, in the Navigation group, click the **Link to Previous** button to deselect it.

▶ **3.** In the Header & Footer group, click the **Page Number** button, and then click **Format Page Numbers** to open the Page Number Format dialog box. In the Number format list, "1, 2, 3, …" is selected. You need to indicate that you want this section to begin with page number 1.

▶ **4.** Click the **Start at** option button in the Page numbering section to select it. The Arabic numeral one (1) appears in the Start at box.

▶ **5.** Click **OK** to close the dialog box, and then scroll down to view the footers in the rest of the document. The page numbering in section 3 starts with page 1 on the page containing the heading "1. Executive Summary" and proceeds consecutively through the document to page 5.

▶ **6.** Close Header and Footer view, and then save the changes to the document.

Changing the Footer and Page Layout for Odd and Even Pages

Most professionally produced books and reports are printed on both sides of the paper and then bound. The blank space on the inside of each page, where the pages are bound together, is called the **gutter**. When you open a bound book or report, odd-numbered pages appear on the right, and even-numbered pages appear on the left. Often, the headers and footers for odd-numbered pages contain text that is different from the headers or footers for the even-numbered pages.

Bailey wants to follow these standards in the NP_WD_10_Report document. Specifically, she wants you to use the page layouts shown in Figure 10–38.

Figure 10–38   Page setup for odd and even pages

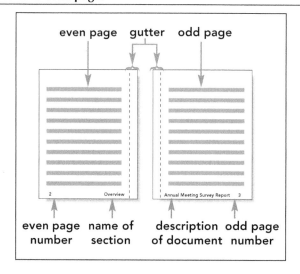

To do this, you'll use the following guidelines:

- Set the gutter to one-half inch. This will cause the text on odd pages to shift to the right (one-half inch in this case), leaving a wider margin on the left, and the text on even pages to shift to the left (again, one-half inch), leaving a wider margin on the right. When the even and odd pages are printed back-to-back, the gutters line up on the same edge of the paper, thus leaving room for the binding.

- Change the location for page numbers so it's different on odd and even pages. In a page layout that distinguishes between odd and even pages, the page numbers are usually printed near the outside edge of the page rather than near the gutter to make them easier to see in a bound copy. On odd pages, the page numbers appear on the right; on even pages, the numbers appear on the left.

- Enter different text for the footers on odd and even pages. In many books, the section title is in the header or footer of odd pages, and the book or chapter title is in the header or footer of even pages. Sometimes this text is shifted toward the gutter (just as page numbers are shifted toward the outer edge). Bailey wants the odd-page footers to contain the text "Annual Meeting Survey Report") and the even-page footers to include the section title (for example, "Overview") closer to the gutter.

First, you'll increase the size of the gutter to allow enough room to bind the report without obscuring any text. To make this change, you'll use the Page Setup dialog box.

To specify a gutter margin in the document:

1. On the second page of the document (numbered page i, with the heading "Contents"), position the insertion point before the heading "Contents." On the status bar, note that the total number of pages in the document is 8, and the current page is page 2.

2. On the ribbon, click the **Layout** tab, and then in the Page Setup group, click the **Page Setup Dialog Box Launcher** ⊡ to open the Page Setup dialog box.

3. Click the **Margins** tab, and then change the setting in the Gutter box to **0.5"**.

4. Near the bottom of the dialog box, click the **Apply to** arrow. You can choose to apply the settings in this dialog box to the current section, to the whole document, or from this point forward.

▶ **5.** Click **This point forward**. Now, the gutter margin will be applied to the remainder of the report—all the pages except the title page.

▶ **6.** Click **OK**. The Page Setup dialog box closes, and the gutter margin increases to one-half inch.

Because the document is not yet set up for odd and even pages, the gutter margin is the left margin on all of the pages. On the status bar, notice that the document now contains nine pages. This is because the increase in the left margin pushed some text onto subsequent pages.

When you set up a document to be printed on odd and even pages, headers and footers on the current page remain, but they are removed from every other page. So if the current page is an odd page, the headers and footers on all the odd pages remain but are removed from all of the even pages. You will set up the document to print on odd and even pages now.

To change the page setup for printing odd and even pages:

▶ **1.** Make sure the insertion point is still before the "C" in the "Contents" heading.

▶ **2.** Open the Page Setup dialog box again, and then click the **Layout** tab.

▶ **3.** In the Headers and footers section, click the **Different odd and even** check box. Now the footers on the odd pages of the document will differ from those on the even pages.

You want this change applied to both the current section—section 2, which contains the front matter—and the next section—section 3, which contains the body of the report. Because you positioned the insertion point on the page containing the table of contents, you can change the Apply to setting so that the odd-even formatting is applied from this point forward.

▶ **4.** At the bottom of the dialog box, click the **Apply to** arrow, click **This point forward**, and then click **OK**. On the status bar, the number of total pages in the document is now 10. On the current page, which is now page 3 according to the status bar and therefore an odd page, the gutter margin is still on the left.

▶ **5.** Scroll so that you can see the footer on page i (page 3 on the status bar) and the top of page ii (page 4 on the status bar), and then click anywhere on page 4. The indicator on the status bar shows that this page is page 4, which is an even page. Because it is an even page, the gutter margin is on the right. Note that the footer on page i, an odd page, has not changed.

▶ **6.** Scroll down so that you can see the footer on page ii (page 4). The footer you created no longer appears on this page, an even page.

When you applied the setting for odd and even pages, an additional page was added to the document. You'll examine the document to see what happened.

To view the document in Multiple Page view:

▶ **1.** On the ribbon, click the **View** tab, and then in the Zoom group, click the **Multiple Pages** button. The Zoom level changes so that you can see three pages across the screen at a time.

▶ **2.** Click anywhere on the title page. The page number indicator on the status bar shows that the insertion point is on page 1 of 10.

▶ **3.** Click anywhere on the Contents page. The page number indicator on the status bar shows that the insertion point is on page 3 of 10.

The first page of a document formatted for odd and even pages is always an odd page—a right page. However, you numbered the second page in the document—the Content page—as page i, which is also an odd page. A document cannot have two odd-numbered pages in a row. To fix this, an additional blank page is automatically added between the title page and the Contents page. The total page count on the status bar includes this hidden blank page.

The blank page after the title page is part of the document. When you print the document, your printer will include a blank page after the title page. Also, if you save the document as a PDF file, a blank page will appear after the title page. This is exactly what you want in a document that will be printed on both sides of each page—the blank page ensures that the back of the title page remains blank. If the document did not include this blank page, then the Contents page would be printed on the back of the title page, turning the Contents page (which is set up to be an odd page) into an even page. The remaining odd and even pages would also be reversed.

Now that you have specified that odd and even pages will be set up differently, you can add footer text and format page numbering differently in the odd and even footers.

To format footers differently for odd and even pages:

▶ **1.** Click anywhere on the page containing the Contents heading (page i). Page 3 of 10 appears on the status bar.

▶ **2.** Change the Zoom level back to **120%**, and then on the ribbon, click the **Insert** tab.

▶ **3.** In the Header & Footer group, click the **Footer** button, and then click **Edit Footer**. The label "Odd Page Footer -Section 2-" appears on the left side of the footer area. In the right margin, the footer contains the page number "i." The insertion point is to the left of the page number. This is the odd page footer in the second section of the document. Because this is an odd page, you'll leave the page number at the right and insert the document name at the left.

▶ **4.** Type **Annual Meeting Survey Report**, and then press **TAB** twice. The text you typed moves to the left margin.

▶ **5.** On the Header & Footer Tools Design tab, in the Navigation group, click the **Next** button. The footer on the next page, labeled "Even Page Footer -Section 2-," appears on the left side of the footer area, and the insertion point is at the left margin in the footer.

▶ **6.** In the Header & Footer group, click the **Page Number** button, point to **Bottom of Page**, and then click **Plain Number 1**. A page number field appears above the blank paragraph in the footer, displaying the page number "ii."

Now you need to add "Annual Meeting Survey Report" to the odd pages in section 3 because you unlinked the sections earlier.

▶ **7.** In the Navigation group, click the **Next** button. The insertion point appears to the left of the page number field in the next section footer. The label in this footer is "Odd Page Footer -Section 3-." Note that in the Navigation group, the Link to Previous button is not selected.

▶ **8.** Type **Annual Meeting Survey Report**, and then press **TAB** twice.

▶ **9.** In the Navigation group, click the **Next** button. The even page footer on page 6 (numbered page 2) of the document appears. This is the first even page in Section 3. In the Navigation group, the Link to Previous button is still selected. Even though you removed the link between sections 2 and 3, after you applied formatting for odd and even pages, a link was reestablished between the even pages. Therefore, when you added the page numbers to the even pages, they were added to the even pages in section 3 as well.

▶ **10.** Close Header and Footer view.

After you have finished setting up a long document, you should scroll through to make sure the page breaks are in logical places.

To review the document and adjust page breaks:

▶ **1.** Press **CTRL+HOME**, and then scroll down the document examining the page breaks until you see the bottom of page 5 (numbered page 1) and the top of page 6. The bulleted list that starts at the bottom of page 5 contains only three items, and the automatic page break moved the last bulleted item to the next page. It would be better if this short list appeared on one page.

▶ **2.** In the heading "2.2. Survey Goals," position the insertion point before "Survey."

▶ **3.** Click the **Insert** tab, and then in the Pages group, click the **Page Break** button. The heading "2.2. Survey Goals" moves to page 6.

▶ **4.** Continue scrolling through the document to examine the page breaks. The rest of the page breaks are fine.

▶ **5.** Save the changes to the document.

Inserting a Style Reference into a Footer

Often in long reports, the section title appears in the footer on even pages. For example, on an even page that includes the heading "4. Participants," you would insert the heading "Participants" in the footer. Rather than manually entering a heading in each footer, you can insert the StyleRef field in the footer to pick up the first heading of whatever heading level you specify that appears on the page. The StyleRef field inserts text formatted with the style you specify. Like many of the Word features you've used in this module, style references are useful because they allow Word to update information automatically in one part of a document to reflect changes made in another part of a document.

Bailey wants you to format the footer on each even page so it includes the first Level 1 heading on the page. When you do this, if an even page does not contain a Level 1 heading, the most recent Level 1 heading from a prior page will be inserted. To do this, you'll insert a style reference to the Heading 1 style.

To insert a style reference to the section title into the footer:

▶ **1.** Scroll up to page 6 (numbered page 2), and then click anywhere on page 6.

▶ **2.** On the Insert tab, in the Header & Footer group, click the **Footer** button, and then click **Edit Footer**. The insertion point appears to the left of the page number on page 6.

▶ **3.** Press the → key to move the insertion point to the right of the page number field, and then press **TAB** twice to position the insertion point at the right margin in the footer.

▶ **4.** On the ribbon, click the **Insert** tab. Recall that to insert a field, you must use the command on the Quick Parts menu.

▶ **5.** In the Text group, click the **Explore Quick Parts** button ▤ ▾, and then click **Field** to open the Field dialog box.

▶ **6.** Click the **Categories** arrow, and then click **Links and References**.

▶ **7.** In the Field names box, click **StyleRef**. Next, you'll indicate the style to which the StyleRef field code should refer.

▶ **8.** In the Style name box, click **Heading 1** (the style applied to the main headings in the document). See Figure 10–39.

Figure 10–39 | Field dialog box after selecting the StyleRef field and the Heading 1 style

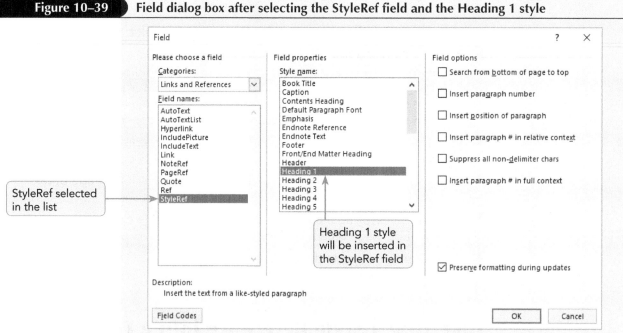

StyleRef selected in the list

Heading 1 style will be inserted in the StyleRef field

▶ **9.** Click **OK**. The Field dialog box closes. The heading "Overview" appears in the footer on page 6 (numbered page 2). Although this heading does not appear on page 2, it is the most recent heading before this page that is formatted with the Heading 1 style.

▶ **10.** Scroll up to see the three Level 2 headings on page 6, and then scroll up until you see the "2. Overview" heading on page 5.

▶ **11.** Scroll down to view the middle of page 8 (numbered page 4), which is the next even-numbered page. The heading "4. Participants" appears in the middle of this page.

12. Scroll to view the bottom of page 8. The footer contains the heading "Participants."

13. Scroll up so that you can see the footer on page 4 (numbered page ii). It contains the "Executive Summary" heading, which is the first heading on page 5 that is formatted with the Heading 1 style. This appears because neither page 4 nor any of the pages before page 4 contain text formatted with the Heading 1 style.

14. Scroll down so that you can see the footer on page 6 (numbered page 2), and then click in the footer, if necessary.

15. On the ribbon, click the **Header & Footer Tools Design** tab, and then in the Navigation group, click the **Link to Previous** button to deselect it.

16. Scroll back up so that you can see the footer on page 4 (numbered page ii), right-click **Executive Summary** in the footer, and then on the shortcut menu, click **Edit Field**. The Field dialog box opens showing the current settings for this field.

17. In the Style name list, click the **Front/End Matter Heading** style, and then click **OK**. The text on the right side of the footer changes to "List of Figures," which is the heading on this page that is formatted with the Front/End Matter Heading style.

18. Close Header and Footer view, and then save the changes to the document.

The report is now set up so Bailey can print the document on both sides of the page and bind it at the gutter margin, like a book.

Inserting Nonbreaking Hyphens and Spaces

In addition to page breaks, you should also look through your document for awkward line breaks. For example, the paragraph below the heading "2.1. Survey Overview" on page 5 of the document contains the hyphenated word "e-survey," and it is split onto two lines, which makes it a little difficult to read. Although this isn't a serious problem, readers might be confused to see "e-" at the end of a line. To prevent Word from breaking a hyphenated word over two lines, you need to use a **nonbreaking hyphen**, also called a **hard hyphen**, which is a hyphen that does not allow the word or phrase containing it to break between two lines. To insert a nonbreaking hyphen, you use the Special Characters tab in the Symbol dialog box. By contrast, a **breaking hyphen**, or **soft hyphen**, is a hyphen that allows the word containing it to appear on different lines. To insert a soft hyphen, you simply press the hyphen key on your keyboard.

To insert nonbreaking hyphens in "e-survey":

1. Scroll to the bottom of page 5 in the document (numbered page 1).

2. In the paragraph under the heading "2.1. Survey Overview," at the end of the second line, click after "e-".

3. Press **BACKSPACE** to delete the breaking hyphen. The "e" becomes joined to "survey," and the word "esurvey" appears on the next line. Now you'll insert the nonbreaking hyphen.

4. On the ribbon, click the **Insert** tab.

> **5.** In the Symbols group, click the **Symbol** button, and then click **More Symbols**. The Symbol dialog box opens with the Symbols tab selected.

> **6.** Click the **Special Characters** tab. A list of special symbols appears. See Figure 10–40.

Figure 10–40   Special Characters tab in the Symbol dialog box

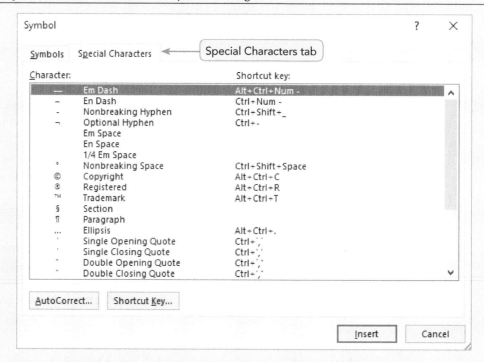

> **7.** Click **Nonbreaking Hyphen**, click **Insert** to insert the hyphen into the document at the location of the insertion point, and then click **Close**. The Symbol dialog box closes, and the word "e-survey" now contains a nonbreaking hyphen.

TIP

You can also press CTRL+SHIFT+_ to insert a nonbreaking hyphen.

Another important special character is the nonbreaking space. A **nonbreaking space** is a space that does not allow the words on either side of it to break over two lines. For example, the phrase "10 KB" (where KB stands for kilobytes, as in a 10 KB file) might be hard to read or distracting if the "10" appears at the end of one line and "KB" appears at the beginning of the next line. To avoid this problem, you can insert a nonbreaking space between the "10" and the "KB."

In the paragraph you just revised, the word "March" now appears at the end of one line and the year "2021" appears at the beginning of the next line. It would be better to keep these words together on one line.

To insert a nonbreaking space:

> **1.** In the paragraph under the heading "2.1. Survey Overview," click at the end of the fourth line (after the space after "March"), and then press **BACKSPACE**. The space after "March" is deleted, and "March2021" appears at the beginning of the next line.

> **2.** On the Insert tab, in the Symbols group, click the **Symbol** button, and then click **More Symbols**.

▶ **3.** In the Symbol dialog box, click the **Special Characters** tab.

▶ **4.** In the Character list, click **Nonbreaking Space**, click **Insert**, and then click **Close**. A nonbreaking space appears between "March" and "2021" at the beginning of the second to last line. The nonbreaking space is indicated with a small, open circle.

▶ **5.** Save the changes to the document.

Creating an Index

Bailey wants you to create an index to help readers locate information in the report. Refer to the Session 10.3 Visual Overview for more information about indexes. To create an index, you first mark the words and phrases in the document that you want to appear as entries in the index. Then you compile the index to create the list of terms you marked along with the pages on which the marked terms appear.

Marking Index Entries

When you mark an index entry, you select the word or phrase you want to appear in the index, and then use the Mark Index Entry dialog box to refine the entry. When you mark an index entry in your document, Word inserts a field code that appears if you display nonprinting characters.

When you mark entries, you can mark only the selected term as an entry or you can mark all instances of the selected term throughout the document as entries. To create a useful index, you need to think carefully about the terms or concepts a user might want to find in the document. Then you need to decide if you want the index to list the page number of one instance of that term, the page numbers of a few individual instances, or all the page numbers on which the term appears. To mark just the selected instance of a term as an index entry, you click Mark in the Mark Index Entry dialog box. To mark all instances of the selected term in the document as index entries, you click Mark All in the Mark Index Entry dialog box.

To create the index for the NP_WD_10_Report, you'll start by marking the main entries for the index.

REFERENCE

Marking Index Entries and Subentries

- Select the word or phrase you want to mark as an index entry.
- On the References tab, in the Index group, click the Mark Entry button to open the Mark Index Entry dialog box; or press ALT+SHIFT+X to open the Mark Index Entry dialog box.
- If necessary, edit the entry in the Main entry box, and then, if desired, type an entry in the Subentry box.
- In the Options section, make sure the Current page option button is selected.
- Click Mark to mark this occurrence, or click Mark All to mark every occurrence in the document.
- Click Close.

To start creating the index, you'll mark "WAPC" at the point where it appears in parentheses after the full name of the organization as an index entry. You don't need to mark every instance of "WAPC" as entries because someone who looks up this term probably wants to know what it stands for.

To mark one instance of the main index entry "WAPC":

▶ **1.** On page 5 (page 1 in the footer), in the paragraph below the heading "2. Overview," in the first sentence, select **WAPC**. You will add the selected term to the index.

TIP

You can also press ALT+SHIFT+X to open the Mark Index Entry dialog box.

▶ **2.** On the ribbon, click the **References** tab, and then in the Index group, click the **Mark Entry** button. The Mark Index Entry dialog box opens. The term you selected, "WAPC," appears in the Main entry box, and the Current page option button is selected in the Options section of the dialog box. This ensures that the current page of this entry will appear in the index.

▶ **3.** Click **Mark**. In the document, the field code {XE "WAPC"} appears next to the selected term "WAPC." See Figure 10–41.

| **Figure 10–41** | **"WAPC" marked as an index entry** |

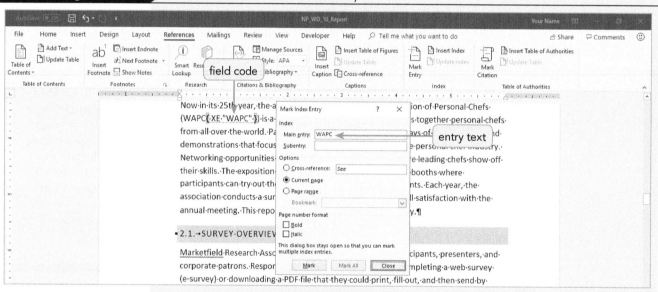

Trouble? If you can't see the field code that was inserted, drag the dialog box by its title bar to reposition it.

Next, you'll mark the phrases "focus group" and "exposition hall" as index entries. You want to mark every instance of these phrases as entries because someone who looks these terms up in the index would want to see where they are referenced.

Note that you do not need to close the Mark Index Entry dialog box to work in the document.

To mark additional index entries in the report:

▶ **1.** Click anywhere in the document, and then in the paragraph below the heading "2. Overview," in the sixth line, select **exposition hall**.

▶ **2.** Click in a blank area of the Mark Index Entry dialog box. The text in the Main entry box changes to "exposition hall."

▶ **3.** Click **Mark All** in the Mark Index Entry dialog box. Word searches the document for every occurrence of "exposition hall" and marks the first occurrence of the phrase in each paragraph. In the document, you can see that Word has inserted the field code {XE "exposition hall"} next to the selected phrase.

▶ **4.** Click in the document, and then press CTRL+END to move to the end of the document. In the last paragraph, the first instance of "exposition hall" is marked as an index entry, but the second instance of the phrase in the paragraph is not.

Marking Subentries

A high-quality index contains subentries as well as main entries. Subentries are indented in a list below the main entry. For the survey report, Bailey wants "respondents" to be a main entry with subentries of "corporate patrons," "participants," and "presenters," and she wants every instance marked.

To create subentries in an index:

▶ **1.** Scroll back to page 5 (page 1 in the footer) so that you can see the heading "2.1. Survey Overview" and the last five lines of the paragraph above this heading.

▶ **2.** In the first sentence of the paragraph below the heading "2.1. Survey Overview," select **participants**.

▶ **3.** Click in a blank area of the Mark Index Entry dialog box. The word "participants" appears in the Mark entry box.

▶ **4.** Select the text in the Main entry box, press **DEL**, and then type **respondents**.

▶ **5.** Click in the **Subentry** box, type **participants**, and then click **Mark All**. All instances of "participants" are marked as subentries under the main entry "respondents." In the XE field code that was inserted, notice the main entry "respondents" appears, followed by a colon and then the subentry. In the paragraph above the heading, both instances of "participants" are marked as subentries. For subentries, when you mark all instances, every instance in the document is marked, not just the first instance in each paragraph. See Figure 10–42.

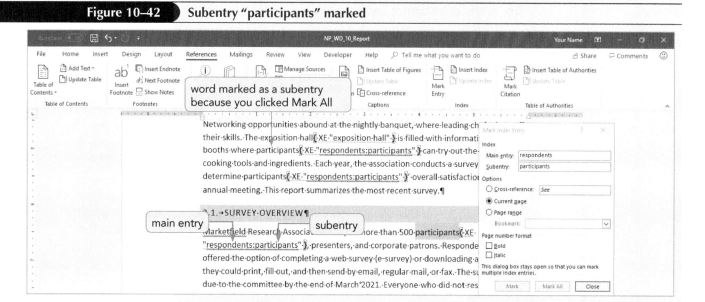

Figure 10–42   Subentry "participants" marked

Now you need to mark "presenters" and "corporate patrons" as subentries for "respondents."

▶ **6.** Click in the document, and then in the first sentence in the first paragraph below the heading "2.1. Survey Overview," select **presenters**.

▶ **7.** Click in a blank area in the Main Index Entry dialog box, and then replace the text in the Main entry box with **respondents**.

▶ **8.** Click in the **Subentry** box, type **presenters**, and then click **Mark All**.

▶ **9.** In the document, in the first sentence in the first paragraph below the heading "2.1. Survey Overview," select **corporate patrons**.

▶ **10.** Mark all instances of **corporate patrons** as a subentry in the index to **respondents**.

You also need to mark all instances of the word "respondents" so that page numbers will appear next to that entry.

▶ **11.** Scroll to page 7 in the document (marked page 3 in the footer), and then in the paragraph below the heading "2.4. Response Information," in the second line, select **respondents**.

▶ **12.** Mark all instance of "respondents" as a main entry in the index.

Creating Cross-Reference Index Entries

You create cross-reference index entries to tell readers to look at a different index entry to find the information they seek. For example, in the NP_WD_10_Report document, the phrase "annual meeting" is frequently used. However, someone searching for this concept in the index might search instead for the phrase "meeting, annual." You can create an index entry for "meeting, annual" and insert a cross-reference to the main entry "annual meeting."

REFERENCE

Creating a Cross-Reference Index Entry

- Select the word or phrase you want to cross-reference. If that word is not already marked as a main entry, mark all instances of that word as a main entry.
- On the References tab, in the Index group, click the Mark Entry button to open the Mark Index Entry dialog box; or press ALT+SHIFT+X to open the Mark Index Entry dialog box.
- Delete any text in the Main entry box, and then type the term you want to be listed as a main entry.
- In the Options section, click the Cross-reference option button, and then after "See," type the main entry you want to reference.
- Click Mark.
- Click Close.

You will mark every instance of "annual meeting" as a main entry, and then create a cross-reference to the main entry "annual meeting" next to the entry "meeting, annual."

To create a cross-reference index entry:

1. Scroll to the top of page 5 to display the paragraph below the heading "1. Executive Summary," and then in that paragraph, in the third line, select **annual meeting**.

2. Mark all instances of the phrase "annual meeting" as a main entry in the index.

3. In the Main Index Entry dialog box, edit the entry in the Main entry box so it is **meeting, annual**.

4. In the Options section of the dialog box, click the **Cross-reference** option button. The insertion point appears to the right of the word "See" in the Cross-reference box.

5. Type **annual meeting** and then click **Mark**. You can't click Mark All because a cross-reference entry appears only once in the index and doesn't include a page number. In the document, a field code for the "meeting, annual" entry appears before or after the field code for the main entry "annual meeting." See Figure 10–43.

Figure 10–43	Cross-reference entry created

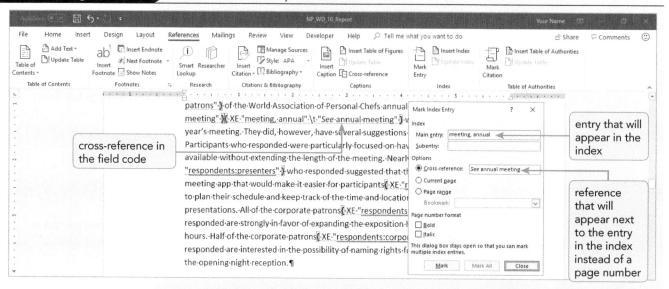

Trouble? The cross-reference field code might appear before the field code marking "annual meeting" as a main index entry. This will not cause any problems with the index.

6. In the Mark Index Entry dialog box, click **Close**.

Creating an Index Entry for a Page Range

In addition to main entries and subentries that list individual pages, sometimes you'll want to include an index entry that refers to a range of pages. For example, you could create an entry for the "Overview" heading and refer users to the range of pages that contain all of the information under this heading. To do this, you first create a bookmark marking the page range you want to index, and then you create an index entry to this bookmark.

You need to create an index entry for the section "Overview." This entry will span a range of pages.

To create an index entry with a reference to a range of pages:

▶ **1.** Switch to Outline view, and then, if necessary, scroll so that you can see the heading "2. Overview."

   Trouble? If the Level 1 headings aren't visible, click the Show Text Formatting check box in the Outline Tools group on the Outlining tab to deselect it.

▶ **2.** Next to "2. Overview," click the **plus sign** symbol ⊕. The entire "2. Overview" section is selected, including its subsections.

▶ **3.** On the ribbon, click the **Insert** tab, and then in the Links group, click the **Bookmark** button. The Bookmark dialog box opens.

▶ **4.** Type **OverviewBookmark** as the bookmark name, and then click **Add**. A bookmark to the selected text is created.

▶ **5.** Close Outline view, click the **References** tab, and then in the Index group, click the **Mark Entry** button. The Mark Index Entry dialog box opens and "Overview" appears in the Main entry box. Because the text is black and selected in the Main entry box, it is hard to read on the orange background.

▶ **6.** Edit the text in the Main entry box so it is all lowercase.

▶ **7.** Click the **Page range** option button, click the **Bookmark** arrow, and then click **OverviewBookmark**.

▶ **8.** Click **Mark** to mark this index entry. The document scrolls to show the last sentence in the selected page range and the index field code that indicates that this is the end of the page range.

▶ **9.** Click in the document, and then scroll up one line so you can see the whole index entry. See Figure 10–44.

Figure 10–44   Page range entry created

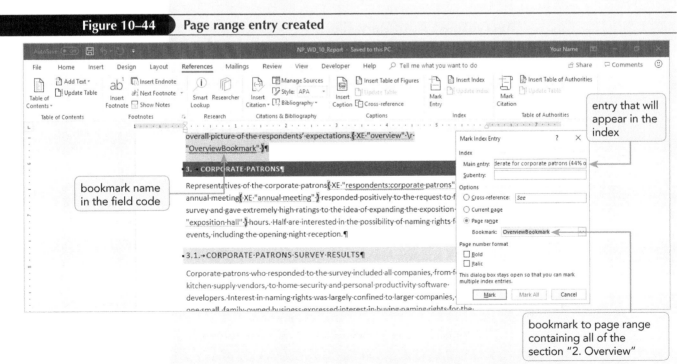

▶ **10.** In the Mark Index Entry dialog box, click **Close**.

▶ **11.** Save the changes to the document.

Using the AutoMark Feature

When you use the Mark All command, only the exact spelling and capitalization that you select is marked throughout the document. So when you marked all instances of "respondents," the word "Respondents" was not marked. (However, if a word includes an apostrophe, the word is marked; for example, *respondents'* would be marked.) One way to handle this is to create an AutoMark file, also called a concordance file. An AutoMark file contains a two-column table listing all the variations of a word that you want marked as the entry in the index in the left column, and the way the main entry should appear in the index in the right column. Then you reference the AutoMark file, and every instance of the words listed in the first column are marked as index entries.

If you want, you can create an AutoMark file as an alternative to using the Mark Index Entry dialog box to mark all instances of terms as index entries. Then after you mark the terms in the document using the AutoMark file, you can review the document and mark additional terms using the Mark Index Entry dialog box.

REFERENCE

Using the AutoMark Feature

- Create a new document, and then insert a two-column table.
- In the left column, type a variation of the main index entry.
- In the right column, type the main index entry.
- Save the document.
- In the document containing the index, on the References tab, in the Index group, click the Insert Index button to open the Index dialog box.
- Click the AutoMark button to open the Open Index AutoMark File dialog box, navigate to the location of the AutoMark file, click it, and then click Open.

To create an AutoMark file:

1. Scroll to page 7 (marked page 3 in the footer) so that you can see the headings "2.3. Survey Coordinator" and "2.4. Response Information" and the paragraphs below those headings. In the paragraph below the heading "2.4. Response Information," in the third line, "annual meeting" is marked as an index entry. However, in the paragraph below the heading "2.3. Survey Coordinator," in the fourth line, "Annual Meeting" is not marked as an index entry.

2. Scroll to the bottom of page 5 (marked page 1 in the footer) so that you can see the last paragraph on the page. In the third line, "Respondents" is not marked as an index entry even though you had marked all instances of "respondents."

3. Create a new, blank document, and then create a table consisting of two columns and two rows.

4. In the first cell in the first row, type **Annual Meeting**. This is the variation of the index entry.

5. Press **TAB**, and then type **annual meeting**. This is the marked index entry. The word "annual" was autocorrected so that the first letter is uppercase.

6. Point to **Annual** so that the **AutoCorrect Options** box ⬚ appears.

7. Point to the **AutoCorrect Options** box ⬚ so that it changes to the **AutoCorrect Options** button ⬚▾, and then click the **AutoCorrect Options** button ⬚▾. A menu appears.

▶ **8.** On the menu, click **Stop Auto-capitalizing First Letter of Table Cells**. The menu closes, and the word you typed is changed back to all lowercase. The insertion point is still in the second cell in the first row.

▶ **9.** Click in the first cell in the second row, type **Respondents**, and then press **TAB**. The insertion point moves to the second cell in the first row.

▶ **10.** Type **respondents**.

▶ **11.** Save the document as **NP_WD_10_AutoMark** in the location specified by your instructor, and then close the file. The NP_WD_10_Report file is the current document.

Now that you have created your AutoMark file, you need to access it from within the NP_WD_10_Report document. You can't do this from the Mark Index Entry dialog box; you need to use the Index dialog box.

To access the AutoMark file and mark the AutoMark entries:

▶ **1.** On the ribbon, click the **References** tab, and then in the Index group, click the **Insert Index** button. The Index dialog box opens with the Index tab selected.

▶ **2.** Click **AutoMark**. The Open Index AutoMark File dialog box opens. It is similar to the Open dialog box.

▶ **3.** Navigate to the location where you saved the NP_WD_10_AutoMark file, click **NP_WD_10_AutoMark** to select it, and then click **Open**. All words in the document that match the words in the first column in the table in the AutoMark file are marked as main entries, using "annual meeting" and "respondents" as the entries. On page 5 (marked page 1 in the footer), in the paragraph below the heading "2.1. Survey Overview" an index field code appears next to "Respondents," marking the word with the entry "respondents."

▶ **4.** Scroll to page 7 (marked page 3 in the footer) so that you can see the heading "2.3. Survey Coordinator" and the paragraph below it. In the fourth line of the paragraph, an index field code appears next to "Annual Meeting," marking it with the entry "annual meeting."

▶ **5.** Press **CTRL+HOME** to move to the beginning of the document. Because the AutoMark file marked every instance of "Annual Meeting" as an index entry, that phrase was marked on the document title page. However, that instance of the phrase should not be included in the index, so you will delete the field code.

▶ **6.** Above the list of names on the title page, select **{ XE "annual meeting" }**, and then press **DEL**. Now when you create the index, that instance of "annual meeting" will not be included.

Compiling an Index

After you mark all the desired index entries, subentries, cross-references, page-range references, and AutoMark entries, you're ready to **compile** the index—that is, you're ready to generate the index using the marked entries. Most often, indexes appear at the end of books, reports, or long documents.

Compiling an Index

- Move the insertion point to the location where you want to insert the index.
- Hide the field codes.
- On the References tab, in the Index group, click the Insert Index button.
- Select the desired options for controlling the appearance of the index.
- Click OK.

You'll compile the index on a new page at the end of the document. You need to create that new page. First, you need to hide the field codes. If the field codes are displayed when you compile the index, words are moved and may appear on different pages.

To create a new page for the index:

1. Scroll so that you can see the bottom of page 5 (marked page 1 in the footer) and the top of page 6 (marked page 2 in the footer). The index entry field codes on page 5 (marked page 1) have caused some of the last paragraph on page 5 to appear on page 6, and the page break you inserted after this paragraph means that the rest of page 6 is blank. Also note on the status bar that there are now 11 pages in the document.

2. Click the **Home** tab on the ribbon, and then, in the Paragraph group, click the **Show/Hide** button ¶ to hide nonprinting characters and the field codes. With the field codes hidden, the entire paragraph at the bottom of page 5 now fits on that page, and page 6 is now filled with text. Also, there are now 10 pages in the document.

3. Press **CTRL+END**. The insertion point moves to the last paragraph in the document, which is the empty paragraph above the endnotes on page 10 (marked page 6 in the footer). This is an even page in the document.

4. Insert a Next Page section break, and then scroll to the new page in the document. The empty paragraph and the endnotes were moved to the new page. On the status bar, the new page is page 11. In the footer, the new page is page 1.

5. At the top of page 11, with the insertion point in the blank paragraph at the top of the new page, type **Index**, and then press **ENTER**.

6. Format **Index** with the Front/End Matter Heading style.

   At the bottom of page 11, the footer contains the wrong page number.

7. Scroll to the bottom of page 11, and then double-click in the footer area. The Header & Footer Tools Design tab appears and is selected.

TIP

If two odd pages or two even pages in a row are created when you insert a Next Page section break, undo the action, click the Breaks button in the Page Setup group on the Layout tab, and then click Even Page or Odd Page on the menu to create a new page of the type you specified.

8. In the Header & Footer group, click the **Page Number** button, and then click **Format Page Numbers**. The Page Number Format dialog box opens.

9. In the Page numbering section, click the **Continue from previous section** option button, and then click **OK**. The dialog box closes, and the page number in the footer changes to 7.

10. On the Header & Footer Tools Design tab, in the Close group, click the **Close Header and Footer** button.

An index is usually the last item in a document. However, your document contains endnotes that appear at the end of the document. When you created the new page, the endnotes moved to that page as well. You need to change the location of the endnotes so that they appear at the end of the previous section.

To change the location of the endnotes:

1. Scroll to page 10 (marked page 6 in the footer), and then click anywhere in the last paragraph on the page.

2. On the ribbon, click the **References** tab, and then in the Footnotes group, click the **Dialog Box Launcher** ⬚. The Footnotes and Endnotes dialog box opens. The Endnotes option button is selected, and End of document appears in the Endnotes box.

   Trouble? If the Endnotes option button is not selected, click it.

3. Click the **Endnotes** arrow, and then click **End of section**.

4. At the bottom of the dialog box, click **Apply**. The endnotes now appear at the end of the current section, after the last paragraph on page 10.

Now you are ready to compile the index.

To compile the index:

1. Press **CTRL+END**. The insertion point appears in the blank paragraph below the "Index" heading on page 11.

2. On the ribbon, click the **References** tab, and then in the Index group, click the **Insert Index** button. The Index dialog box opens with the Index tab selected. In the Formats box, From template appears, indicating that the index will be formatted using the document's template styles, and in the Columns box, 2 appears, indicating that the index will be arranged in two columns. See Figure 10–45.

Figure 10–45   Index dialog box

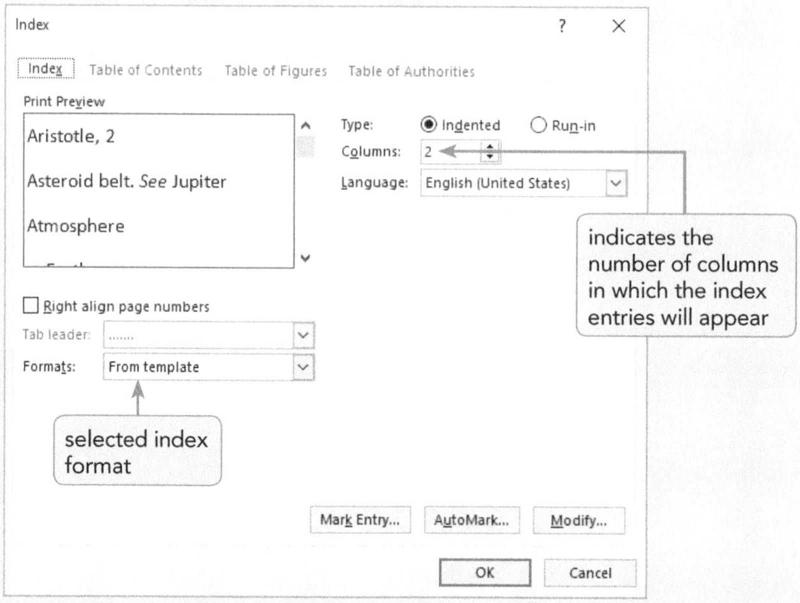

3. Click **OK**. The dialog box closes, and the index is compiled. See Figure 10–46.

Figure 10–46   Index for the NP_WD_10_Report document

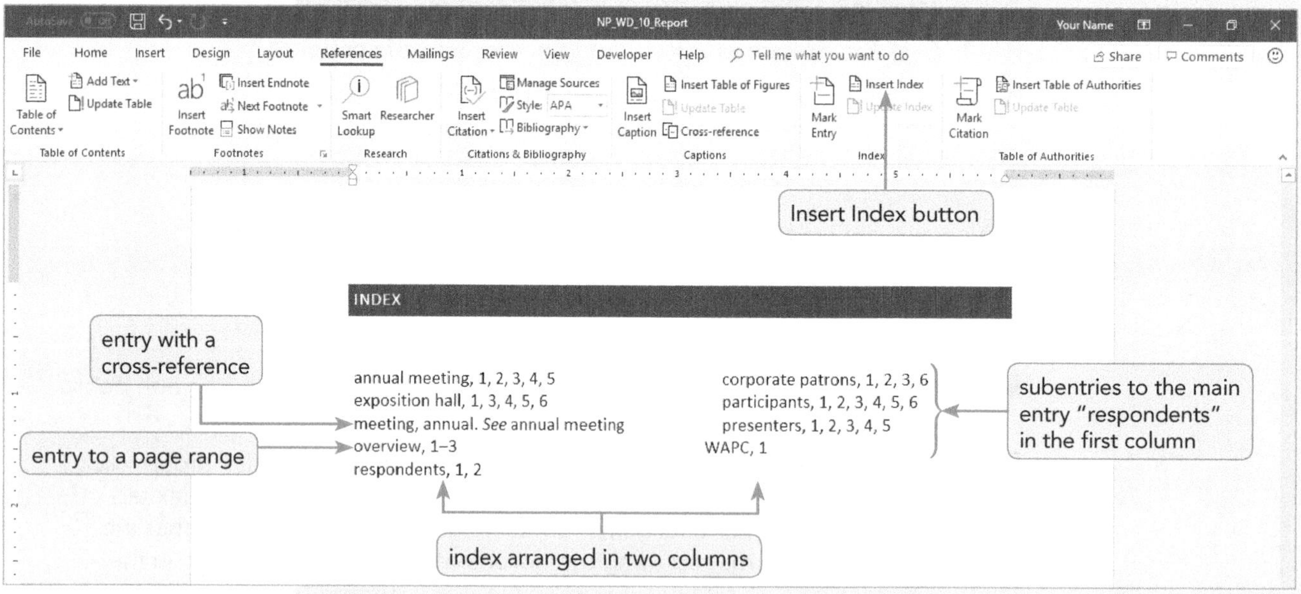

The column break in the Index is not in the best position. The main entry "respondents" should be in the same column as its subentries. You will update the index in the next section, so you will wait to see what effect the update has on the index before you fix this issue.

Updating an Index

After an index is compiled, you can still make changes to it, including adding new entries. To update an index, you click the Update Index button in the Index group on the References tab. This is similar to updating a table of contents. Likewise, if you created a table of figures or a table of authorities, you could click the appropriate Update button in the Captions or Table of Authorities group on the References tab.

Bailey asks you to add one more entry to the index. You'll mark the entry and then update the index to include the new entry.

To create a new index entry and then update the index:

▶ **1.** Scroll up to page 6 (page 2 in the footer), in the paragraph below the "2.3. Survey Coordinator" heading, in the first line, select the phrase **Marketfield Research Associates**.

▶ **2.** On the References tab, in the Index group, click the **Mark Entry** button, and then in the Mark Index Entry dialog box, click **Mark All**. The phrase is marked as an index entry, and the nonprinting characters and the field codes are toggled back on. Now you need to update the index.

▶ **3.** Close the Mark Index Entry dialog box, and then hide the nonprinting characters so that the page numbers will be correct.

▶ **4.** Press **CTRL+END**, and then click anywhere in the index. The entire index field is selected.

TIP

You can also right-click the index field, and then click Update Field on the shortcut menu to update the index.

▶ **5.** On the ribbon, click the **References** tab, and then in the Index group, click the **Update Index** button. The entry "Marketfield Research Associates" is added to the index. Notice that the "respondents" entry shifted to the second column, so you no longer need to add a column break to the index.

Your index is short but representative of the type of entries that would appear in a full index. Of course, to create a proper index, you would need to carefully examine each page to identify important terms or phrases that should be marked as index entries.

You have made many changes to the document, so you need to update the table of contents.

To update the table of contents:

▶ **1.** Go to page 3 in the document so that you can see the table of contents, and then click anywhere in the table of contents. The entire table of contents field is selected.

▶ **2.** On the References tab, in the Table of Contents group, click the **Update Table** button. The Update Table of Contents dialog box opens.

▶ **3.** Click the **Update entire table** option button, and then click **OK**. The table of contents is updated to include the numbered headings, the "Index" heading, and the updated page numbers.

Creating a Table of Figures

A table of figures is a list of the captions for all the pictures, charts, graphs, slides, or other illustrations in a document, along with the page number for each. As with a table of contents, the entries in a table of figures are links to the captions to which they refer. You can click an entry in a table of figures to jump to that caption in the document.

To create a table of figures:

▶ **1.** Scroll to page 4 in the document, display nonprinting characters, position the insertion point in the blank paragraph below the heading "List of Figures," and then hide nonprinting characters again.

▶ **2.** On the ribbon, click the **References** tab if necessary, and then in the Captions group, click the **Insert Table of Figures** button. The Table of Figures dialog box opens with the Table of Figures tab selected. See Figure 10–47.

Figure 10–47 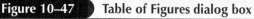 Table of Figures dialog box

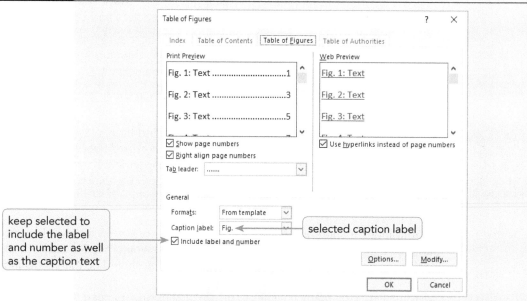

keep selected to include the label and number as well as the caption text

selected caption label

Notice that Fig. appears in the Caption label box. This is the correct label for the figures in this document. Below the Caption label box, the Include label and number check box is selected. This must be selected in order for the label "Fig." and the figure number to be listed as well as the caption text.

Trouble? If Fig. does not appear in the Caption label box, click the Caption label arrow, and then click Fig.

▶ **3.** Click **OK**. The table of figures is generated, as shown in Figure 10–48.

Figure 10–48 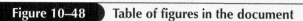 Table of figures in the document

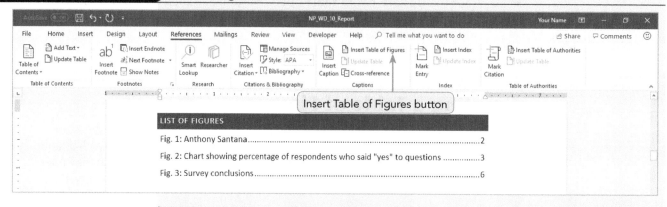

Insert Table of Figures button

LIST OF FIGURES

Fig. 1: Anthony Santana 2
Fig. 2: Chart showing percentage of respondents who said "yes" to questions 3
Fig. 3: Survey conclusions 6

▶ **4.** Save the document.

Creating a Table of Authorities

Besides tables of contents and lists of figures, Word can also generate other lists. When creating legal documents, you may have to create a table of authorities, which is a list of references to cases, statutes, or rules. Similar to other Word-generated lists, a table of authorities includes the page numbers on which the references appear. To create a table of authorities, first mark all the citations (references) by clicking the References tab, click the Mark Citation button in the Table of Authorities group to display the Mark Citation dialog box, select the appropriate category (Cases, Statutes, Rules, Treatises, and so forth), and then click Mark or Mark All. Then you can generate the table of authorities by clicking the Insert Table of Authorities button in the Table of Authorities group on the References tab. To update a table of authorities after adding more citations to a document, click the Update Table button in the Table of Authorities group on the References tab.

Updating Fields Before Printing

Many of the elements you have added to the NP_WD_10_Report document, such as the cross-references and the table of contents, include fields. As you know, you should always update fields in a document before printing to ensure you are printing the most current information in the document. Instead of manually updating the fields, you can set Word to automatically update fields before printing. By default, the option to update fields before printing is turned off.

Bailey wants you to print the document. Before you do, you'll set the option to update the fields before printing.

Note: If your instructor does not want you to print the document, read, but do not execute the following steps.

To change the options to update fields before printing and print the document:

1. On the ribbon, click the **File** tab, scroll down, and then in the navigation pane, click **Options**. The Word Options dialog box opens.

2. In the navigation pane, click **Display**, and then click the **Update fields before printing** check box under "Printing options" to select it, if necessary.

   Trouble? If the Update fields before printing check box is already selected, do not click it.

3. Click **OK** to close the dialog box. Now you will print the document. Because the fields will be updated, you need to make sure the nonprinting characters are hidden so the index is updated correctly.

4. Hide nonprinting characters, click the **File** tab, and then in the navigation pane, click **Print**. The Print screen appears in Backstage view.

5. Click the **Print** button. The Update Table of Contents dialog box opens, prompting you to update the table of contents. The Update page numbers only option button is selected.

6. Click **OK**. The dialog box closes, and the Update Table of Figures dialog box opens with the Update page numbers only option button selected.

▶ **7.** Click **OK**. The dialog box closes, and the document prints. Next, you should turn off Update fields before printing so you leave Word in the same state you found it when you started this module.

▶ **8.** Click the **File** tab, scroll down, and then in the navigation pane, click **Options** to open the Word Options dialog box.

▶ **9.** In the navigation pane, click **Display**.

▶ **10.** If the Update fields before printing check box was not selected prior to you completing this set of steps, click the **Update fields before printing** check box to deselect it.

   Trouble? If the Update fields before printing check box was already selected prior to you completing this set of steps, do not click it to deselect it.

▶ **11.** Click **OK**.

Checking Compatibility

Bailey plans to send the final version of the survey report to the other board members. Because they do not all have the most recent version of Word, she asks you to check the document for features that are not compatible with earlier versions of Word.

To check compatibility with earlier versions of Word:

▶ **1.** On the ribbon, click the **File** tab. The Info screen opens in Backstage view.

▶ **2.** Click the **Check for Issues** button, and then click **Check Compatibility**. The Microsoft Word Compatibility Checker dialog box opens. Several issues were found. See Figure 10–49.

Figure 10–49 | **Microsoft Word Compatibility Checker dialog box**

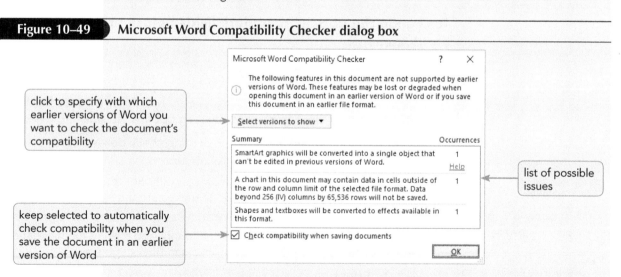

You'll inform Bailey of these incompatibilities so she can decide if she wants to save the document in an earlier format.

▶ **3.** If the **Check compatibility when saving documents** check box is not selected, click it. Now the Compatibility Checker will run automatically if you try to save the document in an earlier version of Word.

▶ **4.** Click **OK**.

Encrypting a Document

To **encrypt** a file is to modify the data structure to make the information unreadable to anyone who does not have the password. When you encrypt a Word document, you assign a password to the file. When you create passwords, keep in mind that they are case sensitive; this means that "PASSWORD" is different from "password." Also, you must remember your password. This might seem obvious; but if you forget the password you assign to a document, you won't be able to open it.

REFERENCE

Encrypting a Document

- Click the File tab to open the Info screen in Backstage view.
- Click the Protect Document button, and then click Encrypt with Password.
- In the Encrypt Document dialog box, type a password in the Password box, and then click OK to open the Confirm Password dialog box.
- Retype the password in the Reenter password box.
- Click OK.

Bailey asks you to encrypt the report to prevent any unauthorized readers from opening it.

To encrypt the document:

▶ **1.** On the ribbon, click the **File** tab. The Info screen opens in Backstage view.

▶ **2.** Click the **Protect Document** button, and then click **Encrypt with Password**. The Encrypt Document dialog box opens. Here, you'll type a password.

TIP

To remove the password, delete the password in the Encrypt Document dialog box, and then click OK.

▶ **3.** Type **Report** in the Password box. The characters appear as black dots to prevent anyone from reading the password over your shoulder.

▶ **4.** Click **OK**. The Confirm Password dialog box opens.

▶ **5.** Type **Report** again, and then click **OK**. The dialog box closes, and a message appears next to the Protect Document button on the Info screen, indicating that a password is required to open this document.

Now, when you save the file, it will be in an encrypted format so that it can't be opened except by someone who knows the password. (Normally, you would use a stronger password than "Report." But for the purpose here, you'll keep it simple and easy to remember.)

PROSKILLS

Decision Making: Creating Strong Passwords You Can Easily Remember

In a world where sharing digital information electronically is an everyday occurrence, a password used to encrypt a document is just one more password to remember. When deciding on a password, you should consider a strong password that consists of at least eight characters using a combination of uppercase and lowercase letters, numbers, and symbols. However, this type of password can be difficult to remember, especially if you have to remember multiple passwords. Some people use the same password for everything. This is not a good idea because if someone ever discovered your password, they would have access to all of the data or information protected by that password. Instead, you should come up with a plan for creating passwords. For example, you could choose a short word that you can easily remember for one part of the password. The second part of the password could be the name of the file, website, or account, but instead of typing it directly, type it backwards, or use the characters in the row above or below the characters that would spell out the name. Or you could split the name of the website and put your short word in the middle of the name. Other possibilities are to combine your standard short word and the website or account name, but replace certain letters with symbols—for example, replace every letter "E" with "#," or memorize a short phrase from a poem or story and use it with some of the substitutions described above. Establishing a process for creating a password means that you will be able to create strong passwords for all of your accounts that you can easily remember.

Making a Document Read-Only

You can make a document **read-only**, which means that others can read but not modify the document. There are two ways to make a document read-only. You can mark the document as final, or you can set the document to always open as read-only. If you mark a document as final, the next time the file is opened, it will be read-only. If you turn off the read-only status, make changes, and then save and close the file, it will no longer be marked as final. If a document is set to always open as read-only and you turn off the read-only status to make changes, the next time the document is opened, it will still be marked as read-only.

Bailey asks you to try both ways of making the document read-only.

To mark the document as final and to always open as read-only:

1. On the Info screen in Backstage view, click the **Protect Document** button, and then click **Mark as Final**. A dialog box opens indicating that the document will be marked as final and saved.

2. Click **OK**. The dialog box closes and another dialog box opens, telling you that the document was marked as final.

3. Click **OK**. The dialog box closes, a message is added next to the Protect Document button telling you that the document has been marked as final, and "[Read-Only]" appears next to the document title in the title bar.

4. In the navigation pane, click the **Back** button ⊖ to exit Backstage view. The ribbon is collapsed, a yellow MARKED AS FINAL bar appears below the collapsed ribbon, the Marked as Final icon appears on the status bar, and "Read-Only" appears in the title bar. See Figure 10–50.

Figure 10–50 | **Document marked as final**

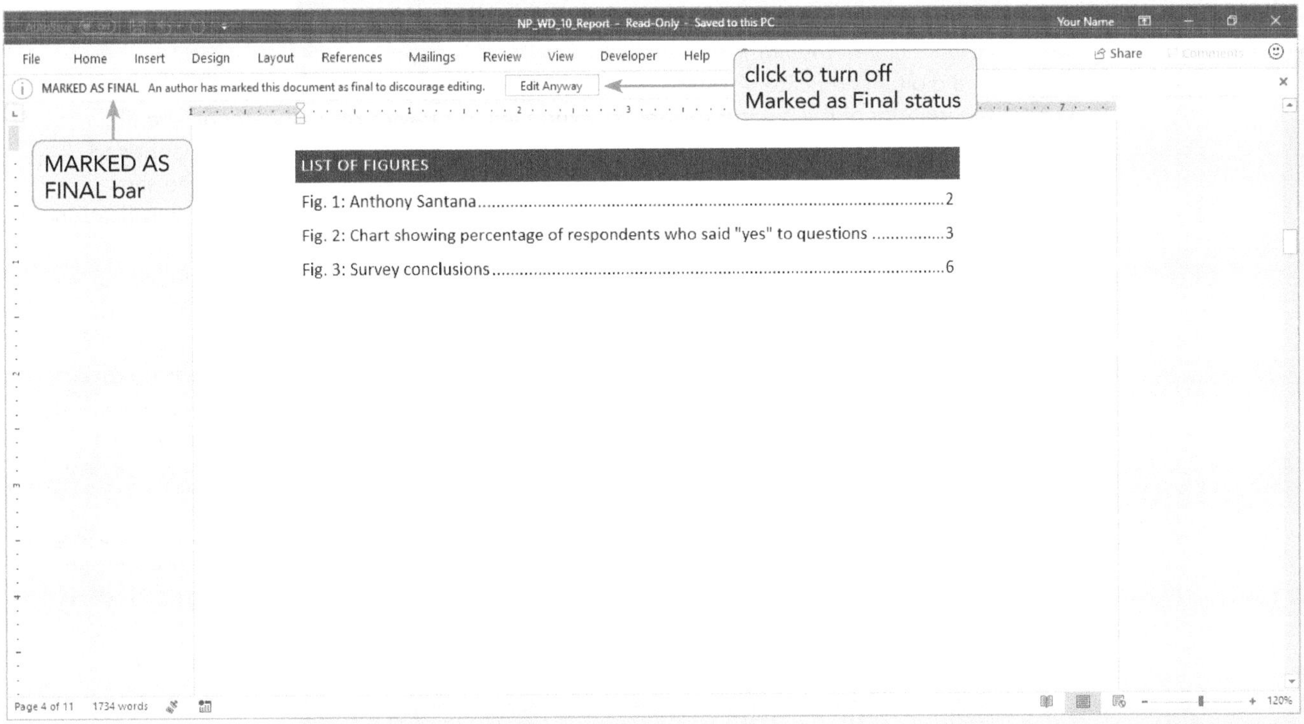

NP_WD_10_Report - Read-Only - Saved to this PC · Your Name

File Home Insert Design Layout References Mailings Review View Developer Help

MARKED AS FINAL An author has marked this document as final to discourage editing.   Edit Anyway ← click to turn off Marked as Final status

MARKED AS FINAL bar

LIST OF FIGURES

Page 4 of 11   1734 words

5. Close the NP_WD_10_Report file, and then reopen it. The Password dialog box appears.

6. In the Password box, type **Report**, and then click **OK**. The document opens, and the yellow MARKED AS FINAL bar appears.

7. In the MARKED AS FINAL bar, click **Edit Anyway**. The bar disappears, and the ribbon is displayed.

8. Save the document, close it, and then reopen it, typing **Report** in the Password box when asked. The yellow MARKED AS FINAL bar does not appear.

9. Click the **File** tab, click the **Protect Document** button, and then click **Always Open Read-Only**. Additional text added below the Protect Document button name tells you that the document has been set to read-only.

10. In the navigation pane, click **Save**.

11. Close, and then reopen the document. A dialog box opens telling you that the author would like you to open this as read-only and asking if you want to open as read-only. If you click Yes, the document will open with the yellow bar at the top again. If you click No, the document will open without the yellow bar at the top and you will be able to edit it.

12. Click **No**. The document opens. The yellow bar is not at the top and the ribbon is available.

13. Save the changes to the document, close it, and then reopen it. The same dialog box appears asking if you want to open the document as read-only. The Always open as read-only status stays applied to the file unless you change it on the Info screen in Backstage view.

14. **sam** Click **Cancel**. The document does not open.

INSIGHT

Adding a Digital Signature to a Document File

A **digital signature** is an electronic attachment not visible in the file that verifies the authenticity of the author or the version of the file by comparing the digital signature to a digital certificate. A **digital certificate** is a code attached to a file that verifies the identity of the creator of the file. When you digitally sign a document, the file is marked as read-only. If anyone removes the read-only status to make changes to the document, the signature is marked as invalid because it is no longer the same document the signatory signed. You can obtain a digital certificate from a certification authority.

To add a digital signature to a document, click the Protect Document button on the Info screen in Backstage view, click Add a Digital Signature, and then click OK. If the Get a Digital ID dialog box opens, telling you that you don't have a digital ID and asking if you would like to get one from a Microsoft Partner, that means no digital certificate is stored on the computer you are using. If you click Yes, your browser starts, and a webpage opens listing certificate authorities from whom you can purchase a digital certificate. Note that you cannot add a digital signature to a master document; you must unlink all the subdocuments first.

If you or your company has access to a Rights Management Server or you are using Office 365 with RMS Online, you can restrict access to a document so that others can read it but not make any changes to it or copy or print it. To do this, click the Protect Document button, and then use the Restrict Access command.

You have completed the survey report for Bailey. The skills you learned in this module will be extremely useful as you create long documents for school and in the workplace.

REVIEW

Session 10.3 Quick Check

1. What type of page numbers are typically used in front matter?
2. What happens when you change the "Start at" page number in a section?
3. Explain what a gutter margin is.
4. How do you insert a heading in a footer using a field code?
5. Why would you use a nonbreaking hyphen or a nonbreaking space in a document?
6. What are the four types of entries you can create using the Mark Index Entry dialog box?
7. What is an AutoMark file?
8. When a document is marked as final, can it be edited?

Review Assignments

Data Files needed for the Review Assignments: NP_WD_10-2.docx, Support_WD_10_Alonzo.docx, Support_WD_10_Marie.docx

The annual meeting of the World Association of Personal Chefs (WAPC), which brings together personal chefs from all over the world, has traditionally been held at midrange resorts in order to encourage the highest possible attendance. Although the results of the survey the WAPC Annual Meeting Committee conducted indicated that most participants, presenters, and corporate patrons were satisfied with the most recent annual meeting, the committee members are considering switching to biennial meetings at more upscale locations. The committee hired Marketfield Research Associates to conduct another survey to find out if WAPC members would rather attend a meeting only every other year (biennially) but at more upscale resorts—and therefore at a higher cost—or if they would prefer to continue to attend annual meetings at a more moderate cost per meeting. Bailey Lawrence, along with Alonzo Garza and Marie Choi, created the documents that will become the master document and the subdocuments for the report on the new survey. It's your job to compile the report as a master document and then perform the necessary revisions, such as creating an index. Complete the following steps:

1. Start Word, create a new, blank document, switch to Outline view, and then save the document as **NP_WD_10_Report2** in the location specified by your instructor.
2. Type the following as Level 1 and Level 2 headings as an outline.

   Recommendations
   Background
     Survey Background
     Response Rates
   Summary
   Corporate Patrons
   Participants
   Presenters

3. Move the Level 1 heading "Background" with its subordinate text below the "Summary" heading, and then move the Level 1 heading "Recommendations" below the Level 1 heading "Presenters."
4. Insert the following as body text under the Level 1 heading "Recommendations" (including the period): **The WAPC Annual Meeting Committee recommends switching to biennial meetings held for four days.** Save your changes, and then close the document.
5. Open the document **NP_WD_10-2.docx** from the Word10 > Review folder included with your Data Files. Add your name in the blank paragraph below the name "Marie Choi" on the title page, and then save it as **NP_WD_10_Master2** in the location specified by your instructor.
6. On page 1, select the "Table of Contents" heading, and then create a new style named **TOC** that is based on the current formatting of that heading but has Body Text as an outline level.
7. Convert the sections beginning with the headings "Survey of Corporate Patrons," "Survey of Participants," and "Survey of Presenters" into individual subdocuments. Save your changes to the master document so that the subdocuments are saved as individual files.
8. Open the file **Support_WD_10_Alonzo.docx**, which is located in the Word10 > Review folder, save it as **NP_WD_10_Alonzo** in the same folder that contains the file NP_WD_10_Master2, and then close the file NP_WD_10_Alonzo. In the NP_WD_10_Master2 document, insert the **NP_WD_10_Alonzo** file as a subdocument in the Body Text paragraph above the "Survey of Corporate Patrons" heading.

9. Open the file **Support_WD_10_Marie.docx**, which is located in the Word10 > Review folder, save it as **NP_WD_10_Marie** in the same folder that contains the file NP_WD_10_Master2, and then close the file NP_WD_10_Marie. At the end of the NP_WD_10_Master2 document, in the last blank paragraph, insert the **NP_WD_10_Marie** file as a subdocument. Save the master document.

10. In Outline view, use the Show Level button to display the first two levels of headings. Position the insertion point in the "Survey of Corporate Patrons" heading, and then add automatic numbering to all the section headings using the same style on the Multilevel List menu that you used in the module steps. Change the style of the Level 2 headings (headings formatted with the Heading 2 style) so the period is replaced with a dash (hyphen). Modify the formatting of the Front/End Matter Heading style and the TOC style so that the headings with those styles applied are not numbered.

11. Save the changes to the document.

12. Make sure you saved the changes to the document, and then save the document as **NP_WD_10_Biennial** in the location specified by your instructor.

13. In the NP_WD_10_Biennial document, unlink all five subdocuments. Save the changes to the document.

14. Starting from the end of the document, delete all the section breaks in the document (do not delete the manual page break after the paragraph after the "Table of Contents" heading), and delete the blank paragraph above the heading "5 Survey of Presenters" and the blank paragraph above the heading "3 Survey of Corporate Patrons." Add Next Page section breaks before the headings "Table of Contents" and "1 Executive Summary."

15. On page 5, replace the yellow highlighted placeholder text "[Chart 1]," "[Chart 2]," and "[Chart 3]" with pie charts. For each chart, do not change the text in cell B1, type **Responded** in cell A2, and type **Did not respond** in cell A3. After adding the following data, remove rows 4 and 5 in the spreadsheet from the chart:

Chart 1:

Responded **23%**

Did not respond **77%**

Chart 2:

Responded **80%**

Did not respond **20%**

Chart 3:

Responded **94%**

Did not respond **6%**

16. For each chart, make the following format changes:

a. Remove the chart title.

b. Change the style to Style 7, and change the color scheme to Colorful Palette 3.

c. Change the position of the legend so it is on the right side of the chart.

d. Resize each chart object so it is 2.5" high and 4.5" wide (using the Shape Height and Shape Width boxes in the Size group on the Chart Tools Format tab).

e. Center each chart horizontally in the paragraph.

17. Insert **Figure 1: Percentage of corporate patron respondents** as a caption below the first pie chart. Insert **Figure 2: Percentage of participant respondents** as a caption below the second pie chart. Insert **Figure 3: Percentage of presenter respondents** as a caption below the third pie chart that reads.

18. In the paragraph below the heading "2-2 Response Information," replace the yellow highlighted placeholders for the cross-references with cross-references to the pie charts using only the figure label and number.

19. In the paragraph below the heading "2 Overview," insert an endnote after the last period in the paragraph. Type **WAPC members Brad Welke and Jana Saadi assisted as well.** (including the period).

20. Restrict editing in the document by not allowing users to change the theme and allowing only changes marked with tracked changes. Do not require a password.

21. In the paragraph below the heading "1 Executive Summary," in the last sentence, change the "50%" to **60%**.

22. Remove the editing restrictions so that users are allowed to make changes without having them tracked. Do not remove the restriction for changing the theme.

23. Use the Document Inspector to remove comments, revisions, and versions.

24. Use the Accessibility Checker to identify the elements that could cause problems for people who use assistive devices. Add the following alt text to the three charts:

    Figure 1 **Chart illustrating that only 23% of corporate patrons responded to the survey**

    Figure 2 **Chart illustrating that 80% of participants responded to the survey**

    Figure 3 **Chart illustrating that 94% of presenters responded to the survey**

25. Center the title page between its top and bottom margins.

26. In the front matter, insert lowercase Roman numeral page numbers right-aligned in the footer, with page i starting on the Table of Contents page. Remove the link to the first section (the title page), and then remove the page number on the title page.

27. Insert Arabic numerals as page numbers right-aligned in the footer on the rest of the pages of the report, with page 1 starting on the page containing the heading "1 Executive Summary."

28. Set up all the pages except the title page so that they have a 0.5" gutter.

29. Set up all the pages except the title page so odd and even pages have different formatting.

30. Set up footers so that the odd-page footers include the document title **Biennial Meeting Feasibility Survey** at the left margin and the page number at the right margin. In the section of the document numbered with Arabic numerals, set up even-page footers so that the page number is at the left margin and a style reference to the Heading 1 style is at the right margin. In the section of the document numbered with Roman numerals, set up even-page footers so that the page number is at the left margin and a style reference to the Front/End Matter Heading style is at the right margin. (*Hint*: Review the even-page footers to make sure the even-page footers in the section containing the Arabic page numbers include a reference to the Heading 1 style, and that the even-page footer in the section containing the Roman numeral page numbers include a reference to the Front/End Matter style. Break the link between the previous sections if needed.)

31. At the end of the document (before the end note), insert a new, blank paragraph, and then insert a Next Page section break. Type **Index** in the blank paragraph on the new last page, and then press ENTER. Format "Index" with the Front/End Matter Heading style, and then modify the footer on this page so that the page number is correct and so that the field references the Front/End Matter Heading style.

32. Change the location of the endnotes so that they appear at the end of the section before the section that contains the "Index" heading.

33. In the paragraph below the heading "6 Recommendations," change the hyphen at the end of the second line between "two" and "day" to a nonbreaking hyphen. (*Hint*: If the hyphen between "two" and "day" does not appear at the end of the line, check to make sure the gutter margin of all of the sections except for the section containing the title page is still set to 0.5".) In the paragraph below the heading "2-2 Response Information," at the end of the second line, change the space between "(see" and the cross-reference to Figure 2 to a nonbreaking space.

34. Review the document for bad page breaks, and then insert a page break before the heading "4-2 Participant Focus Group Responses." Select the page break you inserted, and apply the Normal style to that paragraph.

35. Create the following index entries:

    a. Mark the first instance of "WAPC" in the body of the report. (Do not mark this text on the title page.)

    b. Mark every occurrence of "participants," "corporate patrons," and "presenters" as subentries to the main entry "respondents." Then mark every occurrence of "respondents."

    c. Mark every instance of "upscale" as a main index entry. Create "opulent" as a cross-reference index entry to the main entry "upscale."

d. Bookmark the section "2 Overview" (including the two subsections) with a bookmark named **OverviewSection**, and then mark the bookmark as a page range index entry under the main entry "overview." (*Hint*: Make sure you change the text in the Main entry box so that it is "overview" and not "Overview.")

e. Create an AutoMark file named **NP_WD_10_NewAutoMark** that contains the entries shown in Figure 10–51, and then mark the AutoMark entries.

Figure 10–51   Data for NP_WD_10_NewAutoMark file

participant	participants
Participants	participants
Participant	participants
corporate patron	corporate patrons
Corporate patrons	corporate patrons
Corporate patron	corporate patrons
presenter	presenters
Presenters	presenters
Presenter	presenters

36. Move the insertion point to the end of the document, below the heading "Index." Hide nonprinting characters, and then generate the index.

37. Mark every instance of "biennial" as a main index entry. Hide nonprinting characters, and then update the index. (*Hint*: Click the Layout tab, click the Breaks button in the Page Setup group, and then click Column.)

38. Display nonprinting characters, click before the blank paragraph mark below the heading "List of Figures" in the front matter, and then press ENTER. (*Hint*: If the paragraph containing the section break is formatted with the Heading 1 style, undo the last action, position the insertion point before the paragraph mark, and then press ENTER.) Hide the nonprinting characters, and then in the first empty paragraph below the "List of Figures," insert a table of figures.

39. With the nonprinting characters hidden, insert a table of contents below the "Table of Contents" heading in the front matter using the Custom Table of Contents command on the Table of Contents menu.

40. Encrypt the document using the password **Biennial**. If requested, update the fields before printing, and then print the document. If you changed the Printing option in the Word Options dialog box to update the fields before printing, change it back.

41. Mark the document as Always open read-only, save it, and then close it.

Case Problem 1

APPLY

Data Files needed for this Case Problem: NP_WD_10-3.docx, Support_WD_10_Background.docx, Support_WD_10_Market.docx, Support_WD_10_Summary.docx

Bradford Estate Bradford Estate was established in 1727 on 85 acres in Westerly, Rhode Island. The estate, located on the coastline, was the summer residence of various families for more than 250 years. The mansion contains 16 rooms and was completed in 1754. The estate has been neglected for the past 50 years, and last year, the nonprofit group The Friends of Bradford Estate was established to prepare a plan to modernize the facilities and market the estate as a viable location for small conferences and events. Members of the group have written drafts of the various parts of the business plan for the estate in preparation for requesting a loan. They asked you to help put the final document together and format it. Complete the following steps:

1. Open the document **NP_WD_10-3.docx** from the Word10 > Case1 folder included with your Data Files, and then save it as **NP_WD_10_Plan** in the location specified by your instructor.

2. On the title page (page 1), in the blank paragraph below "Prepared By," type your name.

3. On page 1, in the blank paragraph above the "List of Tables" heading, type **Contents**, and then press ENTER. Apply the Headings style to the "Contents" paragraph, and then create a new style named **Contents** based on the custom Headings style, but with an outline level set to Body Text.

4. Open the files **Support_WD_10_Background.docx**, **Support_WD_10_Market.docx**, and **Support_WD_10_Summary.docx**, which are located in the Word10 > Case1 folder, and then save them as **NP_WD_10_Background**, **NP_WD_10_Market**, and **NP_WD_10_Summary**, respectively, in the same folder in which you saved NP_WD_10_Plan. Close these three files.

5. In the NP_WD_10_Plan document, in the blank paragraph above the heading "Index," insert the files **NP_WD_10_Summary**, **NP_WD_10_Background**, and **NP_WD_10_Market**, in that order, as subdocuments.

6. Show Level 1 headings in Outline view, and then add automatic numbering to all headings formatted with the Heading 1 style using the style in the first column in the last row on the Multilevel List menu. Modify the heading numbers by replacing the period after the heading number for level 1 with **)** (a close parenthesis). Remove the numbering from the custom Contents and Headings style definitions.

7. Save the changes to the master document, and then save the document as **NP_WD_10_PlanFinal** in the location specified by your instructor.

8. Unlink the three subdocuments, and then save the document again.

9. Delete the Continuous section break on page 6. Delete the two Continuous section breaks on page 4. Delete the two Continuous section breaks on page 2, and then restore the "II) Background" heading by placing the insertion point before the word "Background" at the end of the third paragraph on the page, pressing ENTER, and then applying the Heading 1 style to the "Background" paragraph. Finally, delete the Continuous section break below the "List of Tables" heading on page 1.

10. On page 4, replace the placeholder text "[INSERT COLUMN CHART]" with a column chart based on the data in the table above it. Do not type the column headers in cells A1 and B1. (*Hint*: When the spreadsheet opens, click in the document behind it, and then scroll the document so that you can see the table.)

11. Remove the chart title and the legend, change the color scheme to Colorful Palette 4, and then use the Shape Height and Shape Width boxes in the Size group on the Chart Tools Format tab to change the dimensions of the chart object to 2.8" high and 5" wide. Center the chart horizontally on the page.

12. Add captions to the two tables in the document using the label "Table." Do not add any descriptive text to the table captions. Make sure the numbering format is 1, 2, 3,… and the caption appears above the table. (Note that table captions appear above tables by default.) Center the paragraph containing the captions horizontally on the page.

13. Add a caption to the chart using the label "Figure." After the space following the figure number in the caption, add **Projected number of events in 2022** as the descriptive text.

14. Add cross-references where indicated to the two tables and to the chart, using only the label and number.

15. Insert Next Page section breaks before the "Contents," "I) Summary," and "Index" headings. Insert an ordinary page break before the "List of Tables" heading. Insert another ordinary page break on page 5 before the second paragraph after the "IV) Market Analysis" heading so that that paragraph and the bulleted list after it move to the next page.

16. Center the text on the title page between its top and bottom margins.

17. Set up the pages (except the title page) as odd and even pages, with a 0.5" gutter.

18. Insert page numbers in the front matter using lowercase Roman numerals center-aligned at the top of the page, with page i starting on the "Contents" page, and then remove the page number on the title page. (You might need to reinsert the page numbers in the front matter after changing the format.) Start Arabic numeral page numbering with page 1 on the page containing the "I) Summary" heading (page 5 on the status bar). If necessary, correct the page number on the last page (the page with the "Index" heading) so it continues from the previous section.

19. On page i (page 3 on the status bar), unlink the footer from the previous section, type **Bradford Estate Business Plan**, and then center it horizontally in the footer.

20. On page 2 (page 6 on the status bar), insert a style reference in the footer so that the Heading 1 text appears. Center the text in the footer.

21. On page 2 (page 6 on the status bar), unlink the even page footers from the previous section. Then in the footer of page ii (page 4 on the status bar), edit the field in the footer so that the text formatted with the Headings style appears.

22. In the third bulleted item below the heading "IV) Market Analysis," replace the hyphen in "25-mile" with a nonbreaking hyphen.

23. In the first paragraph below the heading "V) Market Size," replace the space between "$210" and "million" with a nonbreaking space.

24. Mark every occurrence of "events" as a main entry in the index.

25. Create a cross-reference index entry for the word "bookings" to the main entry "events."

26. In Outline view, click the plus sign symbol next to "IV) Market Analysis," press and hold SHIFT, click the plus sign symbol next to "VI) Projected Bookings," and then bookmark the selected three sections with a bookmark named **Market**. Mark the bookmark as a page range index entry under the main entry **market**.

27. Create an AutoMark file named **NP_WD_10_PlanAutoMark** stored in the location specified by your instructor. Add the terms **event**, **Events**, and **Event** as entries in the left column of the table, and add **events** as the main entry in all three rows in the right column, and then mark those entries using the AutoMark file.

28. Position the insertion point in the paragraph below the "Index" heading, and then compile the index using the default settings. Remember to hide nonprinting characters before compiling the index.

29. Insert the table of contents using the Custom Table of Contents command. Remember to hide nonprinting characters before creating the table of contents.

30. Below the "List of Tables" heading in the front matter, before the paragraph mark, insert a list of all the tables. (*Hint*: In the Table of Figures dialog box, change the option in the Caption label box.)

31. Mark the document as final, and then close it.

CREATE

Case Problem 2

There are no Data Files needed for this Case Problem.

Preparing a Group Report   Your instructor will divide your class into workgroups of three to six students and will appoint a workgroup leader or have each workgroup select one. Each workgroup will collaborate to prepare a document that explains how specific Word features can be useful in the workplace. The group can decide if each member of the group needs to provide a description of a separate feature or if group members are allowed to collaborate. The final document needs to contain a description of at least three different features of Word along with explanations of their uses in the workplace. Complete the following steps:

1. Conduct a planning meeting to discuss how the workgroup will accomplish its goals, and how it can make all the sections consistent in style and format.

2. Create an outline for the document. The first heading should be **Introduction**, and this should be followed by a paragraph that describes the report.

3. Plan the document's overall formatting. Choose an appropriate theme. Decide if you want to use the default heading styles or modify the heading styles. Also, decide how you want to format figures, including how you want text to wrap around these elements. You will use two-sided printing, so plan the headers and footers accordingly.

4. Create a new document to be used as the master document for the report, and then save it as **NP_WD_10_Features** in the location specified by your instructor. Create a title page, and then set up headings for the table of contents and the index. Add the "Introduction" heading and paragraph. On the title page, if you are completing one document as a group, on the title page, type **Prepared by:** and then add each group member's name in a list sorted in alphabetical order by the group members' last names. If each member of the group is completing a separate document, type **Prepared by:** followed by your name, and then type **Group Members:** and add each group member's name in a list sorted in alphabetical order by the group members' last names (including your own name).

5. Each feature should appear in its own section on a new page. Each feature description should include at least one screenshot. (*Hint*: Use the Screen Clipping command on the Screenshot menu in the Illustrations group on the Insert tab.) Do not include captions or cross-references at this point. Format each section according to the formatting plan created in Step 3, and then protect each section for tracked changes (without a password).

6. Each group member should review the documents written by the other members of the group. Make at least one edit per document (the changes should be marked with revision marks), and then pass each document file along to the next group member so that all of the group's changes are made in a single copy of each document file. When everyone is finished, each workgroup member should have a copy of his or her document file that contains edits from all the members of the workgroup.

7. Retrieve the file for your section, unprotect the document, and then accept or reject the edits made by the other workgroup members. Discuss each section with the other group members as necessary until you all agree on the final status of all the sections.

8. Insert the prepared documents as subdocuments, and then format the document consistently according to the formatting plan you agreed on in Step 3. Add figure captions and cross-references.

9. Save the changes to the master document. Then, save the file as **NP_WD_10_FinalReport** in the location specified by your instructor, and unlink the subdocuments.

10. In the NP_WD_10_FinalReport document, remove the section breaks inserted when the subdocuments were inserted or created, and then add Next Page, Odd Page, or Even Page section breaks as needed so that you can set up different headers, footers, and page numbering for the title page, the front matter, and the body of the document.

11. Set up the document so the pages are formatted as odd and even pages. Create appropriate headers or footers for the odd and even pages. Make sure you include page numbers, the document title, and section names in the headers and/or footers.

12. Insert the table of contents.

13. Mark appropriate index entries (make sure you have at least eight entries in the index), and then compile the index.

14. Review the document on the Print screen in Backstage view, and then make any necessary changes to ensure that your document looks polished and professional. Save the changes to the document.

15. Change the setting to update fields before printing, and then print the document. Print on both sides of the document pages, if possible.

16. Change the setting to update fields before printing back to its original setting, if necessary, and then close the document.

INDEX

A

Accessibility Checker pane, WD 10-47

active cell, **WD 10-32**

adding
- alt text, WD 1-49–1-54
- border to the flyer, WD 1-55–1-56
- custom paragraph border, WD 8-19–8-22
- digital signature to document file, WD 10-83
- document properties, WD 8-34–8-36
- formulas, WD 3-25–3-27
- headers and footers, WD 3-43–3-47
- numbers to headings, WD 10-20–10-24
- page border, WD 1-54–1-56
- paragraph border, WD 1-45–1-47
- shading, WD 1-45–1-47
- text to text box, WD 4-19–4-21

adjusting track changes options, WD 7-8–7-10

Adobe Dreamweaver, WD 7-45

advanced text formatting, WD 8-9–8-11. *See also* formatting
- applying, WD 8-9–8-11

alignment
- cell content, WD 9-17–9-18
- defined, WD 1-43
- text, WD 1-43–1-44

alternative text (alt text), **WD 1-50**
- adding, WD 1-49–1-54
- options in the Alt Text pane, WD 10-48

Alt Text pane, WD 1-52
- alt text options in, WD 10-48

American Psychological Association (APA) style, **WD 2-28**

anchored, object, **WD 4-12**

applying different page number formats in sections, WD 10-53–10-57

arguments, **WD 9-49**

Associated Press Stylebook, WD 2-28

AutoComplete, **WD 1-10**
- inserting date with, WD 1-10–1-11

AutoCorrect, **WD 1-14**–1-17

AutoFit button, WD 9-17

AutoFit Contents command, WD 9-17

AutoMacro. *See also* macro(s)
- available in Word, WD 8-61
- defined, **WD 8-61**
- recording, WD 8-61–8-63

AutoMark feature, WD 10-72–10-73

AutoMark file, WD 10-72

automatic hyphenation, WD 3-36

automatic sequential numbering, WD 10-20

automating documents using fields, WD 8-38–8-43

B

background fill effect
- applying, WD 7-42–7-43
- defined, **WD 7-42**

Backstage view
- featured templates on the New screen in, WD 5-4
- new options in, WD 1-27
- print settings in, WD 1-26

banded columns, **WD 3-21**

banded rows, **WD 3-21**

beveled edges, **WD 4-32**

bibliography
- creating, WD 2-37–2-49
- displayed in content control, WD 2-46
- as field, WD 2-45
- finalizing, WD 2-48–2-49
- generating, WD 2-45–2-47
- inserting, WD 2-45
- menu, WD 2-46
- selecting style for, WD 2-39
- updating, WD 2-48–2-49

bitmap, **WD 4-53**

block-style letter
- completed, WD 1-9
- continuing to type, WD 1-11–1-12

blog post
- creating, WD 7-47–7-49
- publishing, WD 7-47–7-49

BMP files, WD 4-53

body text, **WD 1-39**
- collapsed in document, WD 3-9
- collapsing and expanding, WD 3-8–3-10
- in new location, WD 3-7

bookmark
- defined, **WD 7-35**
- inserting hyperlink to, WD 7-35–7-39

border(s), **WD 3-2, WD 9-3**
- changing the width of, WD 9-22–9-23
- removing, WD 9-19–9-22

breaking hyphen, **WD 10-63**

browser, **WD 7-45**

building blocks, **WD 5-47**
- properties, editing, WD 8-28–8-29

Building Blocks template, **WD 5-47**

bulleted lists
- creating, WD 1-56–1-59
- defined, **WD 1-56**
- organizing information in, WD 1-56

Bullet Library, **WD 1-57**

business letters, creating, WD 1-9

C

Caption dialog box, WD 10-25

captions, **WD 10-24**
- creating, WD 10-24
- inserting numbered, WD 10-24–10-27

category, **WD 10-18**

cell(s)
- active, WD 10-32
- applying custom formatting to, WD 9-25–9-27
- changing margins, WD 9-23–9-24
- merging, WD 3-27–3-29, WD 9-6–9-10

rotating text in, WD 9-10–9-11
- splitting, WD 9-6–9-10

cell content, aligning, WD 9-17–9-18

cell margins
- changing, WD 9-23–9-24
- defined, **WD 9-23**

centered text, **WD 1-43**

changing
- character spacing, WD 5-18–5-20
- footer and page layout for odd and even pages, WD 10-57–10-61
- outline level of a heading, WD 10-7
- theme colors, WD 5-11–5-12
- theme fonts, WD 5-12–5-14

character(s)
- nonprinting, WD 1-6
- special, WD 4-9–4-11
- typographic, WD 4-9, WD 4-10

character spacing
- changing, WD 5-18–5-20
- changing in Font dialog box, WD 5-19
- defined, **WD 5-18**

character style, **WD 2-22, WD 5-20**

chart(s). *See also* graph(s)
- after excluding row 5, WD 10-35
- creating, WD 10-31
- defined, **WD 10-30**
- inserting, WD 10-30–10-39
- selected in the Errors section of the Accessibility Checker pane, WD 10-47

Chart Elements menu, WD 10-37
- legend submenu on, WD 10-37

Chart Tools Design tab, WD 7-35

Check Box content controls, **WD 9-29**
- inserting, WD 9-42–9-45

checking
- compatibility, WD 10-80
- documents for accessibility, WD 10-46–10-49
- document with the Document Inspector, WD 10-44–10-46
- for tracked changes, WD 7-19

checklist, for formatting default Word document to match MLA style, WD 2-29

chevrons, **WD 6-2**

citation(s), **WD 2-28, WD 2-44**
- creating, WD 2-37–2-49
- MLA style selected and insertion point positioned for new, WD 2-40
- selecting style for, WD 2-39

Citation dialog box, WD 2-41

clip art, WD 4-42

clipboard
- cutting or copying and pasting text using, WD 2-12–2-15

Clipboard pane, **WD 2-13**, WD 2-14
- items in, WD 2-14

color. *See also* font colors, applying
- fill, WD 4-32
- outline, WD 4-32

column(s), **WD 4-3**

balancing, WD 4-53–4-54
- banded, WD 3-21
- deleting, WD 3-18–3-19
- formatting text in, WD 4-7–4-9
- inserting in table, WD 3-17–3-18
- widths, changing, WD 3-19–3-20

column chart. *See also* chart(s)
- spreadsheet containing sample data for, WD 10-32

Columns dialog box, WD 4-7

column widths
- adjusting, WD 3-20
- changing, WD 3-19–3-20
- moving gridlines to change, WD 9-11–9-17

Combine feature, **WD 7-11**

combining, documents, WD 7-10–7-15

Combo Box content control, **WD 9-28**

comma-separated values (CSV) file, **WD 6-44**

comment(s), **WD 2-5**
- attached to document text, WD 2-8
- displayed in document, WD 2-6
- restricting editing to allow only, WD 10-39–10-43
- working with, WD 2-7–2-10

Compare feature, **WD 7-11**

comparing, documents, WD 7-10–7-15

compatibility, checking, WD 10-80

compiling index, **WD 10-74,** WD 10-74–10-76

compressing, pictures in document, WD 8-11–8-14

concordance file, WD 10-72

constants, **WD 9-48**

content controls, WD 9-30–9-31
- Check Box, WD 9-29, WD 9-42–9-45
- Combo Box, WD 9-28
- Date Picker, WD 9-29, WD 9-36–9-38
- Drop-Down List, WD 9-28
- grouping, WD 9-51–9-52
- list, WD 9-39–9-42
- Plain Text, WD 9-28
- Repeating Section, WD 9-45
- Rich Text, WD 9-28
- text, WD 9-31–9-36
- understanding, WD 9-30–9-31

contextual tab, **WD 1-49**

continuous section break, **WD 4-3**

converting text to table, WD 6-44–6-48

copying, **WD 2-12**
- building block to another document or template, WD 8-29–8-31
- macros to another document or template, WD 8-59–8-61
- style to another document or template, WD 8-32–8-34
- text, WD 2-12–2-15

copyright laws, WD 4-37

cover page, inserting, WD 3-47–3-48